REALbasic
The Definitive Guide

SECOND EDITION

REALbasic
The Definitive Guide

Matt Neuburg

Beijing · Cambridge · Farnham · Köln · Paris · Sebastopol · Taipei · Tokyo

Preface

How This Book Came to Be Written

Back in the 1960s, when I first started working with computers, a program was simply the instructions necessary to accomplish a single task, usually a calculation of some sort. The program had a completely fixed idea of what this task was going to be; to run the program meant to perform the task uninterrupted, and no more. For example, suppose I had some pairs of numbers representing points in the Cartesian plane and I wanted to integrate the area under these points. I would write a program to carry out this task, and run it; the program would read in the numbers, perform the calculation, spit out the answer, and stop.

In the late 1970s, I got hold of a personal computer. This made a big difference to how I interacted with the computer. Up until then, I had clumsily created my program on paper and transcribed it onto punch cards, which I handed to the computer's guardians, who ran it at their convenience, usually some time during the night when CPU time was cheap; I'd come in the next day and receive a printout of the results, usually showing that there was a bug in the program, whereupon the whole cycle would begin again, with me tweaking the program and running it again, and so on over a period of weeks until I finally got it to work. But now, suddenly, there were no computer guardians: the computer was *mine*! I worked interactively with the computer, entering the program, running it, fixing a bug, running it again, for as long as I liked and whenever I liked. Nonetheless, the concept of what a program was remained essentially unchanged.

In 1984 came the Macintosh, and everything got stood on its head. This computer had a graphical user interface—a *GUI*. Instead of programs, there were applications. An application, when you started it up, didn't crunch away at some set task and then stop. In fact, it didn't do anything at all. It just sat there and waited for the user to do something, such as type some text, or click a button with the mouse. An application was all about interacting with the user. It all sounded very novel and intriguing, until it came to programming the Macintosh. As soon as I looked into this, one thing became very clear to me: I wasn't going to be able to do it. The management of the

GUI was far too daunting a task, requiring programming techniques and detailed knowledge of the computer's inner workings—its *Toolbox*—that were much too complicated and elaborate for me. As far as I was concerned, therefore, the Macintosh wasn't a computer at all; it was just a very expensive toy. It had a lot of GUI bells and whistles, but I couldn't program it. And a computer is to program.

That changed in 1990, with the release of HyperCard 2.0. HyperCard, which Apple at that time bundled for free with every Macintosh, was a customizable GUI framework wrapped around a programming language (except that Apple called it "scripting," because they were afraid that the word "programming" would scare people). If you wanted to be able to enter text in a field, you dragged a text field into the window. If you wanted something to happen when a button was clicked, you dragged a button into the window, and wrote some code saying how it should respond to being clicked. It was easy, and it was powerful, and it caused me to take the Macintosh seriously for the first time, because now, in effect, I could program it. In short order, I was using HyperCard and the Macintosh to let my students drill themselves on Ancient Greek forms and exercises; I went on to apply HyperCard to lots of other purposes, and I still use it all the time.

HyperCard had some shortcomings, to be sure. It didn't generate true applications, but rather made "stacks" that could run only in the presence of HyperCard; still, this was okay, because every Macintosh included HyperCard. The stacks ran rather slowly; still, they ran a lot faster as Macintoshes got faster. The stacks lacked certain Macintosh features, such as color; still, there were workarounds. The fact remained that for certain sorts of tasks, such as storage and retrieval of loosely structured text, HyperCard was absolutely superb; and in general its shortcomings were greatly outweighed by the sheer pleasure and power of being at last able in some sense to program the Macintosh.

What bothered me was that the world of HyperCard was not the world of true Macintosh programming, which had notably failed to rise to HyperCard's level. In 1996, I was editing a magazine devoted to Macintosh programming, and was astonished at how difficult it still was to write even a simple Macintosh application. There were development environments and application frameworks, but even the most basic tasks required of any application, such as putting up a window and responding to the user's mouseclicks, were very complicated and distracting to program.

It appeared that this was due to historical causes dating back to the Macintosh's beginnings. In those days, the Macintosh's designers had wanted programmers, who were coming ultimately, after all, from the pre-Macintosh non-GUI world, to feel that the application was in full charge of the computer; but at the same time they wanted Macintosh programs to conform to certain standards of appearance and behavior. So the Toolbox consisted of lots of little utility routines, while the onus of stringing these routines into standard patterns was left upon the program's shoulders. The result was that the Macintosh programmer was being forced to juggle every niggling rise and fall of the mouse button. For example, a programmer could not be concerned simply with a high-level notion such as what the program should do when the user closed a certain window. The program itself had also to do the busywork of interacting with the user, as well as making the window actually close; and it was the programmer's job to make sure it did this. If the user clicked in the window's go-away box, the program's event loop, which was supposed to be asking repeatedly to be notified of any user actions, would receive a MouseDown event; the program was then expected to notice that the mouse was in the go-away box, and to ask the Toolbox to watch the mouse button and, when it was released, to report whether the cursor was still in the go-away box, and if it was, then the program must give the necessary commands to close the window. This song and dance was an invariable pattern—that is, *every* mouseclick in *any* window's go-away box in *any* program would *always* cause the window to be closed; yet the sequence was not in any sense automatic from the programmer's point of view. Multiply this instance by many hundreds, and you'll have an idea of what programming the Macintosh was like. Macintosh programs had come to consist mostly of material that was more or less boilerplate, merely to initiate all the right Toolbox actions at all the right moments, so as to manage the standard interface elements and behaviors. The irony was that, despite the standardization of these universal conventional features of the interface, it was still up to all individual programs—and therefore all individual programmers—to handle the details, even though they were all doing it in just the same way as one another;* so far from being in charge of the computer, therefore, the programmer had become its slave.

I found this situation frustrating, daunting, and ridiculous. In HyperCard, remember, I could drag a button into a window, write some easy code to give it functionality, and presto, I had a working button in a HyperCard stack. Why couldn't I do the very same thing to get a working button in a standalone application? This, it seemed to me, was the Holy Grail of Macintosh programming.

Then along came REALbasic, and suddenly, the Grail appeared.† REALbasic was easy to learn and easy to use; like HyperCard, it took care of the interface and permitted me to create a working application quickly and with very little programming, but unlike HyperCard, it created genuine standalone applications with a truly standard and Mac-like interface. From almost the moment I started working with REALbasic, there was a sort of meeting of the minds between me and it. I soon found that I had become something of a REALbasic disciple. Watching users writing to the REALbasic mailing list, posing questions and describing difficulties they were having—often the same questions and the same difficulties—I realized that what was playing them false wasn't some failure on REALbasic's part, but the lack of a reasoned and instructive explanation of the concepts, and of a compendious guide to

---

* For a superb introduction to the sorts of things a Macintosh program must do just to exist, from maintaining memory to managing windows, see *http://www.mactech.com/macintosh-c/classic-online.html*.

† For more about HyperCard and my celebration of it, see *http://db.tidbits.com/getbits.acgi?tbart=04075*. For my initial response to REALbasic, see *http://db.tidbits.com/getbits.acgi?tbart=05043*.

the techniques, that the user needed in order to work with REALbasic with satisfaction and facility. This book is my attempt to supply that lack. I have written the book that I myself wished to read—and indeed I do read it. I keep it by me whenever I'm using REALbasic. I have studied it in cafés, in bed, and in places you're not supposed to mention in introductions to computer books. I've enjoyed it, I've learned from it, and I've found that it contains the answers to just about all my REALbasic questions. And, from what they've told me, so have many others. I hope you will too.

What REALbasic Is Like

Traditionally, programming means writing code; and writing code is a form of mental activity, somewhat akin (resorting to some analogies with which I'm personally familiar) to solving a British crossword puzzle or translating a passage of Ancient Greek—to reach the solution, you have to juggle a lot of material and make it fit together sensibly. Now, code is text; and a lot of code is a lot of text. The result is that a program of any complexity can be hard to write, hard to read, and hard to understand, because it's hard to keep all that text organized in a way that makes sense—in a way that reflects and reveals what all the parts of the program do and how they fit together. The program is too big for you to hold in your head all at once and to grasp how its parts interact; yet, as with the crossword puzzle or the Greek sentence, it is just this simultaneous interaction of its parts that you need to have in mind in order to solve the problem of writing or understanding the program. Then too, writing a full-fledged application for a modern personal computer with a graphical user interface, such as the Macintosh, requires some particularly complex and even cumbersome programming, because, as explained in the previous section, quite apart from whatever its useful purpose may be, the application must also present and manage all its windows and buttons and menus and other interface features, and must respond correctly to the unpredictable actions of a user wielding a mouse and keyboard.

REALbasic makes it easy to create a working application in a matter of minutes, and helps you, the programmer, keep even large amounts of code well organized, lucid, and easy to modify. The reasons for this may be summarized under three heads, describing three aspects of REALbasic.

First, REALbasic is an *application framework*. REALbasic already knows how to make a working application, as well as how to construct and manage the interface elements, such as windows and buttons and menus, that applications typically need, before you do any programming at all. All you have to do, metaphorically speaking, is to hang the desired pieces on the framework that REALbasic has already provided.

Second, REALbasic is *object-oriented*. The notion of an *object*, in programming, is a powerful and interesting one, which enables a style of programming called object-oriented programming, or *OOP*; we'll have much more to say about this later on. For now, think of OOP as a way of keeping code organized by segmenting it into parts, with each part having a clear, independent functionality. REALbasic enforces OOP, because it is object-oriented from the ground up; it actually makes you keep your code well organized. And REALbasic enforces a particularly natural and easy form of OOP, because it adopts as its primary objects the very elements of your application's interface that you would naturally think of as being objects—windows and buttons and other "physical" items the user will encounter while running your application.*

Third, REALbasic is an *integrated development environment*, or *IDE*. What does this mean? REALbasic is an environment because, figuratively speaking, it's a place where you work as you're programming. It's a development environment because what you're doing in that place is writing (developing) an application. It's integrated because it incorporates the mental aspect of programming, the writing of code, with the physical aspect, the representation of your program's objects. REALbasic shows you your objects as physical entities; for instance, you actually see your application's buttons and windows, and can physically arrange them. And then, because it's object-oriented, REALbasic compels you, and helps you, to associate whatever code you write with some particular object. Your code ends up in neat compartments, because REALbasic's environment consists of compartments. And your code's functionality is organized in a natural way, because those compartments are, in the first instance, the physical items of your application's interface.

You can thus expect your programming activity, as you develop an application with REALbasic, to be of two sorts: mental and physical. And these two aspects will be integrated with each other, thanks to REALbasic's object-oriented programming language and its IDE.

Some of the time, you'll be dictating to REALbasic how you want your application to look. For instance, you might want to say that in a certain window there should be a button of a certain size, with a certain caption, in a certain font. These are physical features of your application, and by and large you'll work with them physically—in essence, you'll "draw" what you want your application to look like. Drag an interface element into a window, and now that window contains that interface element; it's as simple as that. Indeed, in most cases it is possible to design and create a program's entire interface, "drawing" its windows and buttons and text fields and so forth, without writing a single line of code. (The creation of an application can thus easily be shared between a designer who doesn't know how to program and a programmer who has no sense of design.) What's remarkable is that the result is already in some sense a working application: when the application runs, its window appears, and a user can move the window, click its buttons, type and copy and paste text in its text fields, close the window, and even quit the application. That's because REALbasic is an application framework; from the outset, it is already handling all the petty conventional details of getting the interface to interact properly with the user and with the computer.

---

* Some texts insist upon a distinction between object-based programming, which means programming in the presence of objects, and object-oriented programming, which means programming in the presence of polymorphism. I find this distinction artificial; in this book, I just use "object-oriented."

At other times, you'll be dictating the behaviors and calculations that your application is to perform in response to user actions. This is the mental side of working with REALbasic—you're coding. The user has pressed this button—so what would you like to happen? The user is closing this window—so what would you like to happen? Perhaps, when the user chooses the File → Save menu item, the contents of the frontmost window should be saved as a textfile. Perhaps, when the user clicks a Help button, a Help window should appear. All things of this sort you specify by writing code; and at the same time, you'll associate that code physically with the appropriate object, so your code will remain well structured and clear. The code for what happens when a button is pressed is associated with the button; the code for what happens when a window is closed is associated with the window; the code for what happens when a menu item is chosen is associated with the menu item. You write your code in an easy, Basic-like language, which is compiled, not merely interpreted, so it runs quickly. Commonly needed facilities such as display of graphics, file handling, and network communications are built right in, so it's easy to obtain the functionality you're after; additional functionality can be provided through language extensions.

When you're done, you've a remarkably small, remarkably efficient standalone application—not, to be sure, as small or as efficient as if you'd written it in C and explicitly managed the various Toolbox utility routines yourself, but then this was the very thing you were trying to avoid in the first place. The trade-off here is one of ease, not to mention the time it takes (or doesn't take) to create an application with REALbasic, often a matter of mere minutes. For this reason, I find myself reaching for REALbasic to create all sorts of practical utilities. Something to print envelopes with bar codes? Something to count word occurrences in a textfile? Something to look up a dictionary definition on the Internet? Something to play my favorite card game with me? When I want an application of this sort, I don't have to wait for someone else to write it, and I don't have to pay someone else for it—I write it myself, with REALbasic. And REALbasic is not only for private programming; it has been used to create applications of commercial quality.*

REALbasic is also just a truly splendid way to program, or to learn programming. The language is small and simple. In the course of developing an application, it's easy to obtain satisfying partial results early on; this constant satisfaction keeps the programmer motivated, and makes REALbasic a natural candidate for an informal, incremental style of development. Even more impressive is REALbasic's inherent object orientation, which enforces good modern programming techniques, and inculcates, at an almost subconscious level, important higher-level notions such as classes and instances, encapsulation, and inheritance. I've taught REALbasic to children, and have seen them pick up the basics easily in a few days, writing an elementary animation program after a week and an object-oriented Tic-Tac-Toe game after

---

* Some examples are: Nisus Email, from the makers of the wonderful Nisus Writer word processor, *http://www.nisus.com/products/nisusemail/*; Intellinews, from Aladdin, makers of the StuffIt utilities, *http://www.aladdinsys.com/intellinews/*; and Whistle Blower, a server monitor utility, *http://whistleblower.sentman.com/*.

two weeks. I've picked up a C++ textbook which I had formerly found confusing, and understood it clearly and immediately; REALbasic had given me a full grasp of the object-oriented concepts that had previously eluded me. Whether you're a complete beginner or an experienced programmer, whether you treat it as a stepping-stone or as an end in itself, whether you want to create something useful or something fun, REALbasic is a great way to take charge of your Macintosh.

Versions, Editions, and Systems

When I started writing the first edition of this book toward the end of 1998, the current version of REALbasic was 1.0. By the time the manuscript was turned over to the publishers, REALbasic 2.0 had emerged, and the last version of REALbasic of which I was able to take account was 2.1a4. At about that time, by sheer happenstance, development of REALbasic slowed considerably, so after the first edition became available in October 1999, it remained substantially correct for REALbasic 2.1 when the latter appeared in April 2000—a rare circumstance in today's computer world, where printed books are usually left panting in the dust of the constantly evolving software they are trying to describe. REALbasic 2.1.2, which appeared soon after, was primarily a maintenance release, and the book was able to remain current, for all practical purposes, through the mediation of a web page of corrections that I posted at *http://www.tidbits.com/matt/rberrata.html*. In February 2001 the reprinting of the first edition provided an opportunity to correct some typographical errors, to account for some changed URLs, and to relieve readers of some unnecessary worry by deleting one or two outdated bug warnings.

Since then, REALbasic 3.0 has added many helpful features to the IDE, a complete rewrite of the SpriteSurface control, some rationalization of other built-in control class behaviors, better application memory management, greatly improved compilation for Windows, and the ability to compile for—and to run under—Mac OS X. There have also been numerous bug fixes (many of them, I'm proud to say, apparently inspired by criticisms, warnings, workarounds, and explanations in the book's first edition). The sum of these alterations is a substantially new REALbasic; hence this second edition of the book. The latest version of REALbasic available to me before the manuscript left my hands was 3.2.1, and while it is impossible, by the very nature of software and of books, for a printed book to be perfectly coordinated with the software it describes, you can be secure in the knowledge that I did my level best to be accurate right up to the last minute. Some differences between your copy of REALbasic and what this book describes would be no bad thing, if the reason is that some of the bugs mentioned in the book are fixed!

REALbasic itself is also available in two editions, though these are simultaneous, not successive: the difference is that only the higher edition comprises the full Windows compilation and database capabilities. Nowhere in this book do I comment upon this distinction; I simply describe the higher edition. Those with the standard edition should have no difficulty mentally deleting the irrelevant passages, which are very few, consisting mostly of Chapter 22 (on databases) and the various mentions of

Windows scattered throughout. Apart from this, the book applies equally to both editions of REALbasic.

Those who have purchased the higher edition of REALbasic in the expectation of building Windows executables may be disappointed to find that I don't devote much space to discussion of writing Windows-specific code. The truth is that this is not something I know a great deal about. This is primarily a Macintosh book, I'm primarily a Macintosh person, and REALbasic, let's face it, is primarily for writing Macintosh applications. My approach, therefore, is to assume that your application will be running on Macintosh. That is what I describe in detail. When I'm aware of the Windows implementation of a feature differing from the Macintosh implementation, I mention it as a deviation from the Macintosh standard; otherwise, I leave to your experimentation to discover the details about how particular features translate across platforms.

With Mac OS X, the problem is more one of timing. In a sense, the Mac OS X version of REALbasic is primary; to reflect this fact, the screen shots have been redone to reflect the new Aqua interface. Nevertheless, both Mac OS X and Version 3.2 of REALbasic that runs on it and builds for it are very new at the time of this writing. The "classic" REALbasic, which runs on and builds for Mac OS 7.6.1 through 9.x (to which I refer in this book, for want of a better name, as "Mac OS Classic"), is noticeably more mature and reliable. So I have ended up treating this as the standard, with Mac OS X differences treated as deviations from it, where I know about them.

The first edition of this book included, for the benefit of those who, for some unknown reason, persisted in using REALbasic Version 1, an appendix summarizing the differences between it and Version 2. It has not, however, been deemed worthwhile to maintain such backward compatibility in this new edition, precisely because it *is* a new edition. Those who have not migrated to REALbasic 3.2 can continue to use the first edition; meanwhile, the second edition is about REALbasic 3.2, and treats earlier versions of the program mostly as if they never were.

Acknowledgments

Hard as it is to believe, REALbasic was essentially the brainchild of one man, Andrew Barry. Or perhaps this is not so surprising, since why should we expect great software to be designed and produced by committee? I've never met or spoken to Andrew, but I feel as if I know him intimately. From the structure of REALbasic itself and from Andrew's letters to the REALbasic mailing lists, I came to appreciate his profound, original insights into the nature of programming, and to see him as an extraordinary coder, a great teacher, a patient and generous helper, a sharp computer scientist, and something of a philosopher. To know his work has been a deep and abiding pleasure, and I hope that this book can in some measure serve as a sign of my appreciation and gratitude for his gift to the world.

At REAL Software, Inc., first Jannice Faber and then Geoff Perlman saw to it in the early days that I was supplied with a copy of REALbasic; this courtesy was much appreciated. Since then, my relationship with REAL Software has continued to be a pleasure, including some heated arguments which I hope they enjoyed as much as I did, and culminating in their awarding me the 2000 Cubie award as REALbasic Advocate of the Year, a proud honor indeed. Lorin Rivers, the product manager for REALbasic, has overseen various mutually agreeable arrangements. David Grogono has done splendidly the job I'd like to have had, providing technical assistance to users and bringing bugs to the special attention of the programming team; I have benefited from both categories of his work. Programmers Cortis Clark, Joe Strout, and William Yu have shown ingenuity, persistence, and balanced judgment in picking up the work where Andrew Barry left off, and also in providing answers on the REALbasic mailing lists. In this regard, though I greatly appreciate the contributions of all three, I think Joe Strout deserves special mention, for his constant presence on the lists, his patient and generous willingness to provide detailed information about REALbasic's inner workings, and his ability to squash a bug or re-architect an entire REALbasic control class in amazingly short order. He is a presence on the Internet in various other guises as well, and it simply beats me where he gets his energy and his time. In any case, this edition of the book has been the beneficiary of his kindness; whatever I have learned since the first edition about what goes on inside the magic black box that is REALbasic, I have learned by hanging on the words of Joe Strout. To all the team, I hope that this book serves as a token of my gratitude, and that it helps REALbasic to go far in the world, as well it deserves to.

I should like to say a word also about the documentation included with REALbasic (written originally by Geoff, though various hands since then have labored to keep it up-to-date and corrected), along with the release notes provided at each iteration of the development process. My book is, I should make clear, in no sense a mere rehash of this documentation. It is, on the contrary, a thoroughly original work: I have disagreed with the organization and terminology of REAL's documentation, going to great lengths to create better terminology and explanations of my own; I have approached with skepticism and suspicion every assertion in REAL's documentation, and have taken much time confirming or denying each one for myself, in the process finding many downright mistakes and omissions (some of which, of course, were later corrected in REAL's documentation on the basis of the first edition of this book); I have even deliberately ignored the REAL documentation's examples and skipped reading entire passages, so as to approach the subject for myself with an open mind and to guarantee that the book is, except where specified in a footnote, "all my own work." In short, this book documents my own approach to the learning and teaching of REALbasic, as I have come to understand it by experimentation, discussion, and thought. Nevertheless, it is also perfectly obvious that my book simply couldn't exist without REAL's documentation, which made REALbasic remarkably easy for me to learn at the initial stages, and which remains the primary source of facts in detail—there are, indeed, several places in this book where, with no reluctance whatever, I refer the reader to it for further information. So, to all at REAL who have contributed to the documentation and the release notes, a special thanks.

At O'Reilly & Associates, my first thanks go to Tim O'Reilly, my publisher and initial editor, for being willing to take on this book. He's smart and helpful, and it's a pleasure and an honor to work with him. Second, many thanks to the late Frank Willison, my original editor-in-chief. He was smart and helpful, and it was a pleasure and an honor to work with him too. It was through Frank's generosity that I obtained a copy of FrameMaker in which to compose the manuscript, thus enabling the book to move through production much more rapidly and accurately than it otherwise might have done. He also did some smoothing of troubled waters, above and beyond the call of duty. He will be missed.

What makes FrameMaker, for all its faults, a pleasure to work with, is Mike Sierra's brilliant series of templates. Robert Romano redrew the diagrams to make them professional, and provided clear and helpful instructions about them. For the first edition, Nancy Kotary was the production manager, occasional diplomat, and, as ever, a good friend, and Maureen Dempsey provided extensive production support and guided the first edition through its final stages. Cathy Record and Suzanne Axtell assisted greatly with the book's postpublication fate, and treated me to a memorable meal. Rachel Wheeler oversaw the corrected reprint of the first edition. For the second edition, Troy Mott was editor, and made several insightful suggestions that have resulted in a friendlier exposition. Mary Brady was the hard-working production editor; her friendly professionalism was a great comfort, and the book owes its polish and consistency to her and to the sharp eyes and amazing memory of proofreader Norma Emory. To them all, and to the many others who, unbeknownst to us mere authors, mysteriously cause O'Reilly books to see the light of day, thanks.

This book owes a very, very great deal to the users who haunt the REALbasic mailing lists. I learned from what they asked; I learned from what they answered; I learned from what they got wrong; I learned from what they got right; I learned from explaining to them; I learned from what I couldn't explain. In the years I have spent in their virtual company, we have grown together, like the fellow classmates that we are. I should like to thank them, one and all, for letting me play in their sandbox. It would be impossible for me to single out by name all those list members who have made a difference to this book. Some, those from whom I took particular nuggets of information or lines of illustrative code, are thanked in footnotes. But others have helped me in a more general way, probably without knowing it or intending to, just by being the kinds of people they are, knowing the kinds of things they know, and making the kinds of arguments they make. Since they are not mentioned elsewhere, I would like to thank them here: they are Anjo Krank, Fabian Lidman, James Milne, Rudi Muiznieks, Søren Olin, Fabian Rueger, Steve Schacht, James Sentman, Art Urban, Jan Vanderwegen, and Paul Welty. Special mention must go to Seth Dillingham, who generously gave of his time to supply me with his entire archives of the mailing list as I was getting started with the first edition. Thomas Tempelmann and Tonio Loewald performed extensive technical review of the final draft of the first edition, for which I am very grateful; the book was crucially improved through their corrections and suggestions. Ken Hagler also did some sharp-eyed proofreading, saving me from many silly mistakes. For this edition, the book was helped immeasurably by the technical review comments of Apple Computer's Quinn ("The Eskimo!") and of REAL Software's Cortis Clark and David Grogono.

From its readership this book has benefited twice. First, on a personal level, there are all those who, while the book was being written, though anxious for it to be finished and available, did not chastise me for how long it was taking, but cheered and urged me on, and those who, after it was published, took the time to send along words of commendation and appreciation. Their enthusiasm beforehand is what brought this book to life; their insightful response afterward is what made the time and the effort worthwhile. Second, on a critical level, errors were spotted and suggestions both pedagogical and technical were offered by numerous readers, and the simple fact is that if this second edition is an improvement over the first, it would not be so without them. Once again there are too many to mention by name, but I cannot resist citing here, because they are not mentioned elsewhere in the book, George Bate, Joe Brown (several gold stars), Bernd Froehlich, Dave Fultz, Joe Huber, Fabian Lidman, Tony Rich, Donald Siano, Bob Stern, Mark Stubbs, Kem Tekinay, Bob Urschel, James Wilson (several more gold stars), Charles Yeomans, and Andrew Who Is Nice to Bears. I know that there are others whose names I've omitted; I apologize, but I hope at least that when you see what effect you had on this edition you will realize that I listened and was grateful.

Finally, the traditional caveat is in order. Though I have received inspiration and advice from many quarters, nonetheless, someone has to take ultimate responsibility, and it's clear who that is. There may, in this book, be accidental omissions, or areas where my understanding is faulty, or places where I guessed wrong, or points on which I should have taken the advice I was offered but didn't. In short, this is my book, and the errors and shortcomings are my own, and no one else's. I apologize for them, and I hope you'll let me know about them, so that perhaps they can be mended in the future.

How to Contact Us

We have tested and verified all the information in this book to the best of our ability. If you have an idea that could make this book better, please let us know by writing to us at:

O'Reilly & Associates, Inc.
101 Morris Street
Sebastopol, CA 95472
(800) 998-9938 (in the U.S. or Canada)
(707) 829-0515 (international/local)
(707) 829-0104 (fax)

There is a web page for this book, which lists errata, examples, or any additional information. You can access this page at:

http://www.oreilly.com/catalog/realbasic2

To comment or ask technical questions about this book, send email to:

bookquestions@oreilly.com

For more information about books, conferences, software, Resource Centers, and the O'Reilly Network, see the O'Reilly web site at:

http://www.oreilly.com

To contact the author, send email to:

matt@tidbits.com

Most of the code examples in this book can be downloaded as REALbasic files, some of them in expanded form, from the author's web site. The site also contains additional examples too large or elaborate to appear in the book, as well as pages documenting errors and corrections as they accumulate. The site is here:

http://www.tidbits.com/matt/

Conventions

The following typographical conventions are used in this book:

Constant width
> Used to indicate keywords, names of variables and parameters, values (such as string and numeric literals), code, and comments embedded within the code.

Constant width bold
> Used to indicate user input in examples.

Italic
> Used to introduce new terms and to indicate URLs, filenames, and notes to the reader within code blocks.

 This icon indicates a tip, suggestion, or general note.

 This icon indicates a warning or caution.

Beyond This Book

No one volume, not even a great big one like this, can tell you everything you want to know about REALbasic, for the simple reason that it's impossible to guess what you might want to do with REALbasic. REALbasic is a tool to make tools, a program to make programs, and its uses are as various as the needs and desires and imaginations of all its users. So here are a few other resources that you might like to look at.

For REALbasic resources, a good starting place is REAL's own site, *http://www. realsoftware.com/*, especially the "Made with REALbasic" page, *http://www.realbasic. com/realbasic/mwrb.html*, where you can find links to hundreds of downloadable code examples, classes, and model applications from generous users. There is also the REALbasic web ring, *http://nav.webring.yahoo.com/hub?ring=xbasic&list*, a portal to dozens of user-maintained sites. I would also strongly recommend that you consider joining the REALbasic mailing list, which is haunted by people who (for some unknown reason) actually want to help you learn this program: "Operators are waiting to take your call!" Subscription information appears at REAL's site. There is also a Usenet newsgroup, *news://comp.lang.basic.realbasic*.

REALbasic lets you design your own interface, but it has no power whatever to keep you from designing it badly, nor can it cope with every nutty idea you might throw at it. Since REALbasic makes it all too easy to do whatever you like with the interface, you should know something about the principles of good interface design. I particularly recommend *Tog on Interface*, by Bruce Tognazzini (Addison-Wesley, 1992). Also, if you're writing a Macintosh program, you should know how the parts of a Macintosh program are expected to behave. The official word on this topic is Apple Computer's own Human Interface Guidelines, which can be found at *http://developer. apple.com/techpubs/macos8/HumanInterfaceToolbox/HumanInterfaceGuide/humanint-erfaceguide.html*; as this book goes to press, the corresponding Mac OS X resource is available for download only in preliminary form, at *http://developer.apple.com/tech-pubs/macosx/SystemOverview/AquaGuidelines.pdf*.

This book is not a computer science textbook, and although it contains many examples, it is not a compendium of algorithms. If you want to know how to sort, or how to make an interesting data structure such as a binary tree or a doubly-linked list, this book won't tell you. There are many books that do, and although they don't use REALbasic's own language, the principles are identical on any computer and in any language. The granddaddy of all such books is Donald Ervin Knuth's *The Art of Computer Programming*, 3d ed. (Addison Wesley, 1998); a fine practical introduction to algorithms and data structures is Robert Sedgewick, *Algorithms in C++* (Addison Wesley, 1998). To understand computer programs deeply, read Harold Abelson et al., *Structure and Interpretation of Computer Programs*, 2d ed. (MIT Press, 1996).

There are many, many numerical and graphical cookbooks: the best numerics text is William H. Press et al., *Numerical Recipes* (Cambridge, 1992), available online at *http://lib-www.lanl.gov/numerical/bookcpdf.html*; good graphics texts are David Rogers, *Mathematical Elements for Computer Graphics,* 2d ed. (McGraw-Hill, 1989), and the several volumes of the *Graphics Gems* series (Academic Press, 1993–1995).

Another thing this book can't teach in depth is object-oriented design. I do try very hard to give a sense of how to organize your program in an object-oriented way in line with the structure of REALbasic's built-in object model, but as your programs become more complex and you start adding a lot of objects, you've gone beyond REALbasic itself into a world to which many books are already devoted. I particularly recommend Martin Fowler et al., *Refactoring* (Addison Wesley, 1999); its philosophy of both the nature and purpose of object-oriented code and the programmer's day-to-day tasks have proved nothing short of revolutionary in my own life.

Finally, although this book teaches you to program REALbasic, and although it assumes that you will use REALbasic to write Macintosh programs, this book does not teach you to program the Macintosh or how a Macintosh works. The ultimate source on that topic is, of course, the massive *Inside Macintosh*. Much of it is available online, as web pages and as downloadable PDF files; the places to start are *http://developer.apple.com/techpubs/macos8/mac8.html* and its Mac OS X counterpart *http://developer.apple.com/techpubs/macosx/macosx.html*. You can also purchase much of this documentation on CD-ROM or in book form. The Windows equivalent web pages may be found at *http://msdn.microsoft.com/library/default.asp*.

Fundamentals

REALbasic is a development environment, a programming language, an object-oriented hierarchy of classes and subclasses, and an application framework. In Part I, all of these aspects of REALbasic are explained.

You'll be guided through the REALbasic workspace, and learn how to create, edit, and debug your application project there; you'll find the syntax of the REALbasic language summarized, along with a discussion of how its fundamental datatypes are handled; you'll learn what object-oriented programming is, how REALbasic enforces and simplifies object orientation both in its workspace and in its language, how to envision your application in terms of objects, and when and how to create new classes of object; and you'll see how REALbasic structures an application by means of the hierarchy of built-in classes and the event messages it automatically sends them.

The chapters in Part I are:

Chapter 1, *The Workspace*
Chapter 2, *The Basic Language*
Chapter 3, *Objects, Classes, and Instances*
Chapter 4, *Class Relationships and Class Features*
Chapter 5, *Datatypes*
Chapter 6, *Menus*
Chapter 7, *The Architecture of an Application*
Chapter 8, *Debugging and Building*

In this chapter:
- The Project Window
- Editing Windows
- Adding Functionality
- How the Three Editors Relate
- Testing Without Building
- Online Help
- Shortcuts

CHAPTER 1

The Workspace

This chapter introduces the REALbasic workspace, also called the IDE (for *integrated development environment*; see "What REALbasic Is Like" in the Preface). We'll tour the IDE's various windows and talk about what they do and how you work with them. By way of illustration, we'll actually build a working application. So you might want to follow along on your computer, with REALbasic running. You'll discover that writing an application with REALbasic can be almost effortless, involving just a few swift, easy moves on your part, and that the IDE is extremely simple, consisting of a very small number of windows and menus. (Figure 1-1 shows the REALbasic IDE in action. Don't worry, this is not the working application we'll be building in this chapter! If you're curious, it's my Durak card-playing program, which you can download from my web site.)

The Project Window

When you start up REALbasic by opening it from the Finder, two windows occupy the center of your screen, as shown in Figure 1-2.

The rear window is the Project Window. If you close the Project Window, or if you don't see it, you can open it and bring it to the front by choosing Window → Project. The Project Window represents your project, and provides access to its components.

The Project

What is a project? Simply put, it's a REALbasic document file on disk. Every application that you create with REALbasic is represented by, and will ultimately be generated from, a single REALbasic project document. The project file is not, itself, the application you're planning on creating; it's a much smaller file where you tell REALbasic all about that application. With REALbasic, you work on a project file; when it's ready, you tell REALbasic to generate (or *build*) your application from it.

In Figure 1-2, REALbasic was started up directly from the Finder without specifying an existing project file, so a new project has been created automatically. No project

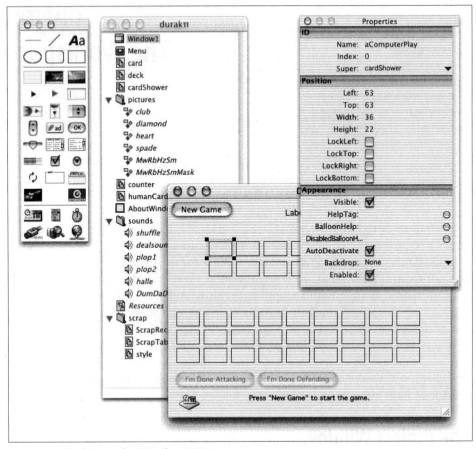

Figure 1-1. Working in the REALbasic IDE

file exists yet; that's why the Project Window's title is Untitled. Once the project is saved to disk, by choosing File → Save, the Project Window will take on the name assigned to the project file. (For instance, one might save this project as *My First Project*.) A project file on disk works like any document file: it can be opened by choosing File → Open within REALbasic, or it can be opened from the Finder, which will also start up REALbasic if necessary; and you can create a new project by choosing File → New. To keep things simple, exactly one project can be open at a time; when REALbasic is running, and you open a project or create a new one, the currently open project will be closed (REALbasic will offer to save it first).

Project Components

The Project Window lists, and provides access to, the components of your project. Such components include one menubar object, plus all the types of window your

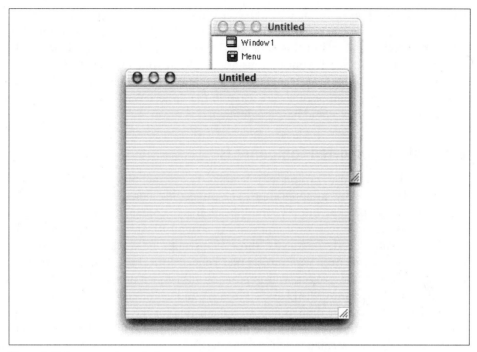

Figure 1-2. A new empty project

application is to be able to show, plus any classes and modules you've created for encapsulating pieces of your code, plus any external files associated with the project.*

The Project Window in Figure 1-2 shows the project's menubar object and one window type, called Window1. REALbasic has created this window type automatically, because in REALbasic's object model, an application usually has a default window type. In a new project, Window1 is your project's default window type.

To access a component of your project, double-click its listing in the Project Window, or select its listing in the Project Window and hit Return. If, in Figure 1-2, you bring the Project Window to the front and double-click Window1, the other window in the figure returns to the front. That's because this other window *is* Window1—or, more properly, it is the Window Editor for Window1 (we'll talk more about Window Editors in a moment). You can hide the Window1 Window Editor in the usual ways (by choosing File → Close, or by clicking its go-away box), and you can make it reappear by again double-clicking Window1 in the Project Window.

---

* External files are discussed in the next section, "External and Imported Components." You needn't concern yourself yet over what classes and modules are. Classes, including windows, are discussed in Chapter 3; modules, and the creation of new classes, are discussed in Chapter 4. Chapter 6 explains how to work with the menubar object. The default window is treated in Chapter 3, Chapter 7, and Chapter 9.

Each project component listing in the Project Window has a contextual menu, which you access in the usual way (by holding down the Ctrl key and then clicking on a listing). The precise contents of this contextual menu depend upon the nature of the component. For Window1, your options are to edit it, which is exactly the same as double-clicking Window1, or to encrypt it (encryption is discussed later in this chapter). If any external components were listed in the Project Window, your options in their contextual menus would be quite different.

External and Imported Components

Some components of your project may be ancillary external files that REALbasic will need in order to build your application. The project file alone is sufficient for creating a minimal application, but if your application is to contain any pictures, sounds, movies, or other resources, or if you want to extend REALbasic's functionality by means of compiled code fragments, those items must be made available through external files, separate from your project file. To alert REALbasic that such a file is to be associated with the project, you *import* the file: either drag-and-drop the file's icon from the Finder into REALbasic's Project Window, or choose File → Import in REALbasic and select the desired file. An italic listing for the file will then appear in the Project Window, showing that the file's contents are available to your project's code.* (Figure 1-1 shows many such italic listings.)

Figure 1-3 shows a schematic of the relationship between REALbasic, a project file, some external files, and the final built application. What this diagram tries to show is that REALbasic and the project file "belong" to one another, like a word-processing application and document. External files are imported into the project, meaning only that the project file maintains an internal reference to them; the contents of the external files are not incorporated into the project. When editing ends, all of these assets are assembled into the independent built application, meaning that their contents *are* incorporated directly into it. The external files are thus not needed by the built application; it is a standalone application. Therefore, once the application has been built for the last time, if you know that you will never edit the project and build the application again, you can throw away the external files.

When you import an external file, you don't really import anything from the external file into the project file; that is, the contents of the external file are not added to the project file. Instead, what happens is merely that an internal reference is created within the project file, pointing to the external file. This means that the external file, even after it has been imported, is still needed in order for you to build your application; therefore it must, throughout the development process, continue to exist where the project file can find it. (The exception is cursors, which are in fact added to the project file when they are imported.)

---

* Each of these types of entity is discussed later, in the chapter describing how to manipulate it in code.

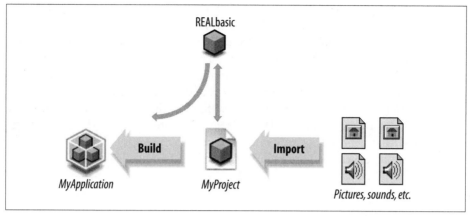

Figure 1-3. The relationship between project, external files, and built application

Rather confusingly, the rules about how the project file's internal references are maintained depend upon the nature of the external file. If the external file is a picture, a sound, or a movie, the reference is maintained in two ways: by its pathname and, if the external file is located at any depth within the same folder as the project file, by a relative pathname. This means that you can move the project file, and the project file will still be able to find the external file using the full pathname, and you can move the folder containing the project file and (at some deeper level) the external file, and the project file will still be able to find the external file using the relative pathname. But if you move just the external file, the project will lose track of it and will no longer work properly. For other kinds of external file, the internal reference is maintained as an alias. This means that you can move the external file anywhere within the same volume and the project will still be able to find it, but if you move the external file to a different volume (and delete the original) the project will lose track of it and will no longer work properly.

It is, however, by no means a disaster for a project to lose track of an external file, since if REALbasic can't find an external file when you open a project, it will simply ask you where it is, offering you a chance to repoint its internal reference. Furthermore, as soon as you show REALbasic where *any* of a project's lost external files are, it will automatically try to find *all* of them there; so a reasonable strategy is to keep all of a project's external files in a single folder, since the penalty for moving that folder is merely to have to show the project where it is, once. Still another option is to keep any external files in the same folder as the project file, because a REALbasic project file will always look for its external files in the same folder as itself, automatically, as a last resort.

An external file's listing in the Project Window can be double-clicked, or you can select it and hit Return, to view the contents of the external file inside REALbasic if this is possible. In the case of a sound, the sound is played. In the case of a picture, the picture is shown. In the case of a movie, the first frame of the movie is shown, along with a movie controller with which you can run the movie but on Mac OS X, movies can't be previewed in this way—at least, it doesn't work on my machine. On the other hand, trying to "open" an AppleScript or a Resource file in this way opens the file in an external editor, not in REALbasic itself; and trying to open an XCMD does nothing. An external file's listing in the Project Window also has a contextual menu where various operations can be performed on it; these include opening or showing the external file itself from the Finder, and viewing or changing the project's internal path to the file. To delete an external file's listing from the Project Window, select it and hit Delete, or choose Delete from the contextual menu; this deletes the listing only (that is, it breaks the association between the project file and the external file), with no effect upon the external file itself.

Folders

If your project contains more than a few components, you may wish to organize them within the Project Window. Unfortunately, this is not simple to do; you cannot, for example, just drag the component listings within the Project Window to rearrange them. You can, however, distribute the components amongst "folders" inside the Project Window. These are not real folders; they have no significance except as organizational and navigational devices. To create a folder within the Project Window, choose File → New Folder. (To change the name of the resulting folder, use its Name entry in the Properties Window, as discussed later in this chapter.) You can drag a component listing into or out of a folder; you can click a folder's disclosure triangle, or double-click its listing, to expand or collapse your view of its contents. (Figure 1-1 contains some folders.)

You can't rearrange component listings inside a folder, any more than you can within the Project Window. Folders do, however, remember the order in which you add items to them—the last item added to a folder is the last item listed within it—and the same is true of the Project Window itself. This means that by dragging component listings into and out of folders, you can eventually achieve the desired order. It can be a clumsy, tedious process, reminiscent of one of those puzzles where you have to slide one square out of the way in order to slide another into place; but it's better than nothing. Personally, I often find it more straightforward to export the whole project as XML, rearrange the items in folders in a text editor, and reimport; XML exporting is discussed later in this chapter.

Editing Windows

It may surprise you to learn at this point that, although you haven't edited your new project at all, you can already build a working application. To do so, you'll probably wish to save the project file if you haven't already; then choose File → Build Application, specify a name for the built application in the dialog (or just accept the default name, AppName), and click the Build button. Note that the application will be created in the same folder as your project file, and that you cannot elect to create it anywhere else. (If you don't save the project file before building, the application is created in the same folder as REALbasic.) Then, in the Finder, look in that folder; lo and behold, there's now an application called AppName (or whatever you decided to name it). Open this icon from the Finder to run the application.

 The Build Application dialog does not warn you before replacing an existing file with the specified name when you hit the Build button (though it will refuse to replace a running application). There's a good reason for this: you can expect to build the same application many times in the course of development, and it would drive you mad to have to jump each time through any more hoops than you must do already (indeed, in time you'll probably resent even the Build Application dialog). So take care when specifying the name of an existing file, as REALbasic will happily (and silently) overwrite it.

One might be tempted to dismiss the resulting application as useless—which, indeed, it is. It does nothing. It consists entirely of an empty window; click the window's go-away box, and it consists of nothing at all. But although it has no functionality, this application is hardly inconsiderable. The application puts up a window; the window redraws itself properly when covered and uncovered by another application's window; the window can be moved or dismissed; the application runs, harmlessly, among the other applications on your computer, and you can switch between applications as usual; the application has two menus, a File menu and an Edit menu; and the File menu contains a Quit item, which works, either by choosing it manually or by hitting Command-Q. (On Mac OS X, the Quit item is in the system's application menu; for example, if your application is called AppName, then there's a Quit AppName item in the AppName menu.)

That's hardly trivial, as anyone knows who has tried to accomplish the same thing by writing and compiling an application from scratch in Pascal or C. But you didn't have to accomplish any of it; REALbasic accomplished it for you. REALbasic is an application framework; it knows how to construct an application. It also knows how to implement the basic elements of an application's interface, as we shall now see.

The Tools Window

Towards the left of the screen in the IDE is a floating window consisting of a couple of dozen icons. This is the Tools Window. If the Tools Window is closed, it can be opened by choosing Window → Show Tools. The orientation of the Tools Window may be toggled between vertical and horizontal by clicking its zoom box. The icons in the Tools Window correspond to types of interface element that you can place into a window of your application (see Figure 1-4).*

---

* To learn the meaning of each icon in the Tools Window, hover the mouse over it (on Mac OS Classic, turn on balloon help first). In REALbasic 3.5, several new icons will be added, and the layout will look somewhat different from Figure 1-4.

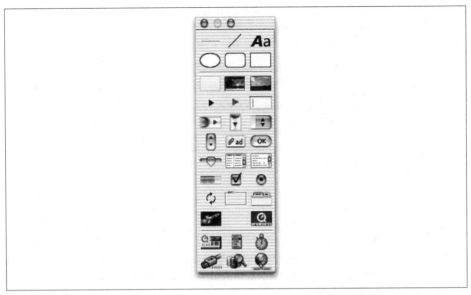

Figure 1-4. The Tools Window

(Time out for some technical talk. An interface element in a window is called a *control*, so the icons in the Tools Window all represent built-in control types. Within REALbasic's class hierarchy, there is also a Control class; most of the icons in the Tools Window represent subclasses of the Control class, but some do not.)

The Tools Window may look like a palette for choosing a tool "mode," as in a draw program, but it isn't; you don't click an icon. All you ever do with the Tools Window is to drag-and-drop an icon from it into a Window Editor, thus adding to the window a control of that type.

Let's try it. Suppose you want your window to contain a button. Click and hold the mouse on the PushButton icon in the Tools Window (it's the one containing the letters OK), and, with the mouse still down, drag the dotted rectangle into the Window1 Window Editor; then release the mouse. At that spot in the window, a button appears, with the caption Untitled.

You have just performed what I like to call the "fundamental act" of REALbasic (illustrated in Figure 1-5): grab a control from the Tools Window, drag it into a Window Editor, and drop it. The change made in the Window Editor will be reflected in the built application. If you choose File → Build Application and run the built application, you'll see that the window now contains a button.

Manipulating Controls

In a Window Editor, you can manually edit the position and appearance of a control. It can be repositioned by dragging it (or by selecting it and then using the arrow

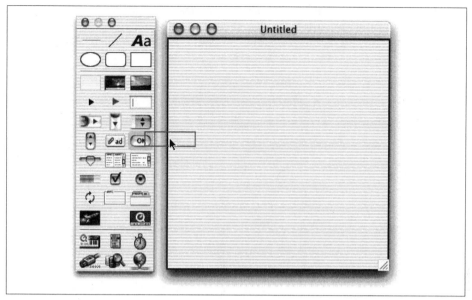

Figure 1-5. The "fundamental act" of REALbasic

keys); most controls can be resized by dragging one of the four selection handles that appear at its corners when it is selected. In the case of a control with a textual component, you can edit the text by typing. For instance, after selecting a button, you can type to replace the caption that appears inside it; hit Return or Enter afterward, to "set" what you have typed as the actual caption. (If you start typing with no control selected, you'll edit the title of the window itself.) In the case of a button, you can also choose from the Font, Size, and Style submenus of the Format menu to change the caption's appearance. If you've been following along with the hands-on example, you might want to experiment with your window's new button; try changing its caption to something meaningful and inviting, such as Push Me.

To help you manipulate controls, Window Editors have the capabilities of a rudimentary draw program. You can select controls by clicking, Shift-clicking, or dragging. You can change the layering order of controls, and align them automatically, through commands in the Format menu. You can copy-and-paste controls, and duplicate them so that the new copies appear evenly spaced. You can remove a selected control by cutting it, or by hitting Delete to clear it completely. Such physical editing methods are similar to those employed by most draw programs, and there's no need to detail them further here. Experimentation will rapidly bring familiarity. A few additional tips appear in the last section of this chapter.

The Properties Window

Another way to edit a control's appearance is by way of the Properties Window, which appears initially to the right of the screen (see Figure 1-6). If the Properties

Window has been closed, it can be opened by choosing Window → Show Properties. The contents of the Properties Window change to reflect whatever is selected in the IDE—not just controls, but also windows and other Project Window listings.

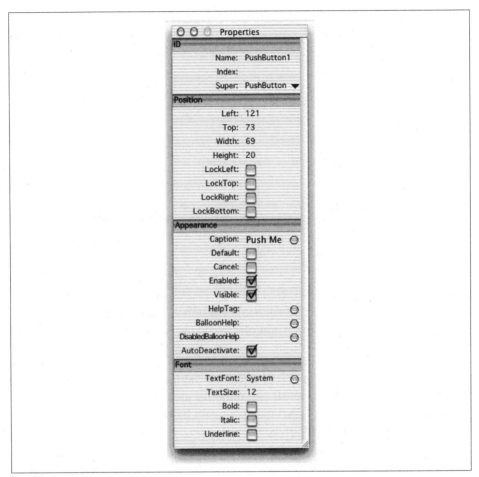

Figure 1-6. The Properties Window

Each line of the Properties Window, except for the outdented bold lines (they are just convenient organizational labels), represents a predefined feature, or *property*, of the selected entity; on the left side of the window is shown the name of the property, and on the right side is shown its value. What properties are listed in the Properties Window depends upon the type of entity that is selected at that moment; each entity type has its own predefined property set. The individual properties will be discussed in later chapters, in connection with each particular type of entity.

The value of a property can be changed by working directly in the Properties Window. The Properties Window is also "live," so if you edit a control physically in its Window Editor, the corresponding values in the Properties Window change

Code Editor is accessed by way of the object's physical avatar—either its Window Editor (in the case of a window), or its listing in the Project Window.

Opening the Code Editor may cause some of the other windows, such as the Properties Window and the Tools Window, to vanish; they reappear when the Code Editor is closed or is no longer frontmost. This behavior, called *autohide*, makes sense, since the Tools Window is useful only when a Window Editor is frontmost, and the Properties Window is useful only with regard to the current selection in the Project Window or the Window Editor. Nevertheless, all this vanishing and appearing of windows may be distracting. You can change REALbasic's auto-hide behavior in the dialog that appears when you choose Edit → Preferences (in Mac OS X, it's REALbasic → REALbasic Preferences). Incidentally, this dialog is also where you set the font and size for code in the Code Editor.

A Code Editor is divided into two parts. On the left is a browser, allowing navigation to each of the snippets of code, or *handlers*, that this Code Editor contains. The actual code appears, and is edited, on the right. Think of a handler as a drawer or a pigeonhole, where a piece of code can be stored. Each Code Editor can have many handlers; on the left, in the browser, you can see all their names, but you can see and work on the code inside only one handler at a time, on the right.

The browser's contents are bundled into categories. Each category listing has a disclosure triangle; to expand or collapse your view of the browser's content, click a disclosure triangle, or double-click a category listing. A window's Code Editor has five top-level categories: Controls, Events, Menu Handlers, Methods, and Properties. These are all categories of handler, except for Properties which is a different category of entity altogether.

Within each category, any existing handlers (or, in the case of the Properties category, any existing properties) are listed by name. In the Controls category, each control in the window is listed, and is itself a category containing that control's handlers. Clicking a handler listing in the browser causes the code of that handler to appear on the right, so you can read and edit it. Once any code has actually been added to a handler, its browser listing on the left becomes bold, as do its containing category listings; this makes it easy to know where the code is. Another option is to "winnow" the listings on the left by clicking the second button at the bottom of the Code Editor window; this toggles between a state where all handlers are listed and a state where the listings for any handlers or controls that lack code (and so are not bold) are omitted.

In Figure 1-7, although Pushbutton1 has some handlers and so does Events, there are no handlers under Menu Handlers or Methods, and no properties under Properties. That's because you haven't defined any; as we shall see, REALbasic provides control handlers and event handlers, but any menu handlers, methods, or properties are supplied by the programmer.

Editing and Executing Code

Let's now enter our code to be executed when the user clicks the button. If you have been exploring the Code Editor browser, arrange it so it looks like Figure 1-7—so that we are working with PushButton1, which is our button, and in particular with the handler called Action, which is the code that runs when the user pushes the button. Then, on the right side of the Code Editor, enter the code so it looks like Figure 1-8. You may have to widen the window to see what you're doing; unfortunately, the Code Editor does not wrap long lines, and you cannot split a long line into multiple lines—REALbasic code has no "continuation character."

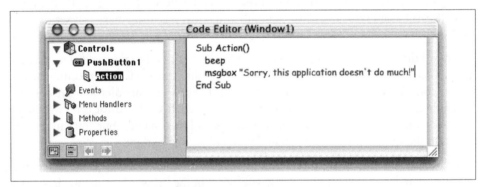

Figure 1-8. Entering code in the Code Editor

As you're typing code, REALbasic tries to guess what you're going to say and shows its guesses by offering to complete the current word in dimmed letters to the right of where you're typing. This is REALbasic's "intelligent typeahead" feature. To accept REALbasic's guess, hit Tab; to reject it, just keep typing. If REALbasic displays ellipsis marks at the end of its guess, that means it can think of more than one alternative for how you might continue typing at that point; if you tab into the ellipsis marks, a list of those alternatives appears, and you can select among them using the up and down arrow keys, accept the current selection by hitting Tab, Return, or right arrow, or hide the list by hitting Esc, Delete, or left arrow. (Or you can use the mouse: click an alternative to accept it, click outside the list to hide it.)

Another "intelligent" feature of code entry is that lines are automatically prettyprinted: REALbasic uses its knowledge of its own keywords and syntactic structures to color-code words and indent lines in such a way as to clarify their linguistic status. So don't indent lines yourself by adding spaces or tabs (in fact, you can't type a tab character into the Code Editor); let REALbasic do it for you.

The desired functionality having been added in the correct place, we can now execute it within the built application. First, you'll probably wish to save the project by choosing File → Save; it's not a bad idea to save your project fairly frequently in REALbasic, and before building is a good time. Now build the application, and open the built application from the Finder to run it. The application puts up a window

Another nice feature of the Language Reference is that it tries to guess from the context what you might be wanting help on. In a Code Editor, select the word `msgBox` and open the Language Reference; you'll see the help page on MsgBox. In a Window Editor, select a PushButton and open the Language Reference; you'll see the help page on PushButton.

Shortcuts

This completes the tour of the REALbasic workspace. What follows is a summary of nonobvious shortcuts for navigating and working in the IDE. Some of them we've met earlier in the chapter; others are new.

To open a window's Window Editor
    If you're in the Project Window, double-click the window's listing; or select the window's listing and hit Return; or bring up the contextual menu associated with the window's listing and choose Edit. If you're in the window's Code Editor, hit Option-Tab, or press the first button at the bottom of the Code Editor window.

To add a control to a Window Editor
    Drag the control's icon from the Tools Window into the Project Window, or copy-and-paste or duplicate an existing control. (In Chapter 3, we will learn that there is another way: you can drag a class listing from the Project Window into the Window Editor.)

In a Window Editor, to select the next control
    Hit Tab. This can be particularly useful when controls obscure one another or are otherwise difficult to select; it works even when the control is located beyond the bounds of the Window Editor and is therefore invisible. It is helpful also as a way of changing what object's properties show up in the Properties Window.

In a Window Editor, while positioning a control, to disable "intelligent" alignment
    Hold Command while dragging the control, or position it using the Properties Window.

In the Properties Window, to "set" a string or number value
    Hit Return or Enter.

In the Properties Window, to cancel a change to a string or number value
    Hit Esc (before hitting Return).

In the Properties Window, to navigate to the next/previous text-editable property
    Hit Tab/Shift-Tab.

In the Properties Window, to set a font property to the System font
    Enter the word "System." The idea here is to give you a way to specify that the object's font should be whatever the System font is on the machine where the application runs; this is needed because you can't know in advance what the System font will be. If you set the font size to 0 it will end up at the default size for whatever platform the application is built for.

In the Project Window, to remove an item
Select it, then hit Delete. Be careful; whatever code is associated with the item is also deleted.

In the Project Window, to rename an item
Select it, then hit Tab. This selects the value of the Name property in the Properties Window, ready for you to type a new name.

In the Project Window, to view an external file
Double-click the item's listing; or select it, then hit Return; or use the item's contextual menu.

In the Project Window, to navigate among project components
Use the up and down arrow keys.

To open a Code Editor
In the case of a class or module, or of a window when the project is running in the IDE, double-click its listing in the Project Window, or select its listing in the Project Window and hit Return.

In the case of a window when the project is not running in the IDE, select its listing in the Project Window, or bring its Window Editor to the front, and hit Option-Tab. Or, double-click within its Window Editor, or select in the Window Editor and hit Return; this causes the Code Editor to appear showing a handler associated with the particular control that was selected (or with the window, if no control was selected).

To toggle between a Window Editor and the corresponding Code Editor
Hit Option-Tab.

In a Code Editor, to navigate quickly to a handler
Control-click to bring up a contextual menu listing the handler.

In a Code Editor, to toggle the focus between browser and code
Hit Shift-Tab. When the browser has focus, up and down arrow keys navigate, and you can hit Delete to remove a property or a handler that wasn't inserted by REALbasic.

In a Code Editor, to resize the browser
Drag the divider bar that separates the two halves. You can drag it all the way to the left to remove the browser completely; the divider bar then appears as a small square in the lower left of the window. You can still navigate among handlers, by using the contextual menu and the history buttons; but unfortunately there's no way to know what handler you're actually in, so this mode is largely useless.

In a Code Editor browser, to expand or collapse a category
Click the category's triangle; double-click the category; or select and hit Command-right-arrow or Command-left-arrow (starting in REALbasic 3.2, it appears that this works only when the browser has the focus).

In a Code Editor, to select a word or a line
Double-click to select a word. Triple-click to select a line. Double-click-drag and triple-click-drag to extend by word or line.

In a Code Editor, to append copied material to the clipboard
Hold Shift while copying or cutting.

In a Code Editor, to copy any visible word to the insertion point
Hold Option and single-click the word. The word to be copied can appear in the code of the same handler, or it can appear on the left side of the window, in the browser, for instance as the name of a property, a control, a method, or an event. The copied word is inserted at the current insertion point or replaces the current selection, without passing through the clipboard. Option-click-drag does not extend the amount of material copied.

In the Language Reference, to alternate between Search and Go
Hold Option.

To accept a proposed "intelligent" typeahead
Hit Tab. If the proposed completion consist of ellipsis marks, this brings up a list of possible completions; up and down arrow keys navigate, Return or Tab or right arrow accepts, Esc or Delete or left arrow dismisses the list.

To change your mind about practically anything
Choose Edit → Undo. REALbasic maintains an effectively infinite Undo list, and you can work your way back to an earlier state by choose Undo multiple times (and then, if you change your mind about changing your mind, you can work your way forward again by choosing Redo multiple times).

CHAPTER 2
The Basic Language

In this chapter:
- Lines and Commands
- Variables and Constants
- Subroutines
- Regulating Flow
- Arrays
- Recursion
- Comments

In Chapter 1 you wrote a working application with REALbasic, where the user can press a button and, in response, hears a beep and sees a little dialog. Just possibly, however, you'd like your application to do a little more than this when the user presses that button. In that case, you're going to need to write some code, using REALbasic's programming language, which (as the name implies) is a form of Basic. In this chapter, you'll start to learn REALbasic's Basic; in fact, you'll learn all there is to know about it, except for the bits having to do with object-orientation. Those bits come in Chapter 3 and Chapter 4.

The name "Basic" is applied to any programming language that descends from the original BASIC (Beginner's All-purpose Symbolic Instruction Code) invented in 1964 by Thomas Kurtz and the late John Kemeny. College courses about computers were new in those days, and BASIC was one of the first computer languages deliberately designed for teaching nonspecialist beginners to program. It gained popularity, in a somewhat bastardized form, in the mid-1970s when it was built in to early personal computers; these computers had tiny memories, but such wizards as Steve Wozniak and Bill Gates ingeniously constructed even tinier BASIC interpreters for them.

The original BASIC was characterized by a small, simple, English-like vocabulary and syntax, surrendering elegance and even convenience to let the user write acceptable code immediately, to shield him from details of implementation, and to protect him from his own mistakes. Even today, Basic dialects typically maintain this traditional spirit of simplicity and safety; but they generally add modern features such as structured programming, and often object-orientation. REALbasic is no exception.*

It could, perhaps, be argued that the fact that REALbasic uses a Basic dialect is neither here nor there. The important aspects of REALbasic are those described in the Preface: its application framework, its object model, and its IDE. The language in which you write code could thus have been just about any computer language

---

* For a history of BASIC, see *http://www.digitalcentury.com/encyclo/update/BASIC.html*. For more information about current Basic dialects for Macintosh, see *http://www.nicholson.com/rhn/basic/*.

capable of expressing and accessing the object model, and REALbasic might easily have ended up as REALc, REALscheme, or REALjavaScript—and there are probably users who wish it had! Basic was probably chosen for its simplicity and its universality, and to give users of a certain Windows programming environment an easy migration path.

The Basic core of the REALbasic dialect, in any case, whatever its merits or demerits as a computer language, is easy to learn, and represents the least of your worries. Just as for those starting to learn Ancient Greek, the Greek alphabet looks unfamiliar at first, but becomes second nature in a day or two and proves almost irrelevant to the real task of learning Greek, so too REALbasic's core of Basic, described in this chapter, should require very little time even for the complete novice, who can then proceed to the really interesting part, the object model, starting in Chapter 3. Those familiar with any Basic dialect or similar language may just quickly skim through this chapter, though I would not advise skipping it altogether, since REALbasic does possess some linguistic peculiarities which, if you're used to some other language, you may find surprising.

Lines and Commands

When speaking of code, we use the term *line* to mean a stretch of text delimited by return characters. In the Code Editor, the return character is invisible, but its effects are evident, because each line really does occupy exactly one physical line. Unlike an ordinary word processor, the code does not "wrap" when it reaches the right edge of the window; a new line begins only when a return character is encountered. (Unlike many other dialects of Basic, REALbasic does not permit you to put more than one line of code onto a physical line, or to split a line into more than one physical line.)

REALbasic is an "imperative" language, meaning that code is composed of commands. Each command appears as a separate line in its handler. The lines of code in a handler represent a sequence of commands, meaning that unless the commands themselves instruct otherwise (and we shall see later in this chapter how they can do this) the lines are executed successively, from top to bottom.

Recall, for instance, our handler from Chapter 1:

```
beep
msgBox "Sorry, this application doesn't do much!"
```

The way these words are arranged into lines is significant in two ways. First, the lines appear in a particular order, which means they are to be executed in that order—first we make a beeping noise, then we put up a dialog. Second, there are two lines, because there are two commands; it would be illegal to combine the two commands into one line, like this:

```
beep msgBox "Sorry, this application doesn't do much!" // error: Unexpected token
```

The error is because you can't have two commands on one line.

It would also be illegal to split up the two lines into three, like this:

```
beep
msgBox // error: Unexpected end of line
"Sorry, this application doesn't do much!" // another error: Statement expected
```

Here, the first error arises because the msgBox command requires more information—okay, says REALbasic, I should put up a dialog, but what should the dialog say? That information belongs to the msgBox command, so it must appear on the same line with it. The second error arises because a phrase in quotation marks is not a command at all, so it can't be on a line by itself.

All of this raises the question of exactly what constitutes a command. To give a simple answer, we might use an analogy to natural language and say that every command is a sentence that has exactly one main verb. beep is a main verb, msgBox is another; they constitute two different commands, and must appear on different lines. Along with each particular main verb must appear any other sentence features demanded by this verb; for example, msgBox also requires a direct object, namely the text that is to appear in the dialog.

The notion of a main verb, while intuitively clear, lacks rigor. We may define it more technically by specifying that every line of REALbasic code must contain exactly one of the following:

- An assignment
- A procedure call
- A declaration
- A flow-control statement
- Nothing

This definition may not sound particularly helpful, if you happen not to know the meaning of its terms; this chapter, though, will provide examples of all of them. In case you're wondering, beep and msgBox are both procedure calls, and an assignment appeared in Chapter 1; that's all we've seen so far. "Nothing" sounds trivial, but becomes significant in connection with comments.

Variables and Constants

A primary feature of any computer language is its ability to associate a name with a value. In this section, we discuss a particular type of name–value association called a *variable*.

Assignment

In REALbasic, as in many computer languages, the association of a name with a value is performed in code by means of the = operator. An *operator* is a symbol, as in arithmetic, used to combine two values or to change a single value. The name goes on the left side of the = operator, the value on the right. For example, we might say:

```
myBirthYear = 1954
thisYear = 2001
```

These are not statements of fact; they are commands. Each line tells the computer to associate with the name on the left side the value on the right. So, as a result of executing these commands, the name myBirthYear ends up having associated with it the numeric value 1954, and the name thisYear ends up having associated with it with the numeric value 2001. Such a command, one whose main verb is the = operator, is called an *assignment*.

Once a name and a value have been associated, the name can be used to denote the value. For example, having executed the preceding statements, we could then perform an arithmetic calculation:

```
myAge = thisYear - myBirthYear
```

This command involves the subtraction operator, which, as one might expect, causes a subtraction to be performed. Here's how REALbasic responds to this command: first, the values associated with the names on the right side are retrieved; then, those values are arithmetically combined (in accordance with the subtraction operator) to give a value for the whole right side; and finally, that value is assigned to the name on the left side. As a result of executing this line in combination with the previous two, the name myAge ends up having associated with it the number 47.

It is perfectly permissible, having assigned a value to a name, to assign a different value to that same name. For instance, in our previous example we got the wrong answer (I'm actually 46), so we could correct it by giving the following command:

```
myAge = myAge - 1
```

There is no circularity here, even though the name myAge is used on both sides of the assignment. That's because the right side is evaluated before assigning the result to the name on the left side; we will end up subtracting 1 from 47 first, to get 46, and then associating 46 with the name myAge. Furthermore, no problem is caused by the fact that the name myAge already had a value associated with it; the old association is forgotten as the new one is made.

We cannot, however, associate just any old value with a particular name, as we shall now see.

Datatypes and Declaration of Variables

In REALbasic, every value is of some one type, called its *datatype*. For instance, a value might be a whole number—an integer. Or, it might be text—a string. Before a name can be associated with a value by means of assignment, there has to be a *declaration* stating the datatype for any value that will be assigned to that name. So, before making any of the assignments in the preceding examples, we would have to declare that the names `myAge`, `thisYear`, and `myBirthYear` are all destined to receive integer values.

In REALbasic code, we perform this declaration by means of a `Dim` statement:*

```
dim thisYear as integer
dim myBirthYear as integer
dim myAge as integer
```

Declarations may be combined, like this:

```
dim thisYear, myBirthYear, myAge as integer, myName as string
```

It is an error to use an undeclared variable name, and it is an error to assign to a variable a value whose datatype is not the datatype for which the variable was declared. Therefore, you must remember to declare every variable before you use it, and you mustn't violate a variable's datatype once you've declared it. In a nutshell: you must say what you're planning to do, and you can do only what you said.

So, for example:

```
dim myName as string
dim thisYear as integer
myName = "Matt" // fine, that's a string value
thisYear = 2001 // fine, that's an integer value
myName = 2001 // error: Type mismatch—can't assign an integer value to a string variable
myName = thisYear // error: Type mismatch—hey, what did I just tell you??
yourName = "Reader" // error: Unknown identifier—we didn't declare a variable name YourName
```

These restrictions may seem very strong, and in practice even maddening; but they accord with the Basic philosophy of protecting you from yourself. REALbasic wants to make sure that it always knows exactly what you mean when you use a name— and that you know that it knows. Also, these rules cause applications built with REALbasic to run faster, because the running application doesn't have to waste any time examining the datatypes of any values—the datatypes of all variables and their values are known in advance.

This discussion deliberately sidesteps the question of what constitutes a name. For example, there might be two things named `myAge`. But REALbasic can tell them apart, according to scoping rules described in Chapter 3; and so the rules still apply to each of them. Properties, which are formally discussed in Chapter 3, are like variables; you must declare them and give them a datatype (although you don't do it in code, and you don't use the word `Dim`), so the rules apply to them as well. Only in Chapter 5 will we see any reason to soften our formulation: it will turn out that a numeric value that is not an integer can be assigned to an integer variable, because

---

* The word `Dim` derives from "dimension," which itself goes back, if memory serves, to FORTRAN. The idea is, I guess, that we are telling the computer to set aside space in its memory for a value of the specified type, and space and dimensionality are the same thing (if you have a Euclidean kind of brain, that is).

they are both numbers, and we will learn that there is in fact a way to permit a name in REALbasic to take on successive values with different datatypes, namely if that name is declared as a variant.

It is not an error to declare a variable and then never use it; it's just a waste (not a very serious one).

It is not an error to declare a variable and then retrieve its value without having assigned it any value; the value will simply be some form of zero, as follows:

- 0 in the case of a number
- The empty string in the case of a string
- false in the case of a boolean
- nil otherwise

Thus, variables in REALbasic are *autoinitialized*, which is a valuable feature. So:

```
dim x, y, z as integer
x = 7
z = x - y // fine; z is now 7, because y is 0
```

Constants

If you know for a fact that you will never need to change the value of a variable, you can save a step by declaring the name in a Const statement instead of a Dim statement. A Const statement consists of the Const keyword followed by an assignment, like this:

```
const thisYear = 2001
```

This performs the declaration of the name and associates a value with that name, all in one move. Afterward, it is illegal to assign a new value to this name. For example, you cannot say:

```
const thisYear = 2001
thisYear = 2002 // error: Expecting an lvalue
```

That's because the name doesn't denote a variable, but is merely a synonym for one particular value. Such a name is called a *constant*. The value denoted by a constant can only be a string or numeric literal.

Aside from saving yourself one line of code, is there any other reason to prefer a Const statement over a Dim statement followed by an assignment? There might be a reason having to do with speed and efficiency. Some language implementations are able to access constant values more quickly than variable values because the substitution is performed before the code actually starts running, but I do not know whether REALbasic is such a language. Chiefly, constants are useful as a way of protecting you from yourself; they permit you to "lock" the value associated with a name, so that in the course of developing and maintaining a large, complicated piece of code, you won't accidentally change that value.

Capitalization of names is not significant in REALbasic code. You can declare a variable as myVar and refer to it subsequently as Myvar with no problem. So too you can say Dim or dim, and Beep or beep (or bEeP). In this book, the following convention has been adopted: in code, except for keywords inserted by REALbasic, all words are minuscule (but usually with internal capitalization), because that's how I most naturally type and read; but in the main text, keywords and names (except for variables) are capitalized, for clarity.

Subroutines

A handler is a sort of pigeonhole in a Code Editor for containing code. The code constituting any one handler must consist of exactly one *subroutine*. A subroutine is a block of code that can be *called* (told to execute) by some other piece of code, or by REALbasic itself. Every subroutine is of one of two types: it is either a *procedure* or a *function*. There are some formal differences between procedures and functions that will be described in this section. The really important difference between them, though, is that a function ends by handing back a result to the code that called it, and a procedure does not; a function is said to *return* a value. In a broad sense, calling a procedure is like giving a command, whereas calling a function is like asking a question, the answer to which is the value returned.

Subroutine Declarations

A procedure and a function are formally distinguished from one another by the lines with which they begin and end. You will never need to type such lines, however; REALbasic always inserts them for you, both when a handler is supplied automatically and when you create one. You can see this in any project by examining the handlers in the Events category of the default window; for example, the window's Open event handler is already declared as a procedure, and its CancelClose event handler is already declared as a function.[*]

A procedure begins and ends with these lines:

```
Sub HandlerName()
    // ... commands go here ...
End Sub
```

A function begins and ends with these lines:

```
Function HandlerName() As ReturnType
    // ... commands go here ...
End Function
```

---

[*] The nature of these handlers, and why they are called *event handlers*, will be revealed in Chapter 3.

In both cases, the first line is the *subroutine declaration*. It gives the name of the subroutine, which will almost always be the name of the handler. (The "almost" is because of menu event handlers, discussed in Chapter 6.) It states, through the use of Sub or Function, whether this subroutine is a procedure or a function; in the case of a function, it also states the datatype of the value the function will be handing back to its caller. The last line is a syntactic statement showing where the subroutine ends. In between go the commands to be executed when the subroutine is called.

In the preceding syntax templates, the subroutine declaration contains parentheses after the handler name. These parentheses will always be present, but they will not always be empty (they are shown as empty in the templates just for clarity). The parentheses must include declarations for any *parameters* that the procedure or function expects. A parameter is a value handed to the procedure or function when it is called. The parameter declarations look like individual variable declarations, but without the Dim keyword, separated by commas.

For example, here is a complete function for calculating the approximate average of two integers:

```
Function average(a as integer, b as integer) As integer
    dim c as integer
    c = (a + b) / 2
    return c
End Function
```

The function is going to return an integer; that is stated by what follows the parentheses in the declaration. What's inside the parentheses is a statement that the function expects to be handed two values when it is called, that each should be an integer, and that within this subroutine the names a and b should be associated with them. For example, suppose that when the function is called, it is handed the values 3 and 5. Then the effect is rather as if we had said, before any of the other commands in the function:

```
dim a as integer
dim b as integer
a = 3
b = 5
```

But, whereas in the case of the Dim statement followed by assignment, we declare the name and datatype and then attach a value to it ourselves, in the case of a parameter in a subroutine declaration we declare the name and datatype and let someone else (the caller of the subroutine) attach a value to it. When the subroutine is called and starts executing, its parameters are like variables that have already been Dimmed and already have values. Actually, a name declared inside the parentheses of a subroutine declaration is rather more like a constant than a variable, in the sense that it is an error to assign to it:

```
Function average(a as integer, b as integer) As integer
    a = 3 // error: Parameters can't be modified
```

(Later in this chapter we shall see how to circumvent this restriction.*)

Within a subroutine, both a variable declared in a `Dim` statement and a parameter declared in the subroutine declaration create names especially for that subroutine and limited to it. The point is an important one: different subroutines cannot "see" one another's internal names. A subroutine MySub and a subroutine YourSub may each declare, using a `Dim` statement or as a parameter, a name `myVar`; but these two `myVar`s have nothing to do with each other—their paths will never cross, as it were, and there will never be any danger of their being confused with each other. Such names are said to be *local* to a subroutine.

Within the body of a subroutine, all `Dim` statements must precede all other nonempty commands; to behave otherwise is an error.†

Return

After a subroutine has executed its last statement, the flow of execution passes automatically back to the code that called the subroutine. But if a `Return` statement is encountered within the body of a subroutine, execution passes back to the caller immediately and any subsequent commands in the subroutine will go unexecuted. The `Return` statement actually has two uses: to terminate execution of the subroutine and, in the case of a function, to state explicitly what value is to be returned to the caller.

In a procedure, a `Return` statement must consist of the single word Return, like this:

```
Sub MySub()
    // ...
    return // this line, if encountered, terminates execution of the procedure
    // ...
End Sub
```

In a function, a `Return` statement must include the value to be handed back to the caller, and that value must be of the datatype specified at the end of the subroutine declaration, like this:

```
Function MyFunction() As integer
    // ...
    return 3 // this line, if encountered, immediately returns the value 3 to the caller
    // ...
End Function
```

---

* Actually, within a subroutine, you can `Dim` a variable with the same name as a parameter and then assign to it. I suspect that the fact that this is possible is a bug; in any case it is a bad idea, because the parameter's original value becomes unavailable.

† But `Const` statements are not subject to this same restriction. I regard this as a bug, and strongly recommend that you voluntarily restrict yourself so that all `Const` statements precede all `Dim` statements. Paradoxical results can ensue otherwise.

It is much faster for REALbasic, each time through the loop, to fetch the value of a local variable than to evaluate a function.

Exit and GoTo

We have seen that it is possible for any of REALbasic's loop structures (meaning While, Do, or For) to be coded in such a way as to provide no escape. In such a situation, the program may repeat some visible action forever; or it may perform *no* visible action forever, in which case it will appear to have become unaccountably inert and unresponsive and is said to be *hung*. Either way, the program has entered an *infinite loop*. Infinite loops are normally undesirable, and the programmer will be careful to avoid them.

But there is another way out of a loop besides having the loop terminate normally, and that is to jump out. The capacity to do this can make an ostensibly infinite loop a perfectly legitimate and useful structure.

There are three ways to jump out of a loop.*

One way to jump out of a loop is by way of the Return statement, which terminates not just the loop, but the entire subroutine.

To jump out of a loop without terminating the entire subroutine, the Exit statement is provided; it causes execution to resume after the first Wend, Loop, or Next statement that follows it. Thus, in the case of nested loops, the Exit statement will jump only out of the innermost loop that contains it. It is an error to use Exit outside the context of a While, Do, or For block.

Finally, REALbasic provides a GoTo statement. GoTo permits execution to jump from anywhere to anywhere within a subroutine. There must be a line consisting of a *label*, a name terminating in a colon. A GoTo statement using that label's name will cause execution to resume immediately following the label. So, for example, the following will display "This is a nice place to visit" twice:

```
Dim beenThereTwice As Boolean
nicePlace:
MsgBox "This is a nice place to visit."
If Not beenThereTwice Then
    beenThereTwice = true
    GoTo nicePlace
End
```

GoTo was once the workhorse of flow control in many programming languages, since all by itself it can implement the equivalent of While, Do, or For, not to mention giving the programmer the ability to leap all over the place at will. This leaping, however, tends to make code difficult to read, debug, and maintain; and a famous letter

---

* Actually, there is a fourth way, which is to raise an exception. Exceptions are discussed in Chapter 8.

by Edsger Dijkstra in 1968 focused discussion so clearly on this point that GoTo is now routinely described as "harmful."*

The presence of GoTo in REALbasic is a nod to "traditional" Basic, and its use is officially deprecated. Nevertheless, there are situations, such as when one wishes to escape from more than one level of nested block, where, in my view, GoTo remains extremely convenient, and not at all harmful.

Arrays

An *array* is a way of associating multiple values of the same datatype with a single name. A particular value to be accessed is specified by an integer in parentheses following the name; this integer is called the *index*. For example, if we have an array of strings called myStrings, then myStrings(1) would be a string value, myStrings(2) would be another string value, myStrings(3) would be yet another string value, and so forth.

There are two chief advantages to being able to talk this way. One is that in computer programming it is very often the case that we can most easily specify arithmetically which of several values we want. Partly this is just a matter of convenience. If myStrings is an array of 100 strings, it is a lot easier to specify the desired string by one name and an index number than to have to maintain 100 names. But also, a notion such as "the next string" is expressible by a simple arithmetic process—incrementing the index—and thus it becomes very easy to perform such a task as visiting every string. So, for example, to set each of our 100 strings to "hello", one can say:

```
for i = 1 to 100
    myStrings(i) = "hello"
next
```

Besides "the next one," there are many other relationships among entities that can be most easily expressed in arithmetic terms. Suppose, for example, we are playing a game on a four-by-four grid; we might designate the 16 squares numerically, as follows:

1	2	3	4
5	6	7	8
9	10	11	12
13	14	15	0

We can now navigate the board arithmetically. Consider a concept like "the square directly below this one, wrapping around if we're in the bottom row"; so, for square 2, we want square 6, and for square 15, we want square 3. Because the squares' names are numbers, as it were, this can easily be expressed in code: given the number of a square, thisOne, the number of the square below it is (thisOne + 4) mod 16. Thus, if information about the game board is stored in arrays, we can easily access

---

* See *http://www.acm.org/classics/oct95/*.

Suppose, for example, that we have a sorted array of strings, sortedArray, and that we wish to know whether it contains a given string, whatStr. We specify that a function findSorted should accept whatStr as a parameter and return an integer that is the index of the matching string in sortedArray, or 0 if no match is found. (We presume, for simplicity, that sortedArray is available without having to be passed as a parameter; for example, it could be a property.) Clearly we could just examine every item of sortedArray in numerical order, until either we find a match or we deduce that whatStr is absent:

```
Function findSorted(whatStr as string) As integer
    dim i, u as integer
    u = ubound(sortedArray)
    for i = 1 to u
        if sortedArray(i) = whatStr then
            return i
        elseIf sortedArray(i) > whatStr then
            return 0
        end
    next
    return 0
End Function
```

The trouble is that this is incredibly wasteful. If the array consists of 10,000 entries, we will have, in the worst case, to loop 10,000 times, performing 20,000 comparisons, before getting an answer.

Our error lies in failing to take full advantage of the fact that the array is sorted. The following alternative approach suggests itself. Look at the middle item of the array. If it's a match, we're done. Otherwise, we know (because the array is sorted) which half of the array contains the match, so do it again with that half. Repeat until either we find a match or we're left with one item that isn't a match. This is called a *binary search*. Since every iteration eliminates half the array, even a large array requires relatively few iterations; with 10,000 entries we will loop only 13 times in the worst case. The notion "do it again with that half" cries out to be expressed recursively.

Here is our function rewritten to be recursive. Imagine that we call it initially with a value of 1 for low and a value of ubound(sortedArray) for hi:

```
Function findSorted(low as integer, hi as integer, whatStr as string) As integer
    dim i as integer
    i = (low + hi) / 2
    if sortedArray(i) = whatStr then
        return i
    end
    if hi <= low then
        return 0
    end
    if sortedArray(i) > whatStr then
        return findSorted(low, i-1, whatStr)
    else
        return findSorted(i+1, hi, whatStr)
    end
End Function
```

Unfortunately, languages not optimized for recursion can deplete computing resources (such as stack space) if the recursion reaches a significant depth; and REALbasic is such a language. The FindSorted example presents no problems until the sortedArray becomes extremely large, but some recursive algorithms will prove impractical in the normal domain of the problem they are intended to solve—not to put too fine a point on it, your application will terminate prematurely as the recursion depth grows too great. Only experimentation will show how great is "too great." While I constantly use and recommend recursion in REALbasic where appropriate, it's a good idea to be ready with a nonrecursive alternative, just in case.

Fortunately, any tail-recursive algorithm can easily be reexpressed as a nonrecursive loop. A recursive algorithm is tail-recursive if it leaves no calculations in suspension when it recurses—in other words, if each recursion call merely redescribes the whole problem. Thus, FindSorted is tail-recursive. Even when a recursive algorithm is not tail-recursive, it can usually be expressed nonrecursively without too much difficulty, by maintaining the results of each partial calculation in an array or other data structure that implements a stack. Here is how, if we had to, we could rewrite Find-Sorted once more, as a nonrecursive version of a binary search (and notice the deliberate use of an infinite loop):

```
Function findSorted(whatStr as string) As integer
    dim i, low, hi as integer
    low = 1
    hi = ubound(sortedArray)
    do
        i = (low + hi) / 2
        if sortedArray(i) = whatStr then
            return i
        end
        if hi <= low then
            return 0
        end
        if sortedArray(i) > whatStr then
            hi = i-1
        else
            low = i+1
        end
    loop
End Function
```

Comments

A *comment* is a part of a line that is ignored by REALbasic. A comment is introduced by a *comment delimiter*; the delimiter and everything after it in the line will be ignored. You have a choice of three comment delimiters:

- The double slash, //
- The single apostrophe, '
- The keyword Rem (short for "remark")

I always use the double slash, as being easiest to see.

If a line consists of only a comment, the comment is ignored and the line consists of nothing: it is an empty line. As was pointed out at the beginning of this chapter, "nothing" is a main verb, meaning that an empty line, and therefore a line consisting of only a comment, is permitted anywhere.

It has become *de rigueur* in books about programming to lecture the reader on the importance of documenting one's code; so please pretend that the lecture appeared at this point (and consult some other book if you actually want to read the lecture). Unfortunately, effective documentation by way of comments is not at all easy in REALbasic, for three reasons:

- REALbasic has no syntax for commenting out a block of lines.*
- REALbasic's Code Editor does not provide automatic wrapping of long lines.
- REALbasic does not permit writing a comment outside a handler's executable code.

The trouble is particularly acute when, as frequently happens, what one wishes to document is not a line of code at all, or even a handler, but rather a noncode entity, such as a property, a control, or a class. One workaround is to create a method handler or handlers consisting entirely of documentation, but this still fails to associate the documentation with the entity it documents. No matter where you put it, documentation is difficult to modify and maintain because of the lack of block comments and line wrapping. What's really needed is that every entity in the IDE should have a "comment window" that pops up on demand and works like a little word processor. Until then, you may find it easiest, as I do, to document your projects using a different application altogether.

---

* I'm thinking here of something like C's /* ... */ construct. REALbasic does, at least, have a provision for commenting out every line in a block individually: select all the lines in question, and choose Edit → Comment Lines. The comment delimiter inserted by this command is the single apostrophe, which I dislike, but it's better than nothing.

CHAPTER 3

Objects, Classes, and Instances

Consider programming as a way of thinking, and code as a way of speaking—a language. The programmer thinks about what the program is supposed to do, and then expresses this in code. An *object* is a programming construct which assists the programmer both in thinking and in speaking about the program, both in organizing and in coding. The program works as if it consisted of autonomous bundles of functionality—the objects. These objects are somewhat like the bundles of reality, the "things," the "objects," in terms of which we perceive and describe the natural world. Thus, the use of objects in programming makes the programmer's thought and speech about the program more natural, which in turn makes programming easier.

What are the objects of which a program is constructed? In general, that's up to the programmer, who, rather like some divinity creating a small universe, dictates both what objects should populate that universe ("Let there be light; let there be the sun; let there be the earth") and what those objects should do and how they should interact ("Let the sun make light to shine upon the earth"). Such power may seem daunting, almost paralyzing, rather than helpful. Where to begin? If there were an easy answer, there wouldn't be approximately six gazillion books about designing object-oriented programs.

REALbasic both enforces object-oriented programming and helps you with object-oriented design. Before you write a line of code, the construction of your program's universe has already been started for you. The program you are contemplating is to be an application; REALbasic is an application framework, and has stocked your program beforehand with objects that mirror the physical elements of an application's interface: windows, buttons, text fields, menu items, and so forth. Such physical elements of the interface are the objects of the "natural world" the user perceives when working with your application, and so they are the very objects in terms of which it is most natural to think and speak about the operation of your program ("This button should react to being pressed by opening that window").

REALbasic's built-in objects are useful and powerful in three ways:

- Conceptually, they organize your program into bundles that reflect the structure of its interface.

- Physically, in the IDE, they act (through their Code Editors) as separate repositories of code.

- Functionally, they supply the programming power of REALbasic's application framework; in other words, not only do they reflect the interface through their structure, they also implement the interface through their hidden programming power, driving the computer and creating physical counterparts for themselves on the screen. For example, windows know how to open and how to draw themselves, buttons know how to be pressed, text fields know how to accept typing, menu items know how to be chosen.

REALbasic's built-in objects may be the only objects your program needs; if your program is fairly simple, that's quite probable. But if your program is more specialized or more complex, you will probably wish to extend REALbasic's objects by modifying them or adding new ones of your own. Either way, you will not be entirely freed from having to make intelligent object-oriented design decisions. At the very least, you will have to construct your program's interface, and you will have to decide how to allocate your code among the objects that implement that interface. To do this efficiently, in a way that makes the program do what you want it to do and as easy as possible to understand, maintain, and alter, you need to draw from two kinds of knowledge: you should understand REALbasic's internal object model and what the built-in objects do; and you should adhere to principles of good object-oriented design.

If this sounds daunting, don't worry; this book is here to help! Throughout this chapter and the rest of Part I, I'll be describing the REALbasic object model, explaining how you work with objects in general and how they fit together to provide the architecture of your application as a whole. The rest of the book provides the details on each of REALbasic's built-in objects.

Messages and Dot Notation

As a programming construct, objects divide a program into pieces. The glue that unites those pieces to form a single working program is the ability of the objects to send one another commands and ask one another questions. The objects are autonomous, but they can communicate; this communication takes place by means of *messages*. In REALbasic code, the sending of a message to an object is expressed by *dot notation*.

Suppose, for example, that we have an object called MyWindow and we wish to tell it to turn blue. We could do this by sending it a TurnBlue message—assuming, of course, that the MyWindow object can accept a TurnBlue message. If it can, then we might say:

```
myWindow.turnBlue
```

This shows the basic dot notation syntax whereby messages are sent: the name of the object is followed by a dot, which is followed by the name of the message.

But how does this syntax fit into the larger syntax of the REALbasic language? The answer is that every message is one of two types, both of which are already familiar to us from Chapter 2: it operates, depending on the particular message, either as a subroutine call or as a variable name. As a matter of nomenclature, it happens that the subroutines that can be called by sending a message to an object are called *methods*, and the variable-like things whose values can be accessed by sending a message to an object are called *properties*. But syntactically and conceptually, they present nothing new. Since we already know how to use subroutine calls and variable names in code, we already know how to use messages as well.

To illustrate, suppose a particular message designates a method. That means the message operates as a subroutine call. As we know, subroutines can be either procedures or functions, so let's suppose this method, TurnBlue, is a procedure. Then, if that procedure takes no parameters, we might say:

```
myWindow.turnBlue
```

If the procedure takes one parameter (perhaps an integer telling how blue the window should turn), we might say:

```
myWindow.turnBlue 32
```

Now let's suppose we have a different method, HowBlue, which is a function taking no parameters (perhaps returning an integer telling how blue the window is). We might say:

```
dim yourBlueness as integer
yourBlueness = myWindow.howBlue()
```

All the other forms of syntax may also be used, as appropriate to a procedure or a function, taking the appropriate number of parameters.

Now, suppose a particular message designates a property. That means the message operates as a variable name. For example, the window might have a property MaxBlueness which is an integer, denoting the maximum blueness this window should allow itself to adopt. Then we might say:

```
myWindow.maxBlueness = 40
```

or:

```
dim theMax as integer
theMax = myWindow.maxBlueness
```

or:

```
myWindow.maxBlueness = myWindow.maxBlueness + 10
```

Thus, aside from dot notation itself, no new syntax is required to send a message to an object, beyond what was already described in Chapter 2.

REALbasic itself also comes with a large number of built-in procedures and functions apparently detached from any object; for example, in earlier chapters, we have already had cause to mention the MsgBox procedure, the Beep procedure, and the Str function. To call these, as we have seen, you just use their names; no dot notation is required. For the sake of completeness, though, and for a rigorous understanding of their ontological status, you might like to consider such built-in procedures and functions to be methods of a sort of supreme, ultimate, universal object—the *global* object.

A thing is global if it is available from everywhere without specifying an object that it belongs to; so, for example, since any code whatever can call the Beep procedure without using dot notation, the Beep procedure is global. So, we can pretend there is a universal object, which we might term REALbasicItself, and that when we say:

```
beep
```

it is really a kind of shorthand for:

```
REALbasicItself.beep // you can't actually say this!
```

This construct is only a pretense; there actually is no REALbasicItself object, and you can't actually send a message to it as in the second example. But there is a sense in which this pretense is accurate, and helps explain the status of REALbasic's built-in procedures and functions: when you call such a procedure or function, you're actually sending a message to REALbasic itself, and accessing one of its methods.

Object Design Philosophy

Methods and properties correspond to the two primary purposes of objects as programming constructs: *encapsulation of functionality* and *maintenance of state*. These two purposes underlie the design of object-oriented code, and an understanding of them will help you to make sense of REALbasic's built-in objects, to appreciate REALbasic's application architecture, to organize your code intelligently, and to know when to create your own objects.

Encapsulation of Functionality

The idea behind encapsulation of functionality is that each object should be the repository of knowledge about how to do all the things appropriate to itself.

Consider, for example, a shoot-'em-up arcade game, where every time the user hits a target, the target explodes, and the score, displayed in a box, increases. Now, we could write such a program without using object orientation at all; it's all just pixels on a screen, after all, and code that controls pixels has the same effect no matter how it's organized. But if we do use object orientation, the very language in which we describe the program, where the nouns are "target" and "score" and the verbs are "explodes" and "increases," suggests that the target and the box containing the score are two different objects, and that it is the target that should contain the code for exploding, and the scorebox that should contain the code for increasing. The target "knows" how to explode; the scorebox "knows" how to increase. In other words, the target object has an Explode method, and the scorebox object has an Increase method.

Messages can be sent to the appropriate objects to instigate the appropriate actions. Instead of exploding the target from elsewhere, we send the target the Explode message, as if to say: explode yourself! Instead of increasing the score from elsewhere, we send the scorebox the Increase message, as if to say: increase yourself! (In fact, our use of the conjunction "and" in describing the program's behavior suggests that it should probably be the target which, as it explodes, tells the scorebox to increase.)

When code is object-oriented, and when the objects encapsulate their appropriate functionality, the objects become more like objects in the real world. It is encapsulation of functionality that gives objects their autonomy. Only the target needs to know how to explode; all other objects can remain blissfully ignorant of the details, secure in the knowledge that they can just say target.explode and all the right things will happen. Moreover, as we develop the program, we can change what an explosion consists of (we can decide to add a sound, for instance) without affecting any code in any other objects; they still just say target.explode. Indeed, the target object may be so autonomous as to have virtually no dependency on the rest of the program; everything the target needs in order to function is inside itself. This makes it easier to write and maintain not only this program, but also any other programs that may need targets; to implement targets in another program, we have only to copy into that program our target object code from this one.

Maintenance of State

The idea behind maintenance of state is that a value needing to be preserved over time should be preserved as part of the object that chiefly operates on it.

Recall that our arcade game is to have a scorebox that knows how to increase itself, and observe that this implies there is a score. Even while the user is busy missing targets, or taking time out to answer the telephone, some object is remembering this score. It makes sense that this object should be the scorebox itself; the jobs of increasing the score, displaying the score, and knowing the score are naturally related. In other words, the scorebox object has a Score property.

Once again, this approach allows other objects to be ignorant of the details, and allows the scorebox to maintain autonomy. When the user hits a target, the score should increase. Let's say that when the user hits a different object (a bad guy), the score should also increase. Both the target object and the bad guy object react to being hit by telling the scorebox to increase itself: scorebox.increase. Neither has to worry about what this means, or what the score is, or how the user will be shown the score. The scorebox, in its turn, doesn't have to worry about who is telling it to increase the score. It just sits there, remembering the score, and when it's told to increase it, it does so, and it both remembers and displays the new score, which is simply the value of its Score property.

To be sure, this example is particularly clear-cut in a way that is sometimes not the case. Interesting questions of philosophy and implementation often arise. That's part of the fun, and the challenge, of designing an object-oriented program.

For example, the target object and the bad guy object don't need to know the score or manipulate it themselves; but what if they did? Should they be permitted to access the scorebox's Score property directly, or should they be required to call one of the scorebox's methods? In other words, is the scorebox not just this value's container, but also its owner and, in some sense, its protector?

Furthermore, it may not always be entirely obvious which is "the object that chiefly operates" upon a certain value. It often seems that direct access to a value needs to be shared among several different objects; should one of these be its container, or its owner and protector, or should the value be spun off into a different object entirely?

Then there is the problem of a value's life cycle. Clearly, if the scorebox object for some reason goes out of existence, yet we still need access to the score, the scorebox was an inappropriate choice of container for the score. At the other extreme, we could make the score permanently and publicly accessible and part of no object at all,* but this seems to defeat the purpose of object-orientation, if there is any object that seems naturally to be the score's owner.

These are all practical and philosophical design decisions with which the programmer must constantly grapple.

Summary

Figure 3-1 represents some of the features of objects we've just discussed: their autonomy, their ability to receive and send messages, their encapsulation of functionality, and their maintenance of state.

Functionality is expressed by methods. State is expressed by properties. Code that is well organized into objects with appropriate methods and properties has several virtues. It is:

Legible
When code in some object says `target.explode`, it's fairly obvious what it's meant to do.

Maintainable
If we decide to modify the code that explodes the target, we know where to find it, and code outside the object remains untouched.

---

* By making it part of a module. Modules are discussed in Chapter 4.

Expandable

If we decide the target needs to be able to do something more, such as move to the left, we know where to put the code.

Portable

If we write another game that uses targets, we can just export our target object code from this program and import it into the other.

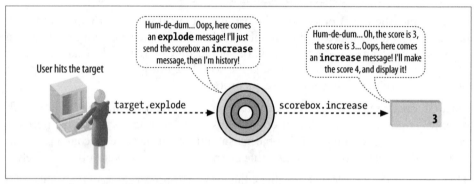

Hum-de-dum... Oops, here comes an **explode** message! I'll just send the scorebox an **increase** message, then I'm history!

Hum-de-dum... Oh, the score is 3, the score is 3... Oops, here comes an **increase** message! I'll make the score 4, and display it!

User hits the target

target.explode

scorebox.increase

3

Figure 3-1. Objects doing their jobs autonomously

Classes and Instances

An object is an abstraction, a way of thinking and speaking. We come now to the details of how objects are actually implemented in the REALbasic programming environment. They appear in two forms: as *classes* and as *instances*. We begin with an explanation of what a class is.

Consider the notion that every object is of some type. The notion of types of object accords intuitively with our ideas of objects in the real world; these two pencils are two different objects, yet they are both pencils. Such a notion implies immediately that our program may have more than one object of the same type; for if this were not possible, and every object were the only one of its kind, the notion of types of object would be superfluous.

The possibility of our program containing more than one object of the same type has both a ready intuitive appeal and an obvious practical value. Returning to our arcade game example, imagine that the user is to be confronted with numerous targets marching across the screen. They look alike, and they behave alike (they explode when hit). It makes perfect sense that we should be able to say and think that each of these targets is a different object (only the one that is hit will explode), yet they are all targets (any one that is hit will explode in the same manner). The same is true of the scorebox; there might be two different scores (how many large targets the user has hit, and how many small targets), each of which is increased individually, and each of which is displayed in a separate box. It makes perfect sense that we should be able to maintain two different scores in two different objects, yet we should be able to say and think that both objects are scoreboxes (each contains a score that it knows how to display and increase).

Figure 3-2 illustrates this notion. The round things, which are marching across the window at the left, are targets. They are different objects; yet they all look identical, because they are all of the same type—each is a target.

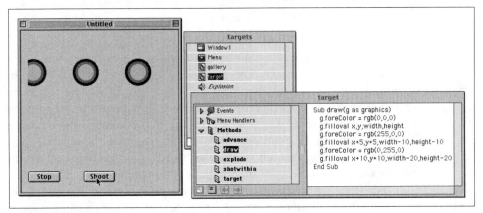

Figure 3-2. A class and several instances of it

Furthermore, *without* the ability to implement multiple objects of the same type, objects threaten to become a hindrance to the organization of our code, rather than a benefit. Suppose our arcade game is to show the user dozens of targets, each of which can be sent the Explode message. If exploding is to be implemented the same way for *every* target, and yet that same code must be written separately in *each* target, imagine what this will mean both for writing the code originally and for changing it later on! The programmer would surely collapse in a state of boredom, frustration, or madness before the program was ever completed. Clearly, in order to do useful object-oriented programming at all, we must have a way to implement object types, and this implementation must include a facility for sharing code, so that all objects of the same type can be sent the same messages and can respond identically to them.

The programming construct that expresses the notion of an object type is called a *class*. Methods and properties that are to be in common for every object of a certain type are placed in the class that represents that type.

For example, if we have a Target class, then we write one Explode method, in the Target class. (And with REALbasic, when I say "*in* the Target class," I really mean *in* it; the Target class will be a listing in the Project Window, and we will double-click that listing to open a Code Editor that belongs just to the Target class, and that's where our code will go.) Now any and all targets in our program will be able to receive the Explode message and will know what to do in response. If we decide to change the way all targets respond to the Explode message (we decide to add a sound to the explosion), we change the code in just one place, the Explode handler in the Target class.

Similarly, if we have a ScoreBox class, then we write one Increase method, in the ScoreBox class, and we create one Score property, in the ScoreBox class. Now any and all scoreboxes in our program will maintain a score, and will know how to increase it.

However, there's an important distinction to be drawn here between the case of a method and the case of a property. For example, every scorebox will have an Increase method (because the ScoreBox class has one), and it will be the same method.[*] On the other hand, every scorebox will have a Score property (because the ScoreBox class has one), and its datatype will be the same (namely, the datatype declared for this property in the ScoreBox class), but its value will be separate, and separately maintained, for each scorebox. In other words, a property is declared in the class, but the individual objects in the program still maintain state individually, so each has its own value for that property. This makes intuitive sense if we consider an object such as a button: clearly any button has a location within its window, so it should have a Top property and a Left property, but we would not want all buttons to be forced to have the same location.

So, a class is an object type, with facilities for sharing code and property declarations among individual objects. Those individual objects, for their part, are called *instances*; and every object is said to be an instance of some class. In our arcade game, each target that the user sees represents a separate instance of the Target class, and each of the boxes showing a different score represents a separate instance of the ScoreBox class.

So, in Figure 3-2, each of the round things in the window on the left represents a separate instance of the Target class. As many targets as you see, that's how many instances of the Target class exist at this moment in the running of the program. There is just one Target class, on the other hand, and you can see it listed in the Project Window.

Whenever a message is sent, it is sent to some particular instance. Returning to Figure 3-1, we can see why this makes sense. A target is a type of object, and any target object needs to know how to explode; but at this moment we're sending the Explode message to this particular target. A scorebox is a type of object, and any scorebox object needs to maintain a score and to know how to increase it; but at this

---

[*] I simplify somewhat. In Chapter 4 we see ways to modify this behavior.

---

moment we're sending the Increase message to this particular scorebox so it will increase its particular score.*

So, in Figure 3-2, each separate round thing in the window on the left was drawn by sending the Draw message to a different instance of the Target class. Each of these different instances drew itself in the same way, though, because the knowledge of how to react to the Draw message is embedded in just one place, the Target class, shown on the right. The Code Window is the Target class's Code Window, and you can see the actual code that each target instance is using to draw itself at every moment.

It may appear at this point that the relationship between classes and instances borders upon the metaphysical. Anyone who knows anything about philosophy will be inclined to suspect that classes and instances are just another way of talking about universals and particulars. Indeed, object-oriented programming seems to fulfill Plato's philosophical program announced in the *Euthyphro* (6e):†

> SOCRATES. Now, you recall that I asked you to explain to me, not this or that particular pious thing, but that Form Itself through which all pious things are pious? You did say, I believe, that it was through one Form that impious things are impious and pious things are pious; don't you remember?
>
> EUTHYPHRO. Yes, I do.
>
> SOCRATES. All right, then; so, explain to me what is this Form Itself, so that by keeping my eyes upon it and using it as a model, I may declare that whatever you or anyone else does that is of this sort, is pious, and that whatever is not, is not.

The problems with Plato's characterization are well known: the Form seems to be a "thing" separate from the particular things of the world around us, the notion "through" is crucial but slippery, and Plato seems to equivocate rather glibly between the Form's being responsible for a thing's being such and such and our ability to know that a thing is such and such; thus, his program is almost certainly doomed to failure as an explanation of how the world works. But he is perfectly accurate about how an object-oriented program works! If an instance is of the Pious type, there really is a separate Pious class that really is responsible for the instance being such as it is.

Fortunately, unlike Plato's Forms and particulars, there is nothing mysterious, metaphysical, or vague about the relationship between classes and instances. And REALbasic makes the relationship especially clear, and the distinction especially sharp, by

---

* Some implementations of object classes permit class properties, whose value is in common for every object of that class. Similarly, some implementations of object classes permit class methods, where a message can be sent to a class without directing it at any particular instance. REALbasic does not have class properties or class methods, but the lack is not a very serious one, because REALbasic allows global properties, global methods, and global instances, as explained in Chapter 4.

† My translation.

locating classes and instances firmly in two different worlds (Plato would have been proud!), as follows.

In the IDE, every object you edit is a class. Every window listed in the Project Window and viewed in a Window Editor is a class. Every control whose icon is shown in the Tools Window is a class. Any new class you create is a class.

In your code, on the other hand, every object to which you send a message is an instance. In fact, your application, as it runs, consists of nothing but a lot of instances, sending messages to one another. And since REALbasic's built-in objects know how to portray themselves on the screen as interface elements, the interface of the running application may be thought of as being composed of instances. The window that appears as the application runs corresponds to an instance. The button contained by the window corresponds to an instance. The menu item you choose corresponds to an instance.

 The principle just enunciated is so important and so fundamental to one's ability to work in REALbasic with fluidity and understanding that I call it *The Golden Rule of REALbasic*. The following mantra serves to summarize the Golden Rule, and repeating it daily (preferably in front of a mirror, though this is not absolutely necessary) is guaranteed to bring enlightenment and to dispel the clouds of confusion: *In the IDE, only classes. In the running application, only instances.*

Figure 3-3 illustrates the Golden Rule. The programmer is shown editing classes; then the application is built and run, and the running application consists of instances, which can receive messages, and some of which are responsible for interacting with the user.

In Chapter 1 it was pointed out, in connection with properties, that editing in the IDE sets up the initial conditions of the application, but then, once the application has actually started running, the code takes over, and has the power to change those properties. A somewhat analogous observation may be made with respect to classes and instances. Editing in the IDE defines the classes for all the objects that will appear in the running application, but it is only as the application starts up, and as the application continues to run, that any instances of those classes are generated, so that messages may be sent to them, so that subroutines may be called, so that the application can actually do anything.

The reader, as programmer, will thus be seriously concerned with how instances are generated (so that there will be something to send a message to) and how they are referred to in code (so that one can specify which object the message is to be sent to). Before we come to this, though, we round out our discussion of classes by providing a road map of the internals of a class.

The Application Class

As your application starts up, the Application class (or a subclass of it, if you've created one) is instantiated once, automatically. This single instance persists throughout the lifetime of the application. You cannot instantiate the Application class (or its subclass) in code.

Because an instance of it is absolutely guaranteed to exist uniquely and at all times, the Application class is an appropriate repository for methods and properties that are to be available always from anywhere (*globally*). Global methods and properties are taken up in Chapter 4. Other features of the Application class are discussed in Chapter 7.

The Default Window Class

Every application has either one default window class or none. To determine which is the default window class, choose Edit → Project Settings and, in the resulting dialog, use the Default Window popup; you can specify any existing window class, or "<none>".

If there is a default window class, an instance of it is generated automatically as the application starts up, just after the Application class is instantiated. This also instantiates the controls within the window, as we shall see. There is nothing special about the default window instance; it's just a convenience so your application has something to get started with, if you like. Nor does the default window class behave specially in any other way. Your code can generate further instances of it, and any instance of it can be destroyed, just as with any window class, by closing the window.

Control Classes

Controls are instances contained by windows. Basically, the rule is that you cannot instantiate a control in code, and you don't need to worry about doing so: a window will automatically instantiate all the controls it contains, when it itself is instantiated. (The rule is actually slightly more complicated than this; as we shall see later in this chapter, once a control has been instantiated by its containing window, the instance can be cloned to make another instance.)

Menu Items

Items in menus at the top of the screen are instances of the MenuItem class (or of a subclass of the MenuItem class). You cannot instantiate a MenuItem; instead, you set up your MenuItems in the Menu Editor, and they are automatically instantiated as your application starts up. (As with controls, I am deliberately ignoring for the present the matter of cloning MenuItems.) MenuItems are discussed in Chapter 6.

Noncontrol Classes

If an instance is not contained in a window, is not a MenuItem, is not the Application class instance, and is not the initial default window class instance, it does not exist until your code in the running application explicitly generates it. This is done in one of two ways.

One way is for your code to call a function that creates and returns an instance of the class. Quite a number of such functions are provided. For example, the GetFolderItem function takes a file's pathname, expressed as a string, and returns an instance of the FolderItem class that corresponds to that file; so, given a file *myFile* in a folder *myFolder* on a disk *myDisk*, we might say:

```
dim f as folderItem
f = getFolderItem("myDisk:myFolder:myFile")
```

Since GetFolderItem is a function returning a FolderItem, we must call it in a context where a value of type FolderItem is expected. In this example we have assigned the value to a variable declared as being of this type.

The second way to make a new instance is with the New operator. This operator must be accompanied by the name of the class of which a new instance is to be made; it instantiates the class and returns the instance just as a function does. Let's suppose your project has a window class, MyOtherWindow. Then you could say:

```
dim w as myOtherWindow
w = new myOtherWindow
```

This causes an instance of the MyOtherWindow class to be generated; typically, indeed, a MyOtherWindow window will visibly appear in the running application.

Like a function, the New operator returns a value, so it must be used in a context where a value of the particular class type is expected. In this example, we have assigned it to a variable declared as being of this type.[*]

In the case of window classes only, there is a third way to make an instance, discussed in the next section.

Referring to Instances

Once your application is running and some instances have been generated, much of the action will be precipitated by your code calling methods, and getting and setting properties—in other words, by sending messages to instances.

Many of REALbasic's built-in methods, as was pointed out earlier, are global, but many of them belong to some particular class, and the only way you can call these is by sending a message to an instance of that class. The same is true for methods that

---

[*] The syntax of New must be modified if the class being instantiated has a constructor; this is explained in Chapter 4.

you write: you can write global methods (as will be explained in Chapter 4), but for the most part, in line with the considerations presented in "Object Design Philosophy" earlier in this chapter, you'll write them as method handlers in some class, and the only way you can call such a method is by sending a message to an instance of that class.

Exactly the same thing is true for properties. Many of REALbasic's built-in classes have properties, and you will often need to retrieve the value of such properties, as a way of obtaining information; for example, getting a window's Top and Left properties tells you where it is on the screen. You'll also frequently want to change the value of such properties; for example, setting a window's Top and Left properties is how you move the window. And of course you'll frequently have properties you've created yourself, and though you can make global properties, more often you'll declare the property in some particular class, and then you'll want to get or set the property's value, in code, and the way you get and set a class's property in code is by sending a message to an instance of that class.

Now, we already know the syntax by which your code will send a message to an instance—dot notation. As explained earlier in this chapter, what appears after the dot will be the name of a property or method, and the syntax of the dot notation expression as a whole is the same as that of a variable name or a subroutine call.

But what about what comes *before* the dot? This is where you tell REALbasic what instance to send the message to. You do this by providing a *reference* to the desired instance—a name or other expression that specifies the instance in question.

The ability to provide a reference to an instance is thus of crucial importance. To repeat: In REALbasic's object-oriented programming environment, making things happen is largely a matter of sending messages to instances. If you can't send a message to an instance, you can't make any of its method handlers execute, or get or set any of its properties. And you can't send a message to an instance if you can't say what instance it is. Thus, it is crucial to know how to refer, in code, to any desired instance. It is not too much to say (and I do often say it) that 99% of the art of writing REALbasic code lies in knowing *how to obtain a reference to an instance*. That's what the rest of this chapter is about, so pay attention!

Being able to provide a reference to an instance is important for another reason: an instance with no way to refer to it is useless and in fact will cease to exist; see "Destruction of Instances," later in this chapter. For certain instances, REALbasic sees to it that there is always a reference, and therefore that the instance will persist—in particular, with the Application instance and the MenuItem instances, and for windows and their controls. But otherwise it is up to the programmer to see to it that there is some way for an instance, once generated, to be referred to, for as long as it is needed.

One way to be perfectly certain of this is to maintain a name, so let's talk about that first.

Maintaining a Name

A very typical way to refer to an instance in code is to use the name of a variable or property to which that instance has been assigned. Once such an assignment has been made, then as long as that variable or property persists, and as long as some other value is not assigned to the variable or property, this name can be used as a reference to the instance.

For example, recall from the previous section that a FolderItem instance was generated by saying:

```
dim f as folderItem
f = getFolderItem("myDisk:myFolder:myFile")
```

After this assignment, f refers to a FolderItem instance, and can be sent messages appropriate to a FolderItem. For example, a FolderItem has a Delete method, so we could say:

```
f.delete
```

This would send the Delete message to the FolderItem instance to which f refers, which would respond by executing the FolderItem class's Delete method (which happens to mean that it would delete a file, though for the purpose of the example that's unimportant).

Let's do it again, for good measure. Recall that earlier we generated a window class instance by saying:

```
dim w as myOtherWindow
w = new myOtherWindow
```

Afterward, w refers to the instance just generated, and we can use w to keep referring to this same window instance, sending it messages such as these:

```
w.top = 50
w.title = "This is fun!"
```

A variable's scope and lifetime are very limited, though. Variables stop existing when their subroutine finishes executing, and they can be referred to only from within that subroutine. If we wish to maintain a reference to an instance for longer than a single subroutine, and to be able to use that reference from elsewhere, we may prefer to assign the instance to a property; a property is itself part of an instance of a class, and persists as long as *that* instance does. (If this gives you a vision of instances stored in properties stored in instances stored in properties stored in instances, you're absolutely right.)

Be warned: merely declaring a variable or property has nothing to do with instances! It doesn't generate an instance, and it doesn't make a reference to an instance. Thus, just after this Dim statement, f is not a reference to a FolderItem at all:

```
dim f as folderItem
```

The declaration says that the variable f is to be of the FolderItem type, but until you have actually gotten hold of an actual FolderItem instance and assigned this FolderItem instance as a value to f, f does not refer to a FolderItem instance *and must not be sent any messages*. If you were to say this:

```
dim f as folderItem
f.delete // oh, no! error: NilObjectException
```

an exception would be raised, meaning that your application would terminate prematurely (unless you are prepared to catch the exception, as described in Chapter 8). I will have more to say on this topic later in the chapter.

Functions as References

A number of built-in REALbasic functions return an instance. Also, it is possible for you to write such a function. Since the result of a function is substituted for the function call, the function call itself is a reference to an instance. Under certain circumstances, that will be the only reference you need.

For example, on rare occasions, an instance is maintained so briefly that it doesn't require a name at all. Consider the task of deleting a file on disk given its pathname. We could say:

```
dim f as folderItem
f = getFolderItem("myDisk:myFolder:myFile")
f.delete
```

But if *all* we wish to do with this file is delete it, there is no need for such elaborate measures; we're not going to refer to this FolderItem ever again, so the name f is not required later on, and it certainly isn't required as an intermediary just so we can send an instance the Delete message. Rather, we can create the instance and send it the Delete message all in one line; we lose all ability to refer to the instance immediately afterward, but we don't care:

```
getFolderItem("myDisk:myFolder:myFile").delete
```

Windows are another good example of where it can be easier to get a reference as the result of a function. It happens that REALbasic maintains a list of window instances for us, and we can consult this list by calling the Window function. To do so, we hand the Window function the index of the window we want, where the index number corresponds to the layering order of windows from front to back (that is, window(0) is the frontmost window). This is useful particularly when the order of windows is what we are concerned with. For example, let's suppose that our application has three windows showing. And suppose we have a menu item, Toggle Front Two, which brings the second window to the front. How can we know which *is* the second window? We could maintain a name for each window and keep a list of the windows in order, changing the list each time the user brings a different window to the front. But this would be tedious and a waste of effort, because the Window function already exists. To get a reference to the second window, it is sufficient to speak of `window(1)`. Since the Show method brings a window to the front, the way to bring the second window to the front is simply to say:

```
window(1).show
```

Paradoxically, sometimes we are forced to set aside a name for an instance even though we don't need it. For example, the Window function (and the Self function and the global instance name, which we shall come to in a moment) may be enough to ensure that we will be able to obtain a reference to a window without maintaining a name for it. But all the same, we are often compelled, when we wish to instantiate a window class using `New`, to assign the result to a name anyway! That's because we cannot say simply:

```
new myOtherWindow // error: Statement expected
```

The `New` operator returns a result, and we must do something with that result. The simplest option is to assign that result to a variable; but this means we must go to all the trouble of declaring that variable beforehand and performing the assignment even though we may have no intention of using this variable ever again:

```
dim w as myOtherWindow
w = new myOtherWindow // and that may be the last we'll ever hear of w
```

Self

Code can obtain a reference to the instance that is actually running that code by way of the Self function. It may not be obvious to you what class this will be an instance of, so just follow this rule: in whatever class's Code Editor the Self function appears, the result of Self will be an instance of that class. It may also not be obvious to you what instance of that class will be running the code (unless there is just one instance of the class, of course); but that's exactly why use of the Self function is such an important technique—the programmer, writing code in a class, may have no idea what instance will actually execute that code and when, and doesn't need to know.

For example, suppose that, in our arcade game, when a target receives the Explode message, one of the things it ultimately does is to vanish, and that the way it does this is by setting its own Visible property to `false`. The programmer, writing the Explode method handler in the Target class, therefore wants to set this Target instance's Visible property to `false`. But which instance is that? The programmer has no notion which target the user will hit, or even of how many targets there may be at the time; how can the message be sent to the correct Target instance? Use of the Self function solves the problem:

```
self.visible = false
```

That line appears within the Target class's Code Editor, so Self means a Target instance. In particular, it means the Target instance that actually executes the line. Since the line appears in the Target class's Explode method, the instance is the

---

Target instance that is running the Explode method. But the only way a method can be executing is if an instance is sent a message that calls it. So the Target instance running this code is obviously the Target instance to which the Explode message was sent. And that's the very instance that should vanish.

For an event handler of a control in a window, the rule about the Code Editor means that Self returns a reference to the window instance. This means that Self has a second use: it acts as a line of communication between a control and the window that contains it. If you drag a PushButton from the Tools Window into a Window Editor, and make its Action event handler go like this:

```
msgBox str(self.width)
```

and run the project and press the button, the dialog will display the width of the window, not the button. The button's Action event handler is edited in the window's Code Editor, so Self means the window. (To access the button's Top, you could say `me.top`; see "Me," later in this chapter.)

When sending a message to the instance returned by Self, it is permitted, as a kind of shorthand, to omit `self` altogether. In this syntax, only the name of the message appears. (Personally, I must admit to wishing that this shorthand didn't exist. In my opinion, it only confuses things: it makes code harder to read, and it puzzles beginners, who can't figure out why sometimes they can access a certain property, control, or method and sometimes they can't.)

This explains the technique outlined in Chapter 2, where the reader was invited to test the use of subroutines by calling a window's method handler from a button's Action event handler by name alone. On page 43, when we said `msgbox str(average(3,5))`, this use of `average` was really a shorthand for `self.average`; we were actually sending a message to Self, the window instance containing the button.

In order to understand how it can be possible to omit `self`, you need to know how REALbasic resolves names. So that's the next topic.

Resolution of Names

REALbasic figures out what you mean when you use a name by searching the namespaces in a definite order:

1. If the context is that of a method call, REALbasic looks among its own built-in global methods.

2. If the context is that of a variable name, REALbasic looks among the local variables.

3. REALbasic looks among the members of the class of which an instance would be returned by Self.

4. REALbasic looks among any global methods or properties that you've defined in a module, as explained in Chapter 4.

REAL Software, Inc., have asked me to warn you that the name resolution order is officially undocumented and therefore subject to change. I'm glad of this, since it is a very peculiar order, and has some confusing ramifications. My purpose in this section is not to encourage you to take any sort of deliberate advantage of the name resolution order, but rather to point out some of the problems it can cause you.

You can define a local variable called msgbox, but you can never refer to it, because msgbox always means the global method. On the other hand, if you define a method handler called MsgBox in a window, you can refer to it; msgbox still means the global method, but self.msgbox means the method handler. But built-in properties (and built-in constants) behave quite differently. A window has a built-in Top property; you can define a variable called Top in window code and still refer to it separately from the built-in Top property:

```
dim top as integer
top = 0 // sets the variable
self.top = 40 // sets the built-in property
```

On the other hand, if you create a window property Top, you can never refer to the window's built-in Top property; it becomes absolutely unavailable, and that's bad because now you've killed a piece of REALbasic's built-in functionality (you can't move the window vertically, or find out where it is). The fact that REALbasic doesn't prevent you from declaring a property that overrides a built-in property of a class is probably to be considered a bug—especially since REALbasic does prevent you from declaring a method handler that overrides a built-in method of a class.

Referring to Controls

A control instance is generated automatically by the instantiation of its containing window, so you are given no chance to capture a reference to it as a name. Therefore, it has a name already—the value of its Name property in the Properties Window. We may speak of this as the control instance's *global name*. The instance can be referred to in any context, by chaining its global name to a reference to the window, using dot notation:

```
theWindow.theControl.theMessage
```

Since code within a window's Code Editor can obtain a reference to the window using the Self function, the Self function enables such code to refer to any control within the same window. For example, suppose a window contains two PushButton instances, named PushButton1 and PushButton2, and we wish the first, when pushed, to disable the second (by setting its Enabled property to false). The Pushbutton1 Action event handler (in the window's Code Editor) can say:

```
self.pushButton2.enabled = false
```

Furthermore, self as a message recipient can be omitted; therefore, in actuality it suffices to say:

```
pushButton2.enabled = false
```

But to speak of a control in a different window, we need an explicit reference to the window:

```
isEnabled = w.pushButton2.enabled
```

A completely different way to obtain a reference to a control in a window is through the window's Control function. The parameter is a zero-based index value specifying the desired control (the order of the controls is the order set in the Format → Control Order dialog). To learn the upper bound of this parameter, subtract 1 from the window's ControlCount property. For example, the following routine interrogates a window to learn how many of its controls are instances of PushButton (or subclasses thereof):*

```
dim  i, j, u as integer
u = myOtherWindow.controlCount - 1
for i = 0 to u
    if myOtherWindow.control(i) isa pushButton then
        j = j + 1
    end
next
msgbox "MyOtherWindow has " + str(j) + " buttons."
```

Me

Code within a control's event handlers in a window class's Code Editor can obtain a reference to the control instance that is actually running that code by way of the Me function (not to be confused with the Self function, which refers, in such code, to the containing window).

As far as I can tell, the Me function is merely a convenience; it makes code easier to read and write, but it doesn't do anything for you that you couldn't already do. Every control instance already has a unique name, and there is no possibility that you're not going to know this name, so you could always have gotten a reference to the control without Me.

For example, let's suppose that we have some code inside PushButton1's Action event handler that moves PushButton2 to a position underneath PushButton1. Then we can say (omitting self for the sake of brevity):

```
pushButton2.left = pushButton1.left
pushButton2.top = pushButton1.top + pushButton1.height + 2
```

There isn't really any problem with this; but it seems sort of silly for PushButton1 to be talking about itself as pushButton1, and it makes it less obvious what the code is supposed to do. This is clearer:

```
pushButton2.left = me.left
pushButton2.top = me.top + me.height + 2
```

---

* For IsA, which reports whether an instance is of a given class, see Chapter 4.

Also, you could then later change the name of PushButton1 or copy-and-paste this code into a different button, and this code would still successfully refer to it.

Me and Self differ only within the event handlers of a control in a window's Code Editor. In other contexts, they may be used interchangeably. It is not, however, permitted to omit me in the way that one may omit self. Indeed, it would be a mistake to do so, because in the situation where Me and Self differ, REALbasic will assume that what's omitted is self, which means the window, not the control. For example, suppose PushButton1 says:

```
pushButton2.top = top + height + 2 // oops
```

PushButton2 promptly vanishes, because it has just been placed lower than the bottom edge of the window.

The Window Global Instance Name

Window instances can be referred to in a special way: you use the window's class name as an instance name. You may do this for only one instance of each window class (obviously, since you could not use the same name to refer to more than one instance!). We shall call this name, which is the same as the window's class name, its *global instance name*. So, for example, if the default window class of your project is Window1, you can refer to one instance of it as window1.

The global instance name may seem like a strange thing: you're abusing the syntax of the language, speaking of an instance by using the name of a class. However, the device is actually rather a clever one. Window instances persist even if you have not maintained a name to refer to them (see "Maintaining a Name," earlier in this chapter); through the global instance name, all your window classes can have one instance to which nevertheless you always possess a reference.

There is a tricky rule associated with using global instance names. The way you instantiate a window class so as to be able to refer to that instance using the global instance name is *not* to use New. Instead, you just refer to the instance by its global instance name even though the instance doesn't exist. This doesn't cause an error; rather, the window class will automatically be instantiated, and your reference starts working immediately as a way of speaking of this new instance. In other words: whenever you use a window's global instance name at a time when no instance by that name exists, an instance by that name is generated. This is called *implicit instantiation*.

So, for example, let's say your project has a window class, MyOtherWindow, and let's say that no implicitly generated instance of MyOtherWindow exists. Then you can say:

```
myOtherWindow.title = "Info"
myOtherWindow.left = 20
```

The first line instantiates MyOtherWindow, assigns the new instance the global instance name myOtherWindow, and sets the value of the new instance's Title property, all in one move. The second line sets the value of the same instance's Left property; it doesn't implicitly generate a new instance of MyOtherWindow, because an instance with the global instance name already exists (the one generated by the first line).

Now, on the one hand, it's clear enough why implicit instantiation exists. If it didn't, the global instance name would be useless, because how would you (or REALbasic) know which instance of this window class the global instance name refers to? With implicit instantiation, it is possible to be very clear about this, because at every moment either there is or there isn't an instance of the window class to which the global instance name refers. If there is, that's the one. If there isn't, a new instance of the window class is generated, and this new instance becomes the one.

But although implicit instantiation may be explicable, it still tricks many REALbasic beginners—and not-so-beginners. Misuse of the syntax, which is all too easy, will cause a window instance to be created accidentally. Moreover, if there is already an instance of this window class, the new window may be created directly on top of the old one, so that the programmer, running and debugging the application, thinks it *is* the old one; an extra window has been created, and the programmer doesn't even know it. This is the source of many strange phenomena.

For example, let's suppose that the window class MyOtherWindow contains a button PushButton1. And let's suppose that you say:

```
dim w as myOtherWindow
w = new myOtherWindow
myOtherWindow.title = "Hello" // oops
w.pushbutton1.caption = "Press Me"
```

The window appears, and its titlebar changes, but the button's caption doesn't change. What's gone wrong? Nothing; but what you said isn't what you meant. Here are the consequences of this code. First, an instance of the MyOtherWindow class is created, using New, and a window appears; that instance is w. Then, a *second* instance of the MyOtherWindow class is created, using implicit instantiation, so a second window appears, hiding the first; that instance is myOtherWindow. The second window's title is changed to Hello. Finally, the first window's button's caption is changed to Press Me, but you can't see this, because the second window is in the way!

A more subtle error is to use the global instance name where a class name was intended. Suppose, for example, you wish to know whether the frontmost window is an instance of the MyOtherWindow class. You can get a reference to the frontmost window as window(0), so you might be tempted to say:

```
if window(0) = myOtherWindow then // oops
```

If there is no instance of MyOtherWindow with the global instance name, this expression will generate one, by implicit instantiation. The problem is that you asked the wrong question; you asked whether two instances were the same instance. What you wanted to know was:

```
if window(0) isA myOtherWindow then
```

Now `myOtherWindow` is just a class name, because `IsA` takes a class name; and no implicit instantiation takes place.*

A window instantiated by using `New` does not receive the global instance name, regardless of what name you use to maintain a reference to it. Suppose that a subroutine were to create an instance of the MyOtherWindow class in this way:

```
dim myOtherWindow as myOtherWindow
myOtherWindow = new myOtherWindow
```

The window thus created does not receive the global instance name, because implicit instantiation was not used. It's true that the name `myOtherWindow` refers to the window just created, but it's still just a name that you're maintaining (here, it's a local variable name). So if another subroutine were later to say:

```
myOtherWindow.pushbutton1.caption = "Press me"
```

this would create a second window, by implicit instantiation, rather than referring to the first.

The default window class is a special case. If your project has a default window class, then when that window is automatically instantiated as the application starts up, that instance is assigned the global instance name. So if your default window class is Window1, and if the automatically created window is still present, then when you say:

```
window1.top = 100
```

no new window is created; the default window is moved.

The Truth About Controls

The term *control* is used in two ways in REALbasic. In general, a control is an instance that is contained in a window. The window automatically generates the instance, when the window itself is instantiated. You can make a control from any programmer-defined class (except a window class), by dragging the class's listing from the Project Window into a Window Editor.

There is also a built-in Control class; an instance of a subclass of the Control class can exist *only* as a control (that is, it must be contained in a window). REALbasic supplies many built-in Control subclasses; all of these are represented by icons in the Tools Window. A few icons in the Tools Window also represent built-in classes that are not Control subclasses. You can make a control from any class represented in the Tools Window, by dragging its icon into a Window Editor.

When you make a control by dragging into a Window Editor, what are you really doing? Let's suppose that what you drag is the PushButton icon from the Tools

---

* For `IsA`, see Chapter 4. The equality test with instance names is discussed later in this chapter.

Window. This icon represents a class—the built-in PushButton class. In dragging it into a Window Editor, you are not making a new class, because the PushButton class already exists; but you cannot be generating an instance, either, because what you edit in the IDE are classes. What you're actually doing is editing the *window* class, telling it to contain an instance of the PushButton class. Let's suppose this is the Window1 Window Editor. You're saying to the Window1 window class: "I want there to be a control that is an instance of the PushButton class. This instance is going to be your responsibility, Window1! You contain it. So, part of your job is to instantiate the PushButton class whenever you yourself are instantiated."

This makes perfect sense, because it captures our intuitive notion of window types. Let's say you're writing an email application, and one of your window types is for composing a new email message, and has a Send button in the upper right. You want the user to be able to work on several new messages at once. Therefore, more than one of these email composition windows may have to be open; in object terms, there will have to be more than one instance of this window class. So each of those windows should have a Send button in the upper right, because they are the same type of window.

That is precisely what will happen. You have one window class representing this type of window. You use the Window Editor to help describe this class to REALbasic. Part of the way you do this is to drag a PushButton icon from the Tools Window into this window class's Window Editor. This lets REALbasic know that the window is to contain a PushButton instance. You also use the IDE to describe the PushButton instance's initial properties. For example, you might dictate that its Caption property should be "Send". And the position and dimensions of the button's representation in the Window Editor also set the initial values of the instance's Top, Left, Width, and Height properties. Now each time a window of that class is instantiated in your running application, it instantiates a PushButton and initializes its properties. Thus, each window of this type that actually appears when your application runs will contain a button, at that position, with those dimensions, and with the caption Send.

Nor is it just a matter of how the Send button will *look*; there's also the matter of how it will *behave*. If you give the Send button some functionality in its Action event handler in the window's Code Editor, you expect that the Send buttons in all instances of this window type will exhibit this same functionality. And so they do. But why? Not because you've edited the PushButton class; after all, not every Push-Button does this. Nor because you've created and edited a PushButton subclass; you haven't. It's because in editing the button's Action event handler within the window's Code Editor, it's the *window* class's code that you're really editing. You're saying to the window class: "Oh, and one more thing: when the user clicks on that PushButton instance you created, here's the code that should be executed."

This explains the fact noted in Chapter 1, that when you double-click a control in a Window Editor to edit its code, it is the *window's* Code Editor that opens. It also explains why, in this code, Self refers to the window, as described earlier in this chapter.

Control Clones and Control Arrays

There is usually no need for you to instantiate any controls in code, because you have already effectively instantiated beforehand all the controls you're going to need, by dragging them into a Window Editor. The window will instantiate them for you, when it itself is instantiated. That's what it means for an instance to be a control, and what it means for it to be contained in a window.

Nonetheless, you *can* instantiate a control in code, provided that an instance of that control exists in that window already (ultimately because you dragged it into a Window Editor). In other words, your code, although it cannot create an instance of a control *ex nihilo*, can *clone* an existing control. The values of properties can differ from clone to clone (for example, different clones of one button can have different positions in the window), but their event handlers in the window's Code Editor are shared.

You don't have to wait to do your cloning until the application runs; you can clone a control manually, in the IDE. We'll see in a moment why you might want to do this. But first, let's pause to discuss the matter of dynamic creation and destruction of controls.

Some newcomers to REALbasic are disappointed at its inability to create controls dynamically that are not clones. But this limitation is not as serious as it may appear, because no rule says that the existing control, the one that is to be cloned, must be visible. In other words, you can't create a control *ex nihilo* while the application is running, but you can certainly make it seem as if you did. As far as the user is concerned, a button can be made to appear in a window where none was previously, and that's all that matters. The truth is that this button existed already, but it was invisible, or was located outside the boundaries of the window. In fact, a common technique is to avoid cloning controls in code altogether, through the use of invisible controls. For example, if you know that you will need up to 10 buttons, you can create 10 buttons in the IDE and make them invisible. (If they will all have the same functionality, they can be clones of a single button, or instances of a single button subclass.) When the application runs, if it needs to present one of these buttons to the user, it just makes it visible.

By the same token, you can't get rid of a clone dynamically when you're done with it—because a control in general cannot be destroyed dynamically.* Again, as a

---

* But MenuItem clones can be destroyed. See Chapter 6.

workaround, you might consider a static set of clones whose items become visible or invisible as necessary. Or, instead of cloning controls at all, you might consider structuring your interface so that each control appears in a separate window; a window can be closed, and this destroys both the window and its controls.

REALbasic assists you to make controls visible and invisible *en masse*; see "Shifting Other Controls" in Chapter 11, and Chapter 18.

Control Arrays

Not just any control can be cloned. To clone a control, the control must be a member of a control array.

A *control array* is a construct for referring to a set of control clones numerically. It is not quite the same as an array of controls. An array of controls would be an array whose elements can refer to *any* control instances of the appropriate type; a control array consists of all the clones of a single control within a single window.

The notation for referring to the various clones within a control array is just like the notation for referring to the elements of any array: you use the array name and an index number, which is zero-based. The array name is the control's global name. For example, there might be three clones of a PushButton instance. The name of the control array is the global name of the original control, which might be pushButton1. The individual clones would then typically be pushButton1(0), pushButton1(1), and pushButton1(2). These names can be used just like any control's global name. For example:

```
window1.pushButton1(2).caption = "Delete"
```

Control arrays lack the functions of normal arrays. You cannot learn their size with Ubound. Also, you cannot use Insert, Append, or Remove on a control array. The really bad part is that you cannot pass a control array as a parameter to a subroutine: you can pass a control (including a control that is part of a control array), and you can pass an array, but you can't pass a control array. This situation becomes a genuine hindrance if we wish to cycle through several different control arrays, doing the same thing to the members of each of them;* there is no general way of doing so, and I regard this fact as a bug.

Nevertheless, control arrays have four great advantages. First, a control array makes it easy for your code to get a reference to a dynamically cloned control. For example, an original button, instantiated automatically by its window, has a global name; it might be pushButton1 (or whatever name you assigned it in the Properties Window). But without control arrays, a clone of this button generated by your code would have no global name in and of itself; it would be up to you to maintain another name that refers to it.

---

* The workaround is to construct normal arrays and use their elements to point to the members of the control array; but at that point the control array itself becomes meaningless.

The second advantage of a control array is that, just like any array, it lets you refer to controls by index number, which is valuable in contexts where arithmetic most conveniently specifies the desired control. To repeat the example from Chapter 2, suppose we are playing a game involving a four-by-four grid; the squares where pieces can go might be represented by Canvas control instances. These Canvas controls are all going to behave identically, so they can be clones of one another. Thus they constitute a control array, and can be referred to as myCanvas(1), myCanvas(2), and so forth up to the 16th square, which is numbered myCanvas(0). This means that the square vertically beneath myCanvas(n) is:

    myCanvas((n+4) mod 16)

The game grid is a good example of why you'd clone a control in the IDE. You know how many myCanvas clones you're going to need, so there is no point generating them dynamically in code; you're creating the clones just to take advantage of the power of control arrays.

The third advantage of control arrays is that they are self-initializing. With an ordinary array, your code must declare the array in some persistent storage, and then initialize it. If this were an array of controls, say an array of 16 Canvas controls, this would involve setting the first element to refer to the first Canvas, the second element to refer to the second Canvas, and so forth. With a control array, the global names myCanvas(0), myCanvas(1), and so on, automatically exist, and automatically refer to the clones.

The fourth advantage of a control array is that a control in a control array knows its own index number within the array. Such a thing would require a lot of work with an ordinary array, but with a control array, it's simply handed to you. This means that even though the code of clones is shared, the actual functionality of each clone can differ depending on the index. That's very powerful. In our game grid, for example, a square represented by a Canvas in a control array can identify the square beneath itself because it knows its own index.

There are two ways to learn the index number of a control that is part of a control array. First, if the code is in one of the control's event handlers in a window's Code Editor, it receives its own index as a subroutine parameter named Index. (This also works for menu event handlers, discussed in Chapter 6.) To take a trivial example, consider a button whose Action event handler contains this code:

    dim i, u as integer
    u = index + 1 // index is handed to us as a parameter
    for i = 1 to u
       beep
    next

Three clones of this button as a control array (let's say they are pushButton1(0), pushButton1(1), and pushButton1(2)) would behave differently when pressed: the

---

variable or property a valid integer, single, or double value (a form of 0); and declaring a variable or property as a boolean assigns it the valid boolean value `false`.

But objects don't work the same way. That's because an object name is merely a pointer; the instance itself has an independent existence (remember?). Declaring a variable or property as an object type uses the name of a class, but it doesn't instantiate that class. Getting an instance and assigning it to the variable or property is up to you. Until you do so, the variable or property has a value, which is `nil`. The value `nil` means merely: "I am supposed to point to an instance, but at the moment I don't." A variable or property whose value is `nil` is a *nil pointer*.

Only an instance can be sent a message; but `nil` isn't an instance. If you send `nil` a message, your application will terminate prematurely.* This means that you must be concerned with not using a nil pointer as the recipient of a message. The name of a variable, the moment that variable is declared as having an object datatype, is a nil pointer. When you `Dim` a variable to an object type, the variable is a nil pointer. If an array has an object datatype, then when that array is declared, all of its elements are nil pointers, and if the array is redimmed to create new elements, the new elements are nil pointers. If a class has a property with an object datatype, then whenever that class is instantiated, that property of the new instance is a nil pointer.

There are several ways to avoid sending a message to a nil pointer. One is simply to be careful. However, accidents will happen, so it is useful to have some programming tricks up your sleeve to make it less likely that you will forget what you're doing and accidentally send a message to a nil pointer.

Since you cannot avoid generating nil pointers, one rule of thumb is to keep those nil pointers as short-lived as possible; the moment you make one, you immediately replace its `nil` value with an instance, if you can. So, for example:

```
dim f as folderItem // f is a nil pointer
f = getFolderItem("myDisk:myFolder:myFile") // f is no longer a nil pointer, you hope
```

is better than:

```
dim f as folderItem
// ... two hundred lines of code, during which f is a nil pointer ...
f = getFolderItem("myDisk:myFolder:myFile")
```

Another device is to test the waters before you dive in, by comparing a value to `nil` before you use its name as a reference to an instance:

```
dim f as folderItem
// ... two hundred lines of code, during which f may or may not have been assigned an instance ...
if f <> nil then
    f.delete // f is an instance, so it's okay to send it a message
end
```

---

* Actually, it will raise an exception (a NilObjectException); you can catch this exception to prevent premature termination, as explained in Chapter 8.

Testing the waters is especially important when your means for assigning an instance to a property or variable may or may not have worked. We've just seen an example. This line:

```
f = getFolderItem("myDisk:myFolder:myFile")
```

will have no effect if *myDisk* or *myDisk:myFolder* doesn't exist (as explained in Chapter 21). Testing f for nil afterward is your way to find this out.

Declaring an array of objects generates multiple nil pointers at once. For some reason, even beginners who understand how to declare a variable and initialize it with an instance value have a tendency to forget that the same thing must be done for every element of an array. Typically, you will iterate through the array, obtaining an instance to assign to each element.

So, for example, imagine that we wish to create an array of Date instances, and then to assign each instance a value by way of its TotalSeconds property (this will all be made clear in Chapter 5). This is not the way:

```
dim d(5) as date
d(1).totalseconds = 1764098908.0 // game over, thank you for playing
```

Before we can send a message to an element of the array, that element must refer to an instance. A For loop lets us create instances easily:

```
dim d(5) as date
dim i as integer
for i = 1 to 5
    d(i) = new date
next
d(1).totalseconds = 1764098908.0 // no problem
```

Assignment Is not Cloning

Scalar values are copied by assignment. When you say:

```
dim this, that as string
this = "Hello"
that = this
this = "Goodbye"
```

then that is "Hello" and this is "Goodbye". The value of this was copied to become the value of that; moreover, the two copies are independent of one another, so afterward, changing this does not affect that.

But when a value whose datatype is an object is assigned to a variable or property, what is copied is merely a pointer. That's because the value in question *is* merely a pointer; the instance itself has an independent existence (remember??). If the source of this value was a variable or property referring to an instance, the result is that *two* variables or properties now refer to the selfsame instance. So, suppose we say this:

```
dim w, w2 as myOtherWindow
w = new myOtherWindow
```

```
w2 = w
w2.top = 50
w.top = 100
msgbox str(w2.top)
```

The dialog box displays "100." But how can that be? We just said that w2's Top property should be 50, and we didn't change it; how did it get to be 100? The answer is that w and w2 are both just pointers, and after the assignment:

```
w2 = w
```

they point to the same thing—a third thing, an instance. Saying:

```
w.top = 100
```

sends a message to that instance. In other words, w and w2 don't have a Top property; they are just names. It's the instance that has a Top property, and in our code there is only one instance. Our code sets that instance's Top property, first to 50, then to 100.

On the other hand, after the assignment:

```
w2 = w
```

you should not imagine that w and w2 are "two names for the same thing." That is a misleading formulation, and can get you into trouble. There are languages, such as C++, that allow you to make two names for the same thing;* but REALbasic doesn't (except through the medium of ByRef parameters), and that's not what's happening here. Rather, w and w2 are names for two different things—two different pointers. It's just that those two pointers *point* to the same thing.

Figure 3-5 schematizes the process of instantiation and assignment: object names are pointers, and the instance has independent existence.

I have seen many REALbasic beginners, and indeed many REALbasic programmers of long standing, absolutely stunned by this behavior. They are used to the intuitive notion that assigning one scalar to another clones the scalar's value, and they expect the same thing to happen with objects. This misunderstanding results in some astonishing code. For example, I often see people do this:

```
dim o, o2 as myClass
o = new myClass
o2 = new myClass
o2.itsProperty = "test"
o = o2
```

This programmer is laboring under three misconceptions. First, he thinks that the last line is copying the value "test" from o2.itsProperty to o.itsProperty. Second, he thinks that after the last line he still has two instances of MyClass. Third, he thinks that he needs the second line to provide an instance to copy o2's properties into.

---

* Confusingly, C++ calls such alternative names "references."

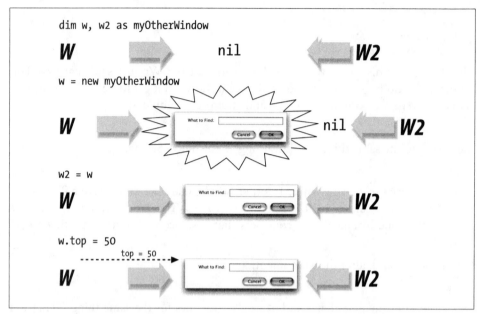

Figure 3-5. Object names are pointers

All three ideas are wrong. The last line causes o to stop being a reference to whatever it used to be a reference to, and to point to the very same instance that o2 points to. There is now only one MyClass instance. It's true that the second line generated an instance of MyClass, and caused o to point to it; but the last line caused o to point to the same instance as o2 instead, so the instance that o originally pointed to now has nothing pointing to it, becomes useless, and goes out of existence. That instance was utterly redundant, born only to die unused.

So, assignment is not cloning; it does not make a second instance with all the same property values as the first. How, then, do you clone an instance? The answer is, you do it the same way Superman gets into his trousers—one leg at a time. If you want the property values of one instance to be copied into the properties of another instance, you must copy them one by one:

```
dim o, o2 as myClass
o = new myClass
o2 = new myClass
o2.itsProperty = "test"
o2.itsOtherProperty = "test2"
// clone o2 into o
o.itsProperty = o2.itsProperty
o.itsOtherProperty = o2.itsOtherProperty
```

To be sure, if this is a class you have created yourself, and if this is something you're going to want to do frequently, you can abstract the cloning code into a method, and you very probably will. But that method must still copy the property values one at a time:

```
Sub clone(o as myClass)
    o.itsProperty = self.itsProperty
    o.itsOtherProperty = self.itsOtherProperty
End Sub
```

Once you are aware that assignment assigns a pointer, you can deliberately take advantage of this fact to achieve some very nice effects. Here are some examples.

Short names

If we have a button named PushButton1 in a window named MyOtherWindow, we can refer to it as `myOtherWindow.pushButton1`. But assignment gives us another way:

```
dim b as pushbutton
b = myOtherWindow.pushButton1
```

This makes subsequent references to our button shorter, and perhaps clearer. It isn't only a lot neater to say `b.top` than `myOtherWindow.pushButton1.top`, it can also make code faster. The reference `myOtherWindow.pushButton1` gives instructions for reaching our button in stages: first go to MyOtherWindow, now go to its PushButton1. The reference b points right at our button in one step. This saves time, and in a loop where the instance is accessed many times, it can save a lot of time. My tests show that the savings is about 25% for this simple example; there are circumstances in which it can be considerably more.

Linked data structures

Many data structures you read about in computer textbooks depend upon pointers to make links. For instance, a stack is a data structure where a simple implementation is for each item in the stack to consist of a value and a pointer to the next item in the stack. Thus, a stack containing the values 1, 4, and 9 would be implemented as 1 plus a pointer to the next item, which is 4 plus a pointer to the next item, which is 9 plus a pointer to nowhere (a nil pointer).

Beginners sometimes wonder how to make this sort of structure in REALbasic; "Where are the pointers?" they ask. The answer is that they are built right in, thanks to assignment. So, to construct the stack in question, we'd start by defining a class (we'll learn how to do this in Chapter 4), which I'll call Stack; let the class have two properties, which I'll call ItsValue and ItsPointer. The datatype of ItsValue is integer. The datatype of ItsPointer is Stack, which really means (as we now know) that its value will be a pointer to a Stack—just the thing we're after. So now we can build the stack:

```
dim s, temp as stack
s = new stack
s.itsValue = 9
temp = s
s = new stack
s.itsValue = 4
```

```
s.itsPointer = temp
temp = s
s = new stack
s.itsValue = 1
s.itsPointer = temp
```

Now s is the first item of the stack, which consists of a chain of linked Stack instances. To show that this is true, we can loop our way down the stack, reporting the value of each item as we go:

```
temp = new stack
temp.itsPointer = s
while temp.itsPointer <> nil
    temp = temp.itsPointer // traverse one link
    msgbox str(temp.itsValue)
wend
```

The complete Stack class appears in the last section of Chapter 4.

Multiple references

If we have an instance and a reference to it, and we assign the reference to a second reference, we have two references to the same instance. This means we can do things to the instance by way of either reference. If this isn't what you intended, it's a bug in your program; but often it's exactly what you intended, and a great convenience.

To take a traditional sort of example, suppose we have various sorts of widgets (imaginary things that we sell), each of which has a price that fluctuates very often. And suppose we have orders from customers, which remain open until we are ready to fulfill them, and that we don't calculate the total on an order until we are ready to close it—that is, the price of each type of widget on an order is the price at the moment the order closes.

You might think that this means at order-closing time we must look up the current price of each widget in the order in some sort of database. But instead we can let pointers be our lookup. Let each widget type be represented by a reference to an instance of the Widget class; we'll call this the master list of widget types. Let an order be an object having as one of its properties an array of Widgets, denoting the widgets on that order. To describe the order, assign to each element of the array one of the instances from the master list. Now any time we change the price of one of the instances in the master list, then in all the open orders for that type of widget, the price changes too—because, for any particular type of widget, the widget reference in the master list and the references to that type of widget in all the different orders all point to the selfsame instance. So the prices of all the widgets in all the open orders are up to date all the time, automatically.

There are some pitfalls associated with multiple references; see "Destruction of Instances," later in this chapter.

Parameters Pass Pointers

When a scalar is passed as a parameter to a subroutine, its value is copied, so that the subroutine receives an independent copy—unless, of course, the subroutine is declared to accept the parameter ByRef:

```
dim s as string
s = "testing"
mungeMyString s
```

Assume that MungeMyString is not declared to accept its parameter ByRef. Then whatever MungeMyString may do, one thing is certain: after the call to Munge-MyString, the value of s will not have changed. That's because s is passed by value, meaning that MungeMyString receives a copy of s's value.

Object references are passed by value too. So when an object reference is passed as a parameter to a subroutine, it is copied. But what's copied is a pointer! That's because an object reference's value *is* a pointer; the instance itself has an independent existence (remember???). So the subroutine ends up having access to the very same instance that the original object reference pointed to, just as with assignment. The subroutine can change the instance's property values, and these changes will be reflected back in the calling routine.

For example, suppose we have a subroutine that goes like this:

```
Sub moveMyWindow(theWindow as window)
    theWindow.top = 100
End Sub
```

Now we'll call the subroutine, as follows:

```
dim w as myOtherWindow
w = new myOtherWindow
w.top = 50
moveMyWindow w
```

Afterward, w.top is 100; MoveMyWindow does indeed move the window that is handed to it as a parameter.

Now, you might say: aha! Objects are passed by reference! But no: objects are normally passed by value, just like scalars; the difference is that with objects, the value passed is itself a reference. So, you may ask, what happens if you *do* pass an object by reference? I mean, since a subroutine that receives an object as a parameter by value can already change that object's property values, what further ability can it possibly gain by receiving that object by reference? The answer is that now you're passing a reference by reference, and so the subroutine now has the ability to change the reference—that is, to repoint the pointer.

To show why this is useful, here's an example involving Picture objects; these are not formally treated until Chapter 11, but the idea will be clear enough. A Picture object is created with a call to the built-in NewPicture function, specifying the height, width, and depth of the picture; then it is possible to draw into the picture. Let's say I have a variable declared as Picture, and I want it to contain a drawing. But I don't want to do the drawing myself; I want to hand the variable to a subroutine and let the subroutine do the drawing, so that I end up with a reference to the completed picture.

Name the subroutine DrawMyPicture, and let it take a single parameter which is a Picture. Then I can say:

```
dim p as picture
p = newpicture(100,100,16)
drawMyPicture p
// ... do something with p ...
```

After the third line, p points to the Picture instance containing the drawing, and I can use it as I please.

Now let's suppose this is not quite what I wanted DrawMyPicture to do. You notice that in the second line I created the Picture object myself. But let's say I don't know what the height and width and depth of the picture should be, and I don't want to know. Instead, that should be part of DrawMyPicture's job; it should create the picture and draw into it. So, I want to be able to say:

```
dim p as picture
drawMyPicture p
// ... do something with p ...
```

We can imagine that DrawMyPicture must look something like this:

```
Sub drawMyPicture(whatPicture as picture)
    dim theWidth, theHeight, theDepth as integer
    // ... figure out size of picture ...
    whatPicture = newpicture(theWidth, theHeight, theDepth) // error
    // ... draw into the picture ...
End Sub
```

There's just one problem: we get an error ("Parameters can't be modified"). The solution is to declare DrawPicture such that whatPicture is ByRef:

```
Sub drawMyPicture(byRef whatPicture as picture)
    dim theWidth, theHeight, theDepth as integer
    // ... figure out size of picture ...
    whatPicture = newpicture(theWidth, theHeight, theDepth)
    // ... draw into the picture ...
End Sub
```

This works, and shows how passing an object reference by reference can be useful.

But now let's turn up the heat still further. Instead of declaring p as a local variable, let's suppose p is a property. In this scenario, our main routine selects a Picture property and hands it to DrawMyPicture to create the actual picture and draw into it. So now our main routine goes like this:

```
drawMyPicture p // p is a property: error
// ... do something with p ...
```

Now there's a new problem; we get another error ("Reference parameters can only be local variables"). We have run smack into one of REALbasic's strangest limitations: you can't pass a property ByRef. What are we to do? If we declare DrawMyPicture so that its parameter is not ByRef, we can pass a property but we can't set it with NewPicture. If we declare DrawMyPicture so that its parameter is ByRef, we can set it with NewPicture but we can't pass a property.

The solution is to rearchitect the property so that it is itself a pointer—in other words, we're going to pass a pointer to a pointer. This sounds obscure, but it's quite simple. We create a class, which I'll name PicturePtr, consisting of a single Picture property named ItsPicture. Let the property p be a PicturePtr, not a mere Picture. Now here is DrawMyPicture:

```
Sub drawMyPicture(whatPicture as picturePtr)
    dim theWidth, theHeight, theDepth as integer
    // ... figure out size of picture ...
    whatPicture.itsPicture = newpicture(theWidth, theHeight, theDepth)
    // ... draw into the picture ...
End Sub
```

The parameter no longer needs to be ByRef. We pass (by value) an object, which is a PicturePtr. This means that DrawMyPicture receives a pointer to the PicturePtr instance, and therefore has complete access to all that instance's properties. A PicturePtr has a Picture property. Therefore DrawMyPicture has complete access to the Picture, and can assign to it.

This technique of devising a class that itself functions as a pointer is of wide utility in REALbasic, and will be taken up again in Chapter 4.

Comparison Tests Identity

Object comparison differs from scalar comparison. For one thing, concepts like "greater than" and "less than" are largely meaningless when applied to objects; REALbasic won't complain, but the results of the comparison won't be of any use to you. Therefore, the main comparison you're likely to use on an object reference is equality comparison with another object reference, or with nil. The purpose of comparison with nil has already been explained: it's to determine whether a reference is a nil pointer. So it remains only to talk about equality comparison between instances.

Equality comparison between two instances asks whether they are the selfsame instance, not whether they have the same "value" (whatever that would seem to mean). For example, beginners are often misled into writing code of this sort:

```
dim d1, d2 as date
d1 = new date
d2 = new date
// ... set d1 to a particular date ...
// ... set d2 to a particular date ...
if d1 = d2 then // this will never succeed!
```

The trouble here is that the programmer is subconsciously equivocating on the notion of a "date." A Date object is a way of expressing a date. The programmer wants to know whether both Date objects are expressing the same date (for example, are they both August 10, 1954?). But that's not what equality between object references tests; it tests only whether the references are to the selfsame instance, and we know they are not, because we saw them created as two separate instances. (How to test whether two Date objects express the same date is irrelevant here, and is explained in Chapter 5.)

Again, consider the FolderItem `desktopFolder.child("test")`, which denotes a file called *test* on the desktop. The condition in this line:

```
if desktopFolder.child("test") = desktopFolder.child("test") then
```

is `false`, because two separate instances are formed by the two separate function calls on the two sides of the comparison. (It's true that those two instances provide access to the same file on disk, but that's irrelevant.)

On the other hand, after executing the following:

```
dim f, g as folderItem
f = desktopFolder.child("test")
g = f
```

the variables `f` and `g` point to identically the same instance, and so the boolean expression in this line:

```
if f = g then
```

is `true`.

Destruction of Instances

We know how instances are born; but how do they die? The short answer is that, in general, you're not supposed to worry about this. REALbasic does its best to shield you from problems of instance destruction. Those problems are intimately related to memory management; and one of REALbasic's great strengths is that it manages memory for you.

The core of REALbasic's memory management system is a principle called *garbage collection*. This states that REALbasic will see to it that an instance will go out of existence all by itself when appropriate, and the memory that it used to occupy will be cleared. In particular, REALbasic uses a style of garbage collection called *reference counting*; this states that an instance is destroyed as soon as there is no way at all for code to refer it. Internally, the implementation is that every instance is accompanied by a property, its reference count, invisible to the programmer, which is incremented every time a reference is assigned to point to that instance, and decremented every time such a reference ceases to point to the instance or ceases to exist. You can manually cause a reference to cease to point to an instance, by setting its value to `nil`; otherwise, a variable goes out of existence automatically when its subroutine terminates execution, and a property goes out of existence automatically when the instance that owns it goes out of existence. An instance is destroyed when its reference count drops to zero. (Actually, the programmer can get access to an instance's reference count, through the built-in Runtime object; this is discussed in Chapter 8.)

For example, if a subroutine instantiates a FolderItem, assigning it to a variable declared within that subroutine and not assigning it to any other name, then once the subroutine has finished executing, the FolderItem instance is no longer pointed to by any name at all. Therefore, the instance is useless and it will be destroyed. On the other hand, if a subroutine instantiates a FolderItem, assigning it to a property, and if the instance containing the property lives on after the subroutine has finished executing, the FolderItem instance is still pointed to by the property name, and will persist as long as the instance containing the property persists.*

Some instances seem to work differently. Chief among these are window instances. Windows have a life of their own, as it were, because they are fundamental features of the interface. If a window vanished just because your code stopped talking about it, the user would see a lot of unpleasant action on the screen! So, it seems that windows persist in defiance of the garbage-collection rules. However, that isn't really true, because even if your code maintains no name by which to refer to a window, there are ways to retrieve a reference to it—for example, by calling the Window function.

On the other hand, windows are certainly special in this sense: since they don't die automatically, your code has to have a way to kill them. Therefore, windows accept a Close message as a way of telling an instance to die. This has a secondary effect: all the window's controls are also destroyed. If an instance is a control in a window class, it is brought into existence automatically when the window is instantiated, and is destroyed automatically when the window is destroyed. (And recall that *any* class that appears in the Project Window or Tools Window, even if it is not a subclass of the built-in Control class, can be instantiated as a control contained by a window, by dragging it into a Window Editor.) Similarly, consider a property of a window class, whose datatype is an object class: after the window is instantiated, the property does not automatically point to any instance (it's up to your code to cause it to do so); but once it does, if there are no other persistent references to the instance pointed to by that property, then when the window is destroyed, the instance pointed to by that property is destroyed. Thus, windows are an important device for easy management of instance lifetimes.

On the whole, you're just supposed to have faith in REALbasic's memory management and not be particularly conscious of it. There are, however, two exceptional situations. One is when you want to prevent yourself from running short of memory by

---

* The whole thing is rather like the haunting short story, "Do You Love Me?" by Peter Carey. The world has been taken over by the Cartographers, who with their elaborate lists of everything have essentially usurped God's task of upholding all things by the word of his power. As the story ends, whatever and whoever is not loved by someone, is ceasing to exist. In effect, it's a world with garbage collection! See Peter Carey, *The Fat Man in History and Other Stories* (Faber and Faber, 1980).

releasing an object's memory right now. This comes up particularly when a reference to an instance is a property, and you know that the instance containing this property isn't going to go out of existence any time soon; you can sever the property from the instance that it points to by setting it to nil, and if this is the last reference to that instance, the instance is immediately destroyed.

A common mistake is forgetting that a reference is not the only reference to an instance. I've been working with REALbasic for years, and I *still* sometimes get this wrong! For example, suppose C is a property declared as MyClass, which has a Picture property P, and that C already points to an actual instance of MyClass. Here, for some reason, we choose to work with c.p through a secondary pointer:

```
dim pp as picture
c.p = newpicture(100,100,16) // c is a property and has been instantiated
pp = c.p
// ... do things with pp ...
pp = nil // free up the memory—not!
// ... more code ...
```

Setting pp to nil doesn't free up the memory occupied by the Picture, because c.p is still pointing to it. A better approach might have been for the secondary pointer to point at C:

```
dim cc as myClass
cc = c
cc.p = newpicture(100,100,16)
// ... do things with cc.p ...
cc.p = nil
// ... more code ...
```

The other situation where you need to take a hand in REALbasic's memory management is when you've created a circular reference. Suppose we have two classes, A and B, and that A has a property ItsB, which is of datatype B, and that B has a property ItsA, which is of datatype A. Now we create instances of A and B and point their properties at one another:

```
dim a as A, b as B
a = new A
b = new B
a.itsB = B
b.itsA = A
```

After this subroutine finishes executing, neither the A instance nor the B instance can be referred to, because our only references to them, the variables a and b, have ceased to exist; but the A instance and the B instance both persist anyway. The reason is that there is still a reference to the B instance (the A instance's property), and there is still a reference to the A instance (the B instance's property). To release the memory, you needed to set one of those properties to nil before the subroutine finished executing. The situation looks artificial when presented in skeletal form, but in fact it is quite prone to arise in object-oriented programming and when you're using data structures that form closed loops of pointers (such as doubly linked lists or circular queues).

CHAPTER 4

In this chapter:
- New Classes and Inheritance
- Casting
- Overriding
- Class Interfaces
- Events and New Events
- The Class Hierarchy
- Global Members
- Advanced Class Features
- Example Classes

Class Relationships and Class Features

Chapter 3 outlined the REALbasic object model, explaining what classes and instances are, and how you work with them in REALbasic. We saw that in the IDE you edit classes; then the running program generates instances and sends messages between them. We talked about the message-sending mechanism, how instances are generated, and how your code can refer to the instance it wants to send a message to. Now we're going to talk about the notion of classes in more depth, and in particular about relationships between classes, other class features, and how to do things with classes. Also discussed are modules, which provide methods, properties, and constants that are available from anywhere. The chapter ends by describing a few useful example classes that you can make in the comfort and safety of your own home.

Most object-oriented programming languages, along with a mechanism for making classes, also provide a means of expressing relationships among classes. There are three such relationships in REALbasic:

- A class may be a type of some other class. When two classes are related in this way, the first is said to be a *subclass* of the second, and the second is said to be the *superclass* of the first. For example, if you have a Triangle class, you might also have an Isosceles class, where Isosceles is a type of Triangle. Isosceles is then a subclass of Triangle, and Triangle is the superclass of Isosceles. A class can have many subclasses (for example, Triangle might also have a Scalene subclass), but every subclass has exactly one immediate superclass. The subclass–superclass relationship is sometimes called "Is-A," because every instance of the subclass also is an instance of the superclass; for example, every Isosceles is a Triangle. This sort of relationship also brings with it the notion of *inheritance*, meaning that a subclass is everything the superclass is, and then some. For example, a Triangle has three sides; so does an Isosceles, but it adds a rule that two of the sides are equal.

- A class may be declared to qualify as also being some other class, without inheritance, and without the other class having any real existence; the other class is just a name. The first class is said to *implement* the second, and the second class is not a real class at all, but a *class interface*. For example, we might have reason to want a Triangle, a Face, and a StopSign to be DrawableThings, as a matter of nomenclature, but to have nothing else in common. A class can implement multiple class interfaces, and can implement class interfaces even if it is a subclass, so this is also a way of getting around the rule that says a subclass can't have more than one immediate superclass. We may think of this as an "Also Is-A" relationship.

- A class may have a property whose datatype is some other class. For example, there might be a Point class and a Line class; you could define the Line class as having two Point properties (because two points determine a line). This relationship, especially when the bond between the class and the properties is felt to be particularly strong, is sometimes called "Has-A." So here, a Line has two Points and just wouldn't be a Line without them, and perhaps our program doesn't use Points except as features of a Line; that's a good solid Has-A relationship. Another kind of "Has-A" relationship is where a class has a property that is of a different class, and also provides all the methods for working with that property; this is called a *wrapper*. An example appears later in this chapter.

What classes you create for your project, and in particular how you set up the relationships among them, is a matter of design—object-oriented design. Your project ends up with an internal architecture of classes. There will be a class hierarchy: A and AA are subclasses of B, B and BB are subclasses of C, and so forth. Cutting across this hierarchy you might have some class interfaces, giving AA and BB some special extra commonality. D might operate only as a property of A, encapsulating functionality or building a data structure. The principles of object-oriented design are a mixture of science, art, philosophy, and expediency; it's a big subject, too big for this book. But the first step is to understand REALbasic's object model, how classes can relate and what you can do with these relationships; that's what this chapter is about.

Relationships among classes in REALbasic, especially the class hierarchy, are not merely a convenience of design; they are crucial. REALbasic's application framework provides a hierarchy of built-in classes before you write any code at all; and adding to that hierarchy is how you take advantage of the built-in functionality of those classes. For example, you might want a class that acts just like a built-in Push-Button but does a few things in addition. To get it, you'd make a subclass of Push-Button. That's what the next section is about.

New Classes and Inheritance

To create a new class, choose File → New Class. A listing for the new class will appear in the Project Window. If you immediately hit the Tab key, you'll be transported to the Properties Window, ready to give the new class a meaningful name.

If the new class you want to create is a window class, you choose File → New Window instead. Window classes can't be subclassed, so they are not the sort of thing this chapter is primarily about.

When you create a new class, you may declare it to be a subclass of some other class, by setting, in the Properties Window, the new class's Super. To do so, you choose from a popup menu which lists all subclassable built-in classes and all classes you've added to this project.* This specifies your new class's superclass, and thus makes your new class a subclass of that other class. It is also possible to specify that a class is to be a subclass of no other class; to do this, choose "<none>" in the Super popup (this is the default when you create a new class).

As we've already said, a subclass relates to its superclass through the medium of *inheritance*. Simply put, this means that an instance of the subclass also is an instance of the superclass ("Is-A"). More formally, the subclass has all the same methods and properties as the superclass, and an instance of the subclass can be sent all the same messages as an instance of the superclass. Furthermore, in the case of one of REALbasic's built-in classes that receives events as part of the application framework, a subclass receives those events as well. Subclassing is thus a quick and easy way to take advantage of an existing class's functionality. And most of REALbasic's built-in classes are part of its application framework, meaning that their functionality includes powerful stuff like displaying interface items on the screen or communicating over the Internet; so the ability to subclass such classes means that you can make some very powerful subclasses.

 Unfortunately, aside from the Super listing in the Properties Window, the nature of the relationship between subclass and superclass is not in any way reflected in the IDE. Looking at a subclass's Code Editor, you are not shown what methods and properties it inherits from the superclass; to find out, you have to look at the superclass (or its documentation). Nor is there any way to learn what are the subclasses of a given class. In short, the REALbasic IDE doesn't make inheritance easy to use. This is one of the worst aspects of the IDE's interface.

If a subclass is like its superclass, why make a new class at all? What makes a subclass a different class from its superclass? Basically, it's that you can add to a subclass members that its superclass lacks. A subclass is its superclass and then some. In the case of REALbasic's built-in classes, the ability to add to the subclass is crucial, because you can't modify the built-in classes; the way you take advantage of the functionality of one of REALbasic's built-in classes while customizing its structure and functionality is to make a subclass of it and customize that.

For example, recall the arcade game described in Chapter 3. There, we imagined a ScoreBox class, which would have a Score property, and would know how to display

---

* For a list of what built-in classes can be subclassed, see "The Class Hierarchy" later in this chapter.

its value in a window. Also, the ScoreBox class would have an Increase method, which would increment the value of the Score property. Let's actually implement the ScoreBox class.

To do so, we'll take advantage of a built-in Control class called a StaticText, which already has the following useful functionality: it displays in its containing window the value of its own Text property. We can't modify the StaticText class, so we make a subclass of it: we create a new class, name it ScoreBox, and designate StaticText as its Super. Then, in the ScoreBox class's Code Editor, we give it a Score property which is an integer, and an Increase method, which goes like this:

```
Sub increase()
    self.score = self.score + 1 // increment the score
    self.showScore // display the score
End Sub
```

We have postponed the question of how the ScoreBox will actually display its score in its containing window, by giving that job to an unwritten subroutine. Let's write it. It will be a method handler, as we know. A StaticText always displays its own Text property, so it suffices to set the Text property to the value of the Score property. The Text property is a string, while the Score property is an integer, so we must also convert. Here is ScoreBox's ShowScore method handler:

```
Sub showScore()
    self.text = str(self.score)
End Sub
```

Finally, let's think about what happens when a window containing a ScoreBox instance first opens. That instance's score is autoinitialized to 0, which seems acceptable. But we also want to make sure it is displayed. Among the Events listed in Score-Box's Code Editor is the Open event. An Open event handler, if we choose to write one, is automatically called by REALbasic when the control is instantiated. That's an appropriate moment to start displaying the score. Here is ScoreBox's Open event handler:

```
self.showScore
```

That's all there is to it! Let's try it out. Drag the ScoreBox listing from the Project Window into a Window Editor. A new control appears in the Window Editor; select it. Looking at the Properties Window, you can see that although this control is named StaticText1 by default, its Super listing says that it is indeed a ScoreBox instance. So StaticText1 should know how to accept the Increase message. Let's see if it does. Drag a PushButton from the Tools Window into the Window Editor; double-click it in the Window Editor to access its Action event handler in the window's Code Editor, and give it this code:

```
staticText1.increase
```

Run the project in the IDE. There's a number in the window! It's zero! And every time you press the button, the number increases!

It's simple, almost trivial; yet, for the reasons explained in Chapter 3, it's tremendously powerful. The score is now maintained, appropriately, by the object that primarily operates on it; other objects can call a ScoreBox's Increase method without worrying about what this does or what the score is; the ScoreBox, for its part, doesn't care who is calling it; and a project can contain multiple ScoreBox instances, each maintaining a separate score, yet all behaving identically.

We've seen that the code for the ScoreBox class's behavior doesn't live in the window's Code Editor; it lives in the ScoreBox class's own Code Editor, which you access by double-clicking the ScoreBox class's listing in the Project Window. All ScoreBox instances will look to this code for their behavior, and if you change this code, all ScoreBox instances will henceforward display the new behavior. Let's prove to ourselves that this is true. (If the project is running in the IDE, you'll have to kill it first, so that you can modify the project.) Start by dragging the ScoreBox listing from the Project Window into the Window Editor again. Now the window has two Score-Box instances, StaticText1 and StaticText2. Change the PushButton's Action event handler to read:

```
staticText1.increase
staticText2.increase
```

Run the project and push the button repeatedly; both ScoreBox instances behave identically (and they increment together, since they both started at zero and both receive the Increase message when we push the button; I remind you, however, that they maintain independent scores). Now, in the ScoreBox class's Increase method, change this line:

```
self.score = self.score + 1 // increment the score
```

to this:

```
self.score = self.score + 2 // increment the score
```

Immediately run the project again, and push the button. Sure enough, now the number increases by two every time, in both ScoreBox instances. Notice that you didn't have to do anything horrible and clumsy like delete the ScoreBox control instances from the window and replace them with new ones; an instance takes on the altered class behavior immediately.

Behind the simplicity of this example lurks the power of inheritance. The ScoreBox instance can receive the Score message because we gave the ScoreBox class a Score property; but it can receive the Text message because the ScoreBox class's superclass, StaticText, has a Text property. The ScoreBox instance can receive the Increase message because we gave the ScoreBox class an Increase method handler; but it has an Open event handler, which is called automatically by REALbasic, because that's how REALbasic has defined its superclass, StaticText. Most impressive of all, we have created a working interface element without knowing anything about how to drive the Macintosh Toolbox, simply by subclassing a built-in class that does know how.

Casting

The existence of subclasses and inheritance complicates the question of what class a given instance is an instance of. Is a ScoreBox instance a ScoreBox, or is it a StaticText? This depends on what the meaning of "is" is.[*] At bottom, a ScoreBox instance is clearly a ScoreBox; ScoreBox is its *final class*.[†] Still, since a ScoreBox is a kind of StaticText (for that is what subclassing means), a ScoreBox instance is a StaticText instance as well; an instance of a subclass is also an instance of the superclass. And you can carry this on up the hierarchy of classes. StaticText is a subclass of RectControl, and RectControl is a subclass of Control. So a ScoreBox instance is also a RectControl instance and a Control instance.

This fact must often be taken into account when manipulating instances and references to instances. That's what this section is about.

We begin with this important fact: A subclass instance is acceptable in a context where an instance of the superclass is expected. We've already seen that this is true; a ScoreBox can talk about self.text because Self, a ScoreBox instance, is acceptable as a recipient of the Text message, where a StaticText instance is expected. Similarly, if we have a ScoreBox called TheScoreBox in our window, REALbasic will not complain if we say this:

```
dim s as staticText
s = theScoreBox
```

The reason this works is that, by the terms of its declaration, assignment to s is legal if the value being assigned is a StaticText; and TheScoreBox *is* a StaticText, by virtue of the fact that it is a ScoreBox (because ScoreBox is a subclass of StaticText).

But the reverse is not true; and for the selfsame reason. If our window contains a control called TheStaticText whose final class is StaticText, you cannot say this:

```
dim s as scoreBox
s = theStaticText // error: Type mismatch
```

Similarly, you cannot send the Increase message to an instance whose final class is StaticText; a StaticText knows nothing of the Increase message. The reason is simple: a StaticText is not a ScoreBox.

The criterion that REALbasic uses to determine what you can do with a reference is the declared type of the *reference*—not the class of the instance to which the reference really points. Consider the following:

```
dim s as staticText
s = theScoreBox // fine
theScoreBox.increase // fine
s.increase // error: Unknown identifier
```

---

[*] Insert your own Bill Clinton joke here.

[†] I have coined this term based on a suggestion by Quinn.

Even though s is pointing to a ScoreBox instance, TheScoreBox, and even though it is fine to send the Increase message to TheScoreBox under its own name (theScoreBox.increase), yet the reference s has been declared as a StaticText, so it cannot accept messages that a StaticText doesn't know about. In general terms, we're allowed to treat a subclass instance as a superclass instance, but a reference declared as the superclass cannot be treated as if it refers to an instance of the subclass, even if it *does* refer to an instance of the subclass. (In technical terms, REALbasic does its type-checking at compile time.) This situation is illustrated in Figure 4-1.

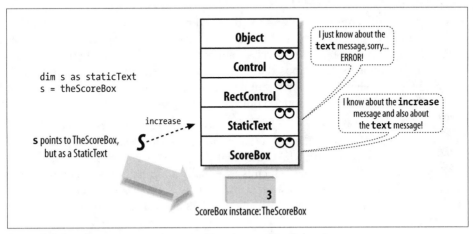

Figure 4-1. Legal messages to an instance depend upon the reference's type

In that case, what's the *good* of being allowed to treat a subclass instance as a superclass instance? Why would I ever say:

```
dim s as staticText
s = theScoreBox
```

if I cannot then treat s as a ScoreBox? Part of the answer is that it can be useful and powerful to have a reference accept a value of more than one datatype indifferently. For instance, we might have an array that we intend to populate with StaticTexts and ScoreBoxes. We cannot declare the array as of type ScoreBox, because then no element can accept a StaticText value. But if we declare the array as of type StaticText, then an element can be a StaticText or a ScoreBox (or any other subclass of StaticText).

This raises the question of how we would know, once our array is populated, what class any given element actually is. The datatype of the reference we know already, since we declared it; but is there any way to tear this mask away and see the class of the instance? Unfortunately, REALbasic provides no way to ask an instance point-blank what its final class is. But it does provide a way to ask an instance whether it is (in any sense) an instance of a *particular* class. This is done by using the IsA operator, which takes a reference and a class name, and returns a boolean reporting whether the instance pointed to by the reference is in fact an instance of the proposed class. Some examples will show both the syntax and the result:

```
dim theTruth as boolean
dim s as staticText
s = theScoreBox
theTruth = (theScoreBox isA scoreBox) // true
theTruth = (theScoreBox isA staticText) // true too
theTruth = (s isA staticText) // true
theTruth = (s isA scoreBox) // true too
theTruth = (s isA theScoreBox) // legal and true!
```

To sum up: The IsA operator ignores the declared type of the reference; it looks only at the actual instance pointed to, and returns true if the proposed class is that instance's final class or one of that class's superclasses. In the case of controls only, IsA also returns true if the proposed class is the control's global name, even though that name is not what one normally thinks of as a class name (this is essentially the same syntax used with New to clone a control, as described in Chapter 3).

So, if a reference declared as the superclass is pointing to an instance of the subclass, we can *learn* that it is the subclass. What's more, we can *treat* it as the subclass—provided we explicitly inform REALbasic that that's how we want it treated. This is done through the use of *casting*, which is essentially a means of disguising one class as another so that REALbasic will see a message as appropriate. A reference to an instance is cast as a different class by using the class name as a function operating on the reference:

```
dim s as staticText
s = theScoreBox
s.increase // error, remember?
scoreBox(s).increase // fine!
```

As we know, the third line doesn't work, because REALbasic refuses to look behind the mask of the reference's declared datatype; s has been declared as a StaticText, and REALbasic's attitude is, "That's all I know, and all I need to know." But we are more adventurous than REALbasic is, so we do look behind the mask! We use casting to tell REALbasic what we saw. By casting, we compel REALbasic to disbelieve the reference's declared datatype, and to treat the value of s as a ScoreBox, willy-nilly; since a ScoreBox can receive the Increase message, REALbasic doesn't complain. What we're doing here is nullifying REALbasic's strict compile-time type-checking; we're saying, "I know I declared s as a StaticText, but trust me, when the code actually runs, s will be pointing to a ScoreBox." In particular, we are *casting down*: we reveal to REALbasic that a reference declared as a superclass is actually pointing further down the hierarchy, at a subclass.

But be warned: REALbasic *does* trust you when you cast; it obviously has no way to check in advance whether the instance really will be what you claim it will, so it simply throws all caution to the winds. So don't betray REALbasic's trust! You can get away with saying this:

```
dim s as staticText
dim c as string
```

```
s = theScoreBox
c = pushButton(s).caption // liar! error: IllegalCastException
```

but your application will terminate prematurely when the last line actually executes and it turns out that s is not a PushButton after all. A common way to prevent this sort of mistake is to wrap casts in an IsA test:

```
dim s as staticText
dim c as string
s = theScoreBox
if s isA pushButton then // nothing can go wrong now
    c = pushButton(s).caption
end
```

Notice that casting doesn't perform any coercion; in other words, it does not transform an instance of one datatype into an instance of another datatype. In fact, it has no effect whatever upon any instances. Casting doesn't turn a sow's ear into a silk purse; it just makes a sow's ear *look* like a silk purse, and even then this works only because the sow's ear really is a silk purse to start with.

Overriding

In the example from "New Classes and Inheritance," earlier in this chapter, we defined ScoreBox, a subclass of StaticText. Every message that ScoreBox can receive is defined either in itself or in its superclass (or in the superclass of that, and so on). The superclass defines some members; the subclass inherits these and adds some more. But in real life we may wish a subclass to *replace* the functionality of a member defined in its superclass. This is called *overriding*. To do this, one simply defines in the subclass a member with the same name as a message that the superclass can receive. Now the message is defined in both the subclass and the superclass.

In making an example, there's no point using ScoreBox to override any of StaticText's members. This is basically the same issue discussed in "Resolution of Names" in Chapter 3: where a built-in class is concerned, to override a property would hide the built-in functionality associated with that property, which is undesirable, and to override a method is forbidden. So we need a superclass and a subclass both of which we ourselves have defined. Let's subclass ScoreBox to make a DoubleScoreBox class. This will be a class that differs from ScoreBox only in that when it receives the Increase message, it increments its score by 2.

Create the DoubleScoreBox class and make it a subclass of ScoreBox. Clear the Window Editor of controls. Drag in a ScoreBox, select it, and give it a more meaningful name—TheScoreBox. Drag in a DoubleScoreBox and name it TheDoubleScoreBox. Drag in a PushButton and have its Action event handler go like this:

```
theScoreBox.increase
theDoubleScoreBox.increase
```

Now it's time to define DoubleScoreBox's Increase method, to override ScoreBox's Increase method. Open DoubleScoreBox's Code Editor and define a method handler Increase, with this code:

```
Sub increase()
    self.score = self.score + 2 // increment the score
    self.showScore // display the score
End Sub
```

Run the project and press the button repeatedly. It works. Let's talk about what's happening.

It's true that our instance TheDoubleScoreBox is a ScoreBox, which defines an Increase method, to increment by 1; but its final class is DoubleScoreBox, which also defines an Increase method, to increment by 2, and that's the one that gets called when we send the Increase message to TheDoubleScoreBox. On the other hand, when TheDoubleScoreBox's Increase method calls self.showScore, DoubleScoreBox has no ShowScore method; but the message is acceptable, because a DoubleScoreBox is also a ScoreBox, and a ScoreBox does define a ShowScore method, which is what gets called. We may summarize by saying that message names are *resolved upward* through the instance's class and its superclasses: first we look in the final class of the instance to see if it accepts the message; only if not do we look at its superclass, and so on. This is illustrated in Figure 4-2.

Our use of the phrase "the instance" may seem surprising, because in the previous section the important thing was the declared datatype of the *reference*. To understand what's happening, separate the message-sending process into two distinct stages. First, REALbasic decides whether the reference can be sent the specified message at all; this is done by resolving the message name upward from the *reference's* declared datatype. If it can, then REALbasic decides which class should actually receive the message; this is done by resolving the message name upward from the *instance's* actual final class. For example:

```
dim s as scorebox
s = theScoreBox
s.increase
s = theDoubleScoreBox
s.increase
```

This increases TheScoreBox's score by 1 and TheDoubleScoreBox's score by 2, even though the reference both times is s, which is declared as a ScoreBox. Do you see why? The fact that the reference s is declared as a ScoreBox means that it can accept the Increase message, so this code is *legal*—and that's all it means. Now we come to the question of what this code will actually *do*; and that depends upon the instance that s points to. When s points to an instance of the ScoreBox class, it is ScoreBox's Increase method that is called. When s points to an instance of the DoubleScoreBox class, it is DoubleScoreBox's Increase method that is called.

The principle here is that all programmer-defined methods are *virtual methods*. That's just technical talk for the very thing we've just been saying: the class of a

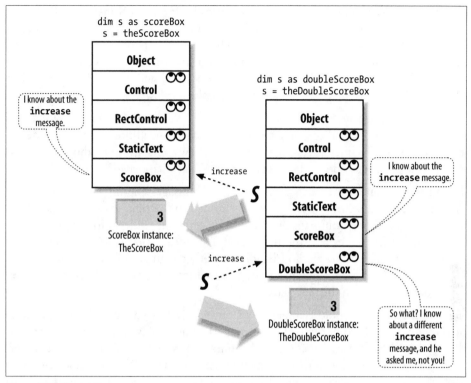

Figure 4-2. Overriding

reference may make it a legal recipient of a message, because that class *can* handle that message; but that fact is no guide as to what class *will* actually handle the message, because the instance may be of a class that overrides it.

Let's look at the matter from a different perspective. Instead of a linear architecture, imagine a situation where one class has two subclasses. We'll take advantage of overriding a virtual method so that it becomes, in effect, a decision-making mechanism. Suppose we're writing a Tic-Tac-Toe game. Every game piece is either an X or an O. But all game pieces have some common behavior. For example, a game piece should know how to draw itself in a given square on the board. Clearly we're going to have a GamePiece class and a Square class. We envision a routine that takes a piece and a square and tells that piece to draw itself into that square, like this:

```
Sub drawPieceIntoSquare(p as gamePiece, s as square)
    p.drawYourselfInto s
End Sub
```

The exact behavior of p is going to depend on whether it is an X or an O. What will it mean, to be an X or an O? Let's make it mean that there is an X class and an O class! Obviously, these are both subclasses of GamePiece. Presume that p is either an X instance or an O instance. If the X class has a DrawYourselfInto method and the O class has a DrawYourselfInto method, then when we send p the DrawYourselfInto message, the right thing will happen automatically. If p is an X instance, X's Draw-YourselfInto will execute; if p is an O instance, O's DrawYourselfInto will execute. What handler will execute depends upon what class this particular instance is during this particular call to our routine. So the class structure becomes a decision-making mechanism! The fact that we can send a message to one higher class as a way of choosing among several lower classes is called *polymorphism*.

However, we've left out a small piece of the puzzle. We define GamePiece. We define X as a subclass of GamePiece, and we give it a DrawYourselfInto method. We define Y as a subclass of GamePiece, and we give it a DrawYourselfInto method. We try to execute the previous code, and we get an error. What's happened?

The answer is that we forgot the first part of the message-sending process. We know that the DrawYourselfInto message will get routed to the right class, the class of the actual instance that p points to. But we also have to make it legal to send the Draw-YourselfInto message to p in the first place! This means that GamePiece must also have a DrawYourselfInto method handler. In other words, in order to take advantage of a virtual method, there has to *be* a virtual method. You can't override something that isn't there in the first place.

Very well; but what should GamePiece's DrawYourselfInto handler do? It's perfectly possible that it will do nothing at all; it might be completely empty! It could be that the whole of X's drawing functionality is contained in its DrawYourselfInto handler, and the whole of O's drawing functionality is contained in its DrawYourselfInto handler. And every GamePiece is going to be an X or an O. Our routine is never going to receive a value for p whose final class is GamePiece; it will always be an X or an O. So GamePiece's DrawYourselfInto handler does nothing, because it will never be called. Is this silly? Not at all. In fact, it's such a common technique that it has a name: GamePiece's DrawYourselfInto handler is said to be *abstract*. It exists only so that X and O can override it, so that a reference declared as GamePiece can be sent the DrawYourselfInto message, taking advantage of polymorphism.

In fact, we can go further. It may be that no instance whose final class is GamePiece will ever be generated throughout the entirety of our program. Not just GamePiece's DrawYourselfInto handler, but the whole GamePiece class, might exist only so that X and O can subclass it and take advantage of polymorphism. Again, this is quite common, and GamePiece is then said to be an *abstract class*. (See the Appendix for a Tic-Tac-Toe game that employs this sort of architecture.)

Class Interfaces

A subclass and its superclass represent one way in which two classes can relate. Both are classes, and the subclass inherits the fullness of the superclass's power, which may be considerable. Compared to this, a *class interface* seems evanescent, almost intangible. A class interface is abstract, and its methods, if any, are abstract. A class interface has no code; it has no properties; you can't make an instance whose final class is a class interface! A class interface is barely a class at all: it's a mere appearance of a class, a skeleton of a class. Yet it adds great power and flexibility to REALbasic's model of object orientation, because it breaks out of the structure of the subclass–superclass hierarchy.

To make a class interface, you choose File → New Class Interface. Just as with a new class, a listing appears in the Project Window, and you can tab into the Properties Window to give your new class interface a meaningful name. But the resemblance ends there. The Name listing is the only listing in the Properties Window; a class interface has no Super, because it has no superclass. The Code Editor has no place for Events, Menu Handlers, or Properties—just Methods—and while you can declare a method, you can't give it any code.

A class cannot have a class interface as its Super; a class does not inherit from a class interface. Instead, to form a relationship between a class and a class interface, you go into the class's Properties Window and edit its Interfaces listing. Here, you simply type the name of the class interface. If you like, the Interfaces listing can include the name of more than one class interface; separate the names with a comma. A class is said to *implement* the class interfaces you list among the Interfaces in its Properties Window.

What does it mean for a class to implement a class interface? We already know part of the answer. A class can have only one Super; but a class can implement more than one class interface, and this is entirely independent of what Super it may have. So implementing a class interface is a separate relationship from inheritance, and it is a relationship that permits a kind of multiple parentage.

But what kind of parentage? The answer lies in what the parent (the class interface) bequeaths to the child (any class that implements it). It bequeaths two things:

The name
> As far as names are concerned, a class interface is just like a superclass. You know that a subclass instance is acceptable where an instance of the superclass is expected. In the same way, an instance of a class that implements a class interface passes the IsA test for the class interface, and is acceptable where an instance of the class interface is expected (which is good, because you can't otherwise make an instance of the class interface).

The method declarations
> A class interface bequeaths to a class that implements it the requirement that that class should declare the same methods that it itself declares. A method declaration in a class interface is thus effectively a rule that a class must obey if it wants the privilege of inheriting the name; it's an abstract virtual method with the power to force an implementing class to override it. Actually declaring the method in the implementing class's Code Editor is up to you (though no law says you have to give it any code).

What are class interfaces for? It was pointed out in "Casting," earlier in this chapter, that the datatype of a reference is like a mask; regardless of the true class of the instance pointed to, the reference can accept only messages appropriate to its datatype. Class interfaces allow a reference to wear an arbitrary mask. You will typically use the power of this arbitrariness to pass instances around in ways that would normally be impossible, because you're cutting across the hierarchy of subclasses and superclasses.

For example, in earlier sections of this chapter we implemented ScoreBox as a subclass of StaticText. But there are other built-in classes that can display text in a window, and these would be equally good candidates as a way of implementing a scorebox type of functionality. Consider an EditField; it automatically displays its Text property, just as a StaticText does. Let's implement a class just like ScoreBox, but based on EditField.

Make a new class, call it EFScoreBox, make it an EditField subclass, give it a Score property which is an integer, and give it code exactly like the ScoreBox's code: the same Open event handler, the same Increase method handler, the same ShowScore method handler. Clear the Window Editor and drag one ScoreBox and one EFScoreBox into it; these will be called StaticText1 and EditField1 by default. Give the window a PushButton and give its Action event handler this code:

```
staticText1.increase
editField1.increase
```

Run the project and push the button several times. It works; both the StaticText and the EditField are incrementing and displaying their score.

Now let's think a moment. From the point of view of the code in the PushButton, there's something silly about this situation. A ScoreBox can accept the Increase message; an EFScoreBox can accept the Increase message. They should, in fact, be the same kind of entity: "things I can send the Increase message to." This sameness should be expressed as a class. We could call it Increaser, and we imagine being able to say something like this:

```
dim i as increaser
// ... set i to point to either a ScoreBox or an EFScoreBox ...
i.increase
```

Under the rules of the class hierarchy, that's impossible. For where might Increaser fit into the hierarchy? Both StaticText and EditField have RectControl as their superclass, and there's nothing we can do about that; those are all built-in classes and we can't access them. We could make Increaser a subclass of StaticText and make ScoreBox a subclass of Increaser; but then EFScoreBox can't be a subclass of Increaser. This impasse is schematized in Figure 4-3.

The solution is to implement Increaser as a class interface, because class interfaces can cut across the hierarchy of subclasses and superclasses. Let's do it. Make a new

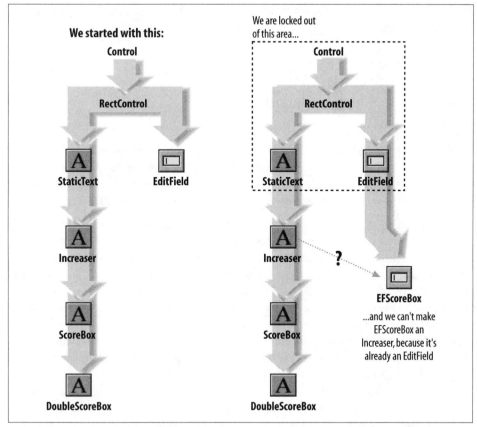

We started with this:

We are locked out of this area...

Control

Control

RectControl

RectControl

StaticText   EditField

StaticText   EditField

Increaser

Increaser

?

EFScoreBox

...and we can't make EFScoreBox an Increaser, because it's already an EditField

ScoreBox

ScoreBox

DoubleScoreBox

DoubleScoreBox

Figure 4-3. Limitations of simple inheritance

class interface and call it Increaser. Go into Increaser's Code Editor and declare a method called Increase. Now select ScoreBox in the Project Window and type **Increaser** into its Interfaces listing in the Properties Window; do the same for EFScoreBox. Now make the PushButton's Action event handler go like this, and run the project:

```
dim i as increaser
i = statictext1
i.increase
i = editfield1
i.increase
```

It works: we've subsumed both our ScoreBox and our EFScoreBox under a single class umbrella. Of course, we're not doing anything very powerful with this capability; but we could. For example, let's turn our PushButton into a *broadcaster*. A broadcaster is an object that sends out a message without caring who receives it: "Whoever has ears to hear, let him hear." As a simplified implementation, we'll make it the case that our PushButton broadcasts to any Increasers in the neighborhood (that is, in the same window as itself). Here is the PushButton's Action event handler now:

```
dim i as increaser
dim c as integer
for c = 0 to self.controlCount-1
    if self.control(c) isA increaser then
        increaser(self.control(c)).increase
    end
next
```

That's quite a remarkable piece of code. We've done the impossible: we've united two utterly distinct classes under a single class heading, and we've used the power of polymorphism to treat them indifferently under that heading, sending instances of each of them the Increase message without knowing or caring what they really are.*

I should pause to describe the more usual implementation of a broadcaster, which is roughly as follows. Start with two class interfaces: let's call them Broadcaster and Recipient. Each defines a communication method; let's say that Broadcaster defines TellRecipient, and Recipient defines HearBroadcaster. The idea is that when the Broadcaster wants to broadcast, its TellRecipient method sends the HearBroadcaster message to a Recipient. There is also some implication that a class implementing Broadcaster has a property whose datatype is Recipient, or perhaps more than one such property, or perhaps a property that is an array of Recipients (I call this an implication because a class interface has no way to require or express it, but the presence of the TellRecipient method helps remind us); this is how it knows who its available recipients are. It then remains to point these Recipient properties at actual Recipient instances, thus hooking together the particular Broadcaster and its particular Recipients; this must be done in code, and when and how to do it is up to the programmer. The power of this architecture is well illustrated by an example I've constructed, too elaborate to describe here, but which you can download from my web site, where either a Scrollbar or a Slider (indifferently) can broadcast to either a StaticText or a ProgressBar (indifferently).

Let's now turn to an example that views class interfaces from a different perspective. Imagine a class that implements a data structure, and provides some methods for manipulating this data structure. There might be several such classes, unrelated and implementing completely different data structures. It ought to be possible to pass an instance of any of these classes to a subroutine, which can then use the methods to manipulate the data structure, without knowing anything about what the nature of the data structure actually is. Class interfaces make this possible.

---

* But if you try this with a DoubleScoreBox in the window, the DoubleScoreBox will misbehave: it will execute ScoreBox's Increase handler, not DoubleScoreBox's Increase handler. That's because ScoreBox is declared as an Increaser and DoubleScoreBox isn't. It's as if class interfaces had the power to disable the virtual method mechanism between superclass and subclass. The workaround is to declare DoubleScoreBox, too, as implementing Increaser; but I regard the fact that this is necessary as a bug.

A powerful example is a Sort routine (a routine that arranges data in order from smallest to largest). If a routine knows how to sort, it knows how to sort anything; it doesn't matter what the type of data is, or how the data are stored. The routine needs just three things:

- It must be possible to refer to the data by index number, and the routine must be told explicitly the lower and upper bounds on this index number.
- It must be possible to learn, given two index numbers, how the corresponding data compare: is one item smaller than, larger than, or identical to the other?
- It must be possible to command that the data for two index numbers be swapped.

The first requirement can be met by the way our routine is called. The other two requirements can be met through a class interface. Suppose we have a class interface, Sortable, which declares a method Compare and a method Swap. Now our routine can be handed as its parameters a lower bound index, an upper bound index, and an instance of the Sortable class. Our routine is secure in the knowledge that it can call this instance's Compare and Swap handlers; and that's all it needs to know! In reality, the Sortable can be an array wrapper, a delimited string wrapper, a List-Box subclass, and so forth; the data to be sorted can be integers, strings, dates, colors, anything at all—if you can decide on a way to compare them, our routine can sort them.*

Events and New Events

Events are the basis of a REALbasic application's ability to interact with the user and to behave in the live, responsive manner that befits a GUI-based application. An event is a message sent only by REALbasic, not by the programmer's code. It is triggered because some predefined occurrence has come to pass—typically some user action, or some action on the part of your code that resembles a user action. It is sent to an instance of a built-in class (or a subclass of such a class) that is predefined to be sent this type of event. When an instance receives an event, its event handler for that event is called. If you, the programmer, want that instance to respond to a predefined occurrence, you write code in the corresponding event handler.

For example, when the user clicks the mouse on an instance of a PushButton (or a PushButton subclass), the instance is sent an Action event. To say what this instance should do when the user clicks the mouse on it, you write code in its Action event handler. If you don't, the button won't respond to being clicked.

---

* This example should help immigrants from the C++ world, seeking the REALbasic equivalent of such devices as multiple inheritance, class templates and pointer-to-function. The example is lifted entirely from Thomas Tempelmann's Sort class, *http://www.tempel.org/rb/#SortInterface*, which is well worth downloading and studying; it certainly opened my eyes as to what class interfaces could do.

Although the programmer writes the event handler code, the event handlers themselves, and the events that call them, belong entirely to REALbasic. The programmer cannot add or remove an event handler. Nor can the programmer create an event; for example, you might wish that REALbasic should send an event to a certain instance every time the user changes the computer's speaker volume, or blows his nose, but that isn't going to happen. You simply have to hope and trust that REALbasic comes equipped with a set of events sufficient to allow your program to implement the kind of responsive functionality you desire for it. For the most part, it probably does; and where it doesn't, you'll have to understand and accept what it cannot do, and implement a workaround or modify your desires accordingly.

Knowing what the predefined occurrences are, and in what order the corresponding events will be sent to what instances, is a crucial part of learning to program effectively with REALbasic, so naturally this book provides lots of details. An overview appears in the section called "Order of Events" in Chapter 7, and then the discussion of each built-in class in Part II and Part III (along with Chapter 6 on menus) provides a complete list of the class's events and the occurrences that trigger them.

Where is the event handler where the programmer is to write code? The situation was simple before we knew about subclasses: drag a PushButton from the Tools Window into a Window Editor, and double-click it to see the PushButton's event handlers listed in the Controls section of the window's Code Editor. Now things have become confusing. We make a subclass of StaticText, called ScoreBox; open ScoreBox's Code Editor and its event handlers are there. Drag a ScoreBox from the Project Window into the Window Editor and double-click it; we're back among the event handlers in the window's Code Editor. Does the event handler code for a ScoreBox go in the class or in the window? Now bring ScoreBox's subclass, Double-ScoreBox, into the story. DoubleScoreBox's Code Editor has event handlers too! Should code for a DoubleScoreBox event handler go into ScoreBox, DoubleScore-Box, or the window? How do events relate to the class hierarchy?

The answer is simple, once you know how an event travels as it is triggered and sent. For purposes of events, pretend that an instance in the window is part of the class hierarchy—in particular, that it's at the bottom of the hierarchy. So, for example, when there's a DoubleScoreBox instance called TheDoubleScoreBox in a window, the hierarchy from top to bottom runs Control, RectControl, StaticText, ScoreBox, DoubleScoreBox, TheDoubleScoreBox. An event is directed ultimately at an instance. But since it is the instance's built-in superclass that is responsible for the fact that the event is being sent to this instance at all, it is the superclass that receives the event first; the event then travels *down* the class hierarchy toward the instance at which it is actually directed, looking for a class that handles the event. At that point, the process comes to an end. By "handles the event," I mean, "contains an event handler bearing the event's name, which has code in it." In a Code Editor, REALbasic signals that an event handler handles an event by making its browser listing bold.

The implication is that event handlers cannot be overridden. If ScoreBox contains code in its Open event handler, the Open event handler in DoubleScoreBox will never be executed, nor will the Open event handler belonging to a DoubleScoreBox instance in a window, because the Open event travels down the class hierarchy, finds that ScoreBox handles it, and stops.

In fact, the IDE enforces this rule by physically preventing you from overriding an event handler. If you put code into any class's event handler, REALbasic actually deletes the corresponding event handler from the Code Editors of its subclasses and superclasses. So, because you wrote code in the Open event handler in the ScoreBox class, you'll find there is no Open event handler in the DoubleScoreBox class or in any ScoreBox or DoubleScoreBox instance in a window! Just the other way, if you write code in the Close event handler of any DoubleScoreBox instance in a window, the Close event handlers in DoubleScoreBox and ScoreBox will vanish.

This means you have to be a little careful about the order in which you put code into event handlers! In the example just given, if we changed our minds and decided we wanted ScoreBox to handle the Close event, we would first have to remove the code from the DoubleScoreBox instance's Close event handler, in order to get ScoreBox even to *have* a Close event handler. This can get very painful when you've got dozens of instances in several different windows, and have to hunt through them all to find the one with code that's preventing you from writing an event handler in a class.

The fact that event handlers can't be overridden seems unfair, because manifestly you might need instances of different classes, or individual controls derived from the same class, to be able to respond differently to an event. For example, both a Score-Box and a DoubleScoreBox presently permit their Score to be autoinitialized to 0. But what if we wanted a ScoreBox's Score initialized to 1 and a DoubleScoreBox's Score initialized to 2? Clearly the place to make this happen is in the Open event handler, before the score is first displayed. But only ScoreBox even has an Open event handler. We could make ScoreBox's Open event handler go like this:

```
self.score = 1
self.showScore
```

But what will we do about DoubleScoreBox?

The best approach, I think, wherever it can be used, is to take advantage of virtual methods. Instead of initializing the Score property directly in an event handler, have the event handler call a method that initializes it. Methods are virtual, so the problem is solved. ScoreBox's Open event handler would then run as follows:

```
self.initScore
self.showScore
```

It is now just a matter of writing InitScore methods in ScoreBox and DoubleScore-Box; obviously, ScoreBox's InitScore method says:

```
self.score = 1
```

and DoubleScoreBox's InitScore method says:

```
self.score = 2
```

But there are situations where this approach isn't so viable. What if we want one particular instance of DoubleScoreBox in one particular window to initialize its Score to 0? We can't put an InitScore method in the instance in the window, because instances in windows don't have method handlers. We could create a special class just for this instance, but that seems extreme. To help us out, REALbasic provides a second way of dealing with the matter—the New Event mechanism.

The New Event mechanism enables code in an event handler to continue handing an event down the hierarchy toward the instance. You define a New Event in a class; its subclasses then inherit the right to handle that event. The only trick is that the class must explicitly trigger the New Event, so that it is sent on down the hierarchy.

So, let's say that in ScoreBox we anticipate the possibility that some ScoreBox subclass or instance may wish to override our initialization of the Score property. To make this possible, we'll propagate a New Event down the hierarchy. In ScoreBox, choose Edit → New Event. The usual subroutine declaration dialog appears, and we name it InitScoreOverride. Drag a DoubleScoreBox instance into the Window Editor, and double-click it. Lo and behold, an InitScoreOverride event handler has appeared among this instance's event handlers in the window! Here, you can put this code:

```
me.score = 0
```

(You must use Me, because that's the DoubleScoreBox; Self is the window, remember?) However, this code has no effect, because the InitScoreOverride event is never triggered. We must take care of that. Go back to ScoreBox's Open event handler, and make it go like this:

```
self.initScore
initScoreOverride
self.showScore
```

The strategy is that we initialize the Score in the normal way, but then we send the InitScoreOverride event down the hierarchy just in case anybody wants to handle it. If nobody does, that's fine. In this particular case, one instance of DoubleScoreBox does handle it, changing the Score to suit its own taste before it is displayed for the first time. The only hard part, which wasn't particularly hard in this case, was deciding just when to trigger the InitScoreOverride event. You have to consider the order in which things are going to happen. Obviously it would have been wrong to do things in this order:

```
initScoreOverride
self.initScore
self.showScore
```

This would allow subclasses and instances to set the Score, but then we return it to its default setting, making InitScoreOverride useless.

The New Event mechanism was of great importance in Version 1 of REALbasic, when virtual methods didn't exist; but now virtual methods do exist, and New Events have been relegated almost to the status of an unused appendix. Nevertheless they do

Modules

A *module* is a global container of methods and properties; these methods and properties belong to no class.

To create a module, choose File → New Module; the module's listing appears in the Project Window. You can then tab into the Properties Window to give the module a meaningful name. But this name, and how you distribute things among modules, is purely a matter of organizational convenience; your code knows nothing about it. (Modules are rather like folders in this respect.) To create methods and properties in a module, double-click the module's listing in the Project Window to open its Code Editor and proceed in the usual way.

To access a module member from code, you just use the member's name, with no reference to the module. For example, a method named MyGlobalMethod, which is a procedure taking no parameters, stored in a module named MyModule, would be called by saying:

```
myGlobalMethod // no mention of MyModule
```

Since module member names are global, a question arises of how they are resolved with respect to the namespace as a whole. The main part of the answer was given in "Resolution of Names" in Chapter 3: the module namespace is consulted last, after REALbasic's built-in functions and after implicitly trying to supply Self. Care should be exercised not to overshadow a module member name with a local name accidentally. For example, if a module contains a property named Prop and you use the name prop in a subroutine where prop has been declared with a Dim statement as a local variable, it is the local variable that will be referred to. If a module contains a property named Prop and you use the name prop in a class containing a Prop property (or a subclass of such a class), it is self.prop that will be referred to. In such situations, there is no way whatever to refer to the Prop in the module.

A module method can refer to other members of the same module by dot notation through the Self function; and if Self is omitted, a module method's references to properties and methods with no dot notation will be resolved by looking in the same module before looking in other modules. This gives modules, if not object-orientation, at least some, er, modularity. Nonetheless, giving two different members in two different modules the same name is probably unwise, since in referring to such members from elsewhere you cannot specify which is meant, and you cannot be certain how the reference will be resolved.

Modules can also contain global *constants*.* A constant is like a property that is initialized in the IDE; its value can be only a literal string, number, or boolean. Aside from the convenience of not having to initialize its value, a global constant's great advantage is that it can be *localized* for the different languages and platforms. This is

---

* For local constants, see Chapter 2.

done by pressing the Add button in the Edit Constant dialog. In Figure 4-4, for example, the constant yes has been localized so as to have the value "Yes" on a U.S. Macintosh but the value "Oui" on a French Macintosh. These settings are consulted at the time you build the application: you specify the desired platform and language in the Build Application dialog.

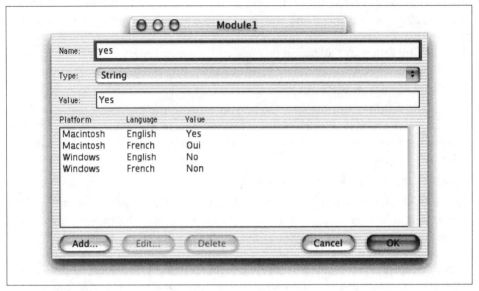

Figure 4-4. Localizing a constant

A constant's value can be accessed in code, by its name; for example:

    msgbox yes

Constant values can also be assigned to properties initialized in the IDE, such as the caption of a button. To do this, the value supplied in the Properties Window must begin with # as a sign that it's the name of a constant and not a literal string. For example, if I initialize the Caption property of a PushButton in the IDE as #yes, the built application will display the button's caption in accordance with the value of the yes constant localized for the platform and language of the build. (To make a string property value start with #, type **#** twice.)

A constant can't have a calculated value. Since unprintable characters can't be expressed in REALbasic except by calculation (see "Strings" in Chapter 5), this might seem to mean that a constant string can't contain an unprintable character. But pasting an unprintable character into the Edit Constant dialog does work. So a workaround is to use some other application (such as BBEdit) to create the string containing the unprintable character, then copy and paste it into the Edit Constant dialog.

A constant value can be used to declare the size of a local array variable, but not an array property (I regard this as a bug). For example, given an integer constant How-Many, you can't declare an array property like this:

```
myArray(howMany) as string
```

The workaround is to declare the array with an arbitrary size (such as -1) and Redim it in code:

```
redim myArray(howMany)
```

The Application Subclass

Modules are the only place where global localizable constants can live. Apart from this, the primary advantage of modules is that they can be exported and reused in other projects—like classes except that they don't need to be instantiated. If you don't need either feature, but simply want globally available methods and properties, consider instead subclassing the Application class.

The Application subclass is automatically instantiated as your application starts up, and a reference to this instance is always available through the App function. Thus, if MyGlobalMethod lived in the Application subclass, it would be called by saying:

```
app.myGlobalMethod
```

The Application subclass offers several major advantages over a module as a repository of global members:

- The Application subclass is sent an Open event, which provides an opportunity for its properties to be initialized.
- There is no possibility that access to members of the Application subclass will be cut off by accidental use of identical local names, because all messages to the Application subclass are explicitly directed to app.
- Modules defeat the purpose of object-orientation, whereas the Application subclass represents a definite "thing" and has a natural right to contain members.

Advanced Class Features

In this section we look at some miscellaneous further topics having to do with classes. Beginners, who may find the details presented here somewhat distracting, may wish to skim this section rather quickly at first, returning to it subsequently as examples arise later in the book or in the course of actual programming.

What's My Window?

Nothing in REALbasic is so important as obtaining a reference to a desired instance, and no instance is so vexing to get a reference to as the window containing a given control. There are three different ways for a control to get a reference to its containing window, depending on the context.

Let's start with code inside a control instance's event handlers. I'm talking here about any code that appears in a window's Code Editor, within its Controls category. Such code can obtain a reference to its containing window by way of the Self function (Chapter 3). This is the only code where Self and Me yield different results; Me returns a reference to the instance itself. So a PushButton instance in a window can refer to the window's title as `self.title` (or simply `title`).

Next, consider code inside the Code Editor of a programmer-defined subclass of the built-in Control class. (ScoreBox, from earlier in this chapter, is an example, because it is a subclass of StaticText, which is a subclass of RectControl, which is a subclass of Control.) Here, Self doesn't refer to the instance's containing window, but to the instance itself. However, the Control class has a Window property that returns a reference to the instance's containing window; the subclass inherits this. So, the Score-Box class can refer to the window's title as `self.window.title` (or `window.title`).

Finally, there is code inside the Code Editor of a programmer-defined class that is *not* a Control subclass. We presume, obviously, that the instance is being used as a control—that is, it is contained by a window. There is only one reliable way for such code to get a reference to the instance's containing window, and that is to use a New Event.

The technique requires some preparation. You have dragged the class's listing from the Project Window into a Window Editor to make a control. You double-click the class's listing in the Project Window to access its Code Editor. Create a New Event: let's call it Owner, and let's have it be a function that returns a Window. Finally, in the Window Editor, double-click the instance to access its event handlers within the window's Code Editor. There is now an Owner event handler; give it this code:

```
return self
```

Code within the class can now refer to the instance's containing window as `owner()`. This device lacks elegance, since we must remember to code an Owner event handler individually for every instance in a window; but this is unavoidable.

Both the Control class's Window property and our Owner New Event have a big drawback: they return an instance of the Window class. That's fine if you want to access a feature of the window common to every window, such as its title; but it's not so good if you want to access a feature particular to the window class containing the instance. For example, if a window contains a button called PushButton1, an instance in the window can refer to `self.pushButton1`, because Self is always the correct window class, and REALbasic knows that this kind of window has a PushButton1. But you can't say `self.window.pushButton1` or `owner.pushButton1`, because the Window class contains no controls. You have to cast to the correct window class. For example, if the type of window containing PushButton1 is a

---

However, there's an easy solution: your subclass has only to override the other superclass method.* In our example, we'd give MySubClass a GreetMe method that *does* take an integer parameter. Now the subclass contains a method whose parameters match those of the call, and everything is fine. Well, not everything. There's still a problem: the functionality you wanted is in the superclass! Luckily, there's a way for code in the subclass to call code in the superclass; that's the next topic.

Class-Directed Messages

Code in a class method can direct a method call at its superclass. This is called a *class-directed message*. The syntax is simple: in a dot notation expression, before the dot, instead of using an instance name, you use a class name. This must be a superclass of the class in which the call appears; in other words, class-directed messages can be directed only up the hierarchy from the class containing the code that's sending the message. This restriction makes sense; a subclass should have the ability to decide how it wants to take advantage of the storehouse of methods it inherits from its superclasses, but it shouldn't be possible to subvert the hierarchy in other ways.

For example, let's go back to our ScoreBox and DoubleScoreBox implementations from earlier in this chapter. It may have occurred to you that there was something inelegant about our implementation of Increase. Here, you recall, is ScoreBox's Increase handler:

```
self.score = self.score + 1
self.showscore
```

Here is DoubleScoreBox's Increase handler:

```
self.score = self.score + 2
self.showscore
```

The routines are near duplicates of each other, and this duplication obscures the essential relationship between DoubleScoreBox and ScoreBox: a DoubleScoreBox is everything that a ScoreBox is, and then some. In particular, a DoubleScoreBox is a ScoreBox that increases its score one more than a ScoreBox does. To capture this fact, we can have DoubleScoreBox increase its score by 1 (it increases its score *one* more than a ScoreBox does), and then call ScoreBox's Increase handler (it increases its score one *more than a ScoreBox* does):

```
self.score = self.score + 1
scorebox.increase
```

---

* It happens that in this example there's another workaround, namely, to cast the instance as a MyClass. This hides from REALbasic the existence of the method that takes the wrong parameters. So, if c is the MySubClass instance, you can say `myClass(c).greetMe(3)`. However, this use of *casting up*, effectively delivering a class-directed message from outside the instance, is probably to be deprecated (though it was quite standard in Version 1 of REALbasic).

In the same way, you can see how class-directed methods solve the problem posed in the previous section. MyClass has one GreetMe method; MySubClass overrides that one and adds another. MySubClass's implementation of the overriding GreetMe can be as simple as calling the overridden GreetMe.

Class-directed messages don't have to have the same name as the method that was originally called, as in these examples. And the method that is called doesn't have to live in the class to which you send the message; it can live in a superclass of that class. Perhaps the best way to envision class-directed messages is to think of them as directed at Me, the instance, but with a proviso as to where resolution of the name should begin. In such a scenario, this line:

```
myClass.greetMe(i)
```

actually means, "me.greetMe(i), but in resolving the name greetMe, skip upward past all classes until you reach MyClass; start resolving upward from there."

Privacy

Object-oriented programming is, in a sense, a way for the programmer to participate in the design of the programming language itself. When we create a class and populate it with members, we are telling other classes how they should speak when they want to communicate with this class.

However, other classes may have the power to speak too freely. We may intend that every instance of the ScoreBox class, for example, should be the "owner and protector" of its own score; when any other class wants to increase a score, it should send the instance an Increase message. But other classes can subvert our intentions, by manipulating the instance's Score property directly:

```
theScoreBox.score = theScoreBox.score + 1
```

It isn't enough to say, since we are writing the code ourselves, that therefore in actual fact no other class *will* speak this way, because we have a "rule" that this is forbidden. Where is this "rule"? If it is just in our own head, it might fall out of our head (we could forget); also, what's in our head is not in the head of some other programmer who might some day come to maintain the project, or to whom we might send an exported class. Self-restraint is no restraint.

REALbasic alleviates such problems by permitting you to declare a member as *private*. This is done by ticking the Private checkbox in the method or property's declaration dialog. The question is then who is allowed to access a private member.* Once a class member is private, it is accessible only from the same class or its subclasses; one instance of a class (or its subclasses) can access a private member of the same instance or another instance of the same class (or its subclasses).

---

* Insert your own Monica Lewinski joke here.

This solves the difficulty with the Score property. If Score is private, then Increase is the only way for outsiders to do anything to the score; Increase is a *setter* for Score. Similarly, if we want outsiders to be able to learn the score, they can't read Score directly, so we must provide a *getter*:

```
Function score() as integer
    return self.score
End Function
```

Experienced OOP programmers will observe that REALbasic's "private" corresponds to C++'s "protected"; total privacy, where not even a subclass can access a private member, is not available in REALbasic, and neither is "friendship," where a class may declare a limited list of other classes that can access its private members.

There is no visual indication in the Code Editor that a method or property is private; you have to double-click its browser listing and inspect its declaration dialog.

Class Properties and Class Methods

A *class property* (sometimes called a *static property*) is a property whose value is shared among all instances of the class. A *class method* (sometimes called a *static method*) is a method that can be called without directing a message at any particular instance of the class (though it does still live in that class). In Chapter 3 it was pointed out that REALbasic lacks class properties and class methods.

This section describes an architecture that helps to compensate for this lack. The idea is to take advantage of the fact that REALbasic permits global instances. We will store a special instance of the class as a property of the Application subclass. This instance will act as a "static" representative of the class; it will function as a master repository of information, and as an instance that can respond to messages in the absence of all other instances.

As an example, let's posit a Widget class whose "static" representative is a Widget instance named WidgetMaster, a property of the Application subclass. We instantiate this property in the Application subclass's Open event, so that the WidgetMaster instance is absolutely global:

```
    self.widgetMaster = new widget
```

Let's say that we wish to be able to ask any Widget how many Widget instances there are. That's like a class property: every Widget instance should give the same answer. The job of WidgetMaster will be to know this answer and to make it available to any Widget instance. Let Widget have a property MasterCount that is an integer. Only WidgetMaster's value for this property will be correct, so to prevent accidents we make MasterCount private. Widget's constructor increments the MasterCount:

```
    Sub widget()
        app.widgetMaster.masterCount = app.widgetMaster.masterCount + 1
    exception
    End Sub
```

The exception line isn't explained until Chapter 8, but the point is that the very first time this constructor is called, the WidgetMaster instance won't exist yet—because it's the instance that's being created! We don't mind this, because we don't want WidgetMaster included in the count anyway; but we have to prevent the application from terminating prematurely, and that's what the exception line does. Widget's destructor obviously just decrements the count:

```
Sub ~widget()
    app.widgetMaster.masterCount = app.widgetMaster.masterCount - 1
End Sub
```

Widget's Count method consults WidgetCount's MasterCount. Thus, Count acts as a mediator to MasterCount; nonwidgets can't get access to MasterCount except indirectly through Count, which acts as a getter:

```
Function count() As integer
    return app.widgetMaster.masterCount
End Function
```

This works beautifully, as we can confirm through the following test:

```
dim w1, w2 as widget
w1 = new widget
w2 = new widget
msgbox str(w1.count) // 2, as expected
```

Furthermore, we can learn the count globally, without a reference to a particular widget instance, by asking WidgetMaster:

```
msgbox str(app.widgetMaster.count)
```

The example could be much extended to demonstrate such powerful techniques as actual instance management being performed by the master instance (a factory architecture), but that would go beyond the scope of this book.

Example Classes

In this section we sketch a few ideas for programmer-defined classes that illustrate useful basic features of classes.

Stack Class

This is the Stack class promised in Chapter 3. A *stack* is a dynamic storage mechanism, where items are added or removed one at a time, and only the most recently added item is accessible (like a stack of plates). You understand that it's completely unnecessary to implement a Stack class from scratch in REALbasic, because REALbasic provides dynamic arrays! So, we could easily implement a stack by using an array, adding items with Append and removing them with Remove. However, the example provides a flexible model that can easily be modified to form other storage mechanisms such as queues, and illustrates the power of object references as pointers to form linked data structures.

Our implementation, you recall, is that each item of the stack will contain a value and a pointer back to the previously added item of the stack; the earliest added item will point to nil. In Chapter 3 these were called ItsValue and ItsPointer, so let's keep those names. We'll make it a stack of strings; so ItsValue is declared as string, and ItsPointer is declared as Stack. The chief actions on a stack are to add (*push*) or remove (*pop*) an item at the front; it's also useful to know whether the stack is empty. The basic implementation, shown in Example 4-1, is a simple matter of manipulating pointers.

Example 4-1. Stack class

```
// stack.push:
Sub push(s as string)
    dim newItem as stack
    newItem = new stack
    newItem.itsPointer = self.itsPointer
    newItem.itsValue = s
    self.itsPointer = newItem
End Sub

// stack.pop:
Function pop() As string
    dim value as string
    value = self.itsPointer.itsValue
    self.itsPointer = self.itsPointer.itsPointer
    return value
End Function

// stack.isEmpty:
Function isEmpty() As boolean
    return (self.itsPointer = nil)
End Function
```

We may test the Stack class as follows:

```
dim st as stack
dim s as string
st = new stack
st.push "hey"
st.push "ho"
s = st.pop() // throw away, just testing
st.push "hey"
st.push "nonny"
st.push "no"
while not st.isEmpty // pop and show whole stack
    msgBox st.pop() // expect "no", "nonny", "hey", "hey"
wend
```

The onus is on the caller not to pop an empty stack; in real life, Pop would probably raise an exception if the stack is empty, as described in Chapter 8. The example is remarkably economical. You might think we'd need two classes, one for the items of the stack and one to represent the stack as whole; instead, the reference that points at the stack is itself just like the items of the stack, but it doesn't store anything in Its-Value.

Array Class

We would like to extend the power of arrays. We cannot subclass an array, because an array is not a class. But we can make a class that has an array as a member and provides an extended interface to it. Such a class is called a *wrapper*. This section presents a class CArray that is a wrapper for a one-dimensional array of strings.

There are several advantages to this class over a normal array. We will be able to define new array operations that ordinary arrays lack: for instance, a Swap function will cause the values of two items to be interchanged, a Reverse function will allow us to sort either ascending or descending, a CopyTo function will copy all items from one array into another, and a Clone method will create a new instance and CopyTo that. Also, it will be easy to subclass CArray to provide for even more specialized types of arrays; imagine, for example, an array that is constantly kept sorted by means of a binary search. Most important, an array wrapper class is a real class, as opposed to an ordinary array in REALbasic, which is neither a class nor a datatype, neither object nor scalar; an array wrapper class is a full citizen and can do things that an ordinary array cannot. For example, you cannot declare an array of array, but you can declare an array of a class that wraps an array; and a class that wraps a multidimensional array can be passed as a parameter to a subroutine (unlike an ordinary multidimensional array).

Example 4-2 gives a sample implementation. We provide wrapper functions for all the standard array operations, using the standard names (except that we cannot name a method Redim because that's a reserved word, so MyRedim is used), plus Set and Get (because we can't overload the assignment operator), plus our various extensions. The private array property is called TheArray; it is declared as being of size -1 initially, but a constructor is provided that lets us create a new CArray instance and Redim it to the desired size in a single command.

Example 4-2. cArray class

```
// cArray.cArray:
Sub cArray()
    // constructor with no parameters
    // do nothing, accept declaration to -1
End Sub

// cArray.cArray:
Sub cArray(size as integer)
    // constructor with one parameter
    self.myRedim(size)
End Sub
```

Example 4-2. cArray class (continued)

```
// cArray.myRedim:
Sub myRedim(size as integer)
    redim self.theArray(size)
End Sub

// cArray.set:
Sub set(index as integer, s as string)
    self.theArray(index) = s
End Sub

// cArray.get:
Function get(index as integer) As string
    return self.theArray(index)
End Function

// cArray.insert:
Sub insert(index as integer, s as string)
    self.theArray.insert index, s
End Sub

// cArray.append:
Sub append(s as string)
    self.theArray.append s
End Sub

// cArray.remove:
Sub remove(index as integer)
    self.theArray.remove index
End Sub

// cArray.ubound:
Function ubound() As integer
    return ubound(self.theArray)
End Function

// cArray.sort:
Sub sort()
    self.theArray.sort
End Sub

// cArray.swap:
Sub swap(index1 as integer, index2 as integer)
    dim s as string
    s = self.get(index1)
    self.set(index1, self.get(index2))
    self.set(index2, s)
End Sub

// cArray.reverse:
Sub reverse()
    dim i, u, u2 as integer
    u = self.ubound()
    u2 = u\2
```

Example 4-2. cArray class (continued)

```
    for i = 0 to u2
        self.swap(i, u-i)
    next
End Sub

// cArray.copyTo:
Sub copyTo(c as cArray)
    dim i, u as integer
    u = min(self.ubound(), c.ubound())
    for i = 0 to u
        c.set(i, self.get(i))
    next
End Sub

// cArray.clone:
Function clone() As cArray
    dim c as cArray
    c = new cArray(self.ubound())
    self.copyto(c)
    return c
End Function

// cArray.display:
Sub display()
    // for debugging
    dim i, u as integer
    u = self.ubound()
    for i = 0 to u
        msgbox self.get(i)
    next
End Sub
```

Here is a brief test routine:

```
    dim a, b, c as cArray
    a = new cArray(4)
    b = new cArray(2)
    a.set(0,"hey")
    a.set(1,"ho")
    a.set(2,"hey")
    a.set(3,"nonny")
    a.set(4,"no")
    msgbox "Here is a:"
    a.display // expect "hey", "ho", "hey", "nonny", "no"
    a.copyTo b
    msgbox "Here is b:"
    b.display // expect "hey", "ho", "hey"
    c = a.clone()
    c.sort
    c.reverse
    c.set(0, "yo")
    c.myRedim(2)
    msgbox "Here is c:"
    c.display // expect "yo", "no", "ho"
```

For example, this code sets b to the value of a rather complicated boolean expression:

```
dim b as boolean
b = (5 > 6) or (not (b and (3 = 2)))
```

If you are coldly logical, you will see at once that b is now true. (If not, you can ask REALbasic to evaluate the expression for you; that's what I did.)

The six comparison operators signify *equals, is less than, is greater than, is less than or equal to, is greater than or equal to,* and *is unequal to.* Notice that the equals comparison operator is identical in appearance to the assignment operator; this can be confusing, though in practice there is no ambiguity as to whether it is being used in the context of an assignment or in the context of a comparison, as those contexts are mutually exclusive. It is legal to write this:

```
dim b as boolean, i as integer
b = i = 2
```

That doesn't assign 2 to i and then to b; it asks whether i is equal to 2 and assigns the resulting boolean value to b. It is common practice in these situations to surround the boolean expression i = 2 with parentheses, for clarity, but this is not required; REALbasic isn't confused, even if you are.

Any values with identical datatypes may be compared; numerical values may be compared even if their datatypes are not identical, because of implicit numerical coercion (see "Coercion of Numbers," later in this chapter). In practice, you will probably limit comparisons to strings, numbers, equality or inequality of booleans, and equality or inequality of class types with nil or with the same class type. It is possible to perform other comparisons with booleans—it turns out that true is greater than false—but personally I have not encountered a use for this. Other comparisons with class types are permissible but essentially meaningless; for instance, given two FolderItem instances, you can ask whether one is greater than the other, but you have no way of knowing what criterion REALbasic is using to determine the answer, so that answer is of no use to you.

Coercion of Booleans

Unlike many computer languages, REALbasic provides no implicit coercion between booleans and other datatypes, meaning that it is an error to use a nonboolean where a boolean is expected, or vice versa. Furthermore, REALbasic provides no function to convert explicitly from a nonboolean to a boolean, or vice versa.

This can make REALbasic code peculiarly clumsy and inelegant. Suppose, for example, that you wish to put up a dialog that reports the value of a boolean variable, myBoolean. You cannot say:

```
msgBox myBoolean // error: Type mismatch
```

Instead, you must resort to laborious periphrasis:

```
if myBoolean then
    msgBox "true"
else
    msgBox "false"
end
```

You may wish to arm yourself with some conversion routines and keep them in a module, where any project can import them and any subroutine can call them; examples appear later in this chapter, under "Variants."

Side Effects

When you use a boolean expression, all its pieces are evaluated right then and there, in order to determine whether the value of the whole expression is true or false. It is important to be conscious of side effects that may accrue when this occurs. Suppose, for example, we have a function DeleteAndCount, which, given a folder, deletes a randomly chosen file from that folder and returns an integer reporting how many files remain in the folder afterward. Then consider the results of the following code:

```
dim b as boolean
b = (deleteAndCount(desktopFolder) = deleteAndCount(desktopFolder))
```

Merely evaluating the boolean expression in the second line to learn whether it is true or false causes two randomly chosen files to be deleted from the desktop, once when the function is called on the left side of the comparison and once when it is called on the right side. As a result, the evaluation yields false even though the two sides of the comparison appear identical; that's because one side returns a number smaller by 1 than the other side, since it deletes an additional file before it counts the files. You have, by the way, no means of knowing *which* side will be evaluated first; it is important not to use expressions in boolean comparisons whose value depends upon the order of evaluation.

On the other hand, the And and Or operators provide an important and helpful guarantee in this regard: they are *short-circuited*, meaning that they evaluate their left-side operand first, and if the result of the operation is then known, they never evaluate their right-side operand at all. Consider, for example, the boolean expression presented here:

```
dim b as boolean
dim f as folderItem
// ... some more code ...
b = f <> nil and f.exists
```

If the FolderItem f is nil, then sending the Exists message to it, in the course of evaluating this boolean expression, will result in premature termination of our application ("Initialization Is Not Instantiation" in Chapter 3). But we are guaranteed by short-circuiting that if in fact f *is* nil, then the second half of the boolean expression will *never* be evaluated, because in that case the value of the entire expression will be known to be false after the first half of the expression is evaluated. Thus, it is perfectly safe to use this boolean expression; and expressions of this sort are commonly used as conditions instead of nested If structures.

 Don't pass a boolean ByRef if you're building for 68K Macintosh. REAL Software, Inc., warns that there is a bug deep in the compiler that causes a crash. In PowerPC builds, there's no such problem.

Strings

A *byte* is a binary number of eight digits in length, so that it lies between &h00 (0) and &hFF (255) inclusive.* A *string* is a sequence of bytes, externally represented as a sequence of text characters. The correspondence between numeric values and character representations is implementation-dependent; a character's underlying numeric value is usually referred to as its ASCII value, though in fact the historical ASCII convention has long been superseded.†

A literal string is delimited in REALbasic by double quotation marks. A literal empty string is represented by two double quotation marks in succession. Double quotation marks may be represented within a literal string as a sequence of two double quotation marks. Thus:

```
msgBox "Hello"  // Hello
msgBox ""  // Dialog is empty
msgBox """Hello"""  // "Hello"
```

Strings have a powerful and efficient internal implementation. Their size can nominally range up to two gigabytes (I say "nominally" because in reality your application will doubtless hit the limit of memory size long before the string size limit is reached). A string of any size can be passed as a parameter to a subroutine without penalty. Furthermore, strings are intended for general use in storing numeric byte sequences and transferring them to disk and over networks; therefore, they may include any byte value, even those that have no "printable" text equivalent, including null (&h00).

On some systems (in Japan, for example), one character of text can be represented internally by a sequence of two bytes, so as to permit representation of more than 256 distinct characters—up to 65,535, in fact (&hFFFF, the maximum unsigned short integer). Such encodings are termed *double-byte* encodings. REALbasic works transparently with these systems, but this means that, unlike with a single-byte system, if

---

* The prefix &h is used in REALbasic to designate a number as hexadecimal (base 16); see "Concatenation and Conversion" and "Numbers," later in this chapter.

† It has been superseded by several different conventions that conflict in a very confusing way. The trouble is that the original ASCII specification provided for only 127 characters, so it has been expanded independently by various institutions for various purposes. For a table of the standard ("MacRoman") ASCII encoding for Macintosh characters, see *http://developer.apple.com/techpubs/mac/Text/Text-516.html*. For a fine discussion of character encoding issues, see *http://mtl.uta.fi/jkorpela/chars.html*.

a string is used to store numeric byte data, the bytes cannot be individually manipulated simply by manipulating text characters. REALbasic therefore provides byte-based versions of many of its string functions; unfortunately, it doesn't provide byte-based versions of all of them.

On a single-byte system, such as a Macintosh with an English-language system, some of the byte-based functions yield identical results, at identical speed, to their character-based equivalents. On the other hand, many of REALbasic's string functions naturally assume that the data being operated on is intended to be considered as text, and therefore maintain an awareness of such textual features as case and diacriticals; such operations are inherently slower than, and may give different results from, those that work on purely numeric values.

For byte-based operations, and for certain other purposes, a memoryblock will often be a faster or more convenient datatype to work with than a string. Memoryblocks provide a way to declare fixed-length strings; to convert between REALbasic strings, C strings, and Pascal strings; to access individual bytes directly by index number; and to treat values indifferently as bytes, short integers, or long integers. Memoryblocks are discussed later in this chapter.

Concatenation and Conversion

Strings are concatenated by using the + operator. The + operator is thus overloaded, since it is also used to indicate arithmetic addition; but there is no danger of confusion, since if even one of the + operator's operands is numeric, it is an error—"Expecting a numeric operand"—for them all not to be numeric.

Conversion between a character's textual and numeric representations is performed with the Asc and Chr functions. The byte equivalents are AscB and ChrB. The Asc function ignores all but the first character of its parameter and converts that character to a number. The Chr function ignores all but the smallest 16 bits of its parameter and converts the resulting number to a string consisting of one character. The reason why Chr considers so many bits is to allow for double-byte systems; ChrB ignores all but the smallest 8 bits of its parameter. Thus:

```
i = asc("h") // 104
i = asc("hello") // 104
s = chr(104) // "h"
s = chr(104 + (256 * 104)) // "hh" on a single-byte system
s = chr(104 + (256 * 104) + (256 * 256 * 104)) // still "hh"
s = chrb(104 + (256 * 104) + (256 * 256 * 104)) // "h"
```

Literal representation of strings involving unprintable characters is impossible; instead, a combination of concatenation and conversion must be used. For example:

```
cr = chr(13) // return character
msgbox "Hello" + cr + "world" // Hello, new line, world
```

String representation of a numeric value is achieved by use of the Str function. Str does not comply with the user's system settings where the decimal separator might not be a period; to achieve such compliance, use CStr instead of Str.

You may not like the Str function's representation of a particular number; indeed, this representation may mislead you. For example, Str may use scientific notation, or it may truncate the number's apparent precision. Also, you may want some specialized form of display, as for currency. To take more control, use the Format function, where you supply a second parameter, a string describing how you want the resulting string to look. The encoding of the formatting string is similar to that of the numeric formatting string used by Microsoft Excel; see the online help for details. But even with Format it is possible to confuse yourself, for instance, by asking for too much precision. So, for example:

```
msgBox str(1234.56) // 1234.56
msgBox str(1234567) // 1.234567e+6
msgBox format(1234567, "#") // 1234567
msgBox str(-1234567.8901234) // -1.234568e+6
msgBox format(-1234567.8901234, "-#.########") // -1234567.8901234
msgBox format(-1234567.8901234, "-#.#############") // -1234567.8901233999059
```

The numeric equivalent of a string that represents a number is obtained with the Val function. All characters of the string that don't look like part of a number, starting with the first such character, are ignored; if the first character of the string doesn't look like part of a number, or if the string is empty, the result is 0. An initial sign character is acceptable; so is a decimal point; so is scientific notation.

```
d = val("123.456") // 123.456
```

Val does not comply with the user's system settings where the decimal separator might not be a period, and where a thousands separator might be legal; to achieve such compliance, use CDbl instead of Val.

The result of Val or CDbl is a double, but it will be coerced implicitly to the numeric type of the reference to which it is assigned. The string may start with "&b" or "&o" or "&h" to signify binary, octal, or hexadecimal; this provides a way to convert the numeric base. See "Numbers," later in this chapter.

Length, Search, Comparison, and Sort

The number of characters in a string is returned by the Len function. The byte equivalent is LenB.

```
i = len("hello") // 5
```

To learn whether one string contains another, use the Instr function. The first parameter is optional, and represents the character position at which the search should begin. The remaining parameters are the containing string and the substring sought within it. Character positions are one-based. The result is an integer—the starting character position at which the substring was found, or 0 if it was not found.

The search ignores the case of characters, and consults the system to learn the case equivalents; if that's not what you want, use the byte equivalent, InstrB.

```
i = instr("hello", "L") // 3
i = instrb("hello", "L") // 0
```

To obtain a version of a string where the first instance or all instances of a substring are replaced with another value, use the Replace or ReplaceAll function. The parameters are the original string, the substring to be sought, and the substring to replace it with. These functions can also be used to delete a substring, by supplying the empty string as the replacement value. The search ignores the case of characters, and consults the system to learn the case equivalents; unfortunately, there are no byte equivalent functions.

```
msgBox replaceAll("hello", "L", "p") // heppo
```

Strings may be compared by using the boolean comparison operators. (The comparison in Select Case is boolean as well.) International case-insensitive ordering is used, which, on an English system, is the same as ASCII order, except for the following rules:*

- Case is absolutely immaterial; a lowercase is treated as if it were the corresponding uppercase.

- Nonbreaking space is sorted together with normal space.

- Guillemets and curly double quotation marks are sorted together with straight double quotation marks.

- Curly single quotation marks are sorted together with the straight single quotation mark.

- Every diacritical variant of a letter is sorted together with the plain uppercase variant of that letter. So, for example, all the uppercase and lowercase diacritical versions of "A" (with an umlaut, with a grave accent, the ligature "Æ", and so forth) are sorted together with "A".

- Things sorted together (except for uppercase and lowercase versions of the same letter, which are considered identical) have an internal order, which in general terms is the ASCII order of their minuscule versions.

Thus:

```
"10" < "9"  // true; "1" is ASCII 49 and "9" is ASCII 57
"hello" < "helloo"  // true; "hello" is shorter
"hello" < "Helloooo"  // true; "hello" is shorter and case is immaterial
"helloo" < "hellp"  // true; "o" sorts before "p"
"héllo" > "hellp"  // true; "e" sorts before "é"
"héllo" < "hf"  // true; "é" sorts with "e" before "f"
"Hello" = "hello"  // true; case is absolutely immaterial
```

---

* See *http://developer.apple.com/techpubs/mac/Text/Text-287.html* and *http://developer.apple.com/techpubs/mac/Text/Text-518.html*.

Another way to compare strings is the StrComp function. It takes three parameters: the first string, the second string, and a mode integer that is 0 or 1 or 2. It returns an integer to indicate the result of the comparison: -1 if the first string is less than the second, 0 if the first string is equal to the second, and 1 if the first string is greater than the second.

When the mode integer is 0, StrComp performs a pure numeric comparison of the bytes constituting the strings. So:

```
i = strComp ("Hello", "hello", 0) // -1; "H" is ASCII 72, "h" is ASCII 104
i = strComp ("Hello", "bellow", 0) // -1; "H" is ASCII 72, "b" is ASCII 98
i = strComp ("Helloooo", "Hello", 0) // 1; "Hello" is shorter
i = strComp ("hello", "Helloooo", 0) // 1; "H" is ASCII 72, "h" is ASCII 104
```

When the mode integer is 1, StrComp uses rules almost identical to those of the boolean comparison operators, but uppercase precedes lowercase:

```
i = strComp ("hallo", "Hello", 1) // 1; "H" is ASCII 72, "h" is ASCII 104
i = strComp ("hello", "Helloooo", 1) // 1; "H" is ASCII 72, "h" is ASCII 104
i = strComp ("héllo", "hollo", 1) // -1; "é" is treated like "e"
```

When the mode integer is 2, StrComp uses a rather complicated lexicographic ordering system. This is based on the rules for boolean comparison, but entities sorted together (such as lowercase, uppercase, and diacritical versions of the same letter) are treated as identical unless all characters that follow them are pairwise identical. So, for example:

```
i = strComp ("hallo", "Hello", 2) // -1; case is ignored, "a" sorts before "e"
i = strComp ("hello", "Helloooo", 2) // -1; case is ignored, "Helloooo" is longer
i = strComp ("héllo", "Helloooo", 2) // -1; case and diacritics are ignored, "Helloooo" is longer
i = strComp ("héllo", "hollo", 2) // -1; "é" is treated like "e"
i = strComp ("Hello", "hello", 2) // -1; now case counts, "H" is ASCII 72, "h" is ASCII 104
```

Table 5-1 summarizes by example the different ways in which REALbasic orders strings.

Table 5-1. Ways of ordering strings

Original	Greater than	StrComp 0	StrComp 1	StrComp 2
héllo	bellow	Hello	bellow	bellow
helloo	hallo	Helloooo	Hello	hallo
hellp	hello	bellow	Helloooo	Hello
Hello	Hello	hallo	hallo	hello
hello	helloo	hello	hallo	héllo
bellow	Helloooo	helloo	hello	helloo
Helloooo	hellp	hellp	hellp	Helloooo
hallo	héllo	héllo	héllo	hellp

Strings may be sorted by loading them into an array and applying the Sort procedure. The sort order is the same as StrComp mode 1. For example:

```
dim myArray(1000) as string
// ... assign values to array items ...
myArray.sort
```

Sorting for Table 5-1 was done using a simple Shell sort algorithm, and the original set of words appeared in the given order but among a much larger set of items. It is purely by luck of the draw that in the greater than comparison, "hello" ended up before "Hello", since the two are equal. Here is the Shell sort algorithm used (the array's Ubound value is bound):*

```
gap = (bound + 1) / 2
while gap > 0
    for i = gap to bound
        j = i - gap
        jg = i
        while j >= 0 and s(j) > s(jg) // or any comparison method
            temp = s(j) // swap
            s(j)= s(jg)
            s(jg) = temp
            jg = j
            j = j - gap
        wend
    next
    gap = gap / 2
wend
```

The reader may be curious about the relative speeds of the various comparison methods. In my not particularly scientific testing, doing 100 sorting repetitions in a built application with the disableBackgroundTasks pragma turned on (see Chapter 8), the results were as follows. REALbasic's native array Sort procedure was fastest (11 ticks), though performance degrades significantly if values are mostly the same. Then, using the Shell sort, come StrComp 0 (12 ticks), boolean comparison (19 ticks), and StrComp 1 (21 ticks)—all of them almost as fast, and the worst only twice as slow. But StrComp 2 is an order of magnitude slower (370 ticks).†

Substrings and Case

To obtain from a string a substring of *count* characters starting at the *n*th character, use the Mid function. The byte equivalent is MidB. The character position is one-based. The syntax is:

```
mid(theString, n, count)
```

---

* Adapted from Brian W. Kernighan and Dennis M. Ritchie, *The C Programming Language*, 2nd ed. (Prentice-Hall, 1988, 2nd ed.).

† On a double-byte system, the relative timings might come out quite differently; I don't know.

So, for example:

```
msgBox mid("Hello out there", 7, 3) // out
```

The Mid function is amazingly forgiving; it cannot be induced to complain. If *count* is omitted, or is too large, all the characters to the end of the string are returned. If n is too large, or *count* is not positive, the empty string is returned. If n is too small (less than 1), the result starts in an imaginary space before the beginning of the string, and characters from that space are thrown away; so for example:

```
msgbox mid("hi", 0, 2) // h
```

The result here is the nonexistent zero character and the first character, "h", with the nonexistent zero character thrown away.

Two further substring functions, Left and Right (and their byte equivalents, LeftB and RightB), are merely a convenient shorthand for effects that can be achieved with Mid. Left is simply Mid with an automatic n value of 1; Right is Mid with an automatic n value of len(*theString*)-*count*+1.

Another way to obtain substrings is in terms of fields. Fields of a string are defined in terms of some substring that acts as a delimiter; if the delimiter occurs n times in the string, the string contains n+1 fields: what precedes the first delimiter, what falls between each successive pair of delimiters, and what follows the last delimiter. To obtain a count of the fields, use the CountFields function:

```
i = countFields("Mississippi", "s") // 5
```

Note that a valuable misuse of CountFields is to count the number of occurrences of a substring! So, in the preceding example, we now know that the target string contains four instances of "s".

To obtain any particular field, use the NthField function. The numbering of the fields is one-based.

```
msgBox nthField("Mississippi", "s", 5) // ippi
```

The search for the delimiter string in both CountFields and NthField ignores the case of characters; there are no byte equivalent functions.

The specialized substring consisting of an original string stripped of leading spaces, trailing spaces, or both, can be obtained with the LTrim, RTrim, and Trim functions.

To perform case changes, use the Uppercase, Lowercase, and Titlecase functions. (Titlecase means that every character is lowercase, except the first character of every word, which is uppercase.)

Extending REALbasic's Abilities

REALbasic's built-in string functions are surprisingly thin, and the question naturally arises of what can be done to supplement them.

A number of useful string functions that REALbasic omits can easily be written in terms of the existing functions. Take, for instance, Delete, which returns a string consisting of a given string stripped of *count* characters starting with character *n*:

```
Function Delete(s as string, n as integer, count as integer) As string
    return left(s,n-1) + mid(s,n+count)
End Function
```

For certain string manipulation functions where REALbasic provides insufficient flexibility, the easiest solution is to resort to an XCMD or a plug-in (see Chapter 32 for more about these). A good example is a case-sensitive find, a serious lack. I particularly recommend the XCMDs by Frédéric Rinaldi, such as FullFind, FullOffset, FullReplace, and FullSort. The plug-ins by Micono have also proven popular.

Another alternative is to take advantage of Macintosh Toolbox functions. For example, the following routine shows how to translate all diacritical characters in a string to normal characters (since this is just an example, I omit explanatory details; see Chapter 32):

```
dim i as integer, s as string
s = "héllö thèrë"
declare function StripDiacritics lib "InterfaceLib" // no line break!
    (s as cstring, i as short, c as integer) as short
i = stripDiacritics(s, lenb(s), 0) // call Mac Toolbox
msgBox s // hello there
```

REALbasic's lack of grep functionality (meaning "regular expressions," which permit complex and powerful find and replace operations) is not so easily remedied. If you're writing an application for your own personal use, it is a simple matter to have it employ Apple events to take advantage of scripting additions, or a scriptable grep package such as PreFab's Text Machine. But this doesn't solve the problem of how to incorporate grep into an application that will run on any machine; for that, a plug-in is probably the best approach.*

With Mac OS X, on the other hand, all your problems are solved. Under the Unix hood are grep and sed and awk and Perl and heaven knows what else, and you can access these through REALbasic's Shell class. All this power is thus at your command—and, more to the point, you are guaranteed that it is at the command of all your users as well.

To give a simple example, imagine that we wish to strip all HTML-type markup from a string. With just REALbasic's built-in string capabilities, this would be tedious; with Perl, it's a snap. In this example, we build a command line that runs a little Perl script:

---

* To learn more about regular expressions, see Jeffrey E.F. Friedl, *Mastering Regular Expressions* (O'Reilly & Associates, 1997). For Rinaldi's XCMDs, see *http://perso.wanadoo.fr/fredric.rinaldi/* and Chapter 32. For Micono's plug-ins, see *http://hp.vector.co.jp/authors/VA009277/rb/index_e.htm*. For Text Machine, see *http://www.prefab.com/textmachine.html*. There is a regular expressions plug-in by Anjo Krank; see *http://www.prnet.de/RegEx/*. In REALbasic 3.5, regular expressions will apparently at last be incorporated into the language (the RegEx classes).

```
dim sh as shell
dim s, orig as string
orig = "I do not <i>like</i> green eggs and <b>ham</b>."
s = "perl -e " // we will supply a perl script
s = s + "'" // here it comes
s = s + "$_ = q{" + orig + "};" // start with orig
s = s + "s/<.*?>//g;" // delete all markup
s = s + "print $_;" // output the result
s = s + "'" // that's the end
sh = new shell
sh.execute(s)
msgbox sh.result // I do not like green eggs and ham.
```

This is already hard enough to read; with a more involved Perl script, you'll probably be happier writing it out to a file and telling the shell to execute from there. For more about the Shell class, see Chapter 31 (though in fact there's little more to know than what you see in this example).*

Converting Between Encodings

As mentioned earlier, the correspondence between numeric byte values and their character representations depends upon the particular implementation. This presents a problem of compatibility across platforms and languages, including the Internet. To ease these difficulties, REALbasic permits you to harness the capabilities of the Text Encoding Converter, which recognizes some 130 different text encodings, some of them with more than one variant, between which it can convert. The Text Encoding Converter used to be a shared library living in the Extensions folder; it has been standard equipment since Mac OS 8.0, and since Mac OS 8.6 it has been incorporated into the system itself.† (It doesn't exist on 68K systems or on Windows.)

There are two built-in classes, TextEncoding (which represents the particular text encodings) and TextConverter (which performs the conversion between them). The technique is as follows:

1. Obtain the desired "from" and "to" TextEncoding instances, by calling GetTextEncoding, GetInternetTextEncoding, or GetFontTextEncoding.

2. Generate from the TextEncoding instances a TextConverter instance, by calling GetTextConverter.

3. Send the TextConverter the Convert message along with the "from" text; the result is the "to" text.

4. If desired, send the TextConverter the Clear message, so that it can be used again with a separate "from" text.

---

* To learn Perl, see Larry Wall, et al., *Programming Perl*, 3rd ed. (O'Reilly & Associates, 2000).
† See *http://developer.apple.com/techpubs/mac/TextEncodingCMgr/TECRefBook-2.html*.

So, for example:

```
dim theFrom, theTo as textencoding
dim theConverter as textconverter
dim s as string
s = "déjà vu"
theFrom = getTextEncoding(0) // MacRoman
theTo = getTextEncoding(&h0201) // ISOLatin1
theConverter = getTextConverter(theFrom, theTo)
s = theConverter.convert(s)
```

The second character has been converted from ASCII 142 to ASCII 233, and the fourth character has been converted from ASCII 136 to ASCII 224. This entire routine could be condensed into a single line, but that line would be too long for the width of this page, and in any case would be hard to read, so I pulled it apart into a series of discrete steps.

If the text to be converted or the converted text is longer than 1024 bytes, the Text-Converter's Convert method will return the empty string. The string to be converted must therefore be broken up and submitted in chunks of 512 bytes or fewer (because if you're converting from a single-byte encoding to a double-byte encoding, that reaches the limit of 1024) and the results reassembled. Do *not* send the TextConverter the Clear message between chunks; send it afterward if you want to convert a separate text.

```
dim i, u as integer, res as string
// ... obtain s, construct theConverter ...
u = len(s)\512
for i = 0 to u
    res = res + theConverter.convert(midb(s,i*512+1,512))
next
theConverter.clear // (if there will be another text later)
s = res
```

To learn the parameter values for GetTextEncoding, consult the REALbasic documentation (the *Language Reference* has an appendix that lists them). Some encodings require a second parameter, and to convert to and from Unicode, you may need a third parameter. Alternatively, you can generate a TextEncoding instance based on the encoding's Internet name; for example, the sixth line of the earlier example could be replaced with this:

```
theTo = getInternetTextEncoding("iso-8859-1")
```

Similarly, in the case of fonts (such as Symbol) which represent non-MacRoman encodings, you can hand their name as a parameter to GetFontTextEncoding to obtain an encoding.

A TextEncoding instance, once generated by one of these three functions, has four read-only properties that you can consult: its Base, Variant, Format, and Internet-Name properties. These correspond to the three GetTextEncoding parameters and the GetInternetTextEncoding parameter, respectively.

When you build your application for Windows, literal strings are converted automatically from MacRoman to WinANSI. Thus, this line:

```
msgbox "déjà vu"
```

puts up a dialog that reads correctly on both Mac and Windows, with no further effort on your part. But of course, this line does not:

```
msgbox "d" + chr(142) + "jà vu"
```

You asked for the character whose numeric value is 142, and that's just what you'll get; only on Macintosh is that character an e-acute.

By the same token, the line separator on Macintosh is the Return character, chr(13); on Windows, it's CRLF, return plus lineFeed, chr(13)+chr(10). If you type a return character as part of a property string value in the Properties window, it will be translated to CRLF when you build for Windows. But in a literal string formed in code, where you must use chr(13) to insert the return character, there is no automatic translation of this to CRLF. If you're doing any cross-platform developing, you will surely want to arm yourself with a localized constant expressing the line separator for both platforms (see "Modules" in Chapter 4).

Numbers

REALbasic has three numeric datatypes: integer, single, and double. An integer may be any whole number between -2147483648 and 2147483647, inclusive. An integer literal has no decimal point. Single and double are both floating-point types; a single is accurate to about 7 decimal digits, a double is accurate to about 15 digits. A floating-point literal has a decimal point, and is assumed to be a double.

Coercion of Numbers

Under certain circumstances, REALbasic performs an *implicit coercion*: it takes a numeric value of one type (integer, single, or double) and changes it to a different type. Care must be taken not to perform such implicit coercion accidentally, as possibly surprising numeric results may ensue. Also, calculations that involve coercion are slower than those that don't. But implicit coercion can be a good thing, since it is REALbasic's only method of numeric coercion.

When a numeric value is assigned to a reference with a numeric datatype, it is implicitly coerced, if necessary, to the declared datatype of the reference. For example, to get the integral part of a floating-point value, you can assign the value to an integer:

```
dim i as integer
i = 123.456 // 123
```

When a floating-point value is coerced to an integer, if the value's integral part is out of range, the result is the maximum positive or minimum negative integer:

```
dim i as integer
i = 2147483648.0 // 2147483647
```

But when a calculated integer value is out of range, it wraps around from the opposite end of the integer range:[*]

```
dim i as integer
i = 2147483647 + 1 // -2147483648
```

Even if you're coercing, the coercion won't take place until after the operation is performed. So we can't avoid the wrapping problem from the previous example by coercing to a double:

```
dim d as double
d = 2147483647 + 1 // -2147483648.0
```

The solution is to coerce *before* the calculation. This can be as simple as using a double literal instead of an integer literal:

```
dim d as double
d = 2147483647.0 + 1.0 // 2147483648.0
```

An operation whose operands are of the same type yields a result of that type. Thus, to perform integer division, just divide two integers; the result of the division is coerced implicitly to an integer:

```
dim d as double
d = 5/2 // 2.0
```

On the other hand, an operation whose operands are of different types causes coercion of the "lower" type operand to the "higher" type before the operation is performed (where double is "higher" than single, and single is "higher" than integer). This fact comes in very handy when you're dealing with integer variables, not literals, and you want to make sure the operation doesn't go out of integer bounds and wrap around. The solution in that case is to coerce the values to doubles by multiplying by 1.0 (before the rest of the calculation):

```
dim d as double
dim i, j as integer
i = 2147483647
j = 1
d = i * 1.0 + j * 1.0 // the answer is correct regardless of what i and j are
```

In fact, this rule means that you can often get away with coercing just one integer to a double:

```
d = i * 1.0 + j
```

---

[*] In earlier versions of REALbasic, you didn't even have to perform a calculation; an out-of-range integer literal was wrapped immediately. So, for example, 2147483648 represented -2147483648. Needless to say, this caused massive confusion (and numerous complaints). In REALbasic 3, this no longer happens; an out-of-range integer literal represents the corresponding double.

But you have to careful of the order of operations (see "Operators," later in this section). In this example, the two integers are multiplied, and the value wrapped to an integer, before 1.0 ever gets involved:*

```
d = i * i * 1.0 // no
d = 1.0 * i * i // yes
```

Bases

Binary, octal, and hexadecimal literals are expressed by preceding the number with &b, &o, or &h, respectively:

```
dim i as integer
i = &hFF // 255
```

To convert from a string representing a binary, octal, or hex number, add the ampersand prefix and use the Val function:

```
dim i as integer, s as string
// ... obtain s; let's say it's "FFA0"
i = val("&h" + s) // 65440
```

The reverse operation, yielding a string, may be performed with the Oct and Hex functions; note that the resulting string does not include the ampersand prefix:

```
s = hex(255) // "FF"
```

There is no corresponding Bin function, but it isn't difficult to write one; the trick is to avoid the pitfall of integers being signed:

```
Function bin(i as integer) As string
    dim s as string
    dim j as integer
    j = i
    if i < 0 then
        j = j + 2147483647 + 1
    end
    do
        s = str(j mod 2) + s
        j = j / 2
    loop until j = 0
    if i < 0 then
        s = "1" + s
    end
    return s
End Function
```

Operators

The four basic arithmetic operators are addition (+), subtraction (-), multiplication (*), and division (/). Order of operations is left to right, multiplication and division

---

* This tip comes from David Grogono of REAL Software.

before addition and subtraction, and things in parentheses before anything else. Multiplication is faster than division.

An integer division operator (\) is also provided. You might think this is superfluous, because integer division can be performed by ordinary division of two integers, but the integer division operator is different: it coerces its operands to integers before the division. Also, some users report that using the integer division operator, even on integer operands, may be faster than normal division:

```
dim d as double
d = 6.0 \ 2.2 // 3.0, as if you had said 6/2
```

Integer division by 1 thus provides a way to coerce singles and doubles to integers on the fly:

```
dim i as integer
dim d, dd as double
d = 6.5
dd = 4.7
i = d \ 1 + dd \ 1 // 10
```

The mod operator obtains the remainder from an integer division; it, too, coerces its operands to integers before the division:

```
dim d as double
d = 7.2 mod 2.2 // 1.0, as if you had said 7 mod 2
```

From a mathematical point of view, REALbasic's mod works incorrectly when the dividend is negative. Properly, the result of mod should always be positive; for example, -7 mod 8 is 1, because it is 1 larger than the next smaller multiple of 8, namely -8. However, REALbasic (like a number of other computer languages) yields -7, the wrong answer. You may wish to write your own function to correct this mistake:

```
Function myMod(i as integer, k as integer) As integer
    return ((i mod k) + k) mod k
End Function
```

Trigonometry and Exponentiation

The six standard trigonometric functions are provided: Sin, Cos, Tan, Asin, Acos, and Atan. There is also Atan2 whose parameters specify a point, so that it's clear what quadrant you're starting in. Angles are expressed in terms of radians, not degrees. Just in case you've forgotten, 360 degrees is 2π radians; if you insist on thinking in degrees, you can define degree versions, as for example:

```
Function sinD(d as double) As double
    return sin(3.141592 * d / 180)
End Function
```

To raise a value to a power, use the Pow function: it raises its first parameter to the power of its second parameter. The Sqrt function is the same as using the Pow function with a second parameter of 0.5. The Exp function is the same as using the Pow function with a first parameter of 2.718281828 (*e*). Hyperbolic trigonometric functions can be derived from Exp.

To take a logarithm, use the Log function. The base is e; in other words, this a natural logarithm, which many computer languages, and anyone who knows any mathematics, would think of as the Ln function. To obtain a logarithm with a different base, divide the natural logarithm by the natural logarithm of the base:

```
Function logBase(d as double, base as integer) As double
    return log(d) / log(base)
End Function
```

Miscellaneous Arithmetic

Numbers may be sorted by loading them into an array and applying the Sort procedure, as for strings.

To take the absolute value of a number, use the Abs function.

There is a random-number generating function, Rnd; it takes no parameters, and provides a pseudorandom double between 0 and 1, exclusive. Thus, to get a pseudorandom double between x and y, exclusive, where y is larger than x, the formula is:

```
dim r as double
r = x + rnd * (y - x)
```

Very commonly, what is wanted is an integer between i and j, inclusive; you can strip the real part of a double by assigning to an integer, obviously, but don't forget to add 1 to j in order to get y:

```
dim r as integer
r = i + rnd * (j + 1 - i)
```

To obtain the lesser or the greater of two numbers, use the Min and Max functions, respectively.

To round a number to the next integer downward, use the Floor function; to round a number to next integer upward, use the Ceil function; to round a number to the nearest integer, use the Round function.

Three binary bit functions are provided: BitwiseAnd, BitwiseOr, and BitwiseXor. They operate on integers, meaning that you have 32 bits to work with; do not forget, though, that integers are signed. Using these operations, it is easy to write routines to set, clear and test a given bit; we number the bits 0 through 31 with 0 as the low-order bit:

```
Function bitSet(i as integer, bit as integer) As integer
    return bitwiseOr(i, pow(2, bit))
End Function

Function bitClear(i as integer, bit as integer) As integer
    return bitwiseAnd(i, bitwiseXOr(&hFFFFFFFF, pow(2, bit)))
End Function

Function bitTest(i as integer, bit as integer) As boolean
    return (i / pow(2, bit)) mod 2 = 1
End Function
```

Bits can be shifted left and right by calling the Toolbox routine BitShift. Another alternative is to multiply or divide by 2, respectively; again, complications appear when the number is negative:

```
if i < 0 then
    i = i + 2147483647 + 1
    i = i \ 2
    i = bitwiseor(i, &h40000000)
else
    i = i \ 2
end
```

To obtain an integer's bitwise complement, add 1 and take the additive inverse. Alternatively, perform an exclusive-or with -1:

```
Function bitwiseComp(i as integer) As integer
    return bitwisexor(i, -1)
End Function
```

Internal Representation

Beginners are often surprised by numeric results that have nothing to do with REALbasic itself, but rather are the outcome of the way computers represent numbers internally. The trouble is basically that numbers exist only in our imagination, so that all internal numeric representation, which has to be physical, is a compromise.

To give a simple example: 1/10 sounds like a definite quantity, but no computer can represent it precisely, because in binary digits it's a repeating decimal of infinite length. This in turn has implications for such concepts as equality; when you multiply 0.1 by 10 and ask whether the result is equal to 1, the computer must decide somehow that even though they are not in fact identical values internally, the difference is so small that you probably don't care. Similarly, in the case of an external representation, such as a string, the computer is rounding before it tells you that 1.0/10 is "0.1". Just to complicate things, the system of internal numeric representation and calculation is different on a 68K Macintosh than on a PowerPC; the 68K doesn't round as cleverly, and will even deny that val("3.01") and 3.01 are the same quantity.

Since these are not REALbasic issues, this book doesn't treat them any further; an awareness of them is the reader's responsibility.* One or two words of advice, however, might not be out of place. If a certain degree of precision is important to you, test for that, rather than for absolute equality. For example:

```
dim d1, d2 as double
// ... obtain d1 and d2
if abs(d1-d2) < 0.0000001 then // close enough
```

---

* For detailed information, see *http://developer.apple.com/techpubs/mac/PPCNumerics/PPCNumerics-2.html*.

A similar approach is to convert to a formatted external representation and back again:

```
dim d1, d2 as double
// ... obtain d1 and d2
d1 = val(format(d1, "-#.#######"))
d2 = val(format(d2, "-#.#######"))
if d1 = d2 then // ...
```

Just the other way, make sure you demand enough precision. Here we clearly aren't getting enough precision, because we started with a poor value of π:

```
msgbox format(sin(3.14159), "#.#######") // 0.0000027
```

This is much closer:

```
dim pi as double
pi = atan(1)*4
msgbox format(sin(pi), "#.##############") // 0.
```

But the truth is that this region of the Sin function is never going to be terribly precise. Fortunately, Sin is periodic, so you can move yourself into a much more precise region:

```
dim pi, x as double
pi = atan(1)*4
x = pi // x can be any value close to pi
if x > pi/2.0 then
    x = pi - x
end
msgbox format(sin(x), "#.####################") // 0.
```

Certain calculations are impossible and will yield an error. Unfortunately, REALbasic doesn't notify you of this, so you have to perform an explicit check; unfortunately again, REALbasic provides no built-in way to check, and it isn't obvious what the best way is. The error emerges in an external representation, so one way of checking is to convert to a string. However, I believe the following test is reliable:*

```
dim d as double
d = acos(2) // NAN (Not A Number); or ...
d = 4.0/0 // INF (divide by zero); or...
d = -4.0/0 // -INF (negative divide by zero)
if d<>d or d=1/0 or d=-1/0 then
    msgbox "error"
end
```

An error-value double coerced to an integer, or an integer divided by zero, yields –2147483648 (negative infinity).

---

* The test for the NAN case comes from Franco Vaccari. The test for the two INF cases comes from David Grogono.

Variants

A *variant* is a datatype with the following remarkable property: a variable, property, or parameter declared as variant is capable of accepting a value of any datatype, either a scalar or an object.[*]

For example, the following is all completely legal:

```
dim v as variant
dim d as date
d = new date
v = d
v = 6
v = "hello"
```

A value passed to a variant can be retrieved by passing it back to the value's original datatype. So:

```
dim v as variant
dim s, ss as string, i, ii as integer, d, dd as date
d = new date
i = d.year
s = d.shortdate
v = s
ss = v
msgbox ss // 2/22/01
v = i
ii = v
msgbox str(ii) // 2001
v = d
dd = v
msgbox dd.shortdate // 2/22/01
```

It works the same way when you pass a parameter, whether handed to a subroutine or returned from a function. Here's a function that just accepts a value and hands it back:

```
Function passThruVariant(v as variant) As variant
    dim vv as variant
    vv = v
    return vv
End Function
```

The effect is the same as before:

```
dim v as variant
dim s, ss as string, i, ii as integer, d, dd as date
d = new date
i = d.year
s = d.shortdate
ss = passThruVariant(s)
msgbox ss // 2/22/01
```

---

[*] Except a Color.

```
ii = passThruVariant(i)
msgbox str(ii) // 2001
dd = passThruVariant(d)
msgbox dd.shortdate // 2/22/01
```

But casting a variant does *not* work:

```
dim v as variant, d as date
d = new date
v = d
msgbox date(v).shortdate // error: IllegalCastException
```

Thus assignment and parameter passing are the only ways to retrieve a variant's value and restore it to its original datatype.

Comparison involving a variant is probably not a good idea, but here are the rules. Comparison between a variant and a nonvariant object (including nil) always fails. Comparison between a variant and an integer can succeed because of implicit coercion (discussed in the next section). Comparison between a variant and a string or boolean is illegal ("Incompatible types"; this is probably a bug). Comparison between two variants tests whether one variant has been assigned to another, not whether two variants have been assigned identical (nonvariant) values.

```
dim v1,v2 as variant
v1 = 1
v2 = 1
if v1 = v2 then // nope
// ...
v1 = v2
if v1 = v2 then // yep
// ...
```

It is possible to learn the datatype of a variant's value, using the VarType function. The result is an integer: 2 means integer, 5 means double, 8 means string, 11 means boolean, 13 means object, 0 means no value.* This is quite remarkable, since it is not otherwise possible to ask a scalar what type it is. As a bonus, since VarType expects a variant parameter, and since anything can be a variant, you can use VarType to learn the datatype of something that is not a variant to start with:

```
dim i as integer
i = 7
msgbox str(vartype(i)) // 2
```

A variant can be tested with IsA, but it turns out to be always a variant, nothing else. Thus, you cannot learn the class of an instance assigned to the variant.

Coercion of Varients

When a variant's value is a scalar, and the variant is assigned or passed to a context where a scalar datatype is expected, the variant will coerce its value implicitly to the

---

* 0 means no value has ever been assigned. A variant that has been set to nil is an object and will yield 13.

recipient's datatype. This works even across boundaries that cannot otherwise be crossed without calling a conversion function, such as passing a number value where a string is expected. It also works across boundaries where there is no built-in conversion function, such as passing a boolean value where a string or a number is expected:

```
dim v as variant
dim s as string
dim i as integer
dim b as boolean

v = true
s = v       // "True"
i = v       // 1

v = false
s = v       // "False"
i = v       // 0

v = 9.5
s = v       // "9.5"
b = v       // true; so too any number except 0

v = "9"
i = v       // 9
b = v       // false; so too any string except "True" (not case-sensitive)
```

There are many ways to take elegant advantage of this facility. For example, the following utility functions convert from a boolean to a number or string:[*]

```
Function boolint(b as variant) As integer
    return b
End Function

Function boolstr(b as variant) As string
    return b
End Function
```

Another utility I've found useful, particularly for debugging, is this one, which accepts a string, number, or boolean and displays it in a MsgBox:

```
Sub display(v as variant)
    msgbox v
End Sub
```

Templates

The most powerful use of variants is to permit a subroutine or class to behave as a *template*. The idea is that the subroutine or class can be handed or can hand back any type of value, indifferently, wrapped up in a variant. In this way, the same

---

[*] These formulations come from Soren Ølin.

subroutine or class can be made to fit a wide range of uses without being rewritten. The onus of worrying about the actual datatype of values being handed back and forth is on the caller. As long as a value is treated consistently from an external point of view, the fact that it is maintained as a variant internally is of no consequence.

As an example, let's return to the Map class developed at the end of Chapter 4, along with its various utility classes. We will greatly increase their usefulness by reimplementing them through variants. For example, Map currently associates names with integers; that's great if we want names associated with integers, as we did when we were using Map to count word occurrences, but what if we want names associated with strings, dates, doubles, CArrays, or Widgets? One and the same Map class can deal with all these datatypes and any others, if it stores its data internally as variants.

Let's start with CArray. Recall that, because CArray was designed originally to wrap an array of strings, we were forced to rewrite the class completely when it turned out that we wanted to wrap an array of Pairs. Clearly this situation is intolerable; if we have to rewrite CArray for every datatype that its array must contain, its portability vanishes and its usefulness is undermined. The solution is to write CArray as a wrapper for an array of variants; now it can be used for strings, Pairs, or anything else whatever. All we have to do is declare TheArray as being an array of variant, and rewrite four of CArray's methods as shown in Example 5-1.

Example 5-1. CArray class rewritten

```
// cArray.set:
Sub set(index as integer, s as variant)
    self.theArray(index) = s
End Sub

// cArray.get:
Function get(index as integer) As variant
    return self.theArray(index)
End Function

// cArray.insert:
Sub insert(index as integer, s as variant)
    self.theArray.insert index, s
End Sub

// cArray.append:
Sub append(s as variant)
    self.theArray.append s
End Sub
```

Now let's turn to IntPtr. This class was created so that a function could return by reference an integer, meaning that the caller would have complete access to that integer in its original place. Clearly we can greatly increase the usefulness of the IntPtr class by generalizing it so that it is not limited to integers. To do so, we substitute for it a VarPtr class consisting of a single property, V, declared as variant. This change has far-reaching consequences. An integer property is autoinitialized to zero; but a variant is autoinitialized to `nil` and can't be used until it has been assigned a value. So VarPtr needs a constructor to give V an initial value:

```
Sub varPtr(v as variant)
    self.v = v
End Sub
```

Proceeding on to Pair, we now rewrite it as consisting of two properties, Key (a string) and Value (a VarPtr). But if Value is now a VarPtr, its constructor expects an initial value for its V, and this means that Pair's constructor has to be changed as well:

```
Sub pair(s as string, v as variant)
    self.key = s
    self.value = new varPtr(v)
End Sub
```

Now let's proceed to the Map class. The effect of the change from IntPtr to VarPtr continues to trickle up. VarPtr requires a value to initialize its V; Pair requires a value to initialize its VarPtr; now Map needs a value to initialize every new Pair. This value will be the same for every new Pair, so it can be maintained as a property of Map, which we'll call Starter, a variant. Map's constructor must be handed this value so it can initialize Starter:

```
Sub map(v as variant)
    pairs = new cArray
    b = new binarySearch(pairs)
    starter = v
End Sub
```

Our classes are now templated, and we are ready to start taking advantage of this. To do so, every caller of a templated class must speak in a slightly new way. Remember, the idea of templating is that a class or function that uses variants doesn't worry about their real datatype; it's the job of the caller to know this, and to be consistent about it. CArray has now been templated, and in this case Map is its caller: Map is using CArray as a utility class so that it (Map) can store Pair instances. Therefore, we have to rewrite Map a little, so that in its dealings with CArray—that is, with its own Pairs property—it remains conscious that CArray is storing Pair instances, even though CArray itself is unaware of this.

All the action happens in Map's Refer method. This is both where new Pair instances are created and stored in the Pairs array, and where existing Pair instances are retrieved from the Pairs array. Creation and storage is easy; Map simply has to obey the new rules for the Pair class's constructor:

```
if not result.found then
    if result.index > pairs.ubound then
        pairs.append new pair(s, starter) // changed
    else
```

```
        pairs.insert result.index, new pair(s, starter) // changed
    end
end
```

Retrieval is a little trickier. The last line of Refer presently reads as follows:

```
return pairs.get(result.index).value
```

But pairs.get() now returns a variant, which has no Value property—until we convert the variant back to a Pair. To do so, let's give Map a little utility method that performs the conversion:

```
Function pair(v as variant) As pair
    return v
End Function
```

Now the last line of Refer can say this:

```
return self.pair(pairs.get(result.index)).value
```

This Value returned by Refer is now a VarPtr, not an IntPtr, so Refer's declaration must be changed too.

BinarySearch must be adjusted in a similar fashion: whenever it retrieves an element from the CArray, CArray thinks of this element as a variant, so BinarySearch must be conscious that this is really a Pair instance and must convert it explicitly in order to get any data out of it. The details are left as an exercise for the reader.

Finally, we consider our main routine, which uses Map to maintain a word count. Our main routine is the caller of Map, and the caller of Map bears the same sort of relationship to Map that Map bears to CArray. Map has now been templated: it stores and retrieves name–value pairs, but it now knows nothing of the datatype of the values in these pairs. It is up to the caller to be conscious of this, both in storage and in retrieval. The storage takes place when a Map instance is created: the caller hands Map's constructor a value of the correct datatype. In our word-counting example, that means an integer; Map will be instantiated like this:

```
m = new map(0)
```

The retrieval takes place in our word-counting routine's Increment method. This now must expect a VarPtr, since that is what Map's Refer function will supply. It then treats this VarPtr's V as an integer—and of course it's absolutely right!

```
Sub increment(vp as varptr)
    vp.v = vp.v + 1
End Sub
```

Collections

A *collection* is a class that implements dynamic storage, rather like an array. And the elements that it stores dynamically are variants, so it's rather like an array of variants.

But each element, besides an index number, may also have a name by which you can refer to it. A collection is thus also somewhat like a map.

You make a Collection instance with New. To append an element, send the instance the Add message, supplying a value for the new element, and optionally a string name for it. So:

```
dim myRect as collection
myRect = new collection
myRect.add 7, "left"
myRect.add 5, "top"
myRect.add 20, "width"
myRect.add 30, "height"
doSomethingWith myRect
```

To obtain the value of a particular element, send the collection the Item message, along with either a name or an index number. The index is one-based! If you supply a name that doesn't match that of any element, an empty variant is returned; to learn whether this has happened, test the variant with VarType to see if you get 0. The collection simply remembers the order in which you added elements, and indexes them successively in that order. If you supply an index number larger than the number of elements, you'll get a runtime error, as with an array. To learn the number of elements in a collection, examine its Count property.

So, presuming that the collection myRect has been initialized as before, here's an example of obtaining values by name:

```
if myRect.item("width") <> myRect.item("height") then
    msgbox "Not a square."
end
```

And here's an example of obtaining values by index (the multiplication by 1 is to cause implicit coercion from a variant to a number before the addition):

```
msgbox "Perimeter: " + str(2*(myRect.item(3)*1 + myRect.item(4)*1))
```

To delete an element, send the collection the Remove message, along with either a name or an index number; the index numbers of subsequent elements are decremented.

Names are not case-sensitive. Nothing prevents your adding an element with the same name as an existing element; in that case, the collection simply has two elements with the same name. You will be able to refer by name to the first of these only.

A common use of collections is to call a subroutine with optional parameters. Pass the subroutine a collection; the subroutine then examines the collection's elements by name to see which ones are present and what their values are. So for instance:

```
if vartype(myRect.item("color")) = 0 then
    msgbox "You forgot to include a color!"
end
```

You can also use a collection as a quick-and-dirty way of returning multiple values from a function, instead of creating a dedicated class to do this.

Collections are best used lightly, for small quantities of data. Retrieval by name is inefficient; REALbasic just cycles through all the items in order, looking for the first one whose name is a match. You can't learn an item's name from its index, or its index from its name. You can't learn the names of all the items. For fast, powerful, customizable storage and retrieval of values by name, you'd want to use a class of your own, such as the Map class already developed in this book.

Dates

A *date* actually means a date-time, to the nearest second. Dates are maintained by the system as an unsigned integer, which is sufficient to assign a unique number to every second from midnight of 1 January 1904 to some time in 2040. REALbasic maintains the date as a double, which extends the range from the year 1 to a much later date (I'm not sure exactly what the limit is, but it seems to be some time in the year 30,000). To provide access to date values in terms more congenial to human beings, dates are implemented in REALbasic as a class, the Date class.

Date Class Properties

A Date instance has Year, Month, Day, Hour, Minute, and Second properties, all integers, which manipulate the instance's underlying date-time value in terms of human notions of a date's components.

So, for example, to form a Date instance denoting 10 August 1954 at 3:00 A.M.:

```
dim d as date
d = new date
d.year = 1954
d.month = 8
d.day = 10
d.hour = 3
d.minute = 0
d.second = 0
```

A new Date instance is automatically assigned the current date-time value from the system clock. This provides a way to learn the current date-time. However, the new instance is not actually set to any value until you access one of its properties. You might thus access a property *only* in order to set the instance (in which case you might well throw away the result). So, for example:

```
dim d as date, i as integer
d = new date
i = d.year // don't really care, just initializing date
```

The actual underlying date-time value of a Date instance is accessible through its TotalSeconds property. Since REALbasic has no native unsigned integer datatype, the TotalSeconds is a double:

```
dim theSecs as double
theSecs = d.totalSeconds // 1597028400.0
```

To view a Date instance's date or time information as a nicely formatted string, use the read-only LongDate, AbbreviatedDate, ShortDate, LongTime, and ShortTime properties. These consult the system to get the details for their formatting, so the results will differ on different machines; on my machine, using the Date instance formed earlier, they yield, respectively:

```
s = d.longDate // Tuesday, August 10, 1954
s = d.abbreviatedDate // Tue, Aug 10, 1954
s = d.shortDate // 8/10/54
s = d.longTime // 3:00:00 AM
s = d.shortTime // 3:00 AM
```

Date Calculations

A common beginner's error is to try to compare two dates directly:

```
dim d1, d2 as date
// ... set d1 and d2 somehow ...
if d1 = d2 then // wrong question
```

This tests whether the two references d1 and d2 point to the same Date instance ("Comparison Tests Identity" in Chapter 3), whereas presumably you wanted to know whether they represent the same date-time value. If that's what you wanted to know, that's what you should have asked:

```
if d1.totalSeconds = d2.totalSeconds then
```

It is possible to perform date arithmetic using the Year, Month, Day, Hour, Minute, and Second properties of a date. For the most part, such arithmetic behaves predictably:

```
s = d.longDate // Tuesday, August 10, 1954
d.year = d.year + 46
s = d.longDate // Thursday, August 10, 2000
```

Things get a little tricky, though, if addition or subtraction of a unit would result in an impossible date. This is a feature, not of REALbasic, but of dates themselves. The system tries to respond sensibly, but there's no way for it to guess whether its notion of what is sensible matches yours. For example:

```
s = d.longDate // Tuesday, August 31, 1954
d.month = d.month + 1 // But there is no September 31!
s = d.longDate // Friday, October 1, 1954
```

Calculation using the TotalSeconds property, on the other hand, has the virtue of being completely predictable; the disadvantage is that you have to do the math:

```
dim d1, d2 as date
dim d as double
```

```
dim i as integer
dim s as string
d1 = new date // current date
i = d1.year // set current date
d2 = new date // start of year 2000
d2.year = 2000
d2.month = 1
d2.day = 1
d2.hour = 0
d2.minute = 0
d2.second = 0
d = (d1.totalseconds - d2.totalseconds) / (60 * 60 * 24)
s = "Your computer has survived the Y2K problem by "
msgbox s + str(d\1) + " days."
```

With a bit of ingenuity you can perform just about any date calculation you can think of. For example, here's a routine that determines whether a date entered by the user as a month number, day number, and year number is valid:

```
Function validDate(m as integer, dd as integer, y as integer) As boolean
    dim d as date
    d = new date
    d.month = m
    d.day = dd
    d.year = y
    return d.month = m and d.day = dd and d.year = y
End Function
```

A concern that occasionally arises is how to convert between a date and an unsigned integer. REALbasic has no unsigned integers, but other programs do, and date values are stored internally as unsigned integers by the Macintosh Toolbox and many other programs. A double that is within the range of an unsigned integer can be converted to an ordinary integer that can be passed where an unsigned integer is expected. In essence, you construct the four bytes that the recipient expects, and pass them, even though REALbasic interprets them one way (as a signed integer) and the recipient interprets them another way (as an unsigned integer):

```
dim secs as double
dim secsint as integer
secs = new date.totalseconds // or any other date
secsint = secs
if secs > 2147483647.0 then
    secsint = secs - 2*2147483648.0
end
```

To generate a date from a unsigned integer, just reverse the procedure:

```
dim secsint as integer
dim secs as double
dim d as date
d = new date
// ... obtain secsint somehow ...
secs = secsint
if secs < 0 then
```

```
        secs = secs + 2*2147483648.0
    end
    d.totalseconds = secs
```

To convert a string to a date, call the ParseDate function, handing it the string and a Date instance. The function returns a boolean reporting whether the conversion was successful, and if it was, the Date instance will correspond to the date described in the string. For example:

```
dim d as date
d = new date
if parsedate("August 10, 1954", d) then
    msgbox str(d.month)
    msgbox str(d.day)
    msgbox str(d.year)
else
    msgbox "That didn't work!"
end
```

REALbasic provides no direct facilities for manipulating dates outside the prescribed range. The system itself lets you range back all the way to 30081 B.C., but I don't know whether and how a REALbasic date can be made to do this. Possible solutions are either to call the Toolbox yourself or to write a class that performs date conversions outside the prescribed range.*

Colors

A Color is a triple of byte values representing the red, green, and blue components of a color; for example, 0,0,0 represents black, 255,255,255 represents white, and 255,255,0 represents yellow. The red, green, and blue components of a color are available through its read-only Red, Green, and Blue properties. Since a color is three bytes, it is in effect a variety of integer (which is four bytes); and internally REALbasic does in fact implement a color as an integer. For this reason, you can't use New to make a new Color; despite my use of the word "properties" here, Color isn't a class. Instead, a new color value can be obtained by using the RGB function, whose parameters are the values of the color's red, green, and blue components:

```
dim c as color
dim i as integer
c = rgb(100, 200, 7)
i = c.red // 100
```

The RGB model of color corresponds to the way the phosphors of a computer screen mix colors, additively. But colors can be generated in other ways, which are better

---

* On the long date-time record, see *http://developer.apple.com/techpubs/mac/OSUtilities/OSUtilities-94.html*. To get started with your own date conversion routines, see Peter Duffett-Smith, *Practical Astronomy With Your Calculator* (Cambridge, 1990).

represented by other color models. The CMY model (a three-color subset of the more widely used four-color CMYK model) corresponds to the way colors are mixed by inks on a printed page; it is subtractive, and is essentially the inverse of the RGB model, since its components, cyan, magenta, and yellow, are the inverses of red, green, and blue. The HSV model (also called HSB) treats colors mathematically, in terms of the human eye's perceptions. The hue component represents the actual color as an angle around the color wheel, ranging from red through yellow, green (one-third of the way around the wheel), blue (two-thirds of the way around the wheel), violet, and back to red; saturation represents how colorful the color is (0 means it is a shade of gray); and value is the color's degree of lightness (ranging from black to white).

A REALbasic color can be described using the CMY and HSV models. It has Cyan, Magenta, and Yellow read-only properties, and it has Hue, Saturation, and Value read-only properties, which are doubles, lying between 0.0 and 1.0 inclusive. A color can be generated using these models, through the CMY function (whose parameters are the values of the new instance's Cyan, Magenta, and Yellow properties) and the HSV function (whose parameters are the values of the new instance's Hue, Saturation, and Value properties).

The fact that the CMY and HSV components are doubles may give a misleading impression of the degree of precision of which they are capable. The truth is that a Color is still a triple of bytes. Each byte can take on only one of 256 discrete values, so the Color as a whole can take on only one of 16,777,216 discrete values. Therefore, when you set a CMY or HSV component, the value of a component may not be exactly the value you assigned. For example:

```
dim c as color
c = hsv (.6667, .999, 1.0)
msgbox str(c.hue)          // 0.6666565
msgbox str(c.saturation)   // 0.9999847
msgbox str(c.value)        // 0.9999847
```

Similarly, you may encounter Macintosh color data that expresses RGB color components as double-bytes, that is, as unsigned short integers (the upper limit is 65535). Since a REALbasic color measures color component values in bytes (the upper limit is 255), all you can do with such data, if you wish to express it as a REALbasic color, is to throw the lower byte away by dividing by 256. For example, I may know that the color I want, a pale red, is represented by RGB values 65535,52851,50737; but with REALbasic I'm not permitted to be so precise:

```
c = rgb(65535/256, 52851/256, 50737/256)
```

Such precision is pointless in any case, since in actual practice sooner or later what you'll do with a color value is to set the color of a pixel in the interface, and the system limits the maximum precision with which a pixel color can be specified to three bytes. (Well, four bytes, actually, because a Macintosh data structure can't consist of an odd number of bytes.) This point is discussed further in Chapter 11.

There are no operators for working with colors; the only way to alter a color is to make a new one and substitute it for the old one. Here's an example that inverts the color of the background of the current window. If you want to try this out, make sure the window's HasBackColor property is checked (set to true).

```
dim c1, c2 as color
c1 = self.backcolor
c2 = rgb(255-c1.red, 255-c1.green, 255-c1.blue)
self.backcolor = c2
```

REALbasic also provides access to a number of system-level color settings, as imposed by the Appearance Manager (or Kaleidoscope, if you're using it), by way of the following functions: TextColor and HighlightColor for text and for highlighting selected text; FrameColor and FillColor for outside edges and inner regions of objects; and DarkBevelColor, LightBevelColor, DarkTingeColor, and LightTinge-Color for giving objects a three-dimensional appearance.[*]

Your application can let the user choose a color by way of the system's own Color Picker dialog. To make the dialog appear, call the SelectColor function. The result is a boolean saying whether the user clicked OK or Cancel; the color itself is returned in a Color parameter that is passed by reference. The color you pass initially is the default when the dialog appears; if the color has no value, the default will be black. The second parameter is the dialog's prompt. Thus:

```
dim c as color
c = rgb(200,0,0)
if not selectColor(c, "Pick a reddish color:") then
    return // user cancelled
end
if c.red < 200 or c.green > 50 or c.blue > 50 then
    msgbox "That's not red enough!"
end
```

Memoryblocks

A *memoryblock* is a class whereby your code allocates a sequence of bytes in memory and manipulates those bytes directly. It has two main uses:

- Because the space for a memoryblock is allocated beforehand, manipulation of its data can be much faster than comparable manipulations on data structures requiring dynamic allocation of memory, such as a string.

---

[*] Unfortunately these REALbasic functions for accessing Appearance colors are largely inadequate. There are many Appearance colors you can't access, and besides, the Appearance Manager doesn't paint with simple colors: it paints with textured "brushes." These brushes are accessible through Toolbox calls, but REALbasic provides no direct access to them. See *http://developer.apple.com/techpubs/macos8/HumanInterfaceToolbox/ AppManager/ProgWithAppearanceMgr/Appearance.97.html.*

- Because the structure of the data within it is arbitrary, a memoryblock can be used to communicate with the system when complex data structures are required. For example, memoryblocks are the way Pascal records (or C structs) and pointers are constructed and parsed when making a Toolbox call, and they are also very helpful in dealing with other structured data such as resources.

Creating a Memoryblock

To create an instance of a memoryblock, you must use the NewMemoryBlock function, at which time you also declare how many bytes of memory you want allocated. REALbasic allocates the memory and zeroes all its bytes. You can then refer to the individual bytes of the memoryblock, rather like referring to items of an array. But don't let the similarity to an array confuse you. Memoryblock indexing is zero-based, but the number you hand to NewMemoryBlock is the total number of bytes, not the highest index; the highest index will be one less than this number. For example:

```
dim m as memoryblock
m = newMemoryBlock(100)
```

Now you have 100 bytes of memory reserved, the first indexed as 0, the last indexed as 99.*

Exchanging Data with a Memoryblock

Data are moved into and out of a memoryblock by means of its Byte, Short, UShort, Long, SingleValue, Ptr, CString, and PString properties. These are accessed by means of an array-like syntax where you specify the byte position at which you want access to begin within the block; the choice of property specifies the way you want the data sized and structured. This sounds rather daunting at first, but examples will show how simple it is.

Let's begin with Byte, Short, and Long. These are all ways of moving data between a memoryblock and a REALbasic integer. A Byte is one byte in length, a Short is two bytes in length, and a Long is four bytes in length. Moreover, on a Macintosh data is stored in this order: high byte first, low byte last. So, let's build a memoryblock out of bytes. Since a byte value is a two-digit hexadecimal value (that is, it's between &h00 and &hFF), we'll speak in hexadecimal, for clarity:

```
dim m as memoryblock
dim i as integer
m = newMemoryBlock(4)
m.byte(0) = &h00
m.byte(1) = &h01
m.byte(2) = &hE2
m.byte(3) = &h40
```

---

* Thanks to John Tsombakos for making this point clear to me.

Our memoryblock now runs: &h00,&h01,&hE2,&h40. Now if we say:

```
i = m.byte(0)
```

we're asking for just one byte, starting at index 0, so i ends up as 0. But if we say:

```
i = m.short(0)
```

we're still starting at index 0, but now we're asking for two bytes, so i ends up as &h0001, which is 1. Finally, if we say:

```
i = m.long(0)
```

we're still starting at index 0, but now we're asking for four bytes, so i ends up as &h0001E240, which is 123456.

Conversely, we could set four bytes at once by saying:

```
m.long(0) = &hABCDEF
```

Then we could investigate each byte, one at a time:

```
i = m.byte(0) // 0
i = m.byte(1) // 171, or &hAB
i = m.byte(2) // 205, or &hCD
i = m.byte(3) // 239, or &hEF
```

A UShort is like a Short, but it is unsigned. To see the difference, consider the following:

```
m.short(0) = -1
i = m.short(0)    // -1
i = m.ushort(0)   // 65535
```

This works because the UShort is being assigned to a REALbasic integer, which consists of four bytes and therefore has room for the UShort's maximum value. There is no ULong because a REALbasic integer is signed and would therefore be incapable of representing half the ULong's values. Conversion between a REALbasic integer and an unsigned long was discussed under "Dates," earlier in this chapter.

On Windows, bytes are stored in the opposite order: low byte first, high byte last. This makes no difference if you store and retrieve data in chunks of the same size (for example, store a Short into a memoryblock and retrieve the same Short later on); but if, as is often the case, you are using a memoryblock to negotiate between chunks of different lengths, you have to be conscious that the same code won't work on both Macintosh and Windows. For example, to build the number 123456 one byte at a time on Windows, the bytes must be arranged in the opposite order from the earlier example:

```
dim m as memoryblock
dim i as integer
m = newMemoryBlock(4)
m.byte(3) = &h00
m.byte(2) = &h01
m.byte(1) = &hE2
m.byte(0) = &h40
i = m.long(0) // 123456
```

A utility function to swap byte values can help in these situations:

```
Sub twiddleBytes(byref m as memoryblock, i as integer, j as integer)
    dim temp as integer
    temp = m.byte(i)
    m.byte(i) = m.byte(j)
    m.byte(j) = temp
End Sub
```

You can then call this utility on one platform but not the other (see "Target Flags and Conditional Compilation" in Chapter 8):

```
dim m as memoryblock
dim i as integer
m = newMemoryBlock(4)
m.byte(0) = &h00
m.byte(1) = &h01
m.byte(2) = &hE2
m.byte(3) = &h40
if targetWin32 then
    twiddleBytes(m, 0, 3)
    twiddleBytes(m, 1, 2)
end
i = m.long(0) // 123456 on both platforms
```

A memoryblock wrapper class might be a more elegant, object-oriented solution, though perhaps at the cost of some speed.

A SingleValue is the standard four-byte representation of a single-precision floating-point number. The encoding involves things like mantissas and exponents that you don't need to know about, especially since the whole point of SingleValue is to shield you from them:*

```
m.singlevalue(0) = 123.456 // &h42F6E979, and never mind why
```

PString and CString are ways of moving data between a memoryblock and a REALbasic string. A PString, which is short for "Pascal string," is formatted as in the Pascal programming language: the first byte tells how long the string is, and then come the bytes representing the characters of the text. A CString is formatted as in the C programming language: first come the bytes representing the characters of the text, and then there is a null byte (that is, a byte whose value is &h00) to signify the end of the string.

To illustrate, we build a string structure out of bytes and retrieve it as a PString or a CString:

```
dim m as memoryblock
m = newMemoryBlock(5)
m.byte(0) = 3 // length byte, we're building a PString
m.byte(1) = 72
```

---

* In REALbasic 3.5, a corresponding DoubleValue will at last be added, along with BooleanValue, ColorValue, and StringValue.

```
m.byte(2) = 105
m.byte(3) = 33
msgBox m.PString(0) // Hi!
m.byte(4) = 0 // end byte, we're building a CString
msgBox m.CString(1) // Hi!
```

Pascal strings and C strings each have their respective advantages. A Pascal string is very fast to operate on, because its length is known immediately; and it can contain a null byte. But it is limited to 255 characters, because its length must be coded in a single byte. A C string can be longer than 255 characters, but it must be traversed to learn its length, and it cannot contain a null byte because this will be taken as marking the end of the string. Thus, if a REALbasic string longer than 255 characters contains a null byte, you can write it into a memoryblock as a CString, but you can't get it back out again; it's like shoving a billiard ball into your mouth.* A utility function will solve the problem, but of course you must know in advance how many bytes to read; in this implementation we assume that reading is to begin at the start of the memoryblock (in REALbasic 3.5, the new StringValue property will make this utility function unnecessary):

```
Function mbToString(m as memoryblock, length as integer) As string
    dim s as string
    while lenb(s) < length
        if m.byte(lenb(s)) = 0 then
            s = s + chrb(0)
        else
            s = s + m.cString(lenb(s))
        end
    wend
    return s
End Function
```

A Ptr is a block of four bytes whose value is the address of another memoryblock. Discussion of Ptr is postponed until Chapter 32.

REALbasic permits you to read memory beyond the bounds of a memoryblock. There are circumstances where this can actually be useful, but if you do it by mistake you're going to get nonsense without knowing why. For example:

```
dim m as memoryblock
dim i as integer
m = newmemoryBlock(2)
i = m.long(0) // legal but unpredictable
i = m.long(5) // ditto
i = m.long(-10) // ditto
```

On the other hand, writing beyond the bounds of a memoryblock could do serious damage, and REALbasic prevents you from doing so:

```
dim m as memoryblock
m = newmemoryBlock(2)
m.long(0) = 4 // error: OutOfBoundsException
```

_____
* Don't try this at home. Or anywhere else.

You can circumvent this restriction with a Ptr, but unless you know what you're doing, don't.

Using Memoryblocks for Speed

As an example of the use of memoryblocks for speed, consider the problem of translating a series of bytes, coded as a string, to their hexadecimal string representation. For instance, if our bytes are the string "Hello", we want to end up with "48656C6C6F", because "H" is ASCII 72, which is &h48, "e" is ASCII 101, which is &h65, and so forth. We can code the solution easily by converting each byte of the string to its hex representation and concatenating it with the solution so far. (The Hex function is not guaranteed to produce a two-character result, so we must be prepared to pad that result with an initial "0" if necessary.)

```
dim s, temp, result as string
dim i, theLen as integer
// make big long string
s = "How doth the little busy bee improve each shining hour"
for i = 1 to 500
    temp = temp + s
next
s = temp
// actual solution begins here
theLen = len(s)
for i = 1 to theLen
    temp = hex(asc(mid(s,i,1)))
    while lenb(temp) < 2
        temp = "0" + temp
    wend
    result = result + temp
next
```

The trouble is that as s becomes long, this method becomes tremendously inefficient and slow. We are dynamically allocating memory for a new string repeatedly, once for every character of the original string. A better solution is to allocate memory for the result, once, using a memoryblock; now we can sweep through the string, filling the memoryblock ourselves and converting it to a string once, at the end. Dynamic allocation of memory is replaced with static allocation, concatenation is replaced with direct assignment, and access to individual bytes becomes very rapid.

```
dim m,mm as memoryblock
dim temp as string
// other stuff as before
m = newMemoryBlock(len(s)*2+1)
mm = newMemoryBlock(len(s)+2)
mm.cstring(1) = s
theLen = lenb(s)
for i = 1 to theLen
    temp = hex(mm.byte(i))
    while lenb(temp) < 2
        temp = "0" + temp
```

```
        wend
        m.cstring(i*2-2)= temp
    next
    result = m.cstring(0)
```

That runs more than 20 times faster, an immense improvement.

Threads

A *thread* is a code execution path that is pursued independently of and simultaneously with other execution paths. Unless you've got multiple processors and a programming language that (unlike REALbasic) knows how to take advantage of them, separate threads do not really execute simultaneously; instead, the computer polls the threads, executing some of one thread before proceeding to execute some of another thread, and so on. But threads do give a fair illusion of simultaneity, and they can be very useful in an object-oriented world such as REALbasic's, because it is not infrequently the case that one wants several objects to act independently at the same time. We say that a thread's code executes *asynchronously*, meaning that while the thread is running, the application does not appear to be busy: the user can still click buttons, type text, and so forth. Unless the thread's activity has some visible counterpart, its code executes, as it were, in the background, almost in secret.

Threads are decently simulated when running the project in the IDE, but the simulation isn't perfect, especially as the IDE is itself a thread. The way to test threads properly is in the built application; never rely on your impressions of their behavior in the IDE as a guide to how they are working.

Creating and Using a Thread

A thread is created as a subclass of the Thread class (the Thread class itself cannot be instantiated). Into the Run event handler of the subclass, you place the code that this thread should execute. Then, when the application runs, you instantiate your Thread subclass; now you can send the instance the Run message. This causes the instance to receive a Run event, which means that its Run event handler is called. Meanwhile, your code that sends the instance the Run message does not pause. Your code just continues on, while the thread's Run event handler proceeds simultaneously and independently; that's what it means to be a thread.

Since the Run event handler takes no parameters, if there are values that you need to communicate to it, you may wish, before sending the Thread instance the Run message, to install those values into properties of the Thread instance, where its Run event handler can find them when it executes (see "Drops" in Chapter 7).

You should not send the same thread instance the Run message twice; this is a meaningless act. You don't really have any way of knowing that the thread is not still running; and in any case a thread's job is to run independently until its Run event handler terminates, and then go out of existence. If you need to perform the same task again, make a new thread instance and send *it* the Run message.

As an example, we will use threads to drive several ProgressBar controls to engage in a race. The project is illustrated in Figure 5-1. The ProgressBars fill simultaneously to the right. Since these are independent simultaneous actions, we'll implement them by having a separate thread fill each ProgressBar. Since these are identical actions, we will need only one Thread subclass.

Figure 5-1. Racing ProgressBars

Drag a ProgressBar into the Window Editor and set its Index to 0 to start a control array. Duplicate the ProgressBar as many times as you like. The ProgressBars will now have names like progressBar1(0), progressBar1(1), and so forth.

Create a Thread subclass; call it Increaser. Each thread needs to know which ProgressBar belongs to it, so give Increaser an integer property called WhatIndex. Give Increaser a constructor, a method called Increaser, which takes one parameter, an integer; this is how we're going to tell each thread which ProgressBar belongs to it, as the instance is created:

```
Sub increaser(i as integer)
    self.whatIndex = i
End Sub
```

Now write Increaser's Run event handler:

```
dim p as progressbar
p = window1.progressbar1(whatindex)
while p.value < p.maximum
    p.value = p.value + 1
wend
```

That's all there is to it. All that remains is to instantiate the thread once for each ProgressBar and set all the instances running. This we'll do in a button. Drag a PushButton into the Window Editor and give its Action event handler this code:

```
const u = 3 // or whatever the maximum ProgressBar Index is
dim t(u) as increaser
dim i as integer
for i = 0 to u
```

```
    t(i) = new increaser(i)    // instantiate and initialize threads
    progressbar1(i).value = 0  // start the ProgressBars at the left
next
for i = 0 to u
    t(i).run // start all the threads running
next
```

The array of Increasers is purely a convenience, so that we can instantiate, initialize, and start running each thread instance by way of loops. The calls to start the threads running come in immediate succession to one another, whereupon the Action event handler terminates; all the work is now being done independently and simultaneously by the threads.

This sometimes surprises beginners who have absorbed the details of "Destruction of Instances" in Chapter 3. It sounds as if, even though t is a local variable that goes out existence, the threads to which it refers live on. That's exactly so. Once a thread starts running, it lives on, irrespective of your code's references to it, until its execution terminates.

This implementation works pretty well, but we are relying upon the thread mechanism itself to behave in a more or less random and evenhanded manner as the threads fill the ProgressBars. We can better ensure such behavior by introducing a delay into Increaser's loop; and to add an element of excitement (assuming you're easily excited), we'll randomize this delay. We'll also randomize the amount of increment a little. The effect feels more like a race:

```
dim p as progressbar
dim i,max as integer
p = window1.progressbar1(whatindex)
while p.value < p.maximum
    p.value = p.value + rnd*4 + 1
    max = rnd*15 + 1
    i = ticks
    while ticks-i < max
    wend
wend
```

As an exercise, you might like to modify the project so that instead of creating the ProgressBar clones in the IDE and hardcoding their maximum Index value, the running application asks the user how many ProgressBars to use, and generates the clones dynamically before starting the race.

Arbitration of Threads

Once a thread is launched, there are now at least two blocks of code running simultaneously. The code that told the thread to start running continues itself to run, and when it is finished, the application as a whole continues to respond to events—in other words, the application itself is a thread. Meanwhile, the actual thread's code, and any code that it calls, is also running. The resulting simultaneity is a somewhat tricky situation. You can no longer be certain of the sequence in which lines of code will be executed, or of how much time will elapse between the execution of one line and the next; it might well be that one line of one thread will execute, and then other code from another thread will execute before we come back to the first thread to execute its next line.

This means that, when threads are about, you must be careful not to write code that could, if the timing fell out in a certain way, be detrimentally interfered with by other code.

Here's an example. In our ProgressBar race, it's sometimes a little hard to tell which ProgressBar has won, because afterward the other ProgressBars continue filling. To make the results of the race clearer, let's say we want all the ProgressBars to stop as soon as one ProgressBar has finished. So, in the thread's loop, instead of examining the Value of our own ProgressBar to see if it has finished, we'll examine the Value of *every* ProgressBar to see if it has finished, and if one of them has, we'll terminate the thread without progressing our own ProgressBar any further. The thread's Run event handler now looks something like this:

```
const u = 3
dim p, p2 as progressbar
dim i,max as integer
p = window1.progressbar1(whatindex)
do
    for i = 0 to u
        p2 = window1.progressbar1(i)
        if p2.value >= p2.maximum then
            return
        end
    next
    p.value = p.value + rnd*4 + 1
    max = rnd*15 + 1
    i = ticks
    while ticks-i < max
    wend
loop
```

But there's a problem. Remember, all the threads are running simultaneously. Consider what might happen during the For loop. Suppose we are the fourth ProgressBar's thread. We examine the first ProgressBar, and it hasn't finished. So we proceed to examine the second ProgressBar, and the third; and meanwhile, perhaps the first ProgressBar's thread increments the first ProgressBar, and now it *has* finished. We continue on, blissfully unaware of this, and increment our own ProgressBar—just what we're not supposed to do. Another thing to worry about is precisely what happens when we change the Value of a ProgressBar. What if, meanwhile, another thread is examining that value? Will we throw off the results of that examination? Will we crash?

The key word here is "meanwhile." Our problem is that, having created threads, which by definition are simultaneous and independent, we now change our minds and want in some measure to undo our handiwork—we find the simultaneity and independence of our threads troublesome, and want to reduce it. We want our threads to be *mostly* independent and simultaneous, but we also would like to be able to arbitrate between threads so that sometimes we are in some control of how they interact. In short, we want to eat our cake and have it too. And, to some degree, we can—with a semaphore.

A *semaphore* is a specially implemented flag. Any thread may raise the flag. If another thread tries to raise the flag when the flag is already raised, it won't be able to; instead, the thread's code will automatically pause until the flag is lowered. Once the flag is lowered, the thread that is asking to raise the flag will be able to, and will do so, and its code will proceed.

Semaphores are purely a voluntary, cooperative device. The idea is that when we come to a piece of code where we know there might be a clash between threads, we raise the flag; when we leave that piece of code, we lower the flag. Of itself, raising the flag does nothing; but if every thread that might clash over whatever it is we're afraid might be clashed over behaves in this same fashion, there will never actually be a clash.

Semaphores are implemented as a class—the Semaphore class. To use one, instantiate a Semaphore at a sufficiently global level, where all the threads that need to cooperate can see it, before the threads start running. To raise the flag (or try to), a thread sends the Semaphore instance the Signal message; to lower it, a thread sends the Semaphore instance the Release message.

You may ask: This sounds like a boolean. So why is a special class needed? Why can't we implement a semaphore ourselves, by setting a boolean to true as a signal and to false as a release? Then any other thread just checks the boolean, and if it's true, it loops until it is false. The trouble is that the boolean flag might not be raised when Thread A checks it, but it might be raised by Thread B before Thread A can raise it. But this is the very difficulty that semaphores are supposed to solve! It follows that you can't make semaphores yourself; the programming language must, at its most basic level, implement them as what is called a *mutex with atomic test-and-set*.

Let's return to our ProgressBars example. We'll place a Semaphore property, named Checking, in the window (because that's a sufficiently global location). In the window's Open event handler, we generate the Semaphore instance:

```
checking = new semaphore
```

Now our Thread class's Run event handler is modified to look like this:

```
const u = 3
dim p, p2 as progressbar
dim i,max as integer
p = window1.progressbar1(whatindex)
do
    window1.checking.signal // take sole access to progressbars
    for i = 0 to u
        p2 = window1.progressbar1(i)
        if p2.value >= p2.maximum then
            window1.checking.release // *
```

```
            return
        end
    next
    p.value = p.value + rnd*4 + 1
    window1.checking.release // *
    max = rnd*15 + 1
    i = ticks
    while ticks-i < max
    wend
loop
```

We raise the semaphore before starting to check the Values of the ProgressBars. The intention is that when we are allowed to raise the semaphore and proceed, we will have sole access to all the ProgressBars. We lower the semaphore, allowing other threads to access the ProgressBars, after we have checked them all and have either incremented our own ProgressBar or quit because the race is over (the lines commented with an asterisk). Always lower any semaphore that you raise! If there is more than one exit path from the block of code protected by the semaphore, as here, lower the semaphore at each exit. If, in this example, we fail to lower the semaphore before the Return line, other threads that may still be running cannot raise the semaphore, cannot proceed, cannot learn the race is over, and cannot terminate.

Another device for managing threads is the CriticalSection. On the face of it, this works just like a Semaphore, except that the relevant messages are Enter and Leave. To illustrate, we'll substitute a CriticalSection for the Semaphore in the previous example. The Checking property in the window is now a CriticalSection, and in the window's Open event handler we instantiate it like this:

```
checking = new criticalsection
```

Our thread class's Run event handler works just the same way as before, except the messages sent to Checking are different; I have added a comment, "it's now a CriticalSection," to indicate the three changed lines:

```
const u = 3
dim p as progressbar
dim i,max as integer
p = window1.progressbar1(whatindex)
do
    window1.checking.enter // it's now a CriticalSection
    for i = 0 to u
        p2 = window1.progressbar1(i)
        if p2.value >= p2.maximum then
            window1.checking.leave // it's now a CriticalSection
            return
        end
    next
    p.value = p.value + rnd*4 + 1
    window1.checking.leave // it's now a CriticalSection
    max = rnd*15 + 1
    i = ticks
    while ticks-i < max
    wend
loop
```

If CriticalSections are interchangeable with Semaphores in this way, what's the difference between them? A CriticalSection has some built-in intelligence. It knows what thread entered it, and it will permit that thread to enter it again without leaving. And it knows how many times that thread has entered it, and it won't let any other thread enter it until the first thread has left it that many times.

So, for example, with a global Semaphore s, once you (a thread) say:

```
s.signal
```

anyone at all (another thread) can say:

```
s.release
s.signal // haha, I stole your semaphore!
```

Semaphores thus have no intelligence; they are a purely cooperative venture. But now let's suppose there's a global CriticalSection c. Once you (a particular thread) say c.enter, only you (the same thread) can say the magic c.leave that will allow others to say c.enter. Also, with a CriticalSection, you could say:

```
c.enter
c.enter
```

Now anyone else who says c.enter will be blocked until you say c.leave *twice*, to balance the two Enter messages. But with a Semaphore s, you would never say:

```
s.signal
s.signal
```

because, the semaphore having been raised in the first line, the second line cannot execute.

Once a thread is launched, you should not imagine that you know anything about how quickly it will execute. Threaded code does not necessarily execute expeditiously; it keeps yielding time to other threads. Threads are therefore usually not the place for code whose speed is of concern. We can slow a thread or pause it, by looping or by trying to raise a raised semaphore, but there is no command to speed up a thread or stop it from yielding time. Nevertheless, in a pinch, there are devices for getting a thread to hog the processor. A threaded routine in which the DisableBackgroundTasks pragma appears will never yield any time at all, for as long as it runs (see "Pragmas" in Chapter 8). And a thread yields time only at the bottom of a looping construct (Wend, Loop, Next), so threaded code without such constructs will run interrupted once it gets started.*

Another common error is to imagine that threads yield to one another in a predictable order. The presence of Semaphores and CriticalSections seems to compound this illusion; people tend to expect that they work like that feature on your telephone where you call your friend's number, the number is busy, but as soon as your friend hangs up the phone the system phones both him and you and connects you.

---

* Thanks to Joe Strout, of REAL Software, for clarifying this.

They don't. If a line of code in a thread attempts to raise a semaphore and fails because the semaphore is already raised, you are not guaranteed that the moment it is lowered, the line will be executed and will succeed. There is not some orderly "queue" of semaphore-raising requests lined up like clients at a men's room urinal. That's not what semaphores do. The effect of a raised Semaphore is negative, not positive: it stops a line of code from executing now; it says nothing about when the line of code will execute. You have to be prepared to tolerate some randomness in this regard. In our ProgressBar racing example, this randomness may not be noticeable, but it is present. You can prove this by instrumenting the code so that each thread records somehow when it executes; you'll see that the threads do not take possession of the semaphore in any regular repeated order.

If such regularity of order is important to you, it is up to you to implement it explicitly. Suppose that in the case of our racing ProgressBars, for example, we want the ProgressBars to advance in constant cyclical order. The window might contain an integer property, WhoMayGo, which is to cycle through the indexes of the ProgressBars; each thread loops until WhoMayGo matches the index of its own ProgressBar, then enters the CriticalSection, taking care to increment WhoMayGo before leaving (the two lines commented with an asterisk do this). The random time delay is now pointless, so we can remove it:

```
const u = 3
dim p as progressbar
dim i,max as integer
p = window1.progressbar1(whatindex)
do
    do // wait for our turn!
    loop until window1.whoMayGo = self.whatIndex
    window1.checking.enter
    for i = 0 to u
        p2 = window1.progressbar1(i)
        if p2.value >= p2.maximum then
            window1.whoMayGo = (window1.whoMayGo + 1) mod (u+1) //*
            window1.checking.leave
            return
        end
    next
    p.value = p.value + rnd*4 + 1
    window1.whoMayGo = (window1.whoMayGo + 1) mod (u+1) //*
    window1.checking.leave
loop
```

There are no facilities for putting a thread to sleep, or for killing one thread from another. Sleeping can be simulated by wasting some time with a While loop, though to be sure this is not quite the same thing. A better simulation is to raise a semaphore that the thread is supposed to check for periodically; the thread tries to signal the semaphore and immediately release it again, but if the semaphore is up, the thread is blocked, effectively sleeping, until the semaphore is lowered. A thread is killed when it says Return or reaches the end of its Run event handler. Killing from outside the thread can be simulated by raising an ordinary boolean flag that the thread can check for periodically; the thread returns immediately if it discovers that the flag is up. Another alternative is to use a Timer, which implements an asynchronous loop or delay while putting less strain on the CPU than a thread does; see Chapter 25.

Every Thread instance has a read-only ThreadID property whose value is a unique integer assigned at instantiation time. This can be useful for both arbitration and debugging of threads.

CHAPTER 6

In this chapter:
- Menu Overview
- Editing Menus
- Special Menu Items
- The Menu-Enabling Moment
- Menu Item Functionality
- Dynamic Menus
- Menu Examples

Menus

Earlier chapters have introduced windows, controls, classes, and subclasses. There is one component of every project that has not yet been discussed—menus. That's what this chapter is about. It describes how menus are created and edited in the IDE, how your application enables menu items, how your application responds when the user chooses a menu item, and how your application modifies its menu items while running.

Menu Overview

Menus are a familiar feature of the Macintosh GUI. When an application is running, the texts of its menus—the File menu, the Edit menu, and so on—appear across the top of the main screen. These are commonly thought of as the *names* of the menus. However, REALbasic uses the term *name* to mean a menu item's unique identifier as seen by the programmer and the code; what the user sees is called the menu or menu item's *text*. Since REALbasic has a project component called a menubar, I refer to the place where the menus appear as "the top of the screen."

On Windows, the menus appear at the top of a window, not the top of the screen. If you are using the multiple document interface (the *MDI*), this window is a containing window, which holds all the document windows of your application, much like a Macintosh screen—though modal and floating windows still appear outside it. (You elect to use the MDI in the Build Application dialog; see "Building" in Chapter 8.) If you're not using the MDI, the menus appear only at the top of the default window or the first window that appears; therefore you should not open a second document window, as it will have no menus (which will look odd to a Windows user), and it may be possible to close the first window and end up with no menus at all (which will cause a Windows user to curse your name). It is possible to open what *looks* like a second window with menus, though, by launching another instance of your own application; this, for example, is how Internet Explorer behaves.

Clicking on a menu causes that menu's items to pop down, so that an item may be chosen. It is also possible for a menu item itself to be a submenu, meaning that it is the source for a further set of menu items that pop down; this creates hierarchical menus (also called cascading menus). To choose a menu item, instead of popping down menu items with the mouse, the user can type on the keyboard the item's Command key equivalent, if it has one; on Windows, these are Ctrl key equivalents. On Windows, menus can also be navigated with the keyboard after pressing the Alt key; in this mode, a menu or menu item can be chosen through its accelerator key, which is different from a Ctrl key equivalent. (For example, Paste on Windows usually has keyboard equivalent Ctrl-V but accelerator key P.)

In REALbasic, the complete set of your application's menus and menu items is called its *menubar*. The project has exactly one menubar, represented by the Menu listing in the Project Window. The menubar contains most of the information about each menu and menu item, such as:

- The physical arrangement of the menus and menu items
- Each menu item's name (used to refer to it in code)
- Each menu item's text (what the user sees)
- Each menu item's Command key equivalent (if it has one) and other properties

The menubar does not, however, contain the functionality to be invoked when the user chooses a menu item; that functionality belongs to your project's classes, as explained later in this chapter.

How Menus Are Enabled

In the running application, a menu item may be either enabled or disabled; a disabled menu item's text is dimmed. Only an enabled menu item can be chosen by the user, whether with the mouse or with its Command key equivalent.* Your application must therefore be concerned with seeing to it that the right menus and menu items are enabled for the current situation. However, your application doesn't do this at just any old time; it won't enable menus whenever it feels like it, some of them now, some of them later, and then walk away, as it were. Instead, any time REALbasic thinks that the enabled state of the menus might be important, it disables *all* menu items, then turns to your application and asks it to describe the enabled state of *all* menu items at that moment. REALbasic does this by sending the EnableMenu-Items event, and the moment is called a *menu-enabling moment*.

For example, when the user clicks the mouse on a menu, before the menu items pop down, there is a menu-enabling moment, so you must say what menu items will be available. Similarly, when the user types a Command key equivalent, before the corresponding menu item is chosen, there is a menu-enabling moment, so you must say whether that menu item is available. And menu-enabling moments arise at certain other times, detailed later in this chapter.

---

* Things on Windows are a bit different; see the end of "The Menu-Enabling Moment," later in this chapter.

Each and every menu item that is to be choosable must be explicitly enabled during each menu-enabling moment; otherwise, it will be disabled. That's important, so I'll say it another way. If your code, during a menu-enabling moment, fails to declare that a particular menu item should be enabled, *that menu item is disabled and cannot be chosen.*

On the other hand, just because menu items must actually be enabled during the menu-enabling moment, that doesn't mean your application cannot make the *decision* as to whether to enable a given menu item outside of the menu-enabling moment. It can make such a decision at any time. It just won't *do* the actual enabling at that time.

For example, your application can, at any time, record the fact that a particular menu item needs to be enabled. It can record this information anywhere it likes; a good place might be in the Tag string property of the menu item itself. The idea is that during the menu-enabling moment, when menu items must be enabled, the application will consult the Tag property of the menu item to learn what to do. For instance, suppose that if a certain button is pressed a certain menu item should thereafter be enabled. The button's Action event handler could say:

```
theMenuItem.tag = "Yes"
```

Then later, during subsequent menu-enabling moments, your code could examine theMenuItem.tag, and would enable this menu item only if it is "Yes".

So, to sum up, the enabled state of menu items must be created anew at every menu-enabling moment, or your menu items will all be disabled and unchoosable. Only the enabling of menu items behaves in this special way. Other features of menu items—their text, their checked state, and so forth—are untouched by REALbasic, so they can be set at any old time. Conversely, your code can take advantage of the menu-enabling moment to do things other than enabling menus, such as checking or unchecking menu items, changing their text, or even performing activities unrelated to menus.

Menu Item Classes

By default, all menu items are instances of the MenuItem class—except for the Quit menu item, which is an instance of the QuitMenuItem subclass of the MenuItem class. You can create subclasses of the MenuItem class, and you can dictate that any menu item be an instance of such a subclass, through the Super popup in the Properties Window.

What makes a MenuItem subclass useful? A menu item that is an instance of a MenuItem subclass is eligible to receive two events (described in detail later in this chapter). One is received during the menu-enabling moment; the menu item might

---

* Unless the menu item is self-enabling; see "Special Menu Items," later in this chapter.

then enable itself. The other is received when the menu item is chosen; the menu item might then perform its appropriate functionality. Clearly, a MenuItem subclass can help make menu items self-enabling and object-oriented. Examples will appear later in the chapter.

Cloning Menu Items

Menu items, like controls, can be cloned. The technique is just as for controls. In the IDE, you create a menu item array. In the running application you can use New with the global name of the menu item, and a new menu item will come into existence. Remarkably, you can also do something with a menu item that you can't do with a control: you can destroy it while the application is running. There will be more about all this later in the chapter.

Editing Menus

As already stated, the physical information about your project's menus and menu items is contained in its menubar. To edit the menubar, double-click the Menus listing in the Project Window; the Menu Editor appears, showing a simulation of the menus as they will appear when the application runs. In the Menu Editor, click on a menu text to reveal its menu items. (See Figure 6-1.)

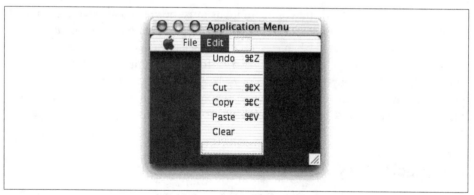

Figure 6-1. The Menu Editor

In the Menu Editor, when any menu or menu item is selected, its properties are listed in the Properties Window. You can type to create or replace the text of a selected menu or menu item; hit Return or Enter to "set" the new text. If you're not in the middle of typing its text, you can remove a selected menu or menu item by hitting Delete. Two dotted outlines show where to create a new menu item or menu: just select an outline and type its text. (A new dotted outline will appear after you hit Return or Enter.) Menus and menu items can be rearranged by dragging. Arrow keys navigate among menus and menu items.

A menu item's name, as listed in the Properties Window, is its global name. Your code will use a menu item's global name to perform such operations as enabling it, changing its text, giving it a checkmark, and so forth. When you create a menu item and provide it with a text, REALbasic supplies a suggested global name based on the text of the containing menu and the text of the item itself. You should feel free to change this name, if you like, to something more descriptive or convenient. But be wary of changing the names of the built-in menu items that appear in the Edit menu of a new project; if you do, you will disable the automatic functionality that accompanies them (more about this later in the chapter).

REALbasic does not supply any global name for a menu, as opposed to a menu item, because your code will have no occasion to refer to it; menu items can be manipulated by your code, but menus themselves cannot be. This means that although menu items can appear and disappear or change their text in the course of the application's running, menus themselves cannot. Programmers accustomed to environments that permit such behavior, such as HyperCard, may find this limitation irritating; but an argument can be made that an application that changes its menus on the fly is confusing and poorly planned.

To create a hierarchical menu, check a menu item's Submenu checkbox; a dotted outline will appear cascading to its right, so you can create the hierarchical menu items. You can't drag menu items of submenus to rearrange them; this bug will be fixed in Version 3.5.

To create a menu item separator, make a menu item's text a single hyphen.

To give a menu item a Command key equivalent, set its CommandKey property value to a single letter; don't actually use the Command key as you type the value. For example, a CommandKey value of A results in a keyboard equivalent Command-A. You can add other modifiers to a keyboard equivalent by typing their name and a hyphen as the CommandKey value; don't include "command" in the name. For example, you might type control-shift-A or option-A, meaning, respectively, Command-Ctrl-Shift-A and Command-Option-A. These will not show up properly in the Menu Editor, but that's just a cosmetic bug; they will work fine. In the running application, you can change a CommandKey property in code, but you can't include a modifier; for example, this doesn't work:

```
myMenuItem.commandKey = "option-A" // doesn't work
```

However, if the menu item already had a modifier, it remains automatically. For example, if MyMenuItem was assigned a CommandKey of option-A in the IDE, then this works:

```
myMenuItem.commandKey = "B" // means Command-Option-B
```

On Windows, the CommandKey value is interpreted as a Ctrl key equivalent, except that Function key values are legal and are correctly seen as not implying the Ctrl key. Alt and Shift are legal modifiers; illegal modifier specifications are ignored. Table 6-1 summarizes.

Table 6-1. Menu item keyboard equivalents on Windows

CommandKey value	Keyboard equivalent on Windows
A	Ctrl-A
F5	F5
Alt-A	Ctrl-Alt-A
Alt-F5	Alt-F5
Shift-A	Ctrl-Shift-A
Option-A	Ctrl-A

The accelerator key for Windows is indicated by an ampersand (&) in the menu or menu item's text before the corresponding letter of the text. Windows users tend to regard accelerators as more important than keyboard equivalents. If you don't include an ampersand, the first letter of the menu or menu item will be used, but you really should include an explicit accelerator key for every menu and menu item. The ampersand will make the underline appear under the next letter of the menu item's text on Windows, will be ignored on Macintosh, and won't itself appear in the menu item's text on either platform. For a literal ampersand in a menu item's text, type two ampersands.

In a cross-platform project, it is likely that at least some Text and CommandKey values will be different on Macintosh and Windows. Both values can be fetched from a localized global constant (page 132), or you can change the value as the application starts up, for example in the Application's Open event handler. For an example, see "Cross-Platform Considerations" at the end of this chapter.

The Bold, Italic, Underline, and Submenu properties are not really properties: they dictate the formatting of the menu item, but your code cannot get or set them. Bold, Italic, and Underline have no effect on Windows.

For the BalloonHelp and DisabledBalloonHelp properties, see Chapter 20.

Three properties—Enabled, Visible, and Checked—can be manipulated only by your code, and do not appear in the Properties Window.

You can export and import a menubar, between the Project Window and the Finder, in the usual ways. If you import a menubar, it replaces the existing menubar.

Special Menu Items

Several menus and menu items behave in a special way. This section gives an overview of how they work.

A new project has three menus: the Apple menu, File menu, and Edit menu.

The Apple menu initially contains no menu items. Any menu items that you add here will appear above a separator line in the Apple menu when the application runs. The primary intent here is to let you add the customary About menu item; you really should add one, since otherwise the application will display an Apple menu that starts with a separator line, which looks odd. On Mac OS X, this menu item appears in the system's application menu; for example, if your application is called App-Name, then this menu item appears at the beginning of the AppName menu. On Windows, there is no Apple menu; this menu item appears instead at the end of your last menu.

The File menu contains a Quit menu item, which is an instance of the QuitMenu-Item class. An instance of the QuitMenuItem class has two germane features:

It is self-enabling.
Unlike other menu items, even if your code fails to enable it, an instance of the QuitMenuItem class will be enabled anyway. Your code can override this during the menu-enabling moment.

It is functional.
It really does quit, by calling the built-in Quit method.

You will not normally remove or disable the QuitMenuItem instance. If you do, you should make sure that your application provides a way to quit! You can do this by calling the Quit procedure yourself. In the IDE, if you accidentally delete the Quit menu item, you can reinstate it by creating a new one and specifying that it be a QuitMenuItem. (More than one menu item may be a QuitMenuItem, but this should probably be considered a bug.)

On Mac OS X, when your application runs, the QuitMenuItem appears in the system's application menu—for example, if your application is called AppName, then this menu item appears at the end of the AppName menu—and its text is adjusted automatically to match your application's name (so, for example, it might say Quit AppName). Both this name and the keyboard equivalent are out of your hands, because this isn't really your menu. On Windows, the QuitMenuItem typically has the text Exit; making it say that is up to you (see "Cross-Platform Considerations" at the end of this chapter).

The Edit menu contains five menu items: Undo, Cut, Copy, Paste, and Clear. The Cut, Copy, Paste, and Clear menu items have two germane features, parallel to those of the Quit menu item:

They are self-enabling.
Unlike other menu items, if your code fails to enable the Cut, Copy, Paste, or Clear menu items, they will be enabled anyway if appropriate. Your code can override this during the menu-enabling moment.

They are functional.
They actually do cut, copy, paste, and clear. Your code can add to or override this functionality.

The default behavior of these menu items revolves around the EditField class and its subclasses. The rule is that when your application runs, if an EditField has the focus, then these items are automatically enabled as appropriate—Paste if there is text on the clipboard; Cut, Copy, and Clear if there is a selection (not just an insertion point) in the EditField—and when chosen, they work as expected. (An EditField has the focus if the user is working in it: it will then contain a selection or a blinking insertion point, and may have a thick colored border outlining it. The focus is discussed in more detail in Chapter 13.)

REALbasic identifies the Cut, Copy, Paste, and Clear menu items, not by virtue of their class, but by their names, which are EditCut, EditCopy, EditPaste, and EditClear. In the IDE, if you rename one of these menu items it loses its default functionality. Just the other way, if you rename or remove one of these menu items, and then create a new menu item in any menu that has one of these names, it will take on the associated default behavior. If you delete the entire Edit menu, you cannot restore it in some automatic way; you must create its menu items manually, giving them the correct names if you want them to have their default functionality.

The Undo menu item has no automatic functionality and is not self-enabling; it is there purely for your convenience. Even if your application does not implement Undo, it is still customary for the Undo menu item to be present (but disabled).

Another menu that behaves in a special way is the Help menu. This should be the last (rightmost) menu. There is, by default, no Help menu in a project's menubar. But under Mac OS 8 and 9, all applications do automatically have a Help menu, which is implemented by the system; it is here that the Show Balloons menu item appears, for example. If you create a menu called Help, menu items that you add to it will appear below a separator line after the Show Balloons menu item in the system's Help menu. On Mac OS X, there is no automatically created Help menu, and there is no penalty for not creating one; if you do, it will be an ordinary menu, containing just the items you put there. On Windows, there is no automatically created Help menu, but you will usually create it, both because your users will expect one and because of the automatic treatment of the About item from the Apple menu, which ends up as the last item of your last menu; the idea here is that your About item will end up on Windows as the last item of the Help menu, a fairly standard convention on that platform.

On Mac OS X, the system's application menu also contains a Preferences menu item for your application. Operations on this menu item are outside of the normal menu item mechanisms: you enable it with a Toolbox call (see Chapter 32) and receive communications from it with Apple events (see Chapter 31). Here, without explanation, is code to enable the Preferences menu item and change its text:*

```
dim menuref as integer, menuid as memoryblock
declare sub EnableMenuCommand lib "CarbonLib" (menu as integer, id as OSType)
enableMenuCommand 0, "pref"
declare sub GetIndMenuItemWithCommandID lib "CarbonLib" // no line break!
```

* I owe this code to Patrick Wynne and Chad McQuinn.

```
    (m as integer, id as ostype, i as integer, byref mn as integer, ix as ptr)
menuid = newmemoryBlock(2)
getindmenuitemwithcommandid 0, "pref", 1, menuref, menuid
declare sub SetMenuItemText lib "CarbonLib" // no line break!
    (m as integer, id as short, s as pstring)
setmenuitemtext menuref, menuid.short(0), "MyCoolApp Prefs..."
```

When the user chooses the Preferences menu item, your Application subclass's HandleMenuItems event can respond:

```
if eventclass = "aevt" and eventid = "pref" then
    // ... respond ...
    return true
end
```

It's disappointing that REALbasic doesn't implement all this for you, in a manner consistent with the rest of its menu handling.

The Menu-Enabling Moment

This section describes in detail what happens during the menu-enabling moment, and enumerates the occasions on which it occurs. (What's described is the situation on Macintosh; the Windows situation is summarized at the end of the section.) Figure 6-2 anticipates the discussion by showing the chain of events as the user chooses a menu item—first the sequence of events that make up the menu-enabling moment (described in this section), then the path of the menu event from object to object (described in the next section, "Menu Item Functionality").

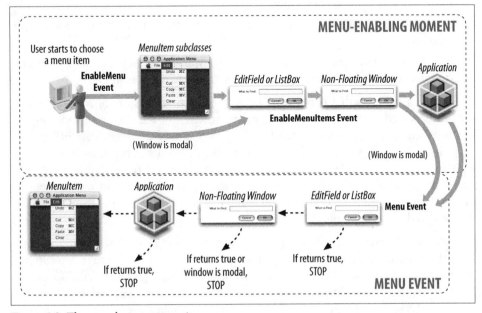

Figure 6-2. The user chooses a menu item

What It Is

The menu-enabling moment is your code's opportunity to dictate the enabled status of menu items. Every time a menu-enabling moment begins, all menu items (except for the few self-enabling menu items discussed in the previous section) are disabled! It is then up to your code to enable them again, as desired, in the course of the menu-enabling moment.

A menu item is enabled by sending it the Enable message, or what amounts to the same thing, by setting its Enabled property to true. A menu item is disabled by the onset of the menu-enabling moment, or by setting its Enabled property to false. It is not an error for your code to enable a menu item at times other than the menu-enabling moment, but it will be disabled again by the onset of the next menu-enabling moment.

What Happens During It

Here is the course of events during a menu-enabling moment. First, all menu items are disabled, except for self-enabling menu items as described in the previous section. Then (this sequence is graphically depicted in the upper part of Figure 6-2):

1. Every menu item that is an instance of a MenuItem subclass receives an Enable-Menu event. This does not happen, though, if the frontmost visible window is modal.

2. If an instance of an EditField or ListBox subclass has the focus, the EnableMenu-Items event is sent to that instance.

3. The EnableMenuItems event is sent to the frontmost visible nonfloating window.

4. The EnableMenuItems event is sent to the Application subclass instance. This does not happen, though, if the frontmost visible window is modal.

So, the event handlers that handle these events are your code's opportunity to enable menu items during the menu-enabling moment. Each of the events sent during the menu-enabling moment is independent; no recipient of an event can prevent an event from being sent to any other recipients. But the order is fixed, so it is possible for a recipient to override an action taken by a previous recipient. For example, the frontmost window might enable a menu item, but the Application subclass might disable it again; or a MenuItem instance might enable itself, but the frontmost window might disable it again.

You should structure your project's menu-enabling functionality in accordance with how the events are sent during the menu-enabling moment. To take an extreme example, if your project has no visible windows, no Application subclass, and no menu items that are instances of the MenuItem subclass, then there will be no place to put an EnableMenuItems event handler, so your application will have no way to enable any menu items (except Quit)! Thus, if your application can ever lack visible windows, you will probably want an Application subclass, or some menu items that are MenuItem subclass instances, because those are places where an EnableMenu-Items event handler can go. If your application has windows, then you know that each window will get an EnableMenuItems event when it is frontmost. So you'll probably have each window's EnableMenuItems event handler enable just those menu items that *that* window knows should be enabled when *it* is frontmost, the menu items that *it* is concerned with—leaving the other menu items in the charge of the other windows, the Application subclass, or whoever is most suitable. And so forth.

How It Is Triggered

The menu-enabling moment is triggered in a number of ways, many of which, surprisingly enough, have nothing to do with the user trying to choose a menu item. The reason has to do with the enabling and disabling of *menus*, as opposed to menu items. It turns out that if all of a menu's items are disabled, that menu is automatically disabled as well; conversely, if at least one of a menu's items is enabled, the menu is enabled. But this effect trickles up from menu items to a menu only during a menu-enabling moment. Now, when certain situations occur, you may wish to enable or disable menus, to signal to the user a change in the underlying set of choices available. REALbasic, anticipating your needs, triggers a menu-enabling moment to cover these situations.

The menu-enabling moment is triggered:

- As the user starts to choose a menu item, by clicking on a menu or by typing a Command key equivalent. (By "a Command key equivalent," I mean any keystroke modified by the Command key; it need not be a Command key combination presently defined for any menu item. Thus the menu-enabling moment can be used to catch Command keystrokes of any kind.)

- As your application starts up.

- After a window becomes frontmost (even if it is invisible). If you instantiate a window invisibly, it is frontmost but invisible. A window that becomes frontmost because a floating window closes doesn't count. If all open windows are closed, there is no newly frontmost window, and there is no menu-enabling moment.

- After your application suspends or resumes. Your application *suspends* or *resumes* when it is already running and ceases to be, or becomes, the frontmost application. When your application suspends, the focus is lost first, so no EnableMenuItems event is sent to the control that had the focus.

- After your code calls the EnableMenuItems method.

REALbasic cannot anticipate *every* occasion when a menu-enabling moment might be needed, so your code can deliberately trigger one by calling the EnableMenu-Items method. This generates the various EnableMenu and EnableMenuItems events as described earlier. Don't call EnableMenuItems from within a menu-enabling moment or you'll cause an infinite loop and your application will terminate prematurely (with a StackOverflowException).

I don't understand why there is a menu-enabling moment when the application suspends, since once the application is in the background, it has no menus to enable. Perhaps this is a bug.

Menu Enabling on Windows

On Windows, all menus (the texts along the top of the window) are always enabled. Therefore the menu-enabling moment occurs only when the user starts to manipulate menus physically, with the mouse or the Alt key; nothing else triggers a menu-enabling moment (and the EnableMenuItems method does nothing). A menu item can *always* be chosen using its keyboard equivalent, regardless of its Enabled property; this may be a bug. On the other hand, under MDI, if all windows are closed, keyboard equivalents stop working altogether, and menus must be chosen physically; this may be another bug. At the start of the menu-enabling moment, the Enabled property of every menu item is set to false and it is up to your code to set it to true if you don't want the menu item dimmed, just as on Macintosh. (See also "Keyboard Communication" in Chapter 19.)

An EditField in a modal or floating window typically won't have the focus during a menu-enabling moment, so it won't receive an EnableMenuItems event: in a modal window you can't use the mouse to choose from a menu, and in a floating window the act of using the mouse to choose from a menu shifts the focus out of the floating window. The user can press the Alt key to access the modal or floating window's private menu (the one containing Close), and this does generate such an event, but you probably won't respond to it because it isn't your menu that the user is accessing.

Menu Item Functionality

This section describes how your application actually does anything when the user chooses a menu item. Apart from some of the default menu items described earlier (in the section "Special Menu Items"), choosing a menu item has no effect whatever unless your code responds. Here's how to make it respond.

Menu Events

When a menu item is chosen, by way of the mouse or a Command key equivalent, REALbasic sends a *menu event*. It is up to your code to handle this menu event, in a *menu event handler*. In a MenuItem subclass, the menu event handler is provided for you, but otherwise creating a menu event handler is up to you. You must decide where to put it, and to do so, you need to understand where menu events are sent.

The sequence resembles, but is not identical to, the sequence of events during a menu-enabling moment:

1. If an instance of an EditField or ListBox subclass has the focus, the instance receives a menu event.
2. The frontmost visible nonfloating window receives the same menu event.
3. The Application subclass receives the same menu event. This does not happen, though, if the frontmost visible window is modal.
4. If the chosen menu item is an instance of a MenuItem subclass, then it receives the same menu event. This does not happen, though, if the frontmost visible window is modal.

On Windows, a modal window behaves like a floating window for purposes of these rules; in other words, a modal window itself does not block or receive any menu events.

During the first three stages, the menu event has the same name as the menu item and will be handled by a menu event handler with that name, which you must create. For the last stage, the menu event goes to the MenuItem subclass's Action event handler, which is already present. Unlike the events during a menu-enabling moment, the menu event is a single event, and any menu event handler that handles it can prevent it from proceeding any further in the chain, by returning true.

Menu Event Handlers

A menu event is handled only by a menu event handler. In a subclass of MenuItem, this handler is already present as the Action event handler. Elsewhere, you create it yourself by choosing Edit → New Menu Handler. A dialog appears containing a popup menu that lists the names of all menu items in your project. (See Figure 6-3.) When you choose an item and hit OK, a menu event handler by that name is created.

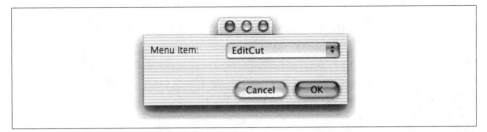

Figure 6-3. The New Menu Handler dialog

The New Menu Handler dialog does not stop you from creating a menu event handler with a name for which a menu event handler already exists. I suppose this should be considered a bug. Also, you can create a menu event handler in a class that is never going to receive a menu event (i.e., it isn't a subclass of Window, Application, EditField, or ListBox). I suppose this should be considered a bug too.

Modifying Default Menu Item Functionality

Knowing how a menu event travels, you can see how to modify or override the built-in functionality of those default menu items that have any (see "Special Menu Items," earlier in this chapter). You modify the functionality by inserting code earlier in the chain. The built-in functionality executes last of all in the chain, so you can prevent it by returning true at any point along the way.

A menu item that is an instance of the QuitMenuItem class will normally call the Quit procedure automatically after its menu event has passed through the chain. You can insert functionality before the Quit procedure is called, at any point along the chain. And you can stop the menu event at any point along the chain, preventing the automatic call to the Quit procedure from ever taking place, by returning true from a menu event handler. (Even if the Quit method is called, that does not necessarily mean that your application will quit; as we shall see in Chapter 7 and Chapter 9, an open window can still prevent the application from quitting by returning true in response to the CancelClose event.)

Menu items named EditCopy, EditPaste, EditCut, and EditClear work differently from all other menu items. Their menu event is not sent to the window, the application, or the MenuItem subclass; it goes *only* to the ListBox or EditField subclass instance with the focus, if there is one. (You can create a menu event handler for the EditCut, EditCopy, EditPaste, or EditClear menu items elsewhere than in a subclass of EditField or ListBox, but this should probably be considered a bug, as such a menu event handler will never be called.)

In the case of an EditField, the menu item's normal functionality will execute automatically, after the menu event has passed through the EditField subclass. You can add to that functionality by inserting an event handler in the EditField subclass. And you can prevent the automatic execution of the item's normal functionality, by returning true from the EditField subclass's menu event handler.

In the case of a ListBox, the EditCopy, EditPaste, EditCut, and EditClear menu items have no predefined functionality, so there is nothing to permit or prevent. If you want a ListBox to respond to these menu items, you must use a ListBox subclass, and you must give that subclass the appropriate menu event handlers. (In "ListBox Copy-and-Paste" in Chapter 23, that's just what we'll do.)

Dynamic Menus

A menu item can be cloned in much the same way as a control. Start by making a *menu item array*. In the IDE, give a menu item an index number of 0. You can manually make more elements of the same menu item array by giving another menu item the same name; REALbasic understands that you want to make a menu item array, and assigns index numbers appropriately.

A menu item can be cloned in the running application; it doesn't have to be an element of a menu item array, but you'll probably prefer that it be one. If it is, then when you use New and the name of the menu item array, a new menu item will be appended to the menu item array; this new menu item copies, and appears right after, what was previously the last element of the array. Elements of a menu item array are referred to by a single global name, and must be distinguished by index number. When chosen, their menu events pass through the same handlers; the index number is passed as a parameter called Index, so your code will know which menu item has actually been chosen. Code in a MenuItem subclass can also use Self (or Me) to refer to the element of the menu item array currently running that code, and can find out that element's index number through its Index property.

A menu item can be destroyed completely by sending it the Close message. This is remarkable, since it can't be done with controls in a window. It would be unusual to destroy a menu item that isn't part of a menu item array, since it can never be restored, and accidentally sending a destroyed menu item a message will prematurely terminate your application.

After creating or destroying a menu item in code, if your code will then continue to work with menu items, it might be helpful to call EnableMenuItems (if you're not in a menu-enabling moment); this can help "set" the change you've just made. But don't do this unnecessarily; experimentation is your best guide.

Menu items can be apparently, though not actually, removed from their menu by making them invisible. This is done through the menu item's Visible property. An invisible menu item can't be seen, and it can't be chosen by means of its keyboard equivalent; it's as if it didn't exist. Here, for example, is the EnableMenu event handler of a MenuItem subclass for menu items that appear only when the user presses the Option key while choosing a menu:

```
me.visible = keyboard.optionKey
me.enable
```

Invisible menu items can be tricky to work with. An invisible menu item can disrupt the ability of subsequent menu items in the same menu to be enabled; the workaround is to enable the invisible menu items, even though they won't be seen. (This bug should be gone in REALbasic 3.5.) Menu items cascading from an invisible menu item are invisible in a physical sense (the user can't see them because the menu item they cascade from isn't there), but if their Visible property is true and they are enabled, they can be chosen by way of their keyboard equivalent;* if the invisible menu item is then made visible, the menu items cascading from it are still

---

* I owe this trick to H. M. van Staveren.

invisible (and can never be made visible), and their keyboard equivalent still works. And there are other quirks too involved to describe here. Nonetheless, invisible items are a valuable and easy way of making menu items come and go; an example appears in the next section.

Menu Examples

To illustrate the basic techniques for working with menus, we'll create the skeleton of a very simple word-processing application, omitting functionality not needed for the example. The project will have just the default window type, Window1, containing an EditField called EditField1. Let's call the application ST (because it's a skeletal version of SimpleText). It will have two dynamic menus: a Font menu, and a Window menu listing all open windows. It will have a Size menu and a Style menu; these, along with the Font menu, will use check marks. It will have a Help menu, partly just to show how this works, and partly because we're going to make this a cross-platform project. We'll work on the Macintosh version first, adding modifications for Windows at the very end.

Creating the Menus

Open the project's Menu Editor.

Click the Apple menu icon. Hit down arrow so you're editing a new menu item, type **About ST...**, and hit Return.

Click the File menu icon. Hit down arrow twice so you're editing a new menu item (not the Quit item!), type **New**, hit Tab several times until the selected Properties Window listing is CommandKey, type **N**, and hit Return. Hit down arrow to edit another new menu item. Type **Open...**, hit Tab several times to edit the CommandKey, type **O**, and hit Return. Hit down arrow to edit another new menu item. Type **Save**, hit Tab several times to edit the CommandKey, type **S**, and hit Return. Hit down arrow to edit another new menu item. Type - (hyphen) and hit Return; this will be a separator. Now drag the Quit menu item to the bottom of the File menu, after the separator.

Leave the Edit menu alone; its default functionality is suitable.

Click the new menu area to the right of Edit. Type **Font** and hit Return. Give the Font menu just one item: make its text **aFont**, and give it an Index value of 0. The idea is that the Font menu items will be entirely composed of a single menu item array; this will be dynamic, because we won't know anything about the fonts until the application is running, so that's all we can do right now.

Create a **Size** menu with items whose texts are **9 Point**, **10 Point**, and **12 Point**. Ideally we'd be more intelligent about this, and there would be more menu items, but this is only an example, remember? For these menu items, we won't accept the default names created by REALbasic; instead, let's give all three menu items the same name, **SizePoint**, so that they have Index values 0, 1, and 2, respectively; this will make it easier to refer to them later.

Create a **Style** menu with items whose texts are **Plain**, **Bold**, and **Italic**. Their CommandKey values should be **T**, **B**, and **I**, respectively. Just for fun, make Bold bold and make Italic italic.

Create a **Window** menu. This will be dynamic, so give it one menu item; its text is unimportant, but let's give it the name **aWindow** and make sure it has an index value of 0.

Create a **Help** menu. Give it one menu item whose text is **ST Guide**.

The Application Subclass

The Application subclass is the recipient of EnableMenuItems events, and of menu events, when no window is present. Therefore it should be responsible for everything that should happen with menus when there is no window. What does that consist of? The Apple menu and the Help menu, because the user should be able to choose from these at any time. The Open and New menu items, since if no window is present the user needs a way to make one, but not the Save menu item, since if no window is open, there's nothing to save. Not the Edit menu; if no window is open, there's nothing to cut or paste. Not the Size or Style menus, since if no window is open, there's nothing to set the size or style of. The Font menu and the Window menu are dynamic and present special problems, so we'll deal with them later.

Create a new class, give it any name you like, and make it a subclass of Application.

Here is the Application subclass's EnableMenuItems event handler:

```
filenew.enable
fileopen.enable
filesave.enable
appleAboutST.enable
helpSTGuide.enable
```

Create menu event handlers for those five menu items. For FileOpen, FileSave, AppleAboutST, and HelpSTGuide, let's just have a simple MsgBox response:

```
msgbox "Not implemented."
```

FileNew needs to make a new window:

```
dim w as window1
w = new window1
```

There are more details connected with the new window; in particular, each new window needs a distinguishing Title. But let's have each window worry about that when it opens.

The Window

Each window's Title will be used as a unique identifier in the Window menu. Therefore, the window needs to be concerned with giving itself a unique Title as it opens.

Here, without comment, is Window1's Open event handler; I'm sure you can think of other algorithms for assigning Titles, but this will do for purposes of the example:

```
dim i, m as integer
for i = windowcount-1 downto 0
    m = max(m, val(replace(window(i).title,"Window","")))
next
self.title = "Window" + str(m+1)
```

What about the Font, Size, and Style menus? These have specifically to do with the EditField in the window; if the focus isn't in that EditField, there's nothing to operate on, and these menus shouldn't even be enabled. So we'll leave them to the EditField itself. (To say that there's nothing else in the window to receive the focus except the EditField is no objection; some day there might be, and besides, the way to be object-oriented is to be object-oriented right from the start.)

The EditField

Our EditField won't receive EnableMenuItems events or menu events unless it is a subclass of EditField. So make a new class; call it EF, and make it a subclass of EditField. Go back to the Window1 Window Editor and make EditField1 an instance of EF.

Open EF's Code Editor. The Font, Size, and Style menu items need to be enabled if the EditField has the focus; otherwise, they should not. Well, the EditField subclass will get an EnableMenuItems event if the EditField has the focus; otherwise, it won't. So we don't have to make any choices, because REALbasic is already making the correct choice for us! (For more about this way of thinking, see "Events Make Choices" in Chapter 7.)

If we get an EnableMenuItems event, therefore, we should enable all the items in the Font, Size, and Style menus. We'll postpone thinking about the Font menu. Here is our first draft of EF's EnableMenuItems event handler:

```
dim i as integer
styleplain.enabled = true
stylebold.enabled = true
styleitalic.enabled = true
for i = 0 to 2
    sizepoint(i).enable
next
```

Not bad, but we've omitted something. If the current selection is bold, the Bold menu item should be checked—and so too for the Italic menu item and all three Size menu items. A perfectly reasonable time to see to this is now, during the menu-enabling moment, while the user might be about to look at the menu items. Without further comment, here's the amended EnableMenuItems event handler:

```
dim i as integer
styleplain.enabled = true
stylebold.enabled = true
```

```
styleitalic.enabled = true
stylebold.checked = self.selbold
styleitalic.checked = self.selitalic
for i = 0 to 2
    sizepoint(i).enable
    sizepoint(i).checked = self.seltextsize = val(sizepoint(i).text)
next
```

We'll learn all about the EditField's SelBold property and so forth in Chapter 13.

The Font Menu

A Font menu must typically be implemented dynamically because we have no way of knowing what fonts will be present when the application runs. We'll assume that the fonts won't change while the application is running; that way, we will need to create the Font menu only once, as the application starts up. So we are now back in the Application subclass, in its Open event handler, ready to create the Font menu.

The Font menu already has one menu item, FontAFont, set up as the first element of a menu item array, ready for us to clone. To create the menu, we consult the built-in functions FontCount and Font to learn the number and names of the fonts. We loop through all the fonts, creating menu items and making their texts the names of the fonts. We must compensate for the fact that the FontCount function counts, but the Font function is zero-based; we must also remember that the 0 item of the menu item array already exists and doesn't need to be created:

```
dim i, u as integer
dim f as menuitem
u = fontcount-1
fontaFont(0).text = font(0)
for i = 1 to u
    f = new fontafont
    f.text = font(i)
next
```

The enabling and checkmarking of the Font menu items can take place back in EF's EnableMenuItems event handler:

```
for i = fontcount-1 downto 0
    fontafont(i).enable
    fontafont(i).checked = self.seltextfont = fontafont(i).text
next
```

The Window Menu

The Window menu is tricky. It must rebuild itself at each menu-enabling moment, as the number or order of windows may have changed in the meantime. We can learn about the windows through the WindowCount and Window functions; as with FontCount and Font, we must remember to compensate for the fact that WindowCount counts but the Window function is zero-based. Let's presume, for simplicity, that we just want the Window menu to list all windows returned by the Window function, in order.* As with the Font menu, we've started with a single menu item in the Window menu, it's called AWindow, and it has an index of 0, ready to be used dynamically.

The Window menu functionality is global but specialized. It's global in the sense that it takes place at a higher level than any windows. This means that we could put the functionality in the Application subclass. It's specialized in the sense that all the menu items of the Window menu do the same thing: the nth menu item shows the name of the nth window, and can be chosen to summon the nth window to the front. So let's package the functionality in a MenuItem subclass.

Make a MenuItem subclass called WindowMI, and go into the Menu Editor and specify that the AWindow menu item should be an instance of WindowMI. Now open WindowMI's Code Editor. When there's a menu-enabling moment, we first want to rebuild the Window menu. So WindowMI's EnableMenu event handler should ask for this to be done. But the EnableMenu event handler will be called repeatedly, once for every menu item in the Window menu; yet we wish to rebuild the Window menu only once per menu-enabling event. The way to take care of this is to do it only for the first menu item:

```
if self.index = 0 then
    self.rebuild
end
```

Let's write WindowMI's Rebuild method. The individual menu items can each take care of their own texts, so Rebuild need only adjust the number of items in the AWindow menu item array. We can't ask the AWindow menu item array how many items it contains at any given moment! So we must maintain this information ourselves; we'll use a private integer property of the WindowMI class called Count, which we'll make zero-based, in imitation of Ubound. We won't destroy any members of the AWindow menu item array; we're in the middle of the menu-enabling moment already, and REALbasic might try to send a destroyed menu item an EnableMenu event and crash the application—and besides, there's no need. If we just make sure there are always enough menu items, each menu item can make itself invisible if it's superfluous. Here is the Rebuild method:

```
dim m as menuItem // throwaway variable
while count < windowCount - 1
    m = new aWindow
    count = count + 1
wend
```

Now we can finish WindowMI's EnableMenu event handler. Remember, this event handler is called for each menu item. If there is a window to correspond to this menu

---

* This isn't quite the standard interface (windows are typically listed in a Window menu in the order in which they were opened), but it is easiest for purposes of illustration. In Chapter 9 it will be shown how to modify the code developed here so that it deals with the possibility of windows that may be present but should not be listed in the Window menu. Tinkering with the order of the menu items, though, is left as an exercise for the reader.

item, the menu item should be visible and take the window's Title as its text; if not, the menu item should be invisible. The menu items are all self-enabling.

```
if self.index = 0 then
    rebuild
end
if self.index >= windowCount then
    self.visible = false
else
    self.visible = true
    self.text = window(self.index).title
end
self.enable
```

The Action event handler of the WindowMI class uses the index of the chosen menu item to bring the corresponding window to the front:

```
window(self.index).show
```

That's all, but for the sake of completeness, here's an alternative implementation where everything happens in the Application subclass; it is less portable, but it may be quicker, and it illustrates the use of the Close message to destroy a menu item.

We use an integer property of the Application subclass, CountWindowMenuItems, to maintain the size of the menu item array. In the EnableMenuItems event handler of the Application subclass (in addition to whatever else is happening there), we adjust the number of Window menu items, and then fix their text and enabled status. We treat the zero item of the menu item array specially, in that when the number of windows changes from zero to one or one to zero, we show or hide the zero item, rather than creating or destroying a menu item:

```
dim u, i as integer
dim m as menuitem
u = max (2, windowcount+1)
for i = countwindowmenuitems downto u
    aWindow(i-1).close
next
u = max (2, countwindowmenuitems+1)
for i = u to windowcount
    m = new aWindow
next
countwindowmenuitems = max (1, windowcount)
if windowCount = 0 then
    aWindow(0).visible = false
    aWindow(0).enabled = false
else
    aWindow(0).visible = true
    u = windowcount - 1
    for i = 0 to u
        aWindow(i).text = window(i).title
        aWindow(i).enabled = true
    next
end
```

The menu event handler for AWindow, also located in the Application subclass, goes like this:

```
window(index).show
```

Cross-Platform Considerations

Now let's make our application work nicely for both Macintosh and Windows. The first step is to open the Menu Editor and go back through every menu and menu item, inserting an ampersand somewhere in its text, so that everything has a keyboard accelerator. So, you should end up with texts like **&File**, **&Open**, and so forth. The ampersands don't show up on Macintosh; on Windows they appear as underlines beneath the next letter.

Next, we grapple with the Quit menu item. On Windows, this should be called Exit, and it should have no Ctrl key equivalent. Let's make the change dynamically as the application starts up; that means this code goes into the Application subclass's Open event handler. We can use the TargetWin32 global boolean to see whether we're running on Windows:

```
if targetwin32 then
    filequit.text = "E&xit"
    filequit.commandKey = ""
end
```

There's one more little problem. On Windows, the AppleAboutST menu item appears as the last item of the Help menu, after the HelpSTGuide menu item. We'd like a separator between these two items. But the separator mustn't appear on Macintosh, because the AppleAboutST menu item isn't part of the Help menu there, so this would make the separator the last thing in the Help menu. The solution is to add the separator in the Help menu after the HelpSTGuide menu item, but give it a name. Let's call it BadHyphen. Now we can delete the separator on Macintosh as the application starts up:

```
if targetwin32 then
    filequit.text = "E&xit"
    filequit.commandKey = ""
else
    badhyphen.close
end
```

The Architecture of an Application

The preceding chapters have explained how to write REALbasic code, and have discussed all the major components of a REALbasic project. The rest of learning REALbasic is just details about how to use particular built-in classes. Such details are the subject of Part II and Part III. That's where you'll find answers to such questions as: What is a checkbox? How do I draw a picture in a window? How does REALbasic connect to the Internet? And so forth.

But one should also give some thought to the larger context in which those details are embedded—namely, the structure and organization of your project's entire code. Details do you no good unless your application works. Properties, methods, lines of code are pointless unless you put them in the right place. The purpose of this chapter is to help you think about your application's overall structure. The subject here is how to organize your code.

In a program written for a GUI-based operating system, that's no small consideration. The joy and the terror of such a program is that it isn't in charge; the user is. Your program can't predict what the user *will* do, so it must be prepared to react sensibly to whatever the user *can* do. Most of the time, your application sits idle, essentially asleep. Then, whenever the user presses a button, types in a field, chooses a menu item, dismisses a window, or performs any other significant action, an event arrives, and your application wakes up and gets to run some code. During that brief time when your application is responding to the user's action, all the right things must happen so that your application is in the proper state as it surrenders control once more and goes back to sleep. Your code needs to be organized in such a way that this will be so.

Object orientation, too, can quickly come to seem more of a hazard than a help to the organization and development of your program. As soon as a project consists of more than a few objects and more than a few lines of code, it threatens to become overwhelming and unmanageable. An event triggered by the user may arrive at one object, which then sends a message to some other object, which causes another event to be sent, which triggers some more code, which calls a handler in a completely different object, and so forth. As a programmer, you no longer understand completely how the program works; you don't remember where all the code is; you become afraid to change any code, lest something that depends upon it should break. In programmer's parlance, your code has become *spaghetti*; wherever you pick it up, it feels like a tangle. This is a bad situation, and should be avoided; and it can be avoided if your code is well organized from the start.

In spite of your project's piecemeal composition, its discrete bursts of activity, and the complexity of the relationships between its objects, it will make sense, work properly, and be easy to maintain, provided you plan and develop its overall shape—its *architecture*—in an orderly fashion. A REALbasic application is composed of snippets of code. Where should those snippets go, and how will they be tied together? The way you answer this question will be reflected in—indeed, it will *be*—your application's architecture.

Remember when the Rubik's Cube craze first swept the country? At the time, an article in *Scientific American* warned that the way to solve it was to look for general principles, which would be useful no matter what state the cube was in; if the sight of someone approaching a cube you'd been working on made you scream, "Don't touch it!" you were going at it the wrong way. So too, if you feel afraid to modify your REALbasic project, something is wrong with your architecture.

Object-oriented design is a major subject unto itself. It is well beyond the scope of this book, and has nothing to do with REALbasic per se. Making your project object-oriented in a way that suits its purpose and your needs and temperament is entirely up to you. In the Preface, I recommend some further reading on the matter; in the Appendix, I demonstrate my own thinking in action; but teaching object-oriented design is neither the purpose nor the place of this book. On the other hand, REALbasic is an application framework, and this framework is organized in a certain object-oriented way before you write a line of code. You should make it your goal to organize your code in a way that *goes with the grain of REALbasic's application framework*. If you don't, things will go badly for you; if you do, your subsequent practical and philosophical expeditions into the higher reaches of object-oriented design will fall neatly into place. In other words, you have to be able to walk before you can run; this chapter is about the principles of walking.

Three Pillars of Zen

Every application is different, of course; but it is nevertheless possible to distill some general principles that will underlie the architecture of a typical well-written REALbasic program. From the smallest and simplest application to the mightiest *magnum opus*, the following three guiding rules will confer order and stability upon your project. Like little Zen koans, concentrating fixedly upon them will bring enlightenment.

- Let the events make the choices.
- Keep scope as narrow as possible but as wide as necessary.
- Handlers are the cloth, references are the thread.

The following sections provide explanations and illustrations of each of these three principles.

Events Make Choices

One of the ways REALbasic's application framework expresses its object orientation is by how it sends your objects events. REALbasic decides where to send each event; you shouldn't fight this decision, but rather welcome it. Your objects are like houses connected by a complex telephone network; as much as possible, you should keep your hands off this network and let REALbasic manage it. When REALbasic sends an object an event, it has already done the switching for you, it has already made the correct phone ring; all you have to do is make sure your code is waiting at the other end, ready to answer.

For example, suppose we are writing a word-processing application. The main window type is the document window, where the user reads and edits text in an Edit-Field. We want the user to be able to bring up a Find dialog, to search for specific text in that field, so we have a menu item, Edit → Find, which causes the dialog to appear. The question now is: how will this menu item be enabled?

We know that four objects can get an event during the menu-enabling moment: the menu item, the EditField, the window, and the Application subclass. Suppose we put enabling code for this menu item in the Application subclass's EnableMenuItems event handler. The code will have to make choices. We don't want the Find menu item enabled if there is no document window. We don't want the Find menu item enabled if there is a document window but it isn't frontmost. We don't want the Find menu item enabled if a document window is frontmost but our EditField doesn't have the focus. We don't want the Find menu item enabled if our EditField has the focus but contains no text.

This situation is bad. We're working too hard, because we're working on a matter that doesn't concern us. We have to find the frontmost window, we have to decide what type it is, we have to look at its fields and figure out which one has the focus, we have to look at a field's contents. We are the Application object, but we're not thinking about the application as a whole. We're drilling down into levels of niggling detail that should be beneath our lofty notice.

Now suppose, just the other way, that the EditField where the user edits the document in the document window is an instance of an EditField subclass, and that the enabling code for the Find menu item is in this subclass's EnableMenuItems event handler. Now we need make hardly *any* choices, because REALbasic has already made them for us. There's no document window present? Then we won't get an event. The document window isn't frontmost? Then we won't get an event. The field doesn't have the focus? Then we won't get an event. In fact, almost the only time we will get an event is exactly on those occasions when we do want to enable the Find menu item! This suggests that this is a good place to put the code: by putting the code here, we're letting the events make the choices for us.

Here's another example. Consider our application's File → New menu item. It creates a new document window in which the user can type some text. When should the user be able to choose this menu item? Just about any time. So the Application subclass *would* be a good place to put the enabling code for *this* menu item, because it will receive an EnableMenuItems event at just about any time. In fact, the only time the Application subclass won't receive an EnableMenuItems event is if the frontmost window is modal; and that's good too, because if a modal window is frontmost, the user needs to work just within that window, and cannot be permitted to create a new document anyway—that, after all, is what it means for a window to be modal. Once more, we're letting the events make all the right choices for us.

Scope

By the *scope* of an entity we mean what other entities are able to see it, and when. You can give a method or property unlimited scope by putting it in a module, but this would violate object orientation. To realize this, just imagine putting *all* your code in a module! The application might work, but the code would be a horrible mess to read, write, and maintain; everything's scope would be too wide. The admonition to keep your scope narrow means: "Don't let any entity see or meddle with another entity it doesn't need to be able to see or meddle with." Paying attention to this admonition will cause your code's functionality to be encapsulated in the appropriate objects.

On the other hand, scope can become *too* narrow. A good example is an event handler, where the code is inaccessible to everyone except REALbasic itself. Suppose more than one event handler in an object needs to be able to perform the same functionality. One option is for the code to be duplicated in both event handlers; but this would pose unthinkable maintenance problems. Instead, that functionality should be promoted, to make its scope less narrow. But don't promote it too far, because scope should still be kept as narrow as possible! The minimum promotion is to put the shared functionality in a method in the same object, where both event handlers can call it. (Of course, if an event handler in another object needs to be able to perform the same functionality, then you have some serious further thinking to do about where that functionality should live.)

For example, consider the code in our word-processing application that responds to the user choosing the File → Save menu item. It writes out the text and style information from the frontmost document window's EditField to the file on disk associated with this window. First, who should respond to the menu event here? The document that is to be saved is the document represented by the frontmost window, so, in keeping with our first koan, we'll put the code into the document window class, in a FileSave menu event handler, and let REALbasic worry about which window is frontmost as it sends the menu event.

Now consider what happens when the user chooses the File → Close menu item or clicks the frontmost document window's close box. If the document is "dirty" (it's been changed since it was last saved), we will presumably put up a dialog asking whether the user wants to save the document before closing. If the user says yes, we must save the EditField's contents. The part of our code that knows how to do this is the same code that responds to the File → Save menu item. Now we'd like to be able to call that same code while responding to the File → Close menu item. But if the document-saving code is inside the FileSave menu event handler, we can't do that, because we can't call an event handler! Therefore, we need to widen the scope of this code. Instead of keeping it in an event handler, we'll promote it into a method, still in the document window class. Let's call this method DoFileSave. Now the FileSave menu event handler merely calls DoFileSave, and the code that responds as the window starts to close can also call DoFileSave if the user wants the document saved.

References Are the Thread

The art of writing a REALbasic application lies in getting references. The minimal unit of scope is the individual handler. Thus, you must make certain that any handler, when it executes, has access to the information it needs in order to do its job. Perhaps this information originates in a different handler or a different object, in which case it may have to be copied to where our handler can get hold of it. Or, it may be globally available, but perhaps our handler still needs to be told where to go to pick it up. The issue becomes one of not only getting but *communicating* references, from one handler to another. This is why our third koan represents handlers as patches, and references as the thread we use to stitch them together into a fine, whole garment.

There are two main ways to communicate a reference in REALbasic: pass it as a parameter, or leave it in a drop. These will now be described in turn.

Parameters

Parameters can be passed when calling a subroutine and, if the subroutine is a function, can be passed when returning as well. Here's an example where parameter passing would be used in our word-processing application. We have a menu event handler that responds when the user chooses File → Open; it puts up a standard File Open dialog, and after the user chooses a file, it creates a new document window, reads the text and style information from that file into the window's EditField, sets the window's Title appropriately, and stores a reference to the file in a property of the window so that the document can later be saved back to the same file. The user needs to be able to do this just about any time, so the FileOpen menu event handler goes into the Application subclass, and initially we put all the functionality into this menu event handler.

Later, however, we get to thinking about what happens when the user opens a file belonging to our application, not with our application, but from within the Finder. This, it turns out, causes the Finder to send an Apple event to our application, which is relayed to the Application subclass instance as an OpenDocument event. Clearly, then, the OpenDocument event handler and the FileOpen menu event handler need to share almost all their functionality—everything, in fact, except for the File Open dialog. So we move this functionality to an Application subclass method called DoOpen. But how will DoOpen know what file to open? The OpenDocument event handler knows, because it receives a FolderItem parameter from REALbasic telling it. The FileOpen menu event handler knows, because it sees, again as a FolderItem, what file the user chose in the File Open dialog. So clearly DoOpen should take a single parameter, a FolderItem, so that either the OpenDocument event handler or the FileOpen menu event handler, when calling it, can give it the information it needs.

Parameter passing, however, is often insufficient in REALbasic. You generally get no opportunity to pass a parameter to an event handler; thus, an event handler (or code called by an event handler) may need some other way to obtain the information it needs. Also, parameters alone don't maintain state; they live only as long as they are being passed from handler to handler. Since the information you'll be passing often will be state information, it ultimately may have to live somewhere else. In such situations, you'll probably use the other technique for communicating references—a drop.

Drops

A *drop* is a technique whereby you leave a value at some agreed-upon location where another routine can pick it up later.* The location will typically be a property, and the problem then becomes merely a matter of deciding on an appropriate scope for this property.

To illustrate, consider a question very frequently asked by beginners. I have a window open, and it gets closed. The next time it opens, I want it to appear in the same position as before. How do I do this?†

Suppose this window is the Find dialog in our word-processing application, which is modal but movable. Since there is only one Find dialog, and it is associated with the application as a whole rather than with any other window, clearly the Application subclass instance would be an appropriate object to remember its position. So we

---

* I have to admit that I chose this term based on my reading of too many spy novels.

† In Chapter 9 a different solution to this problem will be presented, one that I actually like better.

create two integer properties in the Application subclass: FindTop and FindLeft. As the Find dialog closes, it sets `app.findTop` and `app.findLeft` to its own Top and Left property values; when next it opens, it sets its own Top and Left property values based on `app.findTop` and `app.findLeft`. This exemplifies a typical drop; one routine (the Find window's Close event handler) leaves values where they can appropriately be maintained as state, and where another routine (the Find window's Open event handler) expects to find them.

Choosing between a parameter and a drop

Often one must choose between using a parameter and using a drop, and it isn't easy to provide a rule of thumb that will help in making the choice. You will develop your own style, based upon your own experience and your own philosophy of object orientation. I do suspect, however, that experienced programmers, trained by books and teachers to pass parameters and to avoid globals, may feel an aversion to drops, as being somehow ugly or dangerous. I don't think that's a fair assessment, and I find in my own code that although I can often devise elegant, tricky ways to replace a drop with a parameter, the resulting code is sometimes dubious and there's no clear gain in efficiency or neatness. The rest of this discussion, in any case, is intended not to give definite answers—there are none—but to illustrate the thinking process involved in weighing the pros and cons of parameters and drops.

Here's a common REALbasic situation: We want object A to instantiate object B; object B should later hand some information back to object A. How should this handing back be performed? For instance, in our word-processing application, when the user starts to close a document window, if the document is "dirty," we want to offer a chance to save it. So the document window, which we'll call DocWindow (object A) puts up a modal dialog, which we'll call SaveChanges (object B). The SaveChanges dialog has three buttons: Don't Save, Cancel, and Save. How is the document window that put up the dialog going to know which button the user pressed?

The relationship of DocWindow to the SaveChanges dialog is like the relationship of a caller to a function: DocWindow brings the SaveChanges dialog into existence just so the latter can come up with a piece of information and hand it back as it goes out of existence. It would thus be an appropriate expression of this relationship if the SaveChanges dialog could, to all intents and purposes, be a function; the knowledge of what button was pressed could then be the value returned. A window, however, is not a function, and an object does not have some way to return a value as it dies. In Chapter 9 we will see that in fact the SaveChanges dialog can be invoked like a function that returns a value, but this is a mere syntactic elegance. One way or another, DocWindow must know how to get from the SaveChanges window the information it wants; therefore a drop is no less reasonable than a parameter.

Now, the way to invoke a modal dialog in REALbasic is with a window's ShowModal method. The way to destroy a window is with its Close method. The rule about ShowModal is that the code that calls it pauses automatically until the modal window turns itself invisible (with Hide) or destroys itself (with Close); this behavior is what it means for a modal window to be modal. So, I see nothing wrong with the following scenario: The document window creates the SaveChanges dialog with ShowModal (and its code therefore pauses). The ShowModal dialog interacts with the user, who presses a button. The ShowModal dialog places information about what button was pressed into a drop—a property within itself. The ShowModal dialog then turns itself invisible. This permits the document window's code to resume. The document window picks up the information in the drop, and destroys the ShowModal dialog with Close. It's all very nice and neat, and object orientation is not violated. The use of a property within the ShowModal dialog as the drop is appropriate because it maintains the proper relationship: the document window is the master, the SaveChanges window is the servant; the SaveChanges window operates only upon itself, while the document window gets to boss it around, creating it, reaching into its innards to pick up what's in the drop, and eventually killing it.

So, within SaveChanges, the Action event handler of any of the buttons has this form:

```
self.buttonpushed = 1 // or whatever the code for this button is
self.hide // resume after the showModal call
```

And the code in DocWindow might look like this:

```
w = new saveChanges
w.showmodal // pause until SaveChanges hides itself
i = w.buttonpushed
w.close
```

Sometimes the best solution is a mixture of a parameter and a drop; the information is in a drop, but a parameter is used in order to say where the drop is. For example, let's say that our SaveChanges dialog contains some text which is to read: "Save changes to YourDocument?" Except that it won't say "YourDocument"; it will use the name of the actual document. The trouble is that the SaveChanges dialog doesn't know what this is, because it isn't associated with any particular document; it's the document window that invoked the SaveChanges dialog that has this information. So the document window should hand this information to the SaveChanges dialog. How?

Let's consider using a drop. Where might we drop the name of the document where the SaveChanges dialog can retrieve it? Not in a property of the document window; that would beg the question, since the very thing the SaveChanges dialog does not know is what window instantiated it! Very well; how about a property of the Application subclass? That works, but it's terribly ugly; we're violating object orientation. It depends upon a rule that lives only in the mind of the programmer, not in the program itself ("Before instantiating SaveChanges, first drop this information into this property"); it needlessly involves the Application subclass, which doesn't need to know about any of this; and it gives global scope to information that needs to live for only an instant. Clearly, a drop would have to be in the SaveChanges dialog. The process would be just the inverse of how we returned a value from the SaveChanges dialog, and has a nice symmetry: the document window invokes the SaveChanges dialog, sets a SaveChanges property to the name of the document, calls ShowModal so the SaveChanges dialog can interact with the user, retrieves the returned value from a different SaveChanges property, and kills the SaveChanges dialog.

There's nothing really wrong with this, but it leaves us open to error, since once again we have a rule that lives in the mind of the programmer ("After instantiating SaveChanges, then drop this information into this property"), and besides, I feel a little more reluctant to have one object reach right in and set a property of another object than I did to have one object fetch a value from another. We can use a parameter here, and so I lean toward doing so. So, for example, SaveChanges could have a method handler Init, which takes a string parameter; the document window instantiates SaveChanges and calls its Init method, handing it the name of the document, to do with as it pleases.

Now, if we're going to hand SaveChanges information to do with as it pleases, my feeling is, why not go all the way and hand SaveChanges all the information it can possibly want? Instead of Init taking a string parameter, how about having it take a DocWindow parameter? Instead of the document window handing SaveChanges just a string, it could hand SaveChanges a reference to itself! Now the SaveChanges dialog can extract whatever information it likes from the document window. This is a combination of a parameter and a drop; the information SaveChanges wants is inside the DocWindow instance somewhere, but SaveChanges needs a reference to the DocWindow instance in order to know to whom to send a message in order to get that information. In object-oriented programming, this sort of thing is extremely common.

Now our code in DocWindow goes like this:

```
w = new saveChanges
w.init(self) // pass reference to ourself; SaveChanges initializes itself
w.showmodal // pause until SaveChanges hides itself
i = w.buttonpushed
w.close
```

Actually, this can be expressed even more elegantly if Init returns a reference to the SaveChanges instance, like this:*

```
Function init(w as window) As SaveChanges
    // ... use w as desired ...
    return self
End Function
```

In that case, we can reduce the first two lines to one:

```
w = new saveChanges.init(self) // pass reference to ourself; SaveChanges initializes itself
w.showmodal // pause until SaveChanges hides itself
i = w.buttonpushed
w.close
```

---

* I owe this device to David Richards.

Before leaving this example, let me warn you against ingenious solutions where SaveChanges figures out what window invoked it by a process of deduction. After all, one might argue, the only way the SaveChanges dialog can appear is if it is summoned by a document window; therefore, the document window in question is surely the first window behind the SaveChanges dialog; therefore, SaveChanges can obtain a reference to the document window as window(1). The trouble is that this is purely an assumption, and it may not be justified. Suppose there are three dirty document windows open, and the user chooses Quit; things become very complicated, as REALbasic polls each window with the CancelClose event before closing any of them. In this situation, a window that isn't in front may well end up summoning the SaveChanges dialog. Also, as will be pointed out in Chapter 9, an invisible window might be present somewhere in the layering order. The moral is: don't try to substitute some other relationship (here, the order of windows) for the actual relationship (here, the instantiator and the instantiated). Thinking about how to hand information around can be hard work, but don't try to cheat your way out by not handing any information around at all! Your application should run by logic, not by guesswork.

The Application Subclass

A REALbasic application includes exactly one automatically generated instance of the built-in Application class, or its single programmer-defined subclass if there is one. (It is possible to create more than one subclass of the Application class in a project, but this should probably be considered a bug; only the first such subclass will be instantiated.) A reference to this instance is globally available through the App function.

In all probability, the only kind of application that could manage without an Application subclass is one that puts up a single window that is always present and (except for modal dialogs) always frontmost. We've already seen that, from an object-orientation point of view, the Application subclass is frequently the ideal place for global methods and instances, and for maintaining state (see "The Application Subclass" and "Class Properties and Class Methods" in Chapter 4, and "Drops," earlier in this chapter). This section summarizes the Application subclass's place in REALbasic's application framework.

The Application class has two built-in properties:

MouseCursor
Dictates the cursor's appearance (to be discussed in Chapter 20).

ResourceFork
Provides access to any resources in the resource chain, both those placed there by the system and those you've installed in your application through a Resource file (to be discussed in Chapter 21).

The Application instance receives an Open event and a Close event, as the application starts up and quits, respectively. The Open event handler in particular is your earliest opportunity to perform global initializations (examples appeared in "The Font Menu" and "Cross-Platform Considerations" in Chapter 6).

The Application instance receives a Deactivate event when the application suspends (another application comes to the front), and an Activate event when the application resumes (your application comes to the front after suspending); you might wish to respond to these changes. For example, if you raise a global flag when the application suspends, and lower it when it resumes, you can check the flag at any time to learn whether the application is in the background. You can't do this without an Application subclass. (Examples will appear in Chapter 21 and Chapter 23.)

The Application instance receives an EnableMenuItems event during menu-enabling moments, and a menu event when a menu item is chosen. It is thus the best repository for code to enable and respond to menus at the global level. (Details appeared in Chapter 6.)

The Application instance is the sole recipient of Apple events; if your application wants to receive Apple events, an Application subclass will be mandatory (Chapter 31).

The Application subclass is needed if your application has documents that the user is to be able to open from the Finder. When the user opens a document belonging to your application in the Finder, the OpenDocument event is sent to your Application instance; your application has no other way to learn that it should open the document (an example will appear in Chapter 24). Your code can also trigger an OpenDocument event by calling the Application's OpenDocument method.

When the user starts up your application by opening it (not a document) in the Finder, your Application instance receives a NewDocument event. You might wish to respond to this—by opening a blank default document, for example. Your code can also trigger a NewDocument event by calling the Application's NewDocument method.

Order of Events

All execution of your code is ultimately triggered by REALbasic sending an event; events, in turn, are triggered by actions performed by the user or by your code. A knowledge of what events are typically triggered over the lifetime of an application, and when, is useful both for developing your application's architecture and for achieving desired effects at the level of detailed code.

While the application is running, the user can do all sorts of things that will cause events to be sent. Moving or clicking the mouse, typing a key, changing the focus, moving or resizing a window, and so forth, will trigger events destined for controls or windows. Events of that sort, however, being specific to particular built-in classes, are discussed in Part II in connection with each class. The purpose of this section is to provide you with an overall picture of the order of events.

You should not try to memorize the information in this section! In fact, you shouldn't even read it very carefully; just glance over it, so you know it's here, and then consult it like a railroad timetable later on when you actually need it. You'll know you're reading this section too carefully if your eyes glaze over and you have to lie down for an hour or two; in fact, it might be a good idea to lie down now for a bit, just in case.

 REAL Software, Inc., have asked me to impress upon you that the order of events is officially undocumented and therefore subject to change. I describe the facts as observed empirically at the time of writing, but you should not rely too heavily upon the precise details of ordering presented here, since if these do change, your application will break if it depends upon them.

What follows is considerably simplified (believe it or not). I try to show differences between platforms; depending on how gross these differences are, one may regard them as a bug, though perhaps some differences are inevitable just because the platforms themselves manage things differently. Also troublesome are the differences in event order between a built application and the project running in the IDE.

On the menu-enabling moment, see "The Menu-Enabling Moment" in Chapter 6. The concept of Windows under MDI applies to document windows, but not to modal windows since these are outside the MDI.

Imagine a typical application with a default window. The basic sequence as the application starts up runs as follows:

- The Application instance receives an Open event.
- On Windows under MDI, the Application instance receives an Activate event.
- On Windows, the Application instance receives a NewDocument event.
- Each control in the default window receives an Open event. (The order in which the controls receive the Open event is determined through the Format → Control Order dialog.)
- The default window receives an Open event.
- The Application instance receives an Activate event (on Macintosh).
- If the default window has been set as visible, it appears, and receives an Activate event. (On Windows under MDI, this doesn't happen. On Mac OS X, the window receives a Paint event first.) If the default window has been set as invisible, it receives a Deactivate event at this point instead.
- If a control gets the focus, it receives a GotFocus event.

- There is a menu-enabling moment (not on Windows).
- The default window, if visible, receives a Paint event; this completes the drawing of the window. (On Mac OS X, this happens earlier.)
- The Application instance receives a NewDocument or an OpenDocument event (on Macintosh; but in the IDE, this happens earlier, before the Application instance receives the Activate event).

If your application is suspended (a different application comes frontmost):

- On Windows (but not under MDI), the front window receives a Deactivate event.
- The Application instance receives a Deactivate event.
- If the frontmost window contains a control with the focus, the window receives a Paint event to remove the focus ring (not on Windows), and the control receives a LostFocus event.
- The front window receives a Deactivate event (on Macintosh).
- There is a menu-enabling moment (not on Windows). The control is not involved, because it has already lost focus.
- The window receives a Paint event.

If your application is resumed (it comes frontmost after having been suspended):

- The Application instance receives an Activate event.
- The front window receives an Activate event (not on Windows under MDI).
- If the front window has a control with the focus, the control receives a GotFocus event.
- There is a menu-enabling moment (not on Windows).
- Newly uncovered windows get a Paint event.

If a new window is instantiated invisibly:

- On Windows under MDI, the old window receives a Deactivate event.
- Each control in the new window receives an Open event.
- The new window receives an Open event.
- The new window receives a Deactivate event (on Macintosh).
- There is a menu-enabling moment (not on Windows).
- On Windows under MDI, the old window receives a Paint event.

If a new window is instantiated visibly:

- On Windows under MDI, the old window receives a Deactivate event.
- Each control in the new window receives an Open event.

- The new window receives an Open event.[*]
- On Macintosh, if the new window is modal, and on Mac OS X, the new window receives a Paint event.
- If the window that was previously frontmost contains a control that had the focus, that window receives a Paint event to remove the focus ring (not on Windows), and the control receives a LostFocus event.
- The previously frontmost window receives a Deactivate event (not on Windows under MDI).
- The new window receives an Activate event (not on Windows under MDI).
- If the new window contains a control that gets the focus, that control receives a GotFocus event.
- There is a menu-enabling moment (not on Windows).
- The new window and the old window receive Paint events. (But on Macintosh, if the new window is modal, and on Mac OS X, the new window's Paint event was earlier.)

If the user switches between two existing windows:

- The newly frontmost window receives a Paint event (not on Windows or Mac OS X).
- If a control in the old window had the focus, that window receives a Paint event to remove the focus ring (not on Mac OS X), and the control receives a LostFocus event (not on Windows).
- The old window receives a Deactivate event.
- The newly frontmost window receives an Activate event.
- On Windows, if a control in the old window had the focus, the control receives a LostFocus event.
- If the new window contains a control that gets the focus, that control receives a GotFocus event.
- There is a menu-enabling moment (not on Windows).
- Both windows receive Paint events (on Windows under MDI, just the newly frontmost window receives a Paint event).

If a window is closed:

- The window receives a CancelClose event; if this returns true, that's all, and the window does not close.
- If a control in the window has the focus, the window receives a Paint event to remove the focus (not on Windows), and the control receives a LostFocus event.

---

[*] In the IDE, this is followed by some extraneous events: the new window gets a Deactivate event, and there is an extra menu-enabling moment. I regard this as a bug.

- Each control in the window receives a Close event.
- The window receives a Close event, and vanishes.
- If this causes a different window to be frontmost, it receives a Paint event if part of it was uncovered (not on Windows or Mac OS X)
- The new window receives an Activate event.
- The new window's focus-getting control, if any, receives the GotFocus event.
- If a window is still open, there is a menu-enabling moment (not on Windows).
- The newly frontmost window receives a Paint event.

When the Quit procedure is called:

- Each window receives a CancelClose event; if any window returns true, that's all, and the application does not quit.
- The Application instance receives a Close event.
- If the frontmost window has a control with the focus, the window gets a Paint event, and the control gets a LostFocus event.
- For the frontmost window, every control in the window receives a Close event, and the window receives a Close event. It vanishes, and the next window may receive a Paint event. This repeats with the next window, and so on until it has happened for every window.
- On Windows under MDI, the Application instance receives a Deactivate event.

CHAPTER 8
Debugging and Building

This chapter covers topics connected with the final stages of transforming your project into an application: how to do it, figuring out why you can't, figuring out why you can but your application doesn't work anyway, and other considerations leading up to that culminating moment when you declare your application finished.

Compile Errors

Just before you run your project in the IDE or build it into an application, REALbasic pauses to look for errors in your project's code. REALbasic at this moment is *compiling* your code (transforming it into a language that your computer can understand), and so such errors are termed *compile errors*.

If REALbasic discovers a compile error, compiling comes to a halt; you cannot run or build the project. Instead, REALbasic opens the Code Editor where the error was found, selects the line containing the error, and shows beneath that line a popup window describing the error (see Figure 8-1).

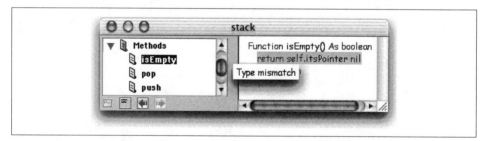

Figure 8-1. A compile error

You can dismiss the popup window by clicking anywhere, and at that point you have to try to figure out, from REALbasic's description, what's wrong with your code. This is not always easy, because REALbasic is thinking like a machine, so its description of the problem may not be of much help to a human being. Even if you understand what the error message *says*, you still must figure out what the problem really

Number of Parameters

REALbasic often has a curious way of complaining that you've omitted a parameter. If a procedure MySub takes two parameters and you supply just one, REALbasic is so nearsighted that it concentrates only on the missing comma:

```
mySub "hello" // error: ',' expected
```

If you foolishly believe REALbasic's explanation and add a comma, you get another unhelpful message:

```
mySub "hello", // error: Unexpected end of line
```

Similarly if you omit a single required parameter:

```
self.theArray.remove // error: Unexpected end of line
```

Here's a particularly uninformative example of the same error message; what REALbasic really means is that this subroutine is a function, so the Return statement must actually return something:

```
Function myFunction() As integer
    return // error: Unexpected end of line
End Function
```

Just the other way, if you give a procedure too many parameters, REALbasic describes it like this:

```
msgbox "hello", "goodbye" // error: Unexpected token
```

When this gets combined with REALbasic's odd way of quibbling over spaces and parentheses, you can really become confused. Wrapping the two parameters in parentheses gets you an even more mysterious result:

```
msgbox ("hello", "goodbye") // error: ')' expected
```

So you try removing the space before the parentheses, and what happens?

```
msgbox("hello", "goodbye") // error: Unknown identifier
```

Define Your Terms

There are a lot of names floating around in a REALbasic project, and you may well become confused about what's what. But REALbasic won't be confused, so if you use a name, but it doesn't designate the thing you think it does, or the kind of thing you think it does, or it isn't a thing that REALbasic can see from this context, REALbasic may well slap your hand.

A trivial example occurs when you use a variable name that hasn't been declared:

```
for i = 1 to 3 // error: Unknown identifier 'i'
```

But sometimes the trouble is that you're not referring to what you think you're referring to. You can't say the following in a button's Action event handler in a window's Code Editor:

```
msgBox caption // error: Unknown identifier 'caption'
```

Even though the button has a Caption property, you're speaking (by implication) of `self`, meaning the window, which has no such property.

Thus, when you get certain error messages, such as "Expecting an lvalue," "Type mismatch," and "Unknown identifier," if the cause isn't immediately obvious, you should look carefully at the datatype of everything involved. This can involve quite a bit of physical hunting through the IDE.

For example, this actually happened to me one day while working on a little word-processing application. I hadn't seen the code in some time, and I had no idea what was supposed to be happening in this line, let alone what might be wrong with it:

```
find.useTM = app.useTM // error: Expecting an lvalue
```

Tracking down the problem was quite an ordeal; until you know what `find`, `find.useTM`, and `app.useTM` are, you have no clue as to what REALbasic really means. In this case, I had to work out that `find` was a window class, open its Window Editor, select various controls there while watching the Properties Window until I found the one whose name was UseTM, study that control's properties, and then open the Application subclass and study *its* properties, before I understood what I had been trying to say when I wrote the code. It turned out that `find.useTM` was a CheckBox (a kind of button), and REALbasic was complaining because you can't assign to an instance's global name. On the other hand, `app.useTM` was a boolean. A CheckBox does have a boolean property, its Value; `find.useTM.value` is what I had intended to assign to.

When you're juggling references to superclasses and subclasses, it's easy to become confused. Here's an example from my early days with REALbasic. In my word-processing application, I wanted to put up a Find dialog in which the user can type some text to search for in the frontmost document window. The Find dialog was modal, and therefore frontmost; and I believed that the second window was a DocWindow containing an EditField named DocWindowEditfield. So I fetched a reference to the second window by means of the Window function, and started blithely talking about it. REALbasic complained:

```
dim w as window
dim s as string
w = window(1)
s = w.docwindoweditfield.text // error: Unknown identifier 'docwindoweditfield'
```

The error message is somewhat opaque, but after a while I got the idea. I had said `w` was a Window, but a Window has no `docwindoweditfield` member. So, I declared `w` as a DocWindow instead, only to hit a different snag:

```
dim w as docwindow
dim s as string
w = window(1) // error: Type mismatch
s = w.docwindoweditfield.text
```

The problem here is that the Window function returns a Window, and you can't assign a superclass to a subclass reference! The fact is, I was right to declare `w` as a

DocWindow, since otherwise I couldn't talk about its controls, but I needed to cast the result of the Window function, since otherwise I couldn't assign it to w:

```
dim w as docwindow
dim s as string
w = docwindow(window(1))
s = w.docwindoweditfield.text
```

For further ways to use names recklessly and confuse yourself hopelessly, see "Resolution of Names" in Chapter 3.

Exceptions

Not every error in your code can be caught during compilation, because some errors depend upon values that won't be known until the application is actually running. From a purely syntactic point of view, there's nothing wrong with this:

```
dim a(4) as integer
dim i as integer
for i = 1 to 5
    a(i) = i
next
```

But the code is doomed anyway, because when it actually runs, the last time through the For loop, it will attempt to talk about a(5)—and there will be no a(5). If you build your application and run it, when this code executes, it puts up a dialog (shown in Figure 8-2) and terminates prematurely. Albeit politely and gently, your application has crashed.

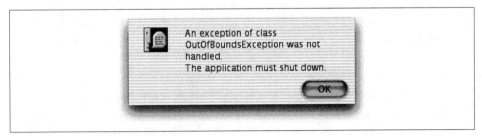

Figure 8-2. A runtime error in the application

If you run the same code in the IDE, the running project still terminates, but things are better in one respect—you learn where in your code this happened. As the running project vanishes, it drops you into the IDE, where a popup window appears below the offending line and describes the error (see Figure 8-3).

This is an example of a *runtime error*, technically known as an *exception*. Most of the time, you'll probably try to eliminate runtime errors from your program in advance, perhaps with the help of the debugger, which is discussed in the next section. After all, a runtime error stops your program dead in its tracks. But it does so only if, as the dialog in Figure 8-2 says, it is "not handled." In this section, we discuss what this

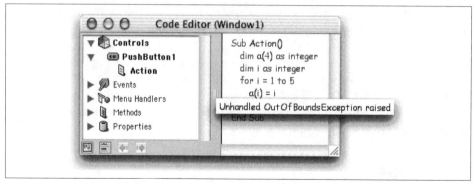

Figure 8-3. A runtime error in the IDE

means. You'll discover how you can have runtime errors without your program necessarily stopping, and how you can, in fact, generate runtime errors intentionally, as a way of communicating between parts of your code.

The Calling Chain

The *calling chain* is the set of event handlers and methods that are currently suspended, waiting for the presently executing subroutine to return. To see what this means, recall that the only reason any code ever runs in REALbasic is because REALbasic sends an event to an instance, and this event is handled by an event handler. Somewhere in its middle, that event handler may call a method, and now it can't proceed until the method returns. Somewhere in *its* middle, the method performs some action that triggers another event, and so another event handler is called; now the method can't proceed until that event handler returns. And so forth. So we can envision the subroutine in which a runtime error occurs as being at the end of some calling chain that started with the original event sent by REALbasic.

Now picture an exception as a message, which is sent from the subroutine where the runtime error occurs up through the calling chain to REALbasic itself. When the message reaches REALbasic, REALbasic doesn't know what to do; all it knows is that something unrecoverable has happened. So it dies, and your application terminates with as much grace as REALbasic can muster.

Exception Blocks

REALbasic terminates because it doesn't know what to do in the face of the runtime error; but your code might know. An *exception block* is a way for your code to *catch* an exception on its way up through the calling chain, to stop it from percolating all the way up to REALbasic (thus preventing the termination), and perhaps to respond to it in some sensible way. By catching the exception, your code may be able to continue running rather than letting your application fall to its metaphorical knees.

The syntax of an exception block is as follows:

```
exception errorParam as errorType
    // ... code goes here ...
```

The $errorType$ is optional; if it is omitted, the $errorParam$ is optional as well. Their use will be explained in a moment. The exception block should always be the last thing in its subroutine, because everything after the Exception line will be seen as part of the exception block. The subroutine may end with several exception blocks, however, and they will be seen as distinct; the reasons why you might want to do this will be clear presently.

If a runtime error occurs in the course of executing a subroutine, execution will abort right then and there, and an exception will start percolating back up through the calling chain. If the subroutine in which the error occurred, or any subroutine anywhere along the calling chain, is found to contain an exception block, the exception stops there, and that exception block will start executing.

Let's begin with a simple example. Suppose the Action event handler for a Push Button goes like this:

```
Sub Action()
    dim f as folderItem
    msgBox "All is well"
exception
    msgBox "Something went wrong"
End Sub
```

When the button is pressed, only the dialog saying "All is well" appears. There was no error, so the exception block is ignored. Now let's cause something to go wrong:

```
Sub Action()
    dim f as folderItem
    f.delete
    msgBox "All is well"
exception
    msgBox "Something went wrong"
End Sub
```

The command f.delete constitutes a case of sending a message to a nil pointer; that's a nil object error. Execution of the main part of the subroutine aborts at that point—but there's no crash. REALbasic generates a NilObjectException, but this exception never percolates all the way up to REALbasic itself, because it is caught in the exception block. The result is that when the button is pressed, the dialog saying "Something went wrong" appears, and that's all; the application then blithely continues running.

RuntimeException and Its Subclasses

The purpose of the $errorParam$ is to permit the exception block to receive the exception itself, as an instance. To be precise, the exception is an instance of the RuntimeException class or a subclass thereof, and you can test its type using IsA. Exceptions generated by REALbasic will be of one of five types, represented by five subclasses of

RuntimeException. Here are the types and the basic reasons each would be generated:

NilObjectException
You tried to send a message to a nil pointer.

OutOfBoundsException
You tried to access an array item using too large or too small an index.

StackOverflowException
The calling chain got too long—because you tried to recurse too deeply, for example.

IllegalCastException
You cast an object to a different class and sent it a message its real class couldn't accept.

TypeMismatchException
You tried to assign to a reference a value of the wrong datatype. This can arise only in situations where the compiler can't determine the value's datatype at compile time, such as when assigning a variant.

There is also an undocumented EndException, which is REALbasic's internal device for aborting the calling chain when you call Quit; if you catch an EndException and prevent it from reaching REALbasic, your Quit call will fail.

So, we can capture the incoming exception and respond differently depending upon its type:

```
Sub Action()
    dim f as folderItem
    f.delete
    msgBox "All is well"
exception err
    if err isA nilObjectException then
        msgBox "I knew this would happen"
    else
        msgBox "I wasn't expecting this"
    end
End Sub
```

However, in order to save us the trouble of testing for each exception type with an If structure, REALbasic lets us write more than one exception block, each of which is destined for only one type of exception. This is what the *errorType* parameter is for. So, the previous example would be equivalent to this:

```
Sub Action()
    dim f as folderItem
    f.delete
    msgBox "All is well"
exception err as nilObjectException
    msgBox "I knew this would happen"
exception
    msgBox "I wasn't expecting this"
End Sub
```

To test that this is working properly, you can introduce a different error, one that is not a NilObjectException:

```
Sub Action()
    dim f as folderItem
    dim a(3) as integer
    a(4) = 10 // error: OutOfBoundsException
    f.delete
    msgBox "All is well"
exception err as nilObjectException
    msgBox "I knew this would happen"
exception
    msgBox "I wasn't expecting this"
End Sub
```

Sure enough, the dialog reads "I wasn't expecting this." The exception was filtered out by the first exception block, so it was the second exception block that caught it and executed.

Raise

One of the things you might like to do when you've caught an exception is to continue passing it on up through the calling chain. In the previous example, suppose we are prepared to ignore most exceptions, but if we get a NilObjectException we would like the application to go ahead and die. The way to do this is with the Raise statement. It takes an instance of the RuntimeException class or a subclass thereof; and we can get a reference to such an instance as the *errorParam*, so we can just turn around and send this on its way up the chain:

```
Sub Action()
    dim f as folderItem
    dim a(3) as integer
    a(4) = 10
    f.delete
    msgBox "All is well"
exception err as nilObjectException
    raise err
exception
    msgbox "Something bad happened, but let's keep running."
End Sub
```

You cannot use Raise to pass an exception from one exception block to another in the same subroutine; if Raise is used in an exception block, the exception proceeds on up through the calling chain.

Custom RuntimeExceptions

Now comes the Really Interesting Part. Since an exception is a subclass of Runtime-Exception, and since we are permitted to subclass RuntimeException ourselves, and since we can send such an exception up the calling chain with Raise, it follows that we can create our own exception types and send them. This provides a powerful, object-oriented way to jump out of running code, without the use of GoTo, and without being restricted to jumping just within the current subroutine; we can raise an exception, and catch it with an exception block in the same subroutine or anywhere up the calling chain.

The only trick here is that since Raise takes an instance, we must remember to generate such an instance, using New. We do not necessarily need a variable to hold the resulting instance, though; we can generate the instance right in the Raise statement. So, if we have subclassed RuntimeException to make the MyException class, we could say:

```
Sub Action()
    raise new myException
exception
    msgBox "Cool, I generated my own exception"
End Sub
```

A custom RuntimeException subclass can have methods and properties, like any subclass. What sort of property would an exception have? Any we like, but since an exception is a kind of error message, the text of the message is an obvious choice! Let's give MyException a string property called Text. Now before we raise the exception we'll attach some text to it. The exception block, when it catches the exception, can retrieve this text and do something with it, such as display it to the user.

In this example, we imagine that it is to be a runtime error to run the program during 2001. If it is 2001, we raise a MyException error, using its Text property to describe the problem:

```
Sub Action()
    dim err as myException
    dim d as date
    d = new date
    if d.year = 2001 then
        err = new myException
        err.text = "Sorry, you can't run this program during 2001!"
        raise err
    end
End Sub
```

We can catch the exception and take appropriate action, in the same subroutine or higher up the calling chain:

```
exception err as myException
    msgBox err.text
    quit
```

The next example illustrates that RuntimeException subclasses can be used to encapsulate functionality, like any other class. It also shows that a RuntimeException instance can be a property instead of a local variable, like any other instance. Finally, the example shows that the instance can even raise itself!

We continue pretending it is to be an error if the program runs within a certain year; but to make things interesting, we suppose that there are several such years. We'll modify the MyException class so that in addition to the Text property, it also has a YearList property that is an array of integers. We'll give MyException a MyException method, a constructor, which initializes YearList:

```
redim yearList(2)
yearList(0) = 2001
yearList(1) = 2002
yearList(2) = 2003
```

And we'll give MyException a CheckYear method, which examines the current year and raises itself if it's an illegal year:

```
dim i, u as integer
dim d as date
d = new date
u = ubound(yearlist)
for i = 0 to u
    if yearlist(i) = d.year then
        text = "Can't run during " + str(d.year) + "!"
        raise me
    end
next
```

We'll store an instance of this class as a global by making it a property of the Application subclass, named YearChecker. In the Application subclass's Open event handler, we'll make sure to generate the instance:

```
yearchecker = new myException
```

Now, at any point in our program's code, we can check the year, and raise an exception if it's a bad year—all in a single line!

```
app.yearChecker.checkYear
```

Earlier it was said that exceptions are a useful device for jumping out of running code. A common case is when a routine must terminate with some sort of *cleanup* operation. For example, suppose that at the start of a routine we set the cursor to the watch (Chapter 20):

```
app.mouseCursor = watchCursor
```

Before exiting our routine, we wish to remove the watch, returning control of the cursor to REALbasic:

```
app.mouseCursor = nil
```

But suppose our routine has many exits. For instance, at various points in the routine we perform some sort of test; if the test fails, we return. But we cannot just return; we must also remember to set the MouseCursor to nil. If we do this manually before every Return statement, the result is inelegant and invites confusion. The best way is to end our routine with an exception block that cleans up:

```
exception err as selfRaiser
    app.mouseCursor = nil
```

Now suppose we've got a global instance of SelfRaiser, a RuntimeException subclass with a Raise method where (guess what) it raises itself. Then we can exit our routine and clean up, at any point, by saying:

```
app.selfRaiser.raise
```

As a bonus, this works even in subroutines called by our routine.

Another powerful technique is to use *assertions*. An assertion is a boolean expression that we hope and believe is true, but if it is false we should terminate. We hand the boolean to a RuntimeException, which raises itself if it is false.

In this example, the exception will both raise itself and catch itself! Create a RuntimeException subclass called Assertion, with a Text property, and with a method Assert, which takes two parameters, a boolean and a string, like this:

```
Sub assert(b as boolean, s as string)
    text = s
    if not b then
        raise me
    end
exception err as assertion
    msgbox err.text
    quit
End Sub
```

Let there be a global instance of Assertion called Assertion, living as a property in the Application subclass. Now at any time our application can assert the truth of an expression; if that expression is false, the application will quit, showing an informative message which we also supply. Often, this takes only one line; for example:

```
// ...
app.assertion.assert((new date).year <> 2001, "App run in illegal year.")
// ...
```

A wise precaution is to sprinkle your application liberally with assertions. You hope that none of them will ever raise an exception, because that means you've got a bug somewhere; but if one of them does raise an exception, it may prevent some worse occurrence (such as an unhandled exception or a crash), and it is accompanied by a dialog that lets you know where the problem is, to help you track down your bug. This approach to error handling is very professional. When your users phone you to report the problem, they'll also be telling you how impressed they are.

The Debugger

Recall how, in the previous section, we used too high an array index and ended up with a runtime error that terminated our running project, as shown in Figure 8-3. Let's suppose now that it's not evident to you *why* this line is problematic. What can you do to track down the source of the trouble more precisely? You can use the debugger. And the debugger is helpful with other kinds of problem as well. For example, even if you don't get a runtime error, perhaps the program is not behaving as expected. You're pretty sure that the trouble lies in a certain subroutine. The debugger can help you obtain some details about just what your code actually does when that subroutine is executing.

Breakpoints and Stepping

REALbasic's debugger is not sophisticated, but at least it's straightforward. To use it, you need to have set a *breakpoint* in your code. In the IDE, select a line where you want to start debugging, and choose Debug → Set Breakpoint. A big red diamond appears, as shown in Figure 8-4. Now run the project in the IDE, and, acting as the user, do whatever you need to do to cause that code to execute. When the breakpointed line is just about to execute, the running project suspends, and REALbasic drops you into the IDE, which is now acting as the debugger.

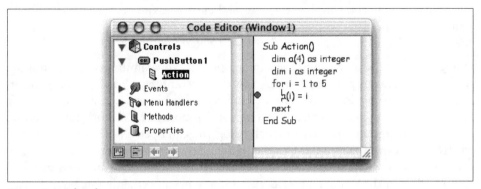

Figure 8-4. A breakpoint

In your code, a green arrow shows the line that is about to execute; initially, of course, this is the breakpointed line. You can now proceed forward through the code in various ways, watching the path of execution by noting where the green arrow goes. Figure 8-5 shows what happens after dropping into the debugger at the breakpoint and then proceeding forward one line, which is called *stepping*.

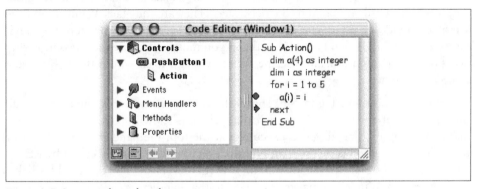

Figure 8-5. Stepping through code

Choosing Debug → Step Over or Debug → Step Into causes execution to advance by a single line; the difference between them is that with Step Over, the green arrow will afterward be located on the next line to be executed in the same subroutine, but with Step Into, the green arrow will afterward be located on the first line of a subroutine called or triggered by the indicated line (if there is one). Choosing Debug → Step Out causes your code to execute until a breakpoint is again encountered, or until the present subroutine returns, whichever comes first. If you use Step Out repeatedly and no breakpoints are encountered, you back all the way out the calling chain and resume running the project. A shortcut to back all the way out the calling chain in a single step is to choose Debug → Run; you'll find yourself back in the running project, unless a breakpoint is encountered on the way up the chain.

You may recall that it is possible to change your code in the IDE while the project is running. In the debugger, you can't do that—well, you can, but the project will usually stop running. You can, however, set and clear breakpoints. (To clear a breakpoint, select the line containing the breakpoint and choose Debug → Clear Breakpoint.) Note that breakpoints don't persist after your project is closed.

While acting as the user within the running project, you can drop yourself into the debugger manually by hitting Ctrl-C. You can't be entirely certain of the point in your code at which you'll drop into the debugger, though, and in any case this trick works only if your code is actually running—it has no effect if the program is sitting idle. In an emergency, such as a modal dialog you can't get rid of, just click any of the IDE's windows, behind those of the running project; you're not in the debugger, but at least now the running project can be killed. In Mac OS X, in an emergency you can usually quit the running project (and if not, you can certainly force-quit REALbasic itself). Unfortunately, there is no code command that drops you into the debugger.

The Debugging Windows

When you fall into the debugger, there are two special debugging windows present. (Actually, these windows are present any time your project is running in the IDE, but they are blank until you fall into the debugger.) They are the Stack Window and the Variables Window. These windows remember their visibility setting from the previous session, so if you don't see one of them, you must have closed it on some earlier occasion; to summon it again, use the Window menu from within the IDE while a project is running.

The Stack Window (see Figure 8-6) shows the calling chain, listing the names of all the handlers currently executing. The calling chain is shown upside down: the handler containing the line about to execute is at the top, the handler that called it or triggered its execution is below that, and the event handler initially called by REALbasic is at the bottom. (In Version 3.5, this order is reversed.) You can double-click a line in the Stack Window to navigate quickly to that handler.

Stack

Window1.Moved
Window1.myWindowMoverMethod
Window1.myReallyDeepMethod
Window1.myDeeperMethod
Window1.myMethod
Window1.PushButton1.Action

Figure 8-6. The Stack Window

The Variables Window gives you some idea of the values of the variables visible to the current subroutine (see Figure 8-7). In this example, the Variables Window shows me that i is 1, and as I step through the code I can watch i increment until it reaches 5, which ought to be enough to help me understand my bug. In fact, the Variables Window even lets you change a value, just like the Properties Window, so I can even alter i as the code proceeds and confirm that preventing it from reaching 5 averts the error.

Objects and arrays can be investigated by pressing a View button in the Variables Window; the result is an Object Window. An Object Window is read-only. Objects that are properties of objects or elements of arrays are shown in an Object Window as hyperlinks; clicking the link brings up another Object Window. Arrays of objects can be displayed as a list of those objects or as a list of some particular property of those objects (use the popup menu at the top of the array's Object Window).

Unfortunately, you can't use the debugger to explore your application freely. The only objects available in the Variables Window are those that are local to the subroutine containing the green arrow, or global in a module. The workaround, if you can plan ahead, is to capture as a local variable any value that you're likely to be interested in. For example, if I need to know what `myOtherWindow.checkBox1.value` is at this moment, the Variables Window won't tell me; but if I have previously captured it as a local variable of this subroutine for debugging purposes, I can examine that variable:

```
tempBoolean = myOtherWindow.checkBox1.value
```

In REALbasic 3.5, clicking a handler name in the Stack Window changes the Variables Window context to that handler.

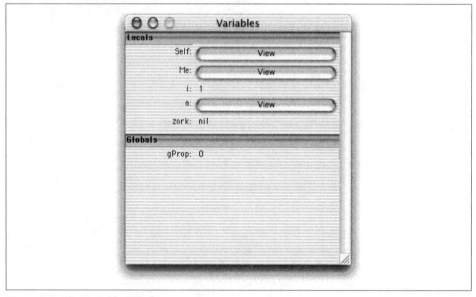

Figure 8-7. The Variables Window

Additional Debugging Strategies

You can supplement REALbasic's native debugging facilities by inserting signals of your own into your code, so that you can learn, as your project runs, what code is executing and what values are being operated on. Such techniques have the advantage of being available even in a built application, and are often more convenient than a breakpoint even when running in the IDE.

One such signal is obviously a MsgBox call, putting up a dialog containing whatever information you're curious about. An occasional word from your application that "I'm starting the MyMethod subroutine" or that "x is currently 6" can be immensely helpful.

On the other hand, sometimes MsgBox is unsatisfactory, because a dialog might be too intrusive. For example, you wouldn't want to put up a dialog in an EnableMenu-Items event handler, because it would appear too often, and would interfere with your ability to choose menu items. If you're examining how a window repaints itself, an extra dialog may cause false results. And a MsgBox dialog within a loop that iterates many times becomes tiresome.

In situations of this sort, sound might be a better cue; this lets the program signal where it is and what it's doing, without clogging up the interface of screen, mouse, and keyboard. Judicious use of calls to the Beep procedure may prove quite sufficient. You can distinguish between different points in the program's code by using a

Minor Options

Before building your application, you should assign it a four-letter creator code, also sometimes referred to as its *signature*. This is done by choosing Edit → Project Settings and typing four letters into the Mac Creator field.

Your application's creator code identifies your application to the Macintosh filesystem, and therefore it should be unique among all Mac applications, so that, for example, double-clicking a document belonging to some other application doesn't open yours by mistake. There is an easy way to find out whether your contemplated creator code is already in use: Apple keeps a database, which you can search online.*

Another concern should be your application's icon. This isn't crucial, and there's nothing wrong with just using the system's default application icon, but having your own icon is better form, better advertising, and easier on the user. (Besides, working on your icon will give you something to do during the periods when you're too exhausted to program.) You can draw an icon using the simple icon editor included in ResEdit, or you can capture art directly from your screen, or you can use a paint program; there are also a number of dedicated tools you can use to help design your icon.† The important thing is that you must end up with an entire icon family; the various icon creation utilities will help with this, or you can paste into a folder's Get Info dialog to have an image converted automatically into an icon family (which you can then edit further with one of the utilities). When your icon is ready, copy the icon family from your icon utility or from a Get Info dialog, and paste it into the Icon box of the Build Application dialog. Alternatively, the icon family can be included in your application through a Resource file, and in certain cases this may be a better option; for example, an 'icns' resource, ID 128, is the only way to give your application a Mac OS X icon. (Your application may also have documents of its own that need icons; this is discussed in Chapter 21, as are Resource files.)

The Name field of the Build Application dialog is where you specify your application's name. Recall the warning in Chapter 1: be careful not to type a name identical to that of any file in the same folder as your project, as this file will be overwritten without notification when you build the application.

The Language popup menu determines how your global constants will be evaluated. Recall that a global constant can have different values for different languages, and that you can also use these values to localize text in the interface (such as button captions). If you choose Default, the language setting will be taken from the Default Language popup in the Edit → Project Settings dialog (which might itself be Default).

---

* See *http://developer.apple.com/dev/cftype/find.html*. There is also a link to a list of all ASCII characters that can be used in a four-letter creator code; any character from &h20 to &hFB is eligible, except for the unprintable &h7F. Ideally, when your application is ready, you should register your creator code (and any associated file type codes) with Apple, so that no one else uses it.

† Some intriguing possibilities are *http://www.mscape.com*, *http://www.iconmachine.com/iconmachine.html* and *http://www.iconfactory.com/ib_home.asp*.

The material in the Get Info group box is where you create your application's 'vers'(1) and 'vers'(2) resources.* The version number is mostly for your own use, but the three version string entries will be visible to the user, so you should give some thought to what you want them to say. Figure 8-8 shows where your entry in the Short Version field might be displayed in a Finder listing; Figure 8-9 shows where your entry in the Package Info and Long Version fields might be displayed in a Get Info dialog.

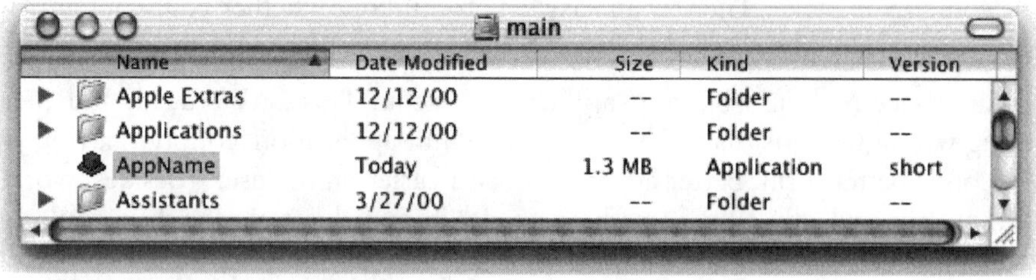

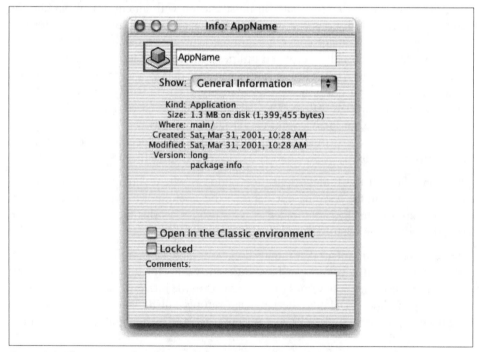

Figure 8-8. The short version string displayed in the Finder

Figure 8-9. The version info and long version strings in a Get Info window

---

* To learn more about these, see *http://developer.apple.com/techpubs/mac/Toolbox/Toolbox-454.html*.

Build Type

A crucial decision is what sort of build you want to produce. You have a choice of three platforms: Macintosh (meaning what I refer to in this book as Mac OS Classic), Mac OS X, and Windows. A Mac OS Classic application can run on any Macintosh with a 68020 processor or better and System 7.6.1 or later, and will run under Mac OS X in the Classic environment. A Mac OS X application can run under Mac OS X, or under Mac OS 8.6 or higher using the CarbonLib extension. You can't build for Mac OS Classic and Mac OS X simultaneously, and if you're going to build for both you should be careful to change the application name before the second build or you'll overwrite the output of the first build. A Windows executable can run on Windows 95 or later. You can build for Windows simultaneously with either of the other two.

When building for Mac OS Classic, you can generate 68K code, which will run on 68K machines and in emulation on PowerPC machines; or, you can generate PowerPC code, which will run natively on PowerPC machines but won't run on 68K machines at all; or, you can produce both types of code in a single application (a so-called "fat" application), which will run natively on both sorts of machine.*

The choice of Mac OS Classic, Mac OS X, and Windows will probably be clear to you, but within the Mac OS Classic category it's worth pausing over the question of whether to build for PowerPC or 68K or both. What you're weighing in making this decision are mostly factors of target audience, speed, and size on disk. If you don't care that your application isn't backward-compatible to those users who have not yet upgraded to PowerPC machines, then there is no reason not to build a PowerPC-only application and have done with it. If you assume that your user has plenty of disk space (not an unreasonable assumption these days), then there is probably no reason not to build a fat application, which will be backward-compatible. If the size of the application is a worry, you might opt for 68K only: REALbasic genuinely compiles your project into Macintosh native code, but it wraps this code in a framework that occupies some room on disk, something around 300K for a 68K application and about 1MB for a PowerPC application (and so about 1.3 MB for a fat application), which is a significant size difference. As for speed, you may well find, depending on how fast your processor is and how intensively or noticeably your application makes speed demands, that there is little benefit in including any PowerPC code in your application at all. Nevertheless, PowerPC code can be significantly faster. And there may be other reasons why your application needs to be PowerPC-native: some features, such as calling shared libraries or performing text encoding conversion (which requires a shared library), are present only on PowerPC; and 68K is sometimes said to be harder to support, since there are various quirky things that don't work well there (problems with ByRef and internal number representation have already been noted).

---

* "68K" designates a processor that is a member of the Motorola 68000 family.

When building for Windows, the choice of Language is still relevant, but 68K/PPC is not. The big decision you have to make is whether or not your executable is to run under MDI, the multiple document interface. If not, then your running executable will appear as separate free-floating windows, which can interleave with any other executable's free-floating windows; your default window will contain your menus. If you elect the multiple document interface, then all your executable's document windows will appear as child windows within a single main parent window; the parent window will hold the menus, and its title will be whatever you have typed in the Caption field.

Heap Size and Memory Management

On Mac OS Classic, the size of your application's RAM heap is a particularly daunting decision. (On Mac OS X and Windows, fixed heaps don't exist, and the application can use as much as necessary of RAM and, through virtual memory, the hard disk. You do still have to think about heap size if your Mac OS X application is to run under Mac OS 8 or 9 with CarbonLib.) Your goal here is mostly to make sure that the heap is sufficiently large for all the objects and data your application is ever going to be maintaining at any single moment. Although the user can, of course, set your application's heap size to anything at all in the Get Info window in the Finder, you are responsible for the default size, and your application can't increase its own heap size while running. Furthermore, you can't count on REALbasic to handle tight memory situations in a graceful or predictable way. There is no built-in exception that tells you automatically that an operation failed because there wasn't enough memory. If your application fills up its heap, you may get a NilObjectException when you try to access an object that REALbasic failed to create because there wasn't enough room; that, at least, could be counted an orderly shutdown. But in some cases, REALbasic will simply misbehave and leave you none the wiser. For example, I have seen REALbasic simply ignore certain graphics commands and proceed as if all was well; and I have even seen REALbasic freeze the computer under tight memory situations (though I believe it is considerably better behaved in this regard than it used to be).

Presuming that your application doesn't freeze, what can you do to prevent it from running out of memory? If the user is allowed to place unlimited demands on your application, such as opening files whose data must be held in memory, discretion is clearly the better part of valor: the heap is finite, so the user *can* do something that will cause the application to run out of memory, and you have no way of knowing that this *won't* happen, so you should assume that, unless you prevent it somehow, it *will* happen. Clearly, catching a NilObjectException, or explicitly testing for nil after creating an object, can be an important safety net. For example, having constructed an offscreen graphics area with the NewPicture function, or having asked for a block of memory with NewMemoryBlock, if the result turns out to be nil, you can recover gracefully: you can put up a dialog warning the user that there isn't enough memory to proceed, and you won't make the mistake of sending the nonexistent instance any messages.

You can also use testing for `nil` as a crude form of "preflighting" a contemplated operation. A reasonable rule of thumb is to require that the heap have twice as much free memory as you are about to request. So, for example, if the user is about to open a file to be read into memory, try using NewMemoryBlock to create a block of memory twice as large. If this fails, you can tell the user you can't read in the file. (If it succeeds, don't forget to set the memoryblock reference to `nil`, to destroy the huge instance you just created for testing purposes!)

To see the value of this approach, put this code into a button's Action event handler, give the same window a StaticText, build the application, run it, and press the button:

```
dim i as integer
dim m as memoryblock
for i = 1 to 1000000 step 1000
    m = newMemoryBlock(i)
    statictext1.text = str(i)
    statictext1.refresh
    if m = nil then
        return
    end
    m = nil
next
```

The routine grabs larger and larger blocks of memory until eventually it asks for more than the heap can supply. The application thus runs out of memory right before your eyes. On my machine, using the default heap size of about one megabyte, the StaticText's display runs up to 530001 and stops. Looking at the application's heap with Memory Mine before pressing the button, there are slightly over 500,000 bytes of free space, so clearly we are getting the sort of answer we'd expect.

An alternative is to use a Toolbox call (as explained in Chapter 32). The following code, run before the button is pressed, reports a value of 514,560 bytes of free space, so once again we are in the right ballpark:

```
declare function FreeMem Lib "InterfaceLib" () as integer
msgbox str(freemem())
```

Various external tools can provide a sense of how much of your application's heap is in use at any given moment. Such tools need not be costly. Metrowerks's Zone Ranger, the demo version of Memory Mine, and Apple's own Macsbug are all free; these can give detailed information about how the heap is being used. The shareware Peek-a-Boo gives a simpler view of the heap, but it's an easy way to create a log showing your application's memory usage over time.* The idea here would be to run the built application, stressing it as much as possible (for example, if it's a word-processor, opening lots of large documents and editing them heavily), and monitoring its heap.

---

* For Zone Ranger, see *http://www.metrowerks.com/tools/software/zoneranger/*. For Memory Mine, see *http://www.adianta.com/files/MMDetailsTxt.html*. For Peek-a-boo, see *http://www.clarkwoodsoftware.com/peekaboo/*.

An internal device for gauging memory use is the built-in Runtime object. This object has a MemoryUsed function which tells you the total memory occupied by objects. So:

```
i = runtime.memoryUsed
```

Unfortunately, it isn't entirely clear how to use this information. Your heap contains at least two other sorts of entity besides the objects whose space is totaled here. First, there is the code and resource overhead of your application as a whole, the memory that is already occupied before your application tries to do much of anything. Second, certain blocks of memory, such as strings, Pictures, and memoryblocks, are not counted by the MemoryUsed function. So the total memory in use is something like the value of the MemoryUsed function, plus all strings, Pictures, and memoryblocks, plus some unknown amount occupied by the code. Thus, you're still largely in the dark about the *total* memory used. Besides, MemoryUsed tells you nothing about how much memory is *unused*. But that is what you wanted to know—not how much memory do my objects occupy, but how much *more* memory can I ask my objects to occupy?

Nonetheless, the MemoryUsed function is able to draw an important distinction that FreeMem and the various external tools cannot. Recall that we were able to obtain a memoryblock of nearly 530,000 bytes, even though FreeMem and the various external heap analysis tools were telling us that only about 514,000 bytes were free. What accounts for this difference? It turns out that in the case of objects (that is, things whose memory usage is measured by MemoryUsed), REALbasic actually allocates and holds more space in the heap than it needs. As memory demands start to climb, REALbasic can give back some of the empty part of this object-space allocation. From the outside, therefore, REALbasic will always appear to have less free space than it really has, because some of the object-space allocation, which is not technically free, is not in fact occupied by objects and can be released at need. The MemoryUsed function, on the other hand, measures the actual object space in use.

Another memory-related concern is whether there's anything wrong with your program that might fill up the heap accidentally, even in normal usage. It's possible that your application may perform an action that grabs some memory and never releases it, so that if this action is performed repeatedly, free memory is gradually consumed. This is the so-called *memory leak*.

One should distinguish carefully whether it is the programmer or REALbasic who is leaking memory. REALbasic's use of memory may not exactly be an open book, but that's no excuse for your behaving unconsciously or irresponsibly; if memory can get tight in your application, and you're using more memory than you need to, you've only yourself to blame. For example, if a memoryblock is a property of a persistent object, and you set it to a large block of memory and never set it to nil, even when you no longer need it, you've effectively robbed yourself of that memory. A more subtle example is this: if you have a reference with an instance assigned to it, and you're going to create a new instance and assign it to that same reference, set the instance to nil first if memory might be tight. The reason is that when you set the instance to nil, if this was the last reference to the old instance, the memory occupied by the old instance is released, so there is that much more room in which to create the new instance. Whereas, if you create the new instance and assign it to the reference in a single line, the evaluation of the righthand side of the assignment takes place before the assignment does—meaning that the new instance is created first (or not, if there isn't room!), and the old instance's memory isn't released until afterward:

```
dim m as memoryblock
m = newmemoryblock(whatOldSize)
// ... do stuff ...
m = nil // don't omit this step!
m = newmemoryblock(whatNewSize)
```

See "Destruction of Instances" in Chapter 3 for more about how your code might fail to release an instance from memory.

On the other hand, REALbasic itself can simply misbehave. If there are no references to an instance and that instance doesn't die, REALbasic's garbage-collection system is falling down on the job, and REALbasic itself is leaking memory; that would be a bug in REALbasic. At various times in REALbasic's history, there have been various memory leaks; many have been fixed, but you may discover that some remain. In these situations, if you can't avoid doing whatever causes the leak, your only option is to write to the management and complain.

REALbasic provides three internal tools for seeing whether memory is being released and objects destroyed. First, in the debugger, an Object Window vanishes when the object it points to is destroyed. So the technique here is to set a breakpoint at some stage that will allow you to drill down from the Variables Window to an Object Window for the object you're interested in. If, as the project resumes running, the Object Window does *not* vanish, you know the object *hasn't* been destroyed.

Second, there is the DebugDumpObjects procedure. You call this procedure, supplying as parameter a string that will become a filename, and your application responds by creating a new textfile (overwriting any existing file of this name) consisting of two things: the amount of the heap currently in use, and a list of the classes of all objects currently instantiated.

Third, the built-in Runtime object gives you the same information as the DebugDumpObjects procedure, and more, without making a log file. We've already seen how its MemoryUsed function reveals the space occupied by objects. Its ObjectCount property tells how many objects there are; you can then refer to these objects by index number. The ObjectClass function takes an index number and returns the class of that object. Here's how to use these functions to populate a ListBox with a list of all objects by class:

```
dim i,u as integer
listbox1.deleteAllRows
u = runtime.objectCount-1
for i = 0 to u
    listbox1.addrow runtime.objectclass(i)
next
```

I believe that the list is in order of instantiation, most recently instantiated objects first. Furthermore, each object has a unique ID, which you can get with the ObjectID function; this allows you to keep track of particular objects. Finally, the ObjectRefs function tells the number of references to an object.

Pragmas

A *pragma* is a code directive to the compiler that makes some difference in the way subsequent code is compiled into the built application. To use a pragma, start a line of code with the #pragma keyword, and follow it with the name of the directive.

The chief pragma is DisableBackgroundTasks:

```
#pragma disableBackgroundTasks
```

The effect is to prevent all code that follows this line, within the same subroutine, until the end of the subroutine, from yielding any time to other threads—meaning other threads of your application and other processes running on this computer. As far as I can tell, this pragma *makes no difference in the IDE*; it comes into effect only in the built application.

Code that runs under the DisableBackgroundTasks pragma will execute as fast as possible, because REALbasic dispenses with its usual rules about being nice to other processes; thus, this is a useful pragma in calculation-intensive situations. It isn't very polite behavior, to be sure, but sometimes you just want your application to hog the CPU ruthlessly, and this is how to make it do so. This pragma also prevents the normal automatic refreshing of the interface, so certain interface elements, such as ProgressBars, will appear frozen unless you refresh them manually.

When a subroutine runs under the DisableBackgroundTasks pragma, subroutines that it calls are unaffected; so you may want to add the DisableBackgroundTasks pragma to those other subroutines as well. Unfortunately, the very act of calling a subroutine adds overhead that can become quite noticeable when there are many repetitions; short of simply not making any subroutine calls, which is usually not desirable and sometimes not practical, there's nothing you can do about this (REALbasic does not have inline subroutines).

DisableBoundsChecking is a pragma that turns off the feature that checks the validity of your index values when you refer to an element of a boolean array, presumably to increase speed of array access. It doesn't apply to any other sort of array.

Target Flags and Conditional Compilation

Your application's code can learn where it is running, and take different actions accordingly, by testing various built-in global boolean flags—the target flags. Debug-Build tells whether you are running in the IDE. TargetWin32 (meaning Windows) and TargetMacOS (meaning Macintosh in general) tell which platform your application has been built for. TargetCarbon, TargetPPC and Target68K permit your TargetMacOS application to learn whether it has been built for Mac OS X, PowerPC, or 68K.

Normally, it will be sufficient to use the target flags as conditions and take action accordingly. (For an example, see "Cross-Platform Considerations" in Chapter 6.) Under some circumstances, however, the ability to execute target-specific code may not be sufficient; there may be code that for some reason must not even attempt to compile when you're building for a certain target. In this situation, you can use *conditional compilation*. Surround your code with the directives #if and #endif, testing in the #if line for a global boolean, such as a target flag or a boolean constant in a module. There is also an #else directive that can be used between them. Thus:

```
#if targetmacos
// ... Mac-only stuff goes here
#endif
```

An example is Apple events. Apple events don't merely not work on Windows; even mentioning Apple events in Windows code will cause the Windows executable to terminate prematurely. If you wrap all code that mentions Apple events in the TargetMacOS conditional compilation test, it won't find its way into the Windows build, and all will be well.

PART II

User Interface

The Macintosh utilizes a graphical user interface (GUI), and you'll probably want your application to take advantage of this. From the user's point of view, the interface is the visual metaphor that most distinctively characterizes your application. From your point of view as a programmer, the interface is your line of communication with the user, operating in both directions: not only will a well-designed interface present the user with good visual cues for navigating your application and viewing information, but also it is the means whereby your application will be aware that the user is giving it commands and interacting with it.

REALbasic makes it easy to construct and manage your application's interface through a number of built-in classes that handle this bidirectional communication—on the one hand, presenting the visual interface to the user by drawing and updating the screen, and on the other hand, receiving communications from the user by way of the mouse and keyboard. These classes include such familiar components of the visual arsenal as windows, buttons, editable text fields, and so forth. Part II describes these classes, explaining how your code can most easily and effectively manage them, to dictate what appears on the screen and to respond to user actions.

Many of these classes have a second purpose quite apart from their onscreen interactive abilities. Through their properties and built-in functionality, they are often your best choice as primary repositories of your application's data; that is, they are, in and of themselves, data structures, often accompanied by useful methods for managing that data. For example, an application displaying styled text in an EditField will usually have no need to maintain the text and style information in a data structure of the programmer's own devising, since the EditField itself is already handling this task.

The chapters are:

Chapter 9, *Windows*
Chapter 10, *Abstract Control Classes*
Chapter 11, *Canvases*
Chapter 12, *Buttons and StaticTexts*

This chapter describes REALbasic's built-in Window class and explains the details of its use.

Figure 9-1 shows some of the standard types of window that REALbasic creates. At the left is the fundamental common or garden type of window, which REALbasic calls a *document window*, where the user would typically work. This one has all the standard window features: a titlebar with a close button, a zoom button, and a Mac OS X minimize button, plus a grow box at the lower right. Next comes a floating window; this is a utility window, and the user can work in the document window even though the floating window is layered in front of it. Finally, at the right, there's a movable modal window; while present, it prevents the user from working in any of the other windows.

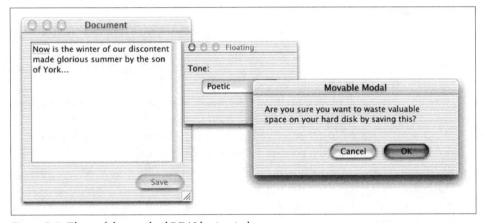

Figure 9-1. Three of the standard REALbasic window types

Certain window-related events and properties are described elsewhere in connection with their topic: on the KeyDown event, see Chapter 13 and Chapter 19; on the DropObject event and on methods relating to drag-and-drop, see Chapter 24; on the EnableMenuItems event, see Chapter 6; on the Paint event, see Chapter 11 (though there is some discussion of it in this chapter as well); on the MouseCursor and BalloonHelp properties, see Chapter 20.

Windows were absolutely revolutionary when they were developed at Xerox PARC during the late 1960s, and it was an astonished world that first was introduced to these marvels of ingenuity in their initial Macintosh implementation in 1984. Windows are so characteristic of and fundamental to the very notion of a graphical user interface that at least one major operating system uses the actual word "windows" in its name.

With time and acquaintance, users of GUI applications have come, by and large, to take windows for granted, concentrating on the interface elements that appear within them and noticing the windows themselves only subconsciously if at all. Yet the primacy of windows remains. In just about any application, they are the basis of the interface, since every visible component of that interface must reside within some window. (On Macintosh, menus are the only exception.)

This primacy of windows, which sets them above and apart from all other interface elements, is expressed in REALbasic by the primacy of window classes as an element of a project. In Part I, several facets of windows were pointed out that make them unique among REALbasic's stock of built-in classes. Here is a quick summary of earlier material about windows; if any of this is unfamiliar, you might want to review before proceeding:

- Every new project is endowed with a window class, by default. Other window classes are created using File → New Window (see Chapter 1).

- Window classes are listed in the Project Window, ranking with programmer-defined classes and modules (see Chapter 1).

- Window classes have their own graphical editor, the Window Editor (see Chapter 1).

- Window classes can "contain" instances of other classes. Such contained instances are called controls. When a window class is instantiated, it automatically instantiates all of its contained controls. Controls within a Window Editor are actually instructions to the window class to perform this instantiation. Code attached to a control instance, edited in the containing window class's Code Editor, actually belongs to the containing window class (see Chapter 3).

- Every project has at most one default window class, which will be instantiated automatically as the application starts up. You use the Project Settings dialog to determine what class this is. All other window instances must be generated through code (see Chapter 3).

- Your code is guaranteed a reference to one instance of every window class, by way of its global instance name. The default window instance is such an instance (see Chapter 3).

- Code within a window's Code Editor can refer to that window as self, which may be omitted as the first element of a dot notation expression (see Chapter 3).

- A window class may be instantiated implicitly merely by using the global instance name, if an instance by this name doesn't already exist. Apart from implicit instantiation and the default window, window classes are instantiated with New (see Chapter 3).

- Your code can learn the number of existing windows through the Window-Count function, and can obtain a reference to any window, in terms of its layering order, by means of the Window function, where the frontmost window is window(0) (see Chapter 3 and Chapter 6).

Window classes cannot be subclassed. This is an inconvenience when you'd like to create a Window class that is like some other Window class you've created except for such and such a feature. But it isn't really a problem if the feature in question is something that can be set in code. For example, the presence or absence of a control can be set in code, because controls can be made visible or invisible.

In the Properties Window, there is a distinction in a window class's Super popup between the Window class and its Applet and Dialog subclasses, but it is not clear that this has much meaning, so perhaps it's a bug. Only the Applet class has a documented distinguishing feature: it can be sent the ShowURL message. But ShowURL is available as a global method in any case, so the Applet ShowURL method is redundant, which seems like a bug too. I suggest you just ignore the Super setting when creating a window class.

For the sake of completeness: the ShowURL method causes the user's browser to try to display the URL that is given as the call's parameter. For example:

```
showurl "http://www.tidbits.com"
```

Window Types

Each window class is of some single type which broadly determines its behavior (modal, nonmodal, floating) and the characteristics of its frame (whether it has a go-away box, whether it is resizable by the user, its general appearance). The type is immutable; it is set in the IDE and cannot be changed in code.*

The property that principally determines a window's type is its Frame. This is an integer from 0 to 7, representing one of eight familiar varieties of window. When you change the Frame property, there is no alteration in the look of the window in the Window Editor—it still has a go-away box, a grow icon in the corner, and so forth; that's because what you're looking at is the Window Editor's window, not the window itself. To experiment with the look of a window type, give a window that type, run the project in the IDE, and show the window.

---

* For some read-only properties, such as a window's Frame, it is not an error to try to set them in code, but it has no effect either. Perhaps the failure of the compiler to complain is a bug.

Modal, Nonmodal, and Floating Windows

There are actually just four basic window types; other types are cosmetic variants of these:

Nonmodal
> The ordinary main window type. Can be dragged by its titlebar,* and can be layered behind other windows. On Mac OS X, this is the only type that can be minimized into the Dock.

Modal
> Not draggable. Wants to be frontmost in its application. I say "wants to be" because you can subvert this layering behavior if you really try. (For example, you can force a nonmodal window to come in front of a modal window. But the modal window still prevents working in the nonmodal window, so this would be a silly thing to do.) Prevents all user operations except working within itself; if the user tries to click in another window of the same application, the system beeps. On Windows and Mac OS X, strict modal behavior is forbidden, so a modal dialog still permits working in another application, like a movable modal dialog.

Movable modal
> Can be dragged by its titlebar. Wants to be frontmost in its application. Does not prevent the user switching to another application, but the system beeps if the user tries to click in another window of the same application.

Floating
> Also known as a *utility window*, *windoid*, or *palette*. Can be dragged by its titlebar. All floating windows are always layered in front of all nonmodal windows. A floating window permits working within another floating window, or within the frontmost nonfloating window, as if that window were actually frontmost. Becomes invisible when the application is suspended—but not on Windows.

Recall from Chapter 6 that when a modal window (including movable modal) is frontmost, the Application subclass instance and MenuItem subclass instances don't receive any menu-related events. On such occasions, the QuitMenuItem is disabled by default—though not on Mac OS X, where resisting quitting is entirely up to the modal window's CancelClose event, which should return true—and in general all menu items should be disabled, except those needed for the user to work directly within the modal window. For example, if a modal window contains an EditField, the EditPaste menu item and so forth should be enabled when the EditField has focus, which is what happens by default.

Recall also that a floating window does not receive any menu-related events; they are passed instead to the first nonfloating window behind it.

---

* Under some Macintosh systems, or if certain third-party extensions are present, a window may also be draggable by its border. But I will just say "titlebar," rather than "titlebar or border."

The Frame Property

Here are the varieties of window type, categorized by Frame setting:

0—*Document Window*

Nonmodal. Has a zoom box, a go-away box, and a grow icon. Any of these can be suppressed by setting the ZoomIcon, CloseBox, or GrowIcon property to false.

1—*Movable Modal*

Movable modal. Has no zoom box, go-away box, or grow icon; the ZoomIcon, CloseBox, and GrowIcon settings are ignored (but not on Windows).

2—*Modal Dialog*

Modal. Has no titlebar. Has no zoom box, go-away box, or grow icon; the ZoomIcon, CloseBox, and GrowIcon settings are ignored.

3—*Floating Window*

Floating. Has a go-away box and a grow icon, which can be suppressed by setting the CloseBox or GrowIcon property to false; has no zoom icon, and the ZoomIcon setting is ignored.

4—*Plain Box*

A document window (the user can switch away from it), but lacks both a titlebar (like a Modal Dialog) and a border. Has no zoom box, go-away box, or grow icon; the ZoomIcon, CloseBox, and GrowIcon settings are ignored. On Mac OS X, looks just like a modal dialog, although it isn't modal. On Windows, this type *is* modal, and not distinguished from a Modal Dialog.

5—*Shadowed Box*

Like Plain Box, but with a slight shadow behind it. But on Mac OS X, it looks like a movable modal window, except that it isn't modal and can be minimized into the Dock.

6—*Rounded Window*

Nonmodal. Has a black titlebar, no border, rounded corners. Has a go-away box, which can be suppressed by setting the CloseBox property to false; has no zoom box or grow icon, and the ZoomIcon and GrowIcon settings are ignored. Under the Appearance Manager, has no windowshade box. On Windows, not distinguished from a Document Window. Unusable on Mac OS X.

7—*Global Floating Window*

Floating. Identical in appearance to Floating Window; its behavior calls for some extra discussion, which follows.

On Mac OS X the CloseBox and ZoomIcon are represented by the close and maximize buttons; these are always present when there's a titlebar, but can be inactive. There's a dot that appears in the close button when the window is "dirty"; you can place or remove this dot by a call to the Toolbox routine SetWindowModified. The line break in the second line here isn't real (the line was too long to fit on this page):

```
dim i as integer
declare function SetWindowModified lib "CarbonLib" // no line break!
   (w as integer, b as boolean) as integer
i = setwindowmodified(window1.macwindowptr, true)
```

On Windows, the CloseBox, ZoomIcon, and GrowIcon properties are reflected in appropriate ways. For example, there is no grow icon, but GrowIcon dictates whether a window can be resized. The ZoomIcon is represented by the minimize and maximize buttons; these cannot appear without a close box (and so setting Close-Box to false when ZoomIcon is true has no effect).

If you're willing to delve a bit into the mysteries of the Macintosh, you can mix and match frame appearances and window behaviors. A window has a MacProcID property, which is an integer; if set to nonzero (in the IDE only), the window will be drawn using the frame appearance corresponding to that MacProcID, but its behavior will usually still be in accordance with its Frame setting. For example, with a Frame of 3 and a MacProcID of 2, you get a floating window with no titlebar or border. On Mac OS X, a Frame of 3 and a MacProcID of 1057 gives a floating window that works like a Mac OS Classic floating window; this is useful to know, since as of this writing REALbasic's floating windows don't always behave properly on Mac OS X. Also on Mac OS X, a Frame of 3 and a MacProcID of 1088 yields a "sheet" (a dialog that pops down from the titlebar of the window that summons it with Show-Modal—see "ShowModal," later in this chapter). Many other useful effects can be achieved in this way.[*]

Global Floating Windows

Global floating windows are rather a remarkable feature of REALbasic. They are windows with the ability to appear in one or all applications other than yours. Indeed, a global floating window doesn't really "belong" to your application at all; its purpose is to function as a "guest" in some other application, so as to give the user a way of communicating with your application, which runs in the background. The user can mouse around in a global floating window (clicking buttons and working with ListBoxes, for example) and can even type into an EditField. Even readers with extensive vocabularies will surely admit that "cool" is an appropriate adjective here.

---

[*] The tip about sheets comes from Jim McKay and Will Cosgrove. For some further possible MacProcID values, see the online help; see also *http://developer.apple.com/techpubs/macos8/HumanInterfaceToolbox/ WindowManager/WindowMgr8Ref/WindowMgrRef.b.html* and *http://developer.apple.com/techpubs/macosx/ Carbon/HumanInterfaceToolbox/WindowManager/Window_Manager/index.html*; or for a more helpful presentation, see the tutorial by Sascha Leib, at *http://www.tietovalta.fi/~sascha/realbug/*. Observe that, as Sascha's tutorial explains, the MacProcID can also be used to access a custom WDEF (window definition); so, for example, you can have a window of arbitrary shape. A parallel effect can be achieved on Windows using Toolbox calls; an example by REAL Software's William Yu, on the REALbasic CD, shows you how.

A global floating window's FloaterProcess property, which can be set only in code, determines which application it will appear in—the four-character creator code of the desired application, or the empty string to mean all applications. (On Windows, this feature is absent; a global floating window can be brought forward of any process.)

A single global floating window cannot be set by means of the FloaterProcess property to appear in, say, exactly two specific applications, but you can easily devise a workaround to achieve the same effect. For example, your code could instantiate the class twice and assign each instance a different FloaterProcess value. The two windows won't be the same window, of course, but nothing prevents you from using code to create the illusion that they are.

Global floating windows are somewhat more limited on Mac OS X: they can only be universal (FloaterProcess does nothing), and you can't give any controls in them the focus. Nevertheless, a universal global floating window with no EditFields or List-Boxes does work acceptably, though you may have to set the AutoDeactivate of all controls to `false`.

Opening and Closing, Showing and Hiding

If a window class is not set to be invisible upon instantiation, then instantiating it causes a physical window to appear on the screen. Because of this connection between the class's instantiation and the appearance of its physical avatar, instantiating a window is also called *opening* the window. For the three ways to instantiate a window, see the beginning of this chapter, and Chapter 3.

It is also possible to destroy a window instance. If the physical window is visible on the screen, then destroying the instance causes the physical window to vanish. Because of this connection between the instance's destruction and the vanishing of its physical avatar, destroying a window instance is also called *closing* the window. The process of closing a window can be initiated in three ways:

- By sending it the Close message in code
- By the user's clicking in the window's go-away box
- By the application quitting

As we shall see, none of these actually closes the window unless the window agrees to be closed.

The fact that a window instance can be explicitly destroyed is rather remarkable, since this is by no means true of instances of every class. In general, while your code is free to instantiate a class, destruction of an instance is usually left to REALbasic's garbage-collection mechanism, which destroys the instance when there are no more references to it. The reason windows are different is that, given the way an application is typically structured, it makes sense for the physical window on the screen to have a life of its own: once opened, it should persist until closed. Since the window on the screen is merely a representation of an instance, the instance persists until explicitly destroyed.

Thus, code may bring a window into existence like this:

```
dim w as window
w = new window1
```

But the local variable w is not absolutely needed in order to obtain a reference to the window, since the Window function can supply that, and the window will still persist even after this subroutine has come to an end and w has gone out of scope.

The behavior of references to a window after it has been sent the Close message is somewhat odd. Let's say we have two window classes, Window1 and Window2. And let's say Window1 has a property, W, whose type is Window2. We create a new instance of Window2 and use W to maintain a name for it:

```
window1.w = new window2
```

This causes Window2 to be instantiated, and a new window appears. Then, we say this:

```
window1.w.close
if window1.w = nil then
    msgbox "it is nil"
else
    msgbox "it is not nil"
end
```

The first line causes the window to vanish, but then the message dialog reads, "it is not nil." That's odd; W has no window to point to, yet it isn't nil? So perhaps it still points to Window2, which is merely invisible. So, we try this:

```
window1.w.show
```

This is the oddest part of all: nothing happens. No new window appears, but we don't terminate prematurely either. Evidently, W isn't nil, but whatever it points to is not an instance that can be used for anything; in effect, W points to a closed window, and a closed window can't be reopened. We cannot, therefore, query W to ascertain whether its window has closed. One workaround is to assign nil to W ourselves when we close the window. Another is to examine W's MacWindowPtr property; if this is 0, the window has closed.*

Invisible Windows

A window's visibility status can be accessed through its boolean Visible property, and can be changed either by setting its Visible property or by sending the window instance the Show or Hide message. The value given to a window class's Visible property in the IDE determines whether the physical window will be made visible at the time the class is instantiated—and even then, a window whose class's Visible property is set to true in the IDE can be brought into existence invisibly, as we shall see. (On Windows, invisible windows are meaningful and well behaved only under MDI.)

---

* I owe this insight to David Fultz.

An invisible window can still be manipulated in code, in all the usual ways—for example, its size and position can be changed, its titlebar text can be changed, its controls can be sent messages, and so forth—but the user sees none of this as it occurs. Also an invisible window is among the windows counted by the WindowCount function and referenced by the Window function. It is even possible for an invisible window to be the frontmost window, in the sense that it can be the window returned by saying window(0). Of course, an invisible frontmost window won't appear to the user to be frontmost, since it won't appear at all; the frontmost visible window will seem to the user to be frontmost absolutely, as indicated by its activated titlebar, the user's ability to work in that window, and so forth. Furthermore, an invisible window, though it can receive events, does not receive any menu-related or mouse-related events. Thus, a frontmost invisible window doesn't interfere with the user's (and the application's) relationship with the frontmost visible window.

The chief use of an invisible window is to maintain state. For example, suppose that the user has made various settings in a window and then closes the window, and that it is desired, if the window is shown again, that it should display the same settings. When we tackled this problem earlier, in Chapter 7, using a Find dialog as our example, we elected to solve it by means of a drop: we captured the Find dialog's settings in global properties as the window closed, and then restored the settings from those properties when the window opened again later on. Another possibility, though, would be not to close the Find window at all, but rather just to hide it. This gives the *illusion* that the window has closed; but it is present, and if it is shown again later, its settings will not have changed.

Such a solution has a certain object-oriented elegance, since it clearly seems appropriate that the window itself should be the object to remember its own settings. On the other hand, one must consider the implications for how other aspects of the application will be implemented. Suppose that the Find dialog, instead of closing, turns invisible as a way of maintaining its settings. If we were also implementing the Window menu as shown in "The Window Menu" in Chapter 6, that implementation would break, because it relies upon an assumption that if there are any windows at all, they are document windows; it is not prepared for the possibility that there is an invisible Find window somewhere in the layering order of windows. There are two problems: we don't want to list the invisible Find window in the Window menu; and, if there is an invisible Find window amongst the windows, the index number of a menu item that the user chooses from the Window menu will not necessarily be the value we should hand to the Window function in order to bring the right window to the front.

However, this is not to say that the invisible Find window is a bad idea—only that it will call for a strategy of distinguishing between window types, which is perfectly acceptable. Suppose, then, that we implement an invisible Find window, but our Window menu must list only document windows. Suppose document windows are of class DocWindow. The following routine, which will probably need to be globally accessible and so should be stored in the Application subclass, returns a reference to the nth DocWindow instance (zero-based), or nil if there is no such window:

```
Function nthDocWindow(n as integer) As docWindow
    dim i,j,u as integer
    if n >= windowcount then
        return nil
    end
    u = windowcount-1
    for i = 0 to u
        if window(i) isa docWindow then
            if j = n then
                return docwindow(window(i))
            else
                j = j + 1
            end
        end
    next
    return nil
End Function
```

Now if we want to implement our Window menu using the WindowMenuItem class from Chapter 6, we modify that class's EnableMenu event handler to look like this:

```
dim w as docwindow
if self.index = 0 then
    rebuild
end
w = app.nthdocwindow(self.index)
if w <> nil then
    self.visible = true
    self.text = w.title
else
    self.visible = false
end
self.enable
```

And the WindowMenuItem class's Action event handler now becomes this:

```
app.nthdocwindow(self.index).show
```

So, having an invisible window on the scene isn't problematic; it just means that your code cannot make certain overly simplistic assumptions.

Let's consider some further circumstances under which an invisible window might be useful. Imagine that your application may at some point need to show a window whose state, when and if it appears, will depend upon actions the user has taken previously. As a simple example, consider a log window, which lists, in an EditField, things the user has done during the present application session. We can instantiate the log window invisibly as the application starts up, and then maintain the log directly in the EditField; if the user asks to view the log, it will then suffice simply to show the log window, which has been ready for viewing all along. Now, this particular example might seem rather artificial, because we could have maintained state in some other way, namely, as a string. But suppose further, when the log window appears, that some of the items listed in the EditField are to be bold. (It doesn't matter what the significance of this would be; perhaps all actions that generated errors are to be bold.) That's something that can't be incorporated into a string, because a string has no style information. We could implement some other sort of data structure to differentiate nonbold text from bold text, but surely at this point we are just making things hard for ourselves, since a styled EditField is *already* just such a data structure! Thus, it is often easiest, when maintaining state, to use a control in an invisible window.

A control in an invisible window is also frequently used as a "scratch pad" to perform operations that require a control but that we do not wish the user to see. Suppose, for instance, that we have an EditField in a visible window, and we desire every occurrence of the letter "e" in that field to turn red. This can be done in code by selecting one instance of the letter "e" and telling the EditField to turn the current selection red, then selecting the next instance of the letter "e," and so forth. (This is discussed in Chapter 13.) The trouble is that if we do this in the visible EditField, the user can see the instances of "e" turning red successively, and there is a disturbing flicker as the EditField is redrawn after each change. A solution is to copy the information from the visible EditField into an EditField in an invisible window, perform the changes there, and then copy the information from the invisible EditField back to the visible one. This causes the user to see the EditField change all at one time.

When a New Window Is Shown

There are clearly two ways to bring a window into existence, yet have it be invisible: the window class's Visible property can be set to false in the IDE beforehand, or the window can be instantiated and then made invisible, even though its class's Visible property is true in the IDE. You might worry that using the second approach would cause the window to appear for a moment and then vanish—but it doesn't.

(Actually, on Windows, both ways cause the window to appear and then vanish. I consider this a bug, and I have not found a good workaround. On the whole, therefore, this section is about Macintosh only.)

It turns out that as a window is instantiated, changes can be made to the window before it is actually shown. The rule seems to be that a newly instantiated window does not appear before the eyes of the user until all code in the current calling chain has finished executing and the application is idle. Thus, your code can instantiate a window and then proceed to alter outward properties of that window, such as its position or its titlebar text, or even its Visible property value, without the user seeing those changes occur.

However, your code can short-circuit this process by sending the window the Show message. This forces the window to appear on the screen right then and there—and subsequent changes to the window may indeed happen visibly. Note that this does *not* occur if your code merely sets the window's Visible property to true; this is one difference between sending the Show message and setting the Visible property.

When a window class is instantiated implicitly by means of its global instance name, the new instance receives the Open event before the line that instantiated the window actually executes. For example, suppose we set up a conflict as to a window's title, by instantiating a window like this:

```
myOtherWindow.title = "Hello" // implicit instantiation
```

but by having MyOtherWindow's Open event handler say this:

```
self.title = "Bonjour"
```

The new window's title will be Hello, proving that first the Open event handler set the window's title, and then the line that instantiated the window changed it.

A new window at the moment of instantiation, or any window to which the Show message is sent, is thereupon made as frontmost as possible. This is the other major difference between sending the Show message and setting the Visible property; the Show message *brings the window to the front*; setting the Visible property does not. Indeed, Show is typically used, even when a window is visible *already*, as the command to bring it to the front. Instantiating a window, or sending a window the Show message, is your code's *only* way to affect the order in which windows are layered.

To be sure, I am deliberately waving my hands with the circumlocution "as frontmost as possible," which is intended to cover various behaviors that complicate the picture, such as: a new document window won't be in front of a floating window; a new modal window will be in front of a floating window, but a floating window can be brought in front of a modal window with Show; and so forth. Rather than trying to enumerate every conceivable combination, I leave it to your common sense and experimentation to discover REALbasic's behavior as the need arises.

ShowModal

The notion of a dialog's being modal means that everything should come to a stop while the dialog is showing, except for the user's interaction with it. Now, suppose we have some code that opens a modal dialog. If that same code then continues running, the modal dialog isn't really modal after all. To see this, think about the purpose of a modal dialog. Typically, code will invoke a modal dialog in order to stop and gather some sort of information from the user that will determine how it should proceed. Clearly, the code cannot do that if it continues running while the modal dialog is up. It needs a way to stop and wait for the modal dialog to be dismissed, when the information has been collected.

The ShowModal method is the solution. ShowModal is like Show with an important difference: when code sends a window the ShowModal message, that window is made frontmost and visible, and *the calling code is then paused* until the window becomes invisible (or closes, since this also makes the window invisible); the calling code then resumes at the next line.

An example of ShowModal in action appeared in Chapter 7, where we talked about how a document window, on the point of being closed, can put up a dialog to ask the user whether or not to save changes. To recapitulate the example: a modal dialog window called SaveChanges has buttons with captions such as Don't Save, Cancel, and Save. The Action event handlers of these buttons all have the following form:

```
self.buttonpushed = 1 // or whatever the number is
self.hide
```

The main code that shows the dialog goes more or less like this:

```
w = new saveChanges.init(self)
w.showmodal
i = w.buttonpushed
w.close
```

The sequence of events is as follows. The main code instantiates and initializes the dialog window, and shows it; then, thanks to ShowModal, it pauses. The user now sees the dialog, and presses one of the buttons. The button's Action event handler is called; it stores a number in a drop, so that the main code can later determine which button was pressed, and then it hides the dialog. This causes the main code to resume execution; it fetches the information from the drop, and proceeds to destroy the dialog window instance. All is now as it was before the dialog window was instantiated; the same code is still executing. The difference is that now this code possesses a number telling it what the user wants to do, and can behave accordingly.

It is possible to tighten this code considerably, effectively turning the modal dialog into a sort of function called by the main code. Instead of the main code showing and destroying the dialog, the dialog's code can do this, within Init. Now Init needn't hand back a reference to the SaveChanges instance; it just hands back the integer result representing the button that was pushed:

```
Function Init(w as window) As integer
    // use w as desired to initialize dialog
    self.showmodal
    self.close
    return self.buttonpushed
End Function
```

The main code just instantiates the dialog and calls its Init handler:

```
i = saveChanges.init(self)
```

Within that one line, the modal dialog is instantiated, shows itself modally, interacts with the user, destroys itself, and reports what button was pushed. The surprise here is that the Init function is able to order the destruction of its own window, with self.close, and yet continue running long enough to hand back the result in an orderly fashion. I take it that REALbasic does not actually destroy a window until its handlers have finished executing.

I should just add, since this is sometimes a source of confusion, that showing a window with ShowModal does not make it a modal window! The window is or isn't a modal window because of its type (see "Window Types," earlier in this chapter). What's special about ShowModal is how it affects the flow of the code. You can show a nonmodal window with ShowModal, but this would be a silly thing to do.

Title, Position, and Size

Your code can get the following properties of a window instance, and can set them to change the window's appearance:

Title
> The text appearing in the window's titlebar.

Top, Left, Height, Width
> The window's position and size, measured in pixels. Top and Left, which determine the window's position, are measured from the top left corner of the main screen; observe that a positive Top value is downward from this origin (unlike the Cartesian coordinates familiar from one's school days). Thus the coordinate value of a window's bottom edge is its Top plus its Height; its right edge is at its Left plus its Width.

MinHeight, MinWidth, MaxHeight, MaxWidth
> These are of interest only if the user is permitted to resize the window by means of a zoom box or grow icon; they dictate the minimum and maximum dimensions that the user can give the window. Your code is not bound by these restrictions, but you should probably try not to violate them, as this may allow the user to violate them too.

FullScreen
> A boolean. If true, the window sizes itself to exactly the dimensions of the screen (if there are multiple monitors, whichever screen contains most of the window). Setting the window's Top, Left, Height, and Width properties then has no effect. The user can still move the window if the titlebar or borders are visible on another monitor, but this can be prevented by making the window Plain.

MenubarVisible
> A boolean. If false, the menu bar disappears whenever the window is frontmost, and reappears when the application suspends or when a window whose MenubarVisible is true becomes frontmost.

REALbasic's notion of the position and dimensions of a window describes the window's content region—that's the *inside*, not the outside, of its titlebar and borders if it has any. The true boundaries of the window, called its *structure* region, may be larger. For example, suppose you're on Mac OS Classic, where a Type 0 window has a border. So, if you give a Type 0 window a Left value of 0, it will not appear to the user to be neatly placed against the left edge of the screen; rather, its left border will be off the screen. If you give it a Left that is the negative of its Width, its right border will still be visible, jutting into the screen from the left.

The situation is further complicated by the presence of the menu bar. It is possible for a window's Top value to be positive, yet for part of the window to be hidden behind the menu bar. It is considered bad form for your code to position a window in such a way.

Unfortunately, REALbasic does not provide direct access to the dimensions of a window's structure region. One solution is just to guess. For instance, in considering how high on the screen to place a window, you know that the menu bar is usually 20 pixels high, and titlebars are usually somewhere around 22 or 26 pixels thick, depending on the window type; so you should probably not make a window's Top less than about 46. However, it is possible, and will sometimes be preferable, to use Toolbox calls to learn accurately the dimensions and position of a window's structure region (see Chapter 32).

To position windows intelligently, your code will need a mental picture of the user's screen arrangement. To obtain this, use the ScreenCount function and the Screen function; you hand the Screen function the zero-based index of the screen you're interested in, and you get back a Screen object whose Top, Left, Width, and Height properties tell you its position and dimensions. A Screen instance also has a Depth property that tells you the screen's color setting as a power of 2. For example, one of my screens has a Depth of 8, meaning it is set for 256 colors (2^8). The origin for the Top and Left is the top left corner of the main screen, obtained as screen(0). Thus, for example, the following routine reports the boundaries of my two screens (top, left, right, bottom):

```
dim i as integer
dim sc as screen
dim s as string
for i = 1 to screencount
    sc = screen(i-1)
    s = s + str(i-1) + ": "
    s = s + str(sc.top) + ", "
    s = s + str(sc.left) + ", "
    s = s + str(sc.height+sc.top) + ", "
    s = s + str(sc.width+sc.left) + chr(13)
next
msgbox s
// 0: 0, 0, 768, 1024
// 1: 35, 1024, 905, 1664
```

You may have reason to position a window off the screen altogether; this is sometimes done as an alternative to an invisible window. Also there are some unusual effects that can be achieved in this way; try positioning a modal window offscreen and see what happens!

You may have noticed that it is not possible to set a window's Top and Left properties in the IDE. Instead, a window determines dynamically its own initial position, based on the value of its Placement property, which is an integer. However, if you don't like this initial position, it's no problem to override it, because your code can reposition the window before it actually becomes visible. Here are the meanings of the different Placement property values:

0—Default
For a document window, if it is the only visible window, then at the upper left of the main screen; otherwise, stacked slightly to the right and downward from the frontmost window.

For a modal window or a Plain or Shadowed box, toward the top center of the main screen.

For a floating window, high at the left edge of the main screen.

1—Parent Window
Stacked downward from the frontmost window. If there is no other window, toward the top center of the main screen.

2—Main Screen
Toward the top center of the main screen.

3—Parent Screen
Toward the top center of the same screen as the frontmost window.

4—Stagger
Like the Default position of a document window.

Events

You may wish to review the section "Order of Events" in Chapter 7, to get a feel for how window events fit into the lifetime of your application.

The following events are received by a window instance in connection with its lifetime:

Open
Sent to a window instance after it comes into existence, after an Open event has been sent to each control in the window, but before the window becomes visible to the user.

CancelClose
Sent to a window instance because the process of closing it has been initiated; for how this happens, see "Opening and Closing, Showing and Hiding," earlier in this chapter. The CancelClose event handler can perform last-minute activities; it can also prevent the window from closing by returning true. (If the application was trying to quit, this will also prevent it from doing so; see Chapter 7.) If it returns false or nothing at all, the closing of the window will proceed. Thus, for example, the CancelClose event handler is the place for a document window to put up its Save Changes dialog, giving the user a chance to save or to prevent the window from closing.

Close

Sent to a window instance just before it is destroyed. The window has returned false (or nothing) from the CancelClose event. Each control in the window has received a Close event. There is nothing now that the window can do to prevent itself from being destroyed.

The following events are received by a window instance in connection with physical alterations:

Activate

Sent to a window instance because the window has come to the front: it has been visibly instantiated, or it has been sent the Show message, or the user has clicked on it when it was not in front, or the application has been resumed. A visible nonfloating window that has received an Activate event and no subsequent Deactivate event is in front.

Deactivate

Sent to a window instance that was previously in front, because it has been made invisible (this includes when a window is instantiated invisibly), or another (nonfloating) window has been brought to the front, or the application has been suspended. A window that has received a Deactivate event and no subsequent Activate event is not the frontmost visible window in the frontmost application. A floating window never receives a Deactivate event.

Moved

Sent to a window instance because it has been moved, either by the user dragging it or by code setting its Top or Left properties. It is too late to prevent the repositioning from taking place.

Resized

Sent to a window instance because it has been resized, either by the user (by its zoom box or its grow icon) or by code. It is too late to prevent the resizing from taking place.

The Moved event is sent if code sets the Top or Left property even if this does not change the property's value, whereas the Resized event is sent only if the Height or Width property value is actually altered. The Resized behavior makes more sense, but the Moved behavior is more typical of how REALbasic events get triggered by code. In any case the difference is confusing and I regard it as a bug.

The following events are received by a visible window instance in connection with the user moving the mouse in relation to its content region. The *content region* here means any part of a window that is not its titlebar, grow icon, or border. These events are received even when the window is not frontmost, but then the content region excludes the area covered by another window of your application. These events are also received even when your application is not frontmost, and then the content region does *not* exclude the area covered by a window of another application. (If a mouse movement event handler does something you'd rather not do if the window or the application isn't frontmost, you can check for those conditions and not do it.*)

MouseEnter

Sent to a window instance because the mouse was outside the content region of the window, and is now within the content region.

MouseMove

Sent to a window instance because the mouse has changed its location within the content region of the window. The event handler is given the mouse's horizontal and vertical coordinates as measured from the top left corner of the window's content region. You can use MouseMove to track the mouse's position within the window; to experiment with this, have an EditField in the window (here named EditField1) and put this line into the MouseMove event handler:

```
editfield1.text = str(x) + "," + str(y)
```

MouseExit

Sent to a window instance because the mouse was within the content region of the window, and is now outside the content region.

The following events are received by a frontmost window instance in connection with the user pressing the mouse button:

MouseDown

Sent to a window instance because the mouse button has been clicked down while the mouse is within the window's content region and not within any clickable control; for example, a button, a ListBox, or an EditField is clickable, but a StaticText is not. The click on a nonfrontmost window that brings it to the front does not trigger a MouseDown event. The event handler is given the mouse's horizontal and vertical coordinates as measured from the top left corner of the window's content region. The MouseDown event handler must return true if you want the window to receive MouseDrag and MouseUp events tracking this click of the mouse.

MouseDrag

Sent to a window instance because the mouse button, having been clicked in such a way as to generate a MouseDown event whose handler returned true, is still down. MouseDrag events are generated more or less continuously while the mouse remains down. The event handler is given the mouse's horizontal and vertical coordinates as measured from the top left corner of the window's content region. The mouse need not actually be within the window's content region. You can use MouseDrag to track the mouse while the mouse button is down. You don't get MouseMove events if you're getting MouseDrag events.

---

* On how to know whether the application is in the background, see "The Application Subclass" in Chapter 7.

MouseUp

Sent to a window instance because the mouse button, having been clicked in such a way as to generate a MouseDown event whose handler returned true, has just been released. The event handler is given the mouse's horizontal and vertical coordinates as measured from the top left corner of the window's content region. The mouse need not actually be within the window's content region.

 In the rare event that you need to know the mouse's position in code not triggered by a MouseMove, MouseDown, MouseDrag, or MouseUp event, a window instance also has MouseX and MouseY properties (read-only), which can be consulted at any time. See Chapter 20; for an example, see Chapter 24.

Code in an event handler can indirectly trigger another event. This can have unintended consequences. For instance, if you reposition a window from within its Moved event handler, you can cause an infinite loop, because this will trigger a Moved event. With a little forethought and experimentation, though, you should be able to prevent problems.

For example, suppose we have a window that we don't want the user to be able to move, even though it has a titlebar. We can't actually prevent the moving of the window, but we can detect its movement in the Moved event handler, and snap it back into place. In doing so, we are moving the window again, and triggering the Moved event handler. But we are in the Moved event handler already! This threatens to become an infinite loop. An easy solution is to raise a flag, move the window, and lower the flag. In this example, the flag is a boolean property of the window, called MeMoved:

```
Sub Moved()
    if not self.meMoved then // user may not move this window!
        self.meMoved = true // a property
        self.top = 100
        self.left = 100
        self.meMoved = false
    end
End Sub
```

Drawing in a Window

A window's controls are automatically redrawn whenever REALbasic becomes aware that this is necessary—because the window has been revealed by another window moving, because the focus has changed and the focus ring needs to be repainted, because a StaticText's text has changed, because code has changed the text of an EditField, and so forth. However, you may find that changes made during the execution of code are not being made visible to the user in a timely fashion. To force changes to appear immediately, send the window the Refresh message; or send it the RefreshRect message, providing the top, left, width, and height values that specify the region of the window to be updated, where the top and left are measured from the top left corner of the window's content region. If what needs updating is an instance of a Control subclass or an area relative to it, you can send the control the Refresh or RefreshRect message instead. The RefreshRect coordinates are then measured from the top left corner of the control (see Chapter 10).

The area of a window behind all controls is its *background*. You are responsible for how a window's background looks. There are three levels, both figuratively and literally, of material a window may use as its background:

A solid color
> To give a window's background a solid color, set its BackColor property to the color and its HasBackColor property to true. REALbasic will maintain the background color for you, with no further effort on your part. If HasBackColor is false, the window's background will be determined by the system (on Mac OS X, it's the stripes; on Mac OS Classic it's a solid color, the same color available through the FillColor function). Colors as a datatype were discussed in Chapter 5.

An existing picture
> To make a window's background be an existing picture, you need to obtain a picture; ways of doing this are discussed in Chapter 11, but an easy way is this: import the picture (such as a PICT, GIF, or JPEG file) into the project; this will cause the picture's name to be listed in the Project Window, and now you can set the window's Backdrop property to that picture (in the IDE, if you like). REALbasic will maintain the background picture for you, with no further effort on your part. The picture is drawn with its top left corner in the top left corner of the content region, and is not resized. If HasBackColor is true, the Backdrop is layered on top of the BackColor.

A picture you draw
> The window's background contains a Graphics property. You can draw into this as you would into any Graphics property. What you draw into the window's Graphics property is layered on top of the Backdrop if there is one.

You can draw into the window's Graphics property at any time, but your drawing will be erased if you don't perform it every time the window receives a Paint event. Whenever any part of a window's content region is about to be redrawn, either because REALbasic has noticed that this is necessary or because the window or a control within it has been sent the Refresh or RefreshRect message, the window's Graphics property is erased, and the window receives a Paint event. The Paint event handler is handed the window's Graphics property, and is expected to redraw its contents. Drawing into a Graphics property is a large topic, and is treated in Chapter 11.

It is important not to cause an infinite loop by doing something within a Paint event handler that in turn causes the window to need updating and triggers a Paint event. This is the same problem discussed at the end of the previous section.

In global floating windows, the drawing of colors using the BackColor or Graphics property of the window or of a Canvas control sometimes does not work properly; the color you see may not be the color you asked for. This is especially the case, I believe, on systems earlier than 8.6, and is a system limitation: it isn't REALbasic's fault. To color a global floating window precisely under these circumstances, draw a picture (dynamically as a Picture object, or beforehand in a graphics application), and use that picture as the window's Backdrop.

CHAPTER 10

Abstract Control Classes

In this chapter:
- Lifetime Events
- Appearance
- Position and Size
- Mouse Movement Events
- Redrawing

This chapter describes two built-in REALbasic classes that the programmer can neither instantiate nor subclass: Control and RectControl. You might wonder: if you can't make an instance of either of these classes, and if you can't make a subclass of either of them, what good are they? The answer is that although *you* can't subclass these classes, REALbasic can, and has. RectControl is a subclass of Control. Every built-in control class is derived from Control, and most are derived from RectControl; and you *can* instantiate or subclass these built-in control classes. (For a diagram, see "The Class Hierarchy" in Chapter 4.)

A class that exists only so that other classes can be derived from it is said to be *abstract*. Its purpose is to express and encapsulate the common functionality of its subclasses. The Control and RectControl classes each receives certain events and has certain methods and properties, and all of their respective subclasses inherit these and have them in common. Thus, this chapter is really about the events, methods, and properties common to control classes.

Each of the built-in Control subclasses—except RectControl, which is abstract—is represented by an icon in the Tools Window. This icon can be dragged into a Window Editor to cause a window class to contain an instance of that control. The window will then instantiate the control automatically when it itself is instantiated. Moreover, this is the *only* way in which these subclasses can be instantiated—even cloning ultimately requires that the original be instantiated in this way. This is what distinguishes control classes from all other classes: control classes can be instantiated *only* as controls contained in windows.

On the other hand, an instance of nearly *any* class *can* be contained in a window class, and *can* be instantiated as a control. Some of the icons in the Tools Window represent ordinary, noncontrol classes; you can drag such an icon into a Window Editor to make a window class contain an instance of that class. For other classes, if you are allowed to subclass the class, you can drag the subclass's listing from the

Project Window into a Window Editor to make a window class contain an instance of that class; or, if an instance of a built-in control class is already in a Window Editor, you can repoint it at a subclass of that control class, using its Super in the Properties Window.* The advantage of this is that the instance will be created and destroyed automatically together with the opening and closing of the window. But that is not what this chapter is about.

Individual control classes are described in various subsequent chapters. Line, ContextualMenu, and all the RectControl subclasses are described in this part of the book; all other control classes are described in Part III. Some functionality common to control classes is discussed elsewhere: on the MouseCursor property and balloon help, see Chapter 20; on drag-and-drop, see Chapter 24. On the Window property, and in general on the problem of referencing a control's containing window, see "What's My Window?" in Chapter 4.

It will help to recall the discussion of controls in Part I. Here is a brief recap. If any of this is unfamiliar, you might want to review the relevant material from Chapter 3 before proceeding:

- Every instance of a control class is contained by some window.

- Your code cannot instantiate a control class *ex nihilo*. Instead, a control is automatically instantiated by its containing window class when the window class is instantiated. It is possible, however, for code within a window class to clone a control that already exists in that window, using New, provided the control is part of a control array.

- Code in an event handler of a control instance (in a window class's Code Editor) can obtain a reference to the instance's containing window using Self, and can obtain a reference to the control instance using Me. Code in the Code Editor of a Control subclass defined by the programmer can obtain a reference to the instance using Self (or Me), and can obtain a reference to the instance's containing window by way of the subclass's Window property.

- A control instance may be referred to using dot notation: a reference to the containing window, a dot, and the global name of the control (its Name property in the IDE). If the reference to the containing window would be self, it may be omitted. If the instance is defined as having an Index value, it is part of a control array, and the index is appended to the global name to specify the instance, as with an ordinary array.

- A reference to a control instance may also be obtained by way of its containing window's Control function.

---

* Windows cannot contain window class instances, for obvious reasons.

Lifetime Events

Every control in a window receives the following events in connection with its lifetime:

Open
> Sent to a control just after it has been instantiated. If (as is usually the case) the control is being instantiated automatically by the instantiation of its containing window class, it receives the Open event before the window does.

Close
> Sent to a control as it is about to be destroyed. This can only be because the control's containing window is about to be destroyed; the window has already received the CancelClose event and has returned `false` (or nothing), and the destruction of the window cannot now be prevented. The control receives the Close event before the window does.

Among controls in a window, the order in which the Open and Close events are received is determined through the dialog that appears when you choose Format → Control Order.

A control's Open event handler is the standard place (apart from the IDE) for initializing features of the control. Its Close event handler typically performs last-minute bookkeeping tasks appropriate to the control's impending destruction. For an example, see Chapter 7, where the controls of a Find dialog initialize themselves when the dialog is instantiated and save their state when the dialog is destroyed.

Since controls receive the Open event before the containing window does, a control cannot initialize itself based on window properties that the window itself has not yet had an opportunity to initialize. The problem is inevitable (it would occur in reverse if Open events arrived in the opposite order), but with some forethought you can get around it. For example, imagine a ListBox subclass that is to initialize its contents based on a string array property (here called TheArray) of its window. Even if the window initializes this array at its earliest opportunity, in its Open event handler, that won't do the ListBox much good, because its Open event handler executes first. Suppose the ListBox's Open event handler goes like this:

```
dim i, u as integer
u = ubound(self.theArray)
for i = 0 to u
    me.addrow self.theArray(i)
next
```

The ListBox appears empty, because TheArray hasn't been initialized when this code runs. And this is only a minor example of the sort of thing that can go wrong; if the window property to be accessed had been an object, we could have gotten a NilObjectException. The cleanest solution here would be for the window to have a separate method that initializes the array, and for the ListBox's Open event handler to begin by calling that method.

Appearance

Every control that is a subclass of RectControl inherits the following properties connected with its appearance:

Visible

A control whose Visible property is set to `false` cannot be seen by the user. It receives no events or messages relating to the focus, keypresses, mouse movement, or the mouse button; in other words, the user cannot type or click in it, and cannot directly affect it in any way or discover its existence. Apart from this, the control can be sent its normal repertoire of messages.

For example, an invisible EditField control still has a Top and a Left, and it still has a Text, which can be changed in code, thus triggering its TextChanged event and its SelChanged event; but sending it the SetFocus message has no effect. Thus, in the example from "Invisible Windows" in Chapter 9 about turning all instances of the letter "e" red, an invisible EditField in the same window as the visible one might be used as a "scratch pad."

The Line control, although not a RectControl, also has the Visible property. A NotePlayer is always invisible. (So are contained instances that are not derived from Control.) It is also possible to position a control outside its window's boundaries as a way of concealing it from the user. Both the Canvas (Chapter 11) and the TabPanel (Chapter 18) provide a convenient way of showing and hiding controls *en masse*.

Enabled

A control whose Enabled property is set to `false` may be visible to the user, but it will usually appear in altered form. It receives no messages or events relating to the focus, keypresses, or the mouse-button; in other words, the user can't type or click in the control. In code, the control can still be sent its normal repertoire of messages, and may still react to these by changing its display, though possibly in a dimmed form.

For example, a disabled ListBox, EditField, or Pushbutton appears dim and flat. As the mouse passes into its region, the control still receives MouseEnter and Mouse-Move events, but clicking in the control has no effect on the control itself, and causes a MouseDown event to be sent to the window, which would not happen if the control were enabled. Changing a disabled EditField's Text property in code changes the displayed text, even though that text is dimmed and can't be selected with the mouse. Changing a disabled ListBox's ListIndex property in code scrolls the list just as if the control were enabled, except that the list is dimmed and there is no selection highlighting.

On the other hand, a disabled StaticText or Rectangle is virtually indistinguishable from an enabled one; indeed, the Enabled property of these classes is `false` by default, and cannot be changed in the IDE, though it can in code.

AutoDeactivate
> A boolean determining whether the control's appearance should change automatically when its containing window switches between being frontmost and being nonfrontmost, in conformity with interface guidelines. If `false`, there will be no change in appearance. The default is `true`.

For example, a StaticText whose AutoDeactivate property is true will have its text dimmed whenever its containing window is in the background.

Position and Size

Every control that is a subclass of RectControl inherits the following properties connected with its position and size:

Top, Left, Height, Width
> These are measured in pixels; Top and Left are measured from the upper-left corner of the window's content region.

LockTop, LockBottom, LockLeft, LockRight
> Boolean properties, stating whether the control's top, bottom, left, and right edge positions are to be considered relative to the corresponding edge of the window when the latter is resized. LockLeft is ignored unless LockRight is true; LockTop is ignored unless LockBottom is true.

To understand the LockTop family of properties, imagine that you have carefully centered an EditField so that its left edge is 10 pixels from the window's left edge and its right edge is 10 pixels from the window's right edge. Now the user widens the window; should the EditField widen to match? Clearly it should; when you originally sized it, you weren't thinking in absolute terms, but in terms relative to the window's size. Now imagine that there's an OK button in the lower-right corner of the window. The user widens the window; should the button move? Clearly it should; when you originally positioned it, you weren't thinking in absolute terms, but in terms relative to the window's bottom and right edges. On the other hand, the button should not be resized—it should just move.

These properties let REALbasic know of your intentions in this regard. If you set a control's LockRight property to true, then when the window is widened or narrowed, the control's right edge will move to remain the same distance from the window's right edge. This will be accomplished by moving the entire control, keeping its width the same; if this isn't what you want, then you should also set the control's LockLeft property to true, which will cause its Left value to remain unchanged when the window is resized. Now you can see why LockLeft is ignored unless LockRight is true. LockBottom and LockTop work in a parallel fashion.

None of these properties restrict what you can do in code to a control's Top, Left, Height, and Width settings; they have to do only with what happens automatically when the window is resized.

Mouse Movement Events

Every control that is a subclass of RectControl, if its Visible is set to true, receives the following events connected with the user's movement of the mouse. The control's *content region* here means the part of the control's region that is within the window's content region—in other words, any part of a control that is not off the window altogether, and is not covered by another REALbasic window. It may, however, be covered by another control in the same window, or by a window of another application.

MouseEnter
> Sent to a visible control instance because the mouse was outside the control's content region and is now within it.

MouseMove
> Sent to a visible control instance because the mouse has changed its location within the control's content region. The event handler is given the mouse's horizontal and vertical coordinates, so this event can be used to track the mouse within the control. The coordinates are measured from the top left corner of the window's (not the control's!) content region.*

MouseExit
> Sent to a visible control instance because the mouse was within the control's content region, and is now outside it.

In the rather silly example illustrated in Figure 10-1, we have a white rectangle, and whenever the mouse passes into this rectangle we want a blue circle to appear under the mouse and to follow it wherever it goes, until it passes out of the rectangle.

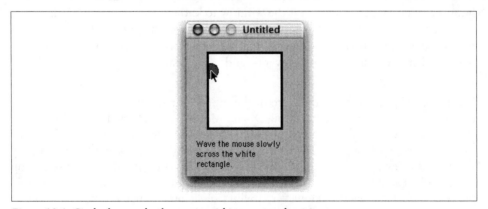

Figure 10-1. Circle that tracks the mouse within a rectangle

---

* But for a Canvas, it's the Canvas's content region. It appears that in REALbasic 3.5 this will change to the control's content region for all RectControls. This makes more sense, but it will break existing code (including the example on this page).

This is achieved by having the blue circle (an Oval control, here called Oval1) be initially invisible, and putting the following code into our Rectangle control's three mouse movement event handlers:

```
Sub MouseEnter()
    oval1.visible = true
End Sub

Sub MouseExit()
    oval1.visible = false
End Sub

Sub MouseMove(X As Integer, Y As Integer)
    oval1.top = y-oval1.height/2
    oval1.left = x-oval1.width/2
End Sub
```

A consequence of the fact that the MouseMove event coordinates are with respect to the top left of the window's content region is that you may or may not, depending on how you intend to use them, have to convert them to be local to the control, by subtracting the control's Top and Left values. Here, there was no need to convert, since the position of the circle is to be dictated in window-based coordinates, which is just what we were handed for the mouse position in the first place.

The ability to detect mouse button events—MouseUp, MouseDrag, and MouseDown—is not in common to all RectControls. Some controls receive them; some don't. In REALbasic 3.5, more controls will get MouseUp and MouseDown events than previously. You'll need to consult the details on the individual control. If a mouseclick falls through to the window (as with a Rectangle or StaticText, or any disabled RectControl), you can catch it, because the window does receive mouse button events. The easiest way for the window to know which control was clicked in is for the control to raise a flag in its MouseEnter event handler and lower it in its MouseExit event handler. Another alternative is to place a Canvas over the control; the Canvas receives mouse button events, and is transparent (so the user won't know it's there).

It is possible to learn about the state of the mouse outside these events. Every control (not just a RectControl) has MouseX and MouseY properties that can be used at any time to ascertain the mouse's position. The coordinates are with respect to the top left of the window's content region; in other words, these properties are merely shortcuts for saying theControl.window.mouseX and so forth. Also, the mouse button can be polled at any time to learn whether it is down, by way of the system.mouseDown property (see Chapter 20). However, polling in a loop is usually not as good as receiving an event, when possible ("Events Make Choices" in Chapter 7).

Redrawing

REALbasic will automatically redraw any portion of a window, including controls, that it discovers needs redrawing, for example because the region was covered by another window and has now been uncovered, or because you've changed in code some feature of a control that corresponds to a visible aspect of the interface. But any control may be sent the Refresh and RefreshRect messages to force such redrawing to occur on the spot. A typical reason for doing so would be that REALbasic is somehow not discovering, or is discovering only belatedly, that it needs to redraw a region; for example, during lengthy code, in order to provide the user with visual feedback, it may be necessary to ask for a control to be redrawn. The downside of a call to Refresh or RefreshRect is that it may result in visible flicker; experimentation may be needed in order to decide whether this is objectionable.

For an example of sending a control the Refresh message, look at the code example in "Heap Size and Memory Management" in Chapter 8, where a StaticText's text is updated continually during a loop, with these lines:

```
statictext1.text = str(i)
statictext1.refresh
```

A StaticText, whenever it redraws, displays its Text property in the window; but merely changing the Text property is not sufficient to redraw the display. Usually what happens is that after the Text property is changed, the StaticText redraws automatically when code yields time to the processor, such as after all code finishes executing and the application lapses into an idle state. But that's not sufficient here, because the loop keeps repeating. So each time through the loop, first we set the StaticText's Text property, then we send the StaticText the Refresh message to force the StaticText to display the new Text value right then and there. If we don't send the Refresh message, the StaticText's appearance does not change until the entire routine has ended.

What's actually being redrawn when you send a control the Refresh message is some region of the window. In the case of the Refresh message, this will be the whole content region of the control. In the case of the RefreshRect message, it will be whatever region you dictate, giving its left, top, width, and height values; these values are measured from the top left corner of the control, but the specified region does not have to lie entirely or even partially within the control's content region—you're simply referring to a region of the window in terms of the position of the control. Recall from Chapter 9 that a Refresh or RefreshRect message, instead of being sent to an individual control, can be sent to an entire window. This redraws the controls within the window. When a Refresh or RefreshRect message is sent to a control or a window, the window receives a Paint event. Redrawing a window and redrawing a control are thus essentially the same act.

CHAPTER 11
Canvases

The Canvas control class is REALbasic's way of letting the programmer display a custom image within a window. Canvases are probably the most versatile and powerful of REALbasic's built-in control classes, because in effect they let you build your own piece of the interface. A Canvas subclass could be used to simulate a PushButton, a StaticText, a ListBox, and many other existing classes and often is used as the basis for constructing variants on such classes.

From the programmer's point of view, the chief sources of a Canvas's great power and versatility are as follows:

- A Canvas permits your code to take direct control over drawing within its region.

- A Canvas receives both mouse movement and mouse button events.

- A Canvas can be scrolled, and can scroll other controls along with it.

- A Canvas can overlay another control, invisibly if desired, in such a way as to let its powers and those of the other control supplement one another.

A Canvas and a window's background have much in common. A Canvas does not have a BackColor or a HasBackColor property, so it lacks a window's simplest level of just displaying a solid color as its rearmost layer. But it has both a Backdrop and a Graphics property, and you use these to draw into a Canvas and into a window's background in identical fashion. Also, a Canvas and a window receive some similar events. The treatment of window backgrounds at the end of Chapter 9 was rather sketchy; the expectation was that you would come to this chapter to learn how to work with them. So even though this chapter speaks mainly of Canvases, most of it applies equally to window backgrounds.

Drawing ultimately comes down to pixels, and pixels ultimately are just colors. See "Colors" in Chapter 5.

This chapter starts off rather dryly, just listing some events, properties, and methods of some classes that you need to know about. Don't worry about absorbing all these facts at once. They are followed by lots of examples to make everything clear.

Canvas Events, Properties, and Methods

A Canvas is a control that displays an image in a window.

A Canvas is a RectControl, and therefore receives all the events and has all the properties and methods listed in Chapter 10: Open and Close events; Visible, Enabled and AutoDeactivate properties; Top, Left, Height, and Width properties; LockLeft, LockRight, LockTop, and LockBottom properties; MouseEnter, MouseMove, and MouseExit events; and Refresh and RefreshRect methods.

Additionally, a Canvas receives the following events:

MouseDown, MouseDrag, MouseUp
  These are analogous to a window's MouseDown, MouseDrag, and MouseUp events. MouseDown must return true in order to cause MouseDrag and MouseUp events to be sent; otherwise, the click passes through to whatever is behind the Canvas. All three events provide your code with the position of the mouse, relative to the top left corner of the Canvas (not the window).

Paint
  Sent when REALbasic discovers, or is told through Refresh or RefreshRect messages, that part of the Canvas needs redrawing. Your code is expected to respond by maintaining the image in the Canvas's Graphics property.

A Canvas has the following method:

Scroll
  Shifts pixels of the Canvas's image horizontally, vertically, or both. Takes two parameters: the pixel distance to shift rightward (a negative value means leftward), and the pixel distance to shift downward (a negative value means upward). Optionally, takes four more parameters specifying the rectangular region within the Canvas that is to be shifted. If they are present, optionally takes one more parameter, a boolean saying whether controls lying on top of the Canvas should be shifted along with it; the default is true.

A Canvas has the following properties:

Backdrop, Graphics
  The two levels, both literal and figurative, of drawing into a Canvas control. The Backdrop image is behind the Graphics image. Once you point the Backdrop at an instance of the Picture class, that Picture's image is drawn automatically in the Canvas. The Graphics property is an automatically generated instance of the Graphics class; an image to be displayed here must be redrawn by your code on every Paint event.

The Backdrop and Graphics properties involve two classes that have not yet been treated, the Picture class and the Graphics class; so the discussion turns now to these classes—their properties and methods, and the means of instantiating a Picture (you do not explicitly instantiate the Graphics class).

Picture Class

A Picture instance is an independent image object. The image is a *bitmap*, meaning that it consists of a grid of pixels, each pixel representing a color. A Picture instance has the following main uses:

- The Backdrop of a Canvas (or window) is a pointer to a Picture instance.
- A Picture instance is REALbasic's way of storing an image that is not currently being displayed (commonly referred to as an *offscreen picture*).
- A Picture instance's image can be copied very rapidly into a Graphics property, through the latter's DrawPicture method; so a Picture is the source for blitting. To *blit* is to transfer bits quickly from one memory location to another. Moving a block of memory to another location is a labor-intensive operation, which arises frequently in computer programs, and nowhere more so than in connection with images, because images are themselves so memory-intensive; therefore, optimized computer processors and internal routines have been developed to make blitting as fast as possible.
- A Picture instance's pixels can be accessed very rapidly, through its RGBSurface property; so a Picture is the locus for manipulation of single pixels.

A Picture's *depth* is, for some unknown reason, not among its properties; but it is tremendously important. It is a power of two, from 1 to 32; the maximum number of colors the image can have is two raised to this value. For example, a depth of 8 means that the image is set for 256 colors (2^8).

The existence of depth complicates the way colors are handled. For example, suppose you have a Picture with a bit depth of 4. That means the Picture can contain just 16 different colors, but you don't get to say what 16 colors these are. Instead, the 16 colors are chosen for you, and each color you write to this Picture's image is mapped to the nearest of these 16 colors. A Color can represent 2^{24} different values, so unless you are writing into a Picture with a bit depth of 32, the color you get out of a Picture may not be the color you put into it. For example, in a Picture with a bit depth of 16, if you write the color rgb(101,111,121) to a pixel and then read that same pixel, its color turns out to be rgb(99,107,123).

Pictures are memory-intensive data structures. The number of pixels is a measure of area, so it rises as the square of the sides: in comparison to an image of 128 by 128 pixels, an image of 256 by 256 pixels requires not twice but four times as much memory. The depth of an image is the third dimension determining how much memory it occupies; for example, an image of 10 by 10 pixels with a depth of 16 requires only half as much memory as an image of 10 by 10 pixels with a depth of 32. Every eight bits is a byte; thus, a 32-bit image uses four bytes to represent just one pixel, so at that depth, even an image of 128 by 128 pixels, which is quite small physically, requires 64K of memory. These numbers get very large very fast! When you're manipulating pictures, you may need to increase the memory assigned both to REALbasic (so that it can run your project) and to the built application.[*]

Properties

A Picture has the following properties:

Height, Width
> The vertical and horizontal dimensions of the Picture image, in pixels.

Transparent
> An integer, either 0 or 1, stating whether the image is to be displayed transparently; if 1, white pixels in the image will not be drawn, permitting whatever is behind to show through.

Mask
> A second Picture, whose pixels determine the degree of transparency with which the main Picture's image will be drawn: black means opaque, white means completely transparent (not drawn), and shades of gray mean partial transparency.

Graphics
> An automatically generated object of class Graphics. Provides access to the Picture's bitmap. Only a Picture instance generated with NewPicture has a non-nil Graphics property. If and only if a Picture instance has a non-nil Graphics property, your code can modify its image. The techniques for drawing into a Canvas's, Picture's, or window's Graphics property are identical; see "Graphics Class," later in this chapter.

RGBSurface
> An automatically generated object of class RGBSurface. Provides access to single pixels of the Picture's bitmap. Only a Picture instance generated with NewPicture, and with a depth of 32 or 16, has a usable RGBSurface property (it will be nil otherwise). The only thing your code can do with a Picture's RGBSurface property is to access single pixels of the Picture image, but this is extremely fast, much faster than doing the same thing through its Graphics property; see "Speed," later in this chapter.

---

[*] For technical details of internal data structures on the Macintosh relating to color and bitmap images, see *http://developer.apple.com/techpubs/mac/QuickDraw/QuickDraw-198.html*. Recall, from Chapter 9, that your code can obtain the bit depth of any of the user's monitors as the Depth property of a value returned from the Screen function. Not infrequently, it will make sense to give a Picture at least the same depth as that of the user's deepest monitor.

Getting a Picture

We come now to the question of how to obtain an instance of the Picture class. There are five techniques:

Import an image file (IDE)

In the IDE, import an image file (such as a PICT, GIF, JPEG, etc.) into the project. A listing appears in the Project Window, representing this image file. Its name is the global name of a Picture instance that REALbasic will automatically generate when the application starts up. The project maintains the pathname of the file and opens the file automatically when you open the project; but the picture itself will be incorporated into the built application. See "External and Imported Components" in Chapter 1.

Import a Resource file (IDE)

In the IDE, import a file of type 'rsrc' (i.e. a ResEdit file) into the project. The file's resource fork becomes part of your application's resource fork. If it contains any resources of type 'PICT', or any icon family resources such as 'icl8' or 'ics8', or 'cicn', they are accessible from code as Picture instances.

Open an image data file (code)

In code, open an existing image file on disk (such as a PICT, GIF, JPEG, etc.) by sending an OpenAsPicture message to an instance of the FolderItem class denoting that file. This returns a Picture instance.

Open a file's resource fork (code)

In code, open an existing file on disk to access its resource fork by sending an OpenResourceFork message to an instance of the FolderItem class denoting that file. The situation is then parallel to an imported Resource file: if this resource fork contains any resources of type 'PICT', or any icon family resources such as 'icl8' or 'ics8', or 'cicn', they are accessible from code as Picture instances.

Generate a new Picture instance (code)

In code, create a new Picture instance by calling the NewPicture function and assigning the result to a variable or property declared as a Picture. The image is initially blank (white); but you can draw to it by way of its Graphics property. This is the only way to generate a Picture instance that has a non-nil Graphics property, so it is the only way to generate a Picture instance whose image you can modify.

Be careful to distinguish between Picture instances that have a usable Graphics property (made with NewPicture) and those that don't (made from a file); if in doubt, test to see whether the Picture's Graphics property is nil. Users sometimes wonder why the only type of Picture instance with a non-nil Graphics property is one generated with NewPicture. In fact, they sometimes complain of this as a bug. But there is a good reason for it: a picture file may not be initially composed of pixels at all. For instance, a PICT file can be entirely vector-based. So, if you wish to modify an image obtained by one of the first four methods, you should create a Picture instance with

NewPicture; this has a usable Graphics property, and you can now copy the original Picture's image into it (using DrawPicture, as we shall see in the next section). This renders the image into pixels that you can modify.

Graphics Class

The Graphics class is a curious entity: you cannot instantiate it directly, nor can it be subclassed. Instead, it is instantiated automatically as a property of a Picture, a Canvas, or a window. Therefore, this chapter speaks of working with a Graphics property rather than a Graphics instance.

A Graphics property is your means of access to the image itself, stored as a bitmap, a rectangle of actual pixels, each pixel representing a color. To draw a custom image or to modify an existing image, your code must send messages to a Graphics property. The methods and properties of a Graphics property are analogous to features of the Macintosh QuickDraw Toolbox; they let you access individual pixels, draw simple geometric shapes, write text, and copy (blit) an image from a Picture into the Graphics image.

Coordinates of pixels in a Graphics property are measured from its top left corner, which is 0,0. A Graphics property has a Width property and a Height property; for purposes of the material in this chapter, these are simply the Width and Height of the Graphics property's owner—a window, a Canvas, or a Picture—so they might seem redundant, but they can be very convenient ways to access these values. (In Chapter 29 we'll encounter a Graphics property with no owner; its Width and Height will be more than a mere convenience.) The Width and Height values provide a count of pixels, but pixel coordinates are zero-based, so it will sometimes be necessary to subtract 1: for example, in a 100-by-100 Picture, the bottom right pixel is 99,99.

Notice that a Graphics property is *just* pixels; it has no layers or "objects" as in a vector-based drawing program. You could probably use REALbasic to create a simple vector-based drawing program, but maintaining data structures to track the positions and features of the vector objects, and to draw them as pixels, would be up to your code.

Recall that a Canvas (or window) has two layers, which REALbasic handles differently: the rear layer is the Backdrop, a Picture, which REALbasic maintains for you; the front layer is the Graphics, which your code must redraw periodically. To draw into the front layer, you just draw: it's a Graphics property, and that's what a Graphics property is for. To draw into the rear layer, you have two choices; you can set the Backdrop to point at an existing Picture, or you can draw into the Backdrop's Graphics property if its Picture has one. So a Canvas (or window) actually can have *two* Graphics properties associated with it: its own, which is its front layer, and that of its Backdrop, the Picture that is its rear layer. This may seem odd at first, but examples of usage, later in this chapter, will clarify.

Pen-Based Drawing

The drawing of simple geometric shapes (lines, ovals, rectangles, polygons) into a Graphics property is referred to as *pen-based* drawing. This is because we pretend, each time drawing is done, that the computer is holding a rectangular pen of a certain size and color, and draws the shape with it.

The following properties of a Graphics property determine features of any subsequent pen-based drawing into it:

ForeColor
> The color for subsequent pen-based drawing. The default is rgb(0,0,0) (black).

PenWidth, PenHeight
> The pixel dimensions of the "pen" that will draw subsequent geometric shapes. The default is 1,1.

The following Graphics property methods perform pen-based drawing within it; all use the current ForeColor and pen size. Unless otherwise stated, the parameters are left, top, width, height. Negative width or height is permitted.

DrawLine
> Draws a line between the two points designated by its parameters. The parameters are the x and y coordinates of the first point followed by the x and y coordinates of the second point.

DrawRect, FillRect
> Draws the rectangle described by its parameters, respectively the outline only or a solid filled shape.

ClearRect
> For the Graphics of a Canvas or window, draws a filled rectangle of the window's BackColor (or its default background color, if its HasBackColor is false). Otherwise, draws a filled white rectangle.

DrawOval, FillOval
> Draws the oval bounded by the sides of the rectangle described by its parameters, respectively the outline only or a solid filled shape.

DrawRoundRect, FillRoundRect
> Draws the rectangle described by its first four parameters, respectively the outline only or a solid filled shape. Two additional parameters give the width and height of the oval that rounds each of the corners; the extremes are an oval value of 0,0, which yields an ordinary rectangle, and an oval value identical to the width and height of the rectangle, which yields an ordinary oval.

DrawPolygon, FillPolygon
> Draws the polygon described by its parameter, respectively the outline only or a solid filled shape. The parameter is an array of integers, where the zero item is ignored, after which each pair of items describes a point. For example, an array of six items whose values (after the zero item) are 0,0,0,40,40,40 describes an isosceles right triangle with the right angle at the lower left.

Constructing the array for describing a polygon is something of a pain if what you start with is a literal value. Here is a routine that generates it from a string formatted as a comma-delimited list:

```
dim s as string
dim i, u, a(0) as integer
s = "0,0,0,40,40,40"
u = countfields(s,",")
redim a(u)
for i = 1 to u
    a(i) = val(nthfield(s,",",i))
next
g.drawpolygon a
```

Pen-based drawing is slightly tricky, because the pen has thickness. Coordinates in a Graphics plane are measured positively from the top left, which is 0,0; but what these coordinates really represent are the interstices between the pixels. Each physical pixel is a 1-by-1 square. The pen-based drawing commands describe a shape in terms of coordinates, but the pen fills in pixels that have thickness with respect to this shape, in accordance with the current PenHeight and PenWidth. The question is, what happens to this thickness? The problem is that there are two different answers, depending upon what procedure is doing the drawing.

When you draw a framed shape with DrawRect or DrawPolygon, the thickness of the pen extends diagonally down and to the right from the shape you describe. Thus, the width and height of the result will usually be at least one pixel greater than that of the shape you describe—because the pen will usually be at least one pixel wide and one pixel high. It is easiest to see this through a diagram. Figure 11-1 shows a rectangle drawn using DrawRect, with a width and a weight of 4, when the PenWidth and the PenHeight are both 3; the result is actually a 7-by-7 rectangle.

On the other hand, when you draw a filled shape (as with FillRect) or a curved shape (as with DrawOval or DrawRoundRect), all drawing is done inside the region defined by the shape you describe. For instance, the rectangle drawn by this command is a 4-by-4 rectangle no matter how thick the pen is:

```
g.fillrect 1,1,4,4
```

Here's another example; the blue circle and the red square are not the same size:

```
g.penheight = 3
g.penwidth = 3
g.forecolor = rgb(255,0,0)
g.drawrect 1,1,30,30
g.forecolor = rgb(0,0,255)
g.drawoval 1,1,30,30
```

The left and top edges of the square and the circle are the same, but at the bottom and right, the circle is inside the square.

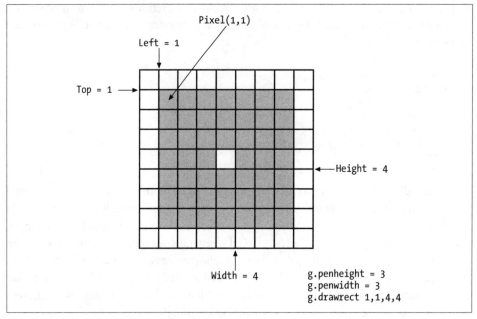

Figure 11-1. How the drawing coordinate system works

String Drawing

The following properties of a Graphics property determine features of any subsequent string drawing into it:

TextFont, TextSize
  The font and size of subsequent string drawing.

Bold, Italic, Underline
  Booleans dictating the style of subsequent string drawing.

TextAscent, TextHeight
  Read-only properties corresponding to the current TextFont and TextSize settings. TextAscent is the height of the tallest letters measured from the baseline. TextHeight is the total of the font's ascent height, its descent height, and its leading space.

The following methods of a Graphics property have to do with drawing strings into it:

DrawString
  Takes three parameters: the text, and the coordinates of a point. Writes the given text, in the current TextFont, TextSize, styles, and ForeColor, with the baseline's left end located at the given point. Optionally, takes a fourth parameter signifying the width at which text should automatically wrap; wrapped text will be left-justified beneath the text's origin point, and you are guaranteed that no pixels of the text will touch an imaginary vertical line at the wrap distance from the origin point.

StringWidth
> A function which, given a string, returns the number of horizontal pixels that the string would occupy in the current TextFont, TextSize, and styles.

StringWidth can be used to calculate where to put the next letter when the style is to change. For example, the following routine writes "RGB" in red, green, and blue:

```
g.textfont = "Geneva"
g.textsize = 24
g.forecolor = rgb(255,0,0)
g.drawstring "R",0,g.textheight
g.forecolor = rgb(0,255,0)
g.drawstring "G", g.stringwidth("R"), g.textheight
g.forecolor = rgb(0,0,255)
g.drawstring "B", g.stringwidth("RG"), g.textheight
```

If what you want to draw is styled text living in an EditField, there is an EditField method, StyledTextPrinter, that helps you. This is often a much better choice than the technique just demonstrated. See "Drawing Styled Text" in Chapter 13.

There is no function, unfortunately, that tells you where the end of the last Draw-String actually was—for example, a StringHeight function that would correspond to StringWidth. This means that if text drawn with either DrawString or StyledText-Printer wraps automatically, you've effectively lost your place within the Graphics bitmap. This is quite a serious problem, and I have no particularly good solution.

Pixels and Pixel Blocks

The following methods of a Graphics property have to do with individual pixels and rectangular blocks of pixels:

DrawCautionIcon, DrawNoteIcon, DrawStopIcon
> Draws the icon with its top left at the given coordinate.

Pixel
> Takes two parameters specifying a coordinate; used to get or set the color of the pixel at that coordinate. Attempting to access a non-existent pixel (outside the bounds of the Graphics property) will raise an exception. A Picture's RGBSurface also has a Pixel method that works just the same way, but is significantly faster; this is an RGBSurface's only method. See "Speed," later in this chapter.

DrawPicture
> Takes three required parameters: a reference to a Picture instance, and the coordinates of a point. Blits the image from that Picture into the Graphics property, with its top left at the given point. Optionally, takes six more parameters, so that its parameters are now a Picture instance and two rectangles; blits the image from the part of the Picture described by second rectangle into the part of the Graphics property described by the first rectangle. If the rectangles are of different sizes, the copied image is scaled.

Use of DrawPicture with the extra six parameters can double the memory requirements of the Picture from which you're copying, if that Picture wasn't generated with NewPicture (that is, if it has a `nil` Graphics property). This is because REALbasic makes a cache copy of the Picture as a speed optimization. If there isn't enough memory for this cache copy, the DrawPicture action fails silently (meaning that the drawing isn't performed and you have no way of knowing it); this might be regarded as a bug. A workaround, for when memory is tight, is discussed later in the chapter ("Fun With Graphics Properties").

Backdrop Property

At last we are ready to display some images! Recall that we can do this in one of two ways: by way of a Canvas's (or window's) Backdrop property, and by way of its Graphics property. This section is about the first of those ways.

The Backdrop property of a Canvas (or a window) couldn't be simpler; it is just a reference to an instance of the Picture class. Once this reference is set, REALbasic automatically displays that Picture's image, with its upper left at the Canvas's (or window's) upper left, and maintains it for you. I will illustrate (to coin a phrase) under five headings, corresponding to the five ways in which a Picture instance can be obtained (as enumerated in "Getting a Picture," earlier in this chapter).

In these initial examples, I set the Canvas's Backdrop property once, presumably when the application starts up. However, it's important to understand that you aren't limited to this. You can set a Canvas's Backdrop property at any time. If the Canvas's Backdrop property is already set to point at a Picture instance, you can set it to point at a different Picture instance. Or, if the Picture instance that the Canvas's Backdrop property is pointing to has a non-nil Graphics property, you can write into that Graphics property to change the Picture's image. Either way, the image displayed by the Canvas will change appropriately. Also, in these examples, I assume that the code belongs to the Canvas instance in the window (for example, it appears in its Open event handler), so I refer to the Canvas as me. But this is just a way of keeping the code short and clear. It's important to understand, once again, that you're not limited to this; you can set and work with a Canvas's Backdrop perfectly well from code outside the Canvas. See "Changing a Backdrop," later in the chapter.

Imported Image File

Figure 11-2 shows a Project Window after importing the file *joconde.jpg* into the project. The name joconde now automatically denotes a Picture instance that can be assigned to a Canvas's Backdrop property.

We now have two choices. If we like, we can assign joconde to a Canvas's Backdrop property right in the IDE, using the Properties Window. If we do, REALbasic helpfully displays the picture in the IDE, as shown in Figure 11-3.

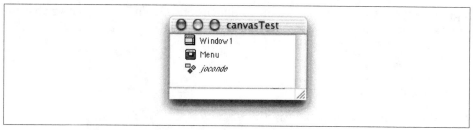

Figure 11-2. Project window listing an imported image file

Figure 11-3. Canvas Backdrop image displayed in the IDE

The other alternative is to perform the assignment in code. Suppose we wish to display this image from the moment the window opens. Then, in the Canvas's Open event handler, we can say:

```
me.backdrop = joconde
```

Either way, when the project runs, the picture is displayed, as shown in Figure 11-4.

Figure 11-4. Image in an application window

The image is cropped because our Canvas isn't large enough to accommodate it; if we like, we can resize and reposition the Canvas dynamically as the application starts up, in response to the Picture instance's dimensions. Again, I'm assuming that the code is in the Canvas's Open event handler:

```
me.backdrop = joconde
self.height = joconde.height + 30
me.width = joconde.width
me.height = joconde.height
me.top = (self.height - me.height) / 2
me.left = (self.width - me.width) / 2
```

Now the picture is fully displayed and nicely centered in the window, as shown in Figure 11-5. No visible flicker arises from assigning the Backdrop and then resizing the Canvas, because the control is not shown until after its Open event handler has finished executing.

Figure 11-5. A Canvas that resizes itself to match its Backdrop

Imported Resource File

Let's presume that a Resource file (that is, a file of type `'rsrc'`) has been imported into the project, and that it contains a `'PICT'` resource whose ID is 1000. Then the Canvas can say this:

```
me.backdrop = app.resourcefork.getpicture(1000)
```

If what you know is the `'PICT'` resource's name, not its ID, you can use GetNamed-Picture instead of GetPicture.

Obtaining an icon resource from the Resource file is similar; the method is GetIcL for a large-icon family, GetIcS for a small-icon family, and GetCicn for a `'cicn'`. So, for example:

```
me.backdrop = app.resourcefork.geticl(-16455)
```

Again, suppose the Canvas is not sized and centered correctly for the picture; the Backdrop is now a Picture instance, so we can check its dimensions:

```
me.backdrop = app.resourcefork.getpicture(1000)
me.width = me.backdrop.width
me.height = me.backdrop.height
me.top = (self.height - me.height) / 2
me.left = (self.width - me.width) / 2
```

Image File at Runtime

Your application can load and display a picture from an image file. For example, imagine that we have not imported any picture file into our project; rather, we know somehow that a JPEG file called *joconde.jpg* is sitting on the user's desktop. Then the Canvas can say this:

```
me.backdrop = desktopFolder.child("joconde.jpg").openAsPicture
```

File Resource at Runtime

Alternatively, suppose there's a file on the user's desktop which is not an image file, but contains a resource of type 'PICT'. The resource can be loaded at runtime. The Canvas could say this:

```
me.backdrop = desktopFolder.child("anyOldFile").openResourceFork.getpicture(1000)
```

Extracting an icon resource from the file is similar:

```
me.backdrop = desktopFolder.child("anyOldFile").openResourceFork.geticl(-16455)
```

The same methods are available as with the application's own resource fork: GetPicture, GetNamedPicture, GetIcL, GetIcS, and GetCicn.

NewPicture

To make a Picture instance from scratch, call the NewPicture function. You supply the width, height, and color depth for the instance. Now you can draw into the new Picture instance's Graphics property, by sending messages to it.

Here is a simple example: in the Canvas's Open event handler, we'll create a Picture instance, assign it to the Backdrop, and then draw a small black rectangle into its Graphics property:

```
me.backdrop = newPicture(100,100,16)
me.backdrop.graphics.forecolor = rgb(0,0,0) // black
me.backdrop.graphics.fillrect 43,37,20,7 // rectangle
```

This gives the result shown in Figure 11-6. Every pixel that we didn't write to is white; the rectangle is filled with black (our ForeColor setting).

The example did not generate a very exciting image, but you should be excited anyway. This fifth technique is not like the others! A Picture instance obtained from a file has no usable Graphics property. That means you can't modify its image. But a Picture instance generated using NewPicture does have a usable Graphics property. That means you *can* modify its image. You can modify it in any way you like; every pixel belongs to you. Perhaps you'd like to see some examples? Read on.

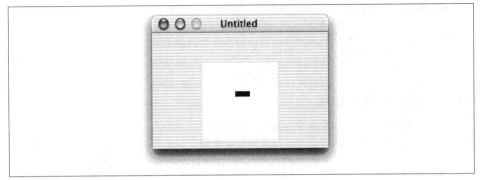

Figure 11-6. Letting the computer construct a drawing from scratch

Fun With Graphics Properties

This section illustrates a few of the devices you can use to form an image, once you have a Graphics property to write to.

Image Transformations

Let's suppose once again that we have imported the file *joconde.jpg* into our project. When the application runs, this will yield a Picture instance. But this Picture instance has a `nil` Graphics property, so we can't modify it. However, suppose we also have a second Picture instance, which was generated using NewPicture. This second Picture instance does have a usable Graphics property. We can use DrawPicture to copy the first Picture's image into the Graphics property of the second. Now, in the second Picture, we have the same image, but we can modify it. If this second Picture instance is a Canvas's Backdrop, the modified image is displayed in our application.

For example, if we like, we can overwrite some of the joconde image's pixels with our black rectangle (see Figure 11-7):

```
me.backdrop = newPicture(100,100,16)
me.backdrop.graphics.drawPicture joconde,0,0
me.backdrop.graphics.forecolor = rgb(0,0,0)
me.backdrop.graphics.fillrect 43,37,20,7
```

In that example, DrawPicture took only three parameters: a reference to the Picture whose pixels we're copying, and the point at which we want to start drawing within our Graphics property. DrawPicture may optionally take six more parameters, and then we can copy just a portion of the original image, and can even scale it as we do so. Here, for example, we scale a portion of the original to four times its initial size (see Figure 11-8):

```
me.backdrop = newPicture(100,100,16)
me.backdrop.graphics.drawPicture joconde,0,0,100,100,40,35,25,25
```

Recall from "Graphics Class," earlier in this chapter, that DrawPicture with the extra parameters doubles the memory requirement of the Picture you're copying from, if

Figure 11-7. Overwriting an image

Figure 11-8. Scaling an image

that Picture wasn't generated with NewPicture. This might not be much of a problem with the small joconde image, but if a Picture occupies several megabytes of memory, the sudden need for several more megabytes might present a serious obstacle. In this example, we're scaling just a small part of the image, so there's a workaround.* We capture the part of the image we're going to scale into a temporary Picture, using DrawPicture without the extra parameters (by means of negative offsets); then we scale from that temporary Picture. Since the temporary Picture was generated with NewPicture, scaling from it does not use any extra memory; the only extra memory involved is the memory occupied by the temporary Picture itself. Here's the scaling routine rewritten to demonstrate the workaround:

```
dim p2 as picture, g as graphics
p2 = newpicture (25, 25, 16)
p2.graphics.drawpicture joconde,-40,-35
me.backdrop = newPicture(100,100,16)
g = me.backdrop.graphics
g.drawpicture p2,0,0,p.width,p.height,0,0,p2.width,p2.height
```

In the next example, we tile a portion of the original image (see Figure 11-9):

---

* I owe my knowledge of this to David Grogono.

```
dim i, j as integer, g as graphics
me.backdrop = newPicture(100,100,16)
g = me.backdrop.graphics
for i = 0 to 75 step 25
    for j = 0 to 75 step 25
        g.drawPicture joconde,i,j,25,25,40,35,25,25
    next
next
```

Figure 11-9. Tiling an image

Alternatively, we can once again avoid the memory demands of the extra cache copy of our original Picture by copying the portion we intend to tile into a temporary Picture first:

```
dim i, j as integer, g as graphics, p2 as picture
me.backdrop = newPicture(100,100,16)
g = me.backdrop.graphics
p2 = newpicture (25, 25, 16)
p2.graphics.drawpicture joconde,-40,-35
for i = 0 to 75 step 25
    for j = 0 to 75 step 25
        g.drawpicture p2,i,j
    next
next
```

Scaling down also automatically performs antialiasing.* This is particularly useful for drawing strings on Mac OS Classic (as opposed to Mac OS X, where strings are anti-aliased automatically). In Figure 11-10, the second Hello was created by drawing it at double size into a double-sized Picture, and then using DrawPicture to scale it down; as a result, the edges of the letters are smoothed with shades of gray.

```
dim p as picture
dim g as graphics
p = newpicture(2*me.width, 2*me.height, 16)
p.graphics.textfont = "Palatino"
p.graphics.textsize = 48
```

---

* This doesn't work on Windows.

```
p.graphics.drawstring "Hello",0,p.height/2
me.backdrop = newpicture(me.width,me.height,16)
g = me.backdrop.graphics
g.drawpicture p,0,0,g.width,g.height,0,0,p.width,p.height
```

Figure 11-10. Antialiased text on Mac OS Classic

Another possibility is to play with the depth setting of our Picture instance. If, when we create it, it has room for only four colors, then drawing into it will reduce the depth accordingly, posterizing the image (Figure 11-11):

Figure 11-11. Posterizing an image

```
me.backdrop = newPicture(100,100,2)
me.backdrop.graphics.drawpicture joconde,0,0
```

Still another possibility is to alter individual pixels. A pixel is referred to by its horizontal and vertical coordinates, and its value is its color. In Figure 11-12, we have altered every pixel by subtracting the value of each color component from 255, thus inverting the image:

```
dim i,j,u1,u2 as integer
dim c as color, g as graphics
me.backdrop = newPicture(100,100,16)
g = me.backdrop.graphics
g.drawPicture joconde,0,0
u1 = g.width - 1
u2 = g.height - 1
for i = 0 to u1
```

```
    for j = 0 to u2
        c = g.pixel(i,j)
        g.pixel(i,j) = rgb(255-c.red, 255-c.green, 255-c.blue)
    next
next
```

Figure 11-12. Inverting an image

And in Figure 11-13 we write the same color to every other pixel, tinting the image:

```
dim i,j,u1,u2 as integer
dim c as color, g as graphics
c = rgb(&hff, &h9c, &h63)
me.backdrop = newpicture(100,100,16)
g = me.backdrop.graphics
g.drawpicture joconde,0,0
u1 = g.width - 1
u2 = g.height - 1
for i = 0 to u1 step 2
    for j = 0 to u2 step 2
        g.pixel(i,j) = c
    next
next
```

Figure 11-13. Tinting an image

Changing a Backdrop

The examples so far have presumed that we are setting the Canvas's Backdrop property once, probably in the Canvas's Open event handler. But of course it can be set or changed at any time, and from code that lives anywhere. There are two techniques: you can reassign the Backdrop property to point at a different Picture instance; or, you can modify the Picture instance to which the Backdrop is pointing already, by way of its Graphics property (if this isn't nil).

Let's try the second technique. We'll invert the image again, but we'll break the example up into two handlers. The Canvas's Open event handler draws the picture normally:

```
me.backdrop = newPicture(100,100,16)
me.backdrop.graphics.drawPicture joconde,0,0
```

The rest of the code we'll put into the Action event handler of a button:

```
dim i,j,u1,u2 as integer
dim c as color
dim g as graphics
g = canvas1.backdrop.graphics
u1 = g.width - 1
u2 = g.height - 1
for i = 0 to u1
    for j = 0 to u2
        c = g.pixel(i,j)
        g.pixel(i,j) = rgb(255-c.red, 255-c.green, 255-c.blue)
    next
next
```

Now the user can press the button to invert the image, and again to return it to normal.

If you're following along by trying out all this code on your computer, you may have noticed (depending on the speed of your computer) that the image took a moment to invert, in response to pressing the button. This sort of access to individual pixels of a Picture's image is much faster if performed by way of the Picture's RGBSurface property than if performed, as here, by way of its Graphics property. See "Speed," later in this chapter.

Animation

As a simple example of animation within a Canvas, let's return to the little black rectangle in the white background. Imagine that we wish to let the user drag this rectangle with the mouse. The Canvas's Open event handler draws the rectangle just as before, but now the position of the rectangle is remembered in two integer properties of the window, OldX and OldY:

```
me.backdrop = newPicture(100,100,16)
me.backdrop.graphics.forecolor = rgb(0,0,0) // black
me.backdrop.graphics.fillrect 43,37,20,7 // rectangle
self.oldX = 43
self.oldY = 37
```

In the Canvas's MouseDown event handler, we check to see if the user's click is within the black rectangle; if it is, we record the relationship between the mouse and the rectangle's top left in two more integer properties of the window, OffsetX and OffsetY, and return true to signal that MouseDrag events should be generated:

```
if x >= self.oldX and x <= self.oldX + 20 then
    if y >= self.oldY and y <= self.oldY + 7 then
        self.offsetx = x-self.oldx
        self.offsety = y-self.oldy
        return true // track the mouse
    end
end
```

In the Canvas's MouseDrag event handler, we erase the existing rectangle, adjust OldX and OldY to record the new rectangle's top left, and draw the new rectangle; this is preceded by a test so that the user can't drag the rectangle out of the Canvas:

```
dim g as graphics
if x > 0 and y > 0 and x < me.width and y < me.height then
    g = me.backdrop.graphics
    g.clearrect self.oldx,self.oldy,20,7
    self.oldx = x-self.offsetx
    self.oldy = y-self.offsety
    g.fillrect self.oldx,self.oldy,20,7
end
```

This works splendidly, and is lots of fun; but if you're trying it on your own computer I hope you noticed an annoying flicker while you were dragging the rectangle. If so, you'll be properly motivated to read the next section, "Canvas Graphics Property," which describes how to do this sort of animation without any flicker, by drawing into the Canvas's own Graphics property instead of the Graphics property of its Backdrop. (Unfortunately for me, but fortunately for you, if you're on Mac OS X, you won't see any flicker. Nevertheless, I assure you that the "Canvas Graphics Property" section is important!)

Before proceeding to that, however, let's give ourselves slightly more of a challenge. We'll do the same animation again, but this time the black rectangle will appear to float over the joconde image. This sounds daunting, but it differs in only two lines of code from the animation we just did.

The Canvas's Open event handler needs just one extra line, to paint the joconde image:

```
me.backdrop = newPicture(100,100,16)
me.backdrop.graphics.drawPicture joconde,0,0
me.backdrop.graphics.forecolor = rgb(0,0,0)
me.backdrop.graphics.fillrect 43,37,20,7
self.oldX = 43
self.oldY = 37
```

The Canvas's MouseDown handler is unchanged:

```
if x >= self.oldX and x <= self.oldX + 20 then
    if y >= self.oldY and y <= self.oldY + 7 then
        self.offsetx = x-self.oldx
```

```
        self.offsety = y-self.oldy
        return true // track the mouse
    end
end
```

In the Canvas's MouseDrag event handler, just one line needs changing. We cannot simply send the ClearRect message to remove the old rectangle, because the rectangle will leave a white trail as it is dragged. Instead, we must replace the black rectangle with the appropriate block of pixels copied from the original joconde image:

```
dim g as graphics
if x > 0 and y > 0 and x < me.width and y < me.height then
    g = me.backdrop.graphics
    g.drawpicture joconde,self.oldx,self.oldy,20,7,self.oldx,self.oldy,20,7
    self.oldx = x-self.offsetx
    self.oldy = y-self.offsety
    g.fillrect self.oldx,self.oldy,20,7
end
```

It works splendidly—except for the flickering. Be patient, we'll fix it.

Limitations of Graphics Methods

After you've worked with Graphics properties a while, you may begin to feel that you're being shortchanged. This is supposedly your chance to access the power of the Macintosh Toolbox's QuickDraw commands, but in fact the methods of a Graphics property represent only a small portion of those commands. You're compelled to work around this, which is annoying because you know that the computer already has facilities for making your life easier, if only you could access them.

For example, in the Odummo game example at my web site—so named because it plays Othello badly, so that I can (usually) win—each game piece is drawn on the board (as shown in Figure 11-14) by a series of Graphics messages:

```
// dropshadow
graphics.foreColor = rgb (90,100,90)
graphics.fillOval 7,7,35,35
// piece interior
graphics.foreColor = fillc
graphics.fillOval 5,5,35,35
// piece outline
graphics.foreColor = hilitec
graphics.drawOval 5,5,35,35
// piece hilite arc, a circle partly covered by two triangles
graphics.drawOval 13,13,19,19
graphics.foreColor = fillc
points(1)=6
points(2)=22
points(3)=39
points(4)=22
points(5)=22
points(6)=39
graphics.fillPolygon points
points(1)=22
```

```
points(2)=22
points(3)=39
points(4)=22
points(5)=27
points(6)=8
graphics.fillPolygon points
```

Figure 11-14. An Odummo game piece, unnecessarily difficult to draw

Things here start out straightforward enough, but then the time comes to draw the small arc within the piece, it turns out that although the Toolbox has a routine for drawing an arc, REALbasic has no corresponding Graphics method; so we have to draw an entire circle and then blot out pieces of it, using polygons filled with the same color as the piece's interior.

If you find yourself frequently being brought up short by such limitations, you may want to write some generalized routines. Another alternative is to look into a third-party plug-in, which extends REALbasic's command set (see Chapter 32). A particularly well known one is Einhugur's QuickDrawLib;* with it, the last sixteen lines of my code would have been reduced substantially to one:

```
framearc 13,13,32,32,0,-90
```

Canvas Graphics Property

Whatever is drawn into a Canvas's Graphics property appears as an image in the Canvas. This image is rendered after the Canvas's Backdrop image, and pixels that have not been written to are not drawn, so the Canvas's Graphics image is effectively layered transparently on top of its Backdrop image (or on top of whatever is behind the Canvas, if it has no assigned Backdrop).

This section describes certain special features of a Canvas's (or window's) Graphics property, as opposed to the Graphics property of a Picture.

Paint Event

The preceding section demonstrated lots of cute tricks for modifying a Canvas's image by way of a Graphics property. But the Graphics property in question belonged to the Canvas's Backdrop, which is somewhat paradoxical, since a Canvas itself has a Graphics property. So why can't we draw directly into *that* Graphics property, and omit altogether the intermediate Backdrop?

---

* See *http://www.einhugur.com/Html/freedl.html*. I wish to thank Björn Eiríksson for making his plug-ins available to me.

We can. But this requires some extra work on our part. Once a Canvas's Backdrop property points to a Picture, the Canvas displays that Picture's image automatically. In particular, it redraws the image whenever the window needs to be redrawn—for example, because another window was covering it and has now been removed, or because it has received a Refresh message (for the Refresh and RefreshRect methods, see Chapters 9 and 10). With the Canvas's Graphics property, exactly the opposite is true: every time the window needs to be redrawn, the Canvas *erases* its Graphics property!

To see this, here's an altered version of an earlier example. We'll have a Canvas's Open event handler write directly to the Canvas's own Graphics property:

```
me.graphics.drawPicture joconde,0,0,100,100,40,35,25,25
```

This is delightfully simple, but there's just one problem: when we run the project, nothing is displayed in the window! What's gone wrong?

The answer is that although we have drawn the *initial* image for our Canvas's Graphics property, we have neglected to *maintain* it. It isn't enough to draw the Graphics property once; we have to draw it *every time it needs redrawing*—because the Canvas erases it every time it needs redrawing. And when is that? At the very least, it's every time the Canvas receives a Paint event. That's what the Paint event is for. It says to your Canvas: "I've just erased your Graphics property, so if you want anything to appear there, draw it now."

Our one-line example will work perfectly if we just move that line out of the Canvas's Open event handler and into its Paint event handler. In fact, the line can be shortened, because REALbasic, knowing that the Paint event handler will probably want to operate on the Canvas's Graphics property, hands it a reference to this property, g:

```
g.drawPicture joconde,0,0,100,100,40,35,25,25
```

Now the image appears, and remains. Every time the Canvas needs redrawing, its Paint event handler is called, and this line is executed. Therefore, from the user's point of view, the image is always there.

Here is the train of events. Whenever REALbasic redraws any portion of a window, it empties the part of the Graphics property of the window, and those parts of the Graphics properties of any Canvases, that intersect the region that needs redrawing. Then it sends a Paint event, first to the window, then to each of these Canvases, which must respond by drawing their respective Graphics properties again. To prevent flicker, REALbasic clips whatever drawing your code performs in response to the Paint event, so that even if your code redraws an entire Graphics property, only those pixels that need redrawing are actually redrawn.

The implication is that we can avoid flicker, and maintain greater control over the redrawing of individual pixels, and redraw faster, if we use the Canvas's Graphics property, rather than its Backdrop. That's what the rest of this section is about.

The Paint event's reference to the Canvas's Graphics property as g is not the same as speaking of theCanvas.graphics or even me.graphics. Do not mix and match reference styles. If your Paint event calls a method that needs to draw into the Graphics property, you should hand that method a reference to g as a parameter.*

Smooth Animation

One reason for preferring to draw in the Canvas's Graphics property, rather than its Backdrop, is that we might want to change the image fluidly, without flicker and with maximum control over the individual pixels. To illustrate, recall the animated rectangle example in which the black rectangle floats over the joconde image ("Animation," earlier in this chapter). We can easily change this so that all the drawing happens in the Canvas's Graphics property, not in its Backdrop.

You may wonder why we do not put the black rectangle in the Canvas's Graphics property and the joconde image, which is unmoving and unchanging behind it, in the Backdrop property. The answer is that no message to the Graphics property alone lets us remove the previous black rectangle during the animation. We have to draw *to* the Graphics property; we cannot erase *from* it, except by using Refresh or RefreshRect which causes the same Backdrop flicker as before.

The Canvas's Open event handler loses its first line, because the Graphics property needs no instantiation from us; references to me.backdrop.graphics become references to me.graphics:

```
me.graphics.drawPicture joconde,0,0
me.graphics.forecolor = rgb(0,0,0)
me.graphics.fillrect 43,37,20,7
self.oldX = 43
self.oldY = 37
```

The Canvas needs a Paint event handler, drawing the joconde image and the rectangle in its current position:

```
g.drawPicture joconde,0,0
g.fillrect self.oldx,self.oldy,20,7
```

In the Canvas's MouseDrag event handler, we write to me.graphics, not me.backdrop. graphics; an additional test at the beginning makes sure that we don't do any drawing unless the mouse has actually moved:

```
dim g as graphics
if self.oldx<>x-self.offsetx or self.oldy<>y-self.offsety then
    if x > 0 and y > 0 and x < me.width and y < me.height then
        g = me.graphics
        g.drawpicture joconde,self.oldx,self.oldy,20,7,self.oldx,self.oldy,20,7
```

---

* Thanks to Steven J. Schaeffer for calling this to my attention.

```
        self.oldx = x-self.offsetx
        self.oldy = y-self.offsety
        g.fillrect self.oldx,self.oldy,20,7
    end
end
```

The Canvas's MouseDown event handler is unchanged:

```
if x >= self.oldX and x <= self.oldX + 20 then
    if y >= self.oldY and y <= self.oldY + 7 then
        self.offsetx = x-self.oldx
        self.offsety = y-self.oldy
        return true // track the mouse
    end
end
```

Try it! You'll see that now you can drag the rectangle over the joconde image with no flicker, because during the drag the only pixels being redrawn are those that our MouseDrag event handler says to redraw.

The thoughtful reader will have noticed that in this example a single pair of lines, the drawing of the joconde image and of the rectangle, appears three times—in the Open event handler, in the Paint event handler, and in the MouseDrag event handler. This typifies a frequent situation: we must draw into the Canvas's Graphics property both in response to the Paint event and in response to some other stimulus. We should abstract the common functionality to a method, because otherwise the code soon becomes difficult to maintain.

At this point we might as well replace our Canvas with a Canvas subclass, which we will call JocoCanvas. The integer properties OldX, OldY, OffsetX, and OffsetY are removed from the window and put into JocoCanvas instead. Now everything is properly object-oriented. We give JocoCanvas a method Redraw, which takes two integer parameters, newx and newy, telling it where to locate the rectangle. Since we need to redraw sometimes the entire joconde image and sometimes just that region of it vacated by the previous location of the rectangle, it also takes a boolean parameter, whole:

```
dim g as graphics
g = self.graphics
if whole then
    g.drawPicture joconde,0,0
else
    g.drawpicture joconde,self.oldx,self.oldy,20,7,self.oldx,self.oldy,20,7
end
self.oldX = newX
self.oldY = newY
g.fillrect self.oldx,self.oldy,20,7
```

Now JocoCanvas's Open event handler goes like this:

```
self.graphics.forecolor = rgb(0,0,0)
self.redraw 43, 37, true
```

JocoCanvas's Paint event handler goes like this:

```
self.redraw self.oldX, self.oldY, true
```

JocoCanvas's MouseDown event handler is exactly the same as the Canvas's Mouse-Down event handler was before:

```
if x >= self.oldX and x <= self.oldX + 20 then
    if y >= self.oldY and y <= self.oldY + 7 then
        self.offsetx = x-self.oldx
        self.offsety = y-self.oldy
        return true // track the mouse
    end
end
```

And JocoCanvas's MouseDrag event handler goes like this:

```
if self.oldx <> x-self.offsetx or self.oldy <> y-self.offsety then
    if x > 0 and y > 0 and x < self.width and y < self.height then
        self.redraw x-self.offsetx, y-self.offsety, false
    end
end
```

The functionality here is unchanged, but it is far better organized.

Scrolling

Another situation where you will prefer to draw to a Canvas's Graphics property rather than to its Background property is when you want to scroll the Canvas image.

A Canvas's Scroll method offsets the image rightward and downward by the number of pixels specified as parameters; these values can be negative, to move the image leftward and upward. The scrolling of the material already visible within the Canvas is very fast and smooth. But no new material appears; for example, if we scroll our image to the left, the existing image moves left, but REALbasic doesn't automatically supply the new part of it that is supposed to have entered from the right. So our code must draw this, and to avoid flicker of the whole image, we should be drawing into the Graphics property.

To make our lives easy, after we send the Canvas the Scroll message, REALbasic sends it a Paint event if any movement of the image actually occurred. To make our lives even easier, our drawing during this Paint event is automatically clipped to the regions that need redrawing; so there is no flicker even if we redraw the whole image, because in fact only the new pixels are actually redrawn. So, the technique is this: scroll the Canvas, and then have its Paint event handler redraw the image at its new location.

To illustrate, let's make a very simple test project. The window has a Canvas and a button. The project has an imported image file (in this example, joconde). The window has two integer properties, JLeft and JTop. The Canvas's Paint event handler draws the whole image at the location specified by JLeft and JTop:

```
g.drawpicture joconde, self.JLeft, self.JTop // window properties
```

Let's first show what *not* to do. In the button's Action event handler, we'll shift the values of JLeft and JTop, and send the Canvas the Refresh message:

```
self.JLeft = self.JLeft-2 // window property
self.JTop = self.JTop-2 // window property
canvas1.refresh
```

Run the project, and press the button repeatedly. The image shifts, but it flickers as it does so, because we're redrawing the entire image. Instead, we should take advantage of the Canvas's ability to scroll. So change the last line of the button's Action event handler:

```
self.JLeft = self.JLeft-2
self.JTop = self.JTop-2
canvas1.scroll -2,-2
```

Try it. No flash! Congratulations, you're scrolling.

That was too easy, so let's implement live scrolling: the user should be able to grab the image with the mouse and drag it within the Canvas, as in Figure 11-15. For the sake of simplicity, we won't worry for now about whether the drag stays within, or drags the image out of, the Canvas.

Figure 11-15. Live scrolling by dragging with the mouse (before and after)

We'll begin with a new Canvas subclass, JocoScroller. It will have four integer properties: JLeft and JTop will designate the top left corner of the joconde image, and OldX and OldY will keep track of the mouse position.

JocoScroller's Paint event handler just draws the image at the current JLeft and JTop coordinates:

```
g.drawPicture joconde, self.jLeft, self.jTop // JocoScroller properties
```

JocoScroller's MouseDown event handler records the position of the mouse and starts tracking it:

```
self.oldX = x
self.oldY = y
return true // track the mouse
```

All the actual work is done in the MouseDrag event handler. If the mouse has not moved, there is nothing to do. If it has, we adjust all four properties and send the Canvas the Scroll message, moving the image to follow the mouse movement:

```
dim diffx, diffy as integer
if x <> self.oldX or y <> self.oldY then
    diffx = x-self.oldX
    diffy = y-self.oldY
    self.jLeft = self.jLeft+diffx
    self.jTop = self.jTop+diffy
    self.oldX = x
    self.oldY = y
    self.scroll diffx,diffy
end
```

That's all, because after we send the Scroll message, REALbasic will send a Paint event and we will redraw the image; this redrawing will be clipped in such a way that we'll be filling in just the new pixels at the edges of the Canvas.

Again, the code could use some reorganization. Our JocoScroller class will be much more powerful if it knows how to scroll itself under any circumstances, not just when dragged with the mouse. So let's abstract the code that actually does the scrolling. We give JocoScroller a method ScrollMe, which takes two integer parameters, x and y:

```
self.jLeft = self.jLeft+x
self.jTop = self.jTop+y
self.scroll x,y
```

Now JocoScroller's MouseDrag event handler goes like this:

```
if x <> self.oldX or y <> self.oldY then
    self.scrollme(x-self.oldx, y-self.oldy)
    self.oldX = x
    self.oldY = y
end
```

That's much better. It's simpler, because we've eliminated a couple of local variables; and it's more object-oriented, because now JocoScroller's MouseDrag event handler thinks only about the properties appropriate to itself (OldX and OldY), while its ScrollMe method maintains the properties appropriate to itself (JTop and JLeft).

In Chapter 15 we'll see how to hook a Canvas to a pair of Scrollbar controls, so that the user can scroll it in the customary fashion.

When continuously animating a scrolling action by means of a loop within a single subroutine, a slight modification of this algorithm is necessary. So, for instance, suppose we want to start with an empty Canvas and press a button to animate the joconde image rising smoothly into it, like a jack-in-the-box. We might expect that it would suffice to use our JocoScroller Canvas, and have the button's Action event handler go like this:

```
canvas1.jtop = canvas1.height // start at the bottom
canvas1.jleft = 0
canvas1.refresh
do // rise one pixel
    canvas1.jTop = canvas1.jTop-1
    canvas1.scroll 0,-1
loop until canvas1.jTop = 0
```

But it doesn't work; the Canvas image vanishes and doesn't reappear. The trouble is that the Paint event is not being sent during the loop. We will have to trigger it ourselves. We can do this with the Refresh method; but that redraws all the pixels and causes flicker. The trick is to use the RefreshRect method. Even if we do this with a zero-size refresh region specified, REALbasic wakes up to the fact that refreshing is necessary, and redraws only the new pixels, in accordance with its usual automatic behavior after a Scroll.* Our button's Action event handler can take advantage of this, and of JocoScroller's new ScrollMe method:

```
canvas1.jtop = canvas1.height
canvas1.refresh
do
    canvas1.scrollme 0,-1
    canvas1.refreshrect 0,0,0,0
loop until canvas1.jTop = 0
```

A Canvas's Scroll method may optionally take four additional parameters specifying the rectangular region of the Canvas that is to be scrolled. This presents no procedural complications as far as the scrolling itself is concerned, but drawing the resulting image afterward in the Canvas's Paint event handler will be a more elaborate affair than merely offsetting some single image, because the resulting image is now "split." One approach might be to draw the entire original image in its original place, then draw the shifted area with its new offset.

Transparency and Icons

An image is transparent if some of its pixels are not drawn, or are not fully drawn; whatever is behind the image is visible wherever the image has transparent pixels. An image can be made transparent in three ways:

- Through a Picture's Transparent property
- Through a Picture's Mask property
- Through the mask information accompanying an icon

These will now be treated in turn.

---

* This technique was first called to my attention by Bob Urschel.

Transparent Property

Using a Picture's Transparent property, only the color white, $rgb(255,255,255)$, can be rendered transparent. If you want to turn some other color of an image transparent, go through all its pixels, turning each white one to some other color (which may be fairly close to white, so that it looks white to the user), and then go through them again, turning white all pixels that you wish to be transparent. The rule is that if a Picture's Transparent property is 1, white pixels are not copied from it when it is copied with DrawPicture into a Graphics property. A Canvas's Graphics property, you remember, is itself transparent: any undrawn pixels are invisible. A Canvas's Backdrop property, on the other hand, is transparent only if the Picture instance to which it points has its Transparent property set to 1.

For example, suppose our project has incorporated into it a Resource file containing a 'PICT' resource with ID 1000 which we wish to display transparently in a window. We create a Picture property, GWorld, to hold the picture in its transparent form.[*] In the Open event handler of the Canvas, we load the image into the Picture property and set the transparency:

```
gworld = app.resourcefork.getpicture(1000)
gworld.transparent = 1
```

Now, in the Paint event handler of the Canvas, we can say:

```
g.drawpicture gworld,0,0
```

Alternatively, we could display the image in the Canvas's Backdrop. Now no GWorld is needed, because the Backdrop is a Picture, whose transparency we can set. Delete the code from the Canvas's Paint event handler, and change its Open event handler to read like this:

```
me.backdrop = app.resourcefork.getpicture(1000)
me.backdrop.transparent = 1
```

Either way, the image is displayed transparently, as shown in Figure 11-16; notice the absence of any white background square behind the image, whereas, if we omit to set the Transparent property to 1, there will be a white background square.

Mask Property

A Picture instance's Mask is another Picture of the same size, each of whose pixels determines the degree of transparency of the corresponding pixel in the main Picture's image. Where the Mask has a black pixel, the main Picture's pixel is drawn normally; where the Mask has a white pixel, the main Picture's pixel is not drawn.

---

[*] Picture instances used to store material so that it can be processed invisibly and rapidly blitted to the screen are often referred to as *offscreen gWorlds*, or simply *gWorlds* (pronounced "gee-worlds"), because this is the Macintosh Toolbox name for such a data structure. Shortly after the movie *Wayne's World* appeared, the monthly CD-ROM that Apple used to send to members of its developer subscription series was entitled "Wayne's gWorld." A lot of geeks collapsed with laughter over that one.

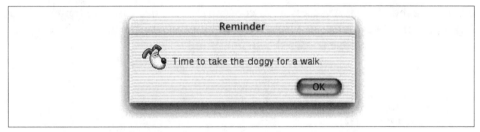

Figure 11-16. Dialog displaying a transparent image

Shades of gray in the Mask cause the main Picture's corresponding pixels to be drawn with partial transparency, blending with what is behind them. By default, every pixel of a Mask is black; otherwise, all images would be invisible!

To draw to a Picture instance's Mask, refer to the Mask's Graphics property and draw into it in the usual way. For example, the following code displays in a Canvas an image that is clipped to an oval shape, as shown in Figure 11-17:

```
dim p as picture
dim h,w as integer
w = joconde.width
h = joconde.height
p = newpicture(w,h,32)
p.graphics.drawpicture joconde,0,0
p.mask.graphics.forecolor = rgb(255,255,255) // completely transparent
p.mask.graphics.fillrect 0,0,w,h
p.mask.graphics.forecolor = rgb(0,0,0) // draw normally
p.mask.graphics.filloval 0,0,w,h
canvas1.backdrop = p
```

Figure 11-17. Masking an image to a solid oval

By drawing the Mask as a succession of concentric ovals, decreasing in both size and brightness (from near-white to black), we can blur the transparency of the clipping oval to achieve a vignette effect, as shown in Figure 11-18:

```
dim p as picture
dim h,w,i as integer
w = joconde.width
h = joconde.height
p = newpicture(w,h,32)
p.graphics.drawpicture joconde,0,0
p.mask.graphics.forecolor = rgb(255,255,255)
p.mask.graphics.fillrect 0,0,w,h
for i = 0 to 15
    p.mask.graphics.forecolor = rgb((15-i)*16,(15-i)*16,(15-i)*16)
    p.mask.graphics.filloval i,i,w-2*i,h-2*i
next
canvas1.backdrop = p
```

Figure 11-18. Masking an image to a blurred oval

Clearly, many interesting effects can be achieved by way of the Mask property; I leave it to your imagination and experimentation to discover them.

Icons

A common type of transparent image is an icon. You don't have to set its Transparent property, and its white pixels are not necessarily transparent. Rather, its transparent region is determined by its mask, which is intrinsic to the icon.

Access to three standard icons is supplied through the Graphics property's Draw-CautionIcon, DrawNoteIcon, or DrawStopIcon methods, which take two parameters telling where to place the icon. For instance, to make a Stop icon appear in a modal dialog, you might have a Canvas in the dialog whose Paint event handler goes:

```
g.drawStopIcon 0,0
```

Alternatively, you can place the icon in the Canvas's Backdrop. But this requires that the Backdrop have a non-nil Graphics property, so you need to create this with NewPicture, and now you'll have to set the Backdrop's Transparent property explicitly:

```
me.backdrop = newpicture(32,32,32)
me.backdrop.transparent = 1
me.backdrop.graphics.drawstopicon 0,0
```

It is also possible to obtain an icon resource from a resource fork, as demonstrated earlier in this chapter, using the GetIcL, GetIcS, and GetCicn methods of a Resource-Fork. These yield Picture instances, so the technique for displaying the icon is just the same as before: you can draw it into a Canvas's Graphics property, or set a Canvas's Backdrop directly to it. Because it comes from an icon, the Picture is already transparent.

Speed

This section presents some basic considerations for making drawing actions appear as fast as possible to the user. What slows down drawing is calculation, meaning scaling, access to single pixels, mathematical transformations, and so forth. Blitting, on the other hand, is very fast. Scroll and DrawPicture (when you're not scaling) use optimized blitting code from the Toolbox, and are virtually instantaneous. Therefore, although one would naturally like to optimize calculation, even better is not to calculate at all—not, that is, at the moment of drawing. Your strategy for speeding up drawing will thus be a combination of speeding up your calculations and performing those calculations at some other time than when the drawing needs to take place.

Prepared Images

If you know in advance that a Canvas is going to be displaying one of several Pictures, the Pictures can perhaps all be prepared in advance; the right one can than be assigned or blitted into a Canvas instantaneously at need.

Recall the example from "Changing a Backdrop," earlier in this chapter, where the user presses a button to invert an image. What slows down the drawing in that example is that we are recalculating the inverted image every time. But this is ridiculous, since there are just two images, and all the button really needs to do is interchange them. We can store a normal and an inverted version of the picture in separate Picture instances, in advance—say, when the application starts up. Suppose these are Picture properties of the window, which we'll call JocoNormal and JocoInverted. In the Canvas's Open event handler, we prepare both Pictures; then we initialize our Backdrop to point at one of them:

```
dim i,j,u1,u2 as integer
dim c as color
dim r1, r2 as rgbsurface
jocoNormal = newPicture(100,100,32)
jocoInverted = newPicture(100,100,32)
jocoNormal.graphics.drawPicture joconde,0,0
me.backdrop = jocoNormal
r1 = jocoNormal.rgbsurface
r2 = jocoInverted.rgbsurface
u1 = joconde.width - 1
u2 = joconde.height - 1
for i = 0 to u1
    for j = 0 to u2
        c = r1.pixel(i,j)
        r2.pixel(i,j) = rgb(255-c.red, 255-c.green, 255-c.blue)
    next
next
```

Now all the button's Action event handler has to do is to point the Canvas's Backdrop property at the other Picture:

```
if canvas1.backdrop = jocoNormal then
    canvas1.backdrop = jocoInverted
else
    canvas1.backdrop = jocoNormal
end
```

Even this causes some slight delay as the application starts up, because it must pause to calculate the inverted image. If an operation cannot be prevented from taking considerable time, you may be able to perform it in advance in a thread. This causes no visible delay, and the user will be unaware of the calculations going on behind the scenes.

When working with prepared pictures, it is not uncommon to use a single property that is an array of Pictures, because then one can access the correct Picture arithmetically, using an index. For example, if Joco were an array of five pictures, we could cycle to the next one easily:

```
jocoNowShowing = (jocoNowShowing + 1) mod 5 // an integer property
canvas1.backdrop = joco(jocoNowShowing)
```

You can also prepare a series of pictures as regions of a single picture, copying the desired region on demand with DrawPicture. An example of this technique appears in Chapter 28.

By the way, turning an invisible Canvas visible and vice versa is a quick, simple, and flicker-free way to substitute one image for another. For example, suppose that clicking on an image should change it to a different image, which reverts when the mouse is released. You could have a visible, enabled Canvas, covered by a second, invisible, disabled one which holds the second image. The visible Canvas's MouseDown event handler turns the invisible Canvas visible, and returns true; its MouseUp event handler turns it invisible again.

Nonflickering Canvas

The reason a Canvas sometimes flickers when it is redrawn is that at the start of the Paint event the Canvas is erased. If the calculations involved in drawing the Canvas are lengthy, the period during which the Canvas is empty is perceptible. The calculation needn't be complicated; it can be something as simple as scaling. For example, if a Picture is, say, 1700 by 1500 pixels, and you use DrawPicture to scale it into a Canvas 170 by 150 pixels, you can see the image go blank and then slowly appear from top to bottom, even on a very fast computer. Redrawing can take place fairly often (though it takes place much less often on Mac OS X), and you probably don't want this sort of effect repeated every time.

Now, let's suppose that you can't avoid performing the calculations at the time of redrawing. Nonetheless, if you could prevent the Canvas from going blank at the start of the Paint event, you wouldn't speed up the actual time needed to complete the drawing, but you would separate that time from the time needed to blit the completed drawing into place, and the latter, as we've already said, is insubstantial. The user would thus perceive the drawing itself as instantaneous.

In this section, I describe a Canvas subclass called a KeeperCanvas, which redraws itself with its current image at the very start of its Paint event handler, so that the time during which the Canvas is empty is imperceptible. KeeperCanvas has a Picture property, P, which will function as a cache for its image. It also defines a New Event, PostPaint. In its Open event handler, it calls a method MakeCache which initializes P. Here is MakeCache; we presume that what's behind the Canvas is a window with a solid background color, so the FillRect call fills P with that color to make it look transparent, like a Canvas:

```
if self.p = nil then
    self.p = newpicture(self.width, self.height, 16)
end
p.graphics.forecolor = self.window.backcolor
p.graphics.fillrect 0,0,self.width,self.height
```

KeeperCanvas's Paint event goes like this:

```
g.drawpicture self.p,0,0
self.makeCache
postpaint
g.drawpicture self.p,0,0
```

Whoever handles the PostPaint New Event—this will be a subclass of KeeperCanvas, or a KeeperCanvas instance in a window—should draw the new image, not into the Canvas's Graphics property, but into P's Graphics property! The result is that P will always contain the Canvas's current image. At the start of the Paint event, the

Canvas's current image is erased, but since P contains a copy of it, we can immediately put it back again and the user never sees the image empty. We then clear P and call the PostPaint New Event, which results in a new image in P. We then draw the new image from P into the Canvas.

Before leaving KeeperCanvas, let's combine it with the principle from the previous section. Basically, we shouldn't be doing any calculation at all unless we have to. But since at any moment the KeeperCanvas already has a cached copy of its own image, it is foolish even to bother performing its PostPaint activity unless the image needs changing. One can think of various architectures to handle this, but a very simple and effective solution, for the sake of example, is to give KeeperCanvas itself a Valid boolean property. Its Paint event now goes like this:

```
g.drawpicture self.p,0,0
if not self.valid then
    self.valid = true
    self.makeCache
    postpaint
    g.drawpicture self.p,0,0
end
```

It is now the responsibility of some other object to set the Canvas instance's Valid property to `false` as a signal that it needs updating.

Pixel Access

Looping over individual pixels can take a long time if you do it in the wrong place. The rule is that pixels are slow in a Canvas, faster in a Picture, fastest in an RGBSurface. On my computer, inverting the color of 10,000 pixels in a Canvas's Graphics property takes well over a second; in a Picture's Graphics property, it takes about a third of a second; in a Picture's RGBSurface, it takes about a thirtieth of a second, which feels nearly instantaneous.

An RGBSurface is a feature only of a Picture instance; so if the image you want to modify is being shown in a Canvas's Graphics property, you'll have to perform your pixel manipulations elsewhere, in a Picture, and blit the results into place.

For an example of using an RGBSurface to loop over every pixel, look at "Prepared Images," earlier in this section. Notice in particular that before the loop begins we have already captured the RGBSurfaces of both the source Picture and the target Picture as references (here, r1 and r2):

```
c = r1.pixel(i,j)
r2.pixel(i,j) = rgb(255-c.red, 255-c.green, 255-c.blue)
```

That's very important for making our loop as fast as possible (in accordance with the principle enunciated in "Short names" in Chapter 3). If you omit to do this, and instead drill your way down to the RGBSurface every time through the loop, you've only yourself to blame if RGBSurfaces don't seem fast to you:

```
c = jocoNormal.rgbSurface.pixel(i,j) // no, no, that's much too slow!
```

Interaction with Other Objects

Various interesting effects can be achieved through the physical relationship between a Canvas and other interface objects. Rather than attempting to enumerate all the possibilities, I will just provide a few brief but vivid examples, in the hope that this will inspire you to further exploration.

Screen Shots

The Pixel property of the built-in System object reports the color of the screen pixel at the corresponding coordinate, at that moment. This provides a way to copy an arbitrary region of the screen.

For example, in the IDE, put a Canvas in a window, and let the following be its Open event handler:

```
dim i,j,u1,u2 as integer
dim x,y as integer
dim r as rgbSurface
me.backdrop = newpicture(me.width, me.height, 32)
r = me.backdrop.rgbSurface
u1 = me.width-1
u2 = me.height-1
x = me.left + self.left
y = me.top + self.top
for i = 0 to u1
    for j = 0 to u2
        r.pixel(i,j) = system.pixel(i+x,j+y)
    next
next
```

Try to guess what will happen when you run the project. Okay, you'll never guess, so just run it. The Canvas displays a screen shot of what's behind the window—it looks as if the window has a hole in it! What happened is that the Open event handler was run before the window had been drawn; the coordinates of the pixels of the Canvas control were known, though, so the pixels copied through `system.pixel` constitute the screen image at those coordinates.

Another sort of screen shot is provided by a window's DrawInto method. This takes three parameters, a Graphics property and the coordinates of a point; it copies the window's content region into the Graphics property, at that point. At present it's very buggy on Mac OS X (it ignores important components of a window such as PushButtons), but it works quite decently on Mac OS Classic.

For example, the rather bizarre Figure 11-19 shows two windows; the second window is a floating window sitting over the first, and contains a Canvas. The image was generated by pressing the button in the first window, whose Action event handler goes like this:

```
self.drawinto(dialog1.canvas1.backdrop.graphics,0,0)
```

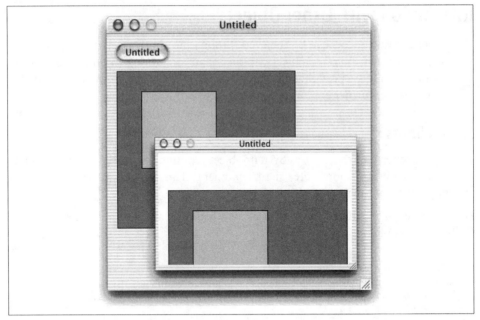

Figure 11-19. A window takes a photo of itself

This feature might be used as a way of masking operations in a window that you don't want the user to see happening. The idea is, during the progress of the operation, to cover the window with a second window containing an image of the first. There is a very slight flicker as the second window appears and disappears, but this may well be preferable to having the user see what's happening in the first window.

For example, recall from Chapter 9 the problem of running through an EditField performing an operation on successive selections. Here we'll turn all instances of the letter "e" bold without the user seeing our progress. The second window consists of a Canvas, and is the same size as the first window. The DrawInto method copies controls but not the background, so we copy our own background color before calling DrawInto; then we show the second window, perform the operation behind it, and hide the second window:

```
dim s as string
dim i as integer
dim e as editfield
dim g as graphics
dim p as picture
dim st,le,sc as integer
e = editfield1
// capture EditField's current state
st = e.selstart
le = e.sellength
sc = e.scrollPosition
// position Window2; its Visible is initially false
window2.top = top
```

```
window2.left = left
p = newpicture(window2.width,window2.height,32)
window2.canvas1.backdrop = p
g = p.graphics
// copy background color
if self.hasBackColor then
    g.forecolor = self.backcolor
else
    g.forecolor = fillcolor
end
g.fillrect 0,0,g.width,g.height
// copy controls
drawInto g,1,1
// show the copy
window2.show
window2.refresh
// do the operation
s = e.text
i = instr(s,"e")
while i > 0
    e.selStart = i-1
    e.selLength = 1
    e.selbold = true
    i = instr(i+1,s,"e")
wend
// restore the EditField's state
e.selstart = st
e.sellength = le
e.scrollPosition = sc
// remove the copy
self.show
window2.close
```

This works particularly nicely if Window2 is a floating window with ProcID 2, because it covers just Window1's content area without deactivating its frame.

Another use of DrawInto might be to create HyperCard-like transitions between one window appearance and another. In this next example, we reveal the new window through a slow "wipe" to the right. The covering window, initially invisible, is named Cover; it consists of a Canvas whose Paint event handler copies into it a Picture property named P. This example illustrates that DrawInto works even if the window is hidden by another window.

```
dim i,t as integer
// create the covering image, position it, and show it
cover.p = newpicture(cover.canvas1.width, cover.canvas1.height, 32)
self.drawinto cover.p.graphics,0,0
cover.left = self.left
cover.top = self.top
cover.width = self.width
cover.height = self.height
cover.show
cover.refresh
// make the new window appearance
```

```
staticText1.text = "Wasn't that amazing?"
statictext1.bold = true
me.caption = "Yes!"
me.enabled = false
// capture the new window appearance in the covering image
cover.p.graphics.clearrect 0,0,cover.p.width,cover.p.height
self.drawinto cover.p.graphics,0,0
// refresh the covering image with a slow wipe
for i = 0 to self.width
    t = ticks
    while ticks-t < 1
    wend
    cover.canvas1.refreshrect i,0,1,cover.canvas1.height
next
// remove the covering image
cover.close
```

Shifting Other Controls

When other controls lie completely on top of a Canvas, the Canvas can be made to move them when it is scrolled; if this moves a control to a position outside the Canvas's boundaries, the Canvas turns it invisible and remembers its location. This is particularly useful as a way of hiding and showing sets of controls *en masse*. A simple example is the "multiple window" shown in Figure 11-20. The figure shows two appearances of a single window; when it looks as in the first picture, pressing the button causes it to look like the second picture, and vice versa.

Figure 11-20. A single window with multiple appearances

Figure 11-21 shows the window's Window Editor in the IDE; the Canvas, which occupies most of the lower part of the window, has four controls lying on top of it. It is this, its state in the IDE, that determines what controls the Canvas will move when it is scrolled. When the application starts up, the Canvas's size must be reduced to hide the lower two controls; here, we also shorten the window.

After that, things are straightforward. The Canvas is scrolled upward in the upper button's Action event handler, and downward in the lower button's Action event

Figure 11-21. How the multiple window is constructed in the IDE

handler; the other controls automatically move along with the scrolling action, turning visible inside the Canvas's boundaries and invisible outside them. The Canvas's background color is changed by its Paint event handler, according to a Color property set by each button. Coordinates in the Canvas are measured, as usual, from the top left of the Canvas control itself. The coding required is minimal:

```
// The window's Open event handler:
self.height = 200

// The Canvas's Open event handler:
me.height = 150
self.bgC = rgb(0,0,255) // a Color property

// The upper button's Action event handler:
self.bgC = rgb(0,255,0)
canvas1.scroll 0,-150
self.refresh

// The lower button's Action event handler:
self.bgC=rgb(0,0,255)
canvas1.scroll 0,150
self.refresh

// The Canvas's Paint event handler:
g.forecolor = self.bgC
g.fillrect 0,0,300,150
self.backcolor = self.bgC // for Mac OS X
```

The last line of the Canvas's Paint event handler, changing the window's BackColor, compensates on Mac OS X for the way the region surrounding a PushButton appears to "punch" through the Canvas to reveal the window color behind it. The StaticText at the top of the window sits over a Rectangle whose color remains constant.

If another control lies only partially on top of a Canvas that is scrolled, weird things can happen. Figure 11-22 shows what happened after three presses of the button on the left, which scrolled a Canvas on the right upward each time. The Canvas has carried with it *three* impressions of the right half of the button (because the button redrew itself in its correct position each time it was pressed). If another window covers and then uncovers this one, forcing the window to refresh, the button and the oval are drawn correctly once again. This behavior should probably not be considered a bug in REALbasic; rather, it has to do with how the Macintosh's drawing routines operate. Visually, a control is merely a rectangular region of pixels within a window; each control takes responsibility for redrawing its own region. When controls overlap, the region drawn by one control is not clipped to avoid incorporating the pixels of the other; if it were, drawing would take far longer. Indeed, this was one of the key insights that made QuickDraw possible in the first place.

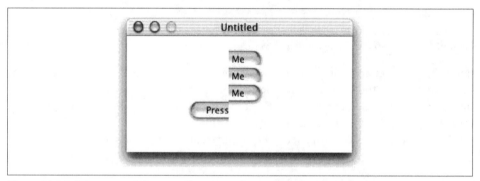

Figure 11-22. When controls lie partially on top of a scrolled Canvas

If a Canvas's Scroll procedure is supplied with the four additional parameters specifying the region that is to be scrolled (which may, of course, specify the entire Canvas), a further parameter may be added specifying whether controls on top of the Canvas are to be shifted along with it. The default is true, but you can set it to false; this scrolls just the Canvas, without moving whatever lies on top of it.

A scrolling Canvas that shifts other controls could be used in conjunction with a Scrollbar control to implement a scrollable "pane" within a window; see Chapter 15. Another way to show and hide controls *en masse* is a TabPanel; see Chapter 18.

Covering Other Controls

If a Canvas is disabled or if its MouseDown event handler doesn't return true, mouseclicks fall through to whatever is behind. By concealing controls behind a

Canvas, it is easy to make it appear that specific parts of the Canvas are responding to clicks, when in reality it is those controls that are responding.

For example, Figure 11-23 shows a thumbnail of an abstract painting. When the black square or the red square is pressed with the mouse, it highlights, returning to normal when the mouse is released. In effect, parts of the image have been turned into virtual buttons, and could perform any desired action in response to being clicked.

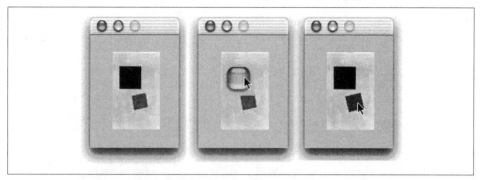

Figure 11-23. Image with objects that respond to a mouse click

For the sake of illustration the two squares are implemented in two different ways. Behind the black square is a button; when the mouse is clicked in the region of the square, the click falls through the Canvas and depresses the button, which automatically redraws itself, in its depressed state, right through the Canvas. The only problem then is to get rid of the apparent button when the mouse is released; so the last line of the button's Action event handler tells the Canvas to refresh itself.

Behind the red square is another Canvas, whose Backdrop image contains the blue square. When the mouse is clicked inside the red square, the click falls through the first Canvas and is received by the second Canvas, whose MouseDown event handler responds by copying its image, with DrawPicture, into the first Canvas's Graphics property, like this:

```
dim c as color
dim g as graphics
g = canvas1.graphics
c = me.backdrop.rgbsurface.pixel(x,y)
if c.red = 0 then // clicked on my blue square
    g.drawpicture me.backdrop,me.left-canvas1.left,me.top-canvas1.top
    return true
end
```

The second Canvas's Backdrop is set as transparent, so its white pixels are not copied, and the Malevich painting is in the first Canvas's Backdrop property, so it remains unaffected. The handler returns true, so that the second Canvas also receives the MouseUp event; its MouseUp event handler tells the first Canvas to refresh itself, thus erasing the blue square.

In that example, the covering Canvas didn't do any work; its job was to display the image. It is also possible, and actually much more common, for a covering Canvas to be used in just the opposite way: it displays nothing at all, so that it is invisible to the user, and it's there to do some work. In particular, the Canvas can receive mouse-related events; it can catch a MouseDown event, for example, and can return true or false to prevent or permit the click falling through to whatever is behind. This can be used to stop an object behind from receiving mouseclicks, or to give the illusion that an object behind does receive mouseclicks.

Figure 11-24 shows some text in a window; when the mouse is clicked anywhere within a certain word, the whole word highlights, until the mouse is released. The

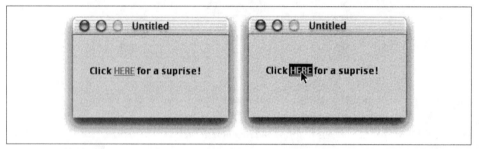

Figure 11-24. Text where one word is a kind of button

text is a disabled EditField with no border, and with a background color matching that of the window. The user seems to be clicking on a word, but in reality what's being clicked on is a Canvas, which sits over the magic word; and it is this Canvas that's doing all the work. The Canvas's MouseDown event handler inverts all the pixels of its Graphics property; since these are the same pixels that constitute the word, the effect is to highlight the word. The MouseDown event handler returns true, which has two effects: first, it prevents the click from falling through to the EditField or the window; second, it causes the Canvas also to receive a MouseUp event, whereupon it refreshes itself and so becomes transparent once more.

a depressed appearance even when it isn't being pressed with the mouse.* (A Bevel-Button can also act like a PopupMenu; for more information, see Chapter 17.) When the mouse is depressed within the BevelButton's region, the BevelButton takes on a depressed or highlighted appearance. When the mouse, having been depressed in the BevelButton's region, is released within that region, the BevelButton is sent an Action event.

A BevelButton receives the following event:

Action
> Sent because the mouse has been depressed and released within the button's region. You are expected to respond by triggering the button's functionality.

A BevelButton has the following properties:

Caption
> Text of the button's caption.

TextFont, TextSize, Bold, Italic, Underline
> Font, size, and style information for drawing the button's caption.

CaptionAlign, CaptionDelta
> For specifying precisely the horizontal position of the button's caption. Caption-Align is an integer whose value can be 0 (left-justified), 1 (right-justified), 2 (system-justified), or 3 (centered). The system-justified setting justifies the caption toward the edge from which it starts: left if the system script is left-to-right, right if the system script is right-to-left. If CaptionAlign is not 3, then CaptionDelta is a nonnegative integer specifying the number of pixels of extra space to be added between the caption and the margin to which it is justified.

Icon
> A Picture instance, to be drawn as the button's icon. On Macintosh, this must be obtained by importing a PICT, or from a PICT file, or from a PICT or icon resource; it cannot be from any other sort of image file, nor can it have been generated with NewPicture, and (worst of all) there is no way to test a Picture instance in code to see if it is the right sort. These restrictions mean that you can't obtain transparency by blitting an image into a Picture and setting the Picture's Transparent property to 1. Transparency of icons works correctly, by way of the icon's mask; but this is cold comfort if you wanted a transparent image larger than an icon—the maximum for a 'cicn' is 64 by 64.

IconAlign, IconDx, IconDy
> For specifying precisely the position of the button's icon. IconAlign is an integer whose value can be 0 (system-justified), 1 (centered), 2 (left center), 3 (right center), 4 (top center), 5 (bottom center), 6 (top left), 7 (bottom left), 8 (top right), or 9 (bottom right). If IconAlign is not 1, then IconDx and IconDy specify the number of pixels of extra space to be added between the picture and the appropriate edge (2–5) or edges (6–9) of the button.

---

* See *http://developer.apple.com/techpubs/mac/HIGOS8Guide/thig-16.html*.

CaptionPlacement

For specifying the caption's position with respect to the icon. An integer. If 1, the icon is ignored; the margins are the left and right edges of the button, and the caption is vertically centered, even if this overwrites the icon. Otherwise, the caption will never overwrite the icon, even if this means that (because there isn't room for it) it must be curtailed or even omitted. Here are the meanings of the values:

2   The margins are the right edge of the icon and the right edge of the button; the caption is vertically centered.

3   The margins are the left edge of the button and the left edge of the icon; the caption is vertically centered.

4   The margins are the left and right edges of the button; the caption is vertically just below the bottom of the icon.

5   The margins are the left and right edges of the button; the caption is vertically just above the top of the icon.

0   System justification, meaning whichever of 2 or 3 causes the icon to be "before" the text.

Bevel

The thickness of the beveled appearance around the outside of the button. Values are 0 (thin), 1 (medium), 2 (thick). (But this has no effect under Mac OS X, where BevelButtons have largely lost their three-dimensionality.)

Under the Appearance Manager, the Bevel property gives access to the various Appearance Manager control definitions. This means that you can use it to make a BevelButton look like a completely different control! For example, assigning a BevelButton's Bevel property a value of 32 turns the BevelButton into a right-pointing DisclosureTriangle. This is largely a useless hack, to be sure, because although the BevelButton now looks like a DisclosureTriangle, it doesn't act like one. Nonetheless, you might like to experiment; it's fun, and a good way to crash your computer.*

Value

A boolean corresponding to whether the button is in its depressed (true) or normal (false) state.

ButtonType

Dictates which of its states (Values) the button will assume when the mouse is released after clicking it:

0   The button returns to whatever state it was in.

1   The button changes state.

2   The button takes on its depressed state.

---

* I owe this discovery to Paul Scott. On Mac OS X, 463 and 464 are fun values to try.

All of these properties can be set in code as well as in the IDE, so many interesting effects are possible. For example, a BevelButton could draw attention to itself as the mouse passes over it by changing its Bevel or its Value setting in its MouseEnter event handler. Similarly, a BevelButton can easily be made to respond visually to a keypress by appearing to depress itself momentarily.

Nonetheless, BevelButtons have some disappointing limitations. For example, you don't get precise control over the caption's vertical position, and you have no control over the background color behind the caption (unless the caption is overwriting the icon). Of course, you could overcome these limitations if your application could create the entire image by drawing to a Picture instance. But it can't. Or can it? It turns out that there's an ingenious workaround, which lets you do just that: place your Picture on the clipboard, and now a BevelButton can use it as its Icon.* Figure 12-3 shows an example: the image is drawn transparently into the BevelButton, and the placement of the text is completely up to us.

Figure 12-3. A better BevelButton

This is implemented as a class, MyPictBevelButton, a subclass of BevelButton, with four public properties:

ThePicture
    The Picture whose image is to appear within the button

TheText
    The button's caption

TheTextFont, TheTextSize
    Font and size information for the button's caption

Clearly we could add lots of other properties, enabling us to customize all sorts of features—the exact position of the picture, the exact position of the caption, the color of the background, and so forth. But this example is deliberately kept simple, since it's just to get you started.

The class defines a New Event, PreOpen. Its Open event handler first calls PreOpen; the instance in the window is expected to set the four public properties. The handler

---

* This brilliant device I owe to Ernesto Giannotta. Cool runnings, indeed.

then draws the picture, pops it into the clipboard, pulls it out again, and sets the Icon from it:

```
dim W, H, i, j as integer
dim g as graphics
dim p,p2 as picture
dim s as string
dim c as clipboard
preOpen // must set theText, theTextFont, theTextSize, thePicture
W = self.width
H = self.height
p = newpicture(W, H, 16)
p.transparent = 1
g = p.graphics
s = self.thetext
// text
g.forecolor = textcolor
g.textfont = self.thetextfont
g.textsize = self.thetextsize
g.drawstring s, (W-g.stringwidth(s))/2, H-g.textheight
// picture
i = (W-self.thepicture.width)/2
j = (H-2*g.textheight-self.thepicture.height)/2
if s = "" then // no text
    j = (H-self.thepicture.height)/2
end
g.drawpicture self.thepicture,i,j
// convert via clipboard
c = new clipboard
c.picture = p
self.icon = c.picture
c.close
```

The sample in Figure 12-3 was generated by dragging a MyPictBevelButton into a window's Window Editor and giving it the following PreOpen event handler:

```
me.thepicture = app.resourcefork.getpicture(1000)
me.theText = "Take a Coffee Break"
me.theTextFont = "Geneva"
me.theTextSize = 9
```

In real life you'd probably want to save the current picture contents of the clipboard (if any) beforehand and restore them afterward. For the clipboard, see Chapter 23.

Placard

A Placard displays itself as a rectangular shape, typically with a beveled edge. It can appear either raised or depressed. A Placard receives the following events:

MouseDown, MouseDrag, MouseUp
These are analogous to a Canvas's MouseDown, MouseDrag, and MouseUp events. MouseDown must return true in order to cause MouseDrag and

MouseUp events to be sent; otherwise, the click passes through to whatever is behind the Placard. All three events provide your code with the position of the mouse, relative to the top left corner of the window (not the Placard).

A Placard has the following property:

Value
    A boolean corresponding to whether the Placard is in its depressed (true) or normal (false) state.

As you can see, a Placard is extremely simple. It performs no automatic display of caption or icon, but of course nothing stops you from placing another control on top of it, such as a StaticText or a Canvas or whatever suits. It also lacks any automatic visual response to being clicked with the mouse, but since it has two states and receives mouse button events, you can easily implement this. For example, to make a Placard behave like a PushButton, create a boolean property called InPlacard, and put the following into the Placard's MouseDown event handler:

```
me.value = true
return true
```

Put this in the Placard's MouseDrag event handler:

```
dim L,T as integer
L = me.left
T = me.top
inPlacard = x-L>0 and y-T>0 and x-L<me.width and y-T<me.height
if inPlacard then
    if me.value <> true then
        me.value = true
    end
else
    if me.value <> false then
        me.value = false
    end
end
```

And put this in the Placard's MouseUp event handler:

```
me.value = false
if inPlacard then
    // ... perform the Action ...
end
```

LittleArrows

A LittleArrows displays itself as two small beveled squares, one above the other; the upper square contains an upward-pointing triangle, the lower square contains a downward-pointing triangle. When the mouse is clicked within either square, the square takes on a depressed appearance; and so long as the mouse remains down and within that same square, the LittleArrows receives a continuous stream of events telling it that the square is being pressed. This goes on until the mouse is released; the appearance of the LittleArrows then returns to normal.

A LittleArrows receives the following events:

Up, Down
Sent once because the mouse has been depressed within the upper or lower square, respectively, and then repeatedly so long as the mouse is still down, whenever it is within that same square.

The typical use of a LittleArrows is in conjunction with the textual display of a number; the user can increment or decrement the number using the LittleArrows. This is often referred to as a *spinner*.

To illustrate, let's create a subclass of LittleArrows called Spinner. For the sake of simplicity, we assume that a Spinner is to be hooked to an EditField (in real life, we might like to generalize this, using a class interface, so that a Spinner could be hooked to a wider variety of control types), and that this EditField is disabled, so the Spinner is the only way to change the value in the EditField (in real life, we would probably wish the EditField to accept direct entry from the user; it would then have to validate such entry, and to notify the Spinner of any changes).

My standard approach with multiple controls of this sort is to define the general behavior in the class and to let the instance in the window initialize properties and hook the particular controls together. Here, Spinner will have a New Event called PreOpen, along with four properties: Value, UpperLimit, LowerLimit (all integers), and Text (an EditField). Its Open event handler says this:

```
preopen
self.text.text = str(self.value)
```

The instance in the window is expected to respond to the PreOpen New Event by setting the properties; for example:

```
me.text = editfield1
me.upperlimit = 10
me.lowerlimit = -10
```

Here is Spinner's Up event handler:

```
#pragma disableBackgroundTasks // prevent watch cursor
dim i as integer
if self.value < self.upperLimit then
    self.value = self.value + 1
    self.text.text = str(self.value)
    self.text.refresh
end
i = ticks
while ticks - i < 3 // don't cycle too fast
wend
```

The Down event handler is parallel.

CheckBox

A CheckBox displays itself as a small shape, usually a square, which either is empty (the box is unchecked) or contains a mark, typically a check mark or an "x" (the box is checked). To the right of the shape there is usually some text (its caption). When the mouse is depressed within the CheckBox's region (meaning the entire region containing both the shape and the caption), the shape takes on a depressed or highlighted appearance. When the mouse, having been depressed in the CheckBox's region, is released within that region, the CheckBox toggles its checked state and is then sent an Action event.

On Windows, the user can tab into a CheckBox and can then toggle it by typing the spacebar.

A CheckBox is typically employed where the user must either accept or reject a certain option. For example, in a Find dialog, the option of a case-sensitive search might be presented as a CheckBox.

A CheckBox receives the following event:

Action
    Sent because the mouse has been depressed and released within the CheckBox's region, in which case its Value is automatically toggled first. Or it might be because the CheckBox's Value has been set (not necessarily changed) in code; this works even if the CheckBox is disabled or invisible.

A CheckBox has the following properties:

Caption
    Text of the button's caption.

TextFont, TextSize, Bold, Italic, Underline
    Font, size, and style information for drawing the button's caption.

Value
    A boolean corresponding to whether the CheckBox is checked (true means it is). Setting the Value in code sets the CheckBox's appearance to match, and the CheckBox then receives the Action event.

RadioButton and GroupBox

A GroupBox displays itself as a rectangle, typically with an etched appearance, usually with some text (its caption) along its top edge. If a GroupBox's caption is the empty string, it is displayed as a simple continuous rectangle (even though it appears as a broken rectangle in the IDE).

A GroupBox's chief function is to group RadioButtons; all RadioButtons whose regions lie completely within a given GroupBox's region are considered by REALbasic to be part of the same group, and REALbasic will see to it that turning any one of them on turns all the others off. At the same time, nothing stops you from using a

GroupBox to enclose other elements; this can be a useful way of cuing the user visually when several controls have related functionality. Just the other way, nothing stops you from making a GroupBox invisible; it will still function to group any enclosed RadioButtons. A disabled GroupBox is drawn dimmed, but it, too, functions normally. (To avoid a bug on Mac OS 8 and 8.1, make sure the GroupBox is also behind the controls it contains.)

On Windows, the user can tab into a RadioButton that's on, and can navigate into (and turn on) any RadioButton using the arrow keys.

If there is only one group of RadioButtons in a window, no GroupBox is needed; the RadioButtons are grouped together automatically. If, on the other hand, *any* RadioButtons in a window are in a GroupBox, then *every* RadioButton in that window should be in some GroupBox, because otherwise a weird effect results—turning on *any* of the RadioButtons that are not within a GroupBox will turn off *all* the RadioButtons that are. Similarly, a GroupBox with RadioButtons should not contain another GroupBox with RadioButtons, because turning on *any* of the RadioButtons within only the former will turn off *all* the RadioButtons in the latter. I regard this behavior as a bug, on two counts: the asymmetry is absolutely wrong, and only RadioButtons that are within all the same GroupBoxes should automatically affect one another.

Figure 12-4 illustrates. Clicking the Mammals button will turn off the Birds button, as expected, but it will also turn off all the Poisonous and Non-Poisonous buttons. But clicking a Poisonous or Non-Poisonous button will have no effect on the Mammals button or the Birds button.

A GroupBox has the following properties:

Caption
     The text of the box's caption.

TextFont, TextSize, Bold, Italic, Underline
     Font, size, and style information for drawing the box's caption.

A RadioButton displays itself as a small shape, usually a circle, which either is empty (the button is off) or contains a mark, typically a smaller circle (the button is on). To the right of the shape there is usually some text (its caption). When the mouse is depressed within the RadioButton's region (meaning the entire region containing both the shape and the caption), the shape takes on a depressed or highlighted appearance. When the mouse, having been depressed in the RadioButton's region, is released within that region, the RadioButton is turned on, and all other RadioButtons in the same group are turned off; the RadioButton is then sent an Action event.

RadioButtons are typically employed where the user must select exactly one of several mutually exclusive items. For example, in a dialog where the user is to specify desired features of a piece of text, the choice between left-aligned, centered, and right-aligned might be made by means of a group of RadioButtons. It is usual for one in each group of RadioButtons to be turned on by default when the buttons appear, so that the user cannot choose nothing at all.

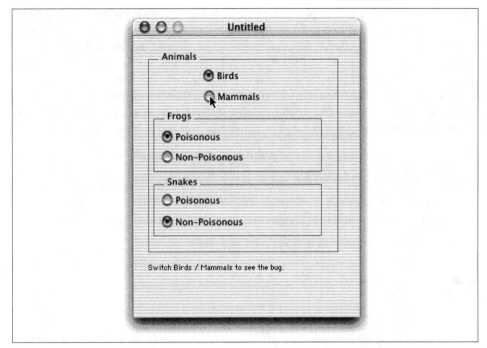

Figure 12-4. GroupBoxes within GroupBoxes don't work

A RadioButton receives the following event:

Action
> Sent because the mouse has been depressed and released within the RadioButton's region, in which case its Value is automatically set to true first. Or it might be because the RadioButton's Value has been set to true (but not necessarily changed) in code; this works even if the RadioButton is disabled or invisible. At the time a RadioButton receives the Action event, you are guaranteed that the Values of all other RadioButtons in the same group will have been set to false, whether or not they are enabled or visible.

A RadioButton has the following properties:

Caption
> Text of the button's caption.

TextFont, TextSize, Bold, Italic, Underline
> Font, size, and style information for drawing the button's caption.

Value
> A boolean determining whether the RadioButton is on (true means it's on). Setting the Value in code sets the RadioButton's appearance to match, and, if the Value is now true, the other RadioButtons in its group are turned off, and the RadioButton then receives the Action event.

Astonishingly, neither a GroupBox nor a RadioButton provides any automatic facility for answering your most likely question: within a particular group, which RadioButton is on? In fact, you can't even ask a GroupBox which RadioButtons belong to it; if you knew that, at least you could poll them individually. These omissions are amazing, since it is obvious, from the behavior of GroupBoxes and RadioButtons, that REALbasic knows the answer to these questions. In other words, the automatic behaviors of GroupBoxes and RadioButtons are object-oriented, but this object orientation is not exposed to your code, so you can't take advantage of it.

Here's how I solve this problem. I have a subclass of GroupBox, called MyGroupBox. It has one property, WhichButton, which is a MyRadioButton. And I have a subclass of RadioButton, called MyRadioButton. It has one property, WhichGroupBox, which is a MyGroupBox. MyRadioButton defines New Events called PostAction and PostOpen, so that the instances in the window can do their own thing.

MyRadioButton's Open event handler goes like this:

```
dim i as integer
dim w as window
dim g as myGroupBox
w = self.window
for i = w.controlcount-1 downto 0
    if w.control(i) isa myGroupBox then
        g = myGroupBox(w.control(i))
        if self.left>g.left and self.top>g.top then
            if self.left+self.width < g.left+g.width then
                if self.top+self.height < g.top+g.height then
                    self.whichGroupBox = g
                    exit
                end
            end
        end
    end
next
postopen
```

The idea here is that each MyRadioButton learns automatically, when it is instantiated, which MyGroupBox it belongs to, by looking to see which MyGroupBox's region it is completely within. Of course this doesn't work for nested MyGroupBoxes; I typically avoid these, but in any case the instance in the window is going to receive a PostOpen New Event, so it can always declare its own GroupBox manually, as it were.

Now each MyRadioButton can register itself with its MyGroupBox whenever its Value is made true. So, MyRadioButton's Action event handler goes like this:

```
whichGroupBox.whichButton = self
postaction
```

The result is that I can ask any MyGroupBox which of its MyRadioButtons is on (and I can do this even from within a MyRadioButton's own code, since it knows which MyGroupBox it belongs to). Here's some code for testing; this might be the Action event handler of a PushButton:

```
dim i as integer
dim g as mygroupbox
for i = controlcount-1 downto 0
    if control(i) isa mygroupbox then
        g = mygroupbox(control(i))
        msgbox g.caption + ": " + g.whichbutton.caption
    end
next
```

The dialog will say things like, "Snakes: Poisonous" and "Frogs: Green." Now, *that's* the way RadioButton information should look! It's elegant and easy, and the classes are portable. As a further refinement, I sometimes clump the RadioButtons into control arrays, so that I can refer to them by number.

DisclosureTriangle

A DisclosureTriangle displays itself as a small triangle. It can be facing rightward, leftward, or downward. Normally, it alternates between facing rightward and downward, or else between facing leftward and downward. When the mouse is depressed within the triangle, the triangle takes on a depressed appearance. When the mouse, having been depressed in the triangle, is released within it, the triangle returns to its normal appearance and then rotates to face its alternate direction.

A DisclosureTriangle is typically used to indicate that there is something hidden and to reveal it. The triangle facing rightward (or leftward) is in its "closed" position; the hidden thing is hidden. Clicking the triangle reveals the hidden thing, typically somewhere below the triangle, and the triangle now faces downward, its "open" position. The triangle can then be clicked again to hide the thing, and it returns to its "closed" position.

A DisclosureTriangle receives the following event:

Action
> Sent because the mouse has been clicked and released in the triangle, or because the DisclosureTriangle's Value has been set (not necessarily changed) in code. The triangle has already rotated.

A DisclosureTriangle has the following properties:

Facing
> An integer determining the triangle's default direction: 0 means rightward, 1 means leftward.

Value
> A boolean corresponding to whether the triangle is facing downward (true) or its default position (false). Setting the Value in code triggers an Action event.

StaticText

A StaticText displays itself as text, in a single font, size, style, and color, drawn transparently against whatever is behind. There is no difference in appearance between an enabled StaticText and a disabled one; indeed, a StaticText is disabled by default, and cannot be enabled in the IDE (it can be enabled only in code). This is somewhat odd, since a StaticText does *have* a separate disabled appearance, which is used automatically when its window is in the background; but you can't access this appearance in code.

A StaticText is typically employed for more or less inert or noneditable text within a window. For example, in a dialog asking the user whether to save changes, the text that poses this question would usually be a StaticText.

A StaticText has the following properties:

Caption
> The text. Alternatively, the name Text can be used for this property.

TextFont, TextSize, Bold, Italic, Underline, TextColor
> Font, size, and style information for drawing the text.

TextAlign
> An integer determining the text's horizontal alignment: 0 for left-aligned, 1 for centered, 2 for right-aligned.

Multiline
> A boolean determining the text's wrapping behavior. If true, the text is vertically top-aligned, and will wrap automatically before the StaticText's right edge. But the StaticText won't automatically resize itself vertically to show all the text; and there is no easy way to determine how tall the StaticText would need to be in order to show all of its text. (This is essentially the same problem noted in "String Drawing" in Chapter 11: there's no StringHeight function that tells the height of automatically wrapped text.) If false, the start of the text is vertically centered, and text will vanish off one or both sides if it is too long to fit within the StaticText's width—though it can still be forced to wrap manually, by a return character within the text.

Unlike the caption of a button, a StaticText has a color that you are allowed to specify. Unlike text in an EditField or a Canvas, or the caption of most buttons, a StaticText implements different horizontal alignments. Thus there are certain situations where, despite its apparently primitive nature, a StaticText is invaluable. Also, a StaticText is easily combined with other controls. For example, to make a clickable StaticText, cover it with a Canvas. To make a StaticText with a border, put a Rectangle behind it. In "Miscellaneous Tips" in Chapter 13, I describe the use of a StaticText to implement a centered EditField. In the next section of this chapter, a StaticText is used as a more flexible button caption.

Nonstyled versus styled

A nonstyled EditField displays all its text in a uniform font, size, and style, like a StaticText. A styled EditField can have different fonts, sizes, and styles for different stretches of its text, like a SimpleText document.

Single-line versus multiline

A single-line EditField does not automatically wrap when text is too wide for the field (but you can make it consist of more than one line by means of return characters within its text). It is limited to a maximum of 32K characters. It implements automatic copying and pasting of text, but not styled text.

A multiline EditField wraps text automatically; it includes, optionally, a working vertical scrollbar. It can hold more than 32K characters of text. In a styled multiline field, copying and pasting of styled text works automatically.*

Password

A password EditField displays bullets instead of the letters typed or pasted, and disables the EditCopy and EditCut menu items. Only a single-line EditField can be a password EditField.

Read-only

A read-only EditField permits the user to select and copy text but not to type, and disables the EditPaste, EditCut and EditClear menu items.

Limited

A limited EditField does not permit the user to type or paste text that would cause the number of its characters to exceed a given limit; it beeps if the user tries to do so. (A limited EditField can in fact display more characters than its limit, since you can modify its text freely in code or in the IDE.) Only a single-line EditField can be a limited EditField.

EditField Events, Properties, and Methods

An EditField is a RectControl, and therefore receives all the events and has all the methods and properties listed in Chapter 10: Open and Close events; Visible, Enabled, and AutoDeactivate properties; Top, Left, Height, and Width properties; LockLeft, LockRight, LockTop, and LockBottom properties; MouseEnter, Mouse-Move, and MouseExit events; and Refresh and RefreshRect methods.

On reading text from and writing text to a file on disk, including styled text, see Chapter 21. On drag-and-drop, see Chapter 24. On menu-related events, and on the EditCut, EditCopy, EditPaste, and EditClear menu items and how they interact with an EditField, see Chapter 6.

---

* A multiline EditField is implemented using the WASTE text engine, written by Marco Piovanelli; see *http://www.boingo.com/waste/* and *http://www.cs.dartmouth.edu/~ngm/waste/*. A single-line EditField is implemented using the Toolbox's native TextEdit services, just as SimpleText is, which is why it is limited to 32K characters.

Physical Characteristics

The following properties have to do with an EditField's type and physical characteristics:

Border
> A boolean. If false, no border is drawn around the field. Cannot be set in code.

UseFocusRing
> A boolean. If false, no highlight ring is drawn around the field when it has the focus. If true, a highlight ring is drawn around the field when it has the focus, unless it is the only control in its window that can receive the focus. Cannot be set in code. (Has no effect on Windows, where there are no highlight rings.)

BackColor
> The color of the field, behind the text. If set in code, causes a Paint event to be sent to the window.

Multiline
> A boolean. If true, the field is multiline; otherwise, it is single-line. Can be set in code, but this has no effect.

Styled
> A boolean. If true, the field is styled; otherwise, it is nonstyled. Cannot be set in code.

Scrollbar
> A boolean. If true, a multiline field will have a vertical scrollbar. Ignored if Multiline is false. Can be set in code, but this has no effect.

LimitText
> A nonnegative integer. If nonzero, a single-line field is a limited field. Ignored if Multiline is true. If set in code to nonzero, causes TextChange and SelChange events to be sent, and deletes any characters beyond the limit.

Password
> A boolean. If true, a single-line field is a password field. Ignored if Multiline is true. If set in code, causes TextChange and SelChange events to be sent, and alters its contents from bullets to normal letters or vice versa.

ReadOnly
> A boolean. If true, the field is read-only.

AcceptTabs
> A boolean. Ignored if Multiline is false. If true, and if the field is multiline, typing Tab into the field inserts a tab character (which will appear as a space unless your code intervenes, since there are no automatic columns). Otherwise, typing Tab shifts the focus to the next control in the same window that can receive the focus, if there is one. The "tab order" of controls that can receive the focus is their order within the Format → Control Order dialog. Cannot be set in code.

Focus

For some perspective on how the GotFocus and LostFocus events fit into the larger sequence of events during the life of an application, see "Order of Events" in Chapter 7, and "The Focus" later in this chapter. On menu-related events, see Chapter 6.

An EditField receives the following events relating to the focus:

GotFocus
> Sent to an EditField that previously did not have the focus, when it receives the focus; if a different EditField or a ListBox previously had the focus, it is sent the LostFocus event first. This can happen because:
>
> - The user clicks in or tabs into an EditField that does not have the focus. "Clicks in" means clicks in the text region of the EditField: clicking in the scrollbar of an EditField does not shift the focus and does not send any event to the EditField.
>
> - An EditField in a front window that does not have the focus, is sent the Set-Focus message.
>
> - An EditField is the focus-bearing control in a window, and that window becomes the frontmost visible window.
>
> - An EditField had the focus, the application was suspended, and now the application has been resumed.

LostFocus
> Sent to an EditField that has the focus, as it loses the focus. If the EditField had a focus highlight "ring" around it, this is preceded by a Paint event sent to the window, to remove the ring. If focus is being shifted to another EditField or List-Box, it is sent the GotFocus event afterward. This can happen because:
>
> - The user clicks in or tabs into another control that can receive the focus.
>
> - Some other control in a front window is sent the SetFocus message.
>
> - The ClearFocus method is called.
>
> - The application is suspended.
>
> - The window is hidden or closing, or another (nonfloating) window comes in front of it.

The following method has to do with the focus:

SetFocus
> Causes the EditField to become the focus-bearing control for its window. If the window is a front window, also actually gives the EditField the focus, triggering all the usual events attendant upon a change of focus (Paint, LostFocus, GotFo-cus). Ignored if the EditField is disabled or invisible.

On the UseFocusRing property, see "Physical Characteristics" earlier in this chapter.

"A front window" means a window containing an EditField that is eligible to receive the focus right now. For example, if there are two windows, a document window and a floating window, they are *both* "a front window." (See the Find/Replace dialog example later in this chapter.) Sending the SetFocus message to an EditField in a window that is not a front window does not change the focus, so no GotFocus event is triggered; it may, however, change what control is the focus-bearing control for that window. A control is the focus-bearing control for its window because it is the first control in the Format → Control Order dialog that can receive the focus, or because it has been sent the SetFocus message, or because the user has shifted the focus to it. There's more about all this later in the chapter.

Selection, Text, Font, and Style

An EditField receives the following events connected with its text and selection:

TextChange
> Sent to an EditField after its text has changed. This can happen because:
>
> - The EditField has the focus, and the user types a key that inserts a character or removes characters, or pastes, cuts, or clears text; the SelChange event precedes.
> - The EditField's Text or SelText property is set (not necessarily changed); the SelChange event follows. (But when setting SelText in a single-line Edit-Field, the SelChange event precedes.)
> - The EditField's Paste method is called; the SelChange event precedes.

SelChange
> Sent to an EditField after the starting point or length of its text selection is newly determined. This can happen because:
>
> - The user clicks or drags the mouse, or types an arrow key or other navigation key, in the EditField. If the user also changed the focus, the GotFocus event precedes.
> - The EditField has the focus, and the user types a key that inserts a character or removes characters, or pastes, cuts, or clears text; the TextChange event follows.
> - The EditField's SelStart or SelLength property is set (not necessarily changed).
> - The EditField's Text or SelText property is set (not necessarily changed); the TextChange event precedes. (But when setting SelText in a single-line Edit-Field, the TextChange event follows.)
> - The EditField's Paste method is called; the TextChange event follows.

The following properties have to do with an EditField's text, font, style, and selection:

Text

The entire contents of the field, as a string. When setting, TextChange and Sel-Change events will be sent to the EditField, and a Paint event will be sent to the window; afterward, the font and style of the field's contents will be uniform in accordance with its TextFont and related properties, and the selection point will be before the first character.

TextFont, TextSize, TextColor, Bold, Italic, Underline

Font and style information for the field as a whole. When setting, the style of the field's entire contents changes to match; and if the EditField is multiline, a Paint event will be sent to the window.

In the case of a single-line styled field, if the field is empty, setting has no effect on subsequently typed or pasted text. This is probably a bug; the workaround is to give the field some text before making any changes.

SelStart, SelLength

Used to learn or change what range of characters is currently selected; setting triggers a SelChange event. The values are measured in terms of the underlying bytes of the EditField's Text. A SelStart of 0 means before the first byte, a Sel-Start of 1 means between the first and second bytes, and so forth. A SelLength of 0 means an insertion point rather than a selection. (In a single-line EditField, setting the SelStart zeroes the SelLength; this may be a bug.)

It is not an error to assign SelStart and SelLength values that are negative or larger than the field's text can accommodate, but the resulting behavior is rather complicated; here goes.

If SelStart is assigned a negative value:

- With a single-line field, the selection will be an insertion point after the last character.
- With a multiline field, the selection will start before the first character, and its length will be reduced by the absolute value of the number assigned to SelStart.

If SelStart is assigned a value too large for the number of bytes of the Text, the selection will be an insertion point after the last character.

If SelLength is assigned a negative value:

- With a single-line field, the selection will be an insertion point that number of bytes before the previous SelStart, unless the absolute value of SelLength is greater than that of SelStart, in which case the selection will extend to the end of the field.
- With a multiline field, the old SelStart becomes the *end* of the selection, and the SelLength will be the absolute value of the number assigned to Sel-Length (but not exceeding the old SelStart).

If SelLength is assigned a value too large for the number of bytes after the Sel-Start, the selection will extend to the end of the field.

When getting their values, SelStart and SelLength are always reported as nonnegative integers.

ScrollPosition

Used to learn or change how far downward a multiline field is scrolled, in terms of its lines of text, which are numbered starting from 0. (The ScrollPosition of a single-line field is always 0, and setting it has no effect.) When getting, tells the number of the earliest line any part of which is showing. When set, scrolls the field so that the top of the designated line is at the top; if set with too large a value, scrolls the field to the bottom.

SelText

The text of the current selection, as a string. Setting replaces the selected text with the new text, and afterward the selection is an insertion point following the new text; a TextChange event and a SelChange event are triggered (SelChange first in a single-line field, TextChange first in a multiline field). In a styled Edit-Field, the new text will be in the font and style of the first character of the original selection, or, if there was originally just an insertion point, in the font and style of the preceding character.

SelTextFont, SelTextSize, SelTextColor, SelBold, SelItalic, SelUnderline, SelOutline,
SelShadow, SelCondense, SelExtend

Font and style information for the current selection. The result of setting these properties depends upon the type of EditField: with a nonstyled field, it affects all the text, and dictates the characteristics for subsequently inserted text; with a styled field, it affects only the selected text, or if there is just a selection point, affects any text inserted immediately afterward. In neither case is there any effect on the field's underlying TextFont and so forth, which are used if you set the Text. (SelOutline, SelShadow, SelCondense, and SelExtend do nothing on Windows.)

TextStyleData

The style data for the entire contents of a styled field. Encoded as a string suitable for copying out to the clipboard, a styled-text file, or the TextStyleData of another EditField. Cannot be set directly; use the SetTextAndStyle method.

The following methods have to do with an EditField's text, font, and style:

SetTextAndStyle

Sets the entire Text and the entire TextStyleData. Takes two parameters, the text and the style data, both as strings; the style data will typically come from the clipboard, a styled-text file, or another EditField's TextStyleData property. Triggers a TextChange event, a SelChange event, and a Paint event to the window.

Copy

Captures the selection's text to the clipboard (along with its style information, in the case of a multiline styled field).

Paste

Replaces the current selection with the text on the clipboard (along with the clipboard's style information, in the case of a multiline styled field). Triggers a SelChange event, a TextChange event, and (in the case of a multiline field) a Paint event to the window.

ToggleSelectionBold, ToggleSelectionItalic, ToggleSelectionUnderline, ToggleSelectionOutline, ToggleSelectionShadow, ToggleSelectionCondense, ToggleSelectionExtend

Identical to saying:

```
theEditField.selBold = not theEditField.selBold
```

and so forth.

LineNumAtCharPos

Given a byte number, returns the number of the line containing that character.

CharPosAtLineNum

Given a line number, returns the number of its first byte.

For purposes of LineNumAtCharPos and CharPosAtLineNum, lines are numbered from 0 (as with ScrollPosition), but bytes are numbered from 1. This means that bytes are off by one with respect to the insertion-point positions measured by SelStart; for example, to make a selection begin at the start of the second line, you'd say this:

```
theEditField.selStart = theEditField.charPosAtLineNum(1) - 1
```

The fact that SelStart, SelLength, LineNumAtCharPos, and CharPosAtLineNum are measured in terms of the bytes of the underlying Text, rather than in terms of characters as displayed in the EditField, is rather surprising (and runs counter to REAL's own documentation). If there is a chance that your application will run on a double-byte system, you must be careful not to make any overly simplistic assumptions. For example, you can't simply add 1 to the SelStart as a way of moving the insertion point one character to the right. Perhaps in some future version of REALbasic this will be fixed, but until then it must be regarded as a bug.

Keyboard

An EditField receives the following event connected with the keyboard:

KeyDown

Sent to an EditField that has the focus, when the user types any key (unless it is a Command key equivalent corresponding to an enabled menu item). The event handler is told what key was typed, and may return true to prevent the default response to it. Precedes any resulting SelChange and TextChange event.

A window's KeyDown event works like that of an EditField, so the discussion here is germane. If an EditField has the focus, it gets the KeyDown event, but if it returns false (or nothing), certain keys are then passed on as a KeyDown event to the window; if the EditField returns true, the window receives no KeyDown event. See also Chapter 19.

The Focus

This section discusses the notion of the focus, and shows some examples of its use in connection with EditFields. Since EditFields are our first control where the focus really comes into play, let's start with the basics: what is the focus, and why does it exist?

When the user clicks and drags the mouse in a Canvas, or drags the mouse in a Slider, or clicks the mouse in a PushButton, the period of the user's interaction with the control is well defined as being the time until the mouse is no longer down. But with an EditField, things are different. If, for example, the user types the letter "H" into an EditField, the application subsequently returns to an idle state, and yet the user's interaction with the EditField is not necessarily over. If the user then types the letter "i," it must somehow be directed at that same EditField, despite the interim idle period of the application, and despite the lack of any further explicit indication from the user as to what is to be done with this new letter.

This notion that certain types of user action must automatically address some one particular control, and the need for the identity of this control to persist through the application's idle periods, is expressed, in REALbasic, as *the focus.*

On Macintosh, only two types of control are capable of receiving the focus: EditField and ListBox. Typically, the user can see which control has the focus because it has a focus ring around it, and the user can tab from one focus-bearing control in a window to the next, in the order dictated in the Format → Control Order dialog.

On Windows, things are slightly more elaborate, because more things can get the focus. EditFields, ListBoxes, PushButtons, CheckBoxes, RadioButtons, Sliders, Pop-upMenus, and TabPanels can be sent the SetFocus message, they all receive Get-Focus and LostFocus events (starting in Version 3.5), and they can all be tabbed into, except that a RadioButton can be tabbed into only if it is on. Arrow keys can be used as a Tab substitute, except that one can't arrow-key out of a control where arrow keys have an internal meaning. And a window as a whole can be sent the SetFocus message, removing the focus from any of its controls.

Summary of Rules About the Focus

Distinguish between the focus, plain and simple, and the *focus-bearing control* for a particular window instance. The focus-bearing control is the control that *would* have the focus plain and simple, if its window were brought to the front. REALbasic's own terminology is a bit confusing, because it fails to draw this distinction. For example, sending the SetFocus message to an EditField in a window that is not a front window may make it the focus-bearing control for that window, but it does not give it the focus plain and simple, because that window is not frontmost; on the other hand, the GotFocus event is sent only to an EditField that receives the focus plain and simple.

The rules about the focus may then be summarized as follows:

- A maximum of one control in the application has the focus (plain and simple) at any given moment. A maximum of one control in a window instance is the focus-bearing control for that window instance.

- Neither a disabled nor an invisible control can receive the focus, nor can it be the focus-bearing control for its window.

- When a window is instantiated, whatever control capable of receiving the focus is listed first in its Format → Control Order dialog automatically becomes the focus-bearing control for that window instance. But in a floating window, no control automatically becomes the focus-bearing control.

- The focus-bearing control for a window instance automatically receives the focus (plain and simple) whenever that window instance is frontmost.

    This statement is complicated, but only slightly, by the existence of floating windows. A control in a floating window *can* have the focus; but it doesn't receive it automatically by virtue of the window's frontmost position. Rather, if a floating window is frontmost, the focus-bearing control in the frontmost nonfloating visible window behind it automatically has the focus. Transfer of focus into a floating window must be performed explicitly, such as by a SetFocus message or by a mouseclick.

- On Macintosh, the control with the focus, if its UseFocusRing property is true, and if it is not the only control in its window capable of receiving the focus, is surrounded by a highlight ring, giving the user visual feedback as to where the focus is.

- The focus-bearing control for any window instance can be changed by the SetFocus message. If this is the window with the focus, this also changes the focus plain and simple. The focus plain and simple can also be changed by the user clicking or tabbing to a different control.

- An EditField or ListBox with the focus is the first recipient of KeyDown messages when the user types.

- An EditField or ListBox with the focus receives menu-related events. It is the only recipient of EditPaste, EditCut, EditCopy, and EditClear menu events, and is responsible for enabling those menu items; normally, this happens automatically, but the automatic behavior can be overridden if the control is a programmer-defined subclass (see Chapter 6).

Amazingly, there is no way to ask a control whether it has the focus, nor to ask a window which of its controls is the focus-bearing control, nor to ask REALbasic what control has the focus plain and simple. To some extent you can make up for this by arranging for every EditField or ListBox to store a reference to itself in some property during its GotFocus event. An example appears later in this chapter ("Validation Field").

Order of Focus-Related Events

See "Order of Events" in Chapter 7 for a summary of how focus-related events fit into the train of typical events during the lifetime of an application. To that summary may be added just a couple of situations that don't involve switching windows.

When the user changes the focus within the same window by tabbing from one control to another, the order of events is:

- KeyDown to the first control, same KeyDown to the window
- Paint to the window, LostFocus to the first control
- GotFocus to the second control

When the user changes the focus within the same window by clicking in a different control, the order of events is:

- Paint to the window, LostFocus to the first control
- GotFocus to the second control
- SelChange or Change to the second control (depending on whether it's an EditField or a ListBox)

Controlling the Focus in Code

Two methods change which control is the focus-bearing control for its window:

SetFocus
> Makes the control to which it is sent the focus-bearing control, if it is capable of being the focus-bearing control on that platform. On Windows, can also be sent to a window.

ClearFocus
> A window method. If sent to the window containing the control with the focus, it temporarily causes no control to have the focus. SetFocus or the user clicking can still set the focus; and things return to normal automatically when something happens that usually causes some control to have the focus, such as bringing a different window to the front, resuming the application, and so forth. (I'm not sure how, if at all, ClearFocus differs on Windows from sending SetFocus to a window.)

Floating Find Window

As a simple example of controlling the focus in code, consider a floating window, which is a Find/Replace dialog. (Let's agree to pass over the question of whether this is a wise or even a likely implementation.) For the sake of simplicity, our application has just one document window, DocWindow, containing an EditField, DocField; the floating window is called FindWindow, and contains five controls: FindField, ReplaceField, CancelButton, ReplaceButton, and FindButton. Figure 13-2 shows the two windows, which (again for simplicity) we imagine are both always present.

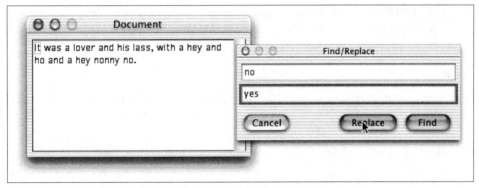

Figure 13-2. Document window and floating Find/Replace window

When the user chooses the EditFind menu item, we want to shift the focus to the Find field in the Find/Replace window, so here is DocField's EditFind menu event handler:

```
findwindow.findField.setFocus
```

In the Find/Replace window, both the Replace button and the Find button are initially disabled; they must be enabled only if there is text in the Find field, since otherwise there is nothing to find. So, FindField's TextChange event handler says:

```
findButton.enabled = me.text <> ""
replaceButton.enabled = me.text <> ""
```

The task of actually doing the finding is identical for the Replace button and the Find button, so it is abstracted into a method handler of the Find/Replace window, DoFind, which is a function returning a boolean. If the find text is not found, DoFind beeps and returns false; if it is found, it selects it and returns true. For the sake of simplicity, finding doesn't wrap in this example: we look only after the end of current selection in FindField. Note that we must compensate for the fact that in string functions such as InStr, the first character of a string is character 1, whereas a selection starting before the first character of an EditField has a SelStart of 0:

```
dim i, start as integer
start = docwindow.docField.selStart + docWindow.docField.selLength + 1
i = instr(start, docwindow.docField.text, self.findField.text)
if i = 0 then
    beep
    return false
else
    docwindow.docField.selStart = i-1
    docwindow.docField.selLength = len(self.findField.text)
    return true
end
```

The Cancel button's Action event handler just returns the focus to the document window:

```
docwindow.docfield.setfocus
```

The Find button's Action event handler calls DoFind (throwing away the boolean result) and returns the focus to the document window:

```
if doFind() then // throw away result
end
docwindow.docfield.setfocus
```

The Replace button's Action event handler calls DoFind, performs the replacement if the result is true, and returns the focus to the document window:

```
if doFind() then
    docwindow.docField.seltext = self.replaceField.text
end
docwindow.docfield.setfocus
```

That's all there is to it. Observe that the user can navigate almost entirely using the keyboard, with no further effort on our part. The EditFind menu item has a keyboard equivalent, which shifts the focus to the Find field in the Find/Replace window, where the user can proceed to type. The user can navigate between the Find and Replace fields by tabbing, and can access the Cancel or Find buttons by using Esc, Command-Period, Return, or Enter, thus returning to the document window. Only the Replace button has no keyboard equivalent, lest the user alter text in the document window by accident; but it would be simple to implement one.

Validation Field

Let's now consider a harder example of controlling the focus in code: a validation field. If the text of a validation field does not meet certain criteria, the user is prevented from shifting the focus away from it. The reason this is hard is that we must combat the user's intentions.

Figure 13-3 shows an example; for simplicity, let's say that only the first three fields are enabled, and that it should be impossible to shift the focus between them unless the current one holds a positive integer.

If the user shifts the focus from one field to another, there is a sequence of two events: LostFocus to the old field, GotFocus to the new field. My approach is to permit the user to make the shift, and in the GotFocus event handler of the new field, to shift the focus back to the first field if it is invalid.

The solution should be as general as possible, so it must be encapsulated in a class, which I will call ValidatorField. Both the old field and new field will have to be instances of this class—the new one so that it can ask the old one whether it is valid, and the old one so that it can answer.

If the user shifts the focus from field A to field B, and field B discovers that field A is invalid and therefore shifts the focus back to field A, we don't want field A to attempt to validate field B; we want to perform the validation only if the *user* is shifting the focus. Therefore, we're going to need a flag. Also, field B needs a way to know which field we just came from, so each ValidatorField must store a reference to

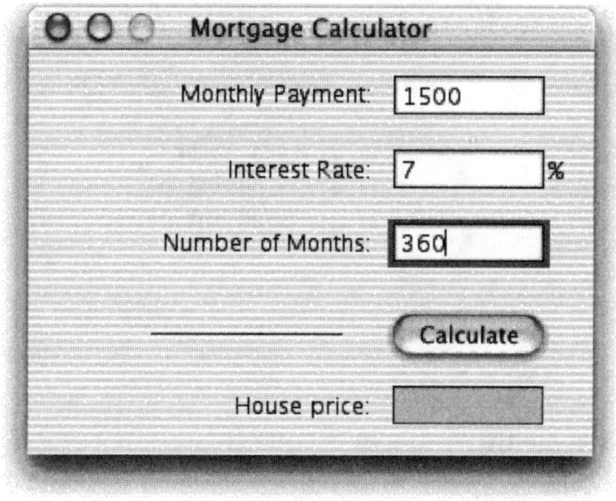

Figure 13-3. Validation fields

itself in a global property when it gets the focus. This reference can also serve as the flag: if it is nil, no validation should be performed. Let's call this property LastField, and let's keep it in the Application subclass. To involve the Application seems to violate object orientation; but we can't record this information in any of the fields, because exactly what we don't know is which field is in question.

We are now ready to code ValidatorField's GotFocus event. We already know that in general it must store a reference to the EditField instance in LastField, so that the *next* field that gets the focus can validate *this* field. But we also know that it must validate the *previous* field. If the previous field turns out to be invalid, we store nil in LastField to prevent *this* field from being validated, alert the user, and switch the focus back to the previous field. Here we go:

```
dim e as validatorField
if app.lastfield = nil or not (app.lastfield isa validatorField) then
    app.lastfield = me
    return
end
if not validatorField(app.lastfield).isvalid then
    e = validatorField(app.lastfield)
    app.lastfield = nil
    msgbox e.message
    e.setfocus
else
    app.lastfield = me
end
```

We have not specified the details of the validation test, IsValid, nor of the alert text to be presented to the user, Message. Instead, we maintain generality of architecture by creating two abstract methods in ValidatorField. IsValid is a function returning a boolean, and just returns true. Message is a function returning a string, and just returns the empty string. Now we can subclass ValidatorField and supply any particular validation test and a message to go with it.

So, in this example, our ValidatorField subclass is called PosIntField. Its IsValid method can go like this:

```
dim s as string
s = me.text
if s = str(val(s)) then          // it is a number
    if val(s) > 0 then           // it is positive
        if val(s) = val(s)\1 then  // it is an integer
            return true
        end
    end
end
return false
```

And PosIntField's Message method can go like this:

```
return "You must enter a positive integer."
```

Now all we have to do is make our three EditFields into PosIntField instances, and we're in business. There may also be some minor points yet to clear up. For example, we don't want validation to take place during the GotFocus event sent when the application resumes, so the Application subclass's Activate event handler should set LastField to nil. And we probably don't want to validate if the user switches windows, so perhaps the window's Deactivate event handler should do the same thing. All this will depend upon the particular context in which the validation fields are used. (Later in this chapter, we'll consider validating as the user enters text into the field rather than as the user leaves it; see "Live Input Validation").

Manipulating Text and Styles

It is often useful to examine an EditField's Text property, but you will not so often have occasion to set it. For one thing, this causes an annoying flicker as the entire EditField redraws itself. For another, it is usually overkill. Typically, you change an EditField's text by selecting just a particular stretch of text and then manipulating the contents of the selection, using SelText, SelTextFont, and so forth.

To select a particular stretch of text means setting SelStart and SelLength. This may require some care. If you set the SelLength, you probably expect it to adopt the value you give it; and if you set the SelStart, you probably expect the SelLength to remain unchanged. But neither will necessarily be the case. In a single-line EditField, setting SelStart has the side effect of setting SelLength to zero. In a multiline EditField, that doesn't happen, but slamming into the end of the text is of particular concern. For example, suppose a multiline EditField contains 10 characters. Consider the following sequence:

```
editfield1.selstart = 0
editfield1.sellength = 7 // but not for long!
editfield1.selstart = 7
editfield1.selstart = 0
```

Afterward, SelLength is 3. Similarly, giving SelStart or SelLength a value that is too small can yield unusual results; for instance, in a multiline field, this code:

```
editfield1.selstart = -1
```

moves the start of the selection to the start of the field and reduces its length by 1.

The rest of this section consists of examples illustrating typical manipulations of an EditField's text and style.

Tickertape Field

To illustrate the basic use of SelStart and SelLength, let's implement a "tickertape" field. The field runs across the top of a window; while the user works elsewhere, a thread causes letters to be removed from the start of the field and added to the end, in such a way that its contents seem to be constantly scrolling to the left (as shown in Figure 13-4). The example is amusingly annoying. It also serves to clear up a serious misunderstanding that beginners sometimes have, by showing that a field does not have to have the focus, nor even be enabled, in order for its selection and contents to be manipulated in code.

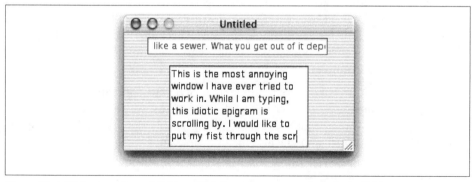

Figure 13-4. Tickertape (upper) field scrolls leftward as user works in lower field

The field is a single-line nonstyled field; it is disabled so that the user can't interfere. The thread's Run handler goes like this:

```
dim s as string
dim theLen, pos, t as integer
dim ticker as editfield
s = "Life is like a sewer. "
s = s + "What you get out of it depends "
s = s + "on what you put into it. "
ticker = window1.tickerField
ticker.text = s // initialize epigram
theLen = len(s)
pos = 1
do // forever
    ticker.selStart = 0
    ticker.selLength = 1
```

```
    ticker.selText = "" // delete first character
    ticker.selStart = theLen
    ticker.selText = mid (s, pos, 1) // append new last character
    ticker.selStart = 0 // keep start of text visible
    pos = pos + 1 // update our idea of next character
    if pos > theLen then
      pos = 1
    end
    t = ticks
    while ticks - t < 20 // wait a bit
    wend
  loop
```

Styled Word Processor

Next, here's an example in which we manipulate text styling, without altering the selection. Suppose we are writing a simple word-processing application. The user is to be able to change the font, size, or style of the currently selected text (or the insertion point), by way of a Font menu, a Size menu, and a Style menu that contains the items Plain, Bold, and Italic.

To implement all this, clearly we will use the SelTextFont, SelTextSize, SelBold, and SelItalic messages, and we will use them in two ways—we will get their values in order to know which menu items should receive a check mark, and we will set them in response to the user's choosing the menu items. The method has already been sketched in "Menu Examples" in Chapter 6.

Our Style menu has three menu items: StylePlain, StyleItalic, and StyleBold. The field where the user edits text is a subclass of EditField. Thus, we can give it an Enable-MenuItems event handler; that event handler will enable the StylePlain, StyleItalic, and StyleBold menu items, and will also include these lines:

```
stylebold.checked = self.selbold
styleitalic.checked = self.selitalic
```

The three menu event handlers for the Style menu, also in the EditField subclass, just set the SelBold and SelItalic properties appropriately:

```
// StyleBold menu event handler:
self.selbold = not self.selbold

// StyleItalic menu event handler:
self.selitalic = not self.selitalic

// StylePlain menu event handler:
self.selbold = false
self.selitalic = false
```

Now let's consider the Font menu (also sketched in Chapter 6). Our EditField subclass's EnableMenuItems event handler puts a check mark next to the correct Font menu item with this line:

```
fontafont(i).checked = self.seltextfont = fontafont(i).text
```

The EditField subclass also contains a menu event handler for FontAFont, consisting of this line:

```
self.seltextfont = fontafont(index).text
```

The implementation of the Size menu is similar.

Styled HTML Editor

Here's an example involving both insertion of text and changing of styles. Suppose our word-processing application is now an HTML editor. The StyleBold menu item, implemented through a menu event handler in the EditField subclass, still turns the selected text bold, but it also inserts "<B>" before the selection, and "</B>" after it— both of them in red, for emphasis. This illustrates nicely the technique of first selecting, then operating on the selection:

```
dim theStart, theEnd as integer
// memorize current position
theStart = self.selStart
theEnd = self.selStart + self.selLength
// make selection bold
self.selBold = true
// select end, insert red "</B>"
self.selLength = 0
self.selStart = theEnd
self.selBold = false
self.selTextColor = rgb(255,0,0)
self.selText = "</B>"
// select start, insert red "<B>"
self.selStart = theStart
self.selTextColor = rgb(255,0,0)
self.selText = "<B>"
```

Word Selection Field

In this next example, we manipulate the selection and its styling to implement a word selection field. The idea is that when the user clicks in the field, the entire word containing the click is automatically selected. To highlight the word still further, we also add some styling and color to it. Figure 13-5 shows the effect; the context is an educational program in which the user is invited to identify a particular word by clicking on it.

The field is a read-only multiline styled EditField. The place to respond to mouseclicks is the SelChange event handler; since we will also be changing the selection in code, a boolean property, SelChanging, protects us from an infinite loop:

```
dim s as string
dim thestart, theend as integer
if selChanging then // avoid infinite loop
    return
end
selChanging = true // raise the flag
```

Figure 13-5. Word selection field

```
s = me.text // memorize relevant facts
thestart = me.selstart
me.selstart = 0 // remove any previous styling
me.sellength = len(s)
me.selbold = false
me.selunderline = false
me.seltextcolor = textcolor
me.sellength = 0 // select where the user clicked
me.selstart = thestart // expand selection to embrace word
do until me.selstart = 0 or mid(s,me.selStart,1) = " "
    me.selstart = me.selstart - 1
loop
theend = me.selstart + me.sellength
do until theend = len(s) or mid(s, theend+1, 1) = " "
    me.sellength = me.sellength + 1
    theend = me.selstart + me.sellength
loop
selchanging = false // lower the flag
me.selbold = true // add styling for emphasis
me.selunderline = true
me.seltextcolor = rgb(200,100,0)
```

Finding Styles

An earlier example showed how simple it is to find text within an EditField; it
amounts to little more than finding in a string. A more vexing problem is that of finding styles. Suppose, for example, we wish to turn all bold text red in a multiline
styled EditField. An obvious technique is to loop over every letter of the field, turning it red if it is bold:

```
dim theLen as integer
theLen = len(theField.text)
theField.selStart = 0
theField.selLength = 1
do
    if theField.selBold then
        theField.selTextColor = rgb(255,0,0)
    end
    theField.selStart = theField.selStart + 1
loop until theField.selStart = theLen
```

This works, but it is slow, and the user can see the selection running through the text from start to finish. If we have a second, invisible field, we can use the technique described in Chapter 9—copy the text and style information into the invisible field, perform the changes there, and then copy the text and style information back again:

```
dim theLen as integer
theField2.setTextandStyle theField.text, theField.textStyleData
theLen = len(theField2.text)
theField2.selStart = 0
theField2.selLength = 1
do
    if theField2.selBold then
        theField2.selTextColor = rgb(255,0,0)
    end
    theField2.selStart = theField2.selStart + 1
loop until theField2.selStart = theLen
theField.setTextandStyle theField2.text, theField2.textStyleData
```

This is faster, but it's still slow.

A much, much faster technique is to dump the TextStyleData into a memoryblock and parse it ourselves to find all the bold stretches of text. On Macintosh, the TextStyleData has the same format as a 'styl' resource, which is a sequence of uniform style runs; the first two bytes tell how many uniform style runs there are, and what follows is that many sets of 20 bytes, of which the first four bytes are the character offset of the start of the run, and the eleventh byte has its 1-bit set if the run has bold styling.* Thus, the following routine turns all bold text red, at lightning speed:†

```
dim i, theRun, theStyles, numStyleRuns as integer
dim theField as editField
dim m as memoryblock
dim s as string
theField = // ... whatever—get reference to field
s = theField.textStyleData
m = newMemoryBlock(len(s)+1)
m.cstring(0) = s
numStyleRuns = m.short(0)
for i = 1 to numStyleRuns
    theRun = 2 + (i-1) * 20
    theStyles = m.byte(theRun + 10)
    if bitwiseAnd(theStyles, 1) = 1 then // it is bold
        theField.selStart = m.long(theRun) // now figure out length
        if i < numStyleRuns then
            theField.selLength = m.long(2 + i * 20) - theField.selStart
        else
            theField.selLength = len(theField.text) - theField.selStart
        end
        theField.selTextColor = rgb(255,0,0) // turn it red
    end
next
```

---

* For more information, see *http://developer.apple.com/techpubs/mac/Text/Text-65.html.*

† The routine is based on examples by Christian Brunel and Doug Holton.

This is extremely fast, but the code is barely legible. If we're going to be doing a great deal of this sort of thing, it will be useful to arm ourselves with classes that can parse, manipulate, and assemble a TextStyleData string. I will describe a set of classes to do this. We begin with ScrapRecord and ScrapTable. ScrapRecord has a constructor which accepts a TextStyleData string, strips off the first two bytes which signify the count of style runs and stores this value in a property called NumStyles, and then appends each style run to an array of ScrapTables:

```
// constructor: accept textstyledata, parse out to scrap style tables
// s is the parameter
dim i as integer
self.numstyles = ascb(midb(s,1,1)) * 256 + ascb(midb(s,2,1))
for i = 1 to self.numstyles
    self.scraptables.append (new scraptable (midb(s, 3 + 20 * (i-1), 20)))
next
```

ScrapTable has properties signifying the different parts of a piece of style run information: Offset, LineHeight, FontAscent, FontFamilyID, CharacterStyle, Size, and RGBColor. These are all integers except for RGBColor, which is a Color, and CharacterStyle, which is a Style (the third class, which we haven't come to yet). ScrapTable's constructor accepts the information for one style run, drops it into a memoryblock property called RawData, and calls its ParseRawData method to parse it:

```
// constructor: given scrap style table, store it and parse it out
// s is the parameter
self.rawData = newmemoryBlock(21)
self.rawData.pstring(0) = s
self.parseRawData
```

Here is ParseRawData:

```
dim r, g, b as integer
self.offset = self.rawdata.long(1)
self.lineheight = self.rawdata.short(5)
self.fontascent = self.rawdata.short(7)
self.fontfamilyID = self.rawdata.short(9)
self.characterstyle = new style (self.rawdata.byte(11))
self.size = self.rawdata.short(13)
r = self.rawdata.ushort(15)\256
g = self.rawdata.ushort(17)\256
b = self.rawdata.ushort(19)\256
self.rgbcolor = rgb(r, g, b)
```

The Style class consists of seven boolean properties: Bold, Italic, Underline, Outline, Shadow, Condense, Extend. Its constructor parses a bitfield to set these booleans:

```
// constructor: parse flag bits into booleans
// i is the parameter
self.bold = bitwiseand(i,&b00000001) > 0
self.italic = bitwiseand(i,&b00000010) > 0
self.underline = bitwiseand(i,&b00000100) > 0
self.outline = bitwiseand(i,&b00001000) > 0
```

```
self.shadow = bitwiseand(i,&b00010000) > 0
self.condense = bitwiseand(i,&b00100000) > 0
self.extend = bitwiseand(i,&b01000000) > 0
```

A method ToString reassembles the data back into a string (left as an exercise for the reader, or download it from my web site if you're completely stumped). Now it's trivial to turn all bold text in an EditField red, in a legible fashion:

```
dim s as scraprecord
dim i,u as integer
s = new scraprecord(editfield1.textstyledata)
u = s.numStyles-1
for i = 0 to u
    if s.scrapTables(i).characterstyle.bold then
        s.scrapTables(i).rgbcolor = rgb(255,0,0)
    end
next
editfield1.settextAndStyle(editfield1.text, s.toString)
```

Nonetheless, it's extremely annoying to be compelled to this sort of expedient, and we'd have to write it all over again if we wanted to do the same thing on Windows, where the TextStyleData is differently encoded. It would be much better if REALbasic itself gave more efficient access to style information.

Scrolling

Scrolling can be used to make an EditField display a particular region of its text. For example, suppose a read-only EditField contains a long text broken into sections; the section titles are listed in a PopupMenu, and the user can select any section title from the PopupMenu to make that section scroll into view in the EditField. (This is actually the implementation of the Help window in my Durak example project, which you can download from my web site.)

The only hard part is deciding initially where the sections are and telling the PopupMenu about them. Here, we assume that any text in bold is a section header. We can thus use the ScrapRecord class to iterate through the text looking for bold style runs. For each such run, we obtain the character position at which it starts; then we give the PopupMenu a new menu item, whose text is the text of the section header, and whose RowTag (a variant associated with each menu item of a PopupMenu) is the character position. This code is the EditField's Open event handler, which begins by loading the text and style information from our application's resource fork, then proceeds to build the PopupMenu:

```
dim s, ss, temp as string
dim si as scraprecord
dim i, u, start, length as integer
s = app.resourcefork.getresource("TEXT", 1000)
ss = app.resourcefork.getresource("styl", 1000)
me.settextAndStyle s,ss
si = new scraprecord(ss)
u = si.numStyles-1
```

```
for i = 0 to u
    if si.scrapTables(i).characterstyle.bold then
        start = si.scrapTables(i).offset + 1
        length = si.scrapTables(i+1).offset - start + 1
        temp = mid(s, start, length)
        popupMenu1.addrow temp
        popupmenu1.rowTag(popupmenu1.listcount - 1) = start
    end
next
popupMenu1.listindex = 0
me.selstart = 0
me.sellength = 0
```

The PopupMenu's job is then extremely simple. When the user chooses a menu item, the PopupMenu tells the EditField to scroll to the line number contained in the corresponding RowTag. This is the PopupMenu's Change event handler:

```
dim lineNum as integer
lineNum = editfield1.lineNumAtCharPos(me.rowTag(me.listindex))
editfield1.scrollposition = lineNum
```

For PopupMenus, see Chapter 17.

Combining EditFields

To combine the contents of two EditFields, select in one and send it the Copy message; then select in the other and sent it the Paste message:

```
// ... select text in EditField1 here ...
editfield1.copy
// ... select in EditField2 here ...
editfield2.paste
```

If the EditFields are multiline styled, style information is copied and pasted seamlessly. The only problem here is that Copy uses the actual clipboard, where the user might have some information already; it is therefore more polite to wrap such use of Copy and Paste in a save-and-restore of the clipboard. Here, for simplicity, we assume that the only thing on the clipboard worth saving is some text:

```
dim c as clipboard, s as string
c = new clipboard
if c.textavailable then
    s = c.text
end
c.close
// ... select text in EditField1 here ...
editfield1.copy
// ... select in EditField2 here ...
editfield2.paste
c = new clipboard
c.text = s
c.close
```

On the clipboard, see Chapter 23.

Reacting to User Input

Most of the time, your code will not need to react to the user's input into an Edit-Field; the whole point of an EditField is that it reacts automatically to such input. But if your EditField does need to implement some additional or nondefault response to user input, there are two chief approaches: you can react after the fact, or intercept the input before it appears as characters in the EditField.

After the Fact

Reacting after the fact is often done through the EditField's TextChange event handler. For example, consider a word-processing application. If the user closes a document window or tries to quit the application, we want to offer a chance to save the document—but only if it is "dirty," meaning that it has been changed since the last time the document was saved. Clearly, we'll want to maintain a boolean property, Dirty, associated with the document. This property will initially be false; the Edit-Field's TextChange event handler will set it to true, because any change to the text will fire a TextChange event, and this in turn means that the document is now dirty; and whatever routine saves the document will reset Dirty to false.

Of course, the TextChange event handler might not be the only place where Dirty needs to be set to true. If the application involves styled text, then perhaps it has a StyleBold menu item, which turns the current selection bold. That won't trigger a TextChange event, so the StyleBold menu event handler needs to set Dirty to true directly. This is something we neglected in implementing StyleBold earlier in this chapter.

Intercepting Input

All user input to an EditField can be intercepted before the EditField changes its text (except for drag-and-drop into a multiline EditField—this is a problem, and probably should be regarded as a bug; see Chapter 24). Typing can be intercepted through the EditField's KeyDown event handler; pasting can be intercepted through the Edit-Field subclass's EditPaste menu event handler. Either event handler can examine the proposed input, and may return true to prevent it from passing to the EditField in the normal fashion. (On the clipboard, see Chapter 23.)

Code Field

Consider a multiline field that does not wrap each line, such as one might use to edit code (see Figure 13-6). REALbasic does not provide an EditField that behaves this way, so we will have to implement it ourselves. To prevent automatic wrapping, this will actually have to be a single-line EditField. But when the user types the Return key in a single-line EditField, its default behavior is to do nothing. So we need to

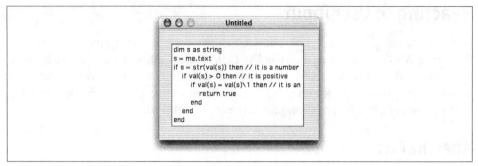

Figure 13-6. Nonwrapping field containing multiple lines

override this behavior; and clearly we need to override it before the fact. So this is a case of using the EditField's KeyDown event handler to intercept input:

```
if key = chr(13) then
    me.seltext = chr(13)
    return true
end
```

Actually, in practice this turns out not to be quite enough: if we type a line longer than the width of the field and hit Return, the visible region of the field doesn't jump left to show us the insertion point. We can mend this with a little song and dance; we type an extra character, then remove it:

```
if key = chr(13) then
    me.seltext = chr(13)
    me.seltext = " "
    me.selstart = me.selstart - 1
    me.sellength = 1
    me.seltext = ""
    return true
end
```

Since this field is for editing code, we might also like to implement tabs within the field. Let's say that when the user types the Tab key, we should insert enough spaces to reach a column number that is a multiple of 4. So now our KeyDown event handler might be like this:

```
dim i, numSpaces as integer
dim s, ret as string
ret = chr(13)
select case asc(key)
case 13
    me.seltext = ret
    me.seltext = " "
    me.selstart = me.selstart - 1
    me.sellength = 1
    me.seltext = ""
    return true
case 9
    if me.sellength > 0 then // refuse to delete current selection
        beep
```

```
        return true
    end
    s = left(me.text, me.selstart)
    for i = len(s) downto 1 // look for prior Return or start of text
        if mid(s,i,1) = ret then
            exit
        end
    next
    for numspaces = (me.selstart - i) mod 4 to 3 // type spaces
        me.seltext = " "
    next
    return true
end
```

In Chapter 15 we'll add a vertical scrollbar to this field.

Live Input Validation

Suppose we have a field in which the user is to enter the two-letter abbreviation for one of the 50 United States. We will force the input to be uppercase, and validate it as the user enters it. (This presents an alternative to validation after the fact, described in "Validation Field," earlier in this chapter.) For simplicity, let's pretend that there are only five states. Our Open event handler initializes a string array property, States, with their abbreviations:

```
dim s as string
dim i,u as integer
s = "AK,AS,ME,MO,NM" // in real life, all 50 abbreviations would go here
u = countFields(s,",")
redim states(u)
for i = 1 to u
    states(i) = nthField(s,",",i)
next
```

The EditField's KeyDown event handler will modify and filter the keys typed by the user. All input is rendered as uppercase, and if the user types a key that cannot represent any of our five states, the field beeps instead of accepting it:

```
dim i, u, start as integer
dim theKey, s, s1, s2 as string
theKey = uppercase (key)
start = me.selstart + 1
s1 = mid(me.text,1,start-1)
s2 = mid(me.text,start+me.selLength,10)
s = s1 + theKey + s2
u = ubound(states)
for i = 1 to u
    if instr(states(i), s) = 1 then
        me.selText = theKey
        return true
    end
next
beep
return true
```

This works perfectly, except that we have accidentally disabled too many keys! Remember, the KeyDown event handler is fed *every* key the user types into the field, including keys used for editing and navigation, such as the arrow keys, the Delete key, the Return key, the Tab key, and so forth. Before our KeyDown event handler does anything else, therefore, it must let these pass through, by returning `false`:

```
dim i, u, n, start as integer
dim theKey as string
n = asc(key)
if n < 32 or n = 127 then
    return false
end
// the rest is as before
```

Since we are validating during typing, we would presumably also need to prevent the user from skirting our validation by pasting. A brute-force approach would be to prevent pasting altogether. If our field is an EditField subclass, the subclass's Enable-MenuItems event handler can just disable the Paste menu item:

```
editpaste.enabled = false
```

In real life, you'd probably use the EditPaste menu event handler to examine the contents of the clipboard and decide whether pasting those contents at the current selection would yield valid input. This is left as an exercise for the reader.

Drawing Styled Text

An EditField has the ability to draw its own text into a Graphics property, wrapping automatically and maintaining the styles. (On Graphics properties, see Chapter 11.) This can save a good deal of time and effort, because drawing wrapped text with changing styles can otherwise be fairly labor-intensive. If you need to draw styled text that isn't in an EditField already, it's worth putting it into one, just to take advantage of this feature. The EditField from which you draw can be invisible.

Drawing styled text from an EditField is an all-or-nothing proposition, so start by making sure that the EditField contains just the text you want to draw. To draw just some of an existing EditField's text, you could use the EditField Copy and Paste methods to get the desired text into an invisible EditField and draw from there; see "Combining EditFields," earlier in this chapter.

Drawing from an EditField is a two-step process. First, send the EditField the Styled-TextPrinter message, handing it a reference to the Graphics property you want to draw into, and the width at which wrapping should take place. This returns an instance of the StyledTextPrinter class. You should not hand the StyledTextPrinter function a Canvas's Graphics property; instead, draw into a Picture's Graphics property, and then blit from the Picture. Next, send the StyledTextPrinter instance the DrawBlock message, giving it the left and top coordinates and the height of a rectangle within which the drawing should take place. (You already provided the width when you generated this StyledTextPrinter instance, remember?) Presto, the drawing is done for you.

Here's an example. We wish to be able to draw into a Canvas called Canvas1. Let the window possess a Picture property, P, to serve as an intermediate repository for the text drawing. The window's Open event handler initializes the Picture:

```
p = newpicture(canvas1.width, canvas1.height, 8)
p.transparent = 1
```

The Canvas's Paint event handler blits the Picture into its own Graphics property:

```
if p <> nil then
    g.drawpicture p,0,0
end
```

Now we are ready to draw some styled text. Suppose the EditField is EditField1. To update the Canvas with the latest version of the styled text from EditField1, we could say this:

```
dim c as canvas, g as graphics
c = canvas1
g = p.graphics
g.clearrect 0,0,p.width,p.height
editfield1.styledtextprinter(g,c.width).drawblock(0,0,c.height)
c.refresh
```

The width you specify when you generate the StyledTextPrinter instance, plus the height you specify when you call its DrawBlock method, make up the maximum dimensions of the rectangle into which text will be drawn. The text is wrapped to the width and clipped to the height. Thus, if the EditField doesn't contain enough text to fill the rectangle, the rectangle simply won't be filled with text, but if the EditField contains too much text for the size of the rectangle, the rectangle will be filled with text, and the excess text won't be drawn.

But then, what if you need to know whether all the text was able to fit into the rectangle? To find out, capture the StyledTextPrinter instance as a separate object, and after sending it the DrawBlock message, examine its EOF property. This is a boolean; if it is true, all the text was drawn in the rectangle.

So, we could rewrite the previous example, as follows:

```
dim c as canvas, g as graphics
dim s as styledtextprinter
c = canvas1
g = p.graphics
g.clearrect 0,0,p.width,p.height
s = editfield1.styledtextprinter(g,c.width) // capture so we can test EOF
s.drawblock(0,0,c.height)
c.refresh
if s.eof then
    msgbox "Yes, all the text fit into the Canvas"
else
    msgbox "Oooops, too much text for this Canvas"
end
```

Very well; suppose, then, that not all the text fit into the rectangle you drew into; what can you do about it? The answer is that you can draw *more* of the text into *another* rectangle! It turns out that after a DrawBlock call, the StyledTextPrinter instance remembers how much of its text fit into the rectangle, and if you send it the DrawBlock message again, with a different rectangle, what it draws is the text that didn't fit into the previous rectangle. In other words, each time you send the Styled-TextPrinter instance the DrawBlock message, it picks up drawing where it left off the last time. The subsequent rectangles do have to be drawn into the same Graphics property, since the StyledTextPrinter is associated with only one Graphics property. However, it shouldn't be very hard for you to think of a technique whereby part of an EditField is drawn into one Canvas and the rest of it is drawn into another. This is left as an exercise.

To illustrate, let's modify the previous example so that it draws only into the left half of the Canvas; if not all the text fits into that half, we draw the rest into the right half of the Canvas. We are thus drawing in two columns:

```
dim c as canvas, g as graphics
dim s as styledtextprinter
c = canvas1
g = p.graphics
g.clearrect 0,0,p.width,p.height
s = editfield1.styledtextprinter(g,c.width\2)
s.drawblock(0,0,c.height)
if not s.eof then
    s.drawblock(c.width\2,0,c.height)
end
c.refresh
```

If, as you draw into subsequent rectangles, you need to make the next rectangle be of a different size, you can. The height is a parameter when you call the DrawBlock method. The width can be changed by setting the StyledTextPrinter's Width property. So, for example, here we draw in two columns, but the first is wider than the second:

```
dim c as canvas, g as graphics
dim s as styledtextprinter
c = canvas1
g = p.graphics
g.clearrect 0,0,p.width,p.height
s = editfield1.styledtextprinter(g,2*c.width\3)
s.drawblock(0,0,c.height)
if not s.eof then
    s.width = c.width\3
    s.drawblock(c.width\3,0,c.height)
end
c.refresh
```

Miscellaneous Tips

A disabled single-line EditField has its text grayed out, but a disabled multiline Edit-Field has normal-looking text, and even a disabled single-line EditField has normal-looking text if the text is changed in code. Some people find this surprising, but I actually rather like it (and the tickertape field example earlier in this chapter took advantage of it). Without this feature, there would be no way to display text in multiple styles that the user can neither edit nor select.

An EditField can only be left-aligned. But sometimes you want the user to be able to edit text in, say, a centered field. For a nonstyled single-line EditField, a reasonable workaround is to show the text as a centered StaticText placed over the EditField. When the EditField gets focus, copy the text from the StaticText into the EditField, and set the StaticText's text to the empty string:

```
me.text = statictext1.text
statictext1.text = ""
```

When the EditField loses focus, reverse the process. The field will appear to be left-aligned while the user is editing it, but centered the rest of the time.

If you find that EditFields just don't meet your needs, you may be able to substitute a plug-in control. Of particular interest is Doug Holton's WASTEfield plug-in, which gives you access to features of the WASTE text engine not implemented by Edit-Fields, such as pictures in fields, text alignment, and line spacing.*

---

* See *http://people.vanderbilt.edu/~doug.holton/basic/plugins/*.

CHAPTER 14

ListBoxes

The ListBox class is a built-in control that maintains a columnar display of brief, individual lines of text—a list. The user can navigate the list and can select a line (or, optionally, more than one line simultaneously), using the mouse or keyboard.

Navigation keys are the up and down arrow keys and the Home, End, Page Up, and Page Down keys. If the user is permitted to select more than one line simultaneously, then Shift-clicking or Shift-up/down arrow selects a range of lines, and Command-clicking selects separate individual lines.

In the Tools Window, the ListBox is represented by two icons; the difference, which is purely a matter of convenience, has merely to do with the ListBox's initial settings in the IDE—either two columns with headings, or one column with no heading.

ListBox Features

Each line of a ListBox is called a *row*. A ListBox also has at least one *column*. The intersection of a row and a column is an individual text item, and is called a *cell*.

Text in a ListBox has only one font and size. Individual cells, however, can receive their own bold, italic, and underline styling. A row may also include a picture (but the row does not expand to display it—in other words, a ListBox is not intended for display of pictures, but small pictures can be used to enhance a ListBox). Figure 14-1 shows a single-column and a multicolumn ListBox; in the multicolumn ListBox, the cells of the first column are bold, and each row includes a fruity picture.

Columns can have headings, which the user can click to sort the rows on that column. A cell can be made to include a checkbox, which the user can click to check or uncheck it; or, a cell's text can be made directly editable by the user. Figure 14-2 illustrates all three features (the user is editing the word "Indescribable").

A ListBox can be *hierarchical*. This involves designating at least one row as a *folder row*, meaning that it is considered to possess subrows. A folder row can be *expanded*

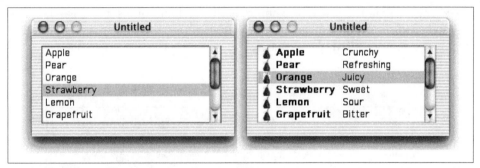

Figure 14-1. Single-column and multicolumn ListBoxes

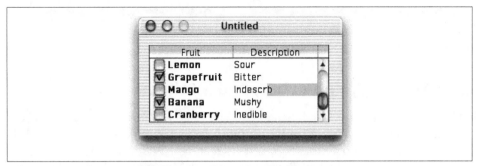

Figure 14-2. ListBox with checkboxes, headings, and editable entries

or *collapsed*; the intention is that when it is expanded, its subrows will be shown, and when it is collapsed, its subrows will be hidden. Figure 14-3 shows a folder row that has just been expanded to reveal three subrows.

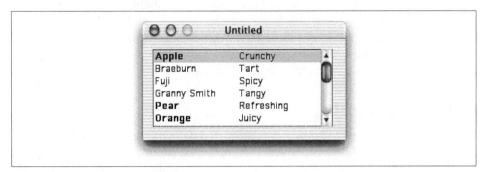

Figure 14-3. Hierarchical ListBox

Optionally, a hierarchical ListBox can display *disclosure triangles* for folder rows. The user can click a triangle as a way of asking for the row to be expanded or collapsed. The triangle of a collapsed row points rightward; the triangle of an expanded row points downward. Such a ListBox is painted rather differently from other ListBoxes: its background is shaded, and a selected row is indicated by highlighting the text of its cells rather than the row as a whole. The first column of a subrow is automatically indented. Figure 14-4 illustrates; a ListBox with disclosure triangles is shown with its first row collapsed, then expanded.

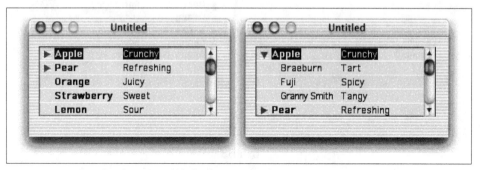

Figure 14-4. Hierarchical ListBox with disclosure triangles

ListBox Events, Properties, and Methods

A ListBox is a RectControl, and therefore receives all the events and has all the methods and properties listed in Chapter 10: Open and Close events; Visible, Enabled, and AutoDeactivate properties; Top, Left, Height, and Width properties; LockLeft, LockRight, LockTop, and LockBottom properties; MouseEnter, MouseMove, and MouseExit events; and Refresh and RefreshRect methods.

For the EnableDrag property, the DragRow event, and drag-and-drop in general, see Chapter 24.

A ListBox can receive the focus; see also "The Focus" in Chapter 13. On the interactions between menu events and a focus-bearing control, see Chapter 6. The EditCopy, EditCut, EditClear, and EditPaste menu items have no automatic behavior with regard to a ListBox, but a ListBox subclass with the focus can enable them and give them functionality; an example appears in Chapter 23.

Contents and Format

A ListBox has the following properties relating to its contents and format:

InitialValue
Initial text for the entire ListBox. Can be set and read only in a dialog box in the IDE. In this dialog, rows are delimited by return characters, and cells are delimited by tab characters.

TextFont, TextSize, Bold, Italic, Underline
Format features of the text of the entire ListBox. Every cell will have the same font and size. If Bold, Italic, or Underline is false, it can be overridden for a particular cell, by way of the CellBold, CellItalic, and CellUnderline properties. Text within a single cell is uniformly styled.

ListCount

The number of rows. Read-only. Row designations are zero-based, so the first row has an index of 0 and the last row has an index of listCount-1. (The maximum number of rows appears to be 32K.)

ColumnCount

The number of columns to be displayed.

ColumnWidths

A string describing the widths of the displayed columns. Ignored if Column-Count is 1. Optional if ColumnCount is 2 or more; the default is for all displayed columns to have equal widths. The string is a comma-delimited list of numbers, each of which is a pixel value, unless it ends with "%", in which case it is a percentage relative to the width of the ListBox's content region. If the list describes fewer than ColumnCount columns, widths of subsequent columns will be equal across the remaining space of the content region. (By a ListBox's "content region," I mean its area exclusive of its scrollbars.)

List

Takes one parameter, a row index. Gets or sets the text of the first cell of that row. The row must exist; otherwise, an exception is raised. Thus, the parameter must not be negative nor exceed listCount-1.

Cell

Takes two parameters, a row index and a column index. (This is the standard order for referring to cells; observe that it is *backward* from the order for referring to point coordinates in Canvases, windows, and so forth!) Gets or sets the text of the designated cell. The first row and the first column have index 0. These two lines are equivalent:

```
me.list(1) = "Hello"
me.cell(1,0) = "Hello"
```

The row must exist, or an exception is raised. The column, however, need *not* exist; that is, the column index can be higher than columnCount-1 (but I'm warned by REAL Software that you should not let it exceed 63). Getting a nonexistent cell yields the empty string; setting a nonexistent cell gives it the designated value even if its column is not displayed.

CellBold, CellItalic, CellUnderline

These take two parameters, as for Cell. A boolean. Determines a cell's individual styling; but setting a cell style to false when the corresponding style for the ListBox as a whole is true has no visible effect.

ColumnAlignment, CellAlignment

The first takes one parameter, a column index; the second takes two parameters, as for Cell. An integer determining the horizontal alignment of a column or cell's text, as follows: 0 or 1 means left; 2 means centered; 3 means right; 4 means decimal-aligned. A nonzero CellAlignment takes precedence over a nonzero ColumnAlignment for the same cell.

ColumnAlignmentOffset, CellAlignmentOffset

Take one and two parameters, respectively, as for ColumnAlignment and Cell-Alignment. An integer dictating how many pixels the text is to be shifted right-ward or (using negative values) leftward from the position dictated by its ColumnAlignment or CellAlignment. A nonzero CellAlignmentOffset takes precedence over a nonzero ColumnAlignmentOffset for the same cell.

RowPicture

Takes one parameter, a row index. A Picture instance. Determines the picture shown behind the row. Setting to `nil` removes the picture.

LastIndex

Read-only. The index of the row most recently added with the InsertRow, AddRow, or AddFolder methods, at the time it was added.

ScrollbarVertical, ScrollbarHorizontal

Booleans determining whether the ListBox should have a vertical and horizontal scrollbar, respectively. Can be set in code!

ScrollPosition, ScrollPositionX

Integers determining the vertical and horizontal scroll position, respectively. The ScrollPosition is the number of the row at the top of the ListBox. The ScrollPositionX is measured in pixels; the maximum is the sum of all column widths minus the width of the ListBox's content region.

A ListBox has the following methods relating to its contents and format:

AddRow

Takes one parameter, a string; creates a new row at the end of the ListBox (or, if called from within the ExpandRow event handler, as the last subrow of the expanded row), and sets the text of its first cell to the string.

InsertRow

Takes two parameters, a row index and a string. Creates a new row at the designated index, and sets the text of its first cell to the string; the index of the existing row with that index is incremented, and so on for all subsequent rows. The row index need *not* designate an existing row; if it is too small or too large, the row will be inserted before or after all existing rows (and you can use LastIndex to find out where it was actually inserted).

RemoveRow

Takes one parameter, a row index; deletes the row at the designated index, decrementing the indices of all subsequent rows. The row must exist; if not, an exception is raised.

DeleteAllRows

Empties the ListBox's contents.

Selection

A ListBox has the following properties relating to its selection:

SelectionType

An integer indicating whether the user is to be able to select more than one row at a time: 0 means no, 1 means yes. Can be set only in the IDE. Even if SelectionType is 0, you can perform multiple selection in code using Selected.

SelCount

The number of currently selected rows. Read-only.

ListIndex

The index of the first selected row. Can be used to learn or to set the selection. A value of -1 means no selection. If set too large or too small, there is no error, and the value will be set to -1. Returns just a single integer, so if SelCount exceeds 1, you'll have to poll every row using Selected to learn what rows are selected; similarly, you must use Selected to perform a multiple selection in code.

Selected

Takes one parameter, a row index; its boolean value corresponds to whether that row is selected. Setting a row's Selected to true does *not* cause any currently selected row to be deselected, so multiple selection is possible even if SelectionType is 0.

Text

The text of the first cell of the selected row; the same as referring to cell(listIndex,0).

A ListBox receives the following events relating to its selection:

Change

Sent to the ListBox because its selection has been newly determined. This happens because:

- The user clicks anywhere in the ListBox, including the already selected line.
- The user employs arrow keys to move the selection highlight.
- The selection is set (not necessarily changed) in code, using ListIndex or Selected.

DoubleClick

Sent because the user has double-clicked in the ListBox. Preceded by a Change event.

Hierarchy

A ListBox has the following properties relating to its being hierarchical:

Hierarchical

Despite its name, does not affect whether the ListBox is hierarchical! A ListBox is hierarchical if any of its rows was created with the AddFolder method. Rather, determines whether the ListBox automatically displays disclosure triangles for rows created with AddFolder, along with an altered background and selection display. Cannot be set in code.

Expanded

Takes one parameter, a row index. If the row was not created with AddFolder, setting has no effect, and the value can never be true. If the row was created with AddFolder, then setting to true triggers an ExpandRow event, and setting to false triggers a CollapseRow event. The row must exist, or an exception will be raised.

A ListBox has the following method relating to its being hierarchical:

AddFolder

Takes one parameter, a string. Identical to AddRow, except that the new row will be a folder row, meaning that it can be affected by the Expanded property, and, if the ListBox's Hierarchical property is true, the new row will have a disclosure triangle.

A ListBox receives the following events relating to its being hierarchical:

ExpandRow

Sent because the Expanded of a row created with AddFolder was previously false and has been set to true. This can happen directly in code, or through the user clicking the row's disclosure triangle if it has one (in which case the triangle has automatically been rotated). *A row added with AddRow or AddFolder within an ExpandRow event handler will become the last subrow of the newly expanded row.* This fact is the key to creating a hierarchical ListBox.

CollapseRow

Sent because the Expanded of a row created with AddFolder was previously true and has been set to false. This can happen directly in code, or through the user clicking the row's disclosure triangle if it has one. In the latter case, the triangle has automatically been rotated, and the row's subrows have not yet been automatically deleted—but they will be. This is an important difference between the behavior of a ListBox whose Hierarchical property is true and one whose Hierarchical property is false; the latter does nothing automatically when it receives a CollapseRow event, but the former deletes the subrows of the collapsed row, after the CollapseRow event has finished executing.

Headings and Sorting

A ListBox has the following properties relating to headings and sorting:

HasHeading

A boolean. Cannot be set in code. If true, headings are present above the columns, and if InitialValue was set in the IDE, its first row will be interpreted as the heading captions.

HeadingIndex

An integer, corresponding to a column. Reports what column the ListBox was most recently sorted on; -1 means not sorted. Setting this property sorts the ListBox on the given column, even if HasHeading is false.

Heading

Takes one parameter, a column index. Gets or sets the heading caption for that column; setting a heading caption to the empty string sets it to its column number. Alternatively, all headings may be set at once by using a parameter of -1 and a tab-delimited string value. Works even if HasHeading is false, but the headings won't be visible.

A ListBox receives the following event related to headings and sorting:

SortColumn

Sent to a ListBox because the user has clicked a heading, or because the ListBox's HeadingIndex property has been set in code. The event handler receives the column number as a parameter; it may return true to prevent the column from being automatically sorted.

The default sort order is by boolean comparison of strings (see Chapter 5); subrows travel with their folder rows and are otherwise ignored.

Checkboxes and Editable Cells

A cell can have its checkbox visible, or can have its text be directly editable by the user, or neither—but not both. A ListBox has the following properties relating to checkboxes and editable cells:

ColumnType, CellType

ColumnType takes one parameter, a column index; CellType takes two parameters, as for Cell. The value is an integer: 0 or 1 means normal; 2 means the cells have a checkbox; 3 means the cells are directly editable. A nonzero CellType overrides a nonzero ColumnType. If a cell is directly editable, its alignment and offset settings are ignored.

CellCheck

A boolean. Takes two parameters, as for Cell. Determines whether the cell's checkbox is checked (true means it is). Works even if the cell's checkbox is not presently visible: the setting is remembered, and will be displayed if the cell's checkbox is shown.

A ListBox receives the following event relating to checkboxes and editable cells:

CellAction

Sent because the user has edited a cell, either by clicking in its checkbox, or by clicking in its editable text and then leaving the cell. "Leaving the cell" means the focus changes or the selection is moved elsewhere in the ListBox. The event handler receives row and column parameters specifying the cell.

Keyboard

A ListBox receives the following event relating to the keyboard (see Chapter 19 for a summary of matters relating to the keyboard):

KeyDown
> Sent to a ListBox that has the focus, when the user types any key (unless it is a Command key equivalent corresponding to an enabled menu item). The event handler is told what key was typed, and may return true to prevent the default response to it. The default response for all but the up and down arrow keys and the Home, End, Page Up, and Page Down keys is for the key to fall through to the window, which in turn is sent a KeyDown event.

Focus

A ListBox has the following property relating to the focus:

UseFocusRing
> A boolean. If true, a highlight ring is drawn around the ListBox when it has the focus, unless it is the only control in its window that can receive the focus. Cannot be set in code.

A ListBox receives the following events relating to the focus:

GotFocus
> Sent to a ListBox that previously did not have the focus, when it receives the focus; if a different ListBox or an EditField previously had the focus, it is sent the LostFocus event first.

LostFocus
> Sent to a ListBox that has the focus, as it loses the focus. If the ListBox had a highlight ring around it, this is preceded by a Paint event sent to the window, to remove the ring. If focus is being shifted to another ListBox or an EditField, it is sent the GotFocus event afterward.

Entering or leaving an editable cell triggers a LostFocus or GotFocus event. This may be a bug.

A ListBox has the following method relating to the focus:

SetFocus
> Causes the ListBox to become the focus-bearing control for its window. If the window is a front window, also actually gives the ListBox the focus. Ignored if the ListBox is disabled or invisible.

For further details, see the discussion of GotFocus, LostFocus, and SetFocus in relation to EditFields, and of the focus in general, in Chapter 13.

Basic ListBox Techniques

This section consists of some simple examples illustrating the basic techniques for manipulating a ListBox's contents and formatting, column display, pictures, and selection.

Contents and Formatting

Let's start by creating the one-column ListBox at the left of Figure 14-1. We could do this by setting the InitialValue in the IDE; but populating a ListBox in code is more common, more challenging, and more important to understand. Let's populate the ListBox in its Open event handler. The list being initially empty, it suffices to add each row:

```
me.addrow "Apple"
me.addrow "Pear"
me.addrow "Orange"
me.addrow "Strawberry"
me.addrow "Lemon"
me.addrow "Grapefruit"
me.addrow "Mango"
me.addrow "Banana"
me.addrow "Cranberry"
```

This lacks elegance and generality, and it is more usual to loop through some other data structure. Here, we start with a delimited string:

```
dim i,u as integer
dim s as string
s = "Apple,Pear,Orange,Strawberry,Lemon,Grapefruit,Mango,Banana,Cranberry"
u = countFields(s,",")
for i = 1 to u
    me.addrow nthfield(s,",",i)
next
```

Imagine now that we wish every other row to be in boldface. That can't be accomplished in the IDE; in code, it's straightforward. We'll use CellBold, remembering to compensate for the fact that the row index, unlike a string field, is zero-based:

```
dim i,u as integer
dim s as string
s = "Apple,Pear,Orange,Strawberry,Lemon,Grapefruit,Mango,Banana,Cranberry"
u = countFields(s,",")
for i = 1 to u
    me.addrow nthfield(s,",",i)
    if i mod 2 = 0 then
        me.cellbold(i-1,0) = true
    end
next
```

Now let's create the two-column ListBox at the right of Figure 14-1. We can use a second delimited string as the source of the second column. Here, we make the first column bold, but we don't yet add the pictures:

```
dim i,u as integer
dim s1,s2 as string
s1 = "Apple,Pear,Orange,Strawberry,Lemon,Grapefruit,Mango,Banana,Cranberry"
s2 = "Crunchy,Refreshing,Juicy,Sweet,Sour,Bitter,Yummy,Mushy,Inedible"
u = countFields(s1,",")
for i = 1 to u
    me.addrow nthfield(s1,",",i)
    me.cellbold(i-1,0) = true
    me.cell(i-1,1) = nthfield(s2,",",i)
next
me.columncount = 2
```

AddRow both creates a row and sets its first cell, but subsequent cells can be set only through the Cell property. If you dislike this asymmetry, you can supply the empty string as the parameter for AddRow, and then use Cell for all the row's cells; but you cannot omit AddRow's parameter altogether:

```
dim i,u as integer
dim s1,s2 as string
s1 = "Apple,Pear,Orange,Strawberry,Lemon,Grapefruit,Mango,Banana,Cranberry"
s2 = "Crunchy,Refreshing,Juicy,Sweet,Sour,Bitter,Yummy,Mushy,Inedible"
u = countFields(s1,",")
for i = 1 to u
    me.addrow ""
    me.cell(i-1,0) = nthfield(s1,",",i)
    me.cellbold(i-1,0) = true
    me.cell(i-1,1) = nthfield(s2,",",i)
next
me.columncount = 2
```

Populating a large ListBox can be slow, especially when doing it for the first time. A common trick is to turn the ListBox invisible before populating it and visible afterward; the ListBox does not vanish and reappear, and the time difference is very great. For example, on my machine, populating a ListBox with the integers from 1 to 30,000 takes more than 300 ticks, but only 50 ticks if the ListBox is turned invisible first.

Column Display

Next we consider the ColumnCount and ColumnWidths properties. What would have happened, in the previous example, if ColumnCount had not been set to 2? If ColumnCount is set in the IDE to 1 and isn't changed, then only the first column is displayed—but after our Open event handler, the second column exists anyway! This means that we can change the ColumnCount value later on, to show the second column. Create a button whose Action event handler reads as follows:

```
listbox1.columncount = listbox1.columncount mod 2 + 1
```

Repeatedly pressing this button causes the second column to vanish and reappear.

What if we want the *first* column to vanish and reappear? Then we keep the ColumnCount at 2, so that the second column will always be shown, and alter the ColumnWidths. If ColumnWidths is the empty string, all columns are shown at identical widths. If fewer widths are supplied than the number of columns, then subsequent columns are shown at identical widths. So here's the Action event handler of a button that can be pressed repeatedly to make the first column vanish and reappear:

```
if listbox1.columnwidths = "" then
    listbox1.columnwidths = "0"
else
    listbox1.columnwidths = ""
end
```

Another way to show and hide columns is by scrolling horizontally. You can do this even if there is no horizontal scrollbar—indeed, that's just when you would do it, since the user cannot interfere with your manipulations. If there are two columns, and ColumnWidths is set at "100%,100%", this code will make the ListBox alternate between displaying just the first column and just the second:

```
if listbox1.scrollpositionx <> 0 then
    listbox1.scrollpositionx = 0
else
    listbox1.scrollpositionx = listbox1.width-15
end
```

The ability of a ListBox to store information in cells that are not shown, and may indeed never be shown, is of great importance, as we'll see later in this chapter.

Pictures

The ListBox at the right of Figure 14-1 shows pictures at the start of each row. Here is the code that adds them; the picture comes from an imported GIF named *ap2*, and this line goes into the For loop in the ListBox's Open event handler, which was presented earlier:

```
me.rowpicture(i-1) = ap2
```

Pictures in a ListBox can be a little tricky. One problem is that the text of the first column shifts rightward somewhat to accommodate a picture in the same row; if only some rows have pictures, this can result in a jagged text layout. Figure 14-5 shows the problem: in the first window, the first two rows have the RowPicture, and their text has shifted rightward, so it doesn't line up with the text of the other rows.

If this isn't what you want, the second window shows a solution, which can actually be achieved in three different ways:

- Let there be three columns, with the fruit names and descriptions placed in the second and third columns.

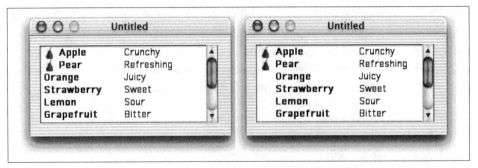

Figure 14-5. Using columns to align text regardless of pictures

- Let there be two columns, but let every row have a picture. The blank picture can be just a small white dot; it isn't visible, but its presence causes the automatic rightward shift in the first column's text.

- Let there be two columns, and let just the first two rows have pictures, but impose offset values upon the text; after some experimentation, I gave the first column a ColumnAlignmentOffset of 21 and the Apple and Pear cells a CellAlignmentOffset of 1.

Another peculiarity of ListBox pictures is their positioning. Because they are expected to be little icons at the left of the row (like the fruit in Figure 14-5), ListBox pictures are vertically centered in the middle of the row and horizontally centered about 12 pixels inward from the left. Nevertheless, with some experimentation, patience, and arithmetic, you can make the image appear anywhere in the row. The image appears behind the text. So you can imagine and achieve some very interesting effects.

For example, in Figure 14-6, it looks as if the cells have borders! This is achieved by a picture in every row. The picture is twice the width of the ListBox, and the placement of the vertical and horizontal line within it was achieved initially by trial and error. To prevent the text in the first column from shifting to the right, there is no text in the first column; the first column is zero pixels wide, and what looks like the first column is actually the second column. Here is the code that generates the picture (a Picture property called VertLine) in the ListBox's Open event handler:

```
dim x,y as integer
x = me.width + me.width/2 - 24
y = 20
vertline = newpicture(me.width*2, 30, 4)
vertline.graphics.drawline x,0,x,vertline.height
vertline.graphics.drawline 0,y,vertline.width,y
```

Unfortunately, since the screen shot in Figure 14-6 was taken, a change has been introduced that prevents this technique from working on Mac OS X.

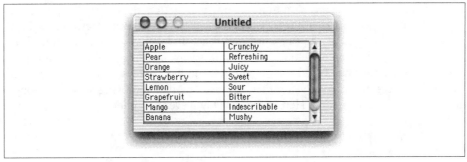

Figure 14-6. Unusual use of pictures

Selection

When the purpose of a ListBox is to present the user with a choice, the user indicates that choice by making a selection within the ListBox; the ListBox will receive a Change event, and then your code can ascertain what that selection was.

The only complication here is that the technique for ascertaining the selection differs depending on how many rows are selected. The following general routine creates a comma-delimited string reporting all the currently selected rows of ListBox1; the idea is to avoid polling individual rows unless we have to, and then to poll as few as possible:

```
dim u,i,ct,fnd as integer
dim s as string
ct = listbox1.selcount
if ct < 2 then
    s = str(listbox1.listindex)
else
    u = listbox1.listcount-1
    for i = listbox1.listindex to u
        if listbox1.selected(i) then
            s = s + "," + str(i)
            fnd = fnd + 1
            if fnd = ct then
                exit
            end
        end
    next
    s = right(s,len(s)-1)
end // now s contains the desired string
```

An interesting problem is how to provide the user with additional selection methods. For example, let's suppose we have a ListBox sorted in alphabetical order. We want the user to be able to type a letter, or a few letters—up to three, let's say—as a way of selecting the first item of the list that starts with those letters. This involves the keyboard, so our code will go into the ListBox's KeyDown event handler.

The only hard part is that we don't know how many letters the user will type. In this implementation, we use two integer properties to track the user's keystrokes: Last-Time records the time of the previous keystroke, and WhatLetter determines how many letters we are presently considering. In this way, a typing "session" can persist until the user either has typed our maximum number of keystrokes or has paused longer than a certain interval. After that, it's just a matter of moving forward through the list until we find a match. Here is the KeyDown event handler:

```
dim diff, max, howmany, index as integer
dim sofar as string
if key < "a" or key > "z" then
    return false // not our problem
end
diff = ticks - self.lasttime
self.lasttime = ticks
if diff < 20 then // more of same session?
    self.whatLetter = (self.whatLetter + 1) mod 3
else
    self.whatLetter = 0
end
max = me.listcount - 1
if self.whatLetter = 0 then // start at beginning
    sofar = ""
    index = 0
else
    sofar = lowercase(left(me.text,self.whatLetter))
    index = me.listindex
end
sofar = sofar + key
howmany = self.whatLetter + 1
do until index = max or lowercase(left(me.cell(index,0),howMany)) >= sofar
    index = index + 1
loop
me.listindex = index
```

Hierarchical ListBoxes

Working with hierarchical ListBoxes is rather tricky, because REALbasic doesn't provide very much assistance. Here's a summary of the main difficulties:

- A row that can possess subrows (a folder row) can be created only with AddFolder, which means that it can be only the last row of the ListBox or the last subrow of a row. There is no InsertFolder method, and no method that converts an existing row into a folder row.

- There is almost no automatic relationship between a folder row and its subrows. It's true that collapsing a folder row does delete its subrows if the ListBox's Hierarchical property is true; but apart from this, a folder row doesn't "possess" subrows in any innate sense—you have to perform this association yourself. You can't ask a row whether it is a folder row; you can't ask a folder row how many subrows it has; you can't ask a row whether it is a subrow, and if so what folder row it is a subrow of.

- A subrow doesn't persist; when a folder row is collapsed, its subrows are destroyed, and it is up to your code to create them anew every time it is expanded. This is possible only in the ListBox's ExpandRow event handler, when that row's Expanded is changed to true.

Sooner or later, you're probably going to want a technique for maintaining a hierarchical ListBox. Rather than simply presenting a completed solution, I develop my approach in stages over the course of this section; the exposition of my reasoning should make the result more comprehensible, and more adaptable to your own needs.

One Folder Row

To begin with, can we get our ListBox to behave hierarchically at all? Let's start with the simplest possible case. We'll take our ListBox of fruits, and we'll suppose that, as with Figure 14-3, the Apple row is to have three subrows that can be shown or hidden. We'll have the ListBox's Hierarchical property be false, and we'll let the user double-click a row as a signal that it should be expanded or collapsed.

Clearly the first step is to modify the Open event handler so that the Apple row is a folder row and the Expand method will apply to it:

```
dim i,u as integer
dim s1,s2 as string
s1 = "Apple,Pear,Orange,Strawberry,Lemon,Grapefruit,Mango,Banana,Cranberry"
s2 = "Crunchy,Refreshing,Juicy,Sweet,Sour,Bitter,Yummy,Mushy,Inedible"
u = countFields(s1,",")
for i = 1 to u
    if i = 1 then // the Apple row
        me.addfolder ""
    else
        me.addrow ""
    end
    me.cell(i-1,0) = nthfield(s1,",",i)
    me.cellbold(i-1,0) = true
    me.cell(i-1,1) = nthfield(s2,",",i)
next
me.columncount = 2
```

Next, the DoubleClick event handler must be written to expand or collapse a double-clicked row:

```
me.expanded(me.listindex) = not me.expanded(me.listindex)
```

The Apple row is now a folder row, so when the user double-clicks it and this line is executed, the ListBox will receive an ExpandRow or CollapseRow event. We must therefore write the event handlers for these events.

The ExpandRow event handler will be called when the Apple row is double-clicked to expand it. What's more, since the Apple row is the *only* folder row, the ExpandRow event handler will be called *only* when the Apple row is double-clicked. The

ExpandRow event handler must respond by adding the subrows, and it must do this by using AddRow. We can model our code after the Open event handler. We know that the Apple row is row 0, so what we need to add are rows starting with row 1:

```
dim s1, s2 as string
dim i,u as integer
s1 = "Braeburn,Fuji,Granny Smith"
s2 = "Tart,Spicy,Tangy"
u = countfields(s1,",")
for i = 1 to u
    me.addrow ""
    me.cell(i,0) = nthfield(s1,",",i)
    me.cell(i,1) = nthfield(s2,",",i)
next
```

In the CollapseRow event handler, the situation is parallel. We know that the event handler won't be called unless we are collapsing the Apple row. Therefore, we must delete the Apple row's subrows, and we know that these are rows 1, 2, and 3:

```
dim i as integer
for i = 3 downto 1
    me.removerow i
next
```

General Single-Depth Hierarchy

We have now succeeded in making one row of a ListBox behave hierarchically. Let's now consider what information unique to our particular situation was hardcoded into it, and what we would have to do to remove this hardcoding and generalize the technique. Clearly our whole implementation revolves around the facts that there is just one row that can be expanded or collapsed and that we happen to know which row this is. The key information turns out to be hardcoded in no fewer than three different places! The Open event handler knows which row is the folder row; the ExpandRow event handler knows what the folder row's subrow texts are; and the CollapseRow event handler knows how many subrows the folder row has. Surely we don't intend to carry on in this manner?! Imagine the difficulties involved as two, three, or a hundred rows are folder rows. Any change in the details, as we develop the project, will require changes in all three handlers; and any change in the ListBox data while the application is running, such as the insertion or deletion of a row, will break the implementation entirely.

Clearly this is totally unacceptable, so at this point there is nothing for it but to take a deep breath and begin all over again.[*] Obviously the information about subrows needs to be stored as data that the application can access while it is running. Optimally, we would like the data for a folder row's subrows to be associated somehow

---

[*] Actually, my response when faced with this sort of impasse is to take a run, a bath, or a nap—sometimes all three. I find that all my best coding is done at these times. This might not work for you, but it is worth trying; if your code fails to improve, at least you'll be fit, clean, and well rested.

with that row. Well, there is a way to do this: we can store the data right in that row, in the ListBox itself! Recall that we are permitted to set the value of cells that are not displayed. Let's give each folder row some extra, hidden cells, containing its subrow information.

To illustrate, it will be sufficient to have two rows be folder rows; if we can generalize to two, we can generalize to a hundred. We return to the ListBox's Open event handler. This time, all the data will be initialized here. We have four strings: the first and second columns, each as a comma-delimited list, and the first and second columns for each row's subrows, each as a semicolon-delimited list of comma-delimited lists. As we build the ListBox's data, we store the subrow information, if any, in the row's third and fourth cells; the user can't see this information, but our other handlers will be able to:

```
dim i,u as integer
dim s1,s2,subRowCol1,subRowCol2 as string
s1 = "Apple,Pear,Orange,Strawberry,Lemon,Grapefruit,Mango,Banana,Cranberry"
s2 = "Crunchy,Refreshing,Juicy,Sweet,Sour,Bitter,Yummy,Mushy,Inedible"
subRowCol1 = "Braeburn,Fuji,Granny Smith;Seckel,Bosc"
subRowCol2 = "Tart,Spicy,Tangy;Tiny,Aromatic"
u = countFields(s1,",")
for i = 1 to u
    if nthfield(subrowcol1,";",i) <> "" then
        me.addfolder ""
        me.cell(i-1,2) = nthfield(subrowcol1,";",i)
        me.cell(i-1,3) = nthfield(subrowcol2,";",i)
    else
        me.addrow ""
    end
    me.cell(i-1,0) = nthfield(s1,",",i)
    me.cellbold(i-1,0) = true
    me.cell(i-1,1) = nthfield(s2,",",i)
next
me.columncount = 2
```

It is now a simple matter to generalize the ExpandRow event handler; it just looks at the third and fourth cells of the current row to obtain the required data:

```
dim s1, s2 as string
dim i,u as integer
s1 = me.cell(row,2)
s2 = me.cell(row,3)
u = countfields(s1,",")
for i = 1 to u
    me.addrow ""
    me.cell(me.lastIndex,0) = nthfield(s1,",",i)
    me.cell(me.lastIndex,1) = nthfield(s2,",",i)
next
```

Similarly, the CollapseRow event handler looks at the third cell of the current row to learn how many rows to delete:

```
dim i,u,numSubRows as integer
numSubRows = countfields(me.cell(row,2),",")
```

```
u = row + 1
for i = row + numSubRows downto u
    me.removerow i
next
```

General Multiple-Depth Hierarchy—First Try

The implementation developed in the previous section works perfectly well, and is quite commonly used. But we must bear in mind that it suffers from a severe limitation: it works only if the hierarchy is just one level deep. What if some of our subrows are to have subrows of their own?

Let's set ourselves a clear goal—to implement a single-column ListBox capable of handling a hierarchy of any desired depth. For example, it should accept and display data such as the following:

```
Fruit
    Apple
        Fuji
        Braeburn
        Granny Smith
    Pear
        Seckel
        Bosc
    Mango
Vegetable
    Broccoli
    Turnip
```

If we can solve this problem, further refinements such as adding columns will be simple. The trouble is that no purely linear data structure, such as the successive cells of a row, can hold the information for that row's subrows *and* any subrows of each of those subrows, and so forth. It is therefore evident that we are going to have to maintain the ListBox's data in some *other* data structure, a data structure of our own devising. And if we're going to do that, we'll want to associate that data structure with the ListBox. This suggests that we should use a ListBox subclass.

Our data structure will itself be a new class, List. It has two properties: a string property, Text, and a property called Subhead, which is an array of Lists. To see how this will work, suppose, first of all, that we have just two items, Fruit and Vegetable. We start with a List object with no Text property (because it is just the root of the list) and whose Subhead array is dimensioned to 2. One List in the Subhead has the Text "Fruit", the other has the Text "Vegetable", like this:

```
Text: (none). Subhead(2):
    Text: "Fruit". Subhead(0)
    Text: "Vegetable". Subhead(0)
```

To add the next level, we dimension appropriately the Subhead array of each first-level List, and assign each item of each Subhead array the appropriate Text:

```
Text: (none). Subhead(2):
    Text: "Fruit". Subhead(3):
```

```
      Text: "Apple". Subhead(0)
      Text: "Pear". Subhead(0)
      Text: "Mango". Subhead(0)
   Text: "Vegetable". Subhead(2):
      Text: "Broccoli". Subhead(0)
      Text: "Turnip". Subhead(0)
```

And so on. In general, then, given a List, we add a subhead by appending to its Subhead array a List with the appropriate Text. So, we create a method handler, AddSub, to do just that:

```
Sub AddSub(s as string)
    dim L as List
    L = new List
    L.text = s
    self.subhead.append L
End Sub
```

A List represents a folder row if its Subhead array is dimensioned to more than 0. The English-like notions "count subheads" and "is a folder" are easier to understand than manipulations of the Ubound function and the Subhead property, so we encapsulate them as functions. We'll call one CountSubs:

```
Function CountSubs() As integer
    return ubound(self.subhead)
End Function
```

The other is called IsFolder:

```
Function IsFolder() As boolean
    return self.countSubs > 0
End Function
```

This completes the List class.

We now turn our attention to the ListBox subclass, which we call ListLister. Clearly, ListLister will need a List property to hold its associated List; we'll call it TheList. Think of ListLister as a graphical representation of TheList.

Initially, ListLister should display TheList's top level. Well, to display a List's top level simply means to run through its Subhead array, getting each subhead's Text and displaying it either with AddFolder or with AddRow, depending on whether or not it is a folder:

```
Sub displayTopLevel(L as List)
    dim i,u as integer
    u = L.countSubs
    for i = 1 to u
        if L.subhead(i).isFolder then
            addfolder L.subhead(i).text
        else
            addrow L.subhead(i).text
        end if
    next
End Sub
```

Expanding any folder row should display the top level of whatever List that row represents. But that is exactly what DisplayTopLevel already does! So we'll put the following into ListLister's ExpandRow event handler. I must warn you, there is a huge bug in this code! If you can't spot it right away, don't worry; we'll stumble over it soon enough:

```
displayTopLevel(theList.subhead(row+1))
```

We are now ready to try out ListLister in action. We drag a ListLister instance into a window and give it the following Open event handler to initialize TheList and display its top level:

```
dim L,L2,L3 as List
L = new List
L.addSub "Fruit"
L2 = L.subhead(L.countSubs)
L2.addSub "Apple"
L3 = L2.subhead(L2.countSubs)
L3.addSub "Fuji"
L3.addSub "Braeburn"
L3.addSub "Granny Smith"
L2.addSub "Pear"
L3 = L2.subhead(L2.countSubs)
L3.addSub "Seckel"
L3.addSub "Bosc"
L2.addSub "Mango"
L.addSub "Vegetable"
L2 = L.subhead(L.countSubs)
L2.addSub "Broccoli"
L2.addSub "Turnip"
me.theList = L
me.displayTopLevel(me.theList)
```

For simplicity, we set this ListLister's Hierarchical property to true; that way, we don't need a CollapseRow event handler, and we're ready to roll. We run the project, and sure enough, the ListBox displays Fruit and Vegetable, just as expected.

So far, so good. We click on the Vegetable triangle; the row expands, and we see Broccoli and Turnip, just as expected. We click on the Fruit triangle; the row expands, and we see Apple, Pear, and Mango, just as expected. We collapse the Fruit row and expand it again—it works. We collapse the Vegetable row and expand it again—and terminate with an OutOfBoundsException.

General Multiple-Depth Hierarchy

So near and yet so far! What went wrong? Our ExpandRow event handler is too simple. It assumes an easy correspondence between the index of the row number being expanded and the index, within TheList, of the List that is to be displayed. But of course there is no such easy correspondence. Everything depends upon the ListBox's current state of expansion. When the Fruit row is collapsed, the Vegetable row has index 1. But when the Fruit row is expanded, the Vegetable row has index 4!

Evidently, we are still missing a major piece of the puzzle. And it is now obvious what that piece is. What we need to know about a given row in order to expand it is what List it represents within TheList. We need a way of *linking back* from each row of the ListBox to the List from which it was generated. How is that possible? Clearly, we're going to have to *give* each row this information when we create it, so that we can ask for it when the time comes to expand the row.

The question is then how to code this backward link. If only every row of a ListBox had a RowTag property, which was a variant, like a PopupMenu! In that case, the List that represents a row could simply hand that row a reference to itself. Unfortunately, there's no such RowTag property. So, in effect, we'll implement it ourselves. Our ListLister will have a new property, an array of Lists, called Links. We'll keep this array synchronized with the displayed rows of the ListBox: given a row number, the Lists array at that index will be a pointer to the List represented by that row. This will require a tiny bit more work, to maintain the synchronization; in particular, we will have to write a CollapseRow handler for ListLister, to remove from the Links array the items corresponding to the subrows that are about to vanish. But on the whole, this implementation will be very easy to write, based on what we already have.

Presume that the Lists array is initially dimensioned to zero. This means that to start with, it will have one element, which is nil. We return to ListLister's Display-TopLevel handler and add just one line; when we insert a row into the ListBox's display, we also insert a pointer at the corresponding position in the Links array:

```
Sub displayTopLevel(L as List)
    dim i,u as integer
    u = L.countSubs
    for i = 1 to u
        if L.subhead(i).isFolder then
            addfolder L.subhead(i).text
        else
            addrow L.subhead(i).text
        end if
        self.links.insert self.lastindex, L.subhead(i) // point back to List
    next
End Sub
```

When using Insert, we must be careful of boundary conditions; we mustn't try to insert at a nonexistent row. Since there is a zero element in the Links array initially, this Insert call will never fail.

The ExpandRow event handler is now easily changed to reach the correct List:

```
displayTopLevel(self.links(row))
```

This works perfectly—as long as we don't collapse any rows. But presumably we will collapse some rows, so the CollapseRow event handler, as I mentioned a moment ago, must remove from the Links array the elements corresponding to the rows that are about to vanish. Which rows are they? Suppose we are collapsing row 0. Row 1 will vanish if it is a subrow of row 0. Now there is a new Row 1. It will vanish if it is a subrow of row 0—or if it is a subrow of the old Row 1. In other words, a row will vanish if its parent, at some remove, is the row that's collapsing. Imagine that we have a way to ask a List whether its parent, at some remove, is a certain other List. Let's call this method IsSubOf. Then we can write the CollapseRow event handler:

```
dim L as list
L = self.links(row)
while self.links(row+1) <> nil and self.links(row+1).IsSubOf(L)
    self.links.remove (row+1)
wend
```

However, the truth is that IsSubOf doesn't exist, and it isn't going to exist unless we have a way to ask a row what its parent is. Our List class will therefore need another List property, Parent. We add a line to List's AddSub method so that it sets the new List's Parent property:

```
Sub AddSub(s as string)
    dim L as List
    L = new List
    L.text = s
    L.parent = self // set the parent
    self.subhead.append L
End Sub
```

Now we can write IsSubOf. Its purpose, you recall, is to let a List answer the question, "Is your parent, at some remove, such and such a List?" It does this by recursing up the parent chain until either it finds the parent in question or runs out of parents:

```
Function IsSubOf(L as List) As boolean
    if self.parent = nil then
        return false
    end
    if self.parent = L then
        return true
    end
    return self.parent.isSubOf(L)
End Function
```

That's all. We have now developed what we set out to develop—a general ListBox subclass that automatically displays hierarchical lists to any depth as the user expands and collapses each folder row. As in Figure 14-7, the user can expand any folder row or rows, in any order and in any combination, and the outline will display correctly.

Other ListBox Features

This section presents a few tips about checkboxes, editable cells, headings, and sorting.

Both checkboxes and directly editable cells are ways of making a cell editable, but a cell can be editable only in one mode at a time: either it can have a checkbox, or it can be directly editable. So naturally the main thing you'd like to do is get around

Figure 14-7. Automatic hierarchical ListBox subclass in action

this limitation. You can, by a simple trick—have one column contain the checkbox and the next column contain the editable text. Thus, in Figure 14-8, the Pear cell apparently has a checkbox and also is directly editable. But there are actually three columns; the first contains no text and is 22 pixels wide, to accommodate the checkboxes; the second holds the fruit names and is editable. Here's the relevant code from the ListBox's Open event handler:

```
me.columncount = 3
me.columnwidths = "22"
me.columntype(0) = 2
me.columntype(1) = 3
```

A curious feature of the implementation of editable cells is that no copy-and-paste functionality is provided. You can't really do much about this, because you have no way to know that the user is working in an editable cell! The trouble is that when the user clicks in an editable cell to start editing, all you get is a Change event, and at that point all you can learn is what *row* the user is in, not what *cell*.

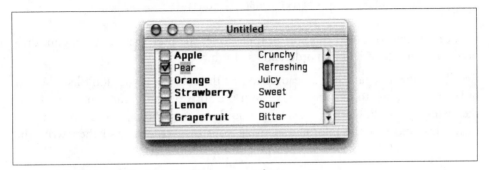

Figure 14-8. Editing a cell with a checkbox, apparently

In any case, although having editable cells is a powerful feature, it isn't the only way to let the user edit the text of a ListBox. Chapter 23 talks about how to implement copying and pasting in a ListBox without the use of editable cells. And it's very easy to couple a ListBox with an EditField and some buttons so that the user can edit a ListBox's contents; an elementary example appears in Chapter 21.

Headings are an interesting feature, but there's one thing to watch out for: they are incompatible with some of the tricks presented earlier in this chapter! For example, if headings appeared in Figure 14-8, they would reveal the secret: there would clearly be three columns.

It's disappointing that the user can't somehow drag a heading boundary to resize that column. Most column-based programs such as Eudora and Excel allow this sort of thing, and your user is likely to expect it and to become frustrated when it doesn't work. The usual solution is place a Canvas over the headings, to intercept mouse-clicks. I'll give a very rudimentary example. Presume that there are exactly two columns, and that the initial ColumnWidths setting is "50,50". Let there be a Canvas over the headings, whose Left is the same as the ListBox's Left. We will allow the user to resize just the first column by dragging. The Canvas's MouseDown event handler detects a click at the right edge of the first column heading:

```
dim cwidth as integer
dim s as string
s = listbox1.columnwidths
cwidth = val(nthfield(s,",",1))
if x > cwidth - 5 and x < cwidth + 5 then
    return true // track the mouse
end
```

The Canvas's MouseDrag event handler changes the width of the first column as the user drags:

```
dim s as string
dim cwidth, length as integer
s = listbox1.columnwidths
cwidth = val(nthfield(s,",",1))
if x < cwidth -1 or x > cwidth +1 then
    length = len(nthfield(s,",",1))
    listbox1.columnwidths = str(x) + mid(s,length+1)
end
```

It's not difficult to extend this sort of thing to let the user resize any column, drag headers to change the column order, and so forth.

Recall that the user can click a heading to sort the column. If you don't like the sort order, you're going to have to intervene in the SortColumn event handler and sort the ListBox yourself. One obvious way to do this is to gather up all the information in the ListBox, sort the information using your own criteria, and then write the sorted information back into the ListBox. But there can be a problem with this approach. When REALbasic sorts, formatting information travels with the cells: a bold cell will be bold in its new position; a checkbox cell will be a checkbox cell in its new position. Also, when REALbasic sorts, it ignores subrows and makes them travel with their folder row—whereas your code has no way even to learn that a row *is* a subrow. So if the ListBox has any formatting complexities of this kind, your code will have to go to a lot of trouble to sort it properly. Thus, it would be nice to find a way to let REALbasic sort the ListBox for you but to trick it into using your sort order.

A way to do this is as follows. Your data is in a certain column. In another, hidden column you maintain some corresponding data whose boolean string sort order is correct for your visible data. When the user asks to sort on your visible data's column, you tell REALbasic to sort on the hidden column instead.

To take a simple example, suppose your ListBox has two columns: the first column consists of words; the second column consists of positive integers, and you want the second column to sort in numerical order. Of course those integers are really strings, so "10" will sort before "2", which isn't what you want. But "02" will sort before "10". (Let's assume, for simplicity, that no integer is longer than two digits.)

So, the ListBox actually has three columns. The first column, column 0, has zero width. The numbers are in column 2. When the user asks to sort on column 2, we translate all the values in column 2 into values in column 0, which will sort correctly, and then we tell REALbasic to sort on column 0, instead. Here is the ListBox's SortColumn event handler:

```
dim i, u as integer
if dontsort then // a boolean property
    return true
end
if column <> 2 then
    return false
end
u = me.listcount-1
for i = 0 to u
    me.cell(i,0) = format(val(me.cell(i,2)),"00")
next
me.headingindex = 0
dontsort = true
me.headingindex = 2 // depress column 2 heading
dontsort = false
return true
```

The DontSort boolean property solves an aesthetic problem: after sorting on column 0, the heading for column 2, which the user clicked on, doesn't have a depressed appearance. So we depress it, and the DontSort boolean prevents an infinite loop.

Possibly, you might like to take advantage of headers as labels but prevent the user from being able to click on one to depress it and sort on that column. A Canvas over the headers that always returns true is one obvious solution. Another is to implement a no-sorting rule right in the SortColumn event handler. A HeadingIndex value of -1 means no sorting:

```
if column <> -1 then
    me.headingindex = -1
end
return true
```

CHAPTER 15

In this chapter:
- ProgressBar
- Slider
- Scrollbar

ProgressBars, Sliders, and Scrollbars

The three built-in control classes, ProgressBar, Slider, and Scrollbar, are variations on a single theme: each provides a visual representation of a numeric value in terms of its position along a scale. They differ, however, in details of appearance and usage:[*]

- A ProgressBar displays a "thermometer," such as might provide the user with visual feedback as to the progress of a time-consuming task.

- A Slider displays a horizontal or vertical "slot" with a "knob"; the user can slide the knob along the slot, like a sliding control on a piece of audio equipment, and can click in the slot to move the knob by a fixed amount.

- A Scrollbar displays a standard horizontal or vertical scrollbar, with arrows at each end and a scroll box (or *thumb*) between. The user can slide the thumb, click the arrows to move the thumb by a small fixed amount, or click the gray areas on either side of the thumb to move the thumb by a larger fixed amount.

The numeric values for these controls must lie between -32768 and 32767. This is because, owing to the way they are implemented by the Macintosh Toolbox, the value is actually a short integer (two bytes).

A ProgressBar, Slider, or Scrollbar is a RectControl, and therefore receives all the events and has all the methods and properties listed in Chapter 10: Open and Close events; Visible, Enabled, and AutoDeactivate properties; Top, Left, Height, and Width properties; LockLeft, LockRight, LockTop, and LockBottom properties; MouseEnter, MouseMove, and MouseExit events; and Refresh and RefreshRect methods.

---

[*] For more information, see *http://developer.apple.com/techpubs/mac/HIGOS8Guide/thig-36.html*, *http://developer.apple.com/techpubs/mac/HIGOS8Guide/thig-21.html*, and *http://developer.apple.com/techpubs/mac/HIGuidelines/HIGuidelines-121.html*.

ProgressBar

A ProgressBar provides visual feedback only; it isn't intended that the user should interact with it directly. Its minimum is automatically 0; you provide a Maximum, and then set its Value to give the thermometer the corresponding length. These are both (short) integers. Typically, you will repeatedly increment the Value to make the thermometer rise from the minimum to the maximum. If the ProgressBar or its window is not going to vanish afterward, you will probably want to reset its Value to 0 at the end, too, so that the user knows that the process is over—though this is less important on Mac OS X, where a partly full ProgressBar is animated but a full ProgressBar is inert.

A ProgressBar can display, instead of a thermometer, a "barberpole" indicator. Like a watch cursor, this merely suggests that activity is proceeding, with no indication of how long it may continue. To display the barberpole, set the ProgressBar's Maximum to 0; the barberpole will appear and will keep spinning automatically until you set the ProgressBar's Maximum to 1 or greater. To display the barberpole frozen, without spinning, make the ProgressBar's Maximum negative (this doesn't work on Mac OS X).

ProgressBars were already used, in a nonstandard way, as the basis for an example in "Threads" in Chapter 5. Here's another, more standard kind of example. Visual feedback is provided while an array of numbers is being sorted, using the algorithm from "Strings" in Chapter 5. There are two ProgressBars, corresponding to the two nested loops:

```
dim gap, bound, temp, i, j, jg as integer
bound = ubound(s)
gap = (bound + 1) / 2
progressbar2.maximum = log(gap) / log(2) + 1
progressbar2.value = 0
while gap > 0
    progressbar2.value = progressbar2.value + 1
    progressbar1.value = 0
    for i = gap to bound
        progressbar1.maximum = bound-gap
        progressbar1.value = progressbar1.value + 1
        j = i - gap
        jg = i
        while j >= 0 and s(j) > s(jg)
            temp = s(j)
            s(j)= s(jg)
            s(jg) = temp
            jg = j
            j = j - gap
        wend
    next
    gap = gap / 2
wend
progressbar2.value = 0
progressbar1.value = 0
```

ProgressBars are very simple, so you might think there wouldn't be anything more to say about them. This is almost true, but they do have two rather finicky points, both of which are illustrated by this example.

First, incrementing the ProgressBars slows down the routine. Without the Progress-Bars, sorting 2000 numbers happens so fast on my machine that you can't even get your finger off the button before it's finished (about four ticks); with them, it takes over a minute! Clearly, you must decide on a compromise as to how much you are willing to delay the calculation in order to represent its state visually. In this case, an obvious approach is to dispense with ProgressBar1 altogether, displaying only the progress of the outer loop with ProgressBar2, whose value changes far less often. To gauge the correctness of this compromise, consider this: as the number of items to be sorted increases to the point where the operation becomes slow enough to warrant providing the user with some feedback (say, 10,000 items or more), the relative difference between the times required to sort with and without the display of ProgressBar2 becomes negligible.

Second, a ProgressBar should pretty well take care of itself, requiring only to be incremented regularly, provided that the Maximum has been wisely determined in advance. In other words (and this is true of Sliders and Scrollbars as well), most of the battle is in choosing a suitable scale. In the previous example, the less arithmetically inclined reader may be somewhat mystified as to the source of the formula for ProgressBar2's Maximum, log(gap)/log(2)+1. The use of logarithms here is straightforward enough, though: we know that gap is to be divided successively by 2, meaning that its size will be reduced by a power of 2 each time through the loop; so, to learn in advance how many loops there will be, we have only to ask gap's size as a power of 2 initially, which is just what a logarithm tells us. The tricky part is adding 1 to this number, to compensate for the fact that we are going to increment ProgressBar2's Value at the outset, before any division has been performed; otherwise, the loop will be performed twice with the ProgressBar at its maximum value, which is confusing for the user.

Slider

A Slider has a Minimum, a Maximum, and a Value, which are (short) integers. Negative values are permitted. Any attempt to set the Value smaller than the Minimum or larger than the Maximum will fail, without error; the Value just becomes the Minimum or the Maximum, respectively.

A Slider also has a PageStep, which is the amount by which the Value will change when the user clicks in the slot; this is an integer, and should be positive, or the Slider will behave incorrectly.

A Slider also has a LineStep property. This is said to be the minimum unit by which the user can change the Value by sliding the knob; however, on my machine, changing the LineStep property has no effect whatever.

On Windows, a Slider can receive the focus, and the user can then type arrow keys to increment or decrement the slider. In this case, the LineStep is the amount by which each use of the arrow key changes the slider's Value.

When the user moves the knob, a ValueChanged event is sent to the Slider. A boolean, LiveScroll, which can be set only in the IDE, determines whether ValueChanged events should be sent continuously while the user is dragging the knob or whether a single ValueChanged event should be sent when the user releases the mouse button.

The ValueChanged event is also sent when the Slider's Value is changed (not merely set) in code. When the Slider's Minimum or Maximum is changed to be larger or smaller, respectively, than its Value, the Value automatically changes as well, to remain within bounds; so this triggers a ValueChanged event too.

Beginners sometimes think that a Slider can only be horizontal. But that's not so! To make a vertical Slider, just adjust its Height to be greater than its Width.

In this example (see Figure 15-1), three sliders represent the red, green, and blue components of a color. A Canvas portrays a swatch showing what the color looks like, and a StaticText gives the color's numeric value. The three sliders have a Minimum of 0 and a Maximum of 255, and their LiveScroll is true so that the color swatch will change continuously as the user slides a knob. All three have a ValueChanged event handler that simply calls a method, Repaint, which is also called by the Canvas's Paint event handler, and which goes like this:

```
dim c as color
dim s as string
s = str(slider1.value)+","+str(slider2.value)+","+str(slider3.value)
statictext1.text = s
c = rgb (slider1.value, slider2.value, slider3.value)
canvas1.graphics.forecolor = c
canvas1.graphics.fillrect 0,0,canvas1.width,canvas1.height
```

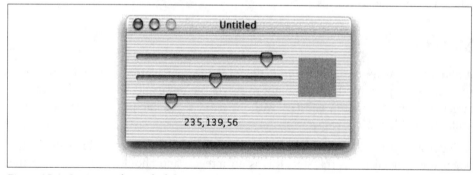

Figure 15-1. Setting a color with sliders

Scrollbar

A Scrollbar is very much like a Slider. It has a Minimum, a Maximum, and a Value, which are (short) integers. Negative values are permitted. The Maximum will usually be greater than the Minimum; if not, the Scrollbar behaves as if disabled (it is dimmed and does not respond to the mouse). Any attempt to set the Value smaller than the Minimum or larger than the Maximum will fail, without error; the Value just becomes the Minimum or the Maximum, respectively.

A Scrollbar also has a LineStep, which is the amount by which the Value will change when the user clicks one of the arrows, and a PageStep, which is the amount by which the Value will change when the user clicks in the gray area; these are integers, and should be positive, or the Scrollbar will behave incorrectly.

A Scrollbar's ValueChanged event and LiveScroll property work just like a Slider's.

As with a Slider, you can make a Scrollbar vertical by adjusting its Height to be greater than its Width. There is also a second Scrollbar icon in the Tools Window, which is vertical to start with. Observe that the smaller dimension of a normal Scrollbar has a customary standard of 16 pixels (and the smaller dimension of a so-called "small scrollbar" has a customary standard of 11 pixels); other sizes will look odd to your users, so you shouldn't deviate from this without good reason.

The major difference between Sliders and Scrollbars is in their usage. Although both a Slider and a Scrollbar represent a number, the Slider's numeric value is explicit— the user thinks of the Slider precisely as a way of setting the number. A Scrollbar, on the other hand, is typically used to shift physically some other element of the interface; the user thinks of the scrollbar, not as a number, but rather in terms of its physical manifestation, the position of the other element of the interface. In short, you'll typically use a Scrollbar when you have some interface element that you want the user to be able to scroll!

It is the task of your code, then, to translate between the Scrollbar's number and the other interface element's scroll position. A good way to approach the problem is first to work out the details of scrolling the interface element *without* a Scrollbar. After that, it should be easy to fit the Scrollbar into the system. The next example will illustrate this principle.

Scrolling Canvas

Recall from Chapter 11 our method for scrolling a Canvas by dragging its image with the mouse. We have a Canvas subclass, JocoScroller, which maintains properties JLeft and JTop. Its Paint event handler draws the image at the JLeft and JTop coordinates:

```
g.drawPicture joconde, self.jLeft, self.jTop // jocoScroller properties
```

The actual work of scrolling is abstracted into a method, ScrollMe, which takes two parameters, x and y:

```
self.jLeft = self.jLeft+x
self.jTop = self.jTop+y
self.scroll x,y
```

This is a good example to start with, because the problem of scrolling is already solved. Figure 15-2 shows JocoScroller, together with a horizontal and a vertical scrollbar. What remains is for us to tie these together in code, so that the scrollbars can do what dragging with the mouse did previously.

Figure 15-2. A scrolling Canvas

Our first problem is that the Scrollbar controls need to assign themselves an appropriate scale. Calculating this scale is easy, provided you maintain a consistent understanding of what the Scrollbar's Value signifies. If the Minimum vertical value is 0, this does not mean that the Maximum is joconde.height! The number 0 is the offset of the image's virtual top, JTop, from its initial position coinciding with the top of the Canvas. When the image is maximally scrolled, it is offset upward enough that its bottom coincides with the Canvas's *bottom*—not with its top. Thus, to get the scale, we must subtract the height of the Canvas from the height of the image. Another way to see this is to consider that if the image were just one pixel taller than the Canvas, the scrollbar would have only two positions—its Maximum would be 1.

So, the vertical Scrollbar's Open event handler goes like this:

```
me.maximum = joconde.height - canvas1.height
```

And the horizontal Scrollbar's Open event handler goes like this:

```
me.maximum = joconde.width - canvas1.width
```

Now we want to write the ValueChanged event handlers for the Scrollbars. This should be simply a matter of calling JocoScroller's ScrollMe method with the right parameters. But ScrollMe's parameters are differences: ScrollMe asks, "How much do you want me to move the image?" This made sense when we were scrolling the image by dragging with the mouse, because only the amount of the drag was important; the relationship between the mouse dragging and the image's new position was relative, and the place where the user clicked the mouse to start the drag was arbitrary. But with Scrollbars, we have a big advantage: a Scrollbar maintains state! This means that the relationship between the Scrollbar's Value and the image's position is absolute. We'd like a different method here, one that asks, "Where do you want me to place the image?"

So let's give JocoScroller a new method and a new way of scrolling itself. We'll call the new method ScrollMeTo; it takes two parameters, x and y, and scrolls in such a way that the image's position is x,y afterward. Since a Canvas's Scroll method is itself relative, ScrollMeTo must work out the parameters for Scroll by comparing the new position to the old position, which lives in JLeft and JTop:

```
dim diffx, diffy as integer
diffx = x-self.jLeft
diffy = y-self.jTop
self.jLeft = x
self.jTop = y
self.scroll diffx, diffy
```

Now, since the Scrollbar's Minimum is 0, the Value numbering is inverted from its physical manifestation: for example, moving a vertical scrollbar's thumb downward means that we want the virtual top of the Canvas's image to move upward. So, what we want the virtual top of the Canvas's image to be is exactly the additive inverse of the Scrollbar's own Value! Also, manipulating a vertical scrollbar must leave the image's horizontal characteristics unchanged, and vice versa. So, the vertical Scrollbar's ValueChanged event handler says:

```
canvas1.scrollmeto canvas1.jleft,-me.value
```

And the horizontal Scrollbar's ValueChanged event handler says:

```
canvas1.scrollmeto -me.value, canvas1.jtop
```

That's all! The Canvas's image can now be scrolled with the scrollbars.

An extra benefit of using Scrollbars is that they limit the extent to which the user can scroll. Recall that when the user was allowed to scroll the image by dragging it with the mouse, we faced the problem of how to limit the scroll distance so as to keep the image within bounds—or rather, we *didn't* face this problem but agreed to leave it unsolved. With Scrollbars, the problem is solved for us, by the interface; the user cannot scroll the image out of bounds, because the thumb cannot be moved off the ends of the Scrollbar.

If we leave in place the user's ability to scroll the image by dragging it with the mouse, it is incumbent upon us to hook the mouse movement to the scrollbars, so that their thumbs move—the Values of the Scrollbars change—to match the position of the image as the user drags. Here's an easy way to do this. Instead of calling ScrollMe directly, JocoScroller's MouseDrag handler now just sets the Values of the Scrollbars, whose ValueChanged event handlers will then automatically trigger the scrolling:

```
if x <> self.oldX or y <> self.oldY then
    window1.scrollbar1.value = window1.scrollbar1.value - (x-self.oldx)
    window1.scrollbar2.value = window1.scrollbar2..value - (y-self.oldy)
    self.oldX = x
    self.oldY = y
end
```

As a final astonishing and delightful benefit, the user is now prevented from dragging the image out of bounds with the mouse! This is because a Scrollbar can never take on a Value outside its Minimum and Maximum range. We have accidentally solved the problem we earlier ignored.

Before leaving this example, let's make it more portable and more general. We will start by expressing the scrollbars as a subclass of the Scrollbar class. We can call this the JocoScrollbar class. JocoScrollbar has one property, MyCanvas, a JocoScroller. Following our usual practice with multiple controls, JocoScrollbar will have a New Event, which I'll call SetCanvas, which will be sent in JocoScrollbar's Open event so that the instance in the window can hook us up to the Canvas by setting MyCanvas.

Now let's do the same for JocoScroller. It will have two JocoScrollbar properties, MyHorizScrollbar and MyVertScrollbar, and a New Event, SetScrollbars, which will be sent in the Open event so that the instance in the window can hook us up to our Scrollbars. As long as we're generalizing, let's make JocoScroller work with any picture; so it will have a Picture property, MyPicture, and a New Event, SetPicture, to be sent in the Open event so that the instance in the window can hook us up to our Picture.

In JocoScroller, references to joconde now become references to myPicture. The Open event sends the SetPicture and SetScrollbars New Events, and the instance in the window responds by setting MyPicture, MyHorizScrollbar, and MyVertScrollbar.

As for JocoScrollbar, the only complication is that its behavior must differ depending on whether its instance is the horizontal or the vertical scrollbar. It can find out which it is by looking to see which is greater, its Width or its Height. So, here is JocoScrollbar's Open event handler:

```
setCanvas // ask instance to hook us to a Canvas
if self.width > self.height then
    self.maximum = self.mycanvas.mypicture.width - self.mycanvas.width
else
    self.maximum = self.mycanvas.mypicture.height - self.mycanvas.height
end
```

And here is JocoScrollbar's ValueChanged event handler:

```
if self.width > self.height then
    myCanvas.scrollmeto -self.value, myCanvas.jtop
else
    mycanvas.scrollmeto mycanvas.jleft,-self.value
end
```

Scrolling Pane

In the preceding example, the object being scrolled was responsible for remembering its previous position, so that the Scrollbar's ValueChanged event handler could work out the difference between the previous position and the new one, as derived from the new Value. Often, it is the Scrollbar itself that simply remembers its own previous Value. The next example will illustrate.

Recall that a Canvas can be scrolled in order to shift other objects sitting on top of it (see "Interaction with Other Objects" in Chapter 11). Let's give the user a Scrollbar as a way of performing this shifting. Imagine that we have a Canvas 300 pixels high, with various other objects on top of it. In its Open event, the Canvas's Height is reduced to 100 pixels, and next to it is a Scrollbar with a Maximum of 200 (the Canvas's Height in the IDE minus its Height in the running application). An integer property, OldValue, is used to remember the Scrollbar's Value. Here is the Scrollbar's ValueChanged event handler:

```
canvas1.scroll 0, self.oldValue - me.value
self.oldValue = me.value
```

Big ListBox

There is a limitation on ListBoxes: they can't hold more than a certain number of rows. You may be able to overcome this limitation satisfactorily by hiding the ListBox's own vertical scrollbar, hooking the ListBox to a Scrollbar control, and "scrolling" the ListBox by rewriting its contents in response to what the user does with the Scrollbar.

To illustrate, here's a way to let a ListBox show values from 95 to 1000000. Presume that the ListBox's height is such that it can display six rows. We remove the ListBox's vertical scrollbar and provide our own Scrollbar control with a LineStep of 1 and a PageStep of 6. The idea is that the ListBox will always hold just six rows of information; whenever the user does something in the Scrollbar, we will respond by changing the values displayed in these six rows so that it looks as if the ListBox has scrolled. For example, if the ListBox is showing the six numbers starting at 1000, then if the user clicks the Scrollbar's up arrow, we will make the ListBox show the six numbers starting at 999; or, if the user clicks the Scrollbar's page-down area, we will make the ListBox show the six numbers starting at 1006.

The Scrollbar will have a Minimum of 1 and a Maximum of 10000. This explains our choice of the range of numbers the ListBox will display; there's an easy formula for converting from a Scrollbar Value to the value to be displayed in the ListBox's first row (multiply by 100 and subtract 5). The Scrollbar's range of values is very large in proportion to its physical height, so its thumb can be used only to make very gross changes. We will take advantage of this fact to detect mouseclicks in the Scrollbar's arrow and page areas: if the Scrollbar's Value changes by 1, it must be because the user has clicked in an arrow, and if the Scrollbar's Value changes by 6, it must be because the user has clicked in a page area, because the user surely couldn't drag the thumb such a small amount. We will use an integer property, CurVal, to remember the Scrollbar's Value so that we can detect, in its ValueChanged event handler, how much it has changed; CurVal is initialized to 1, as is the Scrollbar's Value. We also need a boolean property, Changing, to act as a flag so that the ValueChanged event handler can change the Scrollbar's Value without starting an infinite loop.

The Scrollbar's ValueChanged event handler does all the work. The first problem is to arrive at the value n that should be shown in the first line of the ListBox after "scrolling." There are six special cases. The first two test for a click in one of the Scrollbar's arrows. If we are not at the top or bottom limit for the set of numbers to be displayed, we "scroll" the ListBox by inserting a row at one end and deleting a row at the other; this has the advantage of preserving the current selection intelligently:

```
dim n,i,u,c,v,s as integer
dim extreme as boolean
if self.changing then
    return
end
c = self.curVal
v = me.value
s = val(listbox1.list(0))
n = s
select case v
case c + 1 // down arrow
    if s + 1 <= 999995 then
        n = s + 1
        listbox1.addrow str(s+6)
        listbox1.removerow 0
    end
case c - 1 // up arrow
    if s - 1 >= 95 then
        n = s - 1
        listbox1.insertrow 0, str(s-1)
        listbox1.removerow 6
    end
```

Next we test for a click in the Scrollbar's page-up or page-down area; in that case, we move n up or down by 6:

```
case c + 6 // down page
    n = s + 6
case c - 6 // up page
    n = s - 6
```

You might say: But what if we are displaying numbers starting at, say, 97, and the user clicks in the page-up area? I'm presuming that would be physically impossible; if we're so close to 95, there won't be any page-up area between the thumb and the up arrow.

Next we test for the user sliding the thumb to one extreme or the other. If so, we set a boolean flag for later, and set n according to the standard rule:

```
case me.minimum // thumb slide all the way up
    extreme = true
    n = v*100-5
case me.maximum // thumb slide all the way down
    extreme = true
    n = v*100-5
```

The default case is that the user slides the thumb, and we set n according to the standard rule:

```
else
    n = v*100-5
end
```

Now it's time to "scroll" the ListBox if we are not displaying the correct numbers already:

```
if n <> val(listbox1.list(0)) then
    u = n + 5
    listbox1.deleteallrows
    for i = n to u
        listbox1.addrow str(i)
    next
end
```

Finally, we set the Scrollbar's Value (and the CurVal property). Of course, the user has already changed the Value; but if we make any further change, it will be tiny, and the user won't see the thumb move. We use the standard formula to map from the ListBox display to the Scrollbar's Value; then, if we are at one extreme or the other but we didn't get there from the user sliding the thumb, we add some leeway. The reason for this is that otherwise the Scrollbar's arrows won't work. For example, if the ListBox is displaying starting at 97, then according to the formula the Scrollbar's Value would be 1, but if we allowed that, then clicking the Scrollbar's up arrow would do nothing because the Value can't get any less.

```
self.changing = true
me.value = val(listbox1.list(5)) \ 100
if not extreme then
    if me.value = me.minimum then
        me.value = me.minimum + 2
    end
    if me.value = me.maximum then
        me.value = me.maximum - 2
    end
end
self.changing = false
self.curval = me.value
```

Scrolling Nonwrapping Field

Let's return to the nonwrapping EditField with multiple lines described in "Reacting to User Input" in Chapter 13. Because this field was actually a single-line EditField (to prevent automatic wrapping), it had no vertical scrollbar; let's now try to add one. Our implementation will perforce be rather crude, because, this being a single-line EditField, its ScrollPosition is always 0. REALbasic thus fails to provide the fundamental ability that we most need—to learn from the EditField how far down it is currently scrolled, and to tell it precisely how much to change that amount. Nonetheless, we will be able to do surprisingly well, and the exercise will prove educational.

Before we can do anything, we will need to know how many lines the EditField can show at one time. Since this information will be constant, we obtain it in the Edit-Field's Open event handler and store it in a property, MaxLines. We can learn the height of a line by sending the TextHeight message to a Graphics property (Chapter 11). At the same time, we adjust the height of the EditField (and of the vertical Scrollbar), so that a whole number of lines will always be showing. The Height calculation provides for enough pixels to show MaxLines lines of text, plus a few more pixels to allow for the last line's descent (its TextHeight minus its TextAscent):

```
dim p as picture
dim theHeight as integer
p = newpicture(1,1,1)
p.graphics.textfont = me.textfont
p.graphics.textsize = me.textsize
theHeight = p.graphics.textheight
self.maxLines = me.height\theHeight
me.height = (self.maxLines+1) * theHeight - p.graphics.textascent
scrollbar1.height = me.height
```

In order to manipulate the Scrollbar, we must know how many lines the EditField contains. That's easy; it is one more than the number of return characters in the Edit-Field's Text. This we can learn with the CountFields function. Whenever the field's text changes, then, we need to recalculate the Scrollbar's Maximum. We will have a method handler, RecalcMax, and call it from the EditField's SelChange event handler. When we are not scrolled at all, the first line of text is showing at the top of the field; when we are fully scrolled, the last line of text is showing at the bottom of the field (not its top). Hence, the Scrollbar's Maximum is the number of lines of text, minus the number showing within the field:

```
scrollbar1.maximum = countFields(editField1.text,chr(13)) - self.maxLines
```

This means that if the text hasn't enough lines to exceed the field, the Scrollbar's Maximum will be less than or equal to its Minimum; when this is the case, REALbasic responds by drawing the Scrollbar as if disabled—which is exactly what we want.

When the selection changes, the Scrollbar's Value also may need to change. For example, if the user types the up arrow key, moving the selection toward the beginning of the field, the Value may need to decrease to reflect the current position of the selection. Since we are calling RecalcMax from the SelChange event handler, we may as well include the recalculation of the Scrollbar's Value in RecalcMax as well. We'll use a crude but effective algorithm: the Value will be the line number on which the start of the selection is positioned, again subtracting the number of lines showing in the field. This isn't perfectly right, but it's the best we can do, given that all we can learn is where the selection is; we can't learn what we really need to know, namely, what line is actually displayed at the top of the field:

```
dim s as string
dim n as integer
scrollbar1.maximum = countFields(editField1.text,chr(13)) - self.maxLines
```

```
s = left(editfield1.text,editfield1.selstart)
n = countfields(s,chr(13))
scrollbar1.value = n - self.maxLines
```

Let's now turn to the Scrollbar's ValueChanged event handler, triggered when the user manipulates the Scrollbar. We are once again reduced to devising a hack. We have no direct control over the field's scroll position, so we must set its selection instead. By starting with the selection at the very start of the field and moving it down line by line, we can at least guarantee that any desired line will just scroll into view:

```
dim s as string
dim i,pos,u as integer
s = editfield1.text
editfield1.sellength = 0
editfield1.selstart = 0
pos = 0
u = self.maxLines + me.value - 1
for i = 1 to u
    pos = instr(pos+1,s,chr(13))
next
editfield1.selstart = pos
```

A couple of final tweaks are all that remain. RecalcMax needs to be called at startup, to deactivate the Scrollbar when the text is empty. The Scrollbar's ValueChanged event handler needs to be shut off when the Scrollbar is dimmed. Also, we must use a boolean flag, here called Recalcing, to correct the interplay between the EditField's SelChange event handler, the Scrollbar's ValueChanged event handler, and RecalcMax. The ValueChanged event handler "scrolls" the field by moving its selection; the field's SelChange event handler must not respond to this. RecalcMax changes the Scrollbar's Value; the Scrollbar's ValueChanged event handler must not respond to this.

So, here is the code as it finally stands:

```
// The EditField's Open event handler:
dim p as picture
dim theHeight as integer
p = newpicture(1,1,1)
p.graphics.textfont = me.textfont
p.graphics.textsize = me.textsize
theHeight = p.graphics.textheight
self.maxLines = me.height\theHeight
me.height = (self.maxLines+1) * theHeight - p.graphics.textascent
scrollbar1.height = me.height
self.recalcMax

// The EditField's SelChange event handler:
if not self.recalcing then
    self.recalcmax
end
```

```
// The Scrollbar's ValueChanged event handler:
dim s as string
dim i,pos,u as integer
if me.maximum <= me.minimum or self.recalcing then
    return
end
self.recalcing = true
s = editfield1.text
editfield1.sellength = 0
editfield1.selstart = 0
pos = 0
u = self.maxLines + me.value - 1
for i = 1 to u
    pos = instr(pos+1,s,chr(13))
next
editfield1.selstart = pos
self.recalcing = false

// The RecalcMax method handler:
dim s as string
dim n as integer
scrollbar1.maximum = countFields(editField1.text,chr(13)) - self.maxLines
self.recalcing = true
s = left(editfield1.text,editfield1.selstart)
n = countfields(s,chr(13))
scrollbar1.value = n - self.maxLines
self.recalcing = false
```

To be sure, this is imperfect, even scurrilous. Nonetheless, considering the severity of the limitations imposed upon us, it is remarkable how well we are able to simulate a scrolling nonwrapping EditField with a few lines of code and a little ingenuity.

CHAPTER 16

In this chapter:
- Line
- Shapes
- Separator
- ImageWell
- ChasingArrows
- PopupArrow

Shapes and Decorations

This chapter is about some built-in controls that spice up the appearance of a window, but with which the user is not expected to interact consciously. Several of these display themselves as simple geometric shapes: Rectangle, Oval, RoundRectangle, and Line. These are what I call the *shapes*. The others are standard controls introduced with the Macintosh Appearance Manager: Separator, ImageWell, ChasingArrows, and PopupArrow. I call these the *decorations*. Some examples appear in Figure 16-1.

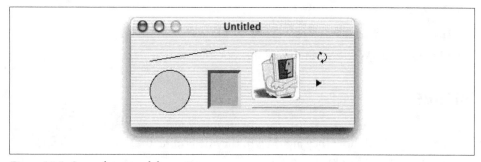

Figure 16-1. Some shapes and decorations

Except for Line, these are all RectControls and therefore receive all the events and have all the methods and properties listed in Chapter 10: Open and Close events; Visible, Enabled, and AutoDeactivate properties; Top, Left, Height, and Width properties; LockLeft, LockRight, LockTop, and LockBottom properties; MouseEnter, MouseMove, and MouseExit events; and Refresh and RefreshRect methods. On drag-and-drop, see Chapter 24.

Since RectControls can detect mouse movements, the shapes and decorations can be animated in interesting ways (an example appeared in Chapter 10). Most of these controls (ImageWell is the exception) do not receive mouseclick events; rather, mouseclicks pass through them to whatever is behind.

Changing the value of a shape's Enabled property does not change its appearance; in fact, shapes are disabled by default, and their Enabled cannot be set in the IDE. (Compare StaticText, Chapter 12.) Changing the value of a decoration's Enabled property does change its appearance (except that ChasingArrows has no disabled appearance in Mac OS X), and decorations are enabled by default.

Line

A Line, being a Control, inherits the Open and Close events and the Refresh and RefreshRect messages; but it is not a RectControl. It has a Visible property but no Enabled property, and receives no events involving the mouse.

Since a Line is not a RectControl, it has no Top, Left, Width, or Height properties. Instead, a Line has positional properties of its own: X1, Y1, X2, and Y2, which represent the coordinates of the start and end points of the line.

A Line also lacks LockLeft, LockTop, LockBottom, and LockRight properties; you can compensate for this in the window's Resized event handler. For example, this Resized event handler keeps a horizontal Line horizontally centered in the window, without changing its length:

```
dim theLength as integer
theLength = line1.x2 - line1.x1
line1.x1 = (self.width - theLength) / 2
line1.x2 = line1.x1 + theLength
```

For a Line's BorderWidth and LineColor properties, see the next section.

Shapes

The remaining properties of the Line, Rectangle, Oval, and RoundRectangle controls have to do with how they are drawn; they determine the instance's fill and outline characteristics, as follows:

- A Line has a BorderWidth and a LineColor.*
- An Oval or a RoundRectangle has a BorderWidth and a BorderColor, plus a Fill-Color.
- A Rectangle has a BorderWidth and a FillColor, but instead of a BorderColor, it has a TopLeftColor and a BottomRightColor, which can be used to give a look of depth or beveling.

---

* These are funny names. A Line can scarcely be said to have a border; and it has no feature called its Line, so how can it have a LineColor? Why aren't these called simply Width and Color? I suspect that the name Width was thought to be too confusing (the programmer might think it refers to the line's horizontal width), and that the name Color is unavailable because it already designates a class.

CHAPTER 17

Menus in Windows

This chapter discusses three built-in control classes that display menus in windows: PopupMenu, BevelButton, and ContextualMenu.

A PopupMenu is a RectControl, and therefore receives all the events and has all the methods and properties listed in Chapter 10: Open and Close events; Visible, Enabled, and AutoDeactivate properties; Top, Left, Height, and Width properties; LockLeft, LockRight, LockTop, and LockBottom properties; MouseEnter, Mouse-Move, and MouseExit events; and Refresh and RefreshRect methods.

A BevelButton is a RectControl too, and it's also a button. For its button-related aspects, see Chapter 12.

PopupMenu

A PopupMenu displays itself as a roughly rectangular region of the window, usually containing some text (its caption), and with an arrow at its right end. (To eliminate the display of the caption, narrow the control to about 20 pixels, which should cause it to consist of just the arrow.) When the mouse is depressed within an enabled Pop-upMenu's boundaries, the PopupMenu takes on a depressed or highlighted appearance and displays a menu. When the mouse is subsequently released, the menu vanishes; if the mouse was released over a menu item, the text of that item becomes the caption, and the next time the menu is shown, that item will have a check mark or some similar indicator next to it. Figure 17-1 shows an example.

On Windows, a PopupMenu is implemented as a combo box. It can receive the focus (see "The Focus" in Chapter 13), and the user can then type letters, arrow keys, and the Enter key to choose a menu item. Accelerators are not used; the user types the start of the desired item's text.

A PopupMenu's properties and methods are almost entirely a subset of those of a ListBox (see Chapter 14). This makes sense, since both a ListBox and a PopupMenu display a column of items from which the user can choose.

Figure 17-1. A PopupMenu in action

Contents and Format

A PopupMenu has the following properties relating to its contents and format:

TextFont, TextSize
Format features of the menu items and the caption.

Bold, Italic, Underline
Format features of the caption only.

InitialValue
Initial text for the entire menu. Can be set and read only in a dialog box in the IDE. In this dialog, menu items are separated by return characters.

ListCount
The number of menu items. Read-only. An item index is zero-based, so the first menu item has an index of 0 and the last menu item has an index of listCount-1.

RowTag
A variant associated with each menu item; the parameter specifies the item index. Intended for use in bindings, but you can use it however you like; see "Scrolling" in Chapter 13 for an example.

A PopupMenu has the following methods relating to its contents and format:

AddRow
> Takes one parameter, a string; creates a new last menu item whose text is the parameter.

AddSeparator
> Creates a new last menu item which is a separator line. The separator line is disabled and cannot be chosen, but it is a menu item and does have an index. (On Windows, the separator is implemented as a hyphen, because there are no genuine separators in combo boxes.)

InsertRow
> Takes two parameters, a menu item index and a string. Creates a new menu item at the designated index, and sets its text to the string parameter; the index of the existing menu item at that index is incremented, and so on for all subsequent items. The index need not designate an existing menu item; if it is too small or too large, the item will be inserted before or after all existing menu items.

RemoveRow
> Takes one parameter, a menu item index; deletes the menu item at the designated index, decrementing the indices of all subsequent items. The item must exist or an exception will be raised.

DeleteAllRows
> Deletes all the menu items.

List
> Takes one parameter, a menu item index; returns the text of that item. The item must exist or an exception will be raised. If the item is a separator, the empty string is returned. Unlike with a ListBox, List is not a property and cannot be used to set an item's text.

Selection

A PopupMenu has the following properties relating to its selection:

ListIndex
> The index of the selected menu item. Can be used to learn or to set the selection. A value of -1 means no selection. Setting causes the text of the menu item to become the PopupMenu's caption; -1 results in a blank caption. Also, there will be a check mark or some similar indicator next to the selected menu item the next time the menu is shown. It is not an error to set the ListIndex too small or too large; it will be set to -1 or to the index of the last item.

Text
> The text of the currently selected menu item, and therefore of the current caption. Read-only.

A PopupMenu receives the following event relating to its selection:

Change
> Sent to the PopupMenu because its selection has been newly determined. This happens because:
>
> - The user pops up the menu and chooses an item other than the current selection.
> - The selection is set (not necessarily changed) in code, using ListIndex.
> - The contents of the menu are changed in code in such a way as to affect the selection; for example, the selected menu item is deleted.

Usage

A PopupMenu should be fairly simple, but complications arise from the necessity to work around the following peculiar and annoying features of REALbasic's implementation:

- The Change event is triggered whenever the selection is set in code, and often when the contents of the menu are changed in code, even if the ListIndex value is not changed.
- The user can pop the menu up and can even rechoose the current selection, without triggering any event at all.
- The initial ListIndex value in the IDE is ignored if the designated menu item does not exist.
- The caption can be dictated only by selection of a menu item.
- The text of an existing menu item cannot be changed.

None of these is so very terrible alone, but taken together they can make PopupMenus extremely tedious to work with. The best solution is: don't use a PopupMenu! Use a BevelButton instead; it doesn't suffer from these difficulties. However, since you might use PopupMenu anyway, I'll illustrate the difficulties and show what you can do to circumvent them.

Initialization

You may wish to initialize a PopupMenu in its Open event handler, rather than the InitialValue dialog of the IDE. The technique in theory should be just like populating a ListBox. So, if the PopupMenu is to list the months of the year, for example, its Open event handler could be something like the following:

```
dim s as string
dim u, i as integer
s = "January,February,March,April,May,June,July,August,September,October,"
s = s + "November,December"
u = countfields(s,",")
for i = 1 to u
    me.addrow nthfield(s,",",i)
next
```

Unfortunately, this PopupMenu is instantiated with no initial caption, regardless of how you set its ListIndex in the IDE. Apparently, REALbasic gets annoyed that at startup the PopupMenu has no items, so the ListIndex just disobeys your setting and silently reverts to -1.

Now, you might think you could get around this by setting the ListIndex in the Open event handler as well. But there's a problem: this triggers a Change event, which is almost certainly not what you wanted at this early stage. So you are compelled to create a boolean flag property (let's call it NoChange) and wrap your setting of the List-Index inside it:

```
dim s as string
dim u, i as integer
s = "January,February,March,April,May,June,July,August,September,October,"
s = s + "November,December"
u = countfields(s,",")
for i = 1 to u
    me.addrow nthfield(s,",",i)
next
self.nochange = true
me.listindex = 0
self.nochange = false
```

And the PopupMenu's Change event handler must begin by aborting if NoChange is true:

```
if self.nochange then
    return
end
```

Changing an item's text

The text of a PopupMenu item cannot be changed directly; for example, you can't say:

```
popupmenu1.list(2) = "Hello" // error:
```

Instead, you must delete the item and replace it with another:

```
popupmenu1.removerow 2
popupmenu1.insertrow 2, "Hello"
```

But this may trigger a Change event, especially if the item being deleted and replaced is the currently selected item; furthermore, if the currently selected item has a higher index than the item being deleted and replaced, the selection will change, meaning that the caption will change, so you may want to set the ListIndex afterward, and *that* will trigger a Change event too. So here is a more general routine for changing a menu item's text; once again, we call upon our boolean property to tell the Change event not to act:

```
dim i as integer
i = popupmenu1.listindex
self.nochange = true
popupmenu1.removerow 2
```

```
popupmenu1.insertrow 2, "Hello"
popupmenu1.listindex = i
self.nochange = false
```

Independent caption

Sometimes, you'd like the initial caption to be an instruction to the user, rather than a menu item that the user can choose. For example, you might want the initial caption of a popup menu of months to be Pick a Month—but you don't want the user to be able to choose a month called Pick a Month. This is not at all easy to arrange. For Pick a Month to be the caption, it *must* be one of the menu items. Therefore, to prevent the user from seeing this menu item in the menu, we must get rid of it between the moment the user clicks the mouse and the moment the menu pops up. But since no event is sent to the PopupMenu when the user clicks the mouse, there is no appropriate PopupMenu event handler in which to do this!

The best workaround I've found is to cover the PopupMenu with a Canvas. The Canvas, which won't be seen by the user, will detect the mouseclick, and will remove the instructional caption from the PopupMenu. We don't want this to trigger a Change event, so the Canvas's MouseDown event handler goes like this:

```
if popupmenu1.text = "Pick a Month:" then
    self.dontchange = true
    popupmenu1.removerow 0
    self.dontchange = false
end
```

This works splendidly—unless the user does not choose any menu item. In that case, we want the caption to read Pick a Month again. Clearly, we need to check the state of the PopupMenu *after* the user releases the mouse. But once again we find that there is no appropriate event in which to do this. If the user hasn't chosen a menu item, no Change event is triggered. And we can't use the MouseUp event of the Canvas, because to get a MouseUp event we must return true in the MouseDown event, which will prevent the mouseclick from falling through to the PopupMenu, so that the user won't be able to choose from the PopupMenu in the first place!

My solution is to spawn a thread; the thread won't actually run while the popup menu is showing, so it can check its Text afterward. Thus, the Canvas's Mouse-Down event handler now goes like this:

```
dim t as watchformouseup
if popupmenu1.text = "Pick a Month:" then
    self.dontchange = true
    popupmenu1.removerow 0
    popupmenu1.listindex = -1
    self.dontchange = false
    t = new watchformouseup
    t.run
end
```

And the thread, WatchForMouseUp, has the following Run event handler:

```
if window1.popupmenu1.text = "" then
    window1.dontchange = true
    window1.popupmenu1.insertrow 0,"Pick a Month:"
    window1.popupmenu1.listindex = 0
    window1.dontchange = false
end
```

In REALbasic 3.5, a PopUpMenu will receive MouseDown and MouseUp events, making an independent caption easier to implement.

BevelButton

On the BevelButton's button features, see Chapter 12.

To make a BevelButton act like a PopupMenu, set its HasMenu property to 1 or 2. You can do this even in code. 1 means the menu will pop up below the button, and adds a popup arrow pointing down; 2 means the menu will pop up to the right of the button, and adds a popup arrow pointing to the right; 0 means that no menu will pop up, and no popup arrow is present (the default).

When the mouse is depressed within the BevelButton's region, if its HasMenu is 1 or 2, it displays a menu. When the mouse is subsequently released, the menu vanishes; if the mouse is released over a menu item, the index of that item becomes the Bevel-Button's MenuValue property, and the next time the menu is shown, that menu item will have a check mark or some similar indicator next to it.

On Windows, the user can depress the BevelButton with the mouse and then type letters, arrow keys, and the Enter key to choose a menu item. Accelerators are not used; the user types the start of the desired item's text.

Contents and Format

A BevelButton has the following methods relating to its menu's contents:

AddRow
 Takes one parameter, a string; creates a new last menu item whose text is the parameter.

AddSeparator
 Creates a new last menu item consisting of a separator line. The separator line is disabled and cannot be chosen, but it is a menu item and does have an index.

InsertRow
 Takes two parameters, a menu item index and a string. Creates a new menu item at the designated index, and sets its text to the string parameter; the index of the existing menu item at that index is incremented, and so on for all subsequent rows. The index need not designate an existing menu item; if it is too small or too large, the item will be inserted before or after all existing menu items.

RemoveRow
> Takes one parameter, a menu item index; deletes the menu item at the designated index, decrementing the indices of all subsequent items. If the item doesn't exist, nothing happens.

DeleteAllRows
> Deletes all the menu items.

A BevelButton has the following property relating to its menu's contents:

List
> Takes one parameter, a menu item index; can be used to get or set the text of that item. When getting, if the item doesn't exist or if it is a separator line, the empty string is returned. When setting, if the item doesn't exist, nothing happens. You can set an item to a hyphen to replace it with a separator.

You can construct and modify the BevelButton's menu even if its HasMenu is 0. There is no way to ask a BevelButton how many items its menu has, so if you need this information you must keep track of it elsewhere.

Selection

A BevelButton has the following properties relating to its menu's selection:

MenuValue
> The index of the currently selected menu item, meaning that there will be a check mark or some similar indicator next to that menu item the next time the menu is shown. Can be used to learn or to set the selection. It is not an error to set MenuValue too large or too small; if too large, the last item will be checked, and if too small, the first item will be checked. There cannot be no selection (that is, there is nothing corresponding to a PopupMenu's -1); a workaround is to set the MenuValue to the index of a separator.

A BevelButton receives the following event relating to its selection:

Action
> If HasMenu is not 0, sent only if a menu item is actually chosen. The MenuValue has already been set.

Usage

A BevelButton's menu cannot be initialized in the IDE, so it must be constructed in code. Its Open event handler is a likely place for this.

You may recall the list of problems from the "PopupMenu" section, earlier in this chapter. Well, you can stop recalling it, because a BevelButton doesn't have any of those problems! It has no ValueChanged event, its MenuValue can be set in the IDE, its caption is completely independent of its automatic menu behavior, and the text of an existing menu item can be changed.

For example, the following code in a BevelButton's Open event handler creates a menu of month names, sets the BevelButton's caption to a prompt, and shows the downward popup arrow:

```
dim s as string
dim u, i as integer
s = "January,February,March,April,May,June,July,August,September,October,"
s = s + "November,December"
u = countfields(s,",")
for i = 1 to u
    me.addrow nthfield(s,",",i)
next
me.caption = "Pick a month:"
me.hasmenu = 1
```

Now the user can choose a month. The caption is not automatically changed when this happens, so if that's the desired behavior, it's up to us to implement it by responding in the BevelButton's Action event handler. For example:

```
me.caption = me.list(me.menuvalue)
```

ContextualMenu

For a contextual menu to appear within a window, you first drag a ContextualMenu icon from the Tools Window into a Window Editor, just as for any other control. This creates a ContextualMenu icon in the Window Editor; but it is merely a placeholder, with no visible physical manifestation in the window of the running application.

A ContextualMenu's menu cannot be initialized in the IDE, so this must be done in code, after the application starts running. Subsequently, some other control, or the window itself, must detect that the user wishes to see the contextual menu. The mouse button should be down at this moment, so this is usually within a Mouse-Down event handler; obviously, this MouseDown event handler must belong to some object that *has* a MouseDown event handler, such as a Canvas or a window. Typically, this event handler calls the IsCMMClick function, which returns a boolean telling whether the user is holding down the Ctrl key, the usual convention for summoning a contextual menu. If IsCMMClick returns true, the event handler will call the ContextualMenu instance's Open method (not to be confused with the Open event!); this causes the instance's menu to be displayed under the mouse. When the mouse is released, if it is over an enabled menu item, the ContextualMenu receives the Action event, including a parameter, which is the text of the menu item chosen.

On Windows, the user, having clicked to make the contextual menu appear, can type letters, arrow keys, and the Enter key to select an item. Accelerators are not used; the user types the start of the desired item's text.

A ContextualMenu is not a RectControl. It is a Control, though, so it inherits the usual Open and Close events. Its methods are basically a tiny subset of those of a PopupMenu.

Contents

A ContextualMenu has the following property relating to its contents:

UseCMM
> A boolean. If `true`, an extra disabled Help item precedes all the other items in the menu.* Why you'd ever want this beats the heck out me; you will probably prefer to leave it set to `false`.

A ContextualMenu has the following methods relating to its contents:

AddRow
> Takes one parameter, a string; creates a new last menu item whose text is the parameter.

AddSeparator
> Creates a new last menu item consisting of a separator line. The separator line is disabled and cannot be chosen, but it does occupy a menu item and does have an index.

DeleteAllRows
> Deletes all the menu items.

Selection

A ContextualMenu has the following method relating to selecting:

Open
> Causes the menu to be shown under the mouse.

A ContextualMenu receives the following event:

Action
> Sent because the menu has been shown and the user has chosen a menu item; the text of the chosen item is supplied as a parameter.

Usage

There are lots of feasible strategies for initializing a ContextualMenu's items. If the ContextualMenu is to have the same set of items throughout the lifetime of the application, you might initialize its items in its Open event handler. Or, if a single ContextualMenu is to have a different set of items depending on what control the mouse is clicked in, you might reinitialize its menu items in each control's MouseEnter event, or even in the very same MouseDown event handler that causes the menu to be

---

* The reason for the disabled Help menu item has to do with the Macintosh's peculiar system-based implementation of contextual menus. This is so that (for example) an application can hook a contextual menu's Help item to an Apple Guide file. But that's not going to happen in a REALbasic application. See *http://developer.apple.com/techpubs/macos8/HumanInterfaceToolbox/MenuManager/MenuMgr8Ref/MenuMgrRef.c.html*.

displayed; alternatively, you could have a different ContextualMenu, each with its own set of menu items, to be displayed by each different control.

In the example shown in Figure 17-2, we use a single ContextualMenu whose menu items are rebuilt in the MouseDown event handler of the control that displays it. Here, the control is a Canvas, which displays the apple and whose MouseDown event handler initializes the ContextualMenu's items before displaying the menu:

```
dim choices as string
dim i,u as integer
if isCMMClick then
    choices = "Pie,Cake,Strudel"
    u = countfields(choices,",")
    contextualMenu1.deleteAllRows // someone else might have initialized
    for i = 1 to u
        contextualMenu1.addrow nthfield(choices,",",i)
    next
    contextualMenu1.open // show the menu
    return true // stop the mouse click from falling through to window
end
```

Figure 17-2. Contextual menu

As soon as you start trying to use ContextualMenus, you will doubtless be struck by the fact that most controls don't receive a MouseDown event. In some cases you can work around this by covering the control with a Canvas, which does receive one, and letting the mouseclick pass through (by returning false) if the Ctrl key is not down. But the interaction between the Canvas and the other control will often not be sufficiently fluid to permit the desired effect.

For example, recall the word-selection field implemented in Chapter 13. Let's suppose that we want the user to be able to Ctrl-click on a word in order to pop up a contextual menu explaining what part of speech it is. The EditField detects a mouseclick by means of its SelChange event; but we cannot send the ContextualMenu's Open message in the EditField's SelChange event handler, because the SelChange event isn't triggered until the mouse is up. But, on the other hand, we can't learn where the user is selecting until the SelChange event is triggered. If we place a Canvas over the EditField, we can intercept the mouseclick in the Canvas's MouseDown event handler, but now we don't know what word the user is selecting; to learn that, we'd have to return from the MouseDown event handler to let the mouse click through to the EditField, and now the Canvas is not in control any more, so it can't show the contextual menu (and once again, we won't get another event until the mouse is up). Things should improve in Version 3.5, where an EditField gets a MouseDown event; but even there, similar problems arise if you try to implement a contextual menu for a ListBox. This sort of thing greatly limits the usefulness of ContextualMenus.

One final point. No law says that the Ctrl key, or even the mouse button, must be down at the time the Open message is sent to a ContextualMenu; nor does the mouse even have to be within the window. For example, it is perfectly possible to send the Open message from the Action event handler of a default button, triggered by hitting the Return key. Even if the mouse is not down or within the window at that moment, the menu will appear beneath it. That, however, is not how a contextual menu is intended to be used! So it is up to your code to exercise voluntary self-restraint and not behave like this.

Alternatives

On the whole, PopupMenus and ContextualMenus are simple, which is nice, but also crude, which isn't. They can't be made hierarchical, they can't display icons, individual menu items can't be disabled or styled, and so forth. It is understandable, then, that you might grow frustrated with these limitations, and be casting about for a substitute control. I can recommend two easy, effective ways to make much better popup and contextual menus. One is an XCMD, Jon Pugh's HierPopUp. The other is Noah Desch's HierPop classes; these are a little more work to use, but they are cross-platform. Both are open source; the HierPopUp XCMD provides Pascal source code, while the HierPop classes are written in REALbasic with ToolBox calls.*

Contextual menus are easiest. Figure 17-3 shows a hierarchical contextual menu generated by Ctrl-clicking on a Canvas, thanks to HierPop.

The code for doing this with HierPopUp is extremely simple, but notice that the y component precedes the x component in the order of HPopupMenu's parameters:

```
dim res, choices as string
if isCMMClick then
    choices = "Apple Types,Fuji,Braeburn,Granny Smith;"
    choices = choices + "Recipes,Pie,Cake,Strudel"
    res = HPopUpMenu(choices, -1, me.top+y, me.left+x) // -1 for no checkmark
    // do something with the result here...
end
```

---

* For the HierPopUp XCMD, see *http://www.seanet.com/~jonpugh/hyperstuff.html*. For the HierPop classes, see *http://wireframe.virtualave.net/files/hierpop.sit*. On XCMDs and Toolbox calls, see Chapter 32.

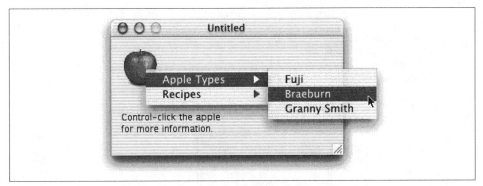

Figure 17-3. Hierarchical contextual menu generated by Toolbox calls

Here is code for generating the same hierarchical contextual menu using the Hier-Pop classes:

```
dim res as string
dim main, types, recipes,dummy as hcMenu
types = new hcMenu
types.items.append new conitem("Fuji")
types.items.append new conitem("Braeburn")
types.items.append new conitem("Granny Smith")
recipes = new hcMenu
recipes.items.append new conitem("Pie")
recipes.items.append new conitem("Cake")
recipes.items.append new conitem("Strudel")
main = new hcMenu
main.items.append new conitem("Apple Types")
main.items.append new conitem("Recipes")
main.items(0).hierarchical = true
main.items(0).hiermenu = types
main.items(1).hierarchical = true
main.items(1).hiermenu = recipes
dummy = main.open(system.mousex, system.mousey)
if dummy <> nil then
     res = dummy.items( dummy.selectedItem ).text
     // do something with the result here...
end
```

Using HierPopUp to implement a popup menu is slightly more involved, because something has to detect the mouseclick. Nonetheless, thanks to BevelButtons, it's still pretty easy, because a BevelButton can be programmatically given a depressed appearance. Figure 17-4 shows the result.

This was achieved using a BevelButton whose HasMenu is 1, so that it has a popup arrow, but which actually has no menu. A Canvas lies over the BevelButton and catches the mouseclick in its MouseDown event handler; it depresses the BevelButton and calls upon HierPopupUp to show the menu, like this:

```
dim choices, res as string
bevelbutton1.value = true
bevelbutton1.refresh
```

```
choices = "January;February;March;April;May;June;July;"
choices = choices + "August,Good Choice!;September;October;November;December"
res = HPopUpMenu(choices, -1, me.top + me.height, me.left)
// do something with the result here...
bevelbutton1.value = false
return true // don't let the click fall through
```

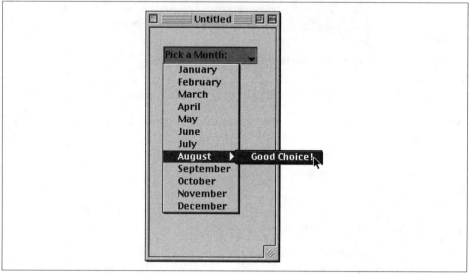

Figure 17-4. Popup menu made with a Canvas, a BevelButton, and an XCMD

You can do the same sort of thing with the HierPop classes, or you can use the included HierButton classes, which are actually Canvas subclasses.

TabPanels

A TabPanel is a built-in control class for showing alternate sets of controls within a window. It displays itself as a rectangular region, at one edge of which there appears a series of text captions (the tabs). When the user clicks on one of the tabs, the set of controls within the TabPanel region is replaced by a different set of controls. Figure 18-1 shows an example.

Figure 18-1. A TabPanel

What's actually happening here is that REALbasic is simply turning one set of controls invisible and another set of controls visible. This is nothing that you couldn't do yourself, in code; however, use of a TabPanel has two advantages:

• The task of maintaining entire sets of controls, turning them all visible and invisible appropriately, is handled automatically by REALbasic.

• The user is presented with a convenient and familiar interface for requesting that the set of visible controls be changed.

On Windows, a TabPanel can receive the focus, and the user can then use arrow keys to switch between its tabs. See "The Focus" in Chapter 13.

Preparation

Preparation of a TabPanel in the IDE, once it has been dragged into a Window Editor, is a two-stage process. First, click on the blank tab (the one containing the ellipsis mark) to bring up the Tab Panel Editor dialog. This is where you create new captions, set the text of captions, and change their order. When you're done, you'll have as many tabs as you have captions. The extra blank tab (with the ellipsis mark) isn't real; it's just a way of bringing up the Tab Panel Editor dialog again. A Tab-Panel with just one tab (besides the ellipsis tab) is disabled at runtime.

Then, back in the Window Editor, you click one of the TabPanel's tabs to bring that panel to the front, and drag onto the panel the controls you want to associate with that tab; do this for each of the tabs. In reality, all the controls within the TabPanel region are now lying on top of one another in what, if you saw them all at once, would be a jumbled mess. But each time you click on a tab in the IDE, REALbasic shows and hides sets of controls, much as will happen in the running application; this allows you to work conveniently, at any given moment, with only the controls associated with one particular tab.

A control must be completely within the bounds of the TabPanel at the time the application is built (or when the project starts running within the IDE) in order for the TabPanel to take charge of its visibility.

Properties and Events

A TabPanel is a RectControl, and therefore receives all the events and has all the properties and methods listed in Chapter 10: Open and Close events; Visible, Enabled, and AutoDeactivate properties; Top, Left, Height, and Width properties; LockLeft, LockRight, LockTop, and LockBottom properties; MouseEnter, Mouse-Move, and MouseExit events; and Refresh and RefreshRect methods.

A TabPanel also has these properties:

TextFont, TextSize, Bold, Italic, Underline
    Font, size, and style information for the captions of the tabs.

SmallTabs
    A boolean; if true, the tabs are slightly smaller than normal. Cannot be set in code.

Facing
    An integer determining which edge of the TabPanel the tabs appear on. The values are 0–3, meaning top, bottom, right, and left, respectively. Cannot be set in code. (Has no effect on Windows.)

Value
    The index of the panel currently showing. Can be set in code, to switch among the panels. The index is zero-based.

REALbasic 3.5 adds a Caption property; for example, `tabpanel1.caption(0)` is the caption of the first tab.

A TabPanel receives this event:

Change
> Sent to the TabPanel because the Value has been changed by the user choosing a different tab, or because the Value has been set (not necessarily changed) in code.

Usage

You can do whatever you like with the Value property and the Change event, but under most circumstances you may very well just ignore them, letting the TabPanel do its work automatically. There is no need, for instance, to respond to the Change event by showing and hiding controls in code; the whole point of the TabPanel is that it takes care of this for you.

A neat device is to make a TabPanel invisible. The user doesn't know it's there, but your code can still change the TabPanel's Value property as a way of showing and hiding sets of controls.* For example, in Figure 18-2, the two StaticTexts and the two EditFields that appear when the second RadioButton is clicked are in the second panel of an invisible TabPanel. The first RadioButton's Action event handler contains this code:

```
tabpanel1.value = 0
```

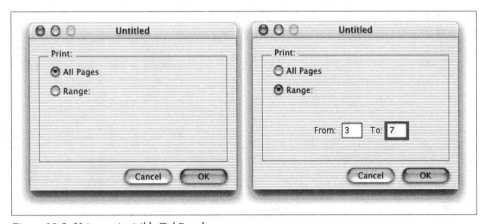

Figure 18-2. Using an invisible TabPanel

and the second RadioButton's Action event handler contains this code:

```
tabpanel1.value = 1
```

---

* This was first pointed out to me by Neil Gillies.

Alternatively, if you want to show and hide sets of controls in the same region, and you don't need the visible TabPanel interface, consider using a scrolling Canvas, as described under "Interaction with Other Objects" in Chapter 11. It's a little more work, but it avoids some potential pitfalls of having all those controls lying invisibly on top of one another. There are fewer of these pitfalls than there used to be, but occasionally one still hears of some unpleasant interaction amongst controls in a TabPanel.

An EditField or ListBox that has the focus in the current panel loses the focus (with the usual LostFocus event) when the TabPanel's Value changes. So if you want the same control to have the focus the next time the user returns to that panel, you have to make this happen yourself, in code. For example, you might capture information about which control has the focus in its LostFocus event handler, and then restore the focus to that control when its panel comes back to the front in the TabPanel's ValueChanged event handler.

CHAPTER 19

In this chapter:
- Keyboard Communication
- Keyboard Object
- UserCancelled

Keyboard

The keyboard is one of the two chief conduits of communication from the user to your application. (The mouse is the other; see Chapter 20.) This chapter summarizes the ways in which keyboard communication can take place. Some of these ways have already been mentioned, though certain details have been postponed until now; others are described here for the first time.

A little terminology is in order at the outset. The Command key, Option key, Shift key, and Ctrl key are *modifier* keys. Other keys are, for lack of a better term, *nonmodifier* keys. Only the nonmodifier keys count as first-class citizens, in the sense that pressing one generates a keydown event at system level; the modifier keys are merely ancillary, their purpose being to alter the meaning of the nonmodifier keys.[*]

On Windows, what REALbasic calls the Option key maps to the Alt key, and what REALbasic calls the Command key maps to the Windows key.

Keyboard Communication

Here are all the ways in which your application might learn that the user has pressed a key:

- The user presses a nonmodifier key and is holding down the Command key. This causes a menu-enabling moment, during which the keypress can be detected, if desired, in any of the resulting EnableMenu or EnableMenuItems events, through the Keyboard object, as explained later in this chapter. If the keypress matches the keyboard equivalent of a menu item that is enabled when the menu-enabling moment is over, a menu event will be generated (see Chapter 6). If the keypress does *not* match the keyboard equivalent of an enabled menu item, the key falls through to the appropriate KeyDown event as described next.

---

[*] I'm not sure what to term the Caps Lock key. In theory, it's a modifier key that doesn't have to be physically held in order to count as being down. Perhaps one should say it's a "dinosaur key," being left over from the days of typewriters. My suggestion is that you just rip it off the keyboard and throw it away.

- The user presses a nonmodifier key and is not holding down the Command key, or is holding down the Command key but the keypress does not match an enabled menu item equivalent, at a time when a ListBox or an EditField has the focus. This causes the ListBox or EditField to be sent a KeyDown event (see Chapter 13 and Chapter 14).

  - Unless a ListBox returns true from its KeyDown event handler, the Up arrow and Down arrow keys and the Home, End, Page Up, and Page Down keys will navigate the selection and scroll the ListBox; any other key will fall through as a KeyDown event sent to the window.

  - Unless an EditField returns true from its KeyDown event handler, most keys will have an effect within the EditField (arrow keys navigate, letter keys insert text, and so forth); but the Function keys, the keypad Num Lock (Clear) key, the Help key, the Esc key, and the Enter and Return keys if the EditField is single-line, and the Tab key if the EditField is single-line or its AcceptTabs property is false, will fall through as a KeyDown event sent to the window.

- The user presses a nonmodifier key and is not holding down the Command key, or is holding down the Command key but the keypress does not match an enabled menu item equivalent, at a time when neither a ListBox nor an Edit-Field has the focus, or when a ListBox or an EditField has the focus but the key falls through as just described. This causes the window to be sent a KeyDown event. Unless the window returns true from its KeyDown event handler, the Tab key shifts the focus, the Return and Enter keys press the Default button, and the Esc key presses the Cancel button. A floating window does not receive Key-Down events unless a control in it has the focus.

- Your code can ascertain the state of the keyboard, by means of the Keyboard object. See "Keyboard Object," later in this chapter.

- Your code can ascertain whether the user has pressed Command-Period since the current event handler started executing, by means of the UserCancelled function. (Not on Windows.) See "UserCancelled," later in this chapter.

On Windows, the Alt key alone, to start navigating the menu with the keyboard, triggers a menu-enabling moment. Ctrl key combinations do *not* generate a menu-enabling moment, and if they match a menu item's keyboard equivalent, they trigger a menu event even if that menu item is not enabled; I regard this as a bug. Alt key combinations, if they match a control's accelerator key, don't generate any event and can't be intercepted; if they don't match a control's accelerator key, they trigger a (quite unnecessary) menu-enabling moment. The window's KeyDown event *precedes* that of an EditField or ListBox on Windows, so returning true from it can have very bad effects—the user won't be able to type in EditFields, for example.

Keyboard Object

The Keyboard object is an "intrinsic" object: it is an automatically generated instance of a class that cannot otherwise be instantiated or subclassed. A reference to this instance is provided by the global instance name Keyboard. A number of read-only properties of this object permit your code to ascertain the state of the keyboard:

AsyncCommandKey, AsyncOptionKey, AsyncShiftKey, AsyncControlKey
>   Booleans stating whether the Command key, Option key, Shift key, or Ctrl key is down at this very moment. AsyncControlKey differs from IsCMMClick (Chapter 17), in that the latter is true only if the Ctrl key is the *only* modifier key being held down.

AsyncKeyDown
>   Takes one parameter, an integer, representing a keycode. Returns a boolean stating whether the key corresponding to that keycode is down at this very moment.

CommandKey, OptionKey, ShiftKey, ControlKey
>   Booleans stating whether the Command key, Option key, Shift key, or Ctrl key was down at the time the current event was triggered.

Polling the keyboard asynchronously works in both Timers and threads, and because these run even when the application is otherwise idle, it works even when your application is in the background.

AsyncCommandKey and Its Friends

Consider the following problem. We have several buttons in a window. We want the user to be able, in effect, to push any of these buttons by means of a Command key equivalent. To help cue the user as to what these equivalents are, we want Static-Texts stating each button's equivalent to appear when the user holds down the Command key, as shown in Figure 19-1.

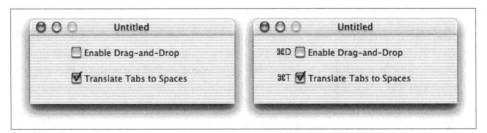

Figure 19-1. StaticTexts that appear in response to a modifier key alone

This problem doesn't arise on Windows, because buttons have accelerator keys which work automatically, and whose value is cued in their captions.

Pressing a modifier key alone does not generate any events. Therefore, in order to learn that the user is holding down the Command key, we will have to be more proactive; we will need to poll the keyboard repeatedly, in a loop. Since the question at each moment is whether the Command key is down at that very moment, this is a job for AsyncCommandKey.

One way to implement such a loop is in a thread. Actually, a Timer would be a *much* better implementation; but since Timers have not yet been discussed (see Chapter 25), a thread will do for the sake of the illustration. The Application subclass could instantiate and launch the thread, whose Run event handler loops forever, watching to see if our window is present and frontmost. If it is, the thread might execute code such as the following:

```
do
    if keyboard.asyncCommandKey then
        if not window1.staticText1.visible then
            window1.staticText1.visible = true
        end
        if not window1.staticText2.visible then
            window1.staticText2.visible = true
        end
    else
        if window1.staticText1.visible then
            window1.staticText1.visible = false
        end
        if window1.staticText2.visible then
            window1.staticText2.visible = false
        end
    end
loop until false // or until the window is no longer frontmost, or whatever
```

The code keeps looping, checking whether the Command key is actually down; it changes the visible state of the StaticTexts accordingly. The extra conditions ensure that this happens only once each time the Command key's state changes, because we don't want the StaticTexts bombarded with unnecessary requests to change their visibility.

AsyncKeyDown

AsyncKeyDown is rather tricky to use. It does not report what key is down; rather, you have to ask it about some one particular key. And you don't ask it by handing it the desired key as a string or as an ASCII equivalent; rather, you must hand it the keycode of the key you want to know about.

For example, to learn whether the D key is down, you would not say this:

```
if keyboard.asyncKeyDown("D") // error!
```

nor would you say this:

```
if keyboard.asyncKeyDown(asc("D")) // wrong key!
```

Instead, you *might* say this:

```
if keyboard.asyncKeyDown(2)
```

CHAPTER 20

In this chapter:
- Mouse Communication
- Polling the Mouse
- Balloon Help
- Cursor

Mouse and Cursor

The mouse is one of the two chief conduits of communication from the user to your application. (The other is the keyboard; see Chapter 19.) The user moves and clicks the mouse; this chapter summarizes the ways in which your application can learn that this has happened. Your application can also respond to the user's positioning of the mouse by popping up balloon help captions that guide the user through the interface; so this chapter also discusses balloon help. In addition, your application can, in a sense, communicate through the mouse back to the user, by changing the appearance of the cursor (the onscreen representation of the mouse); this chapter discusses the cursor as well.

Mouse Communication

This section lists all the ways in which your application is notified automatically, through an event, that the user has performed a significant action involving the mouse. Such actions may be divided into two headings: the user has moved the mouse, and the user has clicked the mouse button.

Mouse Movement

Here are all the ways in which your application might be notified that the user has moved the mouse. The user may move the mouse:

- Into a visible window's content region. The window is sent a MouseEnter event (see Chapter 9).

- Within a visible window's content region. The window is sent a MouseMove event (see Chapter 9).

- Out of a visible window's content region. The window is sent a MouseExit event (see Chapter 9).

- Into the content region of a visible RectControl. The control is sent a Mouse-Enter event (see Chapter 10).

- Within the content region of a visible RectControl. The control is sent a Mouse-Move event (see Chapter 10).
- Out of the content region of a visible RectControl. The control is sent a Mouse-Exit event (see Chapter 10).

Recall that a window's content region is that portion of the window that is not its frame (titlebar, border, grow icon) and that is not covered by another visible REAL-basic window; a RectControl's content region is that portion of the control that is within its window's content region.

Mouseclick

Here are all the ways in which your application might be notified that the user has clicked the mouse button:

- The user clicks the mouse in the menubar at the top of the screen. A menu-enabling moment is triggered; if the user proceeds to choose an enabled menu item, a menu event is sent (see Chapter 6).
- The user clicks and releases the mouse in a window's go-away box. The window is sent a CancelClose event (see Chapter 9).
- The user drags a window by its border. The window is sent a Moved event (see Chapter 9).
- The user drags a window's grow icon or clicks in the window's zoom box. The window is sent a Resized event (see Chapter 9).
- The user clicks in a rear window and brings it to the front. The window is sent an Activate event, and a menu-enabling moment is triggered (see Chapter 6 and Chapter 7).
- The user clicks the mouse in a front window's content region, *not* in a control that intercepts the click. The window is sent a MouseDown event; if the Mouse-Down event returns true, the window will also be sent MouseDrag and Mou-seUp events (see Chapter 9).

  The following controls, if visible and enabled, will intercept a click, preventing it from generating a MouseDown event to the window (or whatever else is behind the control):

  - Canvas, Placard, or ImageWell, if its MouseDown event handler returns true
  - PushButton, BevelButton, LittleArrows, DisclosureTriangle, CheckBox, and RadioButton
  - An EditField's text region
  - An EditField's scrollbar, if the scrollbar is enabled

- ListBox
- Slider and Scrollbar
- A PopupMenu that has menu items (on Windows, even a PopupMenu without menu items)
- A tab of a TabPanel (on Windows, even a panel of a TabPanel)
- A MoviePlayer

- The user clicks the mouse in a visible, enabled Canvas, Placard, or ImageWell in a front window. The control is sent a MouseDown event. If the MouseDown event returns true, the control will also be sent MouseDrag and MouseUp events; otherwise, the MouseDown event falls through to what is behind (see Chapter 11, Chapter 12, and Chapter 16).

- The user clicks and releases the mouse in a visible, enabled PushButton, BevelButton, DisclosureTriangle, CheckBox, or RadioButton in a front window. The control is sent an Action event after the mouse is up (see Chapter 12).

- The user clicks the mouse in a visible, enabled LittleArrows in a front window. The control is sent Up or Down events, depending where the click occurred, for as long as the mouse is down and within that part of the control (see Chapter 12).

- The user clicks the mouse in the text region or the enabled scrollbar of a visible, enabled EditField in a front window. If in the text region, then if this shifts the focus the EditField is sent a GotFocus event while the mouse is down, and the EditField is sent a SelChange event after the mouse is up (see Chapter 13).

- The user clicks the mouse in the text region or the scrollbar of a visible, enabled ListBox in a front window. If in the text region, then if this shifts the focus, the Listbox is sent a GotFocus event while the mouse is down, and the ListBox is sent a Change event after the mouse is up (see Chapter 14).

- The user clicks the mouse in the heading region of a visible, enabled ListBox in a front window. The ListBox is sent a SortColumn event after the mouse is up (see Chapter 14).

- The user clicks the mouse in an enabled, visible Slider or Scrollbar in a front window, in such a way as to change its value; the control is sent a ValueChanged event after the mouse is up or, if its LiveScrolling property is true, each time the value changes with the mouse still down (see Chapter 15).

- The user clicks the mouse in an enabled, visible PopupMenu in a front window and changes the selected menu item; the PopupMenu is sent a Change event after the mouse is up (see Chapter 17).

- The user releases the mouse over an enabled item of a ContextualMenu; the ContextualMenu is sent an Action event after the mouse is up (see Chapter 17).

- The user clicks and releases the mouse in a nonfrontmost tab of an enabled, visible TabPanel in a front window; the TabPanel is sent a Change event after the mouse is up (see Chapter 18).
- The user clicks in a MoviePlayer or its controller or on the image of a movie displayed by the MoviePlayer. The MoviePlayer receives a Stop or Play event (see Chapter 27).

In REALbasic 3.5, the repertoire of controls that receive MouseDown and MouseUp events will be augmented.

Mouseclicks that don't generate any event whatever can often be detected through an appropriately placed Canvas. For example, no event is generated when the user clicks the mouse in the enabled scrollbar of an EditField or ListBox, so you can't learn that the scroll position has been changed. I regard this as unfortunate, but at least a Canvas over the scrollbar can tell you that the user is up to something. For other examples of this kind of skullduggery, see "Covering Other Controls" in Chapter 11, "Other ListBox Features" in Chapter 14, and "Independent caption" in Chapter 17.

On Windows, some of these actions can be performed by means of the keyboard. In certain cases, it might in theory be possible to detect that the keyboard was used and not the mouse; for example, if the user hits the spacebar key to toggle a CheckBox, a KeyDown event passes through the window before the Action event is sent to the CheckBox, and the temporal proximity of these could be used to deduce what has happened. But I don't know that you'd have any reason to draw this distinction.

Polling the Mouse

Your code can ascertain at any time the current position of the mouse and the current state of the mouse button, through the following means:

The system-level MouseX and MouseY properties
These are referred to by way of the intrinsic System object, to which you can get a reference by its global instance name, System. Thus: system.mouseX, system.mouseY. Coordinates are measured from the top left of the main screen.

A window's MouseX and MouseY properties
Coordinates are measured from the top left of the window's content region. The window need not be visible.

A control's MouseX and MouseY properties
Coordinates are measured from the top left of the containing window's content region. The window need not be visible. This is merely shorthand for accessing the window's MouseX and MouseY properties.

The system-level MouseDown property
Referred to by way of the intrinsic System object, as system.mouseDown. A boolean; true if the mouse button is down.

Polling the mouse asynchronously works in a thread or a Timer. But `system.mouseDown` does not seem to work in a Timer when your application is in the background (I don't know why this is). Also, there are situations where the mouse being down stops threads and Timers from working at all (in an EditField, for example).

Balloon Help

Balloon help is a system-level feature that was added in 1991, with the advent of System 7. When balloon help is turned on, which the user can do by choosing Help → Show Balloons, the user can pause the mouse over a window, a control, or a menu item to see a brief caption describing it. Balloon help has not proven a success, and in Mac OS X it is replaced by a "help tag" feature similar to tooltips on Windows: without the user having to ask for it, a text box appears if the mouse hovers over a control for longer than a second or two.

REALbasic implements balloon help through two properties, BalloonHelp and DisabledBalloonHelp. MenuItems and RectControls have both a BalloonHelp property and a DisabledBalloonHelp property; windows cannot be disabled, so they have a BalloonHelp property only. These properties can be set in the IDE or in code. The length of the caption is limited to 255 characters.

The BalloonHelp and DisabledBalloonHelp are supposed to be the text of the help caption when the object is enabled or disabled, respectively. In the past, however, users have found this confusing, so the rule now is that this distinction is followed only if an object has both a nonempty BalloonHelp string and a nonempty DisabledBalloonHelp string. If only one of the strings is nonempty, it will be used both when the object is enabled and when it is disabled. If both the BalloonHelp and the DisabledBalloonHelp strings are empty, no balloon will appear.

The question sometimes arises of how to turn balloon help on and off in code. For example, you might like to have a button whose caption is Show Balloons, so that the user knows that balloon help is available and can access it without going to the trouble of choosing a menu item. There are various XCMDs and plug-ins that can do this, or you can use a Toolbox call. For example, here is the Action event handler of a button that toggles balloon help, changing its own caption to match (see Chapter 32 for the details):

```
declare function HMSetBalloons lib "InterfaceLib" (b as boolean) as integer
dim dummy as integer
if me.caption = "Show Balloons" then
    dummy = hmsetballoons(true)
    me.caption = "Hide Balloons"
else
    dummy = hmsetballoons(false)
    me.caption = "Show Balloons"
end
```

If you like, you can also set up a Declare for HMGetBalloons, which reports whether balloon help is on or off.

On Mac OS X and Windows, the HelpTag property is used instead. If a control's HelpTag string is nonempty, its value will appear in a box when the user hovers the mouse over the control. Objects that can't have help tags, such as windows and MenuItems, lack this property. On Mac OS X, the user can hold down the Command key to show the balloon help text in place of the help tag's text; this is expected to yield a fuller explanation.

Cursor

The *cursor* is the appearance assumed by the screen representation of the mouse's position. One should not underestimate the importance of the cursor in providing the user with helpful feedback. The shape of the cursor, if deftly and consistently manipulated by your application, can communicate with the user on an almost subliminal level, providing an understanding of the current process, clarifying the user's options, and acting as a guide to what's on the screen.

Control over the cursor is distributed throughout your project, as follows:

- Every instance of a Control subclass has a MouseCursor property. Setting this property determines the shape of the cursor when the mouse is over the control in a frontmost window.

- Every window has a MouseCursor property. Setting this property determines the shape of the cursor when the mouse is over the window and the window is frontmost.

- The Application has a MouseCursor property. Setting this property determines the shape of the cursor at all times, *even when your application is suspended.* (This behavior will be fixed in REALbasic 3.5.)

- Sometimes, REALbasic takes control of the cursor's shape. For example, during a lengthy code operation, REALbasic may put up a watch cursor.

Getting a Cursor

MouseCursor property values must be instances of the MouseCursor class. There are three ways to obtain such an instance:

- REALbasic provides three globally available MouseCursor instances, corresponding to three familiar standard shapes: their global names are `WatchCursor`, `IBeamCursor`, and `ArrowCursor`.

- Import into your project a ResEdit file containing a `'CURS'` resource (and nothing else). This will cause the cursor shape to be listed in the Project Window by a name based on that of the ResEdit file; the shape will automatically be instantiated as a MouseCursor instance when your application starts up, and its name in the Project Window becomes the instance's global name. The project stores the cursor resource itself, not merely an alias to the ResEdit file, so you can subsequently throw the ResEdit file away if you wish.

- In code, open a file's resource fork and use the ResourceFork's GetCursor function to specify a 'CURS' or 'crsr' resource. A MouseCursor instance is returned. A 'crsr' is a color cursor, so this is the only way to give your application a color cursor. Commonly, the resource fork will be your application's own; the cursor resources will have been included in a Resource file that has been imported into your project.

In this example, we will cause our application to have a color cursor originating in a Resource file imported into the project. In the Application's Open event handler, the MouseCursor instance is extracted from the resource chain and stored as a Mouse-Cursor property of the Application subclass, Cur1. It is also assigned to the Application's MouseCursor property. When the application is suspended, we must set the Application's MouseCursor property to nil so that it doesn't conflict with the cursor of other applications (this won't be necessary in REALbasic 3.5):

```
// Application's Open event handler:
cur1 = resourcefork.getcursor(1000)
mouseCursor = cur1

// Application's Deactivate event handler:
mouseCursor = nil

// Application's Activate event handler:
mouseCursor = cur1
```

Negotiating the Cursor

The implementation of the relationship amongst the various MouseCursor properties is a little surprising. You might have expected it to work like the scoping of variables, where the more local scope takes precedence over the more global scope—or like virtual methods, where a method lower down the hierarchy overrides a method higher up the hierarchy. Under this scenario, the window's MouseCursor property would govern the mouse only when the cursor was over no control with a non-nil MouseCursor property, and the application's MouseCursor property would govern the mouse only when the cursor was over no window or control with a non-nil MouseCursor property.

In fact, however, it works just the other way round! If the Application's MouseCursor property is non-nil, then the MouseCursor properties of any windows and controls are ignored. If a window's MouseCursor property is non-nil, then the MouseCursor properties of any controls in the window are ignored. This means that you can't assign different MouseCursor properties different values and let the various objects negotiate the cursor's shape amongst themselves automatically as the mouse moves. This, in my view, if not exactly a bug, is still obviously backward. Things are perfectly fine if the only cursors in your project belong to individual controls that don't overlap; you just assign to each control's MouseCursor property its respective cursor, and they never conflict with one another. But as soon as you want cursors to work on more than one level, *you* must resolve any conflicts yourself. This is not difficult, but it is tedious and may require some experimentation.

Let's take a simple example. Suppose we want the cursor to be Cur1 when the mouse is over Window1 and Cur2 otherwise. Since the notion "otherwise" implies that Cur2 must be the Application's MouseCursor, we have a conflict between levels, which we must resolve ourselves. We cannot assign Cur1 to Window1's MouseCursor property and Cur2 to the Application's MouseCursor property, because Cur2 will always override Cur1. Instead, we must assign Cur2 to the Application's MouseCursor property, and change this to Cur1, ourselves, whenever the mouse is over Window1.

In the Application's Open event handler, we obtain the MouseCursor instances and assign them to properties of the Application subclass, as before:

```
cur1 = resourcefork.getcursor(1000)
cur2 = resourcefork.getcursor(1001)
mousecursor = cur2
```

Now let's turn to Window1 for a moment. The cursor is to change when the mouse crosses the physical boundary between the window and its surroundings. We will know when that happens, because the window receives MouseEnter and MouseExit events. So we contemplate writing Window1's MouseEnter event handler like this:

```
app.mousecursor = app.cur1
```

But that's not right. Recall that MouseEnter is sent even if the application is suspended. We don't want Window1 to snatch control of the cursor away from the frontmost application. So Window1 will need to consult a boolean, to learn whether the application is suspended. Let's call this boolean Backgrounded and make it an Application property. Now, the Application's Activate and Deactivate event handlers, in addition to enabling and disabling the cursor, must raise and lower this flag:

```
// Application's Deactivate event handler:
backgrounded = true
mousecursor = nil

// Application's Activate event handler:
backgrounded = false
mousecursor = cur2
```

Now we can write Window1's MouseEnter and MouseExit event handlers:

```
// Window1's MouseEnter event handler:
if not app.backgrounded then
    app.mousecursor = app.cur1
end

// Window1's MouseExit event handler:
if not app.backgrounded then
    app.mousecursor = app.cur2
end
```

This works, but we are still not finished. A likely situation is that the application will be suspended, and then the user will resume it by clicking in Window1. Now the mouse is within Window1, but Window1 never received a MouseEnter event so the cursor is the wrong cursor. We need to catch this situation; in Window1's Activate event handler, we test for the mouse's location using the window's MouseX and MouseY properties:

```
if mousex > 0 then
    if mousey > 0 then
        if mousex < width then
            if mousey < height then
                app.mousecursor = app.cur1
            end
        end
    end
end
```

Starting in REALbasic 3.5, your application relinquishes control of the cursor automatically when it goes into the background; when it resumes, it assumes control of the cursor again, correctly. Thus, the preceding example ends up being far simpler: the Application's Open event sets its MouseCursor to Cur2 at startup, and the window changes the Application's MouseCursor to Cur1 and back to Cur2 in its MouseEnter and MouseExit events, respectively.

Overcoming the Watch

REALbasic has a certain tendency to take control of the cursor's shape away from you. In loops, particularly, it tends to change the cursor to a watch.

You may be able to prevent this behavior in the built application, through the DisableBackgroundTasks pragma (see "Pragmas" in Chapter 8). But I believe this doesn't work on Mac OS X. And anyhow, what if you don't want to disable background tasks?

In that case, you have two alternatives. One is to set a MouseCursor property repeatedly during a loop. For example, during the following code, despite the assignment in the second line, REALbasic displays the watch cursor:

```
dim t as integer
app.mousecursor = arrowcursor // this won't work
t = ticks
while ticks-t < 3600 and not usercancelled
    // hit Command-Period to get out of the loop
wend
app.mousecursor = app.cur1
```

But during this code, REALbasic displays the arrow cursor throughout:

```
dim t as integer
dim c as mousecursor
```

```
c = arrowcursor
t = ticks
while ticks-t < 3600 and not usercancelled
    app.mousecursor = c // fine
    // hit Command-Period to get out of the loop
wend
```

The other alternative is to use the DisableAutoWaitCursor pragma. This pragma is implemented in an unusual way: no matter where it appears in your code, it applies to your entire code. In other words, this pragma simply switches off the automatic watch cursor behavior for this project, and then if you ever want the watch cursor, it is up to you to provide it explicitly. Another unusual feature of this pragma is that it works even when you're just running the project in the IDE.

Animated Cursors

REALbasic makes no automatic provision for animated cursors, but there is no great difficulty: your code simply needs to cycle through the different cursors that constitute the animation. The most elegant way to do this is to define a class whose job is to provide the next cursor in the animation cycle.

Let's call our class AnimCursor. It has two properties: an integer, Which, and a MouseCursor array called Cur, initially dimensioned to 0. AnimCursor has one method handler, a function called NextCur, which returns a MouseCursor:

```
dim i as integer
i = self.which
self.which = (self.which + 1) mod (ubound(self.cur) + 1)
return self.cur(i)
```

Now, suppose we have six cursors, Hand1 through Hand6. To provide easy indexed reference to them, we have an Application property Hand, declared as an AnimCursor. In the Application subclass's Open event handler, we instantiate Hand and initialize its Cur array:

```
hand = new animcursor
redim hand.cur(5)
// ... obtain the six cursor instances somehow ...
hand.cur(0) = hand1
hand.cur(1) = hand2
hand.cur(2) = hand3
hand.cur(3) = hand4
hand.cur(4) = hand5
hand.cur(5) = hand6
```

The animated cursor is now ready for use. It is to cycle through the cursors, providing the animation effect; it's just a matter of repeatedly calling an AnimCursor instance's NextCur function. For example, let's return to the integer sorting routine from Chapter 15. Instead of a ProgressBar, we'll provide feedback to the user by an animated cursor:

```
dim gap, bound, temp, i, j, jg, cur as integer
j = ubound(s)
for i = 0 to j
    s(i) = rnd
next
bound = ubound(s)
gap = (bound + 1) / 2
while gap > 0
    app.mousecursor = app.hand.nextcur() // animate the cursor
    for i = gap to bound
        j = i - gap
        jg = i
        while j >= 0 and s(j) > s(jg)
            temp = s(j)
            s(j)= s(jg)
            s(jg) = temp
            jg = j
            j = j - gap
        wend
    next
    gap = gap / 2
wend
app.mousecursor = nil // all done, reset cursor
```

PART III

Reaching Out

Part II described the ways in which REALbasic interacts with the user. But REALbasic also knows how to reach out beyond the interface world of the screen, the keyboard, and the mouse, into a multitude of places and spaces. It can meddle with the clipboard; it can read and write files; it can make sounds and show QuickTime movies; it can print; it can communicate with other applications by means of Apple events; it can even operate as a client or server over the Internet.

Part III is about these and similar features of REALbasic. In other words, it's about all the miscellaneous stuff that wasn't covered in previous parts of the book! Finally, the last chapter discusses how to extend REALbasic's reach still further, by giving it new commands and letting it call the Toolbox directly.

The chapters in Part III are:

Chapter 21, *Files*
Chapter 22, *Databases*
Chapter 23, *Clipboard*
Chapter 24, *Drag-and-Drop*
Chapter 25, *Time*
Chapter 26, *Sound*
Chapter 27, *Movies*
Chapter 28, *Animation*
Chapter 29, *Printing*
Chapter 30, *TCP/IP Communications*
Chapter 31, *Interapplication Communications*
Chapter 32, *Language Extensions*

In this chapter:
- Getting a FolderItem
- File Types
- File Properties and File Actions
- Arbitrary Data: Binary Streams
- Sequential Data: Text Streams
- Resources
- Predefined Data Formats

Files

This chapter explains how to use REALbasic to work with files on disk. You can access the filing system itself, in order to learn or set such things as the type or date of a file, or to copy, delete, or create a file; and you can read or write the data that a file contains.

Getting a FolderItem

Every reference to a file on disk is performed by way of an instance of the FolderItem class. Conversely, every non-nil FolderItem instance points to some file on disk; the file in question need not actually exist (otherwise, it would be impossible to create a file, since you could not refer to the file you wanted to create!), but in that case its containing folder must exist.

There are five ways to obtain a FolderItem instance, as described in the following sections.

GetFolderItem and GetTrueFolderItem

The first way to obtain a FolderItem instance is to generate it from a standard pathname string. Pathname strings are colon-delimited on Macintosh; for example, if one of my hard disks is called *Power*, then "Power:Applications" is a legal pathname. On Windows, a backslash is the delimiter; for example, "C:\Program files".

The procedure here is to hand the string as parameter to the GetFolderItem function or the GetTrueFolderItem function; a FolderItem is returned. The difference between the two functions is that if the item described by the pathname exists and is an alias, GetFolderItem points to the original, while GetTrueFolderItem points to the alias. And let's please not get into a philosophical discussion of whether the original isn't really the "true" item! GetFolderItem existed first; when it became apparent that its behavior was causing difficulties, a second function was created, and it had to be named *something*, after all.

So, for example:

```
dim f as folderItem
f = getFolderItem("Power:Applications") // on Macintosh
f = getFolderItem("C:\Program files") // on Windows
```

Now, in real life your use of GetFolderItem and GetTrueFolderItem is going to be very limited. Manipulation of pathnames is *not* the proper way to refer to items on disk in REALbasic. (The other four ways discussed in this section are the proper ways.) These functions do not work for pathname strings longer than 255 characters; and in any case, pathname manipulation is a very tricky business. However, there is one perfectly legitimate and extremely valuable use of GetFolderItem: a parameter string consisting of a single item, with no delimiter, is specially interpreted to be relative to your application file (or, in the IDE, your project file). For example, suppose your application is to have a folder named *Users* in the same folder as itself. You can obtain a reference to this folder by saying:

```
dim f as folderItem
f = getFolderItem("Users")
```

The same technique may be used to point to the folder that contains your application file; just hand the empty string to GetFolderItem, like this:

```
dim f as folderItem
f = getFolderItem("")
```

If you're testing this by running in the IDE, it's a good idea to save the project first, since otherwise you'll be pointing to the folder that contains REALbasic, which is probably not what you wanted.

The question sometimes arises of how to point to your application file itself. This is no easy task, because although you can get a pointer to the folder that contains your application file, you don't know your application's *name*—because the user is free to change it! One solution is to doubt whether you really need this information. For example, if you're just trying to look inside your application's resource fork, you don't need a FolderItem at all; you can simply refer directly to app.resourceFork. However, if you really do need your running application's name, one method is the use of an AppleScript:

```
on run{}
    tell app "Finder" to get name of every process where it is frontmost
end run
```

Create this AppleScript in the Script Editor, compile it under a useful name such as *WhoAmI*, and import the compiled script into your project. Now you can call it from code to get your application's name as a string, like this:

```
if app.myName = "" then // a string property, has not yet been initialized
    app.myName = whoAmI()
end
```

If this code appears in the Application subclass's Activate event handler, you will know that your application is frontmost when it calls WhoAmI, so now you've captured your application's name. (This doesn't work on Mac OS X. Another way to get your application's name is to use a Toolbox call to consult the Process Manager; an example appears in Chapter 32.) Once you know your application's name, you can use it to obtain a FolderItem pointing to the application file itself:

```
dim f as folderItem
f = getfolderitem(app.myName)
```

Volumes

To obtain a FolderItem pointing to a mounted volume, or simply to get a list of mounted volumes, use the VolumeCount and Volume functions. VolumeCount counts, but the Volume index is zero-based, so don't forget to compensate accordingly. Volume returns a FolderItem. The zero volume is always the boot volume.

So, for example, to obtain a FolderItem pointing to the boot volume, you can say:

```
dim f as folderItem
f = volume(0)
```

If you know a volume's name already, then you might think that this would be a reasonable use of GetFolderItem. For example, to refer to my disk *Second*, I ought to be able to say:

```
dim f as folderItem
f = getFolderItem("second") // there's a bug in this line!
```

However, this is to be discouraged. In the first place, it's all too easy to make a mistake. I've made one in this code: can you spot it? I haven't obtained a reference to my disk *Second* at all; I've obtained a reference to a file or folder named *Second*, which may or may not exist, in the same folder as my application (or project). The way to avoid this pitfall is to use a colon:

```
f = getFolderItem("second:")
```

But at this point we are relying rather dangerously upon trivia of punctuation. I prefer the following approach:

```
dim f as folderitem, i as integer
for i = volumecount - 1 downto 0
    if volume(i).name = "second" then
        f = volume(i)
        exit
    end
next
```

After that, either f is nil or it points to the disk in question.

Special Folders

On the Macintosh, some folders have a special system status. You can obtain a FolderItem pointing to certain of these folders.

The following read-only global properties return FolderItems pointing to special folders: SystemFolder, DesktopFolder, TrashFolder, AppleMenuFolder, ControlPanelsFolder, ExtensionsFolder, FontsFolder, StartupItemsFolder, ShutdownItemsFolder, ApplicationSupportFolder, PreferencesFolder, and TemporaryFolder. The system actually provides access to about 60 more special folders, but REALbasic unfortunately has no built-in properties that return pointers to them.

A FolderItem instance also has four read-only properties that return FolderItems pointing to special folders on the same disk as itself: DesktopFolder, TrashFolder, SharedTrashFolder, and TemporaryFolder.

So, for example:

```
dim f, ff as folderitem
f = desktopfolder // the boot disk's desktop folder
ff = volume(1).desktopfolder // the second disk's desktop folder
```

I'm not going to delve into the uses of the various special folders, but two deserve special attention.

PreferencesFolder can be important, since if your application needs to store ancillary information where it can be retrieved the next time the application runs, you will probably want to maintain a Preferences file, and the Preferences folder is the place for it.

TemporaryFolder can also be of great value. It points to an invisible folder where your application can create a "scratch" file without the user seeing it. Your application should delete such a file before quitting. A further special function, GetTemporaryFolderItem, may be used to obtain a reference to such a scratch file, so that you don't even have to make up a name for it: you just call GetTemporaryFolderItem, use the resulting FolderItem until you're done with it, and then send it the Delete message.

Not all the special folders have Windows equivalents, but some do, as shown in Table 21-1.

Table 21-1. Mac OS folders and their Windows equivalents

Mac OS	Windows
SystemFolder	System directory, e.g., C:\WINNT\System32
ExtensionsFolder	Same as SystemFolder
PreferencesFolder	Same as SystemFolder
FontsFolder	Fonts directory
DesktopFolder	The user's Desktop directory
StartupItemsFolder	Startup directory in the user's Start Menu
AppleMenuFolder	Programs directory in the user's Start Menu
TemporaryItemsFolder	The user's Temp folder
ApplicationSupportFolder	Windows directory, e.g., C:\WINNT

On Mac OS X, the AppleMenuFolder, ControlPanelsFolder, ExtensionsFolder, StartupItemsFolder, and ShutdownItemsFolder don't correspond to anything. The desktop, trash, and preferences folders refer to the user's desktop, trash, and preferences.

User Dialogs

Another way to obtain a FolderItem is to let the user choose a file or folder, by way of a dialog. REALbasic provides three such dialogs, each of which appears in response to a function call. These are Open and Save dialogs, but they don't actually open or save any files! That's up to your code, after you've called one of the functions. The functions are:

GetOpenFolderItem
Puts up a File Open dialog. Requires one parameter, a string denoting a semicolon-delimited list of file types (see "File Types," later in this chapter). REALbasic ignores the creator part of these file types and considers only their type part; these will be the only types of file the user will be able to choose. The FolderItem returned points to the file chosen by the user; if the user cancels the dialog, nil is returned.

SelectFolder
Puts up a Folder dialog in which the user can browse folders and choose one. The FolderItem returned points to the folder chosen by the user; if the user cancels the dialog, nil is returned.

GetSaveFolderItem
Puts up a File Save dialog. Requires two parameters. The first parameter is a string denoting a semicolon-delimited list of file types (see "File Types," later in this chapter) to appear in the dialog on Windows; for a Macintosh-only application, you can supply the empty string. The second parameter is a string representing the text to appear in the filename field (pass the empty string for an empty field). If the user specifies a filename that already exists in the given folder, the usual negotiation about replacing an existing file takes place automatically. The FolderItem returned points to the file specified by the user, which may or may not exist; if the user cancels the dialog, nil is returned.

It's important to check whether the resulting FolderItem is nil. This tells you that the user cancelled, which might affect how your code should proceed. Also, if you try to send a message to a nil FolderItem, you'll raise an exception. For example, the following code puts up a Save dialog with the name MyFile entered in the filename field, and aborts if the user cancels:

```
dim f as folderItem
f = getSaveFolderItem("","MyFile")
if f = nil then
    return // user cancelled
end
// if we reach this point, f is a valid non-nil FolderItem
```

These dialogs are peculiarly intractable (and I'm told that, after years of complaints, there are plans to replace them in REALbasic 3.5). You cannot add a custom prompt, so the user may not understand what to do; even worse, you cannot specify the *working folder*, that is, the folder to which the dialog will be pointing when it first appears. Where possible, therefore (meaning on Mac OS Classic), I suggest an XCMD to put up file dialogs: a very good one is Frédéric Rinaldi's FullSFPack.[*] FullSFPack uses resources, so to import it into your project, use ResEdit to copy the FSFPGetVol and FSFPGetDir 'DLOG' resources, and the FSFPGetVolDir 'DITL' resource, from the stack into a Resource file. You can copy other resources if you like; these instructions are just what's necessary to obtain an Open dialog, a Choose Folder dialog, and a Save dialog. Import both the stack and the Resource file into your project. Now just follow the instructions in the stack as to the calling syntax; the result is a pathname string you can hand to GetFolderItem. For example, to put up an Open dialog that points initially at a folder called *Power:Applications:* and whose prompt is "Pick a file:", you would say:

```
dim f as folderItem
dim s as string
s = fullsfpack("Get","Power:Applications:", "Pick a file:")
if s <> "" then // user didn't cancel
    f = getFolderItem(s)
end
```

Relative FolderItems

Given a FolderItem instance pointing to an item on disk, you can obtain a second FolderItem instance representing a second item relative to the first by sending the instance the following messages:

Parent
> Returns a FolderItem pointing to the item's containing folder. The Parent of a FolderItem pointing to a volume is nil. For example, if f points at "Power: Applications:", then:
>
>   f = f.parent // f points at "Power:"

Child, TrueChild
> Takes one parameter, a string denoting a filename. If the original FolderItem points to an existing folder, returns a FolderItem pointing to a file within it whose name is the parameter. The difference between them is that if the parameter is the name of an existing alias, Child returns a FolderItem pointing to the original. For example, if f points at "Power:Applications:", then:
>
>   f = f.truechild("SimpleText") // f points at "Power:Applications:SimpleText"
>
> The Child or TrueChild of a valid FolderItem pointing to a file or to a nonexistent item is nil.

---

[*] See *http://perso.wanadoo.fr/frederic.rinaldi/*. If you want dialogs that are Navigation Manager–aware, you could use his FullNavigation stack instead.

Item, TrueItem, Count

Item or TrueItem takes one parameter, an index number. If the original Folder-Item points to an existing folder, then for each different valid index number, the returned FolderItem points to a different item within that folder. I do not know by what criterion items are assigned index numbers—it doesn't really matter. The largest valid index is given by Count, and there is no zero Item: in other words, *Item's index is one-based!* The difference between Item and TrueItem is that if the index number designates an alias, Item returns a FolderItem pointing to the original.

The Count property of a valid FolderItem not pointing to an existing folder is 0. Supplying too large an index to Item or TrueItem yields nil. Supplying too small an index, meaning 0 or less, does *not* yield nil (I regard this as a bug); it yields either a runtime error or a terrible entity that I call a Bad FolderItem, and should be avoided.

Relative FolderItems—not pathnames—are the correct way to navigate the hierarchy of folders and files. For example, to point to the file "Power:Applications:SimpleText", first point f at the volume *Power* as explained already (in the section "Volumes"), and then navigate down the hierarchy:

```
f = f.truechild("Applications").truechild("SimpleText")
```

Just the other way, given a FolderItem f, to obtain a reference to the volume it's on, cycle up the hierarchy:

```
while f.parent <> nil
    f = f.parent
wend
```

Similarly, given a FolderItem f, to talk about a file named *Data* in the same folder, you would speak of f.parent.truechild("Data").

As you're navigating the files in a folder, be aware that some files may be invisible. For example, most folders contain an invisible Icon file; and of course Mac OS X is positively loaded with invisible files. Such files are included in Count and can be referred to with Item. (If you're *trying* to refer to an Icon file, it might be helpful to know that its name is actually "Icon"+chr(13).)

File Types

As part of the Macintosh Finder interface, a file is typologically identified by two four-letter codes: its *type* and its *creator*. The creator code corresponds to the unique creator code of an application; the type code is a document type identifier. Generally speaking, this pair of codes expresses an "ownership" relation: this application "owns" this type of document. However, certain file types, such as 'TEXT' and 'PICT', represent standard public formats that any application can read and write, and others, such as 'pref' (a Preferences file), have no standard format, but identify the file's purpose.

REALbasic operates with file types in two very different ways:

- REALbasic can get or set the type and creator codes of a file pointed to by a FolderItem by means of the FolderItem's MacType and MacCreator properties.
- A REALbasic project can have associated with it certain special named file types; this association is established by way of the File Types dialog that appears when you choose Edit → File Types.

Your project *must* have at least one named file type listed in the File Types dialog if you want your application to be able to put up an Open file dialog with GetOpen-FolderItem, to be able to open files that are double-clicked in the Finder or dragged and dropped onto your application's icon or into one of its windows, or to be able to create documents uniquely associated with itself.

The File Types dialog is shown in Figure 21-1. When you click the Add button, a fur-

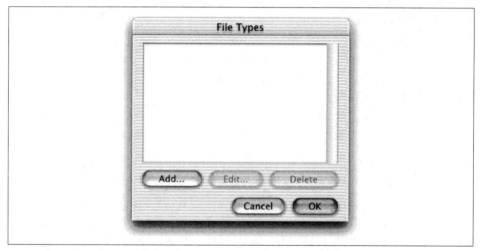

Figure 21-1. The File Types dialog

ther dialog window appears in which you can enter a name, a creator code, and a type code. On Windows, the creator code and type code (and the MacCreator and MacType) are meaningless; Windows uses the extension at the end of a file's name to identify its type, so instead, you can enter a semicolon-delimited list of extensions. The name you give a file type is completely up to you, and on Macintosh it has no meaning outside of your project; but on Windows the user may actually be able to see it (in the Open and Save dialogs, for example). The special code '????' is not actually a type or creator code, but a "wildcard" that matches any type or creator code. In Figure 21-2, I'm creating a named file type, AnyFile, that matches any file's type and creator.

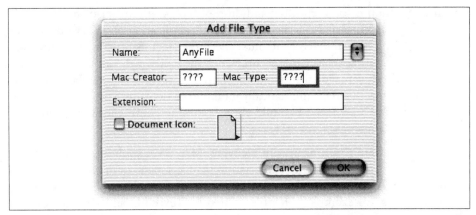

Figure 21-2. Editing a file type

The type/creator pair are ordered backward in this dialog! The standard Macintosh convention lists them in the order type/creator; but the dialog shows creator first, then type. I, however, *do* use the standard Macintosh convention; so, for example, I will say "TEXT/ttxt" to mean creator 'ttxt', type 'TEXT' (a SimpleText file).

At the right of the Name field in the File Types dialog is a popup menu from which you can choose a standard MIME file type. The list is mostly drawn from your system; on Mac OS 9, for example, it comes from the Internet control panel. It also includes special/folder, special/disk, and special/any, for referring to folders, disks, and any file, respectively.

Once you have a file type defined in your project, you refer to it in your project's code *by its name*. For example, the GetOpenFolderItem function requires a parameter that is a string consisting of a semicolon-delimited list of file type names; these are the types of files that can be chosen in the Open File dialog. Beginners often get this wrong, so let me say it again. REALbasic has no provision for referring to type/creator in a single string; the items in the GetOpenFolderItem parameter are not type/creator codes, but names as they have been defined in your project's File Types dialog. Thus, if you want to put up an Open File dialog in which the user can choose any file, you cannot simply say this:

```
f = getOpenFolderItem("????/????") // not an error, but useless
```

Well, you *can* say it, but it won't do any good: the user won't be able to choose any files. Rather, you must have a named file type defined for your project whose type code is '????' and whose creator code is '????', and you must supply GetOpenFolderItem with your declared name for that file type. So, after filling out the dialog as in Figure 21-2, I would be able to say:

```
f = getOpenFolderItem("AnyFile")
```

If your application is to accept drag-and-drop of files, you must also check the File Types dialog's Document Icon checkbox. If your application is to have document types that belong to it uniquely, you must check the Document Icon checkbox, and you will presumably also paste in an icon, which the Finder will automatically assign to any file of the designated creator and type once you've built your application. (The Finder usually gets the idea automatically a minute or two after you build the application; if not, you may have to rebuild your desktop to get this to work.) On drag-and-drop, see Chapter 24.

On Mac OS X, there's a problem with file types. Mac OS X applications often create files with no file type; they use an extension to the file's name to mark its type, as on Windows. But REALbasic doesn't sense a file's extension on Mac OS X, as it does in Windows. Thus, for example, a textfile created by TextEdit can't be included in a REALbasic file type: the file doesn't have a 'TEXT' type code, and REALbasic ignores the *.txt* extension.

File Properties and File Actions

This section discusses how to learn things about files and how to do things to them, as items on disk. Treating a file as a repository of data is discussed in the subsequent sections of this chapter.

File Properties

The following are properties of a FolderItem that relate to the features of the item (file or folder) that it points to, in the context of the Finder interface:

Name
    A string. The name (not the pathname) of the item. If you try to give an item an illegal name (for example, it's too long or contains a colon), there is no error, but the name will not be assigned.

AbsolutePath
    A string. Read-only. The pathname of the item.

Exists
    A boolean. Read-only. Reports whether the item exists on disk.

Directory
    A boolean. Read-only. Reports whether the item is an existing folder.

Locked
    A boolean. Can be used to get or set a file's locked status. A locked file cannot be renamed or deleted, nor can its MacCreator, MacType, CreationDate, ModificationDate, or visibility be changed; an attempt to do so will be ignored. In theory, it cannot be written to either (but, as we shall see, REALbasic does not always correctly obey this rule).

Visible
A boolean. Can be used to get or a set a file or folder's visibility.

Alias
A boolean. Read-only. Reports whether the item is an existing alias file. A FolderItem generated with GetFolderItem, Child, or Item can never return true because aliases are resolved before the FolderItem is returned.

MacCreator, MacType
The item's creator code and type code. Meaningless on Windows. The codes used to describe a folder or disk are shown in the special/folder and special/disk file types. (No, you can't magically turn a file into a folder or a disk by assigning it these codes!)

Type
Read-only. A string reporting the name of the *first* type listed in the File Types dialog corresponding to the file's MacType (or, on Windows, its extension). Regardless of order, the type '????' is matched only if there is no other match. If there is no match at all, the empty string is returned.

CreationDate, ModificationDate
Date instances.

Length, ResourceForkLength
The length, in bytes, of the file's data fork and resource fork, respectively. Read-only. The sum of these values is the size of the file (though it will probably occupy more space on disk, because of the filesystem's rules about minimum block size).

As I've already said ("Relative FolderItems," earlier in this chapter), you must not misuse the AbsolutePath property by taking the string that it yields, modifying the string, and handing the modified string to GetFolderItem as a way of obtaining a different FolderItem. This is unnecessary and unreliable; you should probably use the AbsolutePath property only when debugging, or when you need to pass a pathname, unaltered, in some other context. The way to navigate the folder hierarchy is to use the Parent, Child and TrueChild, Count, and Item and TrueItem properties to obtain one FolderItem based on another. In fact, you don't really even need the Absolute-Path property to learn an item's pathname; you can derive it by cycling up the hierarchy:

```
s = f.name // a string variable
if f.directory then
    s = s + ":"
end
while f.parent <> nil
    f = f.parent
    s = f.name + ":" + s
wend // now s holds the pathname
```

File Actions

The following are FolderItem methods that manipulate the item that a FolderItem points to, in the context of the Finder interface and the folder hierarchy.

Delete
> If the item is an unlocked, nonbusy file or an empty folder, deletes it; ignored otherwise.

CopyFileTo
> Ignored if the item is a folder. Takes one parameter, a FolderItem. If the parameter points to a folder, the item is copied into that folder; if the parameter points to a file, the item is copied so the copy becomes that file. If an item exists at the pathname that the new copy would have, no copying is done.

MoveFileTo
> Takes one parameter, a FolderItem. If the parameter points to an existing folder, the item is copied into that folder. If the parameter points to a nonexistent item, the original item is copied so that the copy becomes that item. If the item is a folder and the parameter points into a different volume, no copying is done. If a file exists at the pathname that the new copy would have, no copying is done. If copying was done, the original item is then deleted.

CreateAsFolder
> If the item does not exist, creates it as a folder; ignored otherwise.

Launch
> Opens the file from the Finder; in the case of a folder, ignored. REALbasic does not wait for the launch to complete, nor does it provide any direct way to learn when the launch is complete.

Certain file actions, such as copying, creating, or deleting a file, may not register immediately, thus throwing off the results of subsequent interactions with the filesystem. I have not been able to work out a rule for when this happens, nor to determine the precise cause, but you can see the problem plainly enough from an example such as this:

```
dim b as binarystream
dim f as folderitem
f = desktopFolder.child("testingtesting")
f.createasfolder
b = f.child("one").createbinaryfile("text")
b.close
b = f.child("two").createbinaryfile("text")
b.close
b = f.child("three").createbinaryfile("text")
b.close
msgbox str(f.count) // 0
```

The three files have been created, but for some reason REALbasic has not yet heard about them, so the result of f.count is wrong. The workaround is to reassert the value of the FolderItem pointing to the folder; this causes REALbasic to update its information about the folder:[*]

```
f = desktopFolder.child("testingtesting") // reassert, force update
msgbox str(f.count) // 3
```

A different sort of problem is that you don't get any sort of result from these commands letting you know what happened; they can fail silently, leaving you none the wiser. The problem is particularly severe with CopyFileTo and MoveFileTo. I regard this situation as a bug.

Recursive Techniques

When manipulating items on disk, recursion often comes into play (see "Recursion" in Chapter 2). For example, you cannot delete a folder that contains items, so to delete a folder you must first delete its items. But what if one of those items is a folder? We are now repeating ourselves, which clearly suggests recursion:

```
Sub deleteAnything(f as folderItem)
    dim i as integer
    if not f.directory then
        f.delete
    else
        for i = f.count downto 1
            deleteAnything(f.trueitem(i))
        next
        f.delete
    end if
End Sub
```

By the same token, you cannot copy a folder, so instead you must create a new folder and then copy the items from the original folder. But what if one of those items is a folder? Recursion again! The following routine assumes that you begin with f1 pointing to a folder and f2 designating a nonexistent folder:

```
Sub copyAnything(f1 as folderItem, f2 as folderItem)
    dim i as integer
    if not f1.directory then
        f1.copyFileTo f2
    else
        f2.createAsFolder
        for i = f1.count downto 1
            copyAnything(f1.trueitem(i), f2.truechild(f1.trueitem(i).name))
        next
    end
End Sub
```

---

[*] I owe this workaround to Steve LoBasso.

Building upon this, we can construct a basic folder reconciliation technique: given two folders, f1 and f2, we copy to f2 anything in f1 that has no counterpart in f2 or is newer than its counterpart in f2:

```
Sub reconcile(f1 as folderItem, f2 as folderItem)
    dim fTarg, fSrc as folderitem
    dim i, d1, d2 as integer
    for i = f1.count downto 1
        fSrc = f1.trueitem(i)
        fTarg = f2.truechild(fSrc.name)
        if not fSrc.directory then
            if fTarg.exists then
                d1 = fSrc.modificationdate.totalseconds
                d2 = fTarg.modificationdate.totalseconds
                if d1 > d2 then
                    fTarg.delete
                end
            end
            fSrc.copyfileto fTarg // fails if we didn't delete counterpart
        else
            fTarg.createAsFolder // if it already exists, no harm done
            reconcile fSrc, fTarg
        end
    next
End Sub
```

Here's one more recursion example. Recall the hierarchical ListBox subclass developed in Chapter 14; it depended on a hierarchical List structure. By recursing into a folder, we can generate this List in such a way as to capture the folder's hierarchical structure of folders and files. This routine should be called initially with f pointing at the desired folder and L representing a new empty List:

```
Sub listAll(f as folderItem, L as List)
    dim i,u as integer
    L.addsub(f.name)
    if f.directory then
        u = f.count
        for i = 1 to u
            listAll(f.trueitem(i), L.subhead(L.countSubs))
        next
    end if
End Sub
```

AppleScript Techniques

The Finder is scriptable, and can do things to files and folders. So, consider driving the Finder rather than manipulating files and folders yourself (for more details, see Chapter 31). For example, an alternative to our recursive technique to delete any file or folder is to ask the Finder to do it. Create this AppleScript:

```
on run {s}
    tell application "Finder" to delete item s
end run
```

(On Mac OS X, I find this works better if you say alias instead of item.) Save the compiled script as *FinderDelete*, and import it into your project. Now, to delete a folder, you call FinderDelete, handing it that folder's pathname:

```
dim s as string
s = FinderDelete("Power:MyFolder")
```

Actually, this moves the folder to the Trash; your AppleScript can empty the trash too, if you like.

Similarly, to copy a folder, you can use this AppleScript:

```
on run {s1, s2}
    tell application "Finder" to copy item s1 to folder s2
end run
```

Save the compiled script as *FinderCopy*, and import it into your project. When you call FinderCopy, the first parameter will be the pathname of a file or folder; the second parameter will be the pathname of the folder into which you want to copy.

Aliases

You should always be conscious of whether you are asking aliases to be resolved or not. Having aliases resolved without your knowledge can be very dangerous! For example, in the DeleteAnything method just given, if Item were accidentally used instead of TrueItem, and if the folder being deleted contained an alias to another hard drive, that hard drive would be erased! To resolve an alias deliberately, on the other hand, just use one of the functions that automatically resolves aliases. So, for example, if f is an alias, here's how to get its original:*

```
if f.alias then
    f = f.parent.child(f.name)
end
```

 REALbasic provides no direct way to *make* an alias! You can work around this omission, but the lack of a native way to perform such an important operation, after all these years, is astounding.

Here's an example of how to make an alias by asking the Finder to make it for you. Start with an AppleScript, which we'll call MakeAlias:

```
on run {orig, loc, newName}
    tell application "Finder"
        make new alias at item loc to item orig with properties {name:newName}
    end tell
end run
```

On Mac OS X, I find that this works better:

```
on run {orig, newLoc, newName}
    tell application "Finder"
```

* This elegant formulation comes from Chad McQuinn.

```
        make new alias file at alias newLoc to alias orig
        set name of result to newName
    end tell
end run
```

To call this, we presume we have one FolderItem pointed at the original file, and another pointed at the nonexistent alias file:

```
dim forig, ftarg, ftargFold as folderitem
dim name,s as string
forig = // whatever
ftarg = // whatever
ftargFold = ftarg.parent
name = ftarg.name
s = makeAlias(forig.absolutePath, ftargFold.absolutePath, name)
```

Arbitrary Data: Binary Streams

The most flexible way to read from or write to a file's data fork is to represent the data fork as a *binary stream*. A binary stream gives you so-called *random access* to the file's data: you can read from or write to any point within the data, and you can access the data in chunks of various sizes, representing various basic datatypes, much as with a memoryblock.

Getting a BinaryStream Instance

To read from or write to a file's data fork as a binary stream, you need an instance of the BinaryStream class pointing to it. There are two FolderItem methods that obtain such an instance:

OpenAsBinaryFile
    You must supply one parameter, a boolean, stating whether you want read/write access (true) or just read access. A BinaryStream instance is returned. You might want mere read access if you know you won't be allowed to write to the file (for example, because it is locked, busy, or on a locked volume) or if you don't want to prevent another program (or another part of your application) from writing to the file.

CreateBinaryFile
    You supply one parameter, which must be a file type name listed in the File Types dialog. A BinaryStream instance is returned. If the FolderItem points to a nonexistent file, the file is created and assigned the corresponding type and creator. If the FolderItem points to an existing file, that file is automatically deleted first, unless it is of the designated file type, in which case its resource fork and data fork are zeroed out.

If either OpenAsBinaryFile or CreateBinaryFile is unable to open the file as instructed, the result will be nil (and if you fail to notice this, you'll get a

NilObjectException when you try to work with the BinaryStream instance). Typical reasons this might happen are:

- CreateBinaryFile received a file type name that wasn't defined in the File Types dialog.
- OpenAsBinaryFile tried to get write access to a busy or locked file.
- CreateBinaryFile tried to delete or zero out a busy or locked file.

Once you have a BinaryStream instance, you read to and write from the file by sending messages to the instance. When you are finished reading and writing data, you want to ensure that other programs, and other parts of your program, can open the file later on; so you want to close the file. To do this, you can send the BinaryStream instance the Close message, or the stream will be closed automatically when the BinaryStream instance is destroyed.

CreateBinaryFile does *not* return nil if the file is busy or locked and the file type parameter is the same as the file's actual type. Instead, it will zero out the file, and will happily permit you to write to it! This is a *major* bug. The workaround is to try OpenAsBinaryFile for write access first; if this fails, don't use CreateBinaryFile.

So, for example, here is a safe way to use CreateBinaryFile:

```
dim f as folderitem
dim b as binarystream
f = // whatever
if f.exists then
    b = f.openasbinaryfile(true)
    b.close // raise exception if failed, close if succeeded
end
b = f.createbinaryfile("text") // now we know this is safe
// ... do stuff here ...
b.close
exception
// ... clean up ...
```

Reading and Writing Data

A BinaryStream points, at all times, to some particular byte within the file's data fork. This is the first byte that will be read or written if the data is accessed at that moment. To learn or set what byte this is, you use the BinaryStream's Position property. The first byte is numbered 0. If you have just opened the file, the Position is 0. If you have just read or written data, the Position is the byte after the last byte read or written. There is also a Position after all existing bytes (since the byte indexing is 0-based, this Position value is the same as the size of the data fork); you can check whether the Position has this value by way of the BinaryStream's EOF property, a boolean. (EOF stands for end-of-file.)

If you write to a BinaryStream when its EOF is true, you append to the file. If you write to a BinaryStream when its EOF is false, you overwrite existing data; if you write more bytes than there are between the starting Position and the end of the file, you also increase the file's size. An attempt to set the Position beyond the end of the file, or to a negative number, will be ignored.

The length of a file's data fork can be accessed through a BinaryStream's Length property. Unlike a FolderItem's Length property, a BinaryStream's Length property can be set. Increasing a BinaryStream's Length appends bytes to the file; the value of those bytes is indeterminate. Decreasing a BinaryStream's Length truncates the file. Setting a BinaryStream's Length to 0 thus deletes a file's data fork while leaving its resource fork intact (and is REALbasic's *only* way to do so).

There are various BinaryStream methods for reading and writing data, depending upon the datatype:

Write, Read
> Write takes a string. Read takes an integer telling how many bytes to read, and returns a string; supplying too large a number reads to the end of the file.

WritePString, ReadPString
> Like Write and Read, but the data is maintained on disk as Pascal strings. WritePString takes a string. ReadPString takes no parameter, because the first byte it encounters will be a length byte telling it how much more data to read.

WriteByte, ReadByte; WriteShort, ReadShort; WriteLong, ReadLong
> Takes or returns an integer; reads or writes one, two, or four bytes respectively. If the file is too short to read the requested number of bytes, 0 is returned.

WriteSingle, ReadSingle; WriteDouble, ReadDouble
> Takes or returns a double; reads or writes four and eight bytes, respectively. If the file is too short to read the requested number of bytes, 0 is returned.

In this example, we delete the fourth character of a file's data (not the third character, because the Position index is zero-based). This shows how to take advantage of the fact that reading and writing can start at any position, and that the length of the file can be altered:

```
dim f as folderItem
dim b as binarystream
dim s as string
f = // whatever
b = f.openasbinaryfile(true)
b.position = 4
s = b.read(b.length) // too big, so this will read to end
b.position = 3
b.write s
b.length = b.length-1 // remove extra character at end
b.close
```

When dealing with numbers in cross-platform data files, you'll need the BinaryStream's LittleEndian property, which affects the order in which bytes are interpreted when reading and writing numbers. Macintosh numbers are "big-endian," meaning the high byte precedes the low byte; Windows numbers are "little-endian," meaning the low byte precedes the high byte (see page 188). You can read numeric data properly only with the same endianity with which it was written. Now, no matter what platform you're on, a BinaryStream's LittleEndian property is false by default; but this is not an issue if the data belongs solely to your program—your program stores the data and then reads it, and since it is consistent with itself, no problem arises. If, however, you want to read a Windows-type file written by some other program, or to write data in such a way that other Windows programs can read it, you'll need to set the BinaryStream's LittleEndian property to true. (Incidentally, the terms "big-endian" and "little-endian" are references to *Gulliver's Travels;* they are not politically incorrect, as some Yahoos have suggested.)

Saving and Restoring Preferences

A binary stream does not let you read delimited data; that's what a text stream is for, as explained in the next section. Rather, with a binary stream, you have to know in advance how many bytes you want to read; or you can read a Pascal string, because it says at the outset how many bytes it consists of; or you can read to the end of the file. In general, you'll regard a file's data as a binary stream when the data is *structured*, meaning that all the pieces of data occur in a known order, and either all the pieces are of known size and quantity or there are pieces that state the size and quantity of other pieces. The structure might, of course, be of your own devising. It could be very short and simple, or it could be quite extensive.

Here's an example. Imagine that your application has exactly one window, which is always open. The user is free to move the window and to resize it. When the application shuts down, you want to save the window's position and dimensions so that you can restore them the next time the application runs. We might store this information as four shorts: the window's Left, Top, Width, and Height. The following routine might be called in the window's CancelClose event handler to save the data into a Preferences file:

```
dim f as folderItem
dim b as binarystream
f = preferencesFolder.child("MyCoolApp Prefs")
b = f.createBinaryFile("MyPref") // type = 'pref', creator = app's signature
b.writeshort self.left
b.writeshort self.top
b.writeshort self.width
b.writeshort self.height
b.close
```

When the application starts up the next time, the window's Open event handler could call the following routine to restore the window's size and position:

```
dim f as folderitem
dim b as binarystream
f = preferencesFolder.child("MyCoolApp Prefs")
if f.exists then
```

```
    b = f.openAsBinaryFile(false)
    self.left = b.readshort
    self.top = b.readshort
    self.width = b.readshort
    self.height = b.readshort
    b.close
end
```

Now let's extend the example. In addition to the window's position and dimensions, we will save and restore the window's contents, which will be a series of strings displayed as a single-column ListBox. The format for this part of the data will be a byte saying how many strings there are, followed by that many Pascal strings. (This is essentially the same as the format of a 'STR#' resource, discussed later in the chapter.) So now the routine from the CancelClose event goes like this:

```
dim f as folderItem
dim i,u as integer
dim b as binarystream
f = preferencesFolder.child("MyCoolApp Prefs")
b = f.createBinaryFile("MyPref") // type = 'pref', creator = app's creator
b.writeshort self.left
b.writeshort self.top
b.writeshort self.width
b.writeshort self.height
b.writebyte listbox1.listcount
u = listbox1.listcount - 1
for i = 0 to u
    b.writePstring listbox1.list(i)
next
b.close
```

And the routine from the Open event handler goes like this:

```
dim f as folderitem
dim b as binarystream
dim i,u as integer
f = preferencesFolder.child("MyCoolApp Prefs")
if f.exists then
    b = f.openAsBinaryFile(false)
    self.left = b.readshort
    self.top = b.readshort
    self.width = b.readshort
    self.height = b.readshort
    u = b.readbyte
    for i = 1 to u
        listbox1.addrow b.readPstring
    next
    b.close
end
```

If you'd like to test the example, here's a small application to wrap it in. As Figure 21-3 shows, the window contains a ListBox, an EditField, and two Push-Buttons, captioned Insert and Delete.

The Insert button adds to the ListBox whatever is in the EditField; here is its Action event handler:

```
listbox1.insertrow(listbox1.listindex+1, editfield1.text)
```

The Delete button deletes the selected row from the ListBox:

```
if listbox1.listindex > -1 then
    listbox1.removerow listbox1.listindex
end
```

Figure 21-3. Saving and restoring window position and data

Though simple, this is a useful application! The user can create and modify a list; the list and the position and dimensions of the window are automatically saved to disk when the application quits, and are restored when it starts up.

Sequential Data: Text Streams

Instead of a binary stream, you can read from or write to a file's data fork by representing the data fork as a *text stream*. Don't be misled by the name: text streams operate on the data fork of *any* file—not just textfiles. A text stream is merely another way of accessing the data. The basic assumption here is that your data is *delimited*: the way you identify each piece of data is that it ends with a special character (usually a return character). Having no fixed length, and being identified only by their last character, the pieces can be found only by searching forward through the data until the delimiter is encountered; this is called *sequential access*.

Unlike a binary stream, a text stream is implemented in REALbasic by two different types of object, one for reading and one for writing.

Reading

To read from a file's data fork by way of a text stream, you need a TextInputStream instance pointing to the data fork, which can be obtained through only one FolderItem method:

OpenAsTextFile
> A TextInputStream instance is returned. Reading will begin at the start of the file.

To read all the data from the file, starting from the current pointer, send the TextInputStream the ReadAll message; a string is returned.

To read just the next piece of data, starting from the current pointer and continuing up to the next delimiter or the end of the file (whichever comes first), send the TextInputStream the ReadLine message; a string is returned. The delimiter will not be included in the resulting string, but the pointer will be moved past it, ready to read another piece of data. The delimiter will usually be a return character, but ReadLine also works correctly in the case of a Windows or Unix file, where the lines are delimited by return-plus-linefeed (CRLF) or linefeed, respectively.

To learn whether there is any more data to read, check the TextInputStream's EOF property. When you're finished with the TextInputStream, you can send it the Close message, to release the file; or the file will be closed when the TextInputStream instance is destroyed.

Typically, the way you'll use a TextInputStream is either to read the whole file at once or to cycle through the file reading a line at a time. So, for example, the following routine reads each line (paragraph) of a file's data into a row of a ListBox:

```
dim f as folderitem
dim t as textInputStream
f = // whatever
t = f.openAsTextFile
while not t.eof
    listbox1.addrow t.readline
wend
t.close
```

At first, it may appear that TextInputStreams are rather restrictive, since you can start reading only at the beginning of any existing data. But they are actually quite versatile, especially because it takes surprisingly little time for a TextInputStream to run through a file and reach a particular piece of data.

Parsing a Mailbox File

As an example, we will use a TextInputStream to parse and display a simple database. So as not to have to create the database, we'll use an existing Eudora mailbox file. For simplicity's sake, our application will worry about only the From field and the text of the mail message. The application is shown in Figure 21-4; a ListBox displays all the From fields in the mailbox, and when the user double-clicks on a row of the ListBox, the corresponding mail message text appears in the EditField.

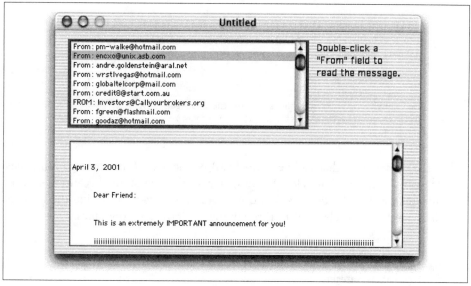

Figure 21-4. Parsing a database with text streams

A Eudora mailbox is a sequential textfile. Every record begins with a line that starts with this phrase:

```
From ???@???
```

The From field is the first line of the record that begins with this phrase:

```
From:
```

The text of the message is preceded by two return characters in a row, and ends when the next record begins or at the end of the file.

To parse the mailbox initially, our application runs through it sequentially, looking for records. Each time it finds a record, it moves forward to the From field and adds this field as a new row to the ListBox; then it moves forward to the start of the message text, and stores, in a hidden cell of the same ListBox row, the number of lines that have been read so far, so that the message text can be retrieved quickly later on:

```
dim f as folderitem
dim t as textInputStream
dim s, ss as string
dim count as integer
f = // whatever
t = f.openastextfile
do
    do
        s = t.readline
        count = count + 1
```

```
    loop until instr(s,"From ???@???") = 1 or t.eof // new record or done
    if t.eof then
        exit // done!
    end
    do
        s = t.readline
        count = count + 1
    loop until instr(s, "From: ") = 1 // got the From field
    listbox1.addrow s
    do
        s = t.readline
        count = count + 1
    loop until s = "" // got the start of the message
    listbox1.cell(listbox1.lastIndex,1) = str(count)
loop until false
t.close
```

When the user double-clicks a line of the ListBox, the text of the corresponding message is loaded into the EditField. We know where the text starts, because we stored this information in a hidden ListBox cell; therefore, to start retrieving the message text, we have only to cycle forward through the mailbox, counting lines:

```
dim f as folderitem
dim t as textinputstream
dim s,ss as string
dim i, count as integer
count = val(listbox1.cell(listbox1.listindex,1)) + 1 // skip blank line
f = // whatever
t = f.openastextfile
for i = 1 to count
    ss = t.readline // cycle forward
next
do
    s = s + ss + chr(13)
    ss = t.readline // acquire lines
loop until instr(ss,"From ???@???") = 1 or t.eof
t.close
editfield1.text = s
```

The significant thing is that retrieval of the message text is quite rapid: the user double-clicks a line, and the message text just appears. If we really needed even faster access, of course, we could parse the data into some other type of structured storage. But the point is that our application is able to work with a common file type, a Eudora mailbox, *directly*, and with a minimum of fuss on our part; and it interfaces with the data remarkably quickly, especially considering that this data is so crudely structured and lives on disk.

Writing

To write to a file's data fork by way of a text stream, you need a TextOutputStream instance pointing to the data fork. There are two FolderItem methods that obtain one:

CreateTextFile

A TextOutputStream instance is returned. If the FolderItem points to a nonexistent file, the file is created; it is assigned the type and creator of your project's defined Text file type (if there is one). If the FolderItem points to an existing file, that file is automatically deleted first, unless it is of your project's defined Text file type, in which case its resource fork and data fork are zeroed out.

AppendToTextFile

A TextOutputStream instance is returned. Writing will begin at the end of the data fork.

To write data using a TextOutputStream, send it the Write message to write a given string, or the WriteLine message to write the given string plus the delimiter. The delimiter is usually the return character; you can change it by way of the TextOutputStream's Delimiter property (but remember, you have no control over a TextInputStream's delimiter). You can send the TextOutputStream the Close message when you're done with it, or the file will be closed automatically when the TextOutputStream instance is destroyed.

CreateTextFile and AppendToTextFile do *not* necessarily return nil if the file is busy or locked. Instead, they may zero out the file, and will then happily permit you to write to it! This is a *major* bug—essentially the same bug noted on page 493, and with the same workaround: try OpenAsBinaryFile for write access first, and if it fails, don't use CreateTextFile or AppendToTextFile.

So, for example, here is a safe way to use CreateTextFile:

```
dim f as folderitem
dim o as textoutputstream
dim b as binarystream
f = // whatever
if f.exists then
    b = f.openasbinaryfile(true)
    b.close // raise exception if failed, close if succeeded
end
o = f.createtextfile // now we know this is safe
// ... do stuff here ...
o.close
exception
    // ... clean up ...
```

TextOutputStreams may seem restrictive, because we can begin writing only at the end of any existing data. But it is not difficult to work around this limitation, as we shall see.

Find-and-Replace

Let's say we have a textfile, and we want to eliminate from it every line (paragraph) containing the word "banner." This means we must modify the file in the middle—something which, at first blush, might seem difficult with a TextOutputStream. But it isn't actually hard at all. If the file is not excessively long, we can just read the entire file, line by line, into a string, eliminating every line containing "banner" as we go along; then we can write the entire string back out:

```
dim f as folderitem
dim t as textInputStream
dim o as textOutputStream
dim s, ss as string
f = // whatever
t = f.openAsTextFile
while not t.eof
    ss = t.readline
    if instr(lowercase(ss),"banner") = 0 then
        s = s + ss + chr(13)
    end
wend
t.close
o = f.createTextFile()
o.write(s)
o.close
```

If the file were very long, we might fear that its contents could not be held in memory as a single string. In that case, we could use a scratch file. The idea is to read from the original and write to the scratch file; this reduces the size of the intermediary string to a single paragraph at a time. When the copying process is over, we then substitute the scratch file for the original. If that's what we're going to do, we should avoid CreateTextFile. We want the scratch file to be just like the original, except for the altered data. But if we open the scratch file with CreateTextFile, we delete its resource fork if it has one, and if the Text file type is different from that of the original file, we will also be changing the file's type and resetting its creation date! We can solve these problems by rejecting the use of CreateTextFile altogether. Instead, we start with a scratch file that duplicates the original, thus maintaining its resource fork and creation date; we then open the scratch file as a binary stream and set the stream's length to zero, which leaves the resource fork intact. Then we append to the data fork (which is now empty) with AppendToTextFile, whose behavior does not depend upon the file's type:

```
dim b as binarystream
dim f,f2 as folderitem
dim t as textInputStream
dim o as textOutputStream
dim ss as string
f = // whatever
f2 = temporaryFolder.child("scratch") // scratch file
f.copyfileto f2
t = f.openAsTextFile
b = f2.openAsBinaryFile(true)
b.length = 0
b.close
o = f2.appendToTextFile
while not t.eof
    ss = t.readline
```

```
    if instr(lowercase(ss),"banner") = 0 then
        o.writeLine(ss)
    end
wend
t.close
o.close
f.delete
f2.copyfileto f
f2.delete
```

Resources

A Macintosh file may store data in its resource fork instead of, or in addition to, its data fork; REALbasic can read and write such data. Additionally, a REALbasic application can read resources from the *resource chain*, a memory-based data structure that includes all of the resources in the application file itself, as well as a number of resources such as fonts and sounds belonging to the system. (Nothing in this section applies to Windows.)

Getting a ResourceFork

Resources are accessed by way of an instance of the ResourceFork class, so your first task will always be to obtain such an instance.

In the case of a file on disk, you have a choice of two FolderItem methods:

OpenResourceFork
  A ResourceFork instance is returned.

CreateResourceFork
  This takes one parameter, the name of a file type defined in the File Types dialog. A ResourceFork instance is returned. If the file does not exist, it is created, with the corresponding type and creator. If the file does exist, its file type is changed to match the file type parameter, and its existing resource fork, if there is one, is wiped out—but its data fork is left intact. (Contrast this with the behavior of CreateTextFile and CreateBinaryStream, which will always destroy the resource fork of an existing file, and will replace an existing file if it has the wrong file type.)

If either OpenResourceFork or CreateResourceFork is unable to open the file, the result will be nil (and if you fail to notice this, you'll get a NilObjectException when you try to work with the ResourceFork instance). Typical reasons why this might happen are:

- The file is busy or locked.
- OpenResourceFork was sent to a FolderItem whose file has no resource fork.
- CreateResourceFork was given a file type that wasn't defined in the File Types dialog.

When you are done with a file's resource fork, you may send the ResourceFork the Close message to close the file; or the file will be closed automatically when the ResourceFork instance is destroyed. Thus, a typical interaction will have the following shape:

```
dim f as folderItem
dim r as resourceFork
f = // whatever
r = f.openResourceFork
// do stuff with resources
r.close
```

Now let's talk about the resource chain. Remember, this is how you examine your own application's resources—though they are mingled in the resource chain with system resources. To read from the resource chain, simply refer to it as app.resourceFork; do not close the ResourceFork instance when finished. Thus:

```
dim r as resourceFork
r = app.resourceFork
// read resources
```

If you include custom resources in your application file, they will be loaded automatically into the resource chain, and your application can read them with app.resourceFork. Thus, custom resources provide a way to package material into your application file which your application can treat as data at runtime, but which the user does not see as separate. To include custom resources in your application, import a file of type 'rsrc' (i.e., a ResEdit file) into your project; this will be seen as a Resource file, meaning that all resources in that file will be incorporated into the built application, and will be available to your code by way of the resource chain. You should be careful about introducing resources of the same type and ID as REALbasic itself will create when it builds the application; you can do this, and your resources will override those that REALbasic would have introduced, but make very sure you know what you're doing in such a case. As a rule of thumb, stick to ID numbers above 15000 if you want to avoid trampling on REALbasic's resources. Your project can have as many Resource files as you like; this gives you a way to reuse resources in different projects without having to copy them from file to file. Also, you can override your own resources; for example, if your project has two Resource files, and if they both contain a resource of type 'yoho' and ID 15000, it is the resource in the second file that will be used.

Starting in Mac OS 9, a new mechanism for including data along with your application was introduced, called a *package*. With a package, what looks to the user like an application is actually a folder containing the application itself along with ancillary files. This has two great advantages. First, your data are files, not resources. Second, your application can write into its own package, essentially storing new information as part of itself. That's very useful, especially since REALbasic does not provide a mechanism whereby an application can write to its own resource fork.*

Here's a simple example. Consider a demo version of an application, which is to expire 30 days after the user first tries it out. One wants the application to be able to store the date when it was first run. A Preferences file won't serve, because the user could easily delete it, thus overcoming the protection system; and an invisible Preferences file isn't nice, because it leaves files lying around that the user doesn't know about. With a package, we store the information as a file inside the "application" itself.

To prepare a package, you should give it the following canonical shape. Start with a folder; let's call it MyApp. Inside this, make a folder named Contents. Inside Contents, make two folders, MacOS and Resources. Put your built application inside MacOS. When your application starts up, it looks for the secret date information inside Resources:

```
dim f as folderitem
f = getfolderItem("").parent.child("Resources").child("MyStuff")
if f.exists then
    // ... read the data ...
else
    // ...store the initial data ...
end
```

The last step is to transform MyApp from a folder to a package; there are a number of utilities available that can do this.† In theory, you should be able to do just the same sort of thing to make the Mac OS X version of a package, which is called a *bundle*; at present, however, I have not found an easy automatic way to do this, and though you can make a bundle by hand using developer tools, it's not for the faint-hearted.

Referring to Resources

Resources are referred to by their type, which is a four-letter string, and by their ID number, which is an integer; optionally, a resource may have a name as well as an ID number. It is this scheme that makes the notion of a resource fork so powerful; in essence, every file becomes a simple random-access data repository. (The emphasis here is on the word "simple"; access to resources becomes inefficient if there are many of them, and there is an absolute limit on how many there can be.)

---

* You may be able to get around this by using the Rinaldi XCMD TextRes (and KillRes). See the footnote on page 482.

† For example, see *http://www.pasoftware.com/products/tape/*.

Usually, you will know in advance the type and ID of the resource you want. In cases of ignorance, however, you can send messages to the ResourceFork to learn more about what resources it contains:

TypeCount
>Returns the number of different resource types in the resource fork.

ResourceType
>Takes one parameter, a zero-based index number; returns a resource type, as a string.

ResourceCount
>Takes one parameter, a string designating a resource type; returns the number of resources of that type.

ResourceID, ResourceName
>These take two parameters, a resource type and a zero-based index number; they return the ID or name, respectively, of the specified resource.

With these messages, you can loop through all the resource types in a resource fork and then through all the IDs (and names) within each resource type, thus supplying yourself with a map of an entire resource fork. For example, make a project consisting of a button and a three-column ListBox, and put this into the button's Action event handler:

```
dim aType as string
dim i, j, imax, jmax as integer
dim f as folderItem
dim r as resourceFork
r = app.resourcefork
imax = r.typeCount - 1
for i = 0 to imax
    aType = r.resourceType(i)
    jmax = r.resourceCount(aType) - 1
    for j = 0 to jmax
        listbox1.addrow aType
        listbox1.cell(listbox1.lastindex,1) = str(r.resourceID(atype, j))
        listbox1.cell(listbox1.lastindex,2) = r.resourcename(atype, j)
    next
next
```

Build the application (because you want to investigate your application, not REALbasic itself), run it, and push the button. You'll see a list of the resources in the resource chain—your application's, along with the system's.

Parsing Resources

The basic ResourceFork methods for operating on resources are these:

GetResource
>Given a type and an ID, returns the resource data as a string.

GetNamedResource
>Given a type and a name, returns the resource data as a string.

AddResource

Takes the data as a string, the type, the ID, and the name of the resource; writes the data as a resource. If the specified resource exists already, it is overwritten.

RemoveResource

Given a type and an ID, deletes the resource.

ResourceLocked, ResourcePreload, ResourceProtected, ResourcePurgeable, Resource-SysHeap

Booleans. Given a type and an ID, used to get or set the corresponding resource attribute. These attributes are critical and should not be altered unless you know exactly what you are doing. (You don't look to me as if you do.)

A resource will typically have some predefined format. Knowing this format, and parsing it, is up to you. (Of course, if you've made up the format yourself, that should be no problem.) For example, consider a resource of type 'STR '. This consists of a Pascal string, possibly followed by further material, which we will ignore. The following routine obtains from a file's resource fork the 'STR ' with ID 128, and converts it to a REALbasic string:

```
dim f as folderItem
dim s as string
f = // whatever
s = f.openResourceFork.getResource("STR ", 128)
s = mid(s, 2, asc(left(s,1)))
```

Sometimes, a memoryblock can help parse the material. Consider how we might parse a 'STR#', which consists of two bytes stating the number of strings, followed by that many Pascal strings. A memoryblock makes it easy to find and gather the Pascal strings, which can then be saved, for instance, as REALbasic strings in an array:

```
dim f as folderItem
dim i,j,idx as integer
dim s as string
dim m as memoryBlock
dim strArray(0) as string
f = // whatever
s = f.openResourceFork.getResource("STR#", 128)
m = newMemoryBlock(len(s)+1)
m.cString(0) = s
j = m.short(0)
redim strArray(j)
idx = 2
for i = 1 to j
    strArray(i) = m.pString(idx)
    idx = idx + m.byte(idx) + 1
next
```

Just the other way, you can build an array of strings into a 'STR#' resource:

```
dim s as string
dim u, i, totalLength as integer
dim m as memoryBlock
dim f as folderitem
```

```
dim r as resourcefork
// assume strArray() holds the strings, starting at index 1
u = ubound(strArray)
for i = 1 to u // make Pascal strings
    s = s + chr(len(strArray(i))) + strArray(i)
next
m = newMemoryBlock(2)
m.short(0) = u
s = chr(m.byte(0)) + chr(m.byte(1)) + s // number of strings
f = // whatever
r = f.openResourceFork
r.addresource(s, "STR#", 128, "")
r.close
```

Here's a different sort of example—a trick for storing a file's data inside your application as a resource. This is useful if your application needs some file to be present, but you don't want the user to be conscious of it (and you can't use a package or don't wish to). Let's take the example of an animated GIF. REALbasic can display an animated GIF by way of a MoviePlayer control in a window (Chapter 27), but the GIF must exist as a separate file, not a resource. The reason is that only the OpenAs-Movie method of a FolderItem can import the GIF while maintaining both its animation and it transparency; if we convert the GIF into a movie beforehand, we lose the transparency, and if we import the GIF as a picture, we lose the animation. Therefore, we will store the data from the GIF file as a resource inside the application, and then, when the application starts up, we'll create it as a file and open that file.

The first problem is to copy the data from the GIF file into a Resource file as a resource. We can actually write a little REALbasic utility to help us with this. Let's call the data, in its resource form, a 'mymo' resource (for "my movie"). The following project prompts us for the GIF, then prompts us for the Resource file, then reads the GIF's data into the Resource file as a 'mymo' resource whose ID is the lowest available integer above 14999 (in case we need to do this for several GIFs). We have previously defined a file type Any as "????/????":

```
dim f1, f2 as folderItem
dim b as binaryStream
dim r as resourcefork
dim i as integer
f1 = getopenfolderitem("any") // the movie file
if f1 = nil then
    return
end
f2 = getopenfolderitem("any") // the Resource file
if f2 = nil then
    return
end
b = f1.openasbinaryfile(false)
r = f2.openresourcefork
r.addresource(b.read(f1.length),"mymo",15000+r.resourcecount("mymo"), f1.name)
b.close
r.close
```

We now import the Resource file into our project, so that its resources are incorporated into the application when it is built. When the application starts up, it re-creates the original GIF files, placing them in the Temporary Items folder where the user will never see them. Our project includes a file type Image/GIF:

```
dim i,n as integer
dim f as folderItem
dim b as binaryStream
for i = app.resourcefork.resourcecount("mymo")-1 downto 0
    f = temporaryfolder.child(app.resourcefork.resourcename("mymo",i))
    b = f.createbinaryfile("image/gif")
    n = app.resourcefork.resourceid("mymo",i)
    b.write app.resourcefork.getresource("mymo", n)
    b.close
next
```

Now the application can open the GIF files from the Temporary Items folder and delete them later; the user will never know they existed.

Predefined Data Formats

So far in this chapter, all writing and reading of data has basically been at the level of individual bytes. You can read and write these bytes as numbers and strings, but interpreting them is ultimately up to you. However, there are some types of data where mere bytes won't do you any good. Therefore, REALbasic also stands ready to translate between a few standard data formats and its own datatypes.

Sounds

A type 1 System 7 sound is a 'snd ' resource. To obtain such a resource as a REALbasic Sound object that REALbasic can play, send a ResourceFork the GetSound message, handing it the resource's ID as a parameter.

If the resource lives in a System 7 sound file (of type "sfil/movr"), you can save a step; send a FolderItem the OpenAsSound message.

Unfortunately, the GetSound message assumes that you know the 'snd ' resource's ID number. Often, this is just what you *don't* know; you know its name instead. In such a case, you'll have to cycle through all the 'snd ' resources, looking for the one with the right name, in order to obtain its ID number. It's easy to see how to do this by adapting the code from the end of "Referring to Resources," earlier in this chapter.

See Chapter 26 for more about sounds.

Pictures

To obtain a 'PICT' resource as a REALbasic Picture object, send a ResourceFork the GetPicture message, supplying the resource's ID, or the GetNamedPicture message, supplying the resource's name.

To obtain an icon resource as a REALbasic Picture object, send a ResourceFork the GetCicn message, supplying the 'cicn' resource's ID, or the GetIcL or GetIcS message, supplying the ID of a large-icon or small-icon family of resources (such as 'icl8' and 'ics8' resources).

To obtain a file's data fork as a REALbasic Picture object, send a FolderItem the OpenAsPicture message. The data can be a PICT file (a BMP file on Windows), or, if QuickTime is present, it can be any type of image data that QuickTime knows how to convert, such as GIF or JPEG. You can also save a Picture object as a PICT file, by sending a FolderItem the SaveAsPicture message, or as a JPEG file, by sending a FolderItem the SaveAsJPEG message. I believe that a PICT file will have SimpleText as its creator, and that a JPEG file will have PictureViewer as its creator, and that you cannot alter this; of course, you can change the creator afterward. If a file of the same name exists, and it is not of the same type, it will be deleted; so be careful.

To let the user choose a folder and format in which to save a Picture object as a file, call the ExportPicture function, which takes a Picture. It puts up a Save File dialog in which the user can choose any file format supported by QuickTime. A boolean is returned, reporting whether the user saved the file. Unfortunately, there is no way to learn where.

A more sophisticated way to save a Picture as a file is by means of a QTGraphicsExporter instance. This works only under QuickTime 4 or later. Start by calling GetQT-GraphicsExporter, specifying a file format; a QTGraphicsExporter instance is returned. Now you can manipulate that instance if you like, and save the Picture by sending the instance the SavePicture message. Unfortunately, you can't manipulate the instance very much; things are best for a JPEG, for which you can specify such features as the compression quality and the target file size, but with other formats you don't get any control. However, you can put up a dialog that gives the user control over settings. So, for example, here's how to save a Picture instance as a TIFF, giving the user a dialog in which to enter settings:

```
dim e as qtgraphicsExporter
dim b as boolean
dim p as picture
dim f as folderitem
f = getsavefolderitem("", "MyPicture.tiff")
if f = nil then // user cancelled
    return
end
p = // whatever
e = getQTGraphicsExporter("TIFF")
b = e.requestSettings
if not b then // user cancelled
    return
end
b = e.savePicture(f,p)
```

See Chapter 11 for more about Pictures; see the online help for more about the QTGraphicsExporter. (A QTGraphicsExporter won't let you save as a GIF; see "Shared Libraries" in Chapter 32 for one solution.)

Movies

To obtain a file's data as a REALbasic Movie or EditableMovie object, send a FolderItem the OpenAsMovie or OpenAsEditableMovie message.

To obtain a 'moov' resource as a REALbasic Movie object, send a FolderItem (not a ResourceFork!) the OpenResourceMovie message, supplying the ID of the resource.

See Chapter 27 for more about movies.

Styled Text

With styled text, you don't really need REALbasic to perform any transformations for you. In a file, the text part of styled text is kept in the data fork, and the style information is kept in a 'styl' resource with ID 128; both of these can be exchanged with a styled EditField simply by using strings. So, for example, to save a styled EditField as a SimpleText file (where the StyledText file type is defined in your project as "TEXT/ttxt"), you could say this:

```
dim f as folderItem
dim b as binaryStream
dim r as resourceFork
f = // whatever
if f.exists then
    b = f.openasbinaryfile(true)
    b.length = 0
else
    b = f.createbinaryfile("styledText")
end
b.write editField1.text
b.close
if f.resourceForkLength = 0 then
    r = f.createResourceFork("styledText")
else
    r = f.openResourceFork
end if
r.addResource(editField1.textStyleData, "styl", 128, "")
r.close
```

Similarly, a styled text file can be read into an EditField by fetching its data fork and its 'styl' resource with ID 128 as strings, and sending the EditField the SetTextAndStyle message with the two strings (text and style) as parameters.

To save you some trouble, REALbasic provides two FolderItem methods for exchanging information between an EditField and a file:

OpenStyledEditField
> Takes one parameter, a reference to an EditField. Reads the FolderItem's `'styl'` resource ID 128 into the EditField's style data and its text data into the Edit-Field's text.[*]

SaveStyledEditField
> Takes one parameter, a reference to an EditField. Creates a new styled text file, with type and creator according to your project's Text file type, and saves the EditField's style data into its `'styl'` resource ID 128 and the EditField's text into its data fork.

Unfortunately, SaveStyledEditField always creates a completely new file; it cannot be used to update an existing file. For this reason, I regard it as fatally flawed.

References to Files

Not uncommonly, you will want to save (in a Preferences file, for example) a reference to a file on disk. The correct way to do this is by means of an `'alis'` resource— an alias. This marvelous device permits the system to keep track of the file referred to even if the file is moved (within the same volume) or if any of its containing folders is renamed.

Unfortunately, REALbasic makes no provision for letting you create an `'alis'` resource directly. This is basically the same problem referred to already: REALbasic doesn't help you make aliases (see "Aliases," earlier in this chapter). One solution is to use a plug-in. Here's a simple example of storing an alias as a resource inside a Preferences file, using Thomas Tempelmann's MacAliasRecord class plug-in:[†]

```
dim f, pref as folderitem
dim a as macAliasRecord
dim s as string
dim r as resourcefork
dim i as integer
f = // whatever
a = new macAliasRecord
i = a.create(nil,f)
s = a.getrecord
pref = preferencesfolder.child("MyCoolAppPrefs")
if pref.resourceForkLength = 0 then
    r = pref.createresourceFork("pref")
```

---

[*] This method is oddly named: what you are opening is a file, not a field. Perhaps OpenAsStyledText would have been better.

[†] See *http://www.tempel.org/rb/*.

```
else
    r = pref.openresourcefork
end
r.addresource(s, "alis", 1000, "")
```

And here, reversing the process, we retrieve the alias from the Preferences file and resolve it:

```
dim f, pref as folderitem
dim a as macAliasRecord
dim s as string
dim r as resourcefork
pref = preferencesfolder.child("MyCoolAppPrefs")
r = pref.openresourcefork
s = r.getresource("alis", 1000)
a = new macAliasRecord
a.setrecord s
f = a.resolve(nil,0)
```

CHAPTER 22

Databases

In this chapter:
- Database Files and Classes
- Schemas
- Displaying Data
- Other Data Sources

The techniques described in Chapter 21 for storing and retrieving data kept in files on disk are fine for most purposes, but sometimes your data calls for the sort of structured storage and flexible access that only a database can achieve.

To see why, you need to know what a database is. In its simplest form, a *database* is merely data kept in the form of a table—a grid of rows and columns, where the information throughout any given column is of a single datatype. A relational database consists of more than one table, and REALbasic databases can be relational; but even a single-table (*flat-file*) database can be very useful. In fact, even the simplest imaginable flat-file database—a two-column table—can be useful. Suppose your application uses a dictionary, a set of word–definition pairs. How will this information be stored as a file? How will you look up information in the file? How will you modify information in the file? These aren't difficult problems to solve, to be sure; but with a database, they are solved for you. In this example, one column consists of words, another consists of definitions; every row is a word–definition pair. End of problem! REALbasic gives you the facilities to add word–definition pairs to the file, to delete word–definition pairs, to see whether a particular word is listed, to look up the definition for a given word, and so forth.

Actually, REALbasic lets you work with databases in two ways. First, it provides a native database file type. Second, if your data is maintained through a SQL server, REALbasic may have the ability to act as a frontend (a *client*) to that server. This chapter uses the native database to discuss REALbasic's various database classes; at the end, there's a list of the other databases with which REALbasic can communicate. The fundamental techniques for working with a data source provided by a SQL server are just the same as those for working with a native database file; the chief differences have to do with how various SQL servers implement SQL itself. Since this matter is implementation-dependent, I can't tell you anything about it; if you're working with a SQL server, consult the documentation for that server. As for REALbasic's native database file, it implements only a small subset of SQL. The online documentation is very clear about what this subset is, and I'm not going to repeat that information here. I'm also not going to try to teach you any SQL! That would be outside the scope of this book.* I'll use a little SQL in my examples, but I'm not going to bother explaining how it works. Actually, as we'll see, it is possible to work with REALbasic's native database using very little SQL.

Database Files and Classes

Databases are manipulated in REALbasic through four classes. The Database class represents the database itself—a table or a collection of tables. The DatabaseRecord class represents one row of the database in the context where you're adding a row of data to a table. The DatabaseCursor and DatabaseCursorField classes are used to peruse and modify existing data.

Database Class

The database itself is represented by an instance of the Database class. In the case of a native database file, this instance corresponds to the file itself. You obtain such an instance in one of three ways:

NewREALdatabase
> Takes a FolderItem pointing to a file, which presumably will not exist; if it does exist, its data will be zeroed out, and you'll be starting fresh with an empty database (and possibly cursing loudly). Returns a Database instance.

OpenREALdatabase
> Takes a FolderItem pointing to an existing database file. Returns a Database instance. If you want the user to be able to choose the file, just use GetOpen-FolderItem; the file type is "Rdb2/RBv2".

Project component
> A database reference can be a component of your project, rather like a picture or a Resource file. You can import a reference to an existing database file by dragging the file from the Finder into the Project Window, or by choosing File → Add Data Source → Select REAL Database. You can also create both a database file and a reference, with File → Add Data Source → New REAL Database. The name of the database in the Project Window is the global name of a Database instance referring to the database file.

Note that, no matter which of the preceding methods you use, the database file remains a separate entity, even after your project is built into an application! It isn't incorporated into the built application. If your application uses a database file that has to exist in advance, the file must be distributed along with the application.

Now let's talk about how you would populate an empty database with tables. There are two ways. If you've imported a reference to the database as a project component,

---

* There's a good online tutorial at *http://www.willcam.com/sql/default.htm*, and there are plenty of SQL books.

double-click the project component, and lo and behold, a window appears where you can add tables. If you double-click a table listing in this window, you can define the table's columns—their names and what kind of data each column holds. (The column structure of a table is called its *schema*. This is a Greek word meaning, "Shhhhh! If anyone ever finds out that a database is just tables of rows and columns, we database experts will be completely out of a job.")

However, defining a database's structure using this editor is the sissy way; and I know none of my readers are sissies. You want to edit the database's structure by speaking SQL to the Database instance, don't you? I thought so. To do so, send the Database instance the SQLExecute message. This takes a string consisting of a SQL command; it does not have to end in a semicolon. In this case, it's going to be a create table command. Here, you'll name each new table; you'll also name its columns and dictate their datatypes. Look in the online reference under Database Class to see your choice of datatypes; which ones are actually supported will depend on what kind of database you're talking to. In the case of a native database file, your choices are: smallint, integer, float, and double; varchar (a string); date and time; and long varbinary (a "blob").

So, for example, let's make a new database file and construct a little table called people, whose columns are lastname, firstname, and age. We'll build the SQL command first, then send it to the database:

```
dim d as database
dim s as string
s = "create table people "
s = s + "(lastname varchar, "
s = s + "firstname varchar, "
s = s + "age smallint, "
s = s + "primary key (lastname))"
d = newrealDatabase(desktopFolder.child("testDB"))
d.sqlexecute s
if d.error then
    msgbox d.errormessage
end
```

It's probably a good idea to check for errors after sending a message to your database. The Database instance's Error property is a boolean indicating whether an error occurred; then you can use the Database instance's ErrorMessage property or its ErrorCode property to retrieve the error as a string or an integer, respectively.

For good measure, let's open the same database a second time and add a second table, called deeds, consisting of two fields, lastname and deed:

```
dim d as database
dim s as string
s = "create table deeds "
s = s + "(lastname varchar, "
s = s + "deed varchar)"
d = openrealDatabase(desktopFolder.child("testDB"))
```

```
d.sqlexecute s
if d.error then
    msgbox d.errormessage
end
```

In real life, if we were going to be working with a database for an extended period, we probably would not keep opening the database like this; we'd maintain a Database reference as a property. That's what I'll do throughout the rest of this chapter: I'll assume that instead of a local d, we've got a Database property d which we've initialized with OpenREALdatabase to point at our database file.

This raises the question of how a database file gets written to. This matter is actually more important when you're using REALbasic as a SQL client. Working with a database is not like working with an ordinary file, because the possibility exists that more than one client will be accessing the database simultaneously. The standard rule for ordinary files on disk is that only one program at a time can have a file open for write access, but with a database, that's too simpleminded—everyone needs write access simultaneously.

So, as soon as you start doing things to a database, those things are maintained in memory until you write them out to the database. To do so, you send the Database instance the Commit message, which writes out all the changes since the last Commit, or else you send it the Close message to indicate that you are completely done with it. If you don't explicitly Close the database, it is written out and closed when the Database instance is destroyed.

As an alternative to Commit, you can cancel all changes since the last Commit by sending the Database instance the Rollback command. This doesn't write anything out; it simply undoes the accumulated internal changes so that the next time you do write something out, those changes won't be among them.

DatabaseRecord Class

To add a row of data to a table, you use an instance of the DatabaseRecord class, which holds one entire row of data at a time. You enter data for every column of the row. Then you hand the DatabaseRecord instance to your Database instance, using the InsertRecord method, telling the Database what table this is to be a row of. The table must exist already.

To add data to a DatabaseRecord instance, the particular property you use depends upon the datatype of the value you want to add: your choices are Column (a string), IntegerColumn, DoubleColumn, DateColumn, and MacPictColumn and JPEGColumn (picture formats). You supply a parameter that is the name of the column, and assign the data for that column. If a column doesn't exist in the DatabaseRecord, it is created; if it does, its value is replaced. Thus, you can use the same instance for successive rows of the same table.

So, we'll add three rows of data to the people table:

```
dim r as databaserecord
dim s as string
r = new databaserecord
r.column("lastname") = "Mouse"
r.column("firstname") = "Mickey"
r.integercolumn("age") = 70
d.insertRecord "people",r
if d.error then
    msgbox d.errormessage
end
r.column("lastname") = "Shakespeare"
r.column("firstname") = "William"
r.integercolumn("age") = 400
d.insertRecord "people",r
if d.error then
    msgbox d.errormessage
end
r.column("lastname") = "Caesar"
r.column("firstname") = "Julius"
r.integercolumn("age") = 2000
d.insertRecord "people",r
if d.error then
    msgbox d.errormessage
end
```

This is rather a boring way to code; the situation calls for a loop. So, for the sake of variety, we'll create the rows of the deeds table using a semicolon-delimited and comma-delimited string:

```
dim r as databaserecord
dim s,ss,cols as string
dim i,j,imax,jmax as integer
s = "Mouse,Steamboat Willy;"
s = s + "Shakespeare,Romeo and Juliet;"
s = s + "Shakespeare,The Taming of the Shrew;"
s = s + "Shakespeare,Richard III;"
s = s + "Caesar,Gallic War;"
s = s + "Caesar,Civil War"
cols = "lastname,deed"
r = new databaserecord
imax = countFields(s,";")
jmax = countFields(cols,",")
for i = 1 to imax
    ss = nthfield(s,";",i)
    for j = 1 to jmax
        r.column(nthField(cols,",",j)) = nthField(ss,",",j)
    next
    d.insertRecord "deeds",r
    if d.error then
        msgbox d.errormessage
    end
next
```

Another approach would be to skip the DatabaseRecord altogether and add records through the Database's SQLExecute method, using the insert command. For example:

```
dim s as string
s = "insert into people "
s = s + "(lastname, firstname, age) "
s = s + "values ('Neuburg', 'Matt', 46)"
d.sqlexecute s
s = "insert into deeds "
s = s + "(lastname, deed) "
s = s + "values ('Neuburg', 'Book about REALbasic')"
d.sqlexecute s
```

DatabaseCursor and DatabaseCursorField Classes

To access your data, send the Database instance a SQL query, using the SQLSelect method. The result is a table, but it is only virtual; you don't access the entire table at once. Instead, you get just one row of this table at a time. Such a row is called a *cursor*, and this cursor is represented by an instance of the DatabaseCursor class, which is what is returned from your call to SQLSelect.

Using the DatabaseCursor instance, you can extract information from, or change information in, the row of the virtual table you are currently looking at. You can move on to the next row by sending the DatabaseCursor the MoveNext message. You'll know when you've traversed every row because the DatabaseCursor's EOF property will be true. When you're finished with the DatabaseCursor, you can send it the Close message to dismiss the virtual table, or it will be closed automatically when the DatabaseCursor instance is destroyed.

When you exchange information with a DatabaseCursor instance, you refer to a particular *field* of the cursor, meaning a column of the row that it represents. The field is an instance of the DatabaseCursorField class. Thus, the actual communication of data from and to cells of the table takes place by means of messages to a Database-CursorField instance. You may not need an explicit reference to a DatabaseCursor-Field instance, though: you will typically just specify a field and get or set that field's data, in a single line of code.

To specify a field (column) of the DatabaseCursor instance by column name, use its Field method. To specify a field by index number, use its IdxField method. *The index is one-based!* The DatabaseCursor also has a FieldCount property that tells how many fields it contains.

Now you have a DatabaseCursorField instance representing one cell, the specified column of the current row. The name of the column is available through the Data-baseCursorField's Name property. The data of the cell is accessed as the Data-baseCursorField instance's StringValue, IntegerValue, DoubleValue, DateValue, MacPictValue, or JPEGValue, corresponding to the types of data you can insert as a column of a DatabaseRecord. The DatabaseCursorField also has a NativeValue which cannot be set, and is a string displaying the actual bytes stored in the database; thus, a NativeValue for any of our age entries would be two characters, because a smallint, like a short integer, is two bytes.

So, for example, let's start by making sure that our data got into the people table. We'll get a virtual table representing the entire people table, and then display the lastname value of each successive row:

```
dim c as databasecursor
c = d.sqlselect("select * from people")
while not c.eof
    msgbox c.field("lastname").stringvalue
    c.movenext
wend
c.close
```

To illustrate more fully, let's peruse all the data from the people table. Pretend we know nothing about the structure of this table. For each successive row, we'll loop through all the fields. For each field, we'll get both the column name and the cell data, and we'll display a row's worth of information at a time:

```
dim c as databasecursor
dim fld as databasecursorfield
dim i,u as integer
dim s as string
c = d.sqlselect("select * from people")
u = c.fieldcount
while not c.eof
    s = ""
    for i = 1 to u
        fld = c.idxfield(i)
        s = s + fld.name + ": " + fld.stringvalue + chr(13)
    next
    msgbox s
    c.movenext
wend
c.close
```

You might be surprised that we were able to extract the age value from each row as a StringValue, since it is in fact an integer. It is certainly true that, since we do happen to know that there is an age column and that it is an integer, we could have written the For loop as follows:

```
fld = c.idxfield(i)
s = s + fld.name + ": "
if fld.name = "age" then
    s = s + str(fld.integervalue) + chr(13)
else
    s = s + fld.stringvalue + chr(13)
end
```

But this was not necessary, because asking for an integer as a StringValue caused the coercion to take place as the value was handed to us.

If, on the other hand, we had asked for a Picture value as a StringValue, we would have received some less than useful data. With pictures, you have to be consistent: if you put the data in as a PICT, you must extract it as a PICT; if you put it in as a JPEG, you must extract it as a JPEG. The field doesn't know what it holds; it's up to you to know. To illustrate, suppose that when we created the people table we included a smallint field jpeg and a long varbinary field picture, and that when we populated the table with data and provided pictures of our people, we set jpeg to 1 if the picture is a JPEG, and 0 if it's a PICT:

```
// ...
r.integercolumn("jpeg") = 0
r.macPictColumn("picture") = mickey
// ... and so forth ...
```

Now, given a DatabaseCursor, we know how to extract the picture:

```
dim p as picture, c as databaseCursor, fld as databaseCursorField
// ...
fld = c.field("picture")
if c.field("jpeg").integervalue = 1 then
    p = fld.jpegValue
else
    p = fld.macPictValue
end
```

To change existing values, send the DatabaseCursor the Edit message, alter the values by way of the DatabaseCursorField, and send the DatabaseCursor the Update message to pass the changes on to the virtual table. Here, we'll double the ages of everyone in the people table:

```
dim c as databasecursor
dim fld as databasecursorfield
c = d.sqlselect("select * from people")
while not c.eof
    c.edit
    fld = c.field("age")
    fld.integervalue = fld.integervalue * 2
    c.update
    c.movenext
wend
c.close
```

Alternatively, you can alter data by using the update command in a SQLExecute message to the Database instance. For example, suppose we discover that the plays of William Shakespeare were actually written by Edward deVere. We can say:

```
dim s as string
s = "update deeds set lastname = 'deVere' where lastname = 'Shakespeare'"
d.sqlexecute s
s = "update people set lastname = 'deVere', firstname = 'Edward' where "
s = s + "lastname = 'Shakespeare'"
d.sqlexecute s
```

A DatabaseCursor is also the way to delete a row: to do so, you send it the Delete-Record message.

After you've worked with DatabaseCursors for a while, you will probably wish there were a better way to navigate the rows of the virtual table. You can only start at the beginning, move forward one row at a time, and reach the end; you can't jump forward to a specified row (you have to issue repeated MoveNext commands), and you can't move backward at all. It appears that in REALbasic 3.5 a new control, the DataControl, will begin to relieve this inconvenience.

Schemas

To report the structure of the database as a whole, a Database has two methods, TableSchema and FieldSchema. They both return DatabaseCursors.

TableSchema returns a virtual table consisting of one column, `tablename`; the values are the names of the tables in the database.

FieldSchema takes a table name, and returns a virtual table consisting of four columns: `columnname`, `fieldtype`, `isprimary`, and `notnull`. `columnname` is the name of a column of the table. `fieldtype` is an integer telling the datatype of values in that column; see the online documentation for the interpretation of this integer. `isprimary` is a boolean telling whether this column is constrained to be the primary key. `notnull` is a boolean telling whether this column is constrained to be not null; a value of `false` means that it's not constrained.

Here's a way to loop over the schema of a database:

```
dim tables,cols as databasecursor
dim fld as databasecursorfield
dim s,tablename as string
tables = d.tableSchema
while not tables.eof
    tablename = tables.field("tablename").stringvalue
    cols = d.fieldSchema(tablename)
    s = tablename + ":" + chr(13)
    while not cols.eof
        s = s + cols.field("columnname").stringvalue + ","
        s = s + cols.field("fieldtype").stringvalue + ","
        s = s + cols.field("isprimary").stringvalue + ","
        s = s + cols.field("notnull").stringvalue + chr(13)
        cols.movenext
    wend
    msgbox s
    tables.movenext
wend
tables.close
```

Displaying Data

So far, nothing has been said about displaying your data. We've been displaying it rather crudely, using MsgBox dialogs; but of course in real life you'll probably want to display it nicely, in a window. Since data is returned from a query as a virtual table, the natural candidate for displaying it is a ListBox, which has rows and columns. You can easily loop over your data, as in the examples, obtaining values and entering them in appropriate cells of a ListBox.

To illustrate, here's the code for a ListBox subclass method that displays a whole table. We assume that the Database d is a property of the ListBox:

```
dim c as databasecursor
dim fld as databasecursorfield
dim i,u as integer
dim table as string
dim firsttime as boolean
firsttime = true
table = // whatever
c = self.d.sqlselect("select * from " + table)
u = c.fieldcount
self.deleteallRows
self.columncount = u
while not c.eof
    self.addrow ""
    for i = 1 to u
        fld = c.idxfield(i)
        if firsttime then
            self.heading(i-1) = fld.name
        end
        self.cell(listbox2.lastindex, i-1) = fld.stringvalue
    next
    firsttime = false
    c.movenext
wend
c.close
```

Alternatively, REALbasic provides the DatabaseQuery control, which acts as an intermediary between a SQL select command and the display of its results in a ListBox. Typically, here's how you'd use a DatabaseQuery control. Drag a DatabaseQuery icon into a Window Editor, to create a control in that window. The icon that appears in the Window Editor is just a placeholder; it doesn't correspond to anything visible when the application runs. You'll also need a ListBox in the same window. Now hold Shift-Command and drag the mouse from the DatabaseQuery to the ListBox, to create a binding. In the dialog that appears, select the first option. Then, when the application runs, set the DatabaseQuery's Database property to a Database instance representing your database, and its SQLQuery property to a string consisting of a SQL select command. Now send the DatabaseQuery the RunQuery message, and presto! It performs the query and displays the results in the ListBox. For example:

```
dim s as string
s = "select * from deeds where deeds.lastname = 'Caesar' order by deed"
databasequery1.database = d
databasequery1.sqlQuery = s
databasequery1.runquery
```

Personally, though, I'm not a great fan of bindings (this is the only place I mention them in this book). They don't do anything you couldn't have done in code; they don't reformat the ListBox in any way, so displaying the right number of columns, attaching appropriate headers, and so forth, is still up to you; and they disable certain ListBox features—for example, once you've displayed data in a ListBox through a binding, you can't sort the ListBox by clicking on a column heading.

Other Data Sources

A Database instance can come from a number of other sources. REAL provides plugins that allow REALbasic to access various sorts of database: OpenBase, CSV, PostgreSQL, DBF, Oracle, ODBC, dtfSQL, and 4D.* Look in the online reference for the correct function to provide a Database instance for the kind of database you'll be talking to. For example, if you have access to an OpenBase server, you'll call Open-OpenBaseDatabase. (Hard to believe, isn't it?) This makes the connection to the OpenBase server and returns a Database instance, which you work with in the usual way. Alternatively, you can choose from the File → Add Data Source submenu to incorporate a reference to a database as a component of your project; with the OpenBase plug-in installed, for example, you'd see an OpenBase Database menu item here. Then you also could work with the database's schema in the editor by double-clicking the database in the Project Window.

To test the CSV plug-in, I made a textfile that looked like this:

```
"Mouse","Mickey",70
"Shakespeare","William",400
"Neuburg","Matt",46
```

Then I was able to extract the data from the first column, as with any DatabaseCursor:

```
dim f as folderitem
dim c as databasecursor
f = getfolderitem("csvexample")
if f = nil or not f.exists then
    return
end
c = opencsvcursor(f)
```

---

* See *http://www.realbasic.com/download/release.html*. On plug-ins and what to do with them, see "Plug-ins" in Chapter 32.

```
while not c.eof
    msgbox c.idxfield(1).stringvalue
    c.movenext
wend
c.close
```

I was also able to try out REALbasic as a frontend to the free single-client version of OpenBase under Mac OS X. First, I used the OpenBase Manager to start up the Company database included with the OpenBase installation. Then, in REALbasic, I created a new project and used the OpenBase Database menu item to specify host localhost and database company; this added the Company database to my Project Window. In my default window, I put a DatabaseQuery and a ListBox, and created a binding between them. In the Properties Window for the DatabaseQuery, I specified Company as the Database and "select description from products" as the SQLQuery. I ran the project in the IDE and presto, there were the products listed in the ListBox, proving that REALbasic could see an OpenBase database and query it.

REAL's native database file format and associated classes are very decent, especially for flat-file data; but many behaviors are not supported (for instance, you can't delete a table or a column), no indexing is provided, and things can get slow as the database grows or your relational or querying needs become complex. Also, REALbasic's internal behavior when it is called upon to interpret SQL is unreliable. Just to give an example of a long-standing bug, if you generate a DatabaseCursor with a SQLSelect command containing an order by clause, any attempt to alter the data with Edit and Update will fail silently.

For an alternative, consider Valentina, a commercial product that comes in the form of a REALbasic plug-in.* It provides your application with very fast, very scalable, fully relational and object-based database capabilities. You'll have some learning to do—nothing in this chapter applies to Valentina, which uses a different set of classes—but it comes with excellent tutorials.

---

* See *http://www.paradigmasoft.com/files/v4rb.html*.

CHAPTER 23

Clipboard

The clipboard, or *scrap* as it is technically known, is where data goes when it is cut or copied, so that it can be pasted later. There is exactly one scrap, and it is available at system level; that's why you can copy from one application and paste into another.

A distinction is sometimes made between the *public scrap* (the system scrap) and the *private scrap* of a particular application. These terms do not necessarily imply that there are actually two different scraps; they have to do more with the format of the scrap data. The question is whether what's on the scrap is intended for public consumption. An application might maintain a private scrap because it needs to be able to copy and paste data in formats unique to itself. It might use the system scrap for this, or it might operate by some other mechanism. Nonetheless, all applications, when they are suspended, are expected to convert their current private scrap data, if any, to a form that other applications can read, on the system scrap. This is to make sure there is a seamless user experience of cutting and pasting *within* an application and cutting and pasting *between* applications.

Scrap data is identified rather like a resource (see "Resources" in Chapter 21), except that the scrap makes available only one instance of any given datatype at a time. The public scrap data formats are, minimally, 'TEXT' and 'PICT', and optionally, 'styl', 'snd ', and 'movv'. Apart from these, scrap data formats may be regarded simply as strings with labels; in other words, a 'yoho' is a string labeled as a 'yoho', but unless we have defined it ourselves, we probably have no idea what on earth it signifies.

The user, when choosing the EditCut, EditCopy, and EditPaste menu items to manipulate text in an EditField, is accessing the scrap in a way that REALbasic handles automatically (see "Special Menu Items" in Chapter 6). And we have also seen that you can move text, or styled text, between an EditField and the scrap with the EditField's Copy and Paste methods ("Selection, Text, Font, and Style" and "Combining EditFields" in Chapter 13). But REALbasic also permits your code to access the scrap directly. You can get or set any scrap datatype by way of a REALbasic string, and you can get or set a scrap 'PICT' by way of a REALbasic Picture instance. That's what the rest of this chapter is about. (On drag-and-drop, which does not involve the clipboard, see Chapter 24.)

Clipboard Class

All of your code's communication with the scrap takes place by way of an instance of the Clipboard class. You obtain this instance with New. When you are done with a Clipboard instance you must send the instance the Close message in the same handler in which it was created.

Four Clipboard properties provide convenient access to the two most common scrap data formats, 'TEXT' and 'PICT':

TextAvailable, PictureAvailable
> Read-only. Booleans reporting whether the scrap contains 'TEXT' or 'PICT' data, respectively.

Text
> The 'TEXT' scrap data, as a string.

Picture
> The 'PICT' scrap data, as a Picture.

Three Clipboard messages provide access to other scrap data formats:

MacDataAvailable
> A boolean. Takes one parameter, a four-character string signifying a data format; reports whether the scrap contains data labeled with this format.

MacData
> Takes one parameter, a four-character string signifying a data format; returns, as a string, the scrap data labeled with this format.

AddMacData
> Takes two parameters, the data as a string, and a four-character string signifying a data format; stores the data onto the scrap, and labels it with this format.

If you are setting scrap data, you should do so only once for any given data format during the lifetime of your Clipboard instance. So, for example, you shouldn't try to set one Clipboard instance's Text property twice. The reason lies in the way the system manages the scrap: if you add to the scrap data in a certain format, and there is already data in that format on the scrap, the system appends the data to the scrap in a way that makes it inaccessible.

The first time you set any scrap data through a Clipboard instance, the scrap is emptied in advance. This is good, because otherwise you'd never be able to put anything on the scrap: for example, the scrap just about always contains 'TEXT' data, so if you couldn't empty the scrap, setting the Clipboard's Text property would add the new data in addition to the old data, making it inaccessible. But it means you need to be careful about the order in which you do things. If the scrap contains both 'TEXT' data and 'PICT' data, for example, and the first thing you do with a Clipboard instance is to set its Text property, you can no longer retrieve the 'PICT' data.

Usage

Here are some examples showing how to work with the clipboard. The clipboard is pretty simple, so the examples are simple too. (Some further examples have appeared earlier; see "BevelButton" in Chapter 12 and "Combining EditFields" in Chapter 13.)

ListBox Copy-and-Paste

Let's begin by implementing copy-and-paste for a ListBox. The ListBox will not have directly editable cells, and for simplicity we will assume that it has just one column and that only one row can be selected at a time. The idea is that the user should be able to select a row of the ListBox and choose Copy, Paste, or Cut, and something reasonable will happen.

We will need a ListBox subclass so that we can receive menu-related events. Let's call it PasteBox. We will implement EditCut, EditCopy, and EditPaste: we will assume that cutting and copying mean that the text of the currently selected row should be placed on the scrap, and that pasting means that a new row, whose text is the text currently on the scrap, should be inserted below the current selection.

The menu items need to be enabled, so in PasteBox's EnableMenuItems event handler we'll put this code:

```
dim c as clipboard
c = new clipboard
if c.textAvailable then // enable only if there's text to paste
    editpaste.enable
end
c.close
if me.listindex > -1 then // enable only if there's a selection to copy
    editcopy.enable
    editcut.enable
end
```

Now we can write the handlers for the three menu events:

```
// EditCopy menu event handler:
dim c as clipboard
c = new clipboard
c.text = me.text
c.close
```

```
// EditCut menu event handler:
dim c as clipboard
dim i as integer
i = me.listindex // do nice stuff with selection
c = new clipboard
c.text = me.text
c.close
me.removerow i
me.listindex = i-1
```

```
// EditPaste menu event handler:
dim c as clipboard
dim i as integer
i = me.listindex+1 // do nice stuff with selection
c = new clipboard
me.insertrow(i,c.text)
c.close
me.listindex = i
```

Show Clipboard

In the previous example, we were interested in only one type of scrap data. Now let's have an example where we are interested in more than one: we'll implement a Show Clipboard command. For the sake of simplicity, we'll limit our clipboard-showing abilities to text, styled text, and pictures; and we will show either a picture or text, but not both. Our clipboard-showing window will have a Canvas lying on top of an EditField: we'll show the Canvas if there is 'PICT' data on the scrap; if not, we'll show the EditField if there is 'TEXT' data.

Here is the code for showing our window, which is called ClipWin and is assumed to be modal and initially invisible:

```
dim c as clipboard
c = new clipboard
if c.pictureAvailable then
    clipWin.editfield1.visible = false
    clipWin.canvas1.backdrop = c.picture
    c.close
    clipWin.showmodal
    return
end
if c.textAvailable then
    if c.macdataAvailable("styl") then
        clipWin.editfield1.setTextAndStyle c.text, c.macdata("styl")
    else
        clipWin.editfield1.text = c.text
    end
    c.close
    clipWin.showmodal
    return
end
c.close
beep // nothing to show
```

Private Scrap

If you implement the copying and pasting of data in a nonstandard format internally, you need to be able to create a version of the data in a standard format as well, so that if the user suspends your application it will be possible to paste the data elsewhere. You'll need an Application subclass so that you can receive the Deactivate event and respond accordingly.

For example, suppose you've been permitting cut-and-paste within your application using the private 'yoho' format. When the application suspends, you need to make the 'yoho' available in a public format. Let's suppose that the best equivalent is 'TEXT'; so, you'll need to convert the 'yoho' to a string, something that can be pasted into other applications as a rough equivalent of whatever was in the 'yoho'. Pretend for a moment that a 'yoho' *is* just text; this will make the conversion minimal (there won't be any). Here is the Application subclass's Deactivate event handler:

```
dim c as clipboard
c = new clipboard
if c.macdataavailable("yoho") then
    c.setText c.macdata("yoho") // ingenious conversion algorithm
end
c.close
```

In real life, of course, you'd need a real algorithm for converting a 'yoho' to a normal string. And you might want to reverse the procedure, converting a 'TEXT' on the clipboard to a 'yoho' when the application is activated.

If you can't think why you'd ever need a private format, let's just return to our List-Box. Suppose the ListBox has multiple selection enabled, and that we want the user to be able to copy and paste more than one row at a time. Clearly, copying me.text into the clipboard's 'TEXT' data will not suffice, because this captures only the first row; we need a data format that can hold the text of all the rows. This is a nonstandard entity, so we will need a nonstandard format. Now, we can call this type of data anything we like; we can call it 'yoho', or 'Rowz', or whatever strikes our fancy. After all, this is data that only our application will access; the message we're leaving on the scrap is intended only for ourselves. But when the user copies and then switches to another application, we must also store a 'TEXT' version of the data on the scrap, so that if the user pastes into another application, something intelligent will be pasted.

Exactly *what* should be pasted is a design decision you'll have to wrestle with on your own. Perhaps it should be whatever text was in just the first cell of the copied row. Perhaps it should be the text from all the cells, separated by spaces, by commas, by tabs, or by return characters. But the point is: don't neglect to put *something* in the 'TEXT' data, because the user is going to be mystified and annoyed if it isn't possible to copy from your application and paste into another.

As a simple example, let's implement a 'yoho' format to hold multiple row data, as text separated by return characters. This implementation is so simple, in fact, that we don't need to perform any conversion in our application's Deactivate event handler: a 'yoho' can simply become a 'TEXT', and if the user pastes into another application, multiple lines of text will be pasted, which is reasonable. Nevertheless, we'll go through all the rigmarole of treating a 'yoho' as private scrap data and "converting" it, because this is what you'd have to do if your private scrap had a more complicated nonstandard format that did require conversion.

So, our application's Deactivate event handler will work as it stands. The line in PasteBox's EnableMenuItems event handler that thinks about enabling the Paste menu item now has to check for our private scrap datatype:

```
if c.textAvailable or c.macdataavailable("yoho") then
```

Here are the other routines from PasteBox. Some common code from the EditCut and EditCopy routines has been moved off into a method handler called DoCopy:

```
// DoCopy method handler:
dim c as clipboard
dim u,i,fnd,all as integer
dim yoho as string
if self.selcount = 1 then
    // copy as TEXT
    c = new clipboard
    c.text = self.text
    c.close
elseif self.selcount > 1 then
    // accumulate multiple selection into yoho format
    all = self.selcount
    u = self.listcount
    do until fnd = all or i = u
        if self.selected(i) then
            yoho = yoho + self.list(i) + chr(13)
            fnd = fnd + 1
        end
        i = i + 1
    loop
    // copy as yoho
    c = new clipboard
    c.addMacData yoho, "yoho"
    c.close
end

// EditCopy menu event handler:
doCopy

// EditCut menu event handler:
dim i,sel as integer
doCopy
// remove selections and delete
for i = self.listcount-1 downto 0
    if self.selected(i) then
        sel = i
        self.selected(i) = false
        self.removerow i
    end
next
// make nice selection
self.listindex = max(0,sel-1)

// EditPaste menu event handler:
dim c as clipboard
```

```
dim yoho as string
dim sel,i,u as integer
// remember initial selection
sel = self.listindex
self.listindex = -1
// get data off clipboard
c = new clipboard
if c.macdataavailable("yoho") then
    yoho = c.macdata("yoho")
elseif c.textavailable then
    yoho = c.text
end
c.close
// remove final return character if any
if mid(yoho,len(yoho),1) = chr(13) then
    yoho = mid(yoho,1,len(yoho)-1)
end
// paste rows after original selection
u = countFields(yoho, chr(13))
for i = 1 to u
    self.insertrow sel+i, nthfield(yoho, chr(13), i)
next
// make nice new selection
self.listindex = sel+1
self.scrollposition = sel
```

In this chapter:
• Beginning a Drag
• Receiving a Drop
• Finder Drop
• Internal Drag-and-Drop
• Limitations and Workarounds

CHAPTER 24

Drag-and-Drop

Drag-and-drop of icons in the Finder goes back to the beginnings of the Macintosh user interface, and certain conventions are now so customary as to be almost subconscious: to copy or move a file to a different folder, drag its icon into the folder; to open a document with a certain application, drag its icon onto the application's icon. But system-level drag-and-drop of data, within an application and from one application to another, was not introduced until about 1994. At first, the technology behind this was called Macintosh Drag-and-Drop; now, it is more often called the Drag Manager.* Drag-and-drop is an intuitive and easy way to move data, and you may well want to consider implementing it in your application.

REALbasic implements drag-and-drop by means of the DragItem class, which works very much like the Clipboard class (see Chapter 23). But don't be misled by this comparison! Drag-and-drop does not use the clipboard; that's one of its advantages. A DragItem is itself the repository of the data being moved; metaphorically, it's like a suitcase, carrying the data inside it from one place to another. Like the Clipboard, a DragItem's data is identified by a format label, such as 'TEXT' or 'PICT'. There can be more than one piece of data, and (unlike the Clipboard) there can be more than one piece of data with the same format.

Three separate situations must be considered:

- You have a control or window, and you want the user to be able to drag data out of it.

- You have a control or window, and you want the user to be able to drop data into it.

- You want the user to be able, in the Finder, to drop file icons onto your application's icon.

---

* See *http://developer.apple.com/techpubs/macos8/InterproCom/DragManager/dragmanager.html*; all the key documents, unfortunately, seem to be available only as PDFs. The Drag Manager SDK is also very helpful: *ftp://ftp.apple.com/developer/Development_Kits/Macintosh_Drag_-_Drop.sit.hqx*. This includes a great debugging application, DragPeeker; you drag something onto its window, and it reports the contents of the DragItem.

Beginning a Drag

Presume you have a control or window, and you want the user to be able to drag data out of it. It turns out that there are three cases, depending on what you want the user to be able to drag from: a multiline EditField; a ListBox; and a class that receives a MouseDown event. These are the only classes from which a drag can be initiated.

Unless the control is a multiline EditField, this will involve obtaining a DragItem and sending it some messages. Without worrying for the moment about where this Drag-Item comes from, let's start by talking about what the possible messages are.

The DragItem

The following DragItem properties can be set as the user starts to drag out of a window or control:

Text, Picture, FolderItem
Pieces of data to be carried by the DragItem.

MacData, PrivateMacData
Pieces of data to be carried by the DragItem; each takes one parameter, a four-character string labeling the data format, and you assign a string value to set the data itself. Data installed with PrivateMacData can't be dropped outside the application.

MouseCursor
The cursor to be displayed during the drag; a MouseCursor instance.

The following methods can be called as the user starts to drag out of a window or control:

NewDragItem
A global method; creates a new DragItem. Takes four parameters describing the drag rectangle, in coordinates local to the window's content region.

AddItem
Creates an additional "row" in the DragItem. Takes four parameters describing an additional drag rectangle, in coordinates local to the window's content region. Any properties set after calling AddItem will affect the new row.

Drag
Tells the DragItem that its data has been loaded, and permits the drag to begin.

The procedure, in general, is as follows. Depending on whether or not this is a List-Box, either you will receive a DragItem as a parameter to your event handler, or you'll create a DragItem with NewDragItem. You will then populate the first "row" of the DragItem with the appropriate kinds of data. If you need additional "rows" of data, you'll call AddItem, and add them. You might set the DragItem's MouseCursor. When you're all done, you'll stand out of the way and cry, "Let the drag begin!"

How you do this depends on whether this is a ListBox: if it is, you do it by returning true; if not, you do it with the Drag method.

Before tackling some actual examples, let's pause to understand AddItem. Think of a DragItem as consisting of multiple clipboard-like structures. What I mean by "clipboard-like" is that one of these structures can hold multiple pieces of data, but the pieces have to be of different formats: at most one 'TEXT', at most one 'PICT', and so on. So, the only way to drag-and-drop two distinct 'TEXT' items or two distinct 'PICT' items is to add a second such structure. You can see that it helps to envision these as "rows," and the format types as "columns": one row can hold at most one item of any given type.

AddItem also offers you the opportunity to define an additional drag rectangle, so that the user, seeing more than one rectangle, gets a sense of dragging more than one thing. But no law says that you have to do this. If you want to add a row of data without adding a drag rectangle, just make the width and height of the new drag rectangle be zero.

All of this raises certain general concerns about how to format your data. Let's say, for example, that you want the DragItem to hold two 'TEXT' items and a 'PICT' item. Clearly you'll need two rows, because you have two 'TEXT' items. But what about the 'PICT'? Should it go in the same row as one of the two 'TEXT' items, or in a third row of its own? If you're planning on receiving and processing the dropped data yourself (the user is dragging and dropping within your application), then it doesn't matter; you're free to arrange the data as you please when the drag begins, because you're free to parse it as you please when the drop occurs. But if the data might be dragged into another application, then you have some hard decisions to make, because you don't control how any particular application will parse the DragItem.

For example, suppose you create a DragItem as follows: a 'PICT', a 'TEXT', a new row, a 'TEXT'. If you drag this into SimpleText or into a multiline EditField, you'll drop both 'TEXT' items in order. But if you drag it into Nisus Writer, you'll drop the second 'TEXT' and then the 'PICT'—the first 'TEXT' is ignored. And if you drag it into Microsoft Word, you'll drop the first 'TEXT' only—the 'PICT' and the second 'TEXT' will be ignored!

Since other applications behave so inconsistently with regard to multiple items and multiple rows, you will probably want to keep your DragItems very simple: basically, one row containing one item.

Multiline EditField

If a control is a multiline EditField, drag-and-drop from within it is already implemented; what's dragged is styled text, meaning a single "row" consisting of 'TEXT' data and 'styl' data.* Drag-and-drop from single-line EditFields is not supported.

---

* Plus two more pieces of data labeled 'FISH' and 'SOUP'. Really.

In a way, both of these things are bad. The lack of drag-and-drop from single-line EditFields is bad, because the user may try to use it, and will be surprised when it doesn't work. The fact that drag-and-drop from a multiline EditField is already implemented is bad, because you can't customize it and you can't turn it off. You don't get access to the DragItem; the whole process is completely out of your hands.

However, there's nothing you can do about this, so there's nothing more to be said. At least it keeps the discussion short.

ListBox

To permit the user to drag from a ListBox, the ListBox's EnableDrag property must be true. You can set its value in the IDE or at any time in code.

When the user starts to drag, if the ListBox's EnableDrag is true, then the ListBox is sent a DragRow event. The DragRow event handler is passed a DragItem instance, named drag, along with the index of the row that the mouse was in as the drag began, named row. Your job is either to forbid the drag or to construct the data to be dragged. The way you do this is either to return false (or nothing), thus forbidding the drag, or else to construct the DragItem and return true. In the latter case, the user will be able to drag, and will see a drag rectangle or rectangles corresponding to the row or rows that were selected. Note that you do *not* use NewDragItem to obtain the DragItem, and that you do *not* send the DragItem the Drag message at the end.

Constructing the DragItem will often consist of as little as setting its Text property; I also find it useful to set the DragItem's MouseCursor property, even if this just means setting it to ArrowCursor. If the ListBox has just one column and doesn't permit selection of multiple rows, the text to be dragged might be just the text of the selected row, and the DragRow event handler could look like this:

```
drag.text = me.list(row)
drag.mouseCursor = arrowCursor
return true
```

If selection of multiple rows is enabled, you might wish the dragged text to be the text of all the selected rows. Assuming you want the DragItem to consist of just one 'TEXT' item, you can separate the pieces of text by some delimiter, such as a return character. In that case, the DragRow event handler could look like this:

```
dim s as string
dim i,u as integer
u = me.listcount-1
for i = 0 to u
    if me.selected(i) then
        s = s + me.list(i) + chr(13)
    end
next
drag.text = left(s,len(s)-1) // remove the last return character
drag.mouseCursor = arrowCursor
return true
```

But how you construct the DragItem is completely up to you, and you're certainly not limited by these suggestions. You're not even limited to text. For example, if the row has a RowPicture, you could add it to the DragItem, as its Picture property. Or, suppose each row of the ListBox represents a file on disk: you could set the DragItem's FolderItem to point to the file that the selected row represents, and the user could then drag from the ListBox to the Finder, as a way of moving or copying a file!

MouseDown Receivers

A Canvas, a Placard, an ImageWell, and a window all have this in common: they receive the MouseDown event. This is what allows a drag to be initiated from within them. To permit the user to drag from one of these objects, its MouseDown event handler must respond to the mouse by creating a DragItem, constructing it, and sending it the Drag message. The DragItem is created with the NewDragItem function, which takes four parameters describing a rectangle. This rectangle is the shape that the user will appear to be dragging. REALbasic doesn't let you drag any other shape of outline, which is a pity, because the system provides routines for letting you define shapes of much greater complexity.*

As a very simple example, let's suppose we have a Canvas containing a red rectangle, drawn with this Paint event handler:

```
g.forecolor = rgb(255,0,0)
g.fillrect 10,10,50,50
```

We will permit the user to drag the red rectangle out of the Canvas. Our Canvas's MouseDown event handler first ascertains whether the mouse is within the red rectangle. If so, it creates the DragItem, describing the drag rectangle's size and position in such a way that it will appear to be the red rectangle's outline; the tricky thing here is that the coordinates local to the Canvas must be converted to coordinates local to the window. Then we draw the red rectangle into a Picture object and assign this to the DragItem's Picture property. Finally, we set the MouseCursor, and start the drag:

```
dim d as dragItem
dim p as picture
if x > 10 and x < 60 and y > 10 and y < 60 then
    d = newDragItem(me.left+10,me.top+10,50,50)
    p = newpicture(50,50,16)
    p.graphics.forecolor = rgb(255,0,0)
    p.graphics.fillrect 0,0,50,50
    d.picture = p
    d.mouseCursor = arrowCursor
    d.drag
end
```

* If this intrigues you (as well it might), look at Matthijs van Duin's Drag Manager examples, which show how to access the relevant Toolbox routines: *http://www.nubz.org/development.html.*

This works perfectly, but it isn't very object-oriented. Both the Canvas's Paint event handler and its MouseDown event handler are drawing the same object in the same way, and we are assuming that there is only one draggable region of the Canvas. We'll come back to this and generalize the example, later in the chapter.

Receiving a Drop

We turn now to the situation in which you have a window or control and you want the user to be able to drop data onto it. Any window or control can receive data by drag-and-drop, but you have to enable it first (except for dropping text onto a multiline EditField). To do so, you must register with the window or control all acceptable types of droppable data, by sending it any of these messages:

AcceptTextDrop, AcceptPictureDrop
> Allows the window or control to receive Text or Picture data, respectively, from a DragItem.

AcceptFileDrop
> Takes one parameter, the name of a file type defined in the File Types dialog (see "File Types" in Chapter 21). File types to specify folders, disks, and any file are included in the File Types dialog. (The file types specifying folders and disks don't work in Mac OS X.) Allows the window or control to receive FolderItem instances of the specified type from a DragItem; the match between a FolderItem and a file type is performed as with the FolderItem Type method.

AcceptMacDataDrop
> Takes one parameter, a four-character string specifying the data format. Allows the window or control to receive data in that format from a DragItem.

Typically, you'll enable a window or control to receive drag-and-drop early in its lifetime—for example, in its Open event handler. If you want the same control to be able to receive drag-and-drop of more than one kind of entity, just send it several of these messages. For example, to allow a control to receive text data, picture data, and two kinds of file whose file types are named Dum and Dee, you'd say this in the control's Open event handler:

```
me.acceptTextDrop
me.acceptPictureDrop
me.acceptFileDrop("Dum")
me.acceptFileDrop("Dee")
```

There's just one tricky bit associated with the AcceptFileDrop message: matching of file types is done in accordance with the rules for the FolderItem Type method (see page 487). This has three important consequences:

- A file's MacCreator makes no difference. For example, if you enable a control to accept drops of SimpleText textfiles, it will accept drops of *any* textfiles.

- The order in which your file types are defined makes a difference. For example, suppose you have two file types, Gum and Garland, which actually denote the same MacType. Then if Gum comes before Garland in the File Types dialog, a file of this MacType, when dropped into your application, will be seen as a Gum, not as a Garland. So if all you say in the control's Open event handler is this:

    ```
    me.acceptFileDrop("Garland")
    ```

    then *no* file drops will be accepted, because even if a file is a Garland, it's seen as a Gum, and you didn't say to accept Gum drops.

- If you're going to permit any file to be dropped ("????/????"), then you must specify *all* your file types! The reason is that you don't get a match on the Any-File type unless there is no match on any other file type you've defined. So, for example, if you've defined file types Snow, Rain, and AnyFile, and all you say in the control's Open event handler is this:

    ```
    me.acceptFileDrop("AnyFile")
    ```

    then your control *won't* receive any Snow drops or Rain drops, because if a file matches one of those types, it doesn't match AnyFile.

All right, then. You've initialized your windows and controls by telling them what kinds of drop they are to receive. After that, when such a window or control receives such a drop, it is sent a DropObject event. The DropObject event handler is given a reference to the DragItem, called obj. The rest is up to you; typically, you'll want to extract the data from the DragItem. Here are the DragItem messages you'll use:

TextAvailable, PictureAvailable, FolderItemAvailable
  Booleans reporting whether the current row of the DragItem contains a piece of data which is, respectively, a Text, Picture, or FolderItem.

MacDataAvailable
  Takes one parameter, a four-character string stating the data format. Returns a boolean, reporting whether the current row of the DragItem contains data with that format.

Text, Picture, FolderItem
  Pieces of data in the current row of the DragItem.

MacData
  Takes one parameter, a four-character string stating the data format. Data in the current row of the DragItem with that format is returned as a string.

DropLeft, DropTop, DropWidth, DropHeight
  The position and size of the drag rectangle, in coordinates relative to the window.

NextItem
  Brings the next "row" of data into view, as it were: afterward, the data-fetching properties apply to this new row. Returns a boolean reporting whether there was in fact another row.

A typical approach is to loop through every row of the DragItem, looking for every type of data that the window or control is registered to receive. Thus, the fullest form of a DropObject event handler would be something like this:

```
do
    if obj.textavailable then
        // do something with the text
    end
    if obj.pictureavailable then
        // do something with the picture
    end
    if obj.folderitemavailable then
        // do something with the folderItem
    end
    if obj.macdataAvailable("yoho") then
        // do something with the Yoho
    end
    // check for any more MacData types here
loop until not obj.nextitem // go on to next row, or stop
```

Often, however, you'll just look for one or two types of data in the first row of the DragItem, and stop. For example, suppose that in a Canvas's Open event handler we have enabled it to accept drag-and-drop of pictures:

```
me.acceptPictureDrop
```

The Canvas's DropObject event handler might look for a 'PICT' and capture it into a Picture property, ThePicture, from which the Canvas's Paint event handler generates its image:

```
if obj.pictureavailable then
    self.thePicture = obj.picture
    me.refresh
end
```

Next, let's consider file drops. Suppose a multiline styled EditField's Open event handler enables it to receive textfiles (defined as "TEXT/????"):

```
me.acceptfiledrop("text")
```

Now the user can drag a textfile from the Finder into the field. In response, the DropObject event handler might show the file's text in the field:

```
if obj.folderitemAvailable then
    obj.folderitem.openStyledEditField me
end
```

Don't forget, though, that the user might drop more than one file at once. If that's acceptable, you'll loop through all the rows of the DragItem, looking for Folder-Items and doing something with them. In this next example, our application's window accepts drag-and-drop of any file or folder. When we get a drop, our DropObject event handler puts up a dialog announcing the total size of all files and folders dropped. We start with a recursive method, FileSize:

```
Function filesize(f as folderitem) As integer
    dim total, i, u as integer
    if not f.directory then
        return f.length + f.resourceForkLength
    else
        u = f.count
        for i = 1 to u
            total = total + filesize(f.trueitem(i))
        next
        return total
    end
End Function
```

Here is the DropObject event handler:

```
dim i as integer
do
    if obj.folderitemavailable then
        i = i + filesize(obj.folderItem)
    end
loop until not obj.nextitem
msgbox "You dropped " + str(i\1024) + "K bytes."
```

Multiline EditFields are a special case. With FolderItems and Pictures, they work in
the usual way. However, you don't have to send a multiline EditField the Accept-
TextDrop message in order to enable text drops; in fact, you can't disable text drops.
And when a text drop does occur, you don't get a DropObject event; so you can't
prevent the drop, or get access to the dropped material. Most of the time, you probably won't care about this, but on those rare occasions when you do care—it's a drag.
However, when a drop occurs in a multiline EditField, the EditField does receive a
TextChange event, and in the TextChange event handler you can learn that what
happened was a drop by testing whether the SelLength is greater than zero; often,
this will provide a sufficient workaround.*

Drag-and-drop into a ListBox will probably involve your wanting to know what row
the DragItem was dropped onto. You can figure this out from the ListBox's
TextHeight and ScrollPosition. Here's a sample implementation, where we insert the
dropped text after the row it was dropped onto, and select it:

```
dim row, h as integer
dim p as picture
if obj.textavailable then
    p = newpicture(1,1,2)
    p.graphics.textfont = me.textfont
    p.graphics.textsize = me.textsize
    h = p.graphics.textheight
    row = me.scrollposition + (obj.droptop - me.top) \ h
    me.insertrow row+1, obj.text
    me.listindex = min(row+1,me.listcount-1)
end
```

---

* I owe this device to Adrian Martin.

Finder Drop

To permit the user to drag files or folders onto your application's icon in the Finder, you need to do three things:

- Define a named file type in the File Types dialog ("File Types" in Chapter 21).
- Check the file type's Document Icon checkbox ("File Types" in Chapter 21).
- Give your project an Application subclass ("The Application Subclass" in Chapter 7).

The first two steps cause REALbasic, when it builds the application, to generate the `'FREF'` and `'BNDL'` resources that will tell the Finder that it should permit drag-and-drop of these types of files.[*] Because you are registering information with the Finder, you may have to rebuild the desktop after building your application; but I find that in recent versions of the system, the Finder catches on almost right away.

You do not actually have to paste in an icon for the file type; in fact, if the file type doesn't belong uniquely to your application, you definitely won't want to do so. For example, to permit a SimpleText read-only file to be dropped on your application's icon, you could create a file type SimpleTextRO, defined as `"ttro/ttxt"`, and check its Document Icon checkbox; but you wouldn't paste in an icon, since the job of dictating the icon for this type of file doesn't belong to you—it belongs to SimpleText.

The last step is so that you can respond to the drop. When the user drops items on your application's icon, the Application subclass receives one OpenDocument event for each item dropped, along with a FolderItem instance, called `item`, that points to it. Typically, what you'll do with a file will be exactly what you would have done if the user had asked to open the file by other means, such as your application's File → Open menu item. There isn't really any standard behavior for responding to folders and disks.

A problem is that you have no way of knowing in advance how many items the user dropped. Suppose, for example, you want to respond to the dropping of multiple items by totaling their sizes. You saw how we did this in the previous section of this chapter, when the items were being dropped into a window or a control: we cycled through the rows of the DragItem until there were no more rows. But now there is no DragItem and there are no rows! You get an OpenDocument event for each item, yes, but which of these OpenDocument events is the last one in the "group"? Users have been complaining about this bug for years, and have devised many ingenious workarounds, typically involving threads or Timers to see whether a certain amount of time goes by without a further OpenDocument event, and assuming that if it does, that was the last item in the group. But that's not really a solution; it's guesswork. A true solution needs to come from REAL: the Finder tells the application, as part of

---

[*] See *http://developer.apple.com/techpubs/mac/Toolbox/Toolbox-450.html*.

the 'odoc' Apple event, how many items there are; the application needs somehow to pass this information on to the OpenDocument event handler.

Internal Drag-and-Drop

Often you'd like a DropObject event handler to be able to distinguish internal drag-and-drop from external drag-and-drop. This might mean you'd like to know when the user drags within a single control, as opposed to dragging out of one control and into another, or that you'd like to know when the user drops from outside your application, as opposed to dragging and dropping entirely within your application, and so forth.

There's an easy trick that makes this possible. When the drag begins, attach to the DragItem some data in a secret format. If the user drags out of your application into another application, or out of a control that knows the secret into a control that doesn't, the receiving application or control won't know about this extra data, or won't know what to do with it (and remember, you can prevent the extra data from being dragged out of your application at all, by marking it as PrivateMacData). If the user drags from another application into your application, or from a control that doesn't know the secret into a control that does, the secret data won't be there, so you'll know the drag is external. If the user drags and drops entirely within your application or between controls that know the secret, the secret data will be there (because you put it there when the drag began), so you'll find it when you receive the drop, and you'll know that this is an internal drag-and-drop.

To illustrate, let's start with a ListBox. We already know how to drag out of a ListBox and how to drag into a ListBox. But what if we want to drag entirely within a ListBox? When the user drags a row out of the ListBox into some other control, such as an EditField, or into some other application, the expectation is probably that the row's text will be copied. On the other hand, when the user drags a row of the ListBox entirely within the ListBox, the expectation is probably that the row will be moved. So you need a way to distinguish these two situations. So, when the user drags from the ListBox, we add to the DragItem, along with the 'TEXT', a secret message to ourselves, an extra piece of data with a special format. When the user drops text into the ListBox, if this extra piece of data is also present, we know that the drag is within the ListBox. Further, we have a use for this extra piece of data: it tells us where the drag started, so that we can remove that row afterward. Here are the three relevant ListBox event handlers:

```
// Open event handler:
me.enabledrag = true
me.accepttextdrop
me.acceptmacDataDrop "tehe"

// DragRow event handler:
drag.text = me.list(row)
drag.macdata("tehe") = str(row) // secret sign, tell where drag started
```

```
    return true

// DropObject Event Handler
dim row, orig, h as integer
dim p as picture
if obj.textavailable then
    p = newpicture(1,1,2)
    p.graphics.textfont = me.textfont
    p.graphics.textsize = me.textsize
    h = p.graphics.textheight
    row = me.scrollposition + (obj.droptop - me.top) \ h
    me.insertrow row+1, obj.text
    me.listindex = min(row+1,me.listcount-1)
    if obj.macdataavailable("tehe") then
        orig = val(obj.macdata("tehe"))
        if orig <= row then
            me.removerow orig
        else
            me.removerow orig+1
        end
    end
end
```

Next, let's return to our earlier Canvas examples and generalize them. We'll make a Canvas containing several drawn objects, any of which can be dragged within the Canvas to move it. Plus, the user can drag a new object into the Canvas from outside the application; the Canvas will then maintain this as one of its own drawn objects.

To implement this, we will give the window a property that is an array of pictures: these are the drawn objects in the Canvas. In the case of an external drag-and-drop, the newly dropped picture will be added to this array. But in the case of an internal drag-and-drop, we obviously don't want to add the dropped picture to the array— we've already got this picture in the array. Thus, we need to distinguish external from internal drag-and-drop.

To make everything nice and object-oriented, each picture should also know its own position within the Canvas. So we'll make a class DraggableThing, which has four integer properties—Left, Top, Height, and Width—and one Picture property, P. We'll give this class a method, DrawYourself, which takes a Graphics instance to draw into, g:

```
    g.drawpicture p,left,top
```

We'll also give it a method Within, which takes two integers, x and y, and returns a boolean:

```
    return x>left and x<left+width and y>top and y<top+height
```

The array of drawn objects will thus be an array of DraggableThings. It's a window property, Pix, and is initially dimensioned to zero.

Here we go. The Canvas's Paint event handler just runs through the Pix array, asking each drawn object to draw itself into the Canvas:

```
dim i as integer
dim d as draggableThing
for i = ubound(pix) downto 1
    d = pix(i)
    d.drawYourself g
next
```

The Canvas's Open event handler creates a couple of DraggableThings, supplies them with pictures (a red square and a blue circle), and pops them into the Pix array, so the Paint event handler will draw them as things start up. It also initializes the Canvas to receive drag-and-drop both of pictures and of our secret format, `'widx'`:

```
dim d1, d2 as draggableThing
d1 = new draggableThing // a red square
d1.p = newPicture(50,50,32)
d1.p.graphics.forecolor = rgb(255,0,0)
d1.p.transparent = 1
d1.p.graphics.fillrect(0,0,50,50)
d1.width = 50
d1.height = 50
d1.left = 10
d1.top = 10
pix.append d1
d2 = new draggableThing // a blue circle
d2.p = newPicture(40,40,32)
d2.p.graphics.forecolor = rgb(0,0,255)
d2.p.transparent = 1
d2.p.graphics.filloval(0,0,40,40)
d2.width = 40
d2.height = 40
d2.left = 20
d2.top = 100
pix.append d2
me.acceptPictureDrop
me.acceptmacDataDrop("widx")
```

The Canvas's MouseDown event handler cycles through every drawn object in the Pix array to see if the mouse is within its boundaries. If it is, a DragItem is loaded up with the drawn object's picture and the secret data, and the drag begins:

```
dim d as dragItem
dim p as draggableThing
dim i as integer
for i = ubound(pix) downto 1
    p = pix(i)
    if p.within(x,y) then
        d = newDragItem(me.left+p.left, me.top+p.top, p.width, p.height)
        d.picture = p.p
        d.privatemacdata("widx") = str(i)
        d.drag
        exit
    end
next
```

Now comes the Canvas's DropObject event handler. We distinguish two cases. If the 'widx' is present, we know that this is an internal drag. The user is moving one of our existing drawn objects in the Pix array—and we know which one, because the 'widx' tells us. (It turns out that 'widx' stands for "which index".) So we change the position for that drawn object. Otherwise, we've got an incoming picture. We add a new DraggableThing to the Pix array, stuff the incoming picture into it, assign it a position, and draw it:

```
dim oldx, oldy, oldw, oldh as integer
dim p as draggableThing
if obj.pictureAvailable then
    if obj.macdataavailable("widx") then // internalDrag
        p = pix(val(obj.macdata("widx")))
        oldx = p.left
        oldy = p.top
        p.left = obj.dropleft - me.left
        p.top = obj.droptop - me.top
        me.refreshrect oldx,oldy,p.width,p.height
        me.refreshrect p.left,p.top,p.width,p.height
    else // make a new draggableThing
        pix.append new draggableThing
        p = pix(ubound(pix))
        p.p = obj.picture
        p.left = obj.dropleft - me.left
        p.top = obj.droptop - me.top
        p.width = obj.picture.width
        p.height = obj.picture.height
        me.refreshrect p.left, p.top, p.width, p.height
    end
end
```

The only tricky part of any of this is that we must convert between coordinates local to the window and coordinates local to the Canvas.

Limitations and Workarounds

A problem with drag-and-drop is that while the user is dragging, the clock is stopped. This means, among other things, that no events are being sent; your application is frozen until the user releases the mouse. You'll see this problem particularly clearly when you're trying to implement drag-and-drop from one control to another within the same window; while the drag is going on, the window cannot respond, as the user passes the mouse over a control, by highlighting that control in the normal way, to signify that the control can accept the drop.

One very simple workaround is to violate the user interface rules, as follows: as the drag begins, you highlight all the places in the window that can accept the drop, even though the mouse is not over any of them yet. It sounds rather skanky, but in practice it looks quite compelling.

For example, suppose we have two Canvases in the same window, and the user is to be able to drag from the first to the second. Behind the second Canvas is a Rectangle with a thick blue border, which is invisible. In the first Canvas's MouseDown handler, we show the Rectangle as the drag begins and hide it when the drag ends, like this:

```
// ... other code as before ...
rectangle1.visible = true
rectangle1.refresh
d.drag
rectangle1.visible = false
rectangle1.refresh
```

Another alternative, if the only drag-and-drop to be permitted is internal to your application, is not to use real drag-and-drop at all; instead, fake it. For the drag rectangle, you could supply a Canvas that moves along with the mouse. Now you're getting events during the "drag," so you can track the mouse's movements, highlighting controls as the mouse passes over them, and so forth. This is rather elaborate, so the details are left to the reader. This sort of thing was, in fact, quite common before system-level drag-and-drop was implemented. However, if you do it now, you may incur the ire of the user, who will be frustrated when trying to drag to another application.

CHAPTER 25

Time

In this chapter:
- Ticks and Microseconds
- Timers
- Yielding Time

Occasions will probably arise when your application needs to concern itself with time. Sometimes you want to know how much time has elapsed between two moments. Sometimes you want to let a certain amount of time elapse before proceeding. This chapter delves into the mysteries of time in REALbasic.

For the current time on the system clock, see "Dates" in Chapter 5.

Ticks and Microseconds

Two functions let you measure the passage of time:

Ticks
> Returns an integer that is the number of ticks (roughly, sixtieths of a second) that have elapsed since the computer was turned on. A tick is rather a gross measure, and may also be slightly inaccurate.

Microseconds
> Returns a double that is the number of millionths of a second that have elapsed since the computer was turned on.

These functions are useful not so much for the actual values they return (since they don't tell you what time it is, in any important sense), but rather for their ability to measure time *intervals* as they elapse. You can use them, for example, to pause for a certain interval. You may recall that in Chapter 5 these lines were used to pause a racing ProgressBar for some random amount of time:

```
max = rnd*15 + 1
i = ticks
while ticks-i < max
wend
```

That's quite a standard approach for pausing. We define how many ticks we want to pause for. Then we learn the current Ticks value, but we don't really care what it is; we only want to keep checking the Ticks value, as the time goes by, until it has increased by the amount of time we want to pause for. Thus, we are guaranteed that we exit the While loop at least that much later than we entered it.

Here's an example of a measuring an interval between events: it's a test to distinguish a single click from a double-click. This code might come from a Canvas's MouseDown event handler; we maintain state in an integer property called LastTicks:

```
dim i as integer
i = ticks - self.lastticks
self.lastticks = ticks
if i < 28 then
    // it's a double-click, so respond...
end
```

The value 28 is artificial, though; the proper way is to consult the system settings to learn the user's preferred double-click interval. You can call the Toolbox routine GetDblTime to do this (see Chapter 32).

Microseconds is better than Ticks for small measures or great accuracy. For example, suppose we have a button that the user is to click twice, as fast as possible, and we wish to report the results quite precisely. This Action event handler determines the interval between the two clicks, using a double property called Micros to maintain state:

```
dim d as double
d = microseconds
if self.micros = 0 then // first click
    self.micros = d
else
    d = d - self.micros
    self.micros = 0
    msgbox "That took you " + format(d/1000000,"#.######") + " seconds."
end
```

Timers

A Timer is a built-in class that executes some code after the lapse of a stated interval. The code in question goes into the Timer's Action event handler. The interval goes into the Timer's Period property, and is an integer measuring thousandths of a second. (That's right, a Timer measures time in yet *another* way: not in ticks, not in microseconds, but in milliseconds.) A Period of 0 or less is meaningless, and is treated as if it were 1.

Getting a Timer

There are two ways to obtain a Timer instance. One is to treat the Timer as a control. Drag the Timer icon (which looks, appropriately, like a stopwatch) from the Tools Window into a Window Editor. Or, create a Timer subclass and drag the subclass from the Project Window into a Window Editor. The icon that appears in the Window Editor has no corresponding physical manifestation when the application runs; it's just a placeholder, signifying that the window will instantiate the Timer automatically when it itself is instantiated.

The other way to obtain a Timer instance is in code, using New. Such a Timer instance must be a property; a Timer that is purely a local variable won't work. You can't enter code into the Timer instance's Action event handler once your application is running, so you'll *have* to use a Timer subclass, so that you can edit its Action event handler in the IDE.

Timer Behavior

A Timer instance's behavior is governed by its Mode property, which is an integer:

- While the Mode is 0, nothing happens; the Timer is off, as it were.
- If the Mode is set to 1, the Timer behaves like an alarm clock: it starts watching the time, and when its Period has elapsed, it resets its Mode automatically to 0 and runs its Action event handler. Such a Timer is *nonperiodic*.
- If the Mode is set to 2, the Timer behaves like the snooze button on an alarm clock: it starts watching the time, and when its Period has elapsed, it *doesn't* automatically reset its Mode to 0—it just runs its Action event handler. If the Mode is still 2 afterward, the Timer now starts watching the time all over again and so on. Thus, its Action event handler runs repeatedly; such a Timer is *periodic*.

A Timer, in its Action event handler, can change its own Mode or its own Period. Of course, if a Timer's Mode is 0, that's not going to happen, because the Timer's Action event handler isn't going to run. But, for example, a Timer whose Mode is set to 1 can, when its Action event handler runs, change itself from nonperiodic to periodic:

```
beep // Hey, that was fun, I think I'll keep doing it
me.mode = 2
```

Actually, in that example, it would have been enough for the Timer to change its own Mode to 1. This overrides the Mode's being automatically reset to 0. Because the Timer keeps doing this, it ends up being periodic, to all intents and purposes:

```
beep // Hey, that was fun, I think I'll keep doing it
me.mode = 1
```

A Timer whose Mode is 2 can change its own Period so that its Action event handler will be called at a different interval next time:

```
beep // Hey, that was fun, I think I'll keep doing it...
me.period = me.period - 100 // ...only faster...
```

And, of course, a Timer whose Mode is 2 can turn itself off by changing its Mode to 0. This is a particularly important device. For example, here's a Timer that beeps ten times and then stops. Of course, each call to the Timer's Action event handler is independent, so state must be maintained in a property; here, we have an integer property, Count, that is autoinitialized to zero:

```
beep // Hey, that was fun, perhaps I'll do it some more
self.count = self.count + 1
if self.count = 10 then
    me.mode = 0 // No, that's enough
end
```

We may say that when a Timer's Mode is 1 or 2, the Timer is *waiting*—it is watching the clock, as it were. If a Timer is treated as a control, and its mode is set to 1 or 2 in the IDE, it starts waiting when it is instantiated. A Timer instantiated with New starts waiting as soon as its Mode is set in code to something other than 0. A Timer can wait, and can run, as long as it exists at all; it does not have to belong to a frontmost window, nor to a visible window, nor (if it's a property) to an instance that has any visible manifestation at all. A Timer goes out of existence in accordance with the normal rules for destruction of instances, and at that point it ceases to do anything at all.

When Timers Run

A Timer is rather like an extremely courteous thread. When it's waiting, a Timer has basically no effect upon the application. When the time comes for it to run, a Timer will keep waiting if any nonthreaded code is running; in other words, REALbasic turns its attention to Timers *only when the application itself is idle*. Once the application is idle, REALbasic calls the Action event handler of any waiting Timer whose Period expired while things were busy.

Busy code prevents a Timer from *running* but does not affect its ability to *wait*. If a waiting Timer's Period does not expire while other handlers are running, then the Timer's Action event handler will be called on time. Even a Timer's own Action event handler does not impair the Timer's ability to wait. For example, suppose a Timer's Period is one second, and suppose its Action event handler takes nine-tenths of a second to execute. If the application is otherwise idle, the Action event handler will still be triggered every second; its own Action event handler has not kept the Timer from keeping an eye on the clock. In this sense, a Timer may be regarded as a fairly accurate timekeeper.

Just the other way, however, a Timer cannot magically skip some calls to its Action event handler just because the application was busy during the moments when they would have fired. A periodic Timer times the interval since it last fired—not the sum of the intervals since it first fired. So, in *this* sense, a Timer is *not* an accurate timekeeper.

An example will clarify. To make a StaticText count down the seconds from ten to zero, you could initialize its Text as "10", and have a Timer with Period 1000, whose Action event handler goes like this:

```
if statictext1.text = "0" then
    me.mode = 0 // all done, stop waiting
```

```
else
    statictext1.text = str(val(statictext1.text)-1)
end
```

We set the Timer's Mode to 2, which gets it going, so that the countdown begins—10, 9, 8—and now suppose, at this instant, that the user presses a button whose Action handler takes a long time to complete, like this:

```
dim i as integer
i = ticks
while ticks - i < 300
wend
```

When the button is pressed, the countdown stops and does not resume until five seconds later—at which point it picks up at 7, then 6, and so forth, still spaced at one-second intervals. The Timer did not magically skip 7, 6, 5, 4, and 3 while the button's Action event handler was running, nor does it afterward compress any of its waiting periods to make up for the time it missed while the button was in charge.

How could you have made the seconds continue ticking off accurately in the background? One way might have been to use a thread, not a Timer; the thread's Run event handler might go like this:

```
dim i,j as integer
for j = 9 downto 0
    i = ticks
    while ticks - i < 60
    wend
    window1.statictext1.text = str(j)
    window1.statictext1.refresh
next
```

The thread keeps running and keeps decrementing the StaticText's display, at intervals of about a second, even while the button's time-consuming Action event handler is executing.

Another alternative is to use the Timer but to maintain state as a way of learning how much time has really elapsed. For example, let's say you don't care whether the StaticText's display keeps decrementing, just so long as when the button's Action event handler is over, the StaticText skips the numbers it missed while the button's Action event handler was running. In other words, you want the StaticText to *look* as if it was keeping count in the background, even though it wasn't visibly changing, during the button's Action event handler.

To do this, you initialize a property when the Timer first runs, and use that property on subsequent runs to learn how much time has really elapsed:

```
dim i as integer
if self.count = 0 then // first time
    self.count = ticks
end
i = 10 - round((ticks-self.count)\60)
```

```
if i <= 0 then // last time
    i = 0
    me.mode = 0
end
statictext1.text = str(i)
```

This technique of doing something special the first and last times a periodic Timer's Action event handler runs is very common indeed.

Timers as Idle Handlers

The fact that a Timer's Action event handler cannot run unless the application is idle should be regarded as a strength, not a weakness. A periodic Timer will trigger its Action event handler repeatedly when the application is idle; this is often exactly what is desired. Readers familiar with HyperCard may recognize a Timer as a cousin of HyperCard's "idle handler."

For example, recall from Chapter 19 how we used a thread to check whether the user was holding down the Command key, so that we could show or hide some StaticTexts accordingly. This was a poor implementation because threads run at erratic rates and slow down the application as a whole, and because the only time we really need to make this check is when the application is idle. A Timer is a much better choice; if its Mode is 2 and its Period is (say) 100, its Action event handler can go like this:

```
if keyboard.asyncCommandKey then
    if not staticText1.visible then
        staticText1.visible = true
    end
    if not staticText2.visible then
        staticText2.visible = true
    end
else
    if staticText1.visible then
        staticText1.visible = false
    end
    if staticText2.visible then
        staticText2.visible = false
    end
end
```

This is simpler than the thread version; there is no need for a loop, since the Timer is periodic, and there is no need for any reference to a particular window, since the Timer can be in the same window as the StaticTexts. Plus, the Timer responds much more briskly to pressing or releasing the Command key than the thread does. Finally, a Timer takes no CPU time while it is waiting; but a thread takes CPU time always, slowing down the application (and the rest of the computer).

Ironically, though, a periodic Timer whose Period is too small will stop being an idle handler and turn into a CPU hog. By "too small," I mean less than about 100. The reason is that if there were no Timers at all, and your application was idle, it would repeatedly yield 5 ticks to other processes; in other words, it would say to the system, "I'm not doing anything, so don't even bother with me for the next 5 ticks." But as Period values fall below 100 (the exact number is 84, if you must know), they become less than 5 ticks, which means that your application can't yield as much time when it's idle as it normally would, so it has more of an effect on the rest of the computer than it normally would. Of course, sometimes you can turn this fact to your advantage. This is the case especially when you want your application to carry on some intensive calculation or repetitious task in the background. By tweaking a Timer's Period, you can obtain enough of the CPU to perform this task with reasonable speed, while yielding enough time to other processes that you don't bog down the application where the user is working.

Yielding Time

A Timer is a two-sided coin. One side of this coin is that the Timer performs some action, when its Action event handler fires. The other side of this coin is that the Timer does nothing whatever when it's waiting. In this section, we concentrate our attention on this second side of the coin—we consider a Timer as a way of deliberately yielding time. This turns out to be one of a Timer's most important uses. With a Timer, the application can continue to receive events, and the user can continue to work, during a lengthy wait or a lengthy process. A thread can serve the same purpose, but a Timer is often a far better implementation.

Think of it this way. A Timer is a kind of loop. But between iterations of the loop, while the Timer is waiting, the application is idle. There is no watch cursor. The user can click buttons and choose menus. Thus, there is a sense in which a Timer runs as a background process, whether your application itself is in the background or not. We may say that a Timer is *virtually asynchronous*—because, although it doesn't actually *run* asynchronously, it *waits* asynchronously.

To see this, imagine looping in the way that a Timer loops, but not in a Timer. For example, you remember how on page 551 we made a Timer count backward from 10. What if we did the same thing in "normal" code? To find out, let's lift the code out of that example and put it in a button's Action event handler. We'll simulate the Timer by using a loop, and we'll simulate its Mode with a local variable:

```
dim i as integer
dim mode as integer
mode = 2
do
    if count = 0 then // first time only
        count = ticks
    end
    i = 10 - round((ticks-count)\60)
```

```
    if i <= 0 then
        i = 0
        mode = 0
    end
    statictext1.text = str(i)
    statictext1.refresh
loop until mode = 0
```

This is horrible. The watch cursor appears, and the user is unable to work: the loop is synchronous. In fact, the loop is *so* synchronous that the window never even gets a chance to repaint itself; we are forced to introduce the Refresh call, or the StaticText doesn't even visibly count down. But now we are refreshing the StaticText constantly, so it flickers constantly. Yet, when we implement the same thing as a periodic Timer, the StaticText counts down asynchronously, and the window refreshes itself naturally, and the user is able to keep working.

The very same thing is true of a nonperiodic Timer. Suppose our application opens with a modal "splash screen" window. We want to show the dialog for four seconds or until the user clicks it—whichever comes first. The way *not* to do this is to put a loop in the splash window's Open event handler that counts four seconds and then closes the window; in that case, we have to force the window into visibility, the loop will be synchronous, the user won't be able to click, the watch cursor will appear, and the Close call in the window's Open event handler will probably crash the application:

```
dim i as integer
show // appear
refresh // really appear!
i = ticks
while ticks - i < 4*60 // oh, no
wend
close // how lucky are you feeling?
```

Instead, let the modal dialog contain a nonperiodic Timer with its Period set to 4000 and its Mode set to 1. The Timer's Action event handler closes the window; so does the window's MouseDown event handler. The Timer waits asynchronously; thus, while the Timer is waiting, the user is perfectly free to click the window to close it earlier than the Timer would do it. And either way, the Close call arrives after the window's Open event handler has finished executing, so all is well.

Similarly, a nonperiodic Timer is often used as a way to call a method handler indirectly, unlinking the method from its caller and letting events arrive in between. Method A doesn't call Method B directly; instead, Method A starts a nonperiodic Timer, and the Timer calls Method B. The effect is the same as a command to yield some time to the system before proceeding with Method B—but REALbasic has no such command, so this is your *only* way to yield some time to the system. Of course, you could do everything in a thread, but then you're just gambling: you don't know when your code will run or how much time it will yield or when. The Timer gives you far more control. Because the Timer's period is short, no delay is apparent to the user, but because Method A comes to an end and the application falls idle for an instant, time is yielded to the system before Method B is called. An example of this technique appears in Chapter 27.

In general, when it occurs to you that what you need is a loop or an elapsed interval during which the user should be free to work or events should be free to arrive, you should reach for a Timer. That's what they're for. I often say that Timers are misnamed: they don't keep time particularly well at all. They're not Timers; they're Yielders.*

* However, there are some user actions that absolutely stop the clock, such as initiating a drag (see Chapter 24) or clicking on a popup menu (see Chapter 17). I have not found any way to yield time during these actions.

Sound

REALbasic can produce four different types of sound. The first three are: a simple beep; a 'snd ' resource (or, what amounts to the same thing, a sound file of type 'sfil', which is simply a way of packaging a 'snd ' resource); and a QuickTime MIDI note. This chapter discusses each of these types of sound.

The fourth way in which REALbasic can produce a sound is as part of a movie. In fact, REALbasic can play a sound *as* a movie: in the presence of QuickTime 4 or later, it can open a sound file in a QuickTime-compatible format (such as AIFF, wav, MP3, or a MIDI file), converting it to a movie on the fly. The sound is then played with a MoviePlayer control; MoviePlayers are the subject of Chapter 27.

On Windows, there's no such thing as a 'snd ' resource; .wav, MIDI, and MP3 files are played as sound files, not as movies.

Beep

To play the system beep sound, call the Beep procedure, like this:*

    beep

Sound Object

REALbasic includes a Sound class; you send an instance of this class the Play message to produce the sound. The question is then how to obtain a Sound instance. There are three ways:

- Import a sound file from the Finder into your project. The project maintains an alias to the sound file until the application is built, so don't throw the sound file away while the project is still under development. The listing in the Project Window is the global name of a sound instance.

---

* This is the shortest section in the book.

- Send a ResourceFork the GetSound message, handing it the ID number of a 'snd ' resource. A Sound instance is returned.

- Send a FolderItem, which points to a sound file, the OpenAsSound message. A Sound instance is returned. This is really just a shortcut for the previous method. (On Windows, though, this is how you play .wav files, MIDI files, and MP3 files.)

For example, we might have a Sound property, called Snd, which is initialized in a window's Open event handler by reading in the sound from a sound file:

```
self.snd = volume(0).child("sound folder").child("loon").openassound
```

Subsequently, the sound can be produced by saying `self.snd.play`.

When a Sound instance is sent the Play message, the sound plays asynchronously, meaning, in effect, that once the sound has been "launched," the application just proceeds about its business, with the sound playing autonomously: code continues to execute, the user is able to interact with the application, and so forth. In fact, a sound can even be sent the Play message while it is currently playing. This is a very useful feature because more than one object might wish to produce the sound more or less simultaneously. For example, you might have a game in which Target objects explode and make a noise; it would be very clumsy if you had to work around some limitation where your Explode sound couldn't be sent the Play message by one Target if another Target was already playing it.

To learn whether a sound is already playing, send it the IsPlaying message, which returns a boolean. You can use this to play a sound synchronously, pausing until the sound is done:

```
operational.play // "I'm completely operational, and all my circuits . . . "
while operational.isplaying
wend
msgbox "The sound is over (but the malady lingers on)."
```

The IsPlaying message returns true if the Sound instance is playing at all, no matter how the reference to it is obtained. For example, suppose a button has this Action event handler:

```
dim s as sound
s = mymindHAL
if not s.isplaying then
    s.play // "Dave . . . my mind is going . . . "
end
```

Imagine that the user pushes this button several times in quick succession. Clearly, the local variable s is different each time; yet it ultimately points to the same Sound instance, so when s is sent the IsPlaying message, it correctly reports whether the sound is playing—and therefore, as intended, the button has no effect if the sound is playing already.

To play a sound repeatedly, send it the PlayLooping message. To stop a sound that is currently playing or looping, send it the Stop message.

MIDI Notes

MIDI notes can be generated through the QuickTime synthesizer, by way of the built-in NotePlayer control.[*]

Since a NotePlayer is a control, it must be instantiated by a window. In the IDE, drag a NotePlayer from the Tools Window into a Window Editor; now the window will instantiate the NotePlayer when it itself is instantiated. The NotePlayer icon that appears in the Window Editor is just a placeholder; it has no physical manifestation in the running application.

The particular MIDI instrument that a NotePlayer will play is determined by its Instrument property, which is an integer from 1 to 128, plus 16385 for the drum kit; a table in the REALbasic documentation tells you the names of the different instruments. To cause a NotePlayer to produce a note, send it the PlayNote message, with two integer parameters: the pitch and the velocity. Pitch is measured in half-steps, with 60 representing middle C.[†] (When you use the drum kit, each "pitch" represents a different percussion instrument.) Velocity is measured on a scale from 0 to 127, and, despite its name, essentially represents how loud the sound will be. There is no duration specification in a MIDI note; instead, the note must be sent a second time, with a velocity of 0, to cause it to cut off.

To play more than one instrument simultaneously, just use multiple NotePlayers. The first corresponds to MIDI channel 1, the second to MIDI channel 2, and so forth.[‡] NotePlayers are limited to QuickTime MIDI; if you want to send and receive MIDI information through a port, you'll need a plug-in.

To get started with MIDI, let's write a routine that permits us to experience the different instrument sounds that the QuickTime MIDI synthesizer can produce. We assume that the window contains a NotePlayer, along with a StaticText so that the instrument's number can be displayed and we can follow along with the REALbasic instrument list as a guide. To make the tune easy to imagine and to write down, I have encoded it as a string of note–duration pairs, with the durations as integers signifying beats. The routine multiplies the durations by a scale factor to get ticks; for each note, it plays the specified pitch with a velocity of 127, pauses the given number of ticks, and then plays the pitch again with a velocity of 0 to cut it off. This routine takes about half an hour to complete, or an hour if you uncomment the third and fourth "bars" for the full experience:

```
dim s,ss as string
dim i,u,j,t,d, note, duration as integer
```

[*] There are many online introductions to MIDI; one that I particularly like is at *http://www.umr.edu/~johns/links/music/midispec.htm*.

[†] For a convenient table of pitch values, see *http://www.midi.org/table4.htm*.

[‡] However, it appears that MIDI channel 10 does not exist; the 10th NotePlayer is MIDI channel 11, the 11th NotePlayer is MIDI channel 12, and that's the end. I owe this information to J. W. van Mook.

```
s = "60,3;55,1;57,3;55,1;65,1;64,1;62,1;60,1;62,3;55,1"
s = s + ";65,1;64,1;62,1;60,1;62,2;55,2;67,7;67,1"
// Uncomment the next two lines for the full experience!
//s = s + ";69,2;67,1;60,1;67,2;65,2;64,2;56,1;57,1;64,2;62,2"
//s = s + ";64,4;65,1;64,1;62,1;60,1;62,4;60,1;59,1;57,1;55,1"
u = countfields(s,";")
for j = 1 to 128
    noteplayer1.instrument = j
    statictext1.text = "Now Playing: Instrument " + str(j)
    statictext1.refresh
    for i = 1 to u
        ss = nthfield(s,";",i)
        note = val(nthfield(ss,",",1))
        duration = val(nthfield(ss,",",2))
        noteplayer1.playnote note, 127
        t = ticks
        d = duration * 25 // tempo
        while ticks-t < d
        wend
        noteplayer1.playnote note, 0
    next
next
```

The foregoing example was easy to write, and is lots of fun to listen to (the first time, anyway), because many of the QuickTime instruments are quite fascinating. As a technique for producing MIDI notes, however, it suffers from serious defects. The worst is that it is synchronous: while the tune is playing, the user cannot do anything else. You might be tempted to solve this by moving all the code into a thread, but the results are disastrous, because the thread, by definition, only executes code now and then, so the timing becomes unreliable. Clearly, we would like to insert into each iteration of the inner loop a call to yield time to other processes and to receive events. REALbasic has no such call; but the notion of a loop that does not interfere with the application's ability to receive events obviously describes a Timer (see "Yielding Time" in Chapter 25).

The rest of this chapter develops an algorithm for Timer-based MIDI playing. Bear in mind, however, that synchronous MIDI playing is always going to sound better! That's because even though we may set a Timer to be called as often as possible (and we will), we cannot guarantee that it will in fact be called that often every time. Even the slightest delay caused by REALbasic's handling of events and yielding time to background processes may be enough to impair the timing of the music. This is one of those situations where we really would like to be able to say: yield just this much time and no more! For best results, build the application (don't run the project in the IDE), use the DisableBackgroundTasks pragma, keep the built application in the foreground, don't have any other processes running, and keep the mouse outside the window.

To develop a Timer-based implementation, we will concentrate on playing asynchronously the same tune from the previous example. The routine will decode the tune into a series of triples: a pitch, a velocity, and a time. The time will not be a duration, but rather will represent a number of ticks from when the tune starts playing; each note in the tune must therefore be represented by two such triples, one to start the note, the other to stop it. The triples will be loaded into three array properties, Notes, Velocities, and Times; the first two are integers, but Times is an array of doubles, for maximum precision—instead of Ticks, we will now think in Microseconds.

The routine itself does not play any notes! That's what the Timer is for. Rather, we decode the tune to fill up the three arrays, and then we initialize two more properties, StartTime (the Microseconds value at the moment we are to start playing) and WhichNote (the index value of the triple currently being processed). Then we start the Timer, which will do the actual playing:

```
dim s,ss as string
dim i,u as integer
dim t as double
s = "60,3;55,1;57,3;55,1;65,1;64,1;62,1;60,1;62,3;55,1"
s = s + ";65,1;64,1;62,1;60,1;62,2;55,2;67,7;67,1"
s = s + ";69,2;67,1;60,1;67,2;65,2;64,2;56,1;57,1;64,2;62,2"
s = s + ";64,4;65,1;64,1;62,1;60,1;62,4;60,1;59,1;57,1;55,1"
u = countfields(s,";")
redim notes(2*u)
redim times(2*u)
redim velocities(2*u)
for i = 1 to u
    ss = nthfield(s,";",i)
    notes(i*2-1) = val(nthfield(ss,",",1))
    times(i*2-1) = t
    velocities(i*2-1) = 127
    notes(i*2) = val(nthfield(ss,",",1))
    times(i*2) = t + val(nthfield(ss,",",2)) * 400000.0
    velocities(i*2) = 0
    t = times(i*2)
next
starttime = microseconds + 200000
whichNote = 1
timer1.mode = 2
```

The Timer is initially off, and has a very small Period—for best results it should probably be set to 1—representing the time slices at which the Timer will check to see whether the NotePlayer needs to be sent a message. The Timer's Action event handler is very simple: it just examines the current Times entry to see if the next note is due to be produced, and, if so, it produces it, increments WhichNote, and keeps doing this until it has produced all notes that are currently due. To finish the tune, we just fall off the end of the array; this generates an exception, which we catch in an Exception block to stop the Timer:

```
while microseconds - starttime >= times(whichNote)
    noteplayer1.playNote notes(whichNote), velocities(whichNote)
    whichNote = whichNote + 1
wend
exception
    me.mode = 0
```

This works splendidly, and we are now ready to tackle our implementation's remaining problems. What are they? For one thing, there are no rests; it is assumed that one note follows another immediately. Also, we have made no provision for sounding more than one note simultaneously (actually, this is the same problem in another guise). Finally, every note is being played with the same velocity (volume), so our tune is not very expressive.

Clearly, we will have to recode our description of the tune. Every note is now a quartet of event descriptors: the note's pitch, its start, its duration, and its velocity. We will recast the start and duration in terms of measures; for example, the beginning of the first measure will be signified by 1.0, the beginning of the second measure by 2.0, and a duration of half a measure by 0.5.

In decoding the tune string to generate the three arrays, we face a new problem: the string does not describe the MIDI events in their temporal order. For example, suppose the first note starts at 1.0 and is 0.5 long, and the second note starts at 1.25 and is 0.1 long. The order of events as we obtain them from the string is: start of the first note, end of the first note; start of the second note, end of the second note. But the Timer's algorithm for running through the arrays assumes that they are temporally ordered; the actual order of these four events needs to be: start of the first note, start of the second note, end of the second note, end of the first note. Thus, code must be added to maintain the Times array in numerically sorted order as we construct it (and the other two arrays along with it).

To demonstrate, I have encoded, with apologies to J. S. Bach, a different tune, one involving notes that overlap and that have different durations and velocities:*

```
dim s,ss as string
dim i,u,j,uu,vel,w as integer
dim t,tempo as double
redim times(0)
redim notes(0)
redim velocities(0)
tempo = 1400000.0
s = "53,1.0,.5,127;48,1.0,.5,127;45,1.0,.5,127;41,1.0,.5,127"
s = s + ";77,1.25,.1,100;65,1.5,.1,100;69,1.5,.1,100"
s = s + ";67,1.75,.1,100;70,1.75,.1,100"
s = s + ";72,2.0,.5,100;69,2.0,.5,100;74,2.5,.5,100;70,2.5,.5,100"
s = s + ";65,2.25,.1,120;62,2.5,.1,120;58,2.75,.1,120"
s = s + ";65,3.0,1.0,120;69,3.0,.5,80;70,3.5,.5,80"
s = s + ";72,3.0,.25,100;77,3.25,.5,100"
s = s + ";75,3.75,.125,100;74,3.875,.125,100"
s = s + ";53,3.25,.1,120;50,3.5,.1,120;46,3.75,.1,120"
s = s + ";65,4.0,.5,100;74,4.0,.1,100;70,4.0,.1,100"
s = s + ";72,4.25,.1,100;69,4.25,.1,100"
s = s + ";53,4.0,.5,120;41,4.25,.1,120"
u = countfields(s,";")
```

---

* No, I'm not going to tell you what the tune is! If you can't read the encoding, you'll just have to run the routine and listen to it.

```
for i = 1 to u
    ss = nthfield(s,";",i)
    for w = 1 to 2
        if w = 1 then // note start
            t = (val(nthfield(ss,",",2))-1.0) * tempo
            vel = val(nthfield(ss,",",4))
        else // note end
            t = t + val(nthfield(ss,",",3)) * tempo
            vel = 0
        end
        uu = ubound(times)
        if t >= times(uu) then
            times.append t
            notes.append val(nthfield(ss,",",1))
            velocities.append vel
        else
            j = uu
            while t < times(j-1)
                j = j-1
            wend
            times.insert j,t
            notes.insert j,val(nthfield(ss,",",1))
            velocities.insert j,vel
        end
    next
next
starttime = microseconds + 200000
whichNote = 1
noteplayer1.instrument = 7
timer1.mode = 2
```

At this point we have practically invented MIDI encoding, so we may as well dispense with the string encoding of the tune altogether and start with a standard MIDI file. REALbasic can then parse and play the file.[*] To keep the example simple, I'll use a very simple MIDI file, consisting solely of note events and channel changes: I artificially skip the file header; in real life, we would have to parse it. Since we are now dealing with channel changes, we will have several NotePlayers in a control array, so that the event's channel number will correspond to the index of the NotePlayer; we have to introduce a fourth array telling the Timer which NotePlayer to send each event to:

```
dim b as binarystream, f as folderitem
dim i, res as integer
dim tempo as double
redim times(0)
redim notes(0)
redim velocities(0)
redim channels(0)
```

---

[*] A convenient and inexpensive way to make MIDI files is to use the brilliant shareware MIDIGraphy, by "Tontata"; see *http://ux01.so-net.or.jp/~mmaeda/indexe.html*. For standard MIDI file format, see *http://www.music-center.com.br/spec_smf.htm* and *http://www.midi.org/table1.htm*.

```
tempo = 450.0
f = // simple standard MIDI file
b = f.openasBinaryFile(false)
b.position = 50 // skip header; in real life, would have to parse it!
while not b.eof
    i = b.readbyte // delta-time
    while i >= 128
        res = res*128 + i - 128
        i = b.readbyte
    wend
    times.append times(ubound(times)) + (res*128 + i) * tempo
    res = 0
    i = b.readbyte
    if i = &hFF then // end-of-song
        exit
    end
    if i >= &h90 and i <= &h9F then // channel change
        channels.append i - &h90
        i = b.readbyte
    else
        channels.append channels(ubound(channels)) // same channel
    end
    notes.append i // pitch
    velocities.append b.readbyte // velocity
wend
starttime = microseconds + 200000
whichNote = 1
b.close
timer2.mode = 2
```

The Timer, timer2, is as before, except that it reads the Channels array to direct each message to the correct NotePlayer; the NotePlayers, representing the different channels, are a control array named N:

```
while microseconds - starttime >= times(whichNote)
    N(channels(whichNote)).playNote notes(whichNote), velocities(whichNote)
    whichNote = whichNote + 1
wend
exception
    me.mode = 0
```

You can see that expanding the example to play genuine MIDI files is only a matter of degree and of details. You would probably introduce at least the ability to respond to events that change the tempo as the tune proceeds; and if the MIDI file contains any other sorts of events, you will have to parse them—if only in order to ignore them. Certain events will *have* to be ignored, because, unfortunately, the NotePlayer control cannot send control change events, such as Damper and Portamento.

CHAPTER 27

Movies

In this chapter:
- Movie Class
- MoviePlayer
- Movie Usage
- Making Movies
- Analyzing Movies

This chapter describes REALbasic's support for movies. The first order of business is to consider what a movie is, since the term has an unexpectedly wide meaning. Figure 27-1 shows a REALbasic window displaying what one normally thinks of as a movie; but the notion, and the technology, can go well beyond this.

Figure 27-1. A movie that looks like a movie

A movie, in the most intuitive and fundamental sense, is time-based sight and sound—an animated succession of images, possibly accompanied by a sound track. Now, this concept masks a number of complex issues: Animated how? How does the timing work? Where is the data stored, and in what format? The user is shielded from these and many other questions thanks to a powerful and self-contained technology, QuickTime. Movies are full of redundant data, because successive images are typically similar to one another; QuickTime sees to it that the data is stored in compressed format, and expands it when the movie needs to be shown. Movies may involve images of varying duration shown at varying rates, and they may call for coordination of multiple tracks, such as sound and video, or several video components;

QuickTime handles these relationships. When a movie is actually shown, an area of a window needs successive images drawn into it, with minimal flicker, and sound must emerge from the speaker; QuickTime takes care of all that too.

Furthermore, QuickTime can accept a wide variety of video, audio, and still-picture formats. Quite apart from the native movie file (of type 'MooV'), which is itself remarkably flexible as to what it can hold and how it is stored, QuickTime can read such formats as animated GIF, PICS, TIFF, AIFF, MIDI, MP3, still-picture GIF, JPEG, and PICT. Thus, in effect, a movie can be a file in any of these formats too. Even more surprising, QuickTime supports user interaction: for example, QuickTimeVR lets the user pan round a scene, and Wired Sprites let the user interact with "hotspots" in a movie, which thus becomes a sort of self-contained mini-application.*

QuickTime's power, by which it reduces so much technology to a deceptively simple "frontend," is at your application's disposal. In a nutshell, whatever QuickTime can play, your application can play. Thus, many varieties of time-based sight and sound can be incorporated into your application. In real life, you probably won't treat still pictures as movies—though it may interest you know that it is QuickTime that is responsible for converting still-picture formats for you when they are opened as REALbasic Picture objects. (So, when you display a GIF, JPEG, or TIFF in a Canvas, as discussed in Chapter 11, you're using QuickTime.) But this still leaves all the various audio and video formats; any of these can be what this chapter calls a movie.

To play a movie, your application will need an instance of the Movie class and a MoviePlayer control to play it. Furthermore, besides playing movies, REALbasic has rudimentary abilities to create movies and to analyze movies into their constituent parts. To create or dissect a movie, you will need an instance of the EditableMovie class and possibly instances of the QTTrack and QTEffectSequence classes. These will all be discussed in turn.

Movie Class

There are four ways to obtain an instance of the Movie class:

- Import a movie file (of type 'MooV') into the project. REALbasic will automatically create a Movie instance when the application starts up; the name under which the movie file is listed in the Project Window is the instance's global name. The project retains an alias to the movie file, so don't throw the file away until the application is built; the built application incorporates the movie.

 This method doesn't always work. When compiling on Mac OS X, I have never gotten it to work. If you're compiling on Mac OS Classic, it might work, but in the past I've found it unreliable.

---

* See *http://www.apple.com/quicktime/*; for a good list of file formats that QuickTime can handle, see *http://www.apple.com/quicktime/samples/file-formats/index.html.*

- Point a FolderItem at a file that QuickTime can open, and send the FolderItem the OpenAsMovie message. A Movie instance is returned.
- Point a FolderItem at a file containing a 'moov' resource, and send the Folder-Item the OpenResourceMovie message, supplying the ID of the resource. A Movie instance is returned.
- Call the global function OpenURLMovie, supplying a string that is the URL of a movie on the Internet. A Movie instance is returned, and can be played as it is downloading across the Internet ("streaming video"). This works only under QuickTime 4 or later.*

If you don't want a movie to accompany your application as a separate file, you may have to do some strategic planning as to how you're going to include it in your application. If importing it into the Project Window works for you, then there's your answer. If not, you can rely on the workaround demonstrated in Chapter 21: you load the file's data into your application as a resource, and then, when the application runs, you reconstruct the file and open it. Be aware that a movie file is a tricky beast; sometimes, the movie data isn't inside the movie file itself. So make sure you start with a cross-platform, single-file version of the movie file, such as you get by saving it as Self-Contained with Apple's QuickTime Player application.

A Movie instance has these properties:

MovieHeight, MovieWidth
　　The dimensions of the image, in pixels.

There are also two other properties, BaseMovieHeight and BaseMovieWidth, but I'm not clear on what they do that's any different from MovieHeight and MovieWidth.

To play the movie, you must first assign it to the Movie property of a MoviePlayer.

MoviePlayer

A MoviePlayer is a RectControl, and therefore receives all the events and has all the methods listed in Chapter 10: Open and Close events; Visible, Enabled, and AutoDeactivate properties; Top, Left, Height, and Width properties; LockLeft, LockRight, LockTop, and LockBottom properties; MouseEnter, MouseMove, and MouseExit events; and Refresh and RefreshRect methods. For drag-and-drop, see Chapter 24.

A MoviePlayer is disabled by default, and cannot be enabled in the IDE. The Enabled state of a MoviePlayer makes no difference to its behavior, except for whether its BalloonHelp or DisabledBalloonHelp text is displayed when balloon help is turned on. (On balloon help, see Chapter 20.) On Mac OS Classic, unfortunately, if a Movie-Player has been assigned a Movie, the user may never see either of these texts;

---

* For instance: `movieplayer1.movie = openurlmovie("http://www.intellisw.com/quandary/static/rhapsody.mov")`. I owe that one to Paul Scandariato.

instead, a generic message appears: "Movie. To play this movie, double-click on it." This is probably a bug; it seems to occur primarily when the movie has a controller, so setting the MoviePlayer's Controller property to 0 may be a workaround of sorts.

Until a MoviePlayer is assigned a Movie, it has no visible manifestation in the built application. Nonetheless, being a RectControl, it has a position and dimensions, and, if its Visible property is true, it receives MouseEnter, MouseMove, and Mouse-Exit events.

A MoviePlayer is assigned a movie by setting its Movie property to a Movie instance. When this is done, then if the MoviePlayer's Visible property is true, and if the movie has a video track, the movie's opening frame is shown until the movie starts playing, or until the MoviePlayer's Position is changed in code.

On Mac OS X, assigning a movie to a MoviePlayer as the window opens fails to show the movie's first frame; the MoviePlayer remains invisible. A simple workaround is to use a nonperiodic Timer to send the MoviePlayer the Refresh message shortly after the window opens. Just the other way, a MoviePlayer may cause a crash if it has a movie when the window closes (or the application quits); a workaround is to set the Movie to nil in the MoviePlayer's Close event handler. (It's expected that these issues will be fixed in REALbasic 3.5.)

If you're going to set any properties of the MoviePlayer, it's a good idea to do this before assigning the MoviePlayer a movie. I think the reason for this is that movies, in a sense, belong to QuickTime, not to your application. When you set a MoviePlayer property, you're storing an instruction that needs to be relayed to QuickTime, and this can't happen until QuickTime is ready to listen. That won't be until the next time the MoviePlayer is assigned a movie—so that's when the property will take effect. Thus, a MoviePlayer property set in code while the Movie property is non-nil will have no immediate visible effect. Another thing to try, to make a MoviePlayer act upon a property change, is to send the window the Refresh message.

Appearance

The following MoviePlayer properties govern its appearance:

Border
    A boolean; if true, a rectangle appears around the outside of the image.

AutoResize
    A boolean; if false, the image (including the controller) will be scaled to fit the MoviePlayer's dimensions; if true, the movie is displayed at its own proper size, without affecting the dimensions of the MoviePlayer control. If set to true, setting to false has no effect once the MoviePlayer has been assigned a movie. (This may be a bug.)

Controller
    An integer, dictating whether a QuickTime movie controller appears, as follows:

0   No controller appears.

1   A "badge" appears within the image. The user can click the badge to show a full controller.

2   A full controller appears.

Even without a controller, the user can double-click a movie image, if there is one, to start it playing, and can single-click it to stop it.

HasStep
A boolean; if true, then if a controller appears, it will have the two "step" arrows at the right end.

Speaker
A boolean; if true, then if a controller appears, and if the movie has a sound track, the controller will have the volume control at the left end.

ControllerHeight, ControllerWidth
Read-only. Integers. ControllerHeight is the height of the movie, from its top to the bottom of the controller, even if the controller is not presently visible. ControllerWidth is the width of the controller, which may be slightly more than the width of the movie image because of the controller's borders. When AutoResize is true, these properties provide the total dimensions of the actual movie image.

Action

There are three ways in which a MoviePlayer can be made to start or stop playing its movie:

- If the movie has a video track, the user double-clicks the image to start it or single-clicks it to stop it.
- The user presses the play/pause button at the left of the controller, if there is one.
- The MoviePlayer is sent the Play or Stop message.

A movie's behavior once it is playing is determined by two MoviePlayer properties:

Looping
A boolean. If false, the movie stops automatically when it reaches the end; if true, the movie keeps playing until it is explicitly stopped.

Palindrome
A boolean. If true, then if Looping is true, the movie plays from beginning to end, then from end to beginning, and so on.* Ignored if Looping is false.

---

* "Palindrome" is really not the right word to describe this. A palindrome is a word or phrase that is identical backward and forward, like "gnu dung" or "Howdy, Madam, I'm Adam Y. Dwoh." A Palindrome movie is (usually) not identical backward and forward! Something that repeatedly travels from start to finish and back again would be better described as "shuttling" or "oscillating."

The following MoviePlayer property expresses its movie's temporal dimension:

Position
> A double. Starts at 0 and increases as the movie plays or as the user moves the controller's thumb rightward. Can be set, whether or not the movie is playing; this may alter what image is currently displayed. You can learn the movie's duration, in seconds, by setting its Position to a ridiculously high number (so that it moves to the end) and then reading its actual Position.

Events

A MoviePlayer receives two events in connection with its movie: Play and Stop, signifying that the movie is about to play or about to stop playing, respectively. If a MoviePlayer sends itself the Play message in its Stop event handler, it cannot be stopped (it will pause very slightly when the user tries to stop it, but it will resume immediately). Similarly, if a MoviePlayer sends itself the Stop message in its Play event handler, it cannot be played (it will advance one frame when the user tries to play it, but it will stop again immediately).

The Play event is sent when:

- The user clicks the play button at the left end of the controller.
- The user double-clicks the image to start playing—after the *second* click.
- The MoviePlayer is sent the Play message.

The Stop event is sent when:

- The user clicks the pause button at the left end of the controller.
- The user single-clicks the image to stop playing.
- The user double-clicks the image to start playing—after the *first* click.
- The user drags the controller's thumb or clicks in its gray area or a step arrow, after the user releases the mouse.
- The MoviePlayer is sent the Stop message.

A MoviePlayer also receives a ControllerSizeChanged event, when the MoviePlayer is assigned a movie. The MoviePlayer might use this to respond to being assigned a movie by resizing the window to accommodate the image if AutoResize is true.

In this example, the MoviePlayer's Open event handler initializes the MoviePlayer, a button's Action event handler lets the user pick a movie file, and the MoviePlayer's ControllerSizeChanged event resizes the window nicely and plays the movie:

```
// MoviePlayer's Open event handler:
me.border = true
me.autoresize = true
me.controller = 0

// PushButton's Action event handler:
dim f as folderitem
```

```
f = getopenfolderitem("movie") // "MooV/????"
if f <> nil then
    movieplayer1.movie = f.openasmovie
end

// MoviePlayer's ControllerSizeChanged event handler:
self.width = me.controllerwidth + 2 * me.left
self.height = me.controllerheight + me.top + 10
me.play
```

Movie Usage

Despite the brilliance of QuickTime, movies are probably an underutilized feature of the Macintosh operating system. One often thinks of a movie as merely a way for the user to view animated information at will, like watching a brief television show; but this is probably because one imagines a movie as a rectangular frame with a controller at the bottom, as in Figure 27-1.

This is indeed a common use of movies. But a movie needn't have a controller; instead of the user, your code can govern when it plays. What's more, if a movie's background is the same color as what's behind it, or if it is an animated GIF that has transparency, it needn't appear rectangular. Finally, movies play asynchronously; the user can continue to work elsewhere while a movie is playing. Thus, all sorts of lively effects can be achieved without seeming to have anything to do with movies.

For example—although this is rather hard to communicate through words and screen shots—Figure 27-2 shows a window containing a button with a constantly dancing, rotating blue arrow pointing to it. When the user clicks the button, the button appears to depress, as usual; but when the user releases the mouse, instead of returning to normal, the button seems to slide suddenly in from the right, following which an animated loudspeaker appears, emitting colorful notes, while an excerpt from the Hallelujah Chorus blares. The result is that the window seems full of lively and surprising objects, but the phrase "QuickTime movie" is very unlikely to cross the user's mind.

Nonetheless, QuickTime is doing nearly all the work. The rotating blue arrow is a looping movie, which plays constantly. The user is able to click the button because movies are asynchronous. A Canvas intercepts the click and turns the button invisible, revealing the first frame of a second movie, which shows the button in its depressed state. Then, when the user releases the mouse button, the Canvas starts the second movie, which shows the button sliding in from the right; when the second movie ends, its Stop event handler shows the real button once again, and also plays the sound and starts the third movie (the loudspeaker). When the third movie ends, its Stop event handler hides it. All three movies are opened from transparent animated GIFs; thus they have no rectangular frame.

Another use for a movie is to play a sound. As mentioned in Chapter 26, QuickTime can open and play sound files in various formats, including AIFF, wav, MP3, and

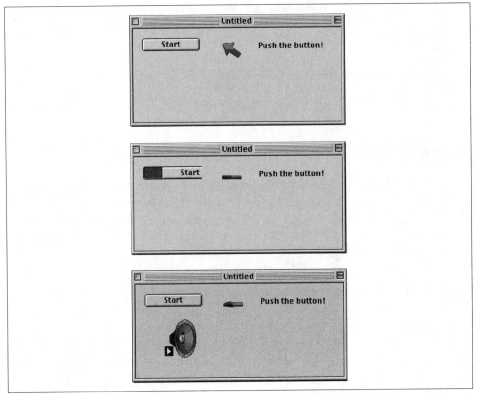

Figure 27-2. QuickTime hellzapoppin

MIDI. Depending on what version of QuickTime is present, you may even be able to perform the conversion on the fly, by sending a FolderItem the OpenAsMovie message. In this example, MoviePlayer1 is invisible; its job is to provide our application's background music, which it gets from a MIDI file:

```
movieplayer1.movie = getfolderitem("brahms.mid").openasmovie
movieplayer1.play
```

The user will be able to work while the music is playing, because QuickTime movies are asynchronous. Again, the idea of a movie will probably never enter the user's head; there's music playing in the background, and that's all.

There are limits, however, to what a QuickTime movie can do. For example, you might wish that a QuickTime movie could be used to animate a sprite within your window: the movie would provide the character's inherent action (a snake wriggling or a rabbit hopping), but your code would provide the locomotion by changing the MoviePlayer's position. But you can't do that, because while a movie is playing, changing the MoviePlayer's position doesn't reposition the image; the image has been positioned by QuickTime once and for all at the time the movie was assigned to the MoviePlayer. This sort of thing sounds much more like a job for a SpriteSurface (Chapter 28).

Making Movies

To construct a movie, you need an instance of the EditableMovie class. This instance is always tied to a file on disk. You can't play the EditableMovie; you have to open the file again to get a Movie instance, and play that.

To obtain an EditableMovie instance, send a FolderItem one of two messages:

CreateMovie
> An EditableMovie instance is returned. The file will be created; if the file exists, it will be deleted and replaced, so be careful.

OpenEditableMovie
> An EditableMovie instance is returned. If the file doesn't exist or isn't a movie file, `nil` is returned.

The next step is to access a track of the movie. This is done by sending the EditableMovie one of two messages:

NewVideoTrack
> Takes three parameters: width and height of the video image, in pixels, and an integer denoting the speed in frames per second. A QTVideoTrack is returned.

Track
> Takes one parameter, a one-based index number. You can learn the number of tracks from the EditableMovie's TrackCount property. A newly created movie (made with CreateMovie) has no tracks. A QTTrack is returned.

QTVideoTrack is a subclass of QTTrack. The main thing you can do with a QTVideoTrack is to add frames to it, by sending it the AppendPicture message and supplying a Picture. In this example, the user is asked for a folder, which is expected to contain a series of PICT files representing the frames of an animation. The files are opened in alphabetical order and combined to create a new movie. The movie is then played. The file represented by the EditableMovie is not closed until the EditableMovie reference goes out of scope (there is, unfortunately, no Close method for an EditableMovie); so the action of opening the file as a movie and playing it is chained to the end of the routine by means of a Timer (see Chapter 25):

```
dim f,f1 as folderitem
dim i,u as integer
dim p as picture
dim m as editablemovie
dim t as qtvideotrack
dim s(0) as string
f = selectfolder
if f = nil then
    return
end
f1 = temporaryfolder.child("myMovie")
m = f1.createmovie
u = f.count
for i = 1 to u
    if f.item(i).mactype = "PICT" then
```

```
        s.append f.item(i).name
    end
next
s.sort
u = ubound(s)
for i = 1 to u
    p = f.child(s(i)).openaspicture
    if i = 1 then
        t = m.newvideotrack(p.width, p.height, 4)
    end
    t.appendpicture(p)
next
timer1.mode = 1
```

And Timer1's Action event handler goes like this:

```
movieplayer1.movie = temporaryfolder.child("mymovie").openasmovie
movieplayer1.play
```

Instead of making all of a movie's frames yourself, you can let QuickTime make some of them for you through one of its many built-in effects. To do this, you first call one of these global functions:

GetQTCrossFadeEffect
A QTEffect instance is returned.

GetQTSmpteEffect
Takes one parameter, an integer specifying the desired effect. For the available effects, see the REALbasic documentation. A QTEffect instance is returned.

Now you make a QTEffectSequence instance, with New. This class has a constructor so that it can take parameters when you use New. The parameters are: the QTEffect instance you got from the previous step; two Pictures to serve as starting and ending frames for the effect; and the total number of frames to be generated.

With the resulting QTEffectSequence instance, you then set its Frame property to some integer to focus on the desired frame, and then get its Image property to obtain the Picture from that frame. You can then stick the Picture into the video track of an EditableMovie. You keep doing that until you've copied out all the frames.

In this example, which is a variation on the previous example, the user is asked for a folder, which is expected to contain a series of PICT files representing the frames of an animation. The first and last files in alphabetical order are opened and an effect is created transitioning between them; the frames of this effect are turned into the frames of a new movie. The picture from the first file isn't included in the effect, so it is added beforehand. The movie is then played, as before:

```
dim f,f1 as folderitem
dim i,u as integer
dim p,p2 as picture
dim m as editablemovie
dim t as qtvideotrack
dim ee as qteffect
dim e as qteffectsequence
dim s(0) as string
```

```
f = selectfolder
if f = nil then
    return
end
f1 = temporaryfolder.child("myMovie")
m = f1.createmovie
u = f.count
for i = 1 to u
    if f.item(i).mactype = "PICT" then
        s.append f.item(i).name
    end
next
s.sort
p = f.child(s(1)).openaspicture
p2 = f.child(s(ubound(s))).openaspicture
ee = getqtsmpteeffect(71)
e = new qteffectsequence(ee,p,p2,20)
t = m.newvideotrack(p.width, p.height, 4)
t.appendpicture(p)
for i = 1 to 20
    e.frame = i
    p = e.image
    t.appendpicture(p)
next
timer1.mode = 1
```

Analyzing Movies

An EditableMovie instance can be analyzed into its constituent parts, by means of
the following properties:

TrackCount
   Number of tracks of the movie. Read-only.

Poster
   Poster image of the movie. A Picture. Read-only.

Duration
   Length of the movie in seconds. A double. Read-only. But because of a bug, this
   is actually an integer and cannot be used for anything.

TimeScale
   Number of units per second into which the movie is analyzable. The default is
   600.

TimeDuration
   Length of the movie in TimeScale units; thus, the product of the Duration and
   the TimeScale. An integer. Read-only.

Position
   Current position of the movie, in seconds. A double. Corresponds to the Posi-
   tion property of a MoviePlayer. Can be set to position the EditableMovie; the
   Picture and EOF properties then apply to the movie in its current position.

TimeValue
Current position of the movie, in TimeScale units. An integer. Like the Position, can be set to position the EditableMovie; the Picture and EOF properties then apply to the movie in its current position.

Picture
Image of the frame at the current position. Read-only.

EOF
Boolean; true if the current position is at (or past) the end of the movie.

Either the Position or the TimeValue can be used to position the EditableMovie; the image at that moment can then be extracted as the Picture property. For example, the following code displays in an ImageWell the image that would appear in a movie one second after the movie's beginning:

```
dim e as editablemovie
dim f as folderitem
f = // whatever
e = f.openeditableMovie
e.position = 1 // or: e.timevalue = e.timescale
imagewell1.image = e.picture
```

But neither Position nor TimeValue is the same thing as a frame. To get down to the level of individual frames, you have to decompose the movie still further, into its tracks. You will thus have a QTTrack instance, probably returned from an EditableMovie's Track function.

A QTTrack or QTVideoTrack instance has the following properties:

MediaType
String indicating whether the track is sound ("soun") or video ("vide").

TrackID
An integer unique to the track within its movie. Read-only.

Enabled
A boolean. Can be set to enable or disable the track.

TimeScale
Integer that can be set to alter the speed at which the track plays (the number of frames per second).

Duration
Length of the track in seconds. A double. Read-only.

TimeDuration
Product of the TimeScale and the Duration. An integer. Read-only.

When creating a video track, as in the two earlier examples, the TimeScale is set initially by the call to NewVideoTrack, and the TimeDuration is simply the number of frames. I find that while actively editing a track, the Duration may not be available (it reads 0);* but this doesn't matter, because you can calculate it by dividing the Time-Duration by the TimeScale.

Since only the TimeScale can be set, it is the means by which a movie's frame rate, and hence its Duration, can be adjusted; but since the TimeScale is an integer, the Duration can take on only certain discrete values. So, for example, given a track consisting of eight frames, we can make the track one second long by giving it a TimeScale of 8, and we can make it two seconds long by giving it a TimeScale of 4, but we cannot make it exactly three seconds long. The solution, of course, is to scale the TimeScale up and repeat frames; so, for example, we can make the track exactly three seconds long if the TimeScale is 600 and each of the eight images is repeated 225 times.

A QTTrack or QTVideoTrack instance has the following methods for walking through its individual frames:

FindFirstSample, FindNextSample
> Respectively, positions the movie at the track's first frame, and advances the movie one frame.

FindFirstKeyFrame, FindNextKeyFrame
> Respectively, positions the movie at the track's first base frame, and advances the movie one base frame.

As you walk through a track's frames, it is the movie as a whole that advances accordingly, so now you can get the frame's image, and so forth. For example, suppose the following code is in a PushButton's Action event handler. We have an integer property, Frame. Pushing the button repeatedly displays successive frames of the movie in an ImageWell; the button disables itself after showing the last frame:

```
dim e as editablemovie
dim f as folderItem
dim q as qttrack
dim i as integer
f = // whatever
e = f.openeditableMovie
q = e.track(1)
q.findfirstsample
for i = 1 to self.frame
    q.findnextsample
next
if e.eof then
    me.enabled = false
end
imagewell1.image = e.picture
self.frame = self.frame + 1
```

---

* This is probably a bug.

Both an EditableMovie and a QTTrack have a read-only DataSize property: you provide a starting time and a length, in seconds, to learn the number of bytes of data in the movie or track during that stretch of the movie. Since both the starting time and the length must be integers, though, the measurement is extremely gross, and I'm not entirely certain what the use of the resulting information would be.

Finally, an EditableMovie also has a UserData property that can be used to access its copyright and similar information; to learn more, consult the REALbasic documentation, under the QTUserData class.

CHAPTER 28

In this chapter:
- Configuring the SpriteSurface
- Basic Sprite Techniques
- Basic Background Techniques
- Improving the Classes
- Intelligent Sprite Behavior
- Responding to Keys
- Intelligent Collisions

Animation

Earlier chapters have mentioned various ways to achieve animated effects in REALbasic: you can redraw parts of a Canvas, for example (Chapter 11), or use a MoviePlayer (Chapter 27). But REALbasic also provides a control class whose primary purpose is animation—the SpriteSurface control. Figure 28-1 shows an example of a SpriteSurface; it's being used to play a little game, PacMan On Mars, which we'll develop later in the chapter. But first, let's start with the basics.

Figure 28-1. PacMan On Mars

A SpriteSurface is a RectControl, and therefore receives all the events and has all the methods listed in Chapter 10: Open and Close events; Visible, Enabled, and AutoDeactivate properties; Top, Left, Height, and Width properties; LockLeft, LockRight,

LockTop, and LockBottom properties; MouseEnter, MouseMove, and MouseExit events; and Refresh and RefreshRect methods. For drag-and-drop, see Chapter 24.

A SpriteSurface is a rectangular area of a window that functions as a "stage" within which animation can take place. A SpriteSurface can contain two sorts of thing:

The background
> An image that fills the SpriteSurface. It can be animated by assigning a different image, or by scrolling.

One or more sprites
> A sprite is an instance of the Sprite class. It has an image, which is drawn transparently in front of the background. It can be animated by changing its position or by assigning it a different image.

A SpriteSurface's behavior may be conceived metaphorically as a sort of silent movie. Think of the SpriteSurface's region in the window as a screen against which the movie is to be projected. The movie consists of a succession of frames; over time, the SpriteSurface is filled with one frame, then with the next, then with the next, and so forth. If these frames differ slightly from one another, animation is achieved. The frames, however, do not actually exist—at least, they don't exist in advance. Rather, the SpriteSurface calculates each frame in real time, before displaying it; the movie is constantly constructing itself.* The SpriteSurface knows when to make its next frame because it receives a NextFrame event. The calculation will consist of doing things to its background and the sprites.

What sorts of things might one do to generate the next frame? One might substitute a different image for the background. One might scroll the background; the parts of the background outside the SpriteSurface's region don't really exist, so as they scroll into view, they can be created, thus effectively altering the background image and scrolling it at the same time. One might add to or subtract from the SpriteSurface's stock of sprites, making sprites appear or disappear from the stage. One might alter the position of some of the sprites; if successive frames alter a sprite's position slightly, the sprite will appear to move smoothly. One might alter the image of some of the sprites; if successive frames alter a sprite's image, the sprite will appear to transform smoothly.

All of this is extremely easy to do, but things are not object-oriented in quite the expected fashion. Only the SpriteSurface receives events; the Sprites themselves receive no events, even though they constitute the "living" part, the "characters," of the animation. This chapter, along with explaining how the SpriteSurface and Sprite classes work, will also present a general object-oriented structure that makes them easier to use.

---

* It's rather like that scene in the Wallace and Gromit film, *The Wrong Trousers*, where Gromit is racing along, constantly laying track just ahead of the very same model train he's riding in.

Configuring the SpriteSurface

A SpriteSurface's "movie" can be generated in two different modes:

Intermittent
> Every once in a while, you send the SpriteSurface the Update message; this causes the SpriteSurface to display its current frame, and to receive a NextFrame event, so it can calculate its next frame.

Continuous
> You send the SpriteSurface the Run message. The SpriteSurface constantly receives NextFrame events, so it constantly calculates its next frame and displays it, at a rate determined by its FrameSpeed property, which is the number of ticks that should elapse between frames (0 means as fast as possible). This continues until the SpriteSurface is sent the Stop message. While the SpriteSurface is running, it becomes the only entity that receives events. However, if the SpriteSurface's ClickToStop property is true, the user can click the mouse anywhere to send the SpriteSurface the Stop message.

A little thought will reveal that if a SpriteSurface's ClickToStop property is false, then once the SpriteSurface is sent the Run message, the only entity that can send it the Stop message is the SpriteSurface itself, from one of its own events—the user can't do it, for example, from a menu item or by pressing a button, because there are no menu events or Action events.

A SpriteSurface has a Depth property, which may be set to 8, 16, or 32, or to 0 to match the depth of the screen automatically. (On screen depth and Picture depth, see Chapter 9 and Chapter 11.) A SpriteSurface is itself mostly just a kind of Picture, so it is memory-intensive in the same way that Pictures are, only more so; as a rough semiofficial formula, the amount of memory occupied by a SpriteSurface may be calculated as follows:[*]

```
dim size as integer
dim s as spritesurface
s = spritesurface1 // or whatever
size = s.depth/8*s.width*s.height + s.depth/8*(s.width+128)*(s.height+128)
```

Basic Sprite Techniques

To create a Sprite instance, use New. To give a SpriteSurface ownership of a Sprite, send the SpriteSurface the Attach message, handing it the Sprite; the SpriteSurface henceforward will draw the Sprite in accordance with the Sprite's various properties. For example, if the Sprite's X is 0 and its Y is 0, then the Sprite's image will visibly appear at the upper left of the SpriteSurface the next time the SpriteSurface draws a frame. To detach a Sprite from its SpriteSurface, send the Sprite the Close message.

---

[*] Thanks to Joe Strout for this formula.

A Sprite has the following properties:

Image
> The Picture displayed as the Sprite image.

X, Y
> The coordinates of the Sprite image's top left, with respect to the top left of the SpriteSurface that owns it.

Priority
> A nonnegative integer; the lower the value, the earlier in the redraw process the SpriteSurface will redraw this Sprite. When there are many Sprites, this can help maintain smoothness of animation, because you can make sure that the Sprites redrawn first are the ones the user is paying closest attention to. Or, you can use this property in a different way: a Sprite image drawn later will appear on top of a Sprite image drawn earlier, if their positions coincide.

A Sprite also has a Group property, whose meaning will be made clear in connection with collisions, later in this section.

Sprite images are drawn transparently against the background, in accordance with the basic rule of Picture transparency, where rgb(255,255,255) is the transparent color (white)—masks have no effect.

Motion

Let's explore some basic strategy for moving a Sprite. Remember, the only event we have to work with is the SpriteSurface's NextFrame event. The key thing to grasp is that a SpriteSurface is rather like a periodic Timer (Chapter 25). The SpriteSurface's NextFrame event is going to be called over and over, just as a periodic Timer's Action event would be; both are at the core of a kind of loop, but it's a loop that can't maintain state. Therefore, state has to be maintained elsewhere. To get a Sprite moving, the SpriteSurface's NextFrame event should make some incremental change in the Sprite's position every time it is called. In this case, the Sprite itself will maintain state, through its X and Y properties. But we still have the problem of getting a reference to the Sprite itself; this will have to be maintained as a property as well.

As a first example, we will cause a Sprite to cross the SpriteSurface from left to right. We start by preparing our properties. We'll give the window a Sprite property, S. The Sprite image is imported into the project as a Picture instance called Pic. A button's Action event handler initializes S, attaches it to the SpriteSurface, initializes the SpriteSurface, and sets it running:

```
s = new sprite
s.image = pic
spritesurface1.attach s
spritesurface1.clickToStop = true
spritesurface1.framespeed = 1
spritesurface1.run
```

The SpriteSurface's NextFrame event handler simply increases the Sprite's X value by 1 each time it is called:

```
s.x = s.x + 1
```

That's it! Run the project and press the button; the Sprite image obligingly appears and moves across the SpriteSurface until it vanishes from sight.

Image Animation

Now let's animate the Sprite's image. To change the image, you assign a Picture to the Sprite's Image property (merely altering the Graphics property of the Picture to which the Sprite's Image property already points won't work). Imagine that we have several pictures which, shown in succession, portray our Sprite character walking to the right. Our button's Action event handler loads the images into a Picture array called Pics:

```
dim f as folderitem
dim i, u as integer
f = getfolderitem("rabbits") // folder full of images
redim Pics(-1)
u = f.count
for i = 1 to u
    pics.append f.item(i).openaspicture
next
s = new sprite
s.image = pics(0)
spritesurface1.attach s
spritesurface1.clickToStop = true
spritesurface1.framespeed = 7
spritesurface1.run
```

An integer property, Which, is used by the SpriteSurface's NextFrame event handler to cycle through the images:

```
which = (which + 1) mod (ubound(Pics) + 1)
s.image = pics(which)
```

The Sprite now walks, but he doesn't get anywhere: his image is animated, but he isn't physically moving across the SpriteSurface. But we already know how to fix that: we simply add a line of this sort to the SpriteSurface's NextFrame event handler:

```
s.x = s.x + 8
```

Exactly how much the Sprite should move to the right on each frame depends on how his feet move in the images we're using.

User Interaction

Let's turn this into a little game—a very, very little game—where the Sprite interacts with the user. The SpriteSurface will show our Sprite. The user will be permitted to click in the SpriteSurface; the Sprite will respond by walking over to where the click occurred. To keep things simple, we'll confine ourselves to purely horizontal walking, as we've been doing. We'll take this opportunity to vary the way we drive the SpriteSurface: instead of sending it the Run message, we'll have a Timer send it the Update message repeatedly. In this way, the window will never be "modal"; the user will always be free to work elsewhere, even when the animation is taking place.

Our button's Action event handler initializes the Picture array as before, but adds a second set of Pictures showing the Sprite walking the other way. (The Reverse method flips a Picture horizontally; it's easy to write, and is not shown.) At the end, we call the SpriteSurface's Update method to show the Sprite image, and stop, waiting for a mouseclick in the SpriteSurface:

```
dim f as folderitem
dim i,u as integer
f = getfolderitem("rabbits")
redim pics(-1)
u = f.count
for i = 1 to u
    pics.append f.item(i).openaspicture
next
for i = 1 to u
    pics.append reverse(pics(i-1))
next
s = new sprite
s.image = pics(0)
spritesurface1.attach s
spritesurface1.clickToStop = false
spritesurface1.update
```

The rest of the action is precipitated by the user clicking in the SpriteSurface. The SpriteSurface doesn't receive mouseclicks, so this task is up to the window. The window's MouseDown event handler returns true, to generate a MouseUp event. The window's MouseUp event handler looks to see if the click is in the SpriteSurface; if it is, it records the click's horizontal coordinate in an integer property, Where, in terms local to the SpriteSurface; then it starts a Timer to drive the animation:

```
if x > spritesurface1.left and y > spritesurface1.top then
    if x < spritesurface1.left + spritesurface1.width then
        if y < spritesurface1.top + spriteSurface1.height then
            where = x - spritesurface1.left // translate coordinates
            timer1.mode = 2
        end
    end
end
```

The Timer's Action event does all the work; the SpriteSurface's NextFrame event does nothing. The reason for this is that when it receives the Update message, the SpriteSurface first shows its current frame, then gets a NextFrame event to generate the frame for the next time the Update message arrives. That's backward; so to avoid this, the Timer generates the next frame, and simply sends the Update message to make the SpriteSurface show it. The Timer's Action event distinguishes three cases: walk right, walk left, or stop. In the last case, it just sets its own Mode to 0, and the action comes to an end. Otherwise, it sets a boolean property, GoRight; calls the Advance method to calculate the next frame; and shows that frame with Update:

```
if where > s.x + s.image.width then
    goright = true
    advance
    spritesurface1.update
elseif where < s.x then
    goright = false
    advance
    spritesurface1.update
else
    me.mode = 0
end
```

The Advance method is very much like the NextFrame event handler from the previous example: it cycles the Sprite's image to the next image, and shifts the Sprite's horizontal position. The only complication is that deciding which is the next image and which way to shift the horizontal position depends on which way we're to walk:

```
dim total as integer
total = (ubound(pics)-1)/2
which = which + 1
if goright then
    which = which mod (total + 1)
    s.image = pics(which)
    s.x = s.x + 8
else
    which = (which mod (total + 1)) + total + 1
    s.image = pics(which)
    s.x = s.x - 8
end
```

Collisions

A SpriteSurface instance receives reports of collisions among its Sprites. The rule is that if two Sprites are "inimical" to each other, and their images in the Surface are touching each other, the SpriteSurface is sent a Collision event, along with references to the two Sprites in question. The concept of Sprites being mutually inimical is implemented through the Sprite class's Group property, which is an integer. Two Sprites are inimical if they have different Group values, except that nonpositive Group values have a special meaning, as follows:

- If a Sprite's Group value is 0, then no Sprite is inimical to it.
- If a Sprite's Group value is negative, then all Sprites are inimical to it.

Unfortunately, there is a problem connected with collisions: you don't get a Collision event until it's too late—the frame has already been drawn. To see what I mean, let's make a simple animation that illustrates collisions. Give a window a SpriteSurface; three Sprite properties named Wall1, Wall2, and Circle; and an integer property called Movement. Let the SpriteSurface's Open event handler go like this:

```
dim p as picture
p = newpicture (20,500,32)
p.graphics.forecolor = rgb(200,0,0)
p.graphics.fillrect 0,0,20,500
wall1 = new sprite
wall1.group = 1
wall1.image = p
me.attach wall1
wall2 = new sprite
wall2.x = spritesurface1.width-20
wall2.group = 1
wall2.image = p
me.attach wall2
p = newpicture (40,40,32)
p.graphics.forecolor = rgb(0,200,0)
p.graphics.filloval 0,0,40,40
circle = new sprite
circle.x = 100
circle.y = 100
circle.image = p
circle.group = 2
me.attach circle
movement = -5
```

If you send the SpriteSurface the Update message, you'll see that we've created two vertical red walls, Wall1 on the left and Wall2 on the right, with a green circle between them. We will now animate the circle to bounce off the walls. Let the SpriteSurface's NextFrame event handler go like this:

```
circle.x = circle.x + movement
```

And let its Collision event handler go like this:

```
if s1 = wall1 or s2 = wall1 then
    movement = 5
else // must be wall2
    movement = -5
end
```

If you run the SpriteSurface, you'll see that the circle now oscillates between the two walls. But upon close inspection, perhaps with the SpriteSurface's FrameSpeed set to some large value such as 10, you can see that, because the circle is moving in large increments, it actually overlaps each wall rather significantly before reversing direction, thus breaking the illusion that the walls are solid and that the circle is bouncing off them. Suppose we try to correct this by repositioning the circle during the Collision event handler so that it no longer overlaps the wall. The Collision event handler now goes like this:

```
if s1 = wall1 or s2 = wall1 then
    movement = 5
else
```

```
    movement = -5
end
if s1 = wall1 or s2 = wall1 then
    circle.x = wall1.x + wall1.image.width + 1
else
    circle.x = wall2.x - circle.image.width - 1
end
```

But it doesn't help. We'd like to use the Collision event as a kind of notification, a warning that we've made two Sprites overlap, so that we can undo the damage before the user sees it. If REALbasic worked that way—and in previous versions, it did!—this routine would make it appear, from the user's point of view, that the circle just barely "kisses" the wall and reverses direction. But it isn't working, because the Collision event arrives after the fact; the frame showing the overlap has already been displayed.

Basic Background Techniques

How the SpriteSurface will look when the window first appears depends upon its Backdrop property, which is a Picture. By default, this is solid black; so if you do nothing else—just drag a SpriteSurface into a window and run the project—you'll see a big black rectangle in the window. The Backdrop may be set to something else in the IDE or in code. The Picture to which the Backdrop is set will be tiled, starting in the upper-left corner, to form the visible background image. If the Picture is larger than the SpriteSurface, only its upper-left portion will be shown.

Here's an example of setting a SpriteSurface's background to a solid color in code, in its Open event handler:

```
dim p as picture
p = newpicture (10,10,32)
p.graphics.forecolor = rgb(255,255,40)
p.graphics.fillrect 0,0,10,10
me.backdrop = p
```

This works no matter what the SpriteSurface's size may be, because the Picture is tiled to fill the background.

To scroll the background, send the SpriteSurface the Scroll message. There are two things to watch out for:

- The Scroll method parameter values are inverted! Positive values mean to the left and upward (as opposed to a Canvas, where positive values mean to the right and downward—see Chapter 11).

- Scrolling the background moves the sprites. Therefore, to hold a sprite still against a scrolling background, it must be moved to compensate.

The reason for both of these things is that the metaphor here is not really scrolling, but panning. You are asked to imagine that there is a big world of sprites with a background image stretching off forever in all directions; the SpriteSurface is merely a window on part of this world, and the Scroll message moves that window. So, scrolling with positive values moves your view of things downward and to the right; as a result, both the background image and the sprites move upward and to the left.

Let's try it. Start with one of our earlier examples where we have a Sprite, S, and a button's Action event gives it an initial image, attaches it to the SpriteSurface, and sends the SpriteSurface the Run message. In the IDE, import a Picture to function as the background; set the SpriteSurface's Backdrop to point to it. Here is a NextFrame event handler that scrolls the background upward and to the left, while the Sprite holds still:

```
me.scroll 1,1
s.x = s.x + 1
s.y = s.y + 1
```

The background image tiles and repeats itself automatically as it scrolls. If we like, we can defeat this automatic behavior and take charge of drawing the new material as it scrolls into view; in essence, we get to construct the background in real time while it's scrolling. This is done through the notion of *tiles*. It turns out that the background is constructed as a grid of squares, each 64 by 64 pixels, with the 0,0 square at the SpriteSurface's upper left to begin with. We are allowed to draw into these squares; our opportunity comes every time the SpriteSurface gets a PaintTile event. Each PaintTile event is accompanied by two integers, xpos and ypos, identifying the tile to which it applies, plus a Graphics property, g, into which we draw the tile. (Since each tile is 64 by 64, any g pixels we draw whose coordinates are smaller than 0 or larger than 63 will result in no visible drawing.)

We get PaintTile events at two times. First, in conjunction with the SpriteSurface's Open event, we get enough PaintTile events to construct the entire background. Thus, we could create the initial background without setting the Backdrop property. Then, whenever we scroll, we get PaintTile events in time to construct any new material as it comes into view.

To help you visualize the tiles, give the SpriteSurface's PaintTile event handler this code:

```
g.forecolor = rgb(255,255,0)
g.filloval 0,0,64,64
g.forecolor = rgb(0,0,0)
g.drawstring str(xpos) + "," + str(ypos), 5, 40
```

The idea is to demarcate each tile by filling it with a yellow circle, and to identify it by writing its xpos and ypos values directly into it. Run the project and start the SpriteSurface. You'll see that the tiles entering from the bottom right have larger and larger "coordinate" values.

You can learn how far the background image has been scrolled by consulting the SpriteSurface's ScrollX and ScrollY position. To see this, put a StaticText in the window, and add these two further lines to the SpriteSurface's PaintTile event handler:

```
statictext1.text = str(me.scrollx) + "," + str(me.scrolly)
statictext1.refresh
```

You'll actually learn two things from this. First, you'll see that the PaintTile event handler fires only when new tiles need to be constructed. Second, you can see the background image's coordinates increasing as it moves up and to the left. Think of these values as telling you the point of the background image currently located at the top left corner of the SpriteSurface.

Improving the Classes

Our next task will be to adapt the SpriteSurface and Sprite classes in such a way as to encapsulate their functionality in a more object-oriented fashion. Right now, this functionality is spread out all over the project: the window maintains the Sprite images and the Sprite, and the SpriteSurface is animating the Sprite. Instead of this, the SpriteSurface should maintain its own Sprites, and the Sprites should animate themselves. Modifying the SpriteSurface and Sprite classes will accomplish this, paving the way for a simple game animation with multiple Sprites, each with an "intelligence" of its own.

We will first design two abstract classes, SmartSurface and SmartSprite. The idea is that we can later subclass these to obtain actual classes with the particular functionality for a specific application.

SmartSprite is a subclass of Sprite. It has two methods: Redraw and Collision. They are both abstract methods; it is up to the subclass of SmartSprite to give them functionality as needed.

SmartSurface is a subclass of SpriteSurface. Its chief purposes are to add properties to SpriteSurface that will make it self-contained, and to function as a dispatcher so that events received by the SpriteSurface are shunted off to the object that should most appropriately respond.

Sprites belong to a SpriteSurface; so SmartSurface will have a property, Sprites, which is an array of SmartSprites. It has four methods. Prepare, Redraw, and Collision are all abstract methods; it is up to the subclass of SmartSurface to give them functionality as needed. The DoAttach method takes one parameter, a SmartSprite called s, and goes like this:

```
self.attach s
self.sprites.append s
```

The power of this architecture comes from SmartSurface's event handlers, which it inherits from SpriteSurface; it deals with these by dispatching the events to the appropriate objects. I'll talk about collisions later in the chapter; for now, let's just look at SmartSurface's NextFrame event handler:

```
dim i,u as integer
// give each sprite a chance to redraw itself
u = ubound(self.sprites)
for i = 1 to u
```

```
    self.sprites(i).redraw(self)
next
// give our subclass a chance to redraw itself
redraw
```

Do you get the idea? To attach a SmartSprite to a SmartSurface, you call DoAttach; this not only attaches the Sprite, but also registers it in the SmartSurface's array of SmartSprites. So now a SmartSurface always knows its own Sprites. When a Next-Frame event comes in, the SmartSurface passes it on to its Sprites, in the form of the Redraw method call. Thus, all the SmartSprites get to do the work that is appropriate to themselves on every NextFrame event, changing their own images, shifting their own positions, and so forth. The Redraw method has a parameter which is a reference to the SmartSurface, so the SmartSprites can get at any SmartSurface properties they may require. The SmartSurface also sends itself the Redraw message, which will be handled by its subclass; the subclass is expected not to misuse this by drawing Sprites, but should perform only those activities appropriate to the Sprite-Surface itself, such as creating Sprites and operating on the background.

Now, all of that has been very wordy to describe, but it makes creating an actual animation very simple. We can now forget about SmartSurface and SmartSprite; they are abstract. Instead, we make a subclass of SmartSurface, which will be the actual SpriteSurface control in the window; and, for each type of Sprite in our game, we make a SmartSprite subclass. These subclasses receive events when work needs to be done *by them*. In this way, object orientation is achieved, so the animation becomes easy to construct.

To see what I mean, let's rewrite an earlier example—the one where the Sprite walks to the right (page 583). No functionality will change; it's the organization that's the important thing. Our project now has a SmartSurface class and a SmartSprite class; these are abstract, so we also need a subclass of SmartSurface, which I'll call MySurface, and a subclass of SmartSprite, which I'll call MySprite. The SpriteSurface in the window is a MySurface. We don't have to give the window any properties! All properties will belong to an appropriate object. There are many possible ways of reorganizing the code, but here's a pretty simple one. The button that sets things going just tells the SpriteSurface to initialize itself, and runs it:

```
spritesurface1.prepare
spritesurface1.run
```

MySurface's Prepare method handler loads the Pictures into a property of MySurface, creates the Sprite image, and assigns its initial image as an instance of MySprite:

```
dim f as folderitem
dim i, u as integer
f = getfolderitem("rabbits")
u = f.count
for i = 1 to u
    self.pics.append f.item(i).openaspicture
next
```

```
self.doattach new mySprite
self.sprites(ubound(self.sprites)).image = pics(0)
self.clickToStop = true
self.framespeed = 7
```

The animation of the Sprite takes place in MySprite's Redraw method handler. This handler receives as parameter a reference to the SpriteSurface, W, so it is able to get at the array of Pictures. The property Which belongs to MySprite:

```
self.x = self.x + 8
self.which = (self.which + 1) mod (ubound(mysurface(W).pics) + 1)
self.image = mysurface(W).pics(which)
```

Do you see now why we went to all this trouble? MySprite has its own Redraw method, so *it* gets to take responsibility for implementing its own behavior as the animation runs. We have achieved true object orientation of Sprites.

Intelligent Sprite Behavior

Now that we have object orientation, each individual Sprite can have properties all its own, to maintain state between NextFrame events. This makes it easy to implement intelligent Sprite behavior.

To illustrate, we'll develop a little game. It will be a PacMan variant, and we'll start with a single imported Picture that holds all the different manifestations of the various Sprites (Figure 28-2).* The Application subclass's Open event dismantles this Picture into a two-dimensional Picture array called Pix:

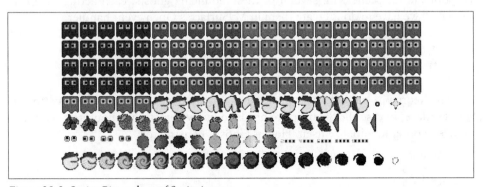

Figure 28-2. SpritesPix, a sheet of Sprite images

```
dim i,j as integer
for i = 0 to 19
    for j = 0 to 7
        pix(i,j) = newpicture(24,24,8)
```

---

* The sheet of images is taken from work done by Alex Metcalf for his Maniac game, and is gratefully reproduced with his permission. Maniac, which afforded me (too many) hours of relaxation while I was writing this chapter, is available here: *http://www.metcalf.demon.co.uk/alex/maniac21.hqx*.

```
        pix(i,j).graphics.drawpicture spritespix,-i*24,-j*24
    next
  next
```

Our project has a SmartSurface class and a SmartSprite class. Our SpriteSurface is a subclass of SmartSurface, MySurface. SmartSprite has two subclasses, Ghost and Pac. The Ghosts will wander around the scene, and the Pac will try to eat them.

We'll start with the ghosts. A ghost will move in a straight line across the stage, but we'll ensure that it will stay in bounds by bouncing off the edge of the SpriteSurface. Further, to make its travel interesting, we'll have it bounce at a random angle each time it strikes the edge. State is maintained in two integer properties of Ghost, Horiz and Vert, which describe the current direction of movement. Here is Ghost's Redraw method (W is the reference to the SmartSurface):

```
if self.x <= 0 then
    horiz = 1 + rnd * 4
elseif self.x + 24 >= W.width then
    horiz = -(1 + rnd * 4)
end
if self.y <= 0 then
    vert = 1 + rnd * 4
elseif self.y + 24 >= W.height then
    vert = -(1 + rnd * 4)
end
self.x = self.x + horiz
self.y = self.y + vert
```

To populate the scene with several of these bouncing ghosts, each acting independently, all we have to do is create them in MySurface's Open event handler:

```
dim i as integer
for i = 1 to 8
    self.doAttach new ghost(self)
next
```

As with Redraw, I pass to the constructors for my SmartSprites a reference to the SmartSurface, in case the SmartSprite needs to know something about its containing surface in order to initialize itself. Here is Ghost's constructor:

```
self.image = app.pix(0,0)
self.x = 5
self.y = 5
self.horiz = -1
self.vert = -1
```

Try it! The ghosts start out from the same point, but because of the calls to the Rnd function, they quickly fan out and are soon bouncing around the surface at various velocities. Our animation is coming to life!

Now let's add to Ghost's sophistication by having its image change as it moves along. Our sheet of Sprite images actually contains five Ghost images, arranged horizontally. Cycling through these will make the ghost appear to be wiggling his ghostly feet (or whatever the wavy lower part of a ghost is called). We'll give Ghost an

---

integer property, Wiggle, and cycle it from 0 to 4 as the ghost moves along. So, Ghost's Redraw method now has some additional lines:

```
wiggle = (wiggle + 1) mod 5
self.image = app.pix(wiggle,0)
```

This is good, but let's go even further. There are actually four rows of images, differing in the direction in which the ghost is looking. We'll choose from these rows, depending on the direction in which the ghost is moving, so that he always appears to be looking where he's going. Since he is usually moving diagonally, we'll let the largest component of his motion dictate the direction he'll look.

```
if abs(horiz) > abs(vert) then // 1 or 3
    if horiz < 0 then
        row = 1
    else
        row = 3
    end
else // 0 or 2
    if vert < 0 then
        row = 0
    else
        row = 2
    end
end
wiggle = (wiggle + 1) mod 5
self.image = app.pix(wiggle,row)
```

But wait, there's still more! The 5 by 4 set of ghost images comes in a choice of four delicious colors. We'll assign each ghost one of these colors, randomly. We'll code the color as an integer from 0 to 3, to be stored as an integer property, MyColor. We choose the color in Ghost's constructor:

```
myColor = rnd * 4
```

Now all we have to do is change the DrawPicture line in the Redraw method to this:

```
self.image = app.pix(mycolor*5+wiggle,row)
```

Responding to Keys

To learn whether a key has been pressed, you are supposed to poll the keyboard by sending the SpriteSurface the KeyTest message, passing it an integer representing the virtual keycode you want to check for. Unfortunately, KeyTest works exactly the same way as the Keyboard class's AsyncKeyDown, and is problematic for exactly the same reason—knowing the keycode doesn't tell you what character has been typed on the user's particular keyboard layout (see Chapter 19). However, we'll ignore this problem for the sake of the example.

We illustrate with our other SmartSprite subclass, Pac. The stage will hold just one Pac instance. The user will be allowed to press any of the four arrow keys, and Pac will respond by changing his direction to match—unless he is already up against a

SpriteSurface edge in that direction, in which case the keypress will be ignored. If the user hasn't pressed a key, and Pac encounters an edge in the direction he is currently moving, he will just stop. Pac's Redraw method received a reference to MySurface as a parameter W, so it will be able to send MySurface the KeyTest message, and it will be able to obtain MySurface's dimensions.

Pac will have three integer properties, Horiz, Vert, and Dir (the purpose of Dir will be clear in a moment). Pac's Redraw method looks like this:

```
if self.x <= 0 and horiz < 0 then
    horiz = 0
elseif self.x + 24 >= W.width and horiz > 0 then
    horiz = 0
end
if self.y <= 0 and vert < 0 then
    vert = 0
elseif self.y + 24 >= W.height and vert > 0 then
    vert = 0
end
if W.keyTest(&h7b) then // left
    if self.x > 0 then
        horiz = -2
        vert = 0
        dir = 2
    end
elseif W.keyTest(&h7c) then // right
    if self.x + 24 < W.width then
        horiz = 2
        vert = 0
        dir = 0
    end
elseif W.keyTest(&h7e) then // up
    if self.y > 0 then
        vert = -2
        horiz = 0
        dir = 3
    end
elseif W.keyTest(&h7d) then // down
    if self.y + 24 < W.height then
        vert = 2
        horiz = 0
        dir = 1
    end
end
self.x = self.x + horiz
self.y = self.y + vert
```

Now let's take care of drawing Pac's image. In the sheet of Sprite images, Pac is the yellow round character with the mouth that opens and closes. Whenever the user succeeds in changing Pac's direction of travel, we'll have Pac face the way he is going; and as he travels, his mouth will open and close. His mouth shouldn't move on every single frame, because that's too fast; instead, Pac's mouth position will change every fifth frame.

So, Pac has three more properties: two integers, Mouth and MouthTimer, and a boolean, Closing. Pac's Redraw method now contains this additional code:

```
mouthtimer = (mouthtimer + 1) mod 5
if mouthtimer = 0 then
    select case mouth
    case 0
        closing = false
        mouth = 1
    case 1
        if closing then
            mouth = 0
        else
            mouth = 2
        end
    case 2
        closing = true
        mouth = 1
    end
end
self.image = app.pix(5+dir*3+mouth,4)
```

Intelligent Collisions

Returning to our abstract classes, SmartSurface and SmartSprite, it is clear that we need to make them respond to collisions in a way that keeps functionality object-oriented. When SmartSurface receives a Collision event, it should notify the two SmartSprites involved in the collision. Here, then, is SmartSurface's Collision event handler:

```
dim ss1, ss2 as smartSprite
// cast down
ss1 = smartsprite(s1)
ss2 = smartsprite(s2)
// give each involved sprite a chance to react
ss1.collision(self,ss2)
ss2.collision(self,ss1)
// give our subclass a chance to react
collision ss1,ss2
```

SmartSurface and SmartSprite both have Collision method handlers, but these are abstract; it's up to their subclasses to implement them as desired.

To illustrate the architecture of object-oriented collisions, we will finish our example by giving Pac the power to eat any ghosts Sprites he encounters. Ghost's constructor sets its Group to 1; Pac's constructor sets its Group to 2. We will leave it entirely to Ghost's Collision method to manage things when there is a collision (Pac's Collision method and MySurface's Collision method will do nothing). Only collisions between a Ghost and the Pac generate Collision events, so Ghost's Collision method is guaranteed that its second parameter is a reference to the Pac instance.

What would we like to have happen if there is a collision? My scenario goes like this: in order for the Ghost to be eaten, the Pac image must be facing the Ghost image, and the Ghost image must fall more or less within the Pac's mouth area; otherwise, the Ghost just bounces nimbly away from the Pac. Here, then, is Ghost's Collision method:

```
dim die as boolean
dim thepac as Pac
dim theX, theY as integer
thepac = pac(s)
theX = thepac.x
theY = thepac.y
// dir is 0 = right, 2 = left, 3 = up, 1 = down
if thepac.dir = 0 and self.x > theX + 12 then
  if self.y > theY - 12 and self.y < theY + 12 then
    die = true
  end
elseif thepac.dir = 2 and self.x < theX - 12 then
  if self.y > theY - 12 and self.y < theY + 12 then
    die = true
  end
elseif thepac.dir = 1 and self.y > theY + 12 then
  if self.x > theX - 12 and self.x < theX + 12 then
    die = true
  end
elseif thepac.dir = 3 and self.y < theY - 12 then
  if self.x > theX - 12 and self.x < theX + 12 then
    die = true
  end
end
if die then
  self.close
else
  horiz = -horiz
  vert = -vert
  self.x = self.x + 2*horiz + 2*thePac.horiz
  self.y = self.y + 2*vert + 2*thePac.vert
end
```

Figure 28-1 shows a screen shot of my final implementation of the game, which I call PacMan On Mars. (I'm not entirely clear on how PacMan wound up on Mars; the news was full of the Mars Lander at the time I was originally writing this game, and this may have influenced what little was left of my judgment.) The window area at the right is used to keep a count of ghosts still alive, and to track the time; implementing this is left as an exercise for the reader, or you can download the game's complete source code from my web site.

CHAPTER 29

In this chapter:
- Page Setup
- Proceeding To Print
- Measurement Problems
- Printing Text

Printing

REALbasic printing is simple. You are presented, in essence, with a blank sheet, a plane of pixels in the form of a Graphics object, like the Graphics property of a Canvas or a Picture; whatever you draw into this will be sent to the printer. This means that, except for some minor details, you already know how to print! The commands for drawing into a Graphics object were presented in "Graphics Class" in Chapter 11; drawing styled text from an EditField was described in "Drawing Styled Text" in Chapter 13. That's essentially all there is to it. REALbasic doesn't give you much assistance in transforming data into the actual pixels of the drawing; on the other hand, since you are in charge of every pixel, there isn't much that you can't do.

The minor details have to do mostly with your interactions with the user, and with the computer's printer driver. You need to be able to present the user with the customary Page Setup and Print dialogs; and in order to position and scale page elements as you print, you need to know the dimensions and resolution of the page you're printing to. That's what the rest of this chapter is about.

Page Setup

Before printing, you should give the user the opportunity to interact with the Page Setup dialog. This is where the user typically gets to make settings such as the size and orientation of the page. It is also your chance to get hold of a properly configured instance of the PrinterSetup class; this is something you'll want to have on hand as you proceed to the actual business of printing.

To put up the Page Setup dialog, first obtain a PrinterSetup instance; you can do this with New. Then, send the PrinterSetup instance the PageSetupDialog message. This causes the standard Page Setup dialog to appear, as appropriate for the currently selected printer. The dialog returns a boolean, reporting whether the user clicked OK or Cancel to dismiss it; if the user cancels, you should not proceed to print.

After the user has interacted with the Page Setup dialog, its SetupString property is a valid string describing the user's settings in the dialog. If you like, you can use the

SetupString's value to bypass the Page Setup dialog during a later round of printing. To do so, save the SetupString's value. Then later, when the user wants to print again, you can create a new PrinterSetup instance with New and set its SetupString from the previously saved value. This should have the same effect as if you had presented the Page Setup dialog and the user filled it out in the same way as before.

A typical scenario, dictated by common sense and the printing interactions with which you're doubtless already familiar, is as follows. Your application has a Page Setup menu item and a Print menu item. The user can choose the Page Setup menu item at any time; in response, you create a PrinterSetup instance and send it the PageSetupDialog message, and if this returns true, you retain the SetupString in a property. If the user chooses the Print menu item, then if you have a SetupString retained from an earlier interaction, you proceed to print; if not, you present the Page Setup dialog first, as if the user had chosen the Page Setup menu item.

Besides the SetupString, a PrinterSetup instance has the following properties:

HorizontalResolution, VerticalResolution
> The number of dots per inch (*dpi*) the printer will print. They are usually the same, though some printers may permit different horizontal and vertical resolution values. All other measurements are in dots, so the resolution values tell you how to convert these to physical units such as inches or centimeters. When you draw to the printer's Graphics object, a pixel of the Graphics object corresponds to a dot of the printer.

Height, Width
> The size of the page's printable region, in pixels. For example, if ps is the PrinterSetup instance, then this code prints the largest rectangle that the printer can fit on one page:
> ```
> g.drawrect 0,0,ps.width-1,ps.height-1
> ```
> The reason 1 must be subtracted from the Width and Height has to do with how a Graphics class wields its "pen"; see Figure 11-1.

PageWidth, PageHeight
> The size of the physical paper, in pixels.

PageLeft, PageTop
> Negative integers describing the left and top "margins"—the distance from the edges of the printable area to the edges of the physical paper.

Left, Top
> The coordinates of the top left of the printable area; always 0,0.

The resolution is the scale factor that allows you to shuttle between pixel measurements and inch or centimeter measurements. For example, suppose PageWidth is reported as 612 and PageHeight is reported as 792, and suppose HorizontalResolution and VerticalResolution are 72. Dividing the PageWidth and PageHeight values by 72 gives 8.5 and 11, which is the paper size in inches.

You cannot set any of these properties; they are all set for you, either when the user fills out the Page Setup dialog or when you set the PrinterSetup's SetupString with a valid string retained from an earlier interaction. There are two further properties, however, which you can set:

MaxHorizontalResolution, MaxVerticalResolution
   The highest resolutions at which you're willing to print. The default is 72. A value of -1 means that you will accept any resolution.

Most commonly, there should not be any reason why you would refuse to obey the user's resolution settings, so you will set MaxHorizontalResolution and MaxVertical-Resolution to -1. Note that you must do this explicitly. If you're going to retain the SetupString, you should set MaxHorizontalResolution and MaxVerticalResolution to -1 *before* presenting the user with the Page Setup dialog; that's because the Page Setup dialog might let the user make resolution settings, and you would not wish the PrinterSetup instance to override these.

Proceeding To Print

To present the user with the Print dialog, call the OpenPrinterDialog function. This takes one parameter—a PrinterSetup instance—which is optional. So, a typical approach is to use the PrinterSetup instance you obtained earlier, either by presenting the user with the Page Setup dialog, or through a SetupString retained from a previous interaction. If you don't provide a PrinterSetup instance, the default settings will be used, but now the user may not be able to set the page size and orientation.

The OpenPrinterDialog function returns a Graphics object. If the user canceled out of the dialog, this Graphics object will be nil, and you should stop. If the Graphics object is not nil, you should proceed to print, meaning you should draw something into it; I find that if the Graphics object is not nil and you don't print, bad things can happen (the computer can crash, for instance). When the Graphics object is destroyed, the page is sent to the printer; typically, you'll receive the Graphics object into a local variable, and when the routine comes to an end, the local variable goes out of scope, the instance is destroyed, and the page prints.

If you wish to learn how the user filled in the Print dialog, the Graphics object that the OpenPrinterDialog function returns has special properties that tell you: its FirstPage and LastPage properties tell you what the user entered into the From and To fields, and its Copy property tells you how many copies the user requested. I find, however, that for some printers at least you can ignore these properties, because the printer driver itself takes care of obeying them for you. For example, the user asked for two copies; you print once, and the printer driver prints two copies. You may have to experiment to determine the correct course of action for a particular printer.

To illustrate a typical overall printing architecture, here's a sketch of an actual utility that prints envelopes and address labels. There's a PrinterSetup property, PS. The Page Setup menu item calls DoPageSetup, which goes like this:

```
dim ok as boolean
dim ps as printersetup
```

```
ps = new printersetup
ps.maxverticalResolution = -1
ps.maxhorizontalResolution = -1
ok = ps.pagesetupdialog
if ok then
    self.ps = ps // store in property
end
return ok
```

The reason DoPageSetup returns a boolean is so that we can call it from DoPrint if necessary and abort if the user cancels. The Print menu item calls DoPrint:

```
dim print as boolean
dim g as graphics
dim s as string
print = true
if ps = nil then
    print = doPageSetup
end
if not print then
    return
end
g = openprinterdialog(ps)
if g = nil then
    return
end
s = getzip()
if s <> "" and not suppressbarcode.value then
    printBarcode(g,s)
end
printRecipient(g)
if not doinglabels.value then
    printReturnAddress(g)
end
```

The various subroutines, PrintBarCode and so forth, draw into g; at the end, g goes out of scope and printing takes place.

The most important thing, before proceeding to print, is to look at the resolution and size settings of the PrinterSetup instance you handed to the OpenPrinterDialog function. The user may have had a chance, in the course of the Print dialog, to set the resolution; so this is your opportunity to discover this final resolution and to take it into account as you print. You can now determine the scale at which you're printing, and can give things the right size and position.

To show you what I mean, here's a rather artificial example. We will go through both dialogs, and then print a page consisting of a grid of one-inch squares. The squares will be the right size and will fill the page, regardless of the resolution at which the user elects to print.

```
dim ps as printersetup
dim i as integer
dim g as graphics
dim b as boolean
```

```
ps = new printerSetup
ps.maxverticalResolution = -1
ps.maxhorizontalResolution = -1
b = ps.pagesetupDialog
if not b then
    return
end
g = openPrinterDialog(ps)
if g = nil then
    return
end
for i = 0 to ps.width step ps.horizontalresolution
    g.drawline i,0,i,ps.height
next
for i = 0 to ps.height step ps.verticalresolution
    g.drawline 0,i,ps.width,i
next
```

Observe that as the resolution rises, the lines that define these squares become thinner. DrawLine draws a line one pixel in thickness, so a line gets thinner as the number of pixels per inch goes up. If this isn't what you want, you need to compensate by scaling the thickness of your lines. For instance, to print a grid of one-inch squares where the bounding lines are the same thickness regardless of the resolution, we could insert these lines just after determining that g isn't nil:

```
g.penheight = ps.verticalResolution / 72
g.penwidth = ps.horizontalResolution / 72
```

If you're printing multiple pages, an extra Graphics method, NextPage, is provided. Sending the NextPage message to the Graphics object causes the Graphics object to dump its present contents to the printer and clear itself, ready for some new drawing. You don't need to send the NextPage message for the last page to be printed.

For instance, this extension of the previous example prints a page of one-inch squares followed by a page of one-inch circles:

```
for i = 0 to ps.width step ps.horizontalresolution
    g.drawline i,0,i,ps.height
next
for i = 0 to ps.height step ps.verticalresolution
    g.drawline 0,i,ps.width,i
next
g.nextpage
for i = 0 to ps.width step ps.horizontalresolution
    for j = 0 to ps.height step ps.verticalresolution
        g.drawoval i,j,ps.horizontalresolution,ps.verticalresolution
    next
next
```

To print without invoking the Print dialog, call the OpenPrinter function. The syntax is just like the OpenPrinterDialog function: you optionally hand it a PrinterSetup instance, and it returns a Graphics instance.

Measurement Problems

You might suppose that the values of a PrinterSetup instance's properties would permit you to print to a precise position on the paper. But idiosyncrasies of individual printers militate against such precision.

For example, on my printer, an extremely aged but stalwart StyleWriter, Height is 752, PageHeight is 792, and PageTop is -15. Since the difference between PageHeight and Height is 40, one would conclude that there is a 15-pixel margin at the top of the page, and a 25-pixel margin at the bottom of the page; but the top margin is actually about 20 pixels, not 15.

These measurements are very disturbing, since the actual margins plus the stated Height sum to rather more than the PageHeight! It appears that my printer feeds the paper, as it prints, more slowly than it should; if I ask it to print a large square, the result is actually a rectangle slightly wider than high, showing that I'm getting somewhat more dots per inch vertically than horizontally.

Similarly, on my printer, Width is 576, PageWidth is 612, and PageLeft is -18. Since the difference between PageWidth and Width is 36, one would think that there is an 18-pixel margin on both sides of the page; but in reality there is a 14-pixel margin on the left and a 22-pixel margin on the right!

The fact that the margins are not identical on both sides may result from how paper feeds into the printer; whatever the cause, the point is that it is impossible to know what the true physical reality will be, so it is impossible (for example) to center a vertical line reliably down the middle of the paper.

Your code can't know about any of this, of course. All you can do is print within the printable area, in accordance with its dimensions and its resolution as the PrinterSetup instance reports them. The moral is: draw no conclusions as to the precise physical interpretation of the printer's measurements. If your program absolutely requires precise physical placement, you can give the user the ability to set some positioning and scaling parameters; the user can then experiment and compensate for the behavior of a particular printer.

Printing Text

Text without styles can be printed with the Graphics property's DrawString method. Styled text contained in an EditField can be printed easily with the EditField's StyledTextPrinter method. Recall that successive DrawBlock messages sent to the same StyledTextPrinter instance cause successive parts of the EditField's text to be drawn; if the NextPage message is sent to the Graphics property between DrawBlock calls, the successive parts of the EditField's text will end up on separate pages.

The text will probably have to be scaled to compensate for the printer's resolution. (I fear that the necessity of this may depend on the particular printer.) If you're using DrawString, that's no challenge at all; just multiply values by the appropriate scale factor.

As an example, here's the PrintReturnAddress method from my envelope-printing utility; g is passed to it as a parameter, and PS and MyAddress are properties:

```
dim s as string
dim x,y as integer
s = myAddress
g.textfont = "Helvetica"
g.textsize = 9 * ps.horizontalResolution / 72
g.bold = false
y = ps.height - 3.5*ps.verticalResolution + g.textheight
x = .2 * ps.horizontalResolution
g.drawstring s,x,y
```

Printing from an EditField is a bit more complicated, because there's no simple command to let you scale up. However, recall that earlier ("Finding Styles" in Chapter 13) we developed utility classes for parsing and manipulating EditField styles; we can use these to scale up. Since this will physically change the contents of the EditField, we copy the real EditField into an invisible or off-window EditField and print from there. So, a skeleton technique might look like this:

```
dim r as scraprecord
dim i,u,thesize as integer
dim leftmargin, rightmargin, topmargin, bottommargin as integer
dim g as graphics
dim s as styledTextPrinter
g = openPrinterDialog(ps) // PS is a property, set previously
editfield2.setTextAndStyle editfield1.text, editfield1.textstyledata
r = new scraprecord(editfield2.textstyledata)
u = r.numstyles - 1
for i = 0 to u
    thesize = r.scrapTables(i).size
    r.scrapTables(i).size = thesize * ps.horizontalResolution / 72
next
editfield2.setTextAndStyle editfield2.text, r.toString
leftmargin = ps.horizontalresolution
rightmargin = ps.width - ps.horizontalresolution
topmargin = ps.verticalresolution/2
bottommargin = ps.height-ps.verticalresolution/2
s = editfield2.styledtextPrinter(g, rightmargin-leftmargin)
s.drawblock(leftmargin, topmargin, bottommargin-topmargin)
while not s.eof
    g.nextpage
    s.drawblock(leftmargin, topmargin, bottommargin-topmargin)
wend
```

The routine arbitrarily establishes one-inch margins to form the rectangle to print into. In real life, it might be nice to add headers and footers to the pages; page numbers would be a good minimum. These are all trivial additions and are left to the reader as an exercise.

Unfortunately, there are times when you want to do more than DrawString or the StyledTextPrinter will permit. Suppose you want to print centered or justified text; you need to know the width of the text before printing, so you can position it correctly. Or, suppose you want to print some wrapped text with further material below it; you need to know how many lines the text occupies and what their total height is. REALbasic doesn't help you with these problems. Basically, you have to get the StringWidth for each character individually, and, if the text wraps, you have to work out the wrapping for yourself.

On the off chance that you might wish to know more about this, I'll go into the details a little. Feel free to skip the rest of this chapter if you don't need any more text-printing ability than is already supplied by REALbasic.

We're going to be using our ScrapRecord class, and we'll need two utility methods to assist us with it. First, a ScrapRecord's idea of a font is a font ID; we need to translate from this to a font name, which we can do by means of a Toolbox call:

```
Function myGetFontName(id as integer) As string
    declare sub GetFontName lib "InterfaceLib" (fid as integer, n as ptr)
    dim m as memoryBlock
    m = newmemoryBlock(256)
    getfontname id,m
    return m.pstring(0)
End Function
```

(On Mac OS X, change "InterfaceLib" to "CarbonLib".) Second, given a Scrap-Record and a character offset within the text, we need to know which of the Scrap-Record's ScrapTables describes the styles for that character (in other words, what style run does this character belong to). This ScrapRecord method tells us:

```
Function whichScrap(pos as integer) As integer
    dim i,u as integer
    u = numstyles-1
    for i = 1 to u
        if scraptables(i).offset > pos then
            return i-1
        end
    next
    return u
End Function
```

Now then. Assume we have an EditField called EditField1, and that we have analyzed its styles into a ScrapRecord, R. Suppose we are considering drawing its character i at position x,y in Graphics g. To do so, we need to set Graphics g's style characteristics to match those of this character; once we've done that, we can use the Graphics's StringWidth method to find out how many pixels wide the character would be. We advance our x position by that amount; before doing so, we can actually choose to draw the character into g or not, depending on whether we're printing or just measuring. This routine is called Advance; its parameters are x (which is ByRef, since this is what we're advancing), y, i, g, and a boolean draw:

```
dim s as scraptable
s = r.scrapTables(r.whichScrap(i))
if s <> prevScrap then
```

```
    g.textfont = mygetfontname(s.fontfamilyID)
    g.textsize = s.size
    g.bold = s.characterstyle.bold
    g.italic = s.characterstyle.italic
    g.underline = s.characterstyle.underline
    g.forecolor = s.rgbcolor
    prevScrap = s
end
if draw then
    g.drawstring mid(editfield1.text,i+1,1),x,y
end
x = x + g.stringwidth(mid(editfield1.text,i+1,1))
```

The clever part of Advance is that it stores a reference to the ScrapTable in a property, so that we change g's style characteristics only when we have to—if they are the same as the last time we were called, we leave them alone. This speeds up the routine tremendously, since changing a Graphics's style characteristics turns out to be extremely slow.

Now we are ready to print. Let's start with the simplest possible case. The following routine prints the contents of a brief styled EditField at an arbitrarily chosen position on the page, without wrapping:

```
x = // whatever
y = // whatever
for i = 0 to len(editfield1.text) - 1
    advance x, y, i, g, true
next
```

Observe that we can use this same routine to learn the width of the material, without actually printing, simply by changing true to false; all we have to do afterward is to subtract x's initial value from its final value. Let's call this *test printing* a line of text. Test printing is a very handy technique. For example, to center a line of multi-styled text, we can test print it and then use our knowledge of its length to print it for real, starting at the correct horizontal position so that it ends up centered.

So far, so good. Now let's think about wrapping. Wrapping involves isolating the individual words of the text. We wish to include on a line as many words as will fit without exceeding a certain maximum width. For the sake of simplicity, let's assume that a "word" simply means a run of nonspace characters, and that the text to be printed contains no huge individual "words" wider than our maximum line width.

We can wrap easily enough by means of a *backtracking* strategy. The idea is to test print one word at a time until we ascertain that we have exceeded our maximum width; if we have, we go back and print for real everything in the line up to but not including that last word, and then wrap.

It is a simple matter to extend the previous example to wrap by backtracking. Assume, for the sake of simplicity, that all the text to be printed will fit on one page, and that it contains no return characters. Assume also that we have already worked out values for the page margins: LeftMargin, RightMargin, TopMargin, and Bottom-Margin. We'll start printing in the top left corner:

```
x = leftmargin
y = topmargin
wordstart = x
wordchar = 0
for i = 0 to len(editfield1.text) - 1
    advance(x,y,i,g,false)
    if mid(editfield1.text,i+1,1) = " " or i = u then
        // did we just exceed the right margin?
        if x < rightmargin then // no, advance the word marker
            wordstart = x
            wordchar = i+1
        else // yes, time to print for real, and wrap
            x = leftmargin
            for j = linestart to wordchar-1 // print for real
                advance(x,y,i,g,true)
            next
            x = leftmargin // wrap!
            y = y + lineheight // new line!
            wordstart = x
            i = wordchar // print that last word as first word of new line
            linestart = i
        end
    end
next
```

Very little now remains to do. We must take account of return characters; if we encounter one, we wrap immediately. Also, each time we move down a line we need to check whether we've reached the end of the page; this can be encapsulated into a little utility routine, LineDown (the parameter y is ByRef, obviously):

```
y = y + lineheight
if y > bottommargin then
    g.nextpage
    y = topmargin
end
```

Here is the result:

```
x = leftmargin
y = topmargin
wordstart = x
wordchar = 0
u = len(editfield1.text) - 1
for i = 0 to u
    advance(x,y,i,g,false)
    ascii = asc(mid(editfield1.text,i+1,1))
    if ascii = 32 or ascii = 13 or i = u then
        // did we just exceed the right margin?
        if x < rightmargin then // no, advance the word marker
            if ascii = 13 or i = u then // print for real, and wrap
                x = leftmargin
```

```
              for j = linestart to i-1
                  advance(x,y,j,g,true)
              next
              x = leftmargin
              linestart = i+1
              lineDown y, lineheight, g, bottommargin, topmargin
          end
          wordstart = x
          wordchar = i+1
      else // yes, time to print for real, and wrap
          x = leftmargin
          for j = linestart to wordchar-1 // print for real
              advance(x,y,j,g,true)
          next
          x = leftmargin // wrap
          wordstart = x
          lineDown y, lineheight, g, bottommargin, topmargin
          i = wordchar // print that word again
          linestart = i
      end
  end
next
```

Let's remember why we went to all this trouble. On the face of it, this technique doesn't seem to accomplish any more than using a StyledTextPrinter; in fact, it's rather worse, since the LineHeight is hardcoded and invariant. Nevertheless, it immediately solves a problem with which REALbasic otherwise provides no help at all: throughout the print process, you know your vertical position. And with slight adaptations (left, as I'm sure you've guessed by now, to the reader as an exercise), it enables you to print centered, right-justified, or even (with more effort) fully justified wrapped styled text. All of this works just the same way if you're drawing text into a Canvas.

CHAPTER 30
TCP/IP Communications

In this chapter:
- Socket Properties, Methods, and Events
- Client
- Server

Communication across a TCP/IP network, such as the Internet, may be performed by way of REALbasic's built-in Socket control. Using a Socket, your application can function as a client or as a server. The two cases work slightly differently, so they are considered separately in this chapter.[*]

If you've never coded for TCP/IP communications before, don't panic. It's just a matter of sending text messages back and forth, like telegrams. The main trick is knowing what message to send when, and how to respond to the messages that you receive. That knowledge is what makes up the *protocol* for the particular sort of communication you're doing. A protocol is simply the list of rules for talking back and forth—a little language, if you will. If you are writing both the client and the server for private use, you can invent your own protocol. If you want to write an application that acts as a client or server for some public standard, you will need to follow the protocol for that standard; for example, if you want your application to speak to or act as a web server, you have to follow the protocol called HTTP.[†]

There are two ways to instantiate a Socket:

- Drag the Socket icon from the Tools Window into a Window Editor; or create a Socket subclass, and drag the subclass from the Project Window into the Window Editor. The window will automatically instantiate the Socket when it is itself instantiated. The icon that appears in the Window Editor has no physical manifestation in the running application; it is just a placeholder.

---

[*] The Serial control (which is not documented in this book, because I had no good way to study it) bears a strong fundamental resemblance to a Socket.

[†] Standard Internet protocols are available in documents called *RFCs* (which stands for "request for comments," because they are always regarded as proposals). A good set of links to repositories of RFCs is *http://www.rfc-editor.org/rfc.html*; a particularly good repository is *http://www.garlic.com/~lynn/rfcietff.htm*. Another very good way to learn a protocol is to run an application that already knows it, and use Interarchy's Show Traffic feature to observe the exchange of messages: see *http://www.interarchy.com/*. This feature is also an invaluable aid in debugging your application.

608

- Instantiate a Socket subclass with New and maintain a reference to it for as long as it is needed.

This chapter uses the second strategy.

Socket Properties, Methods, and Events

This section summarizes the properties, methods, and events of a Socket, in accordance with the stage of communications at which they are typically used. Examples appear later in the chapter.

Connecting and Disconnecting

A Socket has the following properties regarding its network connection:

PPPStatus
An integer (read-only) reporting whether there is a PPP-based dialup network connection. Values are: 0, no PPP; 1, idle; 4, connecting; 5, connected. (Not supported on Windows.)

Address
The IP address (as a string) of the server to which the Socket is to connect as a client.

Port
The port on which the Socket is to connect.

LocalAddress
The IP address (as a string) of the local computer. Read-only. I believe that if LocalAddress is not the empty string, you may pretty reliably conclude that the machine is connected to the Internet.*

RemoteAddress
When the Socket has received the Listen message and an incoming connection arrives, the IP address of the client machine that initiated the connection. Read-only.

A Socket accepts the following messages for connecting and disconnecting:

PPPConnect, PPPDisconnect
Causes the modem to dial up, or to hang up, a PPP-based network connection. (Not supported on Windows.)

Connect
Tells the Socket to try to connect as a client to the server at the Address and Port.

---

* I owe this idea to Chris Parker.

Listen
> Tells the Socket to start listening as a server for an incoming connection on the Port.

Close
> Tells the Socket to stop listening and/or to disconnect.

A Socket receives the following event with respect to connecting:

Connected
> Sent to the Socket because a connection has been established, either because the Socket had received the Connect message and succeeded in connecting, or because the Socket had received the Listen message and an incoming connection arrived.

Receiving Data

A Socket receives the following event when data arrives:

DataAvailable
> Sent when data arrives. The data is appended to the Socket's buffer.

A Socket has the following property with respect to receiving data:

Lookahead
> The current contents of the Socket's buffer.

A Socket has the following methods for reading data:

ReadAll
> Returns the contents of the Socket's buffer, and empties the buffer.

Read
> Takes one parameter, an integer; returns that many characters from the start of the Socket's buffer, and removes them from the buffer.

Sending Data

A Socket has the following method for sending data:

Write
> Takes one parameter, a string. Loads the string into the Socket's buffer, to be sent out over the network.

A Socket receives the following event when sending data:

SendComplete
> Sent when data loaded into the Socket's buffer with the Write message has actually been sent out over the network.

Errors

A Socket receives the following event when the network reports an error:

Error
> Sent because the network has reported an error.

A Socket has the following error-related property:

LastErrorCode
> The number of the most recent error reported by the network.

Yielding

A Socket has the following method for yielding time:

Poll
> Yields time to the Socket so that its properties can update and its event handlers can be triggered.

Client

To use a Socket for client-side communications, your sequence of actions will run something like this:

1. Initialize the Socket's Address property with the IP address of the server, and its Port property with the port number on which the server is listening.

2. Send the Socket the Connect message. When the connection is established, the Socket will receive a Connected event.

3. You will be notified of any incoming responses from the server by means of the DataAvailable event. You will typically extract any complete commands from the incoming data with the Read or ReadAll method.

4. Speak to the server by sending the Socket the Write message.

5. If any error occurs, you will receive an Error event; you can read the error number as the Socket's LastErrorCode property.

6. When finished, send the Socket the Close message to disconnect from the network.

Buffered Read

The chief complication in working with a Socket is that the network is an entity with a life of its own; it supplies or accepts data in quantities and at moments that are of its own choosing. Therefore, a Socket sends and receives data across the network asynchronously, meaning that your code is not in charge of when data arrives or is sent; instead, your code must read and write data by way of the Socket's *buffer*, a block of memory that accumulates data temporarily, until its intended recipient has a chance to extract it. Your code may have to do a little extra work in order to interact properly with this buffer.

For example, let's say that a response arrives from the server, and let's say that it arrives in several pieces. Then the first time you get a DataAvailable event, what's in the buffer is only a piece of the response. And you're not going to get any more of this response until the next DataAvailable event arrives, whenever that may be. So clearly you need to return from the DataAvailable event, so that more of the data can arrive, so that you can accumulate a complete response.

Now let's say that a complete response has accumulated in the buffer. Then your problem is just the converse of before. There's a complete response in the buffer; but is that the only thing in the buffer? Perhaps the server has sent more than one response, and what's in the buffer is your complete response plus the beginning of a different response. This doesn't seem particularly likely, but it's best to make no assumptions whatever about the timing and packaging of data.

Therefore, the strategy for reading data at each DataAvailable event will have to be something like this. We examine the buffer with Lookahead. If there isn't a complete response, we return from the DataAvailable event handler so more data can arrive. If there is a complete response, we extract it from the buffer with Read; any further data in the buffer following our response remains there, forming the start of the next response.

Dictionary Client

To illustrate, we will create a client for a particularly simple protocol: a Dictionary server, used for looking up definitions of words in a dictionary database.* And we will use a particularly simple subset of this protocol's commands: "DEFINE", which asks for the definition of a word, and "QUIT", which says goodbye afterward. We will develop the application in two stages:

1. First, we'll respond manually to communications from the server: we will personally monitor each incoming message as it arrives, and when we see that it has arrived, we'll push one of several buttons to send back the appropriate reply. In this way, we will confirm that the basic logic of our application is working.

2. Then, we'll rewrite the application to be automatic: the application will parse each incoming message and will respond appropriately without human intervention.

I have found this two-stage approach to be particularly helpful when writing communications applications; you don't want your application to become fully automatic

---

* The protocol is defined by RFC 2229. At the time the first edition of this book was published, most people were unaware of this protocol, and there were no Dictionary clients available for Macintosh (to my knowledge); immediately afterward, several Dictionary clients appeared—written in REALbasic. Coincidence? I don't think so.

until you're fairly sure it can negotiate whatever data it may receive, so in the early stages of development, instead of parsing messages from the server in code, we parse them with our brains.

Create a Socket subclass called DictSocket. Give your Window a DictSocket property, named Socket1.

In the Window Editor, create a multiline EditField. This EditField will accumulate everything that arrives in the Socket's buffer, so that we can monitor and respond to incoming communications. Give the DictSocket class an EditField property, TheField, so that it will know where this EditField is.

The window's Open event handler creates the Socket and points TheField at EditField1:

```
socket1 = new dictsocket
socket1.thefield = editfield1
```

Give the DictSocket class a constructor (that is, a method called DictSocket); here, we initialize its Address and Port properties, so that the Socket will know where there is a Dictionary server:

```
me.address = "dict.org"
me.port = 2628
```

DictSocket's Connected, DataAvailable, and Error event handlers simply append text to the EditField so that we can read it. Here is DictSocket's Connected event handler:

```
thefield.text = "Connected: " + chr(13)
```

Here is DictSocket's DataAvailable event handler:

```
thefield.sellength = 0
thefield.selstart = len(thefield.text)
thefield.seltext = me.readall + chr(13)
```

Here is DictSocket's Error event handler:

```
dim s as string
s = str(me.lasterrorcode)
thefield.sellength = 0
thefield.selstart = len(thefield.text)
thefield.seltext = "ERROR: " + s + chr(13)
```

There will be four stages in our communications:

1. Connect to the server.
2. Ask the server for the definition of a word.
3. Disconnect from the server.
4. Disconnect from the network by closing the Socket.

Since we're going to manage all the action ourselves, we will have four buttons in the window, each of which initiates one of these stages. The first button's Action event handler says:

```
socket1.connect
```

The second button's Action event handler says:

```
socket1.write("DEFINE ! penguin" + chr(13) + chr(10))
```

As is typical of an Internet protocol, a command must end with CRLF, that is, chr(13) followed by chr(10). The ! parameter tells the Dictionary server to look up the word in each of its databases in turn, replying as soon as it finds a definition.

The third button's Action event handler says:

```
socket1.write("QUIT" + chr(13) + chr(10))
```

The fourth button's Action event handler says:

```
socket1.close
```

That's all there is to it. Time to play! Connect to the Internet and run the project. Press the first button. When the 220 message comes back from the server, confirming the connection, press the second button. When the definition of "penguin" stops arriving, press the third button. When things have settled down, press the fourth button.

The EditField now contains a record of the communications from the Dictionary server. Since the LF character, chr(10), is invisible (or shows up as a sort of box), I have replaced it with "[LF]" in what follows:

```
Connected:
220 server1.shopthenet.net dictd 1.4.9/rf on Linux 2.0.36 <auth.mime> <442048.30795.
920404208@server1.shopthenet.net>
[LF]
150 1 definitions retrieved
[LF]
151 "Penguin" web1913 "Webster's Revised Unabridged Dictionary (1913)"
[LF]Penguin \Pen"guin\, n. [Perh. orig. the name of another bird,
[LF]    and fr. W. pen head + gwyn white; or perh. from a native
[LF]    South American name.]
[LF]    1. (Zo["o]l.) Any bird of the order Impennes, or Ptilopteri.
[LF]       They are covered with short, thick feathers, almost
[LF]       scalelike on the wings, which are without true quills.
[LF]       They are unable to fly, but use their wings to aid in
[LF]       diving, in which they are very expert. See {King penguin},
[LF]       under {Jackass}.
[LF]
[LF]    Note: Penguins are found in the south temperate and antarctic
[LF]          regions. The king penguins ({Aptenodytes Patachonica},
[LF]          and {A. longirostris}) are the largest; the jackass
[LF]          penguins ({Spheniscus}) and the rock hoppers
[LF]          ({Catarractes}) congregate in large numbers at their
[LF]          breeding grounds.
[LF]
[LF]    2. (Bot.) The egg-shaped fleshy fruit of a West Indian plant
[LF]       ({Bromelia Pinguin}) of the Pineapple family; also, the
[LF]       plant itself, which has rigid, pointed, and spiny-toothed
[LF]       leaves, and is used for hedges. [Written also {pinguin}.]
[LF]
```

```
[LF]   {Arctic penguin} (Zo["o]l.), the great auk. See {Auk}.
[LF].
[LF]250 ok [d/m/c = 1/0/19; 173.000r 30.000u 10.000s]
[LF]

221 bye [d/m/c = 0/0/0; 310.000r 30.000u 10.000s]
[LF]
ERROR: 102
```

This shows the course of communications very clearly:

- When we first connect, we receive a 220 message ending with CRLF.

- When we ask for a definition, we receive a 150 message ending with CRLF; this tells us how many definitions to expect. This is followed by a series of 151 messages containing the definitions, terminated by CRLF, a single period, and CRLF; afterward, there is a 250 message terminated by CRLF. (The protocol tells us that if there had been no match for the word we are looking up, the 150, 151, and 250 messages would have been replaced by a single 552 message saying so.)

- When we log off, we receive a 221 message, terminated by CRLF. We also receive a 102 error, but this isn't actually an error condition; on the contrary, it is our notification that the server has terminated its connection, which is exactly what we asked it to do.

We are now ready to revise our application so that our code, rather than a human being, will determine when and how to interact with the server.

DictSocket needs some more properties so that it can maintain state during the course of the interaction: Query as string, ReceivingDefinition as boolean, Finished as boolean, and NumDefs as integer.

Back in the window, in addition to EditField1, we now have EditField2, a single-line nonstyled EditField in which the user will enter the word to be defined. EditField1 will now hold the definition returned by the server, plus any status messages we care to place there. There is just one button, which the user will press to look up the word in EditField2; its Action event handler does some sanity checks, and then launches things by initializing the Socket's properties, putting up a status message, and telling the Socket to connect:

```
dim s as string
s = editfield2.text // word to be looked up
if instr(s,chr(13)) > 0 or instr(s,chr(32)) > 0 then
    msgbox "Do not type spaces or returns in the word to be defined."
elseif len(s) = 0 then
    msgbox "Enter word to be looked up!"
else
    socket1.query = s
    socket1.receivingdefinition = false
    editfield1.text = "Connecting..."
    editfield1.refresh
    socket1.connect
end
```

The Refresh message to the EditField here and throughout the code is completely unnecessary at this point; but at the end of this section I'm going to describe a different version of this project, with the whole operation synchronously driven by a loop in the button's Action event handler, and at that point, the Refresh messages *will* be necessary. So I've put them in now, so as not to have to do it later.

DictSocket's Connected event handler just posts a status message:

```
thefield.text = "Connected..."
thefield.refresh
```

DictSocket's Error event handler puts up a dialog, except on the 102 error which is not important; it then tries to back out of whatever unpleasant situation has arisen, by closing the connection:

```
dim s as string
s = str(me.lasterrorcode)
if s <> "102" then
    msgbox "ERROR: " + s
end
me.close
```

All the real work is done by the DataAvailable event handler. The challenge here is that this same event handler will have entirely different work to do on different occasions when it is called. We thus end up with an architecture known as an *event loop*, which can be rather tricky to manage. Typically, a series of boolean flags and conditional tests are used to determine what stage things are at, and to respond appropriately. That's what our various Socket properties are for.

Our lowest-level task, and therefore the first thing in the handler, is always to see whether the buffer contains CRLF, because if it does not, we know for certain that we have not yet received a complete message, so we simply stop and wait for more data to arrive. This is the start of the Socket's DataAvailable event handler:

```
dim CRLF, defEnd, reply, lk as string
dim i as integer
CRLF = chr(13) + chr(10)
defEnd = CRLF + "." + CRLF
lk = lookahead
i = instr(lk, CRLF)
if i = 0 then
    return // wait for more data
end
```

Our next concern is to handle situations where we are in the middle of receiving an extended message—one whose completeness is not signaled merely by the fact that it ends in CRLF. In this instance, the only such message is the one that starts with the 150 status line informing us that definitions are on the way; we will signal to ourselves that we are in this situation by means of the ReceivingDefinition boolean flag. While this flag is up, we just keep letting data accumulate in the buffer, until it has all arrived. To be on the safe side, I include two tests for whether the definition has arrived completely. First, I consider whether as many definitions have arrived as were promised in the 150 status line; this number has been stored in the NumDefs property, so I compare this to the number of definition-termination strings in the buffer; second, I consider whether the entire 250 message has arrived. This is the next part of the Socket's DataAvailable event handler:

```
if receivingDefinition then
    if countfields(lk, defEnd) > numdefs then
        i = instr(lk, defEnd + "250")
        if i > 0 then
            i = instr(i+5, lk, CRLF)
            if i > 0 then
```

If all these conditions are met, a complete definition reply has arrived. We extract it from the buffer and present it to the user. (A utility routine, in which we clean up the data cosmetically, is not shown.) We then lower the ReceivingDefinition flag, and initiate the next stage of the conversation by logging off from the server:

```
                reply = read(i+1)
                thefield.text = formatNicely(reply)
                thefield.refresh
                receivingDefinition = false
                me.write("QUIT" + CRLF)
            end
        end
    end
```

All other actions depend on what message has arrived; the choices are couched as a series of ElseIf clauses. If it's the 220 message, we ask the server for the definition. If it's the 150 message, we raise the ReceivingDefinition flag. If it's the 552 message, we log off from the server. If it's the 221 message, we close the connection. Otherwise, something unexpected has happened, so we put up a dialog. In every case, we clear the message from the buffer; also, we keep the user apprised of how things are going with a status message:

```
elseif instr(lk, "220 ") = 1 then
    reply = read(i+1)
    thefield.text = "Looking up word..."
    thefield.refresh
    me.write("DEFINE ! " + query + CRLF)
elseif instr(lk, "150 ") = 1 then
    numdefs = val(nthfield(lk," ",2))
    reply = read(i+1)
    thefield.text = "Receiving definition..."
    thefield.refresh
    receivingDefinition = true
elseif instr(lk, "552") = 1 then
    reply = read(i+1)
    thefield.text = "Not Found."
    thefield.refresh
    me.write("QUIT" + CRLF)
```

```
elseif instr(lookahead, "221 ") = 1 then
    thefield.selstart = 0
    thefield.sellength = 0
    thefield.seltext = "Connection closed. Definition:" + chr(13)
    thefield.refresh
    reply = readall
    finished = true
    me.close
else
    msgbox "unknown: " + readall
end
```

This completes our little Dictionary client; go ahead and try it out! (For some nerdy humor, try looking up "defenestration.")

Before moving on, let's make one small modification. At present, the entire process initiated by the user pressing the button is asynchronous, meaning that while the application is exchanging messages with the server, the user can engage in all sorts of possibly undesirable actions, such as pressing the button again, typing into the second EditField, or quitting the application. We might wish, instead, that the activity should be synchronous: once the user presses the button, the application should become "busy," preventing the user from doing anything else until the exchange with the server is over. But how can we do this, when by their very nature, Socket communications with the network are asynchronous?

The Poll method is designed for this sort of situation. When the Poll message is sent to a Socket, the main execution path remains in the hands of the code that sent it, but the Socket's events are enabled to fire, and its event handlers to run. So, for example, the button's Action event handler can end like this:

```
// ...
    socket1.connect
    socket1.finished = false
    do until socket1.finished
        socket1.poll
    loop
end
```

The Socket's entire action now takes place within a loop in the button's Action event handler. The repeated Poll message permits the Socket to receive and act upon its events, but no other object receives events, and the watch cursor is shown; thus, the action is synchronous. Any event handler that sends the Socket the Close message must now also set Finished to true, as a sign that the conversation is over; this terminates the loop. If I'm not mistaken, the synchronous version is considerably faster than the asynchronous version. I'm guessing that this is because the repeated Poll messages bombard the Socket very densely and persistently, and nothing else is permitted to happen, whereas in our original version the application must spend time between Socket events watching for events in other objects, yielding time to other applications, and so forth.

Buffered Write

In sending large amounts of data, much the same considerations apply as in receiving it, but in reverse. The Socket's Write message merely loads the Socket's buffer; the data is not actually sent until the network is ready to accept it, and the network may accept it only in small packets. In the Dictionary client example, this didn't matter, for two reasons: first, all the packets of data to be sent were already small; and second, we didn't care when the packets were actually sent, since the program's actions were driven entirely by the *arrival* of data.

It is perfectly possible to hand the buffer a lot of data at once; the data will be sent out in packets, and the SendComplete event won't arrive until it has all been sent. But we still may need a way to wait until the SendComplete event does arrive. In this section, I illustrate a technique for doing this. I divide the outgoing data into chunks, and before I use the Write message to hand the Socket the next chunk, I wait until the previous chunk has actually been sent out; to find out when this is, I wait for the SendComplete event to arrive.

How exactly is this going to work? Consider the following scenario. To notify us that the Socket's buffer is empty and ready for a new chunk, we might have its SendComplete event handler raise a boolean flag property:

```
sent = true
```

We could then do all our writing through a method handler, BufferedWrite, which takes one parameter, a string. It lowers the Sent flag, writes the string into the Socket's buffer with the Write message, and then pauses until the Sent flag goes up:

```
sent = false
socket1.write(s)
do // nothing
loop until sent
```

There's just one problem. While BufferedWrite is looping, the SendComplete event cannot arrive; so the thing the loop is waiting for, the raising of the Sent flag, is prevented from happening by the loop itself! Therefore, either BufferedWrite must be implemented as a Timer, or its loop must repeatedly send the Socket the Poll message. In this next example, I'll illustrate both methods of performing a buffered write.

SMTP Client

We will now use REALbasic to send an email message; that is, we will write a simple SMTP client. The conversation with the SMTP server will run as follows:

- Connect to the server; it replies with a 220 message.
- Send the server the EHLO message, supplying your IP address in square brackets; it replies with a series of 250 messages, the last of which is distinguished by having a space after the 250.

- Send the server the RSET message; it replies with a 250 message.

- Send the server the MAIL FROM: message, supplying your return address in angle brackets; it replies with a 250 message.

- Send the server the RCPT TO: message, supplying the recipient's address in angle brackets; it replies with a 250 message.

- Send the server the DATA message; it replies with a 354 message.

- Send the email itself. This consists of any headers, followed by an empty line, followed by the message body, ending with a period on a line by itself. The server replies with a 250 message.

- Send the server the QUIT message; it replies with a 221 message. You get a 102 error and close the Socket.

We start with a Timer subclass, WriteTimer, and a Socket subclass, SMTPSocket. SMTPSocket has a boolean Sent property, and an EditField property, Status, so that it knows where to post status messages; and it has some string properties that are the parts of the outgoing message: Recipient, Subject, and RetAddr. It has a string property WhatsNext; this is a sort of flag, with which we're going to keep track of where we are in the conversation with the server. It has a WriteTimer property called Timer1.

The SMTPSocket class's constructor initializes the port:

```
me.port = 25
```

The SMTPSocket class's SendComplete event handler raises the Sent flag; this is how other objects will learn that a chunk has been sent:

```
sent = true
```

The window has an SMTPSocket property, Socket1, and it instantiates the Socket in its Open event handler:

```
socket1 = new smtpsocket
```

The window consists of various EditFields in which the user enters the message, the addressee, and so forth, and an EditField for status messages from the Socket. It also has a button which initiates the transaction. The button's Action event handler first calls an SMTPSocket routine (not shown), which obtains the body of the message and wraps it, so that its lines are shorter than 72 characters, ending each line with CRLF, and stores the result in the Socket's property, TheData. It then puts up a status message, initializes the Socket properties, and connects:

```
socket1.prepareTheData(editfield1.text)
editfield4.text = "Connecting..."
socket1.sent = false
socket1.recipient = editfield2.text
socket1.subject = editfield3.text
socket1.status = editfield4
```

```
socket1.address = editfield5.text
socket1.retaddr = editfield6.text
socket1.whatsNext = "EHLO"
socket1.connect
```

The Socket's DataAvailable event handler is long but boring. It's an event loop, whose choices are driven by the status flag, WhatsNext. For simplicity, error checking has been omitted; it is assumed that each message from the server arrives as expected, in sequence. Each choice has roughly the same form: put up a status message, clear the input buffer, change the status flag, and talk to the server. Here is the DataAvailable event handler:

```
dim CRLF, lk, dummy as string
dim i as integer
CRLF = chr(13) + chr(10)
lk = lookahead
i = instr(lk, CRLF)
if i = 0 then
    return
end
select case whatsNext
case "EHLO"
    if left(lk,3) = "220" then
        status.text = whatsNext
        status.refresh
        dummy = read(i+1)
        whatsNext = "RSET"
        me.write("EHLO [" + me.localaddress + "]" + CRLF)
    end
case "RSET"
    i = instr(lk, "250 ")
    if i > 0 then
        i = instr(i, lk, CRLF)
        if i > 0 then
            status.text = whatsNext
            status.refresh
            dummy = read(i+1)
            whatsNext = "MAIL"
            me.write("RSET" + CRLF)
        end
    end
case "MAIL"
    if left(lk,3) = "250" then
        status.text = whatsNext
        status.refresh
        dummy = read(i+1)
        whatsNext = "RCPT"
        me.write("MAIL FROM:<" + retaddr + ">" + CRLF)
    end
case "RCPT"
    if left(lk,3) = "250" then
        status.text = whatsNext
        status.refresh
        dummy = read(i+1)
```

```
                whatsNext = "DATA"
                me.write("RCPT TO:<" + recipient + ">" + CRLF)
        end
    case "DATA"
        if left(lk,3) = "250" then
                status.text = whatsNext
                status.refresh
                dummy = read(i+1)
                whatsNext = "SEND"
                me.write("DATA" + CRLF)
        end
    case "SEND"
        if left(lk,3) = "354" then
                status.text = whatsNext
                status.refresh
                dummy = read(i+1)
                whatsNext = "QUIT"
                sendMessage
        end
    case "QUIT"
        if left(lk,3) = "250" then
                status.text = whatsNext
                status.refresh
                dummy = read(i+1)
                whatsNext = "CLOS"
                me.write("QUIT" + CRLF)
        end
    case "CLOS"
        if left(lk,3) = "221" then
                status.text = whatsNext
                me.close
        end
    end
end
```

SendMessage, referred to in the DataAvailable event handler's "SEND" case, is packaged separately to make the code easier to read (and is not shown). It first constructs the message headers, the hardest part of which is building a properly formatted date. It then appends the message and the end delimiter, and packs the whole thing off to BufferedWrite, to be sent to the server.

In our first implementation, BufferedWrite will use our Timer subclass, WriteTimer. The WriteTimer class has these properties: a string, TheData, which must be initialized with the outgoing message; two integers, I and U; and an SMTPSocket, TheSocket, so that the Timer can find the SMTPSocket instance. BufferedWrite merely instantiates and initializes the Timer and starts it running:

```
timer1 = new writeTimer
timer1.period = 10
timer1.theSocket = me
timer1.thedata = s
timer1.mode = 2
```

WriteTimer's Action event handler is a little bit complicated, because it really represents a nest of two different loops: it loops to send successive chunks of TheData, and between those loops it loops until it's time to send the next chunk. The first time through the loop it calculates how many chunks there will be; this calculation depends upon BufferSize, a constant in a module. The actual value of BufferSize doesn't really matter; you could use 2048, you could use 50000. On the next loop it lowers the Sent flag and sends the first chunk of data, and then on subsequent loops it watches until the Socket's SendComplete event has raised the Sent flag; this repeats until the last chunk has been sent, at which point the Timer stops itself. Here is the Timer's Action event handler:

```
if u = 0 then // first time
    u = len(theData) \ buffersize + 1
else
    if not theSocket.sent then // keep waiting
    elseif i = u then // last packet has been sent, done
        me.mode = 0
    else // send next packet
        i = i + 1
        thesocket.sent = false
        thesocket.write(mid(theData,(i-1)*buffersize+1,buffersize))
    end
end
```

This completes the Timer-based implementation of our SMTP client.

In our second implementation, there is no Timer; instead, BufferedWrite itself loops. This is *exactly* the same loop as the Timer was doing, but it's a lot easier to read: instead of using properties I and U to maintain state, we now have local variables, and instead of a comparison and a Mode change to terminate, we have a For loop. The For loop hands the buffer a chunk of the message for it to send to the server, and the Socket then polls itself until the chunk has been sent:

```
dim u,i as integer
u = len(s) \ buffersize + 1
for i = 1 to u
    sent = false
    me.write(mid(s,(i-1)*buffersize+1,buffersize))
    do until sent
        me.poll
    loop
next
```

Server

To use a Socket for server-side communications, your sequence of actions will run something like this:

1. Initialize the Socket's Port property with the port number on which the server is to listen.

2. Send the Socket the Listen message. When an incoming connection is established, the Socket will receive a Connected event.

3. You will be notified of any incoming commands from the client by means of the DataAvailable event. You'll typically clean out the buffer with the Read or ReadAll method.

4. Speak to the client by means of the Socket's Write method.

5. If any error occurs, you will receive an Error event; you can read the error number as the Socket's LastErrorCode property.

6. When finished, send the Socket the Close message to disconnect from the network.

The chief difference between a Socket acting as a server and a Socket acting as a client is that the server Socket is not sent the Connect message and doesn't need any value in its Address property. Instead, the Socket is sent the Listen message; when a client asks to connect to the Socket, the network takes care of establishing the connection.

Web-Based Time Server

As a first example, we will write a server that tells what time it is. The server will be extraordinarily simpleminded: it won't even examine the message sent to it by the client. No matter what that message is, the server will report the time and close the connection.

In order to save ourselves the trouble of writing a corresponding client application, we will use a client application everyone already has—a web browser. Our server will therefore communicate using HTTP, and so its reply to the client will consist of the HTML for a web page that states the time.

We'll use a Socket subclass called ServerSocket. Start with a window that has a ServerSocket property named Socket1. The Window's Open event handler instantiates the ServerSocket; I do this with a method call, because we'll need to do this elsewhere as well:

```
newListener
```

NewListener is a method handler that closes and destroys an existing ServerSocket and replaces it with a new one. If Socket1 points to an existing Socket, we send that Socket the Close message just in case the connection needs closing, and then set the reference to nil to make sure the Socket instance is well and truly destroyed, before creating a new Socket to replace it. In this way we can be quite confident that we won't accidentally create two Sockets on the same port:

```
if socket1 <> nil then
    socket1.close
    socket1 = nil
end
socket1 = new serverSocket
```

Let's turn now to ServerSocket. So as not to let our server be confused with a genuine web server, we will communicate on port 2001. (This is also a port number that

Mac OS X is willing to let us use.) In ServerSocket's constructor, we declare the port number, and start listening for an incoming connection:

```
port = 2001
listen
```

When a client establishes a connection, data appears in the buffer, and we get a DataAvailable event. In HTTP, the arrival of a complete message is signaled by two CRLFs. A complete message having arrived, we proceed to form a reply. In accordance with HTTP rules, this starts with a header (ours is minimal, a status message reporting that all is well) terminated by two CRLFs; we follow this with the HTML for a web page saying what time it is, and send the whole thing back to the client:

```
dim CRLF, s as string
dim d as date
dim i as integer
CRLF = chr(13) + chr(10)
i = instr(lookahead, CRLF + CRLF)
if i = 0 then
    return
end
s = read(i+3) // clear buffer, throw away
d = new date
s = "HTTP/1.0 200 OK" + CRLF + CRLF
s = s + "<html><head><title>Time</title></head>"
s = s + "<body><center><h1>" + d.longtime
s = s + "</h1></center></body></html>"
me.write s
```

In both the SendComplete event handler and the Error event handler, we call the SelfDestruct method handler to close the connection and destroy this Socket. This is how the web browser will know that the complete web page has arrived. I don't like the idea of a Socket instance actually trying to destroy itself, so I start up a Timer to do the job. A boolean property, SelfDestructing, is used to prevent SelfDestruct from being called more than once per Socket instance; I don't really know how likely this is, but since Sockets are asynchronous I'm not taking any chances:

```
if not selfDestructing then
    selfDestructing = true
    window1.timer1.mode = 1
end
```

The Timer has a short Period, let's say 100; all its Action event handler does is call NewListener, and the whole process starts again, with a new Socket instance listening so that someone else can ask us the time.

That's all there is to it! To test this, you can set yourself up with two machines connected locally or across the Internet, or you may even be able to run both the server and a browser on the same machine; in the latter case, you may be able to ask the browser for the "localhost" URL:

```
http://localhost:2001/
```

Presto, the time of day appears displayed in your web browser; and if you ask the browser to reload its page, the time will update itself. I find, in fact, that I'm able to whack away at the Reload button, pushing it every two or three seconds, and the time just keeps updating. We've written an Internet server!

Now, to be quite honest, this example does not display very good HTTP style. It turns out that we really are not supposed to close the connection like this. Instead, we are supposed to examine the header of the incoming message to see whether a Keep-Alive connection has been requested (and it almost certainly will be); if so, we are supposed to let the client close the connection first. To do this, the client needs to know when the entire web page has arrived, so we must provide a Content-Length header.

So here is a slightly more sophisticated version of the server. In the DataAvailable event handler, we examine the incoming command for whether it contains a Keep-Alive header, and we set accordingly a boolean property of the ServerSocket, called KeepAlive. In our reply, we include a Content-Length header, as well as a Content-Type header for good measure:

```
dim CRLF, s as string
dim d as date
dim i as integer
CRLF = chr(13) + chr(10)
i = instr(lookahead, CRLF + CRLF)
if i = 0 then
    return
end
keepalive = instr(lookahead, "Connection: Keep-Alive") > 0
s = read(i+3) // clear buffer, throw away
d = new date
s = "<html><head><title>Time</title></head>"
s = s + "<body><center><h1>" + d.longtime
s = s + "</h1></center></body></html>"
s = "Content-Length: " + str(len(s)) + CRLF + CRLF + s
s = "Content-Type: text/html" + CRLF + s
s = "HTTP/1.0 200 OK" + CRLF + s
me.write s
```

The SendComplete event handler closes the connection only if KeepAlive is false:

```
if not keepalive then
    selfDestruct
end
```

When the client closes the connection, we will get a 102 error; this will trigger the Error event handler, and this is where we will call SelfDestruct and start up a new listening Socket, in good order. I find that this architecture, taking Keep-Alive into account, is even more robust and responsive than before.

Tiny Web Server

Since our little timer server is now speaking decent HTTP, it's easy to take the next logical step and turn it into an actual web server—that is, a program that serves

HTML files from disk. Of course, our web server will be extremely minimal; indeed, it will be downright substandard! But it will allow a user with a browser to read, across a network, an HTML file stored on disk on the server machine.

We really have to make only two changes. One is that we must parse the incoming request to learn what file the client wants. The key element of the request is its second word, which is the pathname of the desired file, delimited by slashes. If it is a slash and no more, the user wants the default file, so we substitute "/default.html". We then parse the pathname to be relative to some base folder that is imagined to be our web site, and we attempt to read the file. If we succeed, we return it, with a 200 header; if we fail, we return a Not Found page, with a 404 header. We also need to do something about requests for images or other non-HTML files; to keep things simple, we refuse to serve them, by artificially generating a Not Found error.

The other change is that, since the HTML file being served could be long, we really ought to break it up and return it in chunks. Well, we know how to do that; we just use the BufferedWrite routine we developed earlier. The Socket's SendComplete event handler must let BufferedWrite know when it's time for the next chunk, by setting a boolean Sent property to true (just as in "SMTP Client," earlier).

Here, then, is the DataAvailable event handler:

```
dim CRLF, s, thePath as string
dim f as folderitem
dim tis as textinputstream
dim i,u as integer
dim notFound as boolean
CRLF = chr(13) + chr(10)
i = instr(lookahead, CRLF + CRLF)
if i = 0 then
    return
end
keepalive = instr(lookahead, "Connection: Keep-Alive") > 0
thePath = nthfield(lookahead," ",2)
s = read(i+3) // throw away
if lowercase(right(thePath,4)) <> "html" then
    thePath = "/nofile" // deliberately cause a Not Found error
end
if thePath = "/" then
    thePath = "/default.html"
end
f = // whatever; this is the base folder for the site
u = countfields(thepath, "/")
for i = 2 to u
    if f <> nil then
        f = f.child(nthfield(thepath, "/", i))
    else
        f = getfolderitem("nofile")
    end
next
if f <> nil and f.exists then
    tis = f.openastextfile
end
```

```
if tis = nil then
    s = "<html><head><title>Oops</title></head>"
    s = s + "<body><center><h1>No Such File"
    s = s + "</h1></center></body></html>"
    notFound = true
else
    s = tis.readall
    tis.close
end
s = "Content-Length: " + str(len(s)) + CRLF + CRLF + s
s = "Content-Type: text/html" + CRLF + s
if notfound then
    s = "HTTP/1.0 404 Not Found" + CRLF + s
    keepAlive = false
else
    s = "HTTP/1.0 200 OK" + CRLF + s
end
bufferedwrite(s)
```

There are some tricky issues surrounding the business of negotiating closure of the connection. The architecture used here involves setting KeepAlive to `false` when a file is not found or is an image, so that the SendComplete event handler will close the connection, and this seems to work well in my tests—meaning that when I ask for a page that contains images, the browser doesn't hang. You may have to experiment a bit. I can assure you that, even though this web server can't serve images or handle multiple connections, you'll get a thrill when you type a URL into your browser and the page appears, served from disk by a tiny REALbasic application!

Multiple Connections

Our little web server works fine, but one of the things that keeps it substandard is that it can't deal with multiple simultaneous requests. The need for this can arise even with a single web page. If a page contains images, the browser can start asking for the images even while the text of the page is still downloading. Multiple Sockets won't help, because REALbasic Sockets can listen on a given port only one at a time. I've tried various workarounds, such as generating a new Socket as soon as the old Socket makes a connection, but I've never found a solution that's completely reliable. What's needed is a listener-dispatcher architecture, where a single listener on a port receives incoming connection requests and hands each one off to a new Socket as they arrive. But REALbasic Sockets are incapable of that.

One solution is a commercial third-party plug-in, SuperSocket, which does use a listener-dispatcher architecture (along with various other Socket enhancements, such as UDP and AppleTalk support).* To illustrate, I'll close with an example that expands our tiny web server so that web pages containing GIFs work properly. We use two SuperSocket classes: TCPListener (the listener-dispatcher) and TCP-Endpoint (the Socket replacement). Our TCPEndpoint subclass is called

* See *http://www.essencesw.com/*.

SuperServerSocket, and our TCPListener subclass, MyListener, has a property which is an array of SuperServerSockets.

On startup, the window initializes a MyListener property: it instantiates the listener and starts it listening on port 2001:

```
listener = new myListener
if listener.listen(2001) then
end
```

When a connection request comes in, MyListener finds an empty slot in its array of SuperServerSockets, creates a new SuperServerSocket, pops it into the array, and hands off the request to it; it then resumes listening automatically. This is taken care of in MyListener's NewConnection event handler:

```
dim s as superServerSocket
dim i as integer
for i = 0 to ubound(sockets)
    if sockets(i) = nil then
        s = new superServerSocket(i)
        sockets(i) = s
        if s.accept(req) then
        exit
    end
next
```

SuperServerSocket's constructor stores the instance's index number in a property; this is how we will destroy the instance later on.

A SuperServerSocket works almost exactly like a ServerSocket. The work is done in the DataAvailable event handler. One change here is that, because of a bug, Super-ServerSocket's Lookahead property isn't working; so we empty the buffer into a string property of our own, called Buffer. The other is that we are now prepared to serve GIFs:

```
dim CRLF, s, thePath as string
dim f as folderitem
dim tis as textinputstream
dim i,u as integer
dim notFound as boolean
dim isGif as boolean
buffer = buffer + readall
CRLF = chr(13) + chr(10)
i = instr(buffer, CRLF + CRLF)
if i = 0 then
    return
end
s = mid(buffer, 1, i+3)
buffer = mid(buffer, i+4, len(buffer))
keepalive = instr(s, "Connection: Keep-Alive") > 0
thePath = nthfield(s," ",2)
if lowercase(right(thePath,4)) <> "html" and lowercase(right(thePath,3)) <> "gif"
then
    thePath = "/nofile" // deliberately cause a Not Found error
end
```

```
isGif = lowercase(right(thePath,3)) = "gif"
if thePath = "/" then
    thePath = "/default.html"
end
f = // whatever
u = countfields(thepath, "/")
for i = 2 to u
    if f <> nil then
        f = f.child(nthfield(thepath, "/", i))
    else
        f = getfolderitem("nofile")
    end
next
if f <> nil and f.exists then
    tis = f.openastextfile
end
if tis = nil then
    s = "<html><head><title>Oops</title></head>"
    s = s + "<body><center><h1>No Such File"
    s = s + "</h1></center></body></html>"
    notFound = true
else
    s = tis.readall
    tis.close
end
s = "Content-Length: " + str(len(s)) + CRLF + CRLF + s
if isGif then
    s = "Content-Type: image/gif" + CRLF + s
else
    s = "Content-Type: text/html" + CRLF + s
end
if notfound then
    s = "HTTP/1.0 404 Not Found" + CRLF + s
    keepAlive = false
else
    s = "HTTP/1.0 200 OK" + CRLF + s
end
write(s)
```

SuperServerSocket inherits a Disconnect method and a Disconnected event, so we are able to close down the connection in good order: either we disconnect ourselves, with the Disconnect method, or we are notified that the client has disconnected, through the Disconnected event. All that remains after that is to destroy the instance. Its index in the listener's array was stored as a property, Index; so:

```
window1.listener.sockets(index) = nil
```

To observe the state of the dynamic SuperServerSocket array, I used a Timer to loop through it and display which elements are non-nil; during a request, the display rises until all pieces of the request have been served, and then falls to zero as expected.

CHAPTER 31

In this chapter:
- Sending Apple Events
- Receiving Apple Events
- Apple Event Classes, Properties, and Methods
- Apple Event Inadequacies
- AppleScripts
- Shell

Interapplication Communications

The Macintosh's system-level mechanism for letting applications communicate with one another is *Apple events.*[*] An application that defines a repertoire of Apple events to which it is prepared to respond is described as *scriptable*. Another application can send to a scriptable application an Apple event from the scriptable application's defined repertoire, to give it a command or to ask for information.

An Apple event is an ingeniously designed package of data, and can express a command or query of astonishing power and complexity. This means, however, that an Apple event is itself a particularly complex data structure. A convenient way to construct and send Apple events without having to deal with the details of their raw structure is through *AppleScript*, a programming language that encodes Apple events as English-like expressions. This, too, is a system-level mechanism; AppleScript code is interpreted and executed as Apple events by way of the system's Open Scripting Architecture, or *OSA*. (The term "AppleScript" properly refers to the language, but I use it also to refer to a script—a self-contained piece of executable code written in that language—so as not to have to talk about an "AppleScript script.")

REALbasic can construct and send raw Apple events. Also, it can incorporate and execute AppleScripts written and compiled in some other milieu, such as Apple's own Script Editor. Through both these means, a REALbasic application can command or query other applications that are scriptable, perhaps as a way of supplementing its own powers with theirs, or in order to exchange data with them. Furthermore, a REALbasic application can receive Apple events; thus, it can itself be scriptable, meaning it can be commanded and queried by other applications that know how to construct and send Apple events.[†]

[*] See *http://developer.apple.com/techpubs/mac/IAC/IAC-2.html*.

[†] To learn more about some of the aspects of Apple events referred to in this chapter, and to see what genuine, full support for Apple events entails, see my earlier book, *Frontier: The Definitive Guide* (O'Reilly & Associates, 1998).

With the advent of Mac OS X, it is possible to communicate with the system itself by way of a *command line*. What you're talking to here is actually the Unix shell in which Mac OS X runs. REALbasic permits your application to access this mode of communication, by way of the Shell class. Since a parallel mechanism exists on Windows (the MS-DOS shell), the Shell class works on Windows as well.

The Shell class is the *only* thing in this chapter that applies to Windows. There are no Apple events or AppleScripts on Windows, and REALbasic provides no direct access to Windows-based interapplication communications mechanisms, such as COM. If your Windows application's code even mentions Apple events, it will crash on startup, so be sure to use conditional compilation, as explained in Chapter 8, to censor any such mentions before they can reach Windows's ears.

Sending Apple Events

In order to send an Apple event, you must construct it; and in order to construct an Apple event, you must know its structure. To find that out, you can intercept and dissect an Apple event as it passes through the system; then you can construct and send the same Apple event using REALbasic's native commands.

There are three main ways to examine the underlying shape of an Apple event:*

- With Capture AE, a Control Panel. Open Capture AE and run an AppleScript anywhere you like; afterward, Capture AE shows the structure of the Apple events corresponding to that AppleScript.

- With Script Debugger, a commercial application very useful for writing and debugging AppleScripts. Within Script Debugger, open the Apple Event Log window and set it to Show Apple Events, with the Format set to AEPrint; then run an AppleScript from within Script Debugger. Afterward, the Apple Event Log window shows the structure of the Apple events corresponding to that AppleScript.

- With the REALbasic IDE's own AE Recorder. Choose Window → Show AE Recorder, then press Record, perform an action, and press Stop. However, this works only for recordable actions of recordable applications. (The AE Recorder is intended for use with REALbasic's "Apple event template" mechanism, which I regard as clumsy and pointless; I don't discuss it in this book.)

Anatomy of an Apple Event

In "AppleScript Techniques" in Chapter 21, it was suggested that one might use an AppleScript to ask the Finder to copy a folder. Let's see how to code this AppleScript

---

* For Capture AE, see *ftp://ftp.westcodesoft.com/OneClick_Scripting_Tools/CaptureAE.sit.hqx*. For Script Debugger, see *http://www.latenightsw.com/sd2.0/index2.html*.

as an Apple event. Given a folder to copy, and another to copy it into, we can form our AppleScript:

```
tell application "Finder" to copy item "HD:folder1" to folder "HD:folder2"
```

If we run the script and capture its anatomy, we get something like the following (this is the display from Capture AE):

```
Process("Finder").SendAE "core,clon,'----':obj {form:name, want:type(cobj),
seld:"HD:folder1", from:'null'()}, insh:obj {form:name, want:type(cfol),
seld:"HD:folder2", from:'null'()}"
```

Let's learn to understand what we're seeing here. First, we're told the addressee of the Apple event, the process to which it was sent—in this case, the Finder. Then comes a very long expression in quotation marks, which is the Apple event itself. It is composed of items separated by commas; here, there are four of them.

The first two items, "core" and "clon", are the Apple event's *class* and *ID*, respectively. These are four-letter strings, much like a file's creator and type codes, that uniquely identify the particular command being given, which in this case is to copy something. The subsequent items are the command's parameters; each parameter is identified by a four-letter name, which is followed by a colon, and then comes its value. In this instance, there are two parameters, whose names are "----" and "insh":

```
'----':
    obj {form:name, want:type(cobj), seld:"HD:folder1", from:'null'()}
insh:
    obj {form:name, want:type(cfol), seld:"HD:folder2", from:'null'()}
```

Every parameter in an Apple event is of some type. In this case, both parameters are *object specifiers*, as is signified by the designator obj. An object specifier picks out some particular object in the target application's world; the object is described in curly braces, in four parts:

form

Tells how the object is being specified. In both these objects, it is being specified by name, as the value "name" informs us.

want

Tells what class of object it is. In this case, the first object is a "cobj" and the second object is a "cfol".

seld

The actual specifier. Here, since the objects are specified by name, these are strings, "HD:folder1" and "HD:folder2".

from

The object's container. This will usually be another object specifier, saying what object the first object is an element of. However, in this example, neither object has any container; they are both at the top level of the container hierarchy, so their from is "null".

Building an Apple Event

Now let's build and send this very same Apple event from within REALbasic. We will need a variable for the Apple event itself, and a variable for each object specifier within it:

```
dim a as appleevent
dim o1, o2 as appleeventobjectspecifier
```

The first step is to construct the two object specifiers. As we shall see, there are several functions that yield an object specifier; which one you use depends upon the way the object is being specified. Here, both objects are specified by name, so we use the GetNamedObjectSpecifier function. This takes three parameters, corresponding to the object's want, its from, and its seld, in that order; when the from is "null", we pass nil:

```
o1 = getNamedObjectDescriptor("cobj", nil, "HD:folder1")
o2 = getNamedObjectDescriptor("cfol", nil, "HD:folder2")
```

Now we build the Apple event itself. This is always a two-stage process. First, we call NewAppleEvent to make an AppleEvent instance, supplying three parameters. The first two parameters are the two parts of the command identifier, here "core" and "clon" (remember?). The third parameter is the creator code of the target application; the Finder's creator code is "MACS":

```
a = newAppleEvent("core", "clon", "MACS")
```

Next, we attach each parameter to the Apple event, by assigning its value to a property of the AppleEvent instance. What property we use depends upon the datatype of the parameter. Since both parameters in this case are object specifiers, we use the ObjectSpecifierParam property. The properties in question all take a parameter that is the Apple event parameter's name; we assign them a value of the appropriate datatype. In this case, the names are "----" and "insh" (remember??), and the values are the object specifiers we constructed earlier:

```
a.objectspecifierparam("----") = o1
a.objectspecifierparam("insh") = o2
```

That's it; the Apple event is built! Now all we have to do is send it. This is done by way of the Send message; a boolean result is returned, but for purposes of this example, we don't care about it:

```
if a.send then // great!
end
```

If you put that code into a button's Action handler, substituting the pathnames of two actual folders, and run the project and press the button, the Apple event will actually be sent to the Finder, which will actually copy the first folder into the second. (But not on Mac OS X, where the Finder hasn't yet achieved this level of scriptability.)

Let's take another example. We'll drive the mail client application Eudora, using two Apple events, to collect all the subjects of all the messages in the In box. We begin by obtaining a count of the messages, using this AppleScript:

```
tell application "Eudora" to count messages of mailbox "In"
```

In Capture AE, this is analyzed as follows:

```
Process("Eudora").SendAE "core,cnte,'----':obj {form:name, want:type(euMB),
seld:"In", from:'null'()}, kocl:type(euMS)"
```

This is very much like the Apple event we sent to the Finder a moment ago, but simpler. The second parameter, "kocl", is a type specifier, as is shown by its type prefix; this is constructed with the MacTypeParam property. Eudora's creator code is "CSOm":

```
dim u, i as integer
dim a as appleevent
dim o1, o2, o3 as appleeventobjectspecifier
o1 = getNamedObjectDescriptor("euMB", nil, "In")
a = newAppleEvent("core", "cnte", "CSOm")
a.objectspecifierparam("----") = o1
a.mactypeparam("kocl") = "euMS"
if a.send then
```

At this point we encounter something new. In the Apple event to the Finder, we simply gave a command; after the Apple event was sent, we stopped caring about it. Here, on the other hand, we are making a query; we expect a result to be returned. The result returned from sending an Apple event is obtained through one of six Reply properties of the same AppleEvent instance that was sent; once again, what property you use depends upon the desired datatype. In this case, we expect an integer, so the ReplyInteger property is used:

```
u = a.replyinteger
```

Now we're ready to construct the second Apple event, whose AppleScript version looks like this:

```
tell application "Eudora" to get subject of message 1 of mailbox "In"
```

Capture AE presents it as follows:

```
Process("Eudora").SendAE "core,getd,'----':obj {form:prop, want:type(prop),
seld:type(euSu), from:obj {form:indx, want:type(euMS), seld:1, from:obj
{form:name, want:type(euMB), seld:"In", from:'null'()}}}"
```

This Apple event has just one parameter, an object specifier; but this object specifier has a from, saying what object it belongs to, and that object specifier has a from as well! Thus, we have a nest of three objects:

```
obj {form:prop, want:type(prop), seld:type(euSu), from:
    obj {form:indx, want:type(euMS), seld:1, from:
        obj {form:name, want:type(euMB), seld:"In", from:'null'()}}}
```

The first object's form is "prop", meaning that we will generate it with the GetPropertyObjectDescriptor function. The second object's form is "indx", meaning that we will generate it with the GetIndexedObjectDescriptor function. The third object's form is "name", meaning, as we already know, that we will generate it with the GetNamedObjectDescriptor function.

To construct the nest of three objects, start with the innermost and work outward. It happens that the innermost object is already constructed by our earlier code, so we won't have to construct it again. In the second object, instead of a hardcoded index of 1, we will pass a variable, i, in a For loop; that's how we'll obtain the subject of each message in turn. Since we are sending the same command each time through the loop, we won't have to keep constructing new AppleEvent instances; we'll just construct the instance once and reuse it, changing its ObjectSpecifierParam property each time:

```
a = newAppleEvent("core","getd","CSOm")
for i = 1 to u
    o2 = getIndexedObjectDescriptor("euMS",o1,i)
    o3 = getPropertyObjectDescriptor(o2,"euSu")
    a.objectspecifierparam("----") = o3
    if a.send then
```

Finally, we capture each result as it arrives; since the subject of a message is a string, we use the ReplyString property. We can conveniently display all the results in a List-Box:

```
            listbox1.addrow a.replyString
        end
    next
end
```

Remote Targets and Send-to-Self

You can send an Apple event to an application running on a machine elsewhere on the LocalTalk network, provided program linking has been enabled on the remote machine. This is identical to constructing and sending an Apple event to an application on the local machine, except that, instead of obtaining the AppleEvent instance by means of the global NewAppleEvent function, you obtain it by sending the NewAppleEvent message to an instance of the AppleEventTarget class that specifies the remote application.

The question is then how to obtain this AppleEventTarget instance. There are two ways:

GetAppleEventTarget
   This brings up the standard Macintosh PPCBrowser dialog, in which the user can choose any application running on any networked machine with program linking turned on. It takes two parameters, a string prompt that will appear at the top of the dialog, and a string prompt that will appear over the list of running applications. An AppleEventTarget is returned, or nil if the user canceled.

   It is also possible for the user to choose an application running on the local machine; this generates a blank and invalid but non-nil AppleEventTarget, so be sure to test for this result. You can do so by means of the AppleEventTarget's Remote boolean property; if it is true, all is well.

NewAppleEventTarget

This takes four parameters, all strings: the application's name, the machine name, the zone name, and the port code. An AppleEventTarget is returned.

To specify the local zone (because, for example, there are no zones), use "*". The port code is like the application's four-letter creator code, but in my testing it also has four more letters, "ep01", and these are required. I don't know what they signify; this may be a bug. You may wish to test for yourself (using GetAppleEventTarget!). I do not know why both the application's name and its creator code are required; this seems redundant.

You then send the AppleEventTarget instance the NewAppleEvent message; it takes two parameters, which are the two strings identifying the Apple event. Now you have an AppleEvent instance, and everything is just the same as in the earlier discussion.

For example, I have hooked my two computers together with an Ethernet crossover cable. I'm sitting at my desktop computer, and I've turned on program linking on my portable. I'll tell the Finder on the portable to open the About This Computer window. This, as a little experimentation with Capture AE shows, is a command identified as "aevt" and "odoc", whose parameter is an object specifier with form "prop", type "abbx", and container nil. Here we go:

```
dim targ as appleeventtarget
dim a as appleevent
dim o as appleeventobjectSpecifier
targ = newappleeventtarget("Finder", "The Flying Brick", "*", "MACSep01")
a = targ.newappleEvent("aevt", "odoc")
o = getPropertyObjectDescriptor(nil, "abbx")
a.objectSpecifierParam("----") = o
if a.send then
end
```

The first time I run this, the remote login dialog appears asking for my username and password. I have to enter these manually, and they must correspond to a user defined on the remote machine as having program linking privileges. On subsequent runs of the same script, no dialog appears because I've already registered with the remote machine. REALbasic provides no way to prevent the dialog from appearing the first time; that is, you cannot somehow supply the username and password in code and bypass the dialog.

For your application to send an Apple event to itself, it should just specify the empty string as the creator code of the target application when it creates the AppleEvent instance. For example:

```
dim a as appleevent
a = newappleevent("matt", "neub", "") // send to self
```

```
a.stringparam("----") = "Well, howdy there, myself!"
if a.send then
end
```

Your application will receive this Apple event and can respond however it sees fit.

 On Mac OS X, at present, a send-to-self Apple event will crash the IDE. It works in the built application, though. Thus, when using send-to-self, you are forced to test by building the application and running it in the Finder.

Why might you want to send yourself an Apple event? For one thing, that's the key to making your application strongly scriptable—and, ultimately, recordable. Suppose your application performs a certain action when the user chooses the File → New menu item. Your FileNew menu event handler, instead of performing that action directly, causes your application to send itself an Apple event; the application then responds to the receipt of that Apple event by performing the action. This means that action is now fully scriptable: its behavior is identical regardless of whether a user chooses the menu item within your application or another application sends that same Apple event to your application as a way of scripting it. This architecture is called *factoring* your application. I'll come back to this in the next section.

Another reason for sending yourself an Apple event is that this is how you call a scripting addition. For example, to perform a "display dialog" within your own application, you could say:

```
a = newappleEvent("syso", "dlog", "")
a.stringParam("----") = "Howdy there!"
if a.send then
end
```

On Mac OS X, nothing will happen. This is not a bug in REALbasic; it's a feature of Mac OS X. For scripting additions to work in your application on Mac OS X, your application must announce to the system that it is willing for them to do so. It does this with a magic incantation involving partly a Toolbox call and partly an initial send-to-self that gets things going. You can make the necessary Toolbox call through a plug-in by Mark Alldritt.* Here is the entire incantation:

```
InstallStandardAEHandlers // the plug-in
a = newappleEvent("ascr", "gdut", "") // the send-to-self
if a.send then
end
```

You say this once; in your Application subclass's Open event would be a good place. After that, scripting additions will work. Your application should *not* accept either the preceding Apple event or any scripting addition send-to-self events; if, as

---

* See *http://www.latenightsw.com/archives/OSAXenFixer1.0.sit.hqx*.

explained in the next section, you have a HandleAppleEvents event handler, then when these events arrive, it should return false or do nothing, to reject them. The events will thus automatically be passed up to the system and on to the scripting addition itself. (Remember not to test in IDE, though; you'll crash if you do.)

Receiving Apple Events

To receive an Apple event originating from another application (or your own), your project must have an Application subclass. The Apple event's arrival will trigger a HandleAppleEvent event, whose handler receives three parameters: the event itself, along with its two identifiers as strings. You then parse and respond to the event. To extract the event's parameters, you use the same properties used for constructing an Apple event. To reply to the Apple event, you set whichever of its Reply properties is appropriate for the datatype of the reply. You must then return true if you handled the Apple event, or false (or nothing) if you reject it; if you return true, the reply will automatically be returned to the originating application.

Three of the four "required" Apple events, "aevt/oapp", "aevt/odoc", and "aevt/quit", are intercepted by REALbasic and do not generate a HandleAppleEvent event. The first two generate a NewDocument event and an OpenDocument event, respectively—see "The Application Subclass" in Chapter 7 and "Finder Drop" in Chapter 24. The third simply generates the Quit command, as if you had given it in code. (In REALbasic 3.5, it is routed to your FileQuit menu handler, as if the user had chosen the Quit menu item.)

 You cannot distinguish between a live user quitting your application and an Apple event telling it to quit remotely. A response to quitting that requires a live user (such as a modal dialog) may make quitting your application remotely impossible.

Apple Event Scriptability

Let's say that I want to define for my application an Apple event of class "your" and ID "name", which returns a string saying what my name is. And let's say further that the sender may optionally attach an integer parameter, named "----" (the main parameter of an Apple event, by convention, is often called "----"), which can be 1 or 2 depending on whether the sender wants my first name or my last name; if this parameter is missing, I'll return my full name.

Here is the Application subclass's HandleAppleEvent event handler:

```
dim i as integer
if not (eventclass = "your" and eventID = "name") then
    return false // sorry, that is the only Apple event we accept
end
i = event.integerparam("----")
```

```
select case i
case 0
    event.replystring = "Matt Neuburg"
case 1
    event.replystring = "Matt"
case 2
    event.replystring = "Neuburg"
else
    return false // sorry, those are the only values we accept
end
return true
```

To test this, I build the application, naming it Snortiblog, and run it. (I was too lazy to assign Snortiblog a creator code, so its creator is "????".) Now, back in REALbasic, I construct another project to send Snortiblog the "your/name" event. If I say this:

```
dim a as appleEvent
a = newappleEvent("your","name","????")
if a.send then
    msgbox a.replystring
end
```

then the response is Matt Neuburg. If I say this:

```
dim a as appleEvent
a = newappleEvent("your","name","????")
a.integerparam("----") = 1
if a.send then
    msgbox a.replystring
end
```

then the response is Matt. If I say this:

```
dim a as appleEvent
a = newappleEvent("your","name","????")
a.integerparam("----") = 2
if a.send then
    msgbox a.replystring
end
```

then the response is Neuburg. It works! We've written an application that can be driven with Apple events.

The example may seem trivial: our application knows how to respond to just one raw Apple event. But there is at least one sort of commonly used program that does very important work in response to the receipt of a single raw Apple event—a CGI application. Such an application is sent a "WWWΩ/sdoc" Apple event by a web server; it is expected to parse the event's parameters and construct a web page, returning it as the ReplyString for the web server to send back to the client.[*]

---

[*] For more about how a CGI application is expected to work, see *http://dev.starnine.com/macoscgis/macoscgis.html*. For a simple REALbasic example, see *http://www.vivaladata.com/downloads/rbcgishell.sea.hqx*.

AppleScript Scriptability

Our application is now scriptable via Apple events, but if we also want it to be scriptable via AppleScript, we must give it an 'aete' resource (ID 0), which maps between Apple event codes and the English-like commands of AppleScript. There are many tools for creating 'aete' resources; in this instance, I'll just use EightyRez, an excellent freeware utility.* Figure 31-1 shows the EightyRez dialog used to define an English-like command, AuthorName, for this Apple event, along with some comments explaining the command to the user. When the built application includes this resource, we can use the Script Editor's File → Open Dictionary menu item to display the dictionary for Snortiblog; as Figure 31-2 shows, the command and its comments appear.

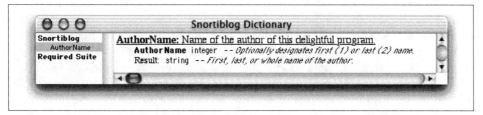

Figure 31-1. Creating an entry in an 'aete' resource with EightyRez

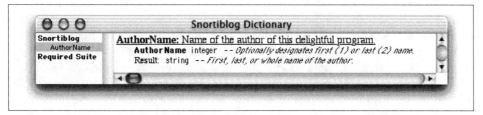

Figure 31-2. How Script Editor's Dictionary window displays the 'aete' resource

---

* See *http://www3.shore.net/~gmcgath/EightyRez.html*. There is a set of ResEdit 'aete' editing resources at *ftp:// ftp.apple.com//developer/Tool_Chest/Interapplication_Communication/AE_Tools_/* or *ftp://ftp.apple.com/developer/Tool_Chest/OS_Utilities/Apple_Events/AE_Tools.sit.hqx*; there is also a HyperCard-based 'aete' editor in the same directory.

Now that our application has an 'aete' resource, it is scriptable via AppleScript. We can type and run the following AppleScript in the Script Editor and receive the expected reply:

```
tell application "snortiblog"
    AuthorName -- or AuthorName 1, or AuthorName 2
end tell
```

Furthermore, if Snortiblog sends itself the "your/name" event (as described earlier in this chapter, "Remote Targets and Send-to-Self"), that action is recordable via Apple-Script. For example, suppose Snortiblog has a Tell → Author menu item, which is handled by a TellAuthor menu event handler that goes like this:

```
dim a as appleEvent
a = newappleEvent("your","name","")
if a.send then
end
```

Now suppose the user opens the Script Editor and presses the Record button, then switches to Snortiblog and chooses the Tell → Author menu item. Back in the ScriptEditor, this script has magically appeared:

```
tell application "Snortiblog"
    activate
    AuthorName
end tell
```

So now the user knows how to script Snortiblog to make it do the same thing that Snortiblog's own Tell → Author menu item does. Thus, if you're going to make your application scriptable through AppleScript, you may as well consider factoring it so that its functionality is heavily made up of send-to-self Apple events—because this essentially makes your application recordable, as well as scriptable, with very little extra effort on your part.

The Object Model

To be fully scriptable in a powerful way, your application may need to support the all-important object model.* This involves analyzing the object specifier parameters of an arriving Apple event. For example, suppose you wanted to write a scriptable word processor; another application could send a "core/getd" Apple event with an object specifier asking your word processor for (let's say) word 2 of window 1. In order to respond appropriately, your application would first need to parse this object specifier into its form, want, from, and seld constituents, so as to learn what information is being requested.

To do this, treat the object specifier as a record. Since the from may be another object specifier, you will have to loop up the container hierarchy until you reach null. The

---

* For a memorable series of articles on designing an application's scriptability, see *http://developer.apple.com/dev/techsupport/develop/issue21/21simone.html* and the subsequent "According to Script" articles referred to at *http://developer.apple.com/dev/techsupport/develop/bysubject/iac.html*.

following HandleAppleEvent event handler code is just a sketch to show that this is possible:

```
dim r as appleeventrecord
if not (eventclass = "core" and eventid = "getd") then
    return false
end
r = event.recordparam("----") // treat it as a record
do // analyze it
    msgbox r.enumeratedparam("form")
    msgbox r.mactypeparam("want")
    msgbox str(r.integerparam("seld"))
    r = r.recordparam("from") // treat its container as a record too
    if r <> nil then
        msgbox "of"
    end
loop until r = nil // loop up the hierarchy
event.replystring = "theWord" // in real life, the requested word goes here
return true
```

If we build the application, run it, and send it an Apple event asking for word 2 of window 1, it puts up a series of dialogs showing that it understands it has been asked for "indx cwor 2 of indx cwin 1." This proves that our application can understand what it is being asked for; in real life, we would then obtain the value of word 2 of window 1 and return it. Of course, this example is highly simplified, because we anticipated that the seld would be a number each time; fully parsing an object specifier is a much more complicated procedure, involving many tests and choices, and is left as an exercise (a very advanced exercise!) for the reader.

Apple Event Classes, Properties, and Methods

This section summarizes the classes and commands available in REALbasic for constructing, sending and receiving Apple events.

Classes

Five classes are associated with Apple events:[*]

AppleEvent
    Used to construct and send, and to receive and parse, an Apple event and its reply.

AppleEventTarget
    Used to specify a remote target of an Apple event.

---

[*] I omit the AppleEventTemplate class. See the REALbasic documentation if this interests you.

AppleEventObjectSpecifier
   The class of an object specifier parameter of an Apple event.

AppleEventDescList
   The class of a list parameter of an Apple event. A list is a series of items; in AppleScript, it is delimited by curly braces.

AppleEventRecord
   The class of a record parameter of an Apple event. A record is a series of named items; in AppleScript, it is delimited by curly braces.

Building and Parsing an Apple Event

The following function constructs an Apple event:

NewAppleEvent
   Returns an AppleEvent instance, so you can fill out its parameters and send it. Takes three parameters: the Apple event's class and ID codes, and the creator code of the target application to which the Apple event is to be sent.

You can also generate an Apple event with the NewAppleEvent method of the AppleEventTarget class. This takes two parameters, the Apple event's class and ID codes. The following functions construct an AppleEventTarget:

NewAppleEventTarget, GetAppleEventTarget
   Returns an AppleEventTarget instance, so that you can send it the NewAppleEvent message and get an AppleEvent instance. The former takes four parameters: the target application's name, its computer name, its zone name, and its port code. (See page 637 for the weird format of the port code string.) The latter puts up the PPCBrowser dialog, and takes two parameters that are prompts for the dialog.

   An AppleEventTarget instance has five read-only properties: Remote (a boolean), and Name, Computer, Zone, and PortType (strings corresponding to the parameters of NewAppleEventTarget).

Among the following AppleEvent properties, those whose names end in Param allow you to fill out an Apple event's parameters or to parse an incoming Apple event; they take one parameter, the four-letter name of the Apple event parameter. Those whose names begin with Reply let you retrieve or generate an Apple event reply; they take no parameter.

StringParam, ReplyString
   Accesses a string parameter of an Apple event or a reply.

IntegerParam, ReplyInteger
   Accesses an integer parameter of an Apple event or a reply.

BooleanParam, ReplyBoolean
Accesses a boolean parameter of an Apple event or a reply.

FolderItemParam
Accesses a parameter of an Apple event as a FolderItem designating a file specifier (`"fss "`).

MacTypeParam
Accesses a parameter of an Apple event as a four-character string designating a type (`"type"`).

EnumeratedParam
Accesses a parameter of an Apple event as a four-character string designating an enumerator (`"enum"`).

ObjectSpecifierParam, ReplyObjectSpecifier
Accesses a parameter of an Apple event or a reply as an AppleEventObjectSpecifier designating an object specifier (`"obj "`).

DescListParam, ReplyDescList
Accesses a parameter of an Apple event or a reply as an AppleEventDescList designating a list.

RecordParam, ReplyRecord
Accesses a parameter of an Apple event or a reply as an AppleEventRecord designating a record.

The following property sets the timeout for an outgoing Apple event:

Timeout
An integer specifying how many ticks the Apple event should wait for a reply before returning (and letting your code proceed). The default is -1, meaning no timeout, in which case your code will pause forever if there is no reply.

An AppleEvent instance has the following methods related to sending the event:

SetNullParam
Takes one parameter, the name of the Apple event parameter; sets that parameter to `null`.

Send
Sends the Apple event, returning a boolean reporting whether the event was sent.

When retrieving a reply parameter with the Reply properties, the datatype one specifies is actually a request that the system should coerce the reply to this datatype if possible. This is a valuable feature when, as not infrequently happens, one does not know in advance the datatype of the reply.

For example, suppose we wish to ask the Finder for the names of whatever files and folders are currently selected. If there is only one item in the selection, a string will be returned; if there is more than one item, a list of strings will be returned. We cannot ask whether the reply is a string or a list, but we can do the next best thing, by making sure it is a list:

```
dim a as appleevent
dim o1,o2 as appleeventobjectspecifier
dim aList as appleeventdesclist
a = newappleevent("core","getd","MACS")
o1 = getPropertyObjectDescriptor(nil, "sele")
o2 = getPropertyObjectDescriptor(o1, "pnam")
a.objectspecifierparam("----") = o2
if a.send then
    aList = a.replyDescList
end
```

Now we certainly have a list, of one or several strings, and can parse it accordingly (as described in the next section).

Records and Lists

An AppleEventRecord or AppleEventDescList instance is obtained from an Apple event parameter with the RecordParam, ReplyRecord, DescListParam, or ReplyDescList properties; or a new instance can be generated with the New operator.

An AppleEventRecord instance is constructed and parsed with exactly the same set of Param properties as an AppleEvent, along with the SetNullParam method.

An AppleEventDescList is constructed with a series of Append methods:

AppendString, AppendInteger, AppendBoolean, AppendFolderItem, AppendRecord, AppendObjectSpecifier, AppendDescList
    These take one parameter; the parameter value is inserted at the end of the list.

An AppleEventDescList is parsed with a series of Item properties, each of which takes one parameter specifying the number of the item to be retrieved:

StringItem, IntegerItem, BooleanItem, FolderItemItem, RecordItem, ObjectSpecifierItem, DescListItem
    These access the value of the list member whose index is the parameter. *The index is one-based.*

Count
    Returns the number of items in the list.

For example, suppose we wish to ask Tex-Edit Plus about the style of the fourth word in the first window:

```
dim a as appleevent
dim o1,o2,o3 as appleeventobjectspecifier
dim aList as appleeventdesclist
dim u,i as integer
```

```
a = newappleevent("core","getd","TBB6")
o1 = getIndexedObjectDescriptor("cwin",nil,1)
o2 = getIndexedObjectDescriptor("cwor",o1,4)
o3 = getPropertyObjectDescriptor(o2, "txst")
a.objectspecifierparam("----") = o3
if a.send then // now what?
```

What is returned is a style record, which is a record consisting of two lists named "onst" and "ofst"—the names of the styles that are set for this stretch of text, and the names of the styles that are not. (The style names are things like "bold", "ital", and so forth.) To retrieve the items of the first list, we can say this:

```
aList = a.replyRecord.descListParam("onst")
u = aList.count
for i = 1 to u
    msgbox aList.stringitem(i)
next
```

Incidentally, the example also shows once again that when retrieving a returned datatype we are actually requesting a coercion. The items in the two lists of a style record are not really strings, but enumerators; however, since enumerators are, in essence, four-character strings, we are able to coerce them to strings and read them.

Building an Object Specifier

The following functions construct and return an AppleEventObjectSpecifier. They differ in the manner by which the object is specified (by name, by number, by position, and so forth). In all cases, the container object is either another AppleEventObjectSpecifier or nil:

GetNamedObjectDescriptor
> The object is specified by name ("name"). Takes three parameters: the class (want), the container object (from), and the name as a string. AppleScript example:
>
> ```
> document "Untitled"
> ```

GetIndexedObjectDescriptor
> The object is specified by number ("indx"). Takes three parameters: the class (want), the container object (from), and the number as an integer. AppleScript example:
>
> ```
> window 1
> ```

GetOrdinalObjectDescriptor
> The object is specified by number ("indx"), but the number is represented by one of the five enumerative constants "firs", "last", "midd", "any ", or "all ". Takes three parameters: the class (want), the container object (from), and the enumerative constant. AppleScript example:
>
> ```
> every process
> ```

GetUniqueIDObjectDescriptor

The object is specified by ID (`"ID  "`). Takes three parameters: the class (`want`), the container object (`from`), and the ID value as a string. AppleScript example:

```
record ID 1
```

GetPropertyObjectDescriptor

The object is specified as a property (`"prop"`). Takes two parameters: the class (`want`), and the four-letter property designator as a string. AppleScript example:

```
name of window 1
```

GetRangeObjectDescriptor

The object is specified by a range (`"rang"`). Takes four parameters: the class (`want`), the container object (`from`), and two objects indicating the start and end of the range. AppleScript example:

```
words 2 thru 4
```

GetTestObjectDescriptor

The object is specified by a boolean expression (`"test"`). Takes three parameters: the class (`want`), the container object (`from`), and an AppleEventObjectSpecifier describing the test; at the moment, this can only be the result of GetStringComparisonObjectDescriptor.

GetStringComparisonObjectDescriptor

A comparison between two strings. Takes four string parameters. The first parameter is the comparison method, which is `"=  "`, `">  "`, `"<  "`, `">= "`, `"<= "`, `"cont"`, `"bgwt"`, or `"ends"` (those last three stand for "contains," "begins with," and "ends with"). The other parameters are the four-letter designator of the comparison's form; the field to be compared; and the value to be compared with. AppleScript example:

```
every process whose name contains "e"
```

Here's how to code that AppleScript as an Apple event to be sent to the Finder:

```
dim a as appleevent
dim o,test as appleeventobjectspecifier
a = newappleEvent("core","getd","MACS")
test = getstringComparisonObjectDescriptor("cont","prop","pnam","e")
o = gettestObjectDescriptor("prcs",nil,test)
a.objectspecifierparam("----") = o
```

Apple Event Inadequacies

There are several common datatypes of Apple event parameters that are not accessible through any AppleEvent property. In some cases you may be able to coerce your way around this problem. For example, an AppleScript could ask Microsoft Excel for the value of a number in a spreadsheet cell, which happens (let's say) to be 98.6:

```
Value of Cell "R1C1" of Worksheet 1 of document 2
```

This is easily constructed and sent as an Apple event from REALbasic, but the reply cannot be retrieved as a double, because there is no ReplyDouble property of an AppleEvent. The workaround is to retrieve the reply as a string:

```
dim a as appleevent
dim o1, o2, o3, o4 as appleeventobjectSpecifier
o1 = getindexedObjectDescriptor("docu", nil, 2)
o2 = getindexedObjectDescriptor("cXLW", o1, 1)
o3 = getnamedObjectDescriptor("ccel", o2, "r1c1")
o4 = getpropertyObjectDescriptor(o3, "pval")
a = newappleevent("core", "getd", "XCEL")
a.objectSpecifierParam("----") = o4
if a.send then
    msgbox (a.replystring)
end
```

Similarly, REALbasic can ask the Finder for an alias to a certain file, but it can't read the reply because there is no ReplyAlias property; furthermore, it can't coerce the reply to a FolderItem because there is no ReplyFolderItem property either, and coercion to a string fails completely. The workaround here is clumsier: coerce the reply to a list, and use the FolderItemItem property of the list. For example:

```
dim a as appleevent
dim o as appleeventobjectspecifier
dim aList as appleeventdesclist
dim f as folderitem
o = getpropertyObjectDescriptor(nil, "sele")
a = newappleEvent("core","getd","MACS")
a.objectspecifierparam("----") = o
a.mactypeparam("rtyp") = "alis"
if a.send then
    aList = a.replydesclist
    f = aList.folderitemitem(1)
    msgbox f.absolutepath
end
```

This yields a valid FolderItem, at least; but a FolderItem is not an alias, and can't be used in the same ways that an alias can.

A large number of common Apple events cannot be constructed and sent at all, because they involve insertion locations ("insl"); REALbasic has no function that generates these. In theory one could work around this by forming an insertion location as a record and coercing it to an "insl", but—guess what?—REALbasic lacks Apple event parameter datatype coercion functionality as well!

For example, in AppleScript one inserts a word in a word processor document by saying this sort of thing:

```
make new word at after word 3 of window 1 with data "hello"
```

REALbasic can't do that, because the notion "at after" has no analogous REALbasic construct. Similarly, REALbasic can't tell Eudora to delete a message, because the AppleScript syntax is this:

```
move message 1 of mailbox "In" to end of mailbox "Trash"
```

REALbasic has no construct for the concept "to end of."

Object specifiers have eight distinct forms for specifying an object, but REALbasic can produce only seven of them. Completely missing is the relative position specifier ("rele"), as in this AppleScript expression sent to a word processor:

```
get word after word 2 of window 1
```

Further, one existing object specifier form, the "test", is so incompletely implemented as to be all but useless. As far as I can tell, it is good only for testing a string property of the designated object; one cannot test for values that aren't strings, values that aren't properties, or values that don't belong directly to the designated object. Here are some typical AppleScript expressions used in querying a scriptable word processor, such as Tex-Edit Plus, each of which involves an object specifier that REALbasic is completely incapable of producing:

```
every word of window 1 whose last character is "e"
every word of window 1 where it ends with "e"
first word of window 1 whose length > 4
```

REALbasic also lacks the ability to set the user interaction level, to append a transaction ID, and to attach "considering" clauses. Also, an important part of communicating via Apple events is receiving and reading any error messages that may be returned; yet REALbasic provides no mechanism for receiving an error message, or for returning one.

These inadequacies, together with a clunky, clumsy syntax, greatly hamstring REALbasic's Apple event facilities. Apple events are one of the Macintosh's greatest distinguishing features, and many wonderful things can be done with them. One can only hope that in some future version, Apple events will be granted a proper implementation, as befits their inherent importance.

In the meantime, I strongly recommend a third-party plug-in, AEGizmo.* I can't say enough in praise of this plug-in. With it, there's very little in the way of Apple events that you can't do.

For example, here's how to use AEGizmo to tell Eudora to move a message to the Trash mailbox, something that REALbasic's own Apple event methods can't do at all. The parameters are formed from a single string, which is basically copied and pasted right out of Capture AE:

```
dim a as appleevent
dim s as string
dim i as integer
a = newappleEvent("core", "move", "CSOm")
s = "'----':obj {form:indx, want:type(euMS), seld:1, from:obj "
s = s + "{form:name, want:type(euMB), seld:"In", from:'null'()}}, "
s = s + "insh:insl{kobj:obj {form:name, want:type(euMB), "
```

---

* By Alex Klepoff. See *http://www.suitesync.com/software/realbasic.html.*

```
s = s + "seld:"Trash", from:'null'()}, kpos:end}"
i = a.buildfromstring(s)
if a.send then
end
```

For the problem of sending Apple events, at least, another workaround when REALbasic's Apple event handling falls short is to use AppleScript. For example, your application can run this AppleScript, with exactly the same effect as the previous example:

```
tell application "Eudora"
    move message 1 of mailbox "In" to end of mailbox "Trash"
end tell
```

The next section of this chapter discusses AppleScripts.

AppleScripts

Your application can run an AppleScript as a way of commanding or querying another application that is scriptable. The first step in letting your application do this is to incorporate the AppleScript into your project. Simply save the script as a compiled script file, then import the file into the project. The project maintains an alias to the script file, so don't delete the script file until the application has been built. The name under which the AppleScript is listed in the Project Window can then be used in your code to run the script.

For example, suppose your script reads as follows:

```
display dialog "Hello from AppleScript"
```

If this script is listed in the Project Window as Hello, then your REALbasic code can say:

```
hello
```

This will cause the AppleScript dialog to appear.

An AppleScript can return a value explicitly, with a Return statement, or implicitly, as the last value set within the script. To capture the value returned by your AppleScript, call it as a function, by appending parentheses:

```
msgbox hello()
```

Regardless of the native AppleScript datatype of the value returned, this value will always be coerced to a string before REALbasic receives it. Knowing this, you may wish to adjust the value within the AppleScript before returning it, so that REALbasic can parse it easily.

If you wish to be able to hand parameters to the AppleScript, you must wrap it in a Run handler. The first line of the handler will be of this form:

```
on run {parameter1, parameter2, ...}
```

For example:

```
on run {what}
    display dialog what
end run
```

I have displayed the parameters as contained in curly braces—not parentheses—because, although you are free to use parentheses, if there are multiple parameters, the Script Editor will change them to curly braces.

This, too, can be called from REALbasic either as a procedure or as a function. Here, we call it as a procedure:

```
hello "Hello"
```

Here, we call it as a function:

```
dim s as string
s = hello("Hello")
```

A parameter handed to an AppleScript may be a string or an integer; the datatype will be maintained (that is, an integer is received by the AppleScript as an integer). No other datatypes are supported.

Since AppleScript is merely a way of sending Apple events by way of an English-like syntax, since most applications that are scriptable by way of Apple events are scriptable by way of AppleScript, and since AppleScript often provides a workaround to some of REALbasic's Apple event shortcomings, one might legitimately wonder why a REALbasic programmer would ever want to construct a raw Apple event at all. Personally, though, I prefer raw Apple events when I can use them, for the following three reasons:

- AppleScripts cannot be edited within REALbasic itself, which makes them rather clumsy to maintain and to interleave with the logic of your native REALbasic code; whereas, the commands whereby raw Apple events are constructed and sent, *are* native REALbasic code.

- If your application is to be scriptable, it must be able to form a raw Apple event anyway, in order to reply to an incoming Apple event.

- Raw Apple events are executed somewhat faster than AppleScripts, though this advantage is considerably less than it was before the advent of Mac OS 8.5.

One counterargument to the first of these three points is that, in a pinch, an AppleScript *can* be constructed dynamically as text, within your application, which can then compile and run the script. One way to do this, on Mac OS X, is through the Shell class (discussed next); another is with Toolbox calls (treated in the next chapter). However, we then run smack into the third point, the issue of speed. A compiled AppleScript file is stored as byte code, and is therefore instantly ready to run. But text takes time to compile; the delay can be quite noticeable. As with everything in the computer world, it's all a matter of deciding what you're willing to trade for what.

Shell

Both Mac OS X and Windows enable communications with the system by means of a command line. On Mac OS X, this command line is accessible to the user through the Terminal application. On Windows, it is accessible to the user through the MS-DOS Prompt or Command Prompt application. REALbasic allows your program effectively to type commands directly into this command line, and to receive the reply, with no intermediate application. This is done through an instance of the Shell class.

To obtain an instance of the Shell class, use New. You can then call the instance's Execute method, handing it a command-line string. To retrieve the result, ask for the instance's Result property. (The Shell class also has an ErrorCode property, for detecting errors, and a TimeOut property, implemented on Windows only, for determining how long you are willing to let a process run.)

For example, on Windows, the following code:

```
dim s as shell
s = new shell
s.execute("dir")
editfield1.text = s.result
```

places into EditField1 a listing of the current directory, which happens to be my Desktop:

```
Volume in drive C has no label.
 Volume Serial Number is 0000-5844
 Directory of C:\Documents and Settings\matt neuburg\Desktop
03/04/2001  10:12a      <DIR>          .
03/04/2001  10:12a      <DIR>          ..
03/04/2001  10:13a                 758 Connect to the Internet.LNK
04/21/2001  06:24p             759,425 AppName.exe
04/10/2001  05:22p             949,255 REALfish.exe
... a lot more stuff you don't need to know about ...
              18 File(s)      8,041,740 bytes
               2 Dir(s)    1,299,709,952 bytes free
```

A roughly parallel example for Mac OS X might be this:

```
dim s as shell
s = new shell
s.execute "ls -la"
editfield1.text = s.result
```

The result is a listing of the top level of my startup drive:

```
total 10288
drwxrwxr-t  33 root     admin     1078 Apr 21 18:51 .
drwxrwxr-t  33 root     admin     1078 Apr 21 18:51 ..
-rw-rw-rw-   1 mattneub admin     6188 Apr  7 15:01 .DS_Store
d-wx-wx-wx   2 root     admin      264 Mar 24 18:26 .Trashes
-r--r--r--   1 root     wheel      142 Feb 25 00:05 .hidden
dr--r--r--   2 root     wheel      192 Apr 21 18:51 .vol
-rwxrwxrwx   1 root     wheel    73728 Jan 24 18:12 AppleShare PDS
```

```
drwxrwxr-x  20 root      admin       636 Apr 19 09:27 Applications
... and so on ...
drwxr-xr-x  10 root      wheel       296 Apr 12 11:45 usr
lrwxrwxr-t   1 root      admin        11 Apr 21 18:51 var -> private/var
```

In "Extending REALbasic's Abilities" in Chapter 5 we saw how to take advantage of the Shell class to process a REALbasic string with Perl. The code was made rather hard to read by the necessity of describing a multiline Perl script as a single-line command. If we know we're going to be doing a lot of this sort of thing, then it quickly becomes more pleasant to construct a Perl executable and just use the command line to run it.

Suppose, for example, I have sitting in */volumes/second/osx/* an executable called *mystrip.pl* which goes like this:[*]

```
#!/usr/bin/perl
$_ = $ARGV[0];
s/<.*?>//g;
print $_;
```

This is the same simple script as before, except that now we can read it. This executable can be called through the shell, handing it the target text as a command-line argument:

```
dim sh as shell
dim s, orig as string
orig = "I do not <i>like</i> green eggs and <b>ham</b>."
s = "/volumes/second/osx/mystrip.pl " + """" + orig + """"
sh = new shell
sh.execute(s)
msgbox sh.result // I do not like green eggs and ham.
```

In an intriguing twist, the shell has the ability to compile and run an AppleScript.[†] Therefore, rather than having to import an AppleScript in advance, you can construct a script on the fly as text, compile it, and run it. The shell command for doing this is osascript; in calling it, you must supply its full pathname. For example:

```
dim script as string
dim s as shell
script = "tell application ""Finder"" to get name of startup disk"
s = new shell
s.execute "/usr/bin/osascript '" + script + "'"
msgbox s.result
```

---

[*] Incidentally, the latest version of BBEdit provides superb Perl editing and debugging support on Mac OS X. See *http://www.barebones.com/bbedit_for_X.html*.

[†] I owe this observation to Kevin van Haaren. For the Toolbox calls to accomplish the same thing on Mac OS Classic, see *http://www.fedora.net/gruber/external_applescripts_in_rb/*, an example by John Gruber and Alex Klepoff that shows you how.

CHAPTER 32

Language Extensions

The REALbasic language and application framework allow the programmer to write, with relative ease, a standard, well-behaved application. But there's a compromise lurking secretly within this fact. Writing an application with REALbasic is easy, because an application written with REALbasic is standard. Or, looking at it the other way round, REALbasic frames a standard type of application and then makes it easy for you to write within that framework. But what if you'd like to step outside that framework?

REALbasic's capacities, though manifold, are necessarily circumscribed. Normally, this is good thing. After all, if you wanted to be able to program the computer to do absolutely anything at all, through direct calls to its system-level routines (its *Toolbox*), you wouldn't be using REALbasic in the first place. REALbasic's whole purpose is to shield you from the intricacies of programming at the Toolbox level; of course, REALbasic itself must call the Toolbox, because that's how applications work, but the access that it gives *you* to the Toolbox is indirect, and involves only the subset of Toolbox functionality that accords with REALbasic's own scheme of how an application is organized and what it does.

But REALbasic can't anticipate everything you might like your application to be able to do. Sometimes, you want to go further than REALbasic's language and classes and methods can take you. Perhaps you want to call a Toolbox routine that no REALbasic class or method will access for you. Perhaps you want a routine to execute more efficiently than REALbasic's language will permit. Perhaps you even want to create your own control class.

One of the most brilliant facets of REALbasic's design is its awareness of its own limitations. Since, by definition, it cannot go beyond these limitations, it provides you with the means to do so. In other words, REALbasic permits itself to be extended.

REALbasic does this in two ways. First, it permits you to make Toolbox calls directly from within your REALbasic code. You do this by means of Declare statements. Second, it permits your code to access various kinds of *code fragment*. A code fragment is essentially a piece of a program—a subroutine—written outside REALbasic, in some other language, such as Pascal, C, or C++. The code is already compiled and ready to run; it's a self-contained object that can't be edited from within REALbasic. The code fragment is in a predefined format that REALbasic understands; so REALbasic is able to hook the fragment's code into its own, and you can call the fragment from within your REALbasic code. REALbasic understands four different code fragment formats:[*]

- Compiled AppleScripts
- XCMDs and XFCNs
- Shared libraries
- Plug-ins

Compiled AppleScripts were discussed in Chapter 31. So along with Declare statements, this chapter talks about XCMDs, shared libraries, and plug-ins.

It is not the place of this chapter to try to teach you how to program the Macintosh by calling the Toolbox. That is a huge subject, treated in many other books, and has nothing to do with REALbasic per se. I'm also not going to teach you any Pascal or C; working with the Toolbox requires an understanding of these languages, but you'll have to get it somewhere else. My purpose in discussing these matters is merely to show you, in general, given a Toolbox routine that you'd like to call, how to get your REALbasic code to interface with that Toolbox routine and call it. By the same token, this chapter doesn't attempt to teach you to write XCMDs, shared libraries, or plug-ins. That would be a huge subject, taking us into the world of other programming languages and environments. The idea here is to describe how to incorporate these code fragments into your project and call them; how they came into existence is another matter.

Direct Toolbox Calls

Calling the Toolbox is not at all difficult, but it takes practice and study when you're starting out. The rewards for calling the Toolbox are very great; it feels miraculous when you reach right past REALbasic into the secret innards of your computer. On the other hand, the penalty for making a mistake is rather severe—the computer will probably crash, at the very least. So, let's prepare ourselves thoroughly before pressing any buttons.

Know Your Enemy

To call a Toolbox routine, you need to know two things:

- What is the syntax for calling this routine?
- In what library is this routine implemented?

---

[*] On code fragments, I recommend Joe Zobkiw, *A Fragment of Your Imagination* (Addison-Wesley, 1995). It's also very instructive on how 68K and PowerPC code interface with each other.

Let's talk about how you will find out the answers to these questions. (The discussion here is about Macintosh; Windows is taken up briefly later in the chapter, page 671.)

Learning about the syntax for calling a Macintosh Toolbox routine is basically just a matter of looking up the relevant discussion in *Inside Macintosh*. You can obtain a volume of *Inside Macintosh* in printed form or as a PDF, or (in most cases) you can just consult it on the Web.

Suppose, for example, we need to know what version of the system the user has. This information is supplied through the Toolbox routine called Gestalt. Now, in actual fact there is no need to call the Toolbox routine Gestalt directly, because REALbasic supplies a function—the Gestalt method of the built-in System object—that calls it for us. But let's pretend, for the sake of the example, that we wish to call Gestalt ourselves, directly. So, to learn about Gestalt, we'd look in the *Operating System Utilities* volume of *Inside Macintosh*.* Here we find the syntax for calling Gestalt expressed in Pascal as follows:

```
FUNCTION Gestalt (selector: OSType; VAR response: LongInt): OSErr;
```

Another way to learn about the syntax of a Toolbox call is to look in the appropriate header file. There are two cases. If you're going to be developing for Mac OS Classic, then if you've got a development environment such as Metrowerks CodeWarrior, you've already got these header files. Otherwise, you can download them from the SDK web page at Apple's developer site; and you should do so, because they are accompanied by the stub library files that you're going to use to answer the second question, what library implements the routine.† If you're going to be developing for Mac OS X exclusively, you can probably manage without these files; you've already got sufficient documentation from when you installed the material on the Developer CD, and the library files are part of the system.

In the Mac OS Classic case, the header files are in *Universal:Interfaces:CIncludes*. The file in question is *Gestalt.h*, and here we find the syntax for calling Gestalt expressed in C:

```
OSErr Gestalt (OSType selector, long * response)
```

In the Mac OS X case, you can use your web browser or online help to arrive at *Developer:Documentation:Carbon:oss:GestaltManager:Gestalt_Manager:index.html*; here we find the syntax expressed more or less the same way. If you're accustomed to programming Mac OS Classic, it's important to confirm that your Toolbox routine really is implemented on Mac OS X! Gestalt is implemented, as it turns out,

---

* See *http://developer.apple.com/techpubs/mac/OSUtilities/OSUtilities-9.html* and *http://developer.apple.com/techpubs/mac/OSUtilities/OSUtilities-18.html*.

† See *http://developer.apple.com/sdk/*, and click on one of the Universal Interfaces links. Or look in *ftp://ftp.apple.com/developer/Development_Kits/*. As of this writing, the latest version of the file you want is *UniversalHeaders3.4.img.bin*.

but many venerable Toolbox routines are not. That's what Carbon is all about: it's a rationalization and reduction of the Toolbox to a smaller number of essential routines ("the minimum required for life," get it?).

Now let's proceed to the question of the library. In the case of Mac OS Classic, the library will mostly be "InterfaceLib", and in the case of Mac OS X, it will almost always be "CarbonLib"; but you need to make sure. The way to do this is to use a utility called PEFViewer. For Mac OS Classic, you can download it;[*] for Mac OS X, it's already on your hard disk, inside *Developer:Applications*. We're going to use PEF-Viewer to peek inside a library file and see whether it "exports" Gestalt.

In the case of Mac OS Classic, we can't look inside the real library file, because no such file exists; the Toolbox routines are hard-wired into the computer's ROM, or made available by the system and its extensions. Therefore, you need to look in a sort of "fake" library file called a *stub library*. A stub library file looks like a shared library file to the extent of containing a resource of the correct type (a 'cfrg' of ID 0), but contains no code apart from the subroutine definitions. The files you want are inside *Universal:Libraries:StubLibraries*. Using PEFViewer, open *InterfaceLib*, and in the resulting window, click the triangle next to its PowerPC listing to reveal the Untitled Loader Section. Double-click this, and then choose View → Exported Symbols. Sure enough, Gestalt is listed. Quit PEFViewer; you're done with it.

In the case of Mac OS X, the actual library file through which the Carbon Toolbox routines are implemented does exist, as part of the system; it's called *CarbonLib*, it's in *System:Library:CFMSupport,* and you can open it and look right inside it with PEF-Viewer. There are three libraries in this file: *CarbonLib, Apple;Carbon;Multimedia,* and *Apple;Carbon;Networking.* Unless you're calling a QuickTime routine or some other such abstruse thing, *CarbonLib* will be the right place to look. Click the triangle next to *CarbonLib*, double-click Untitled Loader Section, choose View → Exported Symbols, and you'll find Gestalt in the list.

We have now confirmed that "InterfaceLib" is the correct library value for calling Gestalt on Mac OS Classic and that "CarbonLib" is correct on Mac OS X.[†]

Declare Your Datatypes

You're going to call a Toolbox routine by means of a Declare statement, which has the following parts:

- The keyword Declare.
- The keyword Sub or Function, depending on whether or not the Toolbox routine returns a value.

---

[*] See *ftp://ftp.apple.com//developer/Tool_Chest/Toolbox/PEF Viewer.sit.hqx*.

[†] Alternatively, if you have CodeWarrior, you are given, in a folder called *Find Library*, some text files that you can search with a batch text processor to learn which one lists a given Toolbox routine.

- The name of the Toolbox routine (usually its actual name, but can be a substitute name of your own choosing if you also use the `Alias` keyword).
- The keyword `Lib`, followed by the name of the library that exports the Toolbox function, as a literal string.
- Optionally, the `Alias` keyword, followed by the real name of the Toolbox routine, as a literal string (see "Who Was That Masked Man?" later in this chapter).
- Parentheses, containing the parameter list for the Toolbox routine; this looks just like the parameter list for a method declaration. The parameter names are just placeholders and are unimportant.
- If the Toolbox routine returns a value, the keyword `As` and the datatype of the returned value.
- Optionally, if you want to be able to call the Toolbox routine on a 68K machine, the keyword `Inline68K`, followed by a machine-language call to the Toolbox routine, as a hex string in parentheses (see "68K," later in this chapter).

Let's consider now where we stand with regard to the rest of our Declare statement in our attempt to call Gestalt.

We know how to type the keyword `Declare`, so that's the first point out of the way. Gestalt is very obviously a `Function`. Its name is `Gestalt`, and we know that its library is `"InterfaceLib"` or `"CarbonLib"`. (So far, this all seems fairly trivial, but I warn you: in a Declare statement, the capitalization of the routine name and the library name are crucial, so don't let me catch you typing `gestalt` or `interfacelib` in your Declare statement, and if you do and it doesn't work properly, don't come to me.)

We don't need an alias (I'll explain later what they are), so at last we come to the parameter list and the return value. And at this point we realize that we have no idea what we're doing, because the datatypes in REALbasic are not the same as the datatypes expressed in Pascal and C when describing the syntax of a Toolbox call. We've got a problem! We need to know how to mediate between REALbasic's datatypes and the datatypes expected by the Toolbox. In fact, this turns out to be just about the entire problem when you're writing a Declare statement and calling the Toolbox.

Here are the main points of working with datatypes when you're writing a Declare statement:

Integers

Integers come in various sizes. A full-fledged REALbasic integer is four bytes (32 bits), which the rest of the world thinks of as a long. You can say `integer` in that case. A short is two bytes (16 bits), and in that case you should say `short`. Beware of making unwarranted assumptions about what the rest of the world means by integer; in particular, a Pascal integer is really a short. You can also say `boolean` to mediate between a REALbasic boolean and an integer functioning as a boolean.

OSType

This is a four-character string expressed as a four-byte integer. (You've seen these a lot in this book, perhaps without knowing it. A file creator code and type code, an Apple event class and ID, the name of an Apple event parameter, and many other four-letter strings we've seen, are all actually OSTypes.) You can say ostype, and REALbasic will mediate between a REALbasic string and an integer.

Addresses

An address in memory is four bytes long. That's an integer.

Strings

A string will certainly not be a REALbasic string, because REALbasic strings are in a private format. The big question is, therefore: is it a Pascal string or a C string? (See "Memoryblocks" in Chapter 5 for more about what this means.) You can say pstring and REALbasic will mediate between a REALbasic string and a Pascal string. You can say cstring and REALbasic will pass a pointer to the first character of a string.

Pointers

This is where things get really tricky. If the Toolbox wants a pointer to an integer, you can pass an integer declared byref. (But a short declared byref doesn't seem to work.) If the Toolbox wants a pointer to the start of a run of text, you can say cstring. If the Toolbox has handed you a pointer to something in memory, that's an address, and you can hand it back as an integer. Otherwise, if the Toolbox wants a pointer to some memory that you're supposed to be maintaining, say ptr and pass a memoryblock. Dereferencing a pointer is a different matter; the solution is to put the integer value of the pointer into a memoryblock with Long and then examine it with Ptr (see "Grasping Handles," later in this chapter). To make a pointer, do just the opposite: set a memoryblock's Ptr to a memoryblock (see "Sharpening Pointers," later in this chapter). This is what a memoryblock's Ptr method is for; you may recall that we postponed discussion of this matter in Chapter 5.

Structs

A struct is always really a pointer to a struct, so you're going to say ptr and pass a memoryblock. Parsing what's in the memoryblock is completely up to you! You will have to analyze the definition of the struct and count bytes to figure out what's where (see "Parsing and Passing Structs," later in this chapter).

Handles

Handles are not usually a problem because what you're holding is just one end of the handle, which is an address—that is to say, an integer. To dereference the handle, treat it as a pointer and dereference it *twice* (see "Grasping Handles," later in this chapter).

FolderItems

To convert between a FolderItem and something the Toolbox can deal with, use its MacVRefNum and MacDirID properties, together with its Name (see "Shared Libraries," later in this chapter).

Windows

The window's MacWindowPtr is a pointer to the window. (On Windows, you'll use the window's WinHWND.) Alternatively, say `windowptr` and pass the window (see "Grasping Handles," later in this chapter).

Controls

A control has a Handle property. Typically, you will declare `integer` and pass the Handle. This works on both Macintosh and Windows.

Movies

Both a Movie and an EditableMovie have a Handle property. Again, you will typically declare `integer` and pass the Handle

Having written the Declare statement for a Toolbox routine, the rule is that you may call it, later in the same handler, in accordance with the declaration. In general, when performing an actual call, you should pass only variables; literals are usually okay, but don't (for example) perform a calculation or fetch the value of a property within the call—get the result of the calculation or the value of the property into a variable, and pass the variable.

The Gestalt example is a fairly simple one, so, as an illustration, we may as well finish it. An OSErr is a short integer; that's an available type. An OSType is an available type. A pointer to a long integer, we've just seen, is an integer declared `byref`. We are ready to write our Declare statement! There's just one little thing: a Declare statement is always very long—too long for the width of this page. So you must pretend that this and all subsequent Declare statements are actually each on a single line of code (and in your real code, they must be so):

```
declare function Gestalt lib "InterfaceLib" // no line break!
    (s as osType, byref i as integer) as short
```

For Mac OS X, instead of `InterfaceLib`, you'll put `CarbonLib`. So too throughout the rest of this chapter.

Now we can write a routine that calls Gestalt. You may recall that we wanted to know what system version the user has. The Gestalt selector for asking about the system version is `'sysv'`. The result indicates whether an error occurred; if it didn't, the result is zero and the answer to our query is in the `byref` integer. The system version is coded as a binary-coded decimal, meaning that it is more legible by a human being if we parse it as a hex string. Here we go:

```
declare function Gestalt lib "InterfaceLib" // no line break!
    (s as osType, byref i as integer) as short
dim s as string
dim i, resp as integer
if gestalt("sysv", resp) <> 0 then
    msgbox "Something went wrong."
    return
end
```

```
s = hex(resp)
for i = len(s) downto 1
    s = left(s,i) + "." + mid(s,i+1)
next
msgbox "You are using System " + s
```

Parsing and Passing Structs

This next example uses the Toolbox function StringToDate to set the value of a Date instance based on a string that describes the desired date. The REALbasic function ParseDate does the same thing, but this example was written long before the Parse-Date function was added to REALbasic, and once again I wasn't about to waste a perfectly good example.

The Pascal calling syntax for StringToDate is as follows:*

```
FUNCTION StringToDate(textPtr: Ptr; textLen: LongInt;
                theCache: DateCachePtr; VAR lengthUsed: LongInt;
                VAR dateTime: LongDateRec): StringToDateStatus;
```

Also, the call to StringToDate must be preceded by a call to InitDateCache:†

```
FUNCTION InitDateCache(theCache: DateCachePtr): OSErr
```

Let's start with InitDateCache. A DateCachePtr is a pointer to a hunk of memory that we are required to maintain, so we declare ptr and we'll pass a memoryblock. An OSErr is a short.

```
declare function InitDateCache lib "InterfaceLib" // no line break!
    (theCache as ptr) as short
```

On to StringToDate. A TextPtr is a pointer to a run of text; that's a cstring. A Long-Int is an integer. A DateCachePtr we know about. A pointer to an integer is an integer passed byref. A LongDateRec is a struct, so we declare ptr and pass a memoryblock. A StringToDateStatus is a short. Here's the Declare statement:

```
declare function StringToDate lib "InterfaceLib" // no line breaks!
    (textPtr as cstring, textLen as integer, theCache as ptr,
    byref lengthUsed as integer, dateTime as ptr) as short
```

Now let's call InitDateCache and StringToDate. We have some preparations to make. The Toolbox is expecting us to maintain two blocks of memory, to which we're going to be passing pointers. From our point of view, these will be memory-blocks. The question is: how large should they be? The header files are more helpful on this than *Inside Machintosh* is. *DateTimeUtils.h*, one of the files in *CIncludes*, seems to suggest that 512 bytes should be large enough for a DateCache. I give it

---

* See *http://developer.apple.com/techpubs/mac/Text/Text-290.html* and *http://developer.apple.com/techpubs/mac/Text/Text-336.html*.

† See *http://developer.apple.com/techpubs/mac/Text/Text-335.html*.

1000 bytes just to be on the safe side. A LongDateRec is 14 shorts, as *DateTimeUtils. h* makes clear:*

```
union LongDateRec {
    struct {
        short                era;
        short                year;
        short                month;
        short                day;
        short                hour;
        short                minute;
        short                second;
        short                dayOfWeek;
        short                dayOfYear;
        short                weekOfYear;
        short                pm;
        short                res1;
        short                res2;
        short                res3;
    } // the rest is unimportant for our purposes
}
```

So, here are our preparations. We make memoryblocks of the requisite size. We initialize the text we're going to convert to a date, and we learn its length because we'll have to pass that information to the Toolbox:

```
dim theLen, lenUsed, i as integer
dim lDateRec, cache as memoryblock
dim d as date
dim theText as string
lDateRec = newMemoryBlock(28)
cache = newMemoryBlock(1000)
theText = "8/10/1954" // or whatever
theLen = len(theText)
```

We are now ready to call the Toolbox, and we do so. Observe how, as advertised, we boldly pass memoryblocks where we declared ptr. Just use the name of the memoryblock as a parameter; what's actually passed is the address of the start of the memoryblock, which is precisely what the Toolbox wants:

```
i = InitDateCache(cache)
i = StringToDate(theText, theLen, cache, lenUsed, lDateRec)
```

The answer is now sitting in our second memoryblock, lDateRec. But this is not a Date; it's some sort of struct. Extracting the information and turning it into something useful is entirely up to us. Consulting the scheme of a LongDateRec, we see that the year, month, and day values will be in the second, third, and fourth shorts of this structure; so we retrieve them and assign them to our Date instance's corresponding properties:

```
d = new date
d.year = lDateRec.short(2)
```

---

* Also, see *http://developer.apple.com/techpubs/mac/OSUtilities/OSUtilities-100.html.*

```
d.month = lDateRec.short(4)
d.day = lDateRec.short(6)
msgBox d.longDate // Tuesday, August 10, 1954
```

Sharpening Pointers

In the next example, we will solve two problems which arose in Chapter 21—to learn our application's name and to find out whether it is frontmost. We will use calls to the following routines:*

```
FUNCTION GetCurrentProcess (VAR PSN: ProcessSerialNumber): OSErr;
FUNCTION GetProcessInformation (PSN: ProcessSerialNumber;
                             VAR info: ProcessInfoRec): OSErr;
FUNCTION SameProcess (PSN1, PSN2: ProcessSerialNumber;
                  VAR result: Boolean): OSErr;
FUNCTION GetFrontProcess (VAR PSN: ProcessSerialNumber): OSErr;
```

A ProcessSerialNumber is a struct, and so is a ProcessInfoRec:

```
declare function GetCurrentProcess lib "InterfaceLib" // no line break!
    (psn as ptr) as short
declare function GetProcessInformation lib "InterfaceLib" // no line break!
    (psn as ptr, processInfoRec as ptr) as short
declare function SameProcess lib "InterfaceLib" // no line break!
    (psn1 as ptr, psn2 as ptr, byref res as boolean) as short
declare function GetFrontProcess lib "InterfaceLib" // no line break!
    (psn as ptr) as short
```

The structure of a ProcessSerialNumber is of interest only because we need to know how big a memoryblock to allot for it; it turns out that it's two long integers:

```
TYPE ProcessSerialNumber   =
    RECORD
        highLongOfPSN:    LongInt;    {high-order 32 bits of psn}
        lowLongOfPSN:     LongInt;    {low-order 32 bits of psn}
    END;
```

On the other hand, we're actually going to have to think about a ProcessInfoRec:

```
TYPE ProcessInfoRec =
    RECORD
        processInfoLength:   LongInt;    {length of process info record}
        processName:         StringPtr;  {name of this process}
        processNumber:       ProcessSerialNumber;
                                         {psn of this process}
        processType:         LongInt;    {file type of application file}
        processSignature:    OSType;     {signature of application file}
        processMode:         LongInt;    {'SIZE' resource flags}
        processLocation:     Ptr;        {address of partition}
        processSize:         LongInt;    {partition size}
        processFreeMem:      LongInt;    {free bytes in heap}
        processLauncher:     ProcessSerialNumber;
```

---

* See *http://developer.apple.com/techpubs/macos8/OSSvcs/ProcessManager/processmanager.html.*

```
    processLaunchDate:    LongInt;        {process that launched this one}
    processActiveTime:    LongInt;        {time when launched}
    processAppSpec:       FSSpecPtr;      {accumulated CPU time}
END;                                      {location of the file}
```

A pointer is four bytes long, so 60 bytes should be enough to hold the Process-
InfoRec; I give it 100 just to be on the safe side. But the size is not the issue; it's the
first two elements of the ProcessInfoRec. We're going to use these to capture the
name of our application. But what are they? The ProcessName is a pointer to a block
of storage; the ProcessInfoLength is the size of that block of storage. So, that storage
too will be a memoryblock; the name of our process could be as long as 32 bytes, so
that's the size I use.

```
dim curPSN, frontPSN, info, thename as memoryblock
dim i as integer
dim s as string
dim res as boolean
curPSN = newMemoryBlock(8)
frontPSN = newMemoryBlock(8)
info = newMemoryBlock(100)
thename = newMemoryBlock(32)
```

Now comes the interesting part. Our ProcessInfoRec is info. We initialize its ProcessInfoLength to the size of info. We initialize its ProcessName to *point* to thename!

```
info.long(0) = 100 // initialize the length
info.ptr(4) = thename // initialize the pointer, pointing to theName
```

We are now ready to call the Toolbox:

```
i = getcurrentprocess(curPSN)
i = getprocessinformation(curPSN,info)
i = getfrontprocess(frontPSN)
i = sameprocess(curPSN,frontPSN,res)
```

That's it! The answer to the question, "What is the name of our process?" is now sitting in thename; it's a Pascal string, so we can extract it with thename.pstring(0). The
answer to the question, "Is our application the frontmost application?" is sitting in
the boolean res.

Grasping Handles

In Chapter 9, it was suggested that you might learn the actual outside dimensions of
your window through Toolbox calls. If we are using Mac OS 8.5 or later, this is particularly simple; a single call to GetWindowBounds will do it. Here is its syntax,
drawn from the header file *MacWindows.h*:[*]

```
OSStatus GetWindowBounds (WindowPtr        window,
                          WindowRegionCode regionCode,
                          Rect *           globalBounds);
```

---

[*] GetWindowBounds was one of the new, rationalized Toolbox calls introduced during the run-up to Carbon.

A little searching with PEFViewer reveals that GetWindowBounds is that *rara avis*, a function defined elsewhere than in *InterfaceLib*; it's in *WindowsLib*. To pass a pointer to a window, we declare windowptr and pass the window. The region code is a short; our value is 32, indicating that we want the window's "structure region." A Rect is a struct, consisting of four shorts; as usual, we declare ptr and pass a memoryblock. Here's the whole routine:

```
declare function GetWindowBounds lib "WindowsLib" // no line break!
    (w as windowPtr, c as short, r as ptr) as short
dim rect as memoryblock, i as integer
rect = newmemoryBlock(8)
i = getwindowbounds(self, 32, rect)
```

Afterward, the window's outer dimensions can be extracted as rect.short(0), rect.short(2), rect.short(4), and rect.short(6), in the order Top, Left, Bottom, Right.

However, that was too easy, so I will show an approach that is more difficult (and therefore more interesting). On Mac OS 8.0 and later, we may obtain the window's outer dimensions with GetWindowRegion:

```
OSStatus GetWindowRegion (WindowPtr        inWindow,
                          WindowRegionCode inRegionCode,
                          RgnHandle        ioWinRgn);
```

The reason this example is interesting is that it requires us to obtain and work with a *handle*—a pointer to a pointer. A handle is a brilliant memory-management device, because it allows the programmer to retain a valid reference to data while allowing the computer to move that data in memory; but it is also rather scary, and saddles the programmer with memory-management tasks, which, if not performed in just the right way, can lead to memory leaks or crashes. Indeed, a very great deal of what goes wrong on a Macintosh is because some programmer mishandled a handle.*

Obtaining the handle is up to us; we are to get it from the system by calling NewRgn. What we end up with is just an address, so we declare NewRgn as returning an integer. Similarly, when we are finished, we must release the memory pointed to by the handle; we do this with DisposeRgn, and again since what we have is an address, we simply pass an integer. Here are the declarations:

```
declare function NewRgn lib "InterfaceLib" () as integer
declare sub DisposeRgn lib "InterfaceLib" (rgnHandle as integer)
```

Here's the declaration for GetWindowRegion; it's in *AppearanceLib*:

```
declare function GetWindowRegion lib "AppearanceLib" // no line break!
    (w as windowPtr, whatRgn as short, rgnHandle as integer) as short
```

---

* For a particularly brilliant explanation of handles, see *http://www.mactech.com/articles/mactech/Vol.12/12.05/Handles2/index.html*; notice the clever logo at the start, symbolizing how a handle works and drawn by *MacTech*'s editor at that time, who was ... well ... modesty forbids. On Mac OS X, where each application gets a large, protected memory space, the importance of handles will likely be diminished.

We are now ready to call the Toolbox. We start by obtaining our handle and calling GetWindowRegion:

```
dim rgn, i, theTop as integer
dim deref as memoryblock
rgn = newrgn()
i = getwindowregion(self,32,rgn)
```

Now comes the really interesting part. Where on earth is our result? It's in the Region—the data structure pointed to by rgn. A Region consists of a short, telling its size as a data structure, followed by four shorts describing its rectangular boundaries as a geometric shape (followed possibly by a lot of other stuff that we don't care about). So, for example, if we want to know the window's structural Top, we need the second short of the Region. But where *is* this Region? It's somewhere off in memory, being maintained by the system. How will we get to it? Keep your shorts on. We have a handle to it: that's what rgn is. So we treat rgn as a pointer, and dereference it to reach the place in memory that it points to; and then we treat *that* place as a pointer as well, to reach the Region. Now we can obtain the second short from that area of memory:

```
deref = newmemoryblock(4)
deref.long(0) = rgn
theTop = deref.ptr(0).ptr(0).short(2)
```

That's all, except for heaven's sake don't forget to release the handle when you're finished with it:

```
disposergn rgn
```

This example shows the great power of memoryblocks as a device for reaching into memory. (This in fact is what they were invented to do; their use as a mechanism for storage and format conversion, as demonstrated throughout this book, is actually a perverse misuse originally discovered by some enterprising REALbasic programmers.) When we use a memoryblock's Ptr property to dereference an address, the result is another memoryblock, *even though we didn't declare it as a local variable!* Thus, we can use *that* memoryblock's Ptr property to dereference the second address, thus winding up at the far end of the handle. And then we can use properties of *that* memoryblock to locate ourselves some number of bytes off that address and pick up some data there. Clearly this power is tremendous; in fact, it's unlimited, since you can also write to an arbitrary address in memory in just the same way, which is a good way to crash the computer if you don't know what you're doing. So have fun, but please, be careful out there.

Who Was That Masked Man?

The optional Alias keyword in a Declare statement is to work around the fact that a Toolbox routine might have the same name as a REALbasic global method. In such a case, you could never call the Toolbox routine, because the global method name will take precedence. Accordingly, your Declare statement declares a fake name for the

Toolbox routine, and then tells REALbasic the real name with the Alias keyword. For example, here's the Gestalt declaration, rewritten to pretend that the Toolbox routine is called Environment:

```
declare function Environment lib "InterfaceLib" alias "Gestalt" // no line break!
    (s as osType, byref i as integer) as short
```

After that, you can call Environment:

```
if environment("sysv", resp) <> 0 then
```

The call to Environment is translated into a call to the Toolbox routine Gestalt. If REALbasic already had a global method called Gestalt, this device would be useful and necessary.

68K

Calling the Toolbox from 68K code is a tricky business, and I can't warn you in detail about all the traps you might encounter. Some of the techniques we've seen may simply not work; in the past, for example, I've had particular difficulty passing booleans back and forth. You'll just have to experiment.

However, you can't experiment at all if you don't know how to call the Toolbox in the first place. The Declare statements we've been using so far won't work! The reason for this is that on 68K there are no libraries. This means that you must supply, as a hex string, the actual machine-language code required to make the Toolbox call. You do this with the Inline68K parameter of the Declare statement.

The trick is then to figure out what the correct value for the Inline68K parameter is. In most cases you can just use the hex values shown in the header file, strung together if there is more than one. For example, the syntax for GetFrontProcess in the *Processes.h* header file reads like this:

```
OSErr GetFrontProcess (ProcessSerialNumber * PSN)
    FIVEWORDINLINE(0x70FF, 0x2F00, 0x3F3C, 0x0039, 0xA88F);
```

It's that "fivewordinline" that concerns us here. The value of the Inline68K parameter is those five words run together as a string. So, on a 68K machine, the Declare statement for GetFrontProcess would look like this:

```
declare function GetCurrentProcess lib "InterfaceLib" // no line break!
    (psn as ptr) as short inline68K("70FF2F003F3C0039A88F")
```

But complications arise when parameters are delivered in unexpected places, such as through special registers. A good example is the Toolbox routine Gestalt. Looking in the header file *Gestalt.h*, we find that the syntax for Gestalt in that file includes this phrase:

```
TWOWORDINLINE(0xA1AD, 0x2288);
```

This seems to imply that the Inline68K value for Gestalt is the string "A1AD2288". But it isn't. Just before the previously quoted phrase in *Gestalt.h*, you'll see this:

```
#pragma parameter __D0 Gestalt(__D0, __A1)
```

That means that the parameters need to be passed in the D0 and A1 registers, respectively, and that the result of the function will be returned in the D0 register. The first word of the machine-language expression, 0xA1AD, calls Gestalt. Afterward, the new value of the second parameter, resp, ends up in the A0 register, which is the wrong place; since the second parameter was passed by reference, its value needs to be in the address pointed to by the A1 register. This is what the second word of the machine-language expression takes care of; 0x2288 means the following in assembly language:*

```
MOVE.L A0, (A1)
```

That is to say, copy the contents of the A0 register into the address pointed to by the A1 register. So, when *Gestalt.h* is included in code, the compiler sees the parameter pragma and creates its object code accordingly; the resulting application puts the parameters in the places where Gestalt expects them, runs the two-word machine-language code, and finds the result waiting in the right spot.

The trouble is that REALbasic knows nothing of all that. Rather, for 68K code, REALbasic simply assumes Pascal passing conventions. In Pascal, space is reserved on the stack for the returned value, and then the parameters are pushed onto the stack in left-to-right order; the called routine is expected to remove the parameters as it uses them, and to leave the result on the stack for the caller to retrieve.

So, when we call Gestalt in our REALbasic code, REALbasic is going to push the parameters onto the stack—which is not where they belong. Therefore, in our machine-language code, before we actually call Gestalt by saying 0xA1AD, we need to pop the parameters back off the stack and into D0 and A1, where Gestalt expects them! This sounds terrifying, but it is really quite easy; we just have to be logical about it. Since REALbasic has pushed the parameters onto the stack in left-to-right order, we will first be popping the second parameter and putting it into the A1 register; we will then be popping the first parameter and putting it into the D0 register. Here we go.

The second parameter is a long. The A7 register points to the top of the stack, so to pop a long from the stack and copy its value into the A1 register, we want to say:

```
MOVEA.L (A7)+, A1
```

which in machine language is 0x225F.

The first parameter is a long as well, so to pop a long from the stack and copy its value into the D0 register, we want to say:

```
MOVE.L (A7)+, D0
```

which in machine language is 0x201F. So, up to and including the call to Gestalt, our Inline68K string now goes like this: "225F201FA1AD".

---

* The easiest way to find this out is to drop into Macsbug and type **DH 2288**.

Next, you recall, comes the 0x2288 after the call to Gestalt, which moves the contents of the A0 register to the address pointed to by the A1 register; this is right, because we set the A1 register to the value of the second parameter, which was a pointer to the place where we wanted the resp value deposited.

But we aren't finished! The result code is now sitting in the D0 register; but REALbasic expects it on the stack. So we need to copy the D0 register onto the stack; we don't have to decrement the stack pointer, because we are copying into a spot that was already reserved on the stack by REALbasic beforehand. The value in the D0 register is a short, so what we want to say is this:

```
MOVE.W D0, (A7)
```

which in machine language is 0x3E80.

So, the complete declaration would look like this:

```
declare function Gestalt lib "InterfaceLib" // no line breaks!
    (s as osType, byref i as integer) as short
    inline68k("225F201FA1AD22883E80")
```

You're probably wondering at this point how I know the machine-language equivalents for all these assembly-language MOVE and MOVEA commands. The answer is that I'm staring at a copy of the reference manual for the 68000 processor.* Since you probably neglected to pick up a copy of this valuable tome during the six minutes when it was on the best-seller list, Table 32-1 shows the commands you are most likely to need:†

Table 32-1. Some common MOVE commands

Assembly language	Machine language
MOVE.L (A7)+, D0	201F
MOVE.L (A7)+, D1	221F
MOVE.L (A7)+, D2	241F
MOVE.W (A7)+, D0	301F
MOVE.W (A7)+, D1	321F
MOVE.W (A7)+, D2	341F
MOVEA.L (A7)+, A0	205F
MOVEA.L (A7)+, A1	225F
MOVE.L D0, (A7)	2E80
MOVE.L A0, (A7)	2E88
MOVE.W D0, (A7)	3E80
MOVE.W A0, (A7)	3E88

---

* *M68000 Family Programmer's Reference Manual*, Motorola, 1989, 2–110ff.

† For this table, for the entire discussion on how to write Inline68K codes, and for the fact that Inline68K works at all in REALbasic, I am heavily indebted to Thomas Tempelmann.

Windows

I'm desperately trying to end this section and get on to something else, but I can see from the advancing mobs of armed ruffians that I won't be allowed to do it without including an example of using a Declare statement on Windows. The Windows Toolbox routines are on the Web, and they even tell you what library to use.* The only hitch is that some routines, those that take strings in particular, may not be implemented under their official names.

As an example, let's call CharLower. This is just about the simplest function in the universe: it converts a string to lowercase. The official syntax is:†

```
LPTSTR CharLower(
   LPTSTR lpsz   // single character or string
);
```

The same page informs us that an LPTSTR is a pointer to a null-terminated string. We know how to pass in a pointer to a null-terminated string: declare cstring and pass a string. Getting the same thing back out again is a bit trickier; we'll have to declare ptr and assign to a memoryblock. The page also says that the library is *User32.lib*. The rule is that in the Declare statement, you should substitute *dll* for *lib*. So we're all set:

```
Declare function CharLower Lib "user32.dll" (lpsz as cstring) as ptr
dim s as string, m as memoryBlock
s = "THIS IS A TEST"
m = newmemoryBlock(len(s)+1)
m = charlower(s)
msgbox m.cstring(0)
```

There's just one problem: when we try to start up the built application on Windows, we are told that there's no such function as CharLower. It turns out that we're supposed to declare this as CharLowerA (the "A" stands for "ANSI," since we're calling the ANSI string version of this function, as opposed to the Unicode version, whose name ends in "W" for "wide"). How on earth we're supposed to know this from the official Microsoft pages beats me; I found it out at a completely different site, one that shows the Declare statement syntax for calling Win32 Toolbox routines from Visual Basic.‡ So, here's the corrected routine:

```
Declare function CharLowerA Lib "user32.dll" (lpsz as cstring) as ptr
dim s as string, m as memoryBlock
s = "THIS IS A TEST"
m = newmemoryBlock(len(s)+1)
m = charlowera(s)
msgbox m.cstring(0)
```

---

* *http://msdn.microsoft.com/library/psdk/portals/win32start_1n6t.htm.*

† *http://msdn.microsoft.com/library/psdk/winui/strings_8t2q.htm.*

‡ *http://www.vbapi.com/ref/c/charlower.html.* Thanks to David Grogono for telling me about this site.

Let's have one more example, for good measure. We'll call GetUserName, because I like to see the computer acknowledge me as master. According to the official page, the syntax is this:[*]

```
BOOL GetUserName(
    LPTSTR lpBuffer,   // name buffer
    LPDWORD nSize      // size of name buffer
);
```

We know that an LPTSTR is a pointer to a buffer; since the Toolbox is going to create the actual string, we'll declare ptr and pass a memoryblock. We're also told that the second parameter is "in/out"; the routine wants to know the size of the buffer, but it will change the value of the variable, setting it to the size of the resulting string. So that's an integer declared byref. We can drop the boolean result into an integer and throw it away. Once again, we must append "A" to the name of the function.[†] Here's the final routine:

```
Declare Function GetUserNameA Lib "advapi32.dll" // no line break!
    (m as ptr, byref n as integer) as integer
dim i,n as integer, m as memoryblock
m = newmemoryBlock(255)
n = 255
i = getusernamea (m, n)
msgbox m.cstring(0)
```

XCMDs

An XCMD (or XFCN) is a code fragment, living in a resource of type 'XCMD' (or 'XFCN'), in a format originally devised about a decade ago for use with Apple's HyperCard scripting environment. An XFCN is indistinguishable from an XCMD, except that an XFCN returns a value; in general, I tend to use the term "XCMD" indiscriminately for both. This format has proven quite useful, so it has gained currency in other programs as well. Because XCMDs have been widespread for such a long time, and especially because of their great popularity in the scripting community, you may well be able to find an already existing XCMD that does what you want.[‡]

XCMDs don't work on Windows. My impression is that they don't work on Mac OS X either, meaning that a REALbasic application compiled for Carbon and running natively under Mac OS X would not be able to use XCMDs. In theory I suppose there could be such a thing as a Carbonized XCMD, but I don't know of any, and I

---

[*] http://msdn.microsoft.com/library/psdk/sysmgmt/sysinfo_9jj9.htm.

[†] http://www.vbapi.com/ref/g/getusername.html.

[‡] Besides HyperCard, programs that support XCMDs include SuperCard, Frontier, 4th Dimension, FoxPro, Director, and MacPerl. Sources of XCMDs include http://www.glasscat.com/hypercard/makeIND.cgi/ XCMD_etc/0002 and http://www.devhq.com/XCMDs/. See also my own "Guide To XCMDs," an index to the best XCMDs available in 1995: http://www.ojai.net/matt/downloads/guideToXCMDs.hqx.

don't imagine there's any great push to write one, since a Carbonized XCMD would not work inside HyperCard (because HyperCard isn't Carbonized).

Not every XCMD works perfectly within REALbasic. There are two generations of XCMD; REALbasic does not run XCMDs of the second generation, which implements a mechanism for defining and displaying windows. Also, XCMDs have access to a number of "callback" procedures, which allow them to query and command HyperCard; but REALbasic is not HyperCard, so it cannot always respond intelligently. A callback that depends upon HyperCard fields, globals, or dialogs, or that tries to send a HyperTalk message for evaluation, will probably not crash, but it won't have the intended effect either.

So, you may have to experiment in order to determine whether a particular XCMD will work properly in your application. But don't hesitate to experiment; people do use many XCMDs within REALbasic, with great success.

To incorporate an XCMD into a REALbasic project, simply import a file containing it. (This will typically be a HyperCard stack.) But REALbasic will incorporate only the first XCMD that it finds in an imported file, so if that wasn't what you were after, you may need to copy each desired XCMD into a separate file with ResEdit and import the files individually. The project maintains an alias to the file, so don't delete the file until the application has been built, at which time a copy of the XCMD's code is incorporated into the application. If the XCMD depends upon other resources, you will have to copy these into a Resource file and import that into the project as well (for an example, and for a discussion of Resource files, see Chapter 21).

The name under which the XCMD appears in the Project Window can be used to call it from your REALbasic code. Every parameter of an XCMD, as well as its result if it has one, is a string.

Here's an example. To supplement REALbasic's sorting facilities, we might want to use Frédéric Rinaldi's FullSort XFCN.* We will sort a list of semicolon-delimited items, sorting on the second comma-delimited item within each item, in reverse ASCII order:

```
dim s as string
s = "hee,Hey nonny no;ha,ho;hi,hey"
msgbox fullsort(s,"D=D","L=;","T=A","C=item 2")
```

The result is this:

```
"ha,ho;hi,hey;hee,Hey nonny no"
```

because in ASCII order, "Hey" precedes "hey" which precedes "ho".

---

* See *http://perso.wanadoo.fr/frederic.rinaldi/*.

Shared Libraries

A *shared library*, also sometimes called a *DLL* (dynamically linked library), is a code fragment in a format defined by the Macintosh PowerPC architecture to enable code to remain on disk except when it is actually needed by an application, and to enable the same code file to be part of multiple applications. If you use a PowerPC Macintosh, you probably have many shared libraries; to see them, use Sherlock to look for files whose type is "shlb". A shared library makes its code available as subroutines (it is said to *export* these subroutines); and on a PowerPC machine, REALbasic can call these subroutines. (Shared libraries are implemented also on some 68K machines by way of the CFM-68K extension, but I believe that REALbasic does not interface with this.)

The syntax for calling a routine in a shared library is a Declare statement, as described in "Direct Toolbox Calls," earlier in this chapter. Use PEFViewer to learn the name of the library; it is this name, not the name of the file, that you will use in your Declare. In order to be located and loaded, the shared library file must be where the Code Fragment Manager expects to find it; basically, this means either that the file must be in the Extensions folder when the computer starts up or else that the file must be in the same folder as your application when your application starts up. When you're developing a project, it isn't clear whether the "same folder" means the same folder as your project or the same folder as REALbasic; I place a copy of the shared library in both places, just to be safe.*

In this example, we will drive the popular image-conversion utility Clip2Gif to take a screen shot and save it as a GIF file.† Since REALbasic provides no native way to create a GIF file, we'll know we're doing something cool. The same effect could be achieved by running Clip2Gif and driving it with Apple events, since Clip2Gif is also scriptable; but that's not what we're going to do. Clip2Gif will never be running! Its code will be loaded directly from disk and called by our project as if it were part of the Toolbox. In effect, Clip2Gif will become an extension to REALbasic's own abilities. We are able to do this because the author of Clip2Gif has designed the application so that it exports certain routines, just like a shared library. However, the Code Fragment Manager still doesn't *see* it as a shared library, so the first step is to make a copy of Clip2Gif and change its type code to "shlb". Give the copy any name you like, and put copies in the same folder as REALbasic and in the same folder as your project.

The code is almost a direct transcription of the example code included with Clip2Gif. We start by asking the user where to save the GIF file:

```
dim f as folderitem
dim filespec, rect, zero as memoryblock
```

---

* I owe this suggestion, and just about everything in this paragraph, to *UncleLiam@aol.com*.

† For Clip2Gif, see *http://www.zdnet.com/downloads/stories/info/0,,MC11335,.html*.

```
dim i, screenshot, ctabhandle as integer
dim fname as string
f = getsaveFolderItem("","myCoolGif.gif")
if f = nil then
    return
end
```

Now we call the Toolbox to convert the FolderItem to an FSSpec. This is an important technique for mediating between REALbasic FolderItems and Toolbox calls that operate on files:

```
filespec = newmemoryBlock(200)
fname = f.name
declare function FSMakeFSSpec lib "InterfaceLib" // no line break!
    (v as short, d as integer, f as pstring, m as ptr) as short
i = fsmakefsspec(f.macvRefNum, f.macDirID, fname, filespec)
```

Next, we call upon Clip2Gif to make a screen shot of a small rectangle in the upper-left corner of the main screen. We will be handed a pointer to the actual image, which we maintain as an integer called screenshot:

```
rect = newmemoryBlock(8)
rect.short(4) = 200
rect.short(6) = 160
declare function GetScreen lib "clip2gif" // no line break!
    (r as ptr, byref p as integer) as short
i = getscreen(rect, screenshot)
```

We now prepare to save the GIF. Clip2Gif wants a color table, so we call the Toolbox to fetch us a handle to the system's default 256-color table:

```
declare function GetCTable lib "InterfaceLib" (id as short) as integer
ctabhandle = GetCTable(72)
```

One more thing Clip2Gif wants is a pointer to zero, to indicate that we don't want a transparent GIF. We construct this, call upon Clip2Gif to save the file, and we're done:

```
zero = newmemoryBlock(4)
declare function ConvertPictToGIFFile lib "clip2gif" // no line breaks!
    (p as integer, f as ptr, int as short, c as ptr,
     d as short, h as integer) as short
i = convertpicttogiffile(screenshot, filespec, 1, zero, 8, ctabhandle)
```

Plug-ins

A *plug-in* is a code fragment compiled into a special format unique to REALbasic and living as a specific resource type in a specific file type. Its purpose will usually be to call the Toolbox, to optimize for speed, or to define a control. To use a plug-in, have a folder called *Plugins* (no hyphen!) in the same folder as the REALbasic application, and place the plug-in file in that folder. The plug-in's functionality will be available to your projects the next time you start up REALbasic. When you build an application, any plug-ins actually used by your project are automatically incorporated into the application.

A plug-in can provide the REALbasic language with a supplementary method, in which case you simply call the method globally in your code as you would any built-in global method. A plug-in can also implement a supplementary REALbasic class. If the class is a control class, the icon for the control will appear in the Tools Window, and you can drag it into a Window Editor as you would any other control. The control will have a repertoire of events, properties, and messages just as if it were a built-in REALbasic control.

Plug-ins do not automatically interface with REALbasic's online help, so in order to know how to use one, you must acquire documentation in some other fashion. Typically, documentation is distributed along with the plug-in.

Plug-ins can be PowerPC-only or 68K; they can be Carbonized; and they can be cross-platform. There are many third-party plug-ins, available as freeware, as shareware, or for commercial purchase; for more information, see the various online resources mentioned in the Preface ("Beyond This Book"). A number of plug-ins have been mentioned in various places in this book, and examples of calling particular plug-ins appeared on page 320, page 512, and page 628.

Writing a plug-in is outside the scope of this book, because it involves coding in an environment other than REALbasic (this will presumably be Metrowerks CodeWarrior), using C/C++. However, let me stress that it can be a very economical way to speed up your code or to give it access to some needed Toolbox routines, so if you know C++, there's no reason to hesitate if you're thinking of writing a plug-in. Start by obtaining the Plug-in SDK; it is available on the REALbasic CD or from the REALbasic web site. When I wrote the first edition of this book, the Plug-in SDK was abstruse and haphazard, and information on writing plug-ins was difficult to come by—it was as if you were expected to learn to write a plug-in by a combination of telepathy, osmosis, experimentation, and guesswork. For this reason, I actually gave an example of how to write a plug-in. Now, however, the SDK has been thoroughly and helpfully revised, and you should find it self-explanatory; so there is no need for any further comment from me. There is also a plug-ins mailing list; you can find out more at REAL's web site.*

---

* As of this writing, the URL for the Plug-in SDK is *http://www.realsoftware.com/files/REALbasicPlug-insSDK. sit*. For the plug-ins mailing list, see *http://www.realsoftware.com/support/internet.html*. REAL maintains a list of available plug-ins at *http://www.realsoftware.com/learn/programmers/Plugin/index.html*.

Growing an Application

The first edition of this book lacked many extras, which, however much I would have liked to include them, were barred by limitations of size and time. Exercises, quizzes, a section on teaching REALbasic to children would all have been nice. But my saddest omission was a reasoned exposition of the entire thought process for the complete development, from start to finish, of an actual application. And readers have told me that they particularly missed this as well. So, in this appendix, I write an entire application—with you, the reader, looking over my shoulder.

What's presented here is just a sample of how I think and work; I don't imagine that this is the only way to think and work, or that it is how you should think and work. Nevertheless, I have learned from years of classroom teaching that the most useful service the teacher can perform for the student is to expose, with candor and clarity, the workings of his or her own mind. Mere facts can be gleaned from any decent reference; simple deductive logic is a matter of practice; ideas are the province of everyone; but the teacher's contribution is a particular *way* of approaching facts, of applying logic, of manipulating and evaluating ideas.

Principles of Approach

Since my way of working may not suit everyone, I should say something at the outset about what that way is. In general, I have found the following to be useful principles:

- Be as object-oriented as you can. The more your logic is a product of the arrangement of your objects, the clearer and simpler the logic of any one handler will be. This will make it easier to understand your own work and to make changes.

- Don't be afraid to change your mind. I don't believe in a strictly compartmentalized development process where first you design, then you code, then you debug; unless you're developing cooperatively with a lot of other people, there's absolutely no need for this, and to have a preconceived design will just

677

hamstring your thinking later on. I do all three simultaneously throughout the development process. I'm not afraid to do something quick-and-dirty, because I know I can come back and clean up later. I don't mind making mistakes along the way, because as long as they're just along the way, I don't see them as mistakes.

- Always have the program do something. By this I mean that you should always have a working program in hand, even if it doesn't yet work the way you want or accomplish your main aim. The fact that REALbasic lets you do this is one of its strongest features, and to fail to take advantage of it is wasteful. For one thing, it's much more satisfying if you can have the program produce some activity; this will keep your spirits up and encourage you to keep working. Also, you might fail to write formal tests into your code as you go along;* so if you are constantly playing with what there is of the program, you are more likely to spot bugs as they arise.

An Example Project: Tic-Tac-Toe

A Tic-Tac-Toe game has always seemed to me an excellent demonstration project. It's an easy game, universally known, where it doesn't much matter if the computer plays randomly. It's interactive in a nice basic way. It involves some elementary graphics, which is good; but apart from this there is almost no user interface, which is also good, because problems of user interface are distracting. And it's useful: no one can really play Tic-Tac-Toe alone, but to play it with a computer passes the time quite pleasantly. When I teach REALbasic to children, the first major milestone I'm aiming at is always a Tic-Tac-Toe game. The particular version presented here was written for a talk I gave at Macworld Expo in January 2001, called "Who's Afraid of Object-Oriented Programming?" This is *not* the way I would organize a Tic-Tac-Toe game example if I were teaching a child! My purpose here was not to keep things on an elementary level, but to answer the time-honored question: "How object-oriented can you get?" As you'll see, the answer is: "Very, very object-oriented!" As I wrote the game, I saved each successive version. So now you can see the entire development process as it actually took place. Everything is as it was, except... You Are There!

Won't You Be My Neighbor?

The project's default window will display the game board, which is a three-by-three grid. Let's call each element of this grid a "space." The user needs to be able to click in a space to play there, and a space needs to be able to display an X or an O. So it sounds as if a space is a kind of Canvas. Furthermore, I'm going to need to be able to

---

* For a wonderful little article on this topic, see *http://members.pingnet.ch/gamma/junit.htm*.

identify each particular space somehow; it would be helpful if these identifiers bore some sort of arithmetic relationship to one another, so this sounds like a control array.

So I create the Space class as a subclass of Canvas, and in the window I make a control array of Space called ASpace, in a three-by-three arrangement. The top left ASpace is ASpace(0); the bottom right ASpace is ASpace(8). See Figure A-1.

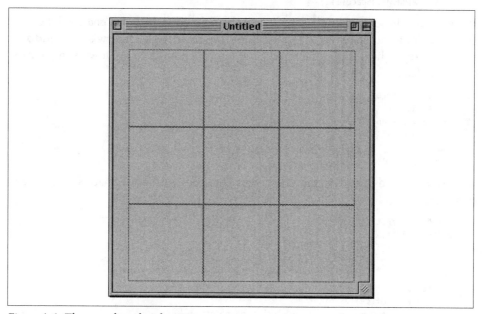

Figure A-1. The game board in the IDE

At the outset, the spaces have a job to do: they should draw the grid lines between themselves. Which spaces should draw grid lines? If a space has a neighbor to its right, it should draw a vertical line at its right edge. If a space has a neighbor below it, it should draw a horizontal line at its lower edge. So a space needs to be able to ask: do I have a neighbor in such and such a direction?

But what on earth is a "direction"? It seems a fairly basic but abstract concept, and we know that it comes in at least two flavors, down and right. This sounds like a class and its subclasses. So I make a Direction class, with no Super; and I create two subclasses of Direction called Down and Right.

Now, a Space needs to be able to learn whether it has a neighbor in a particular direction. It is not, I think, the Space that should know what a neighbor is; the job of the Space is to be clicked on and to be drawn into. So it must be the job of the Direction. So the Direction class gets a NeighborOf method. I'll have this method accept a Space and return a Space; the idea is that we return either the given Space's actual neighbor or nil if there is no neighbor in that direction.

Direction's NeighborOf method is abstract; it's up to the subclasses to implement it. Here is Right's implementation of NeighborOf:

```
dim i as integer
i = s.index // s is the incoming Space parameter
if i mod 3 = 2 then
    return nil
end
return window1.aSpace(i+1)
```

If the Space whose neighbor is sought is at the right edge, its index mod 3 will be 2; in that case, it has no neighbor to the right, and we return nil. Otherwise, we add 1 to the index to get the neighboring Space, and return a pointer to it. Down's implementation of NeighborOf is similar:

```
dim i as integer
i = s.index
if i\3 = 2 then
    return nil
end
return window1.aSpace(i+3)
```

We are now ready to draw the grid lines. This code goes into Space's Paint event handler:

```
dim d as direction
d = new right
if d.neighborOf(me) <> nil then
    g.drawline me.width-1,0,me.width-1,me.height-1
end
d = new down
if d.neighborOf(me) <> nil then
    g.drawline 0,me.height-1,me.width-1,me.height-1
end
```

We run the project, and sure enough, the grid lines appear! See Figure A-2.

Observe what we did *not* do here. We didn't hardcode into a Space any predefined knowledge of what its neighbors are, and we didn't hardcode the difference between down and right into some sort of condition that depends upon a tag. In other words, here is the sort of code we did *not* write:

```
select case me.index
case 0
    if dir = "down" then
        return aSpace(3)
    elseif dir = "right" then
        return aSpace(1)
    end
case 1
    // ... and so on ...
```

Of course, we could have done that, and our code would have worked. But there are several problems with it. For one thing, in my view, that's just plain cheating. Instead

---

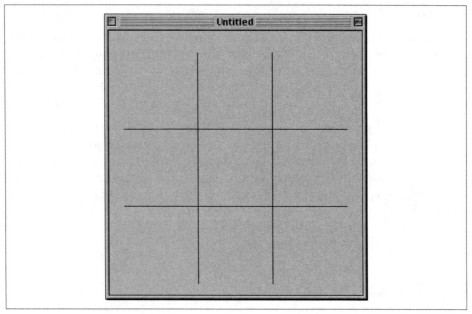

Figure A-2. The grid lines

of making the program do the thinking, you're just telling it the answers! Also, it handcuffs you for the future. The notion of a direction might be needed for more purposes than just drawing these particular grid lines. So it's better for directions to be as general, as abstract, as object-oriented as possible right from the start. If we obey the rule, "Be as object-oriented as you can," these considerations take care of themselves.

The style of programming I use here will, to be sure, look very odd to someone unaccustomed to object-oriented programming. I'm creating a new instance just to send it one message and then throwing the instance away. I do this twice—once with a Right instance, once with a Down instance. I address the instance as a Direction; the virtual method mechanism sees to it that the correct method is called. This seems like merely a roundabout way of accomplishing the same thing I could accomplish with a condition and a tag:

```
if dir = "right" then //...
elseif dir = "down" then //...
```

It is indeed another way of accomplishing the same thing, but it is not merely a roundabout way. It's an object-oriented way. To use an object as a way of packaging functionality—even if that object is simply brought into existence *once*, called, and thrown away—is not roundabout; it's what objects are for. To use the virtual method mechanism as a way of deciding what to do is not roundabout; it's what the virtual method mechanism is for.

Three in a What?

The fundamental concept of Tic-Tac-Toe is a row. What *is* a row? It's a set of three Spaces, and in fact we happen to know that in a three-by-three game there are eight rows, and we can specify them: the three horizontal rows, starting with 0,1,2; the three vertical rows, starting with 0,3,6; and the two diagonal rows. However, we don't *want* to specify them; we want the program to figure out what they are.

Clearly, a row can be expressed as an array of three Spaces. So I make a class Row, with a property TheSpaces, which is an array of three Spaces. And the totality of rows for the game needs to be stored somewhere. So I make a class RowKeeper, with a property TheRows as a zero-sized array of Rows. The window will have a property, TheRowKeeper, and will instantiate this as things start up. I figure RowKeeper should be in charge of making rows, so I give it a method Create, which creates a Row, appends it to the array, and returns a reference to it in case the caller wants to do something with this newly created Row:

```
dim r as row
r = new row
theRows.append r
return r
```

On the other hand, I figure a Row should be in charge of adding a given Space to itself. The Row needs to put the Space into its first available empty slot. I give Row an Add method:

```
dim i as integer
for i = 1 to 3
    if theSpaces(i) = nil then
        theSpaces(i) = s // s is the incoming Space parameter
        return
    end
next
```

Now we wish to populate TheRows; we need a strategy for determining the actual rows of the game. But before starting to work on this strategy, we should prepare a way of seeing if we're generating the rows correctly! In a situation like this, where all the work is going to happen behind the scenes—the RowKeeper and its Rows have no visible correlative in the program's interface—it's important to have some other way of peeking in to see that things are proceeding as planned. I give the Row class a Dump method, which puts up a MsgBox showing the Index numbers of its Spaces:

```
dim i as integer
dim s as string
for i = 1 to 3
    s = s + str(theSpaces(i).index) + ","
next
msgbox mid(s,1,len(s)-1)
```

Next I give the RowKeeper class a Dump method that dumps each row:

```
dim i, u as integer
u = ubound(theRows)
```

```
for i = 1 to u
    theRows(i).dump
next
```

Now I give the window a button I can press as we go along, to call the RowKeeper's Dump method and learn the state of things.

Let's return to the task at hand, which is to populate the Rows. I envision a method that emanates from the individual Spaces—something like this: Start with Space 0. Space 0 looks to the right, and continues looking to the right until he has come to the edge of the game board; all the Spaces that he saw, including himself, constitute a row. Now Space 0 looks down, and continues looking down until he has come to the bottom of the game board; all the Spaces that he saw, including himself, constitute another row. Now Space 0 looks diagonally down and to the right; same thing. Now let's generalize this for all the Spaces. In order for us to derive all the rows in this way, in which directions should each Space look? Well, as we've just seen, a minimum is Right, Down, and DiagRight (meaning diagonally down and to the right). What about Up? No, if a Space is part of a vertical row that extends above him, that row will have been counted already by an earlier Space looking Down. What about Left? No, for the same reason. What about DiagLeft, meaning diagonally down and to the left? Yes! We must look in this direction, because otherwise Space 2 will never discover the diagonal row of which he is a part.

Very well. Our first step is obviously to create two more Direction subclasses, DiagLeft and DiagRight. We can define DiagRight's NeighborOf in terms of the existing Directions Down and Right:

```
dim down as down
dim right as right
down = new down
right = new right
return down.neighborof(right.neighborof(s))
exception
return nil
```

The Exception block takes care of the case of a Space with no neighbor to the right, causing `down.neighborof` to try to operate on a `nil` Space; that will raise an exception, so we catch it and return `nil` because that's the right answer—such a Space has no neighbor down and to the right.

We could define DiagLeft's NeighborOf in terms of the existing Directions Down and Left, if only we had a Left direction. So I make a Left direction, define its NeighborOf, and then define DiagLeft's NeighborOf in terms of it.

So, how would a given Space make its rows? It would gather up the four rows corresponding to each of the four relevant directions. I give Space a MakeRows method:

```
dim d as direction
dim row as row

d = new right
row = self.initiateRow
```

```
self.continueRow(d, row)

d = new down
row = self.initiateRow
self.continueRow(d, row)

d = new diagleft
row = self.initiateRow
self.continueRow(d, row)

d = new diagright
row = self.initiateRow
self.continueRow(d, row)
```

I'm engaging here in a kind of *speculative coding*, a technique you'll see used several more times as this project progresses. The routine is made up almost entirely of calls to other routines that don't exist yet. Treating them as if they did exist helps me think about what routines I need and what they ought to do. Since the routines aren't written yet, I'm not entirely sure what information they might require; so at this stage I tend to pass everything as parameters. Obviously InitiateRow must return a reference to the newly created Row, because the next step is to keep filling that Row. ContinueRow obviously needs to know what Direction to continue in, and it needs a reference to the Row so that it can keep filling it.

Now let's write the Space class's InitiateRow method:

```
dim row as row
row = window1.therowKeeper.create
row.add me
return row
```

That was easy; now what about the Space class's ContinueRow method?

```
dim s as space // and d and row are the incoming Direction and Row
s = d.neighborOf(me)
if s <> nil then
    s.continueContinuingRow(d, row)
end
```

This is getting a bit confusing, but you can see what I'm driving at here. If this Space has a neighbor in the given direction, then it is that neighbor who should add himself to the Row. So I'm imagining yet another Space method, ContinueContinuingRow, which I now proceed to write:

```
dim s as space // and d and row are the incoming Direction and Row
row.add me
s = d.neighborOf(me)
if s <> nil then
    s.continueContinuingRow(d, row)
end
```

Well, I can't help feeling I made that more complicated than I needed to. But that's okay! I can go back and fix it later. "Don't be afraid to change your mind."

At this point we can start to test, using our button in the window. We start shyly and have Space 0 generate just one row:

```
dim d as direction
dim row as row
d = new right
row = aSpace(0).initiateRow
aSpace(0).continueRow(d, row)
window1.therowKeeper.dump
```

Then we get bolder and have Space 0 generate all its rows:

```
aSpace(0).makeRows
window1.therowKeeper.dump
```

Finally we throw all caution to the winds and generate all the rows!

```
dim i as integer
for i = 0 to 8
    aSpace(i).makeRows
next
window1.therowKeeper.dump
```

Things aren't going too badly, but we can see that some of the rows generated in this way are not real rows. For example, Space 0 generates a Row for the DiagLeft direction consisting only of himself, since he has no neighbor down and to the left. And in general, that seems to be a clue as to how to spot these false rows: they won't consist of three Spaces. So, I give Row a HowFull method, which allows us to inquire how many non-nil elements the Row has:

```
dim i as integer
for i = 1 to 3
    if theSpaces(i) = nil then
        return i-1
    end
next
return 3
```

And I give RowKeeper a WinnowRows method that eliminates rows that don't have three Spaces:

```
dim i, u as integer
u = ubound(theRows)
for i = u downto 1
    if theRows(i).howFull < 3 then
        theRows.remove i
    end
next
```

One more test:

```
dim i as integer
for i = 0 to 8
    aSpace(i).makeRows
next
window1.therowKeeper.winnowRows
window1.therowKeeper.dump
```

It works! Now we can use this routine (without the Dump, of course) as the application starts up, to generate the actual rows.

What's My Row?

It seems likely that a Space will need to know what rows it's a part of. The easiest way to give it this knowledge is for the Space class to have a property that is an array of Rows. I'll call this property MyRows; it will be an array of Rows, initially dimensioned to zero. Then every individual Space can maintain a list of its own rows.

I tend to think that the RowKeeper, as master of the situation, should be in charge of assigning the Rows to the Spaces. We can give RowKeeper a method MakeRowPointersFor, where we intend to hand it a reference to a Space, calling it in this manner:

```
window1.therowKeeper.makeRowPointersFor(someSpaceOrOther)
```

Clearly we will need a way to ask a Row whether it contains a given Space. That sounds like a method of the Row class; I'll call it Contains:

```
dim i as integer
for i = 1 to 3
    if theSpaces(i) = s then // s is the incoming Space parameter
        return true
    end
next
return false
```

Now we can write the RowKeeper method MakeRowPointersFor. The incoming parameter is a Space; we run through all the Rows and, if a Row contains the Space, we append a reference to that Row to the end of that Space's MyRows array:

```
dim i, u as integer
u = ubound(theRows)
for i = 1 to u
    if theRows(i).contains(s) then // s is the incoming Space parameter
        s.myRows.append theRows(i)
    end
next
```

So now our opening routine will go like this:

```
dim i as integer
for i = 0 to 8
    aSpace(i).makeRows
next
window1.therowKeeper.winnowRows
for i = 0 to 8
    window1.therowKeeper.makeRowPointersFor(aSpace(i))
next
```

To test whether this is working, we'd like to have a way of asking any particular Space about the Rows in its MyRows array. How can we speak to a particular Space when the application is running? I know—we can click on it! We'll give the Space class a method called DumpRows:

```
dim i, u as integer
u = ubound(myRows)
for i = 1 to u
    myRows(i).dump
next
```

Now if Space's MouseDown event handler returns true, and its MouseUp event handler calls DumpRows, we can click to examine the state of any particular Space's Rows. When we do, we find that things are working correctly.

He Thought About the Game

Let's forget about rows now, and concentrate on a different aspect of Tic-Tac-Toe—the game, by which I mean that quality of alternation that makes a game a game. Player A plays in a space. Player B plays in a space. Player A plays in a space. And so on.

As a first implementation of this alternation, let's have the human be both Player A and Player B. The human will click on a space, and it should show an X. The human will click on another space, and it should show an O. And so forth. This corresponds to my third principle, "Always have the program do something." I really have no idea yet how to teach the computer to decide what Space to play in, or even what such a thing would mean; but I know how to click the mouse! So I start with a case that I can solve, and work upward from there. If I do this correctly, the harder cases are much easier to solve when I come to them. After all, if we can get our program to behave correctly for a human repeatedly clicking, it should be a simple matter to substitute the computer as one of the players. In fact, since alternation is the basic paradigm here, the general overall architecture of the game should really be such that it doesn't matter who is playing—human against human, computer against human, or computer against computer.

We need a Game class to act as master of the situation. I'll have the Window own an instance of this class, and instantiate it when things start up. We also need two instances of the Player class to play in turn; the Game must know who these are, so let's give the Game class two Player properties, which I'll call Player1 and Player2. Since we intend to have two kinds of player, human and computer, and since these will behave quite differently when it is their turn to play, I'll give Player two subclasses, HumanPlayer and ComputerPlayer. Since each Player plays a different piece (an X or an O), we will need two kinds of piece, which is to say, a Piece class and two subclasses, which I'll call X and O. Now, how are we going to get alternation out of this arrangement? Let's build the basis for alternation into the Player class and Piece class themselves. We'll presume that, for a given Game, each Player has a property NextPlayer, which is a pointer to the other Player, and that a Piece has a method

NextPieceToPlay, which returns an instance of the other type of Piece. The Game always needs to be in command of which player is next to play and what piece is next to be played. So the Game class will have a Player property called PlayerToPlay and a Piece property called PieceToPlay. Then the Game class can have a Play method that goes like this:

```
if playerToPlay = nil then
    playerToPlay = player1
else
    playerToPlay = playerToPlay.nextPlayer
end
if pieceToPlay = nil then
    pieceToPlay = new x
else
    pieceToPlay = pieceToPlay.nextPieceToPlay
end
playerToPlay.play(me)
```

Every time the Game class's Play method is called, it changes the value of Player-ToPlay and PieceToPlay. Presto, there's your alternation! And in fact we can consider this part of the problem solved for now. The only thing we have to worry about is the Player class's Play method. But if the player is human, this method will be empty! Everything will simply come to a stop, waiting for the human to click on a Space.

Let's turn, then, to the Space that gets clicked on. Clearly it must adopt the correct Piece as its own: it must display it, and it must continue to display it. Furthermore, a Space needs to know whether it is already displaying a Piece, because if it is, it mustn't do anything when clicked on (otherwise it might allow a click to change an X to an O, which is against the rules). So a Space needs a Piece property, which I call MyPiece.

Space's MouseDown event handler will return true; here is its MouseUp event handler:

```
dim p as piece
if window1.game = nil then // no game in progress, ignore
    return
end
if myPiece <> nil then // can't play here again
    beep
    return
end
// okay, legal to play here
myPiece = window1.game.pieceToPlay
me.refresh
window1.game.play // all done, on to the next player
```

The Refresh command is a signal for the Space to draw the X or O within itself. Clearly we need to add lines to the Space's Paint event handler to take care of this. Here are those additional lines:

```
if myPiece <> nil then
    myPiece.draw(g)
end
```

Again, I'm using speculative coding. Observe how this helps me to organize my classes. How should the Space draw the X or the O? It shouldn't! Instead, I have the Space tell the X or the O to draw itself. In this way, I keep pushing the functionality back until I reach the object I think should be responsible for knowing how to perform it.

Well, I have now reached the object in question. It's time to think about Piece, X, and O. I'll start by making the Piece class abstract; it has a Draw method and a NextPieceToPlay method, but these are just so that its subclasses can override them. The subclasses are X and O. Let's start with X's NextPieceToPlay method. How do you think it goes?

```
return new o
```

Need I tell you how O's NextPieceToPlay method goes? I thought not.

On to X's Draw method. This is something we can refine as we go along; right now, all I care about is that an "x," any representation of an "x," should be drawn. So here it is:

```
g.drawString "x", g.width/2, g.height/2
```

O's Draw method is parallel, except that instead of "x", there's "o".

Believe it or not, we are just about ready to play a game with human against human. All we have to do is have the Game perform some initializations in its constructor. It sets Player1 to an instance of HumanPlayer, and it sets Player2 to an instance of HumanPlayer; then it sets Player1's NextPlayer property to point at Player2, and Player2's NextPlayer property to point at Player1. (Yes, there's a circularity here, and if we aren't careful to break it somehow at the end of each game, we will leak a little bit of memory, because the two Player instances will never be destroyed. But this is a minor issue at this point.)

We run the project and start clicking in Spaces. It works! At every click, either an X or an O appears. The computer knows nothing about how to play Tic-Tac-Toe yet; it can't participate as a player; it doesn't even know when the game is over! But this is a very happy, satisfying moment anyway. I like to fill the development process with happy, satisfying moments of this sort; they are what keeps me going.

Can We Talk?

Instead of just assuming that both players are human—which, after all, will not always be true—let's have the game begin by letting the user say who is to play (human against human, computer against human, or computer against computer). And while we're up, let's have this initialization take place, not when the program starts up (because this means we have to quit and restart in order to play again), but in response to a menu item, New Game. Here is the FileNewGame menu event handler:

```
window1.clearPieces
window1.game = new game
window1.game.start
```

And here is the Game class's Start method:

```
gameSetup.showModal
```

Once again, I am coding speculatively, pushing the responsibility back to something that doesn't even exist yet. My intention is that GameSetup should be a modal dialog; the user will select options here and dismiss the dialog, and it will be the dialog's job to initialize things and start the game.

As for the window's ClearPieces method, it should be obvious how that must go:

```
dim i as integer
for i = 0 to 8
    aSpace(i).clear
next
```

Space's Clear method simply sets its MyPiece property to `nil`. The window could have done this directly, of course, but that wouldn't be object-oriented; the window has no business diving into a Space and manipulating its properties:

```
myPiece = nil
me.refresh
```

Now then, let's proceed to the GameSetup dialog. It has two GroupBoxes, each with two RadioButtons, offering a choice of Human and Computer for Player One and a choice of Human and Computer for Player Two. It has a Cancel button and an OK button. See Figure A-3.

The first RadioButton's Action event handler looks like this:

```
window1.game.player1 = new humanPlayer
enableOK
```

The other RadioButtons are all parallel; the second RadioButton sets Player1 to a new ComputerPlayer, and the third and fourth RadioButtons initialize Player2. The EnableOK method is called by all four RadioButtons; this is a way to make sure that everything is initialized properly before allowing the user to click the OK button:

```
dim b as boolean
b = player1Human.value or player1Computer.value
b = b and (player2Human.value or player2Computer.value)
ok.enabled = b
```

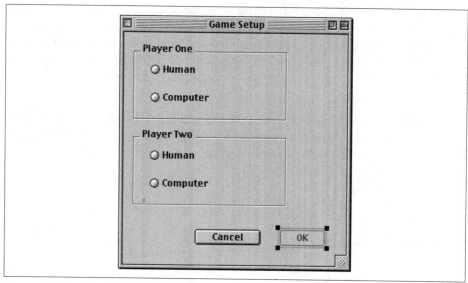

Figure A-3. The GameSetup dialog in the IDE

The OK button points the two Players at each other, closes the dialog, and starts the game:

```
close
window1.game.player1.nextPlayer = window1.game.player2
window1.game.player2.nextPlayer = window1.game.player1
window1.game.play
```

May I Cut In?

Now it's time to permit the computer to become involved in the game. The first step is to move some code out of Space's MouseUp event handler. Recall these lines:

```
myPiece = window1.game.pieceToPlay
me.refresh
window1.game.play // all done, on to the next player
```

These are exactly the lines that the computer needs to execute in order to play in a Space. The trouble is that they are in a place where the computer can't access them. The computer can't click on a Space; it needs to call a method. So we create a Space method, Play, to contain these lines; back in Space's MouseUp event handler, we substitute a call to this Play method.

We have now made it possible for the computer to play; we also need to make it possible for the computer to see. The human knows whether a Space holds a Piece, because an "x" or an "o" is visibly displayed; the computer, on the other hand, must inquire of a Space whether it holds a Piece. The computer could look right at a Space's Piece property, but it's more object-oriented to give the Space class a Has-Piece method that returns a boolean:

```
return myPiece <> nil
```

So, where do things stand now? The game starts; there are two players, one of which is a ComputerPlayer. When it's time for the ComputerPlayer to play, the Game will call its Play method. What should this do? At first, just to make sure everything is working properly, and to give ourselves the satisfaction of playing any sort of game at all against the computer, we can have the computer play randomly:

```
playRandom
```

ComputerPlayer's PlayRandom method chooses a Space randomly from the unoccupied Spaces and plays there. My technique for doing this is to assemble all the unoccupied Spaces into an array, and then choose randomly from the array:

```
dim a(0) as integer
dim i,u as integer
for i = 0 to 8
    if not window1.aSpace(i).hasPiece then
        a.append i
    end
next
u = ubound(a)
i = (rnd * u) + 1
window1.aSpace(a(i)).play
```

That's it! We start up the project, ask for a New Game, and choose human versus computer (or computer versus human). We are able to play alternately against the computer! Of course, the computer plays extraordinarily badly. He has no idea of the purpose of the game, no concept of three in a row. He doesn't even know when he's been beaten and the game is over; he just keeps right on playing, and eventually we hit a NilObjectException when the computer tries to play into an already full board. But that's not important; what's important is that the computer is now involved in the game. That's a major step.

Three in a Row

Let's now teach the computer enough about the purpose of Tic-Tac-Toe that at least he fights back a little: if his opponent gets two in a row, the computer will play into the third square. The logic, which we add to ComputerPlayer's Play method, is to check every row to see if it has two of the opponent's pieces in it, and if so, play in the third Space:

```
dim r as row
dim i, u as integer // and g is the incoming Game parameter
u = ubound(window1.therowKeeper.therows)
for i = 1 to u
    r = window1.therowKeeper.therows(i)
    if r.hasTwo(g.pieceToPlay.nextPieceToPlay) then
        r.theThird.play
        return
    end
next
playRandom
```

The Row class's TheThird method is as follows:

```
dim i as integer
for i = 1 to 3
    if not theSpaces(i).hasPiece then
        return theSpaces(i)
    end
next
```

We turn next to Row's HasTwo method. This has to take a Piece parameter, because the question is not whether the row has exactly two occupied Spaces, but whether it has exactly two Spaces that are occupied by a particular Piece. At this point we realize we've got a problem. HasTwo will receive a Piece parameter, and it will compare this against the Piece of each Space in the row. But how will this comparison work? We cannot use pure equality, because this will always fail; the two instances are different instances. We cannot ask whether they are instances of the same class, because REALbasic provides no way to ask an instance its class. A quick-and-dirty solution is to have a Piece produce some sort of token that *can* be compared using pure equality:

```
if theSpaces(i).myPiece.type = p.type then // p is the incoming Piece
```

Piece will have a Type method; X will implement it like this:

```
return "x"
```

I think it's clear how O will implement the Type method. We are now ready to write the Row class's HasTwo method:

```
dim i, total, empties as integer // and p is the Piece parameter
for i = 1 to 3
    if theSpaces(i).hasPiece then
        if theSpaces(i).myPiece.type = p.type then
            total = total + 1
        end
    else
        empties = empties + 1
    end
next
return (total = 2 and empties = 1)
```

This works splendidly. Having taught the computer to defend, we now teach it to attack. Before worrying about whether its opponent has two in a row, the computer should look to see whether it itself has two in a row, and if so, it should play and win. This is exactly like defending, except that HasTwo's parameter is the other kind of Piece. These lines now appear in ComputerPlayer's Play method:

```
for i = 1 to u
    r = window1.therowKeeper.therows(i)
    if r.hasTwo(g.pieceToPlay) then
        r.theThird.play
        return
    end
next
```

Draw, Partner

Let's now make the drawing of the X and the O look a little nicer. There is going to be a lot of shared functionality here; except for the actual letter being drawn, X's Draw method and O's Draw method will be identical. This suggests that they should both call some common method. I'll have this common method be the Draw method of their superclass, Piece. So, for example, X's Draw method now goes like this:

```
piece.draw(g, "x")
```

Piece now has two Draw methods. One takes a single parameter, the Graphics property into which to draw; this is the method being overridden by X's Draw method and O's Draw method. The other takes two parameters; this is the method being called by X's Draw method and O's Draw method, and its job is to draw a letter in some nice way, such as this:

```
dim h,w as integer // and t is the text to draw, and g is the Graphics to draw into
g.textfont = "sand"
g.textsize = 48
h = g.textheight - g.textascent
w = g.stringWidth(t)
g.drawString t, g.width/2-w/2, g.height/2+h/2
```

Stop the World, I Want to Get Off

Let's now give some attention to our project's last remaining major architectural problem: how to end the game. After every play, we need to look and see if the game is over. If it is, we should do something about it: we should stop playing, we should prevent any further play, and we might like to make it visually clear who has won.

To implement this, I give the Game class a boolean property, GameOver, and I create a new Game method, Continue. From now on, Continue will be the only method that will call Game's Play method. Everyone else who used to call Game's Play method is now changed to call Game's Continue method instead; it goes like this:

```
dim p as piece
p = whoWon
if p <> nil then
    sayWhoWon(p)
    gameOver = true
    window1.refresh
    return
end
if draw then
    sayDraw
    gameOver = true
    window1.refresh
    return
end
play
```

Of course, there are a lot of methods referred to here that aren't written yet. Let's start with WhoWon. This will return a Piece corresponding to the winner, or nil if no one has won yet. It's simply a question of looking through all the rows to see if any of them has three in a row for either type of Piece:

```
dim i, u as integer
dim r as rowKeeper
dim p as piece
r = window1.theRowKeeper
u = ubound(r.theRows)
p = new x
for i = 1 to u
    if r.theRows(i).threeInARow(p) then
        return p
    end
next
p = new o
for i = 1 to u
    if r.theRows(i).threeInARow(p) then
        return p
    end
next
return nil
```

Again, we're referring to a method we haven't written yet: the Row class's method ThreeInARow. Let's write it:

```
dim i, total as integer // and p is the incoming Piece
for i = 1 to 3
    if theSpaces(i).hasPiece then
        if theSpaces(i).myPiece.type = p.type then
            total = total + 1
        end
    else
        return false
    end
next
return (total = 3)
```

The next unwritten method is SayWhoWon. I'll put a StaticText called Message into the window. Now SayWhoWon goes like this:

```
window1.message.text = p.type + " wins!"
```

Similarly, SayDraw goes like this:

```
window1.message.text = "Draw!"
```

The Message text mustn't be left visible when the next game starts, so I add this line to the window's ClearPieces method:

```
message.text = ""
```

Now we can proceed to the Game class's Draw method. Since we know no one has won, it's a draw if the game board is full:

```
dim i as integer
for i = 0 to 8
```

```
    if not window1.aSpace(i).hasPiece then
        return false
    end
next
return true
```

Things are going well, but let me go back to Game's Continue method. I don't like that last line:

```
play
```

Instead of calling Play directly, I'll start up a Timer, which will call Play:

```
theGameContinuer.mode = 1
```

The main reason for this is that I'm getting a little jumpy about the way we keep calling Play. If the computer plays against itself, I have visions that Play is calling Play is calling Play in some terrifying recursion. With the Timer, we step out of this recursion; starting up the Timer causes the entire pending calling chain to terminate, and the Timer itself then starts a new calling chain when it calls Play. The Timer's Period can be very brief; I'll have it be 100.

The computer is now prevented from playing on if the game is over. But we have not enforced the same rule for the human. To do so, we insert these lines within Space's MouseUp event handler:

```
if window1.game.gameOver then
    beep
    return
end
```

To make it even clearer who has won, let's modify the Piece class's Draw procedure so that it marks the Spaces that constitute the win. Traditionally, you're supposed to draw a line through the Spaces, but I think I'll redraw them in a bright color instead. For this to work, Piece's Draw method will need to interrogate the Space that called it, to see if that Space is part of three in a row. So Space's Paint event handler, when it tells its Piece to Draw, must now pass a reference to itself:

```
myPiece.draw(g, me)
```

Here is Piece's Draw method now:

```
dim h,w as integer // and t is the text to draw, and g is the Graphics to draw into
if s.inThreeInARow then // s is the incoming Space parameter
    g.foreColor = rgb(255,0,0)
else
    g.foreColor = rgb(0,0,0)
end
g.textfont = "sand"
g.textsize = 48
h = g.textheight - g.textascent
w = g.stringWidth(t)
g.drawString t, g.width/2-w/2, g.height/2+h/2
```

We also insert a line at the start of Space's Paint event handler, to set the color for drawing the grid:

```
g.forecolor = rgb(0,0,0)
```

Now let's write Space's InThreeInARow method:

```
dim i,u as integer
u = ubound(myRows)
for i = 1 to u
    if myRows(i).threeInARow(myPiece) then
        return true
    end
next
return false
```

It all works splendidly. On the outside, the game is now finished! See Figure A-4.

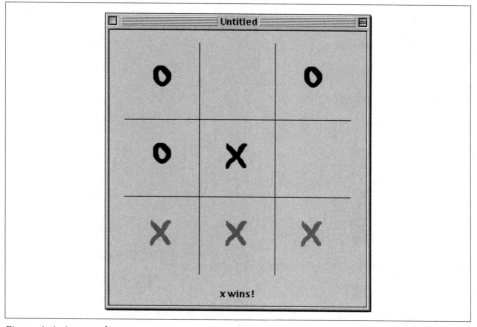

Figure A-4. An actual game

Cleanup

It is not yet time to rest on our laurels. We need to reread all the code and make sure that it's understandable, correct, efficient, and something we'd be willing to show to someone else. At present, I don't quite think it is.

The way we determine what a Row is at startup is particularly skanky. The progressive series of calls within the Space class—InitiateRow, ContinueRow, ContinueContinuingRow—obviously has something wrong with it. And in any case the Space class has no business doing any of this. The master of knowledge about rows is the RowKeeper; that's where everything should happen. RowKeeper's constructor should call its own MakeRows method, which goes like this:

```
dim i as integer
for i = 0 to 8
    makeRowsFor(window1.aSpace(i))
next
winnowRows
for i = 0 to 8
    makeRowPointersFor(window1.aSpace(i))
next
```

MakeRowsFor can now be made cleaner:

```
dim d as direction
dim row as row // and s is the incoming Space parameter

d = new right
row = create
continueRow(d, row, s)

d = new down
row = create
continueRow(d, row, s)

d = new diagleft
row = create
continueRow(d, row, s)

d = new diagright
row = create
continueRow(d, row, s)
```

There is now just one ancillary routine, ContinueRow, which simply embodies the recursion:

```
dim s2 as space // d, row, s1 are incoming Direction, Row, Space
row.add s1
s2 = d.neighborOf(s1)
if s2 <> nil then
    continueRow(d, row, s2)
end
```

Now let's turn once again to X's Draw method, O's Draw method, and Piece's Draw method. Thinking about this a little more, I see that, since "x" is also the result of X's Type method, I could actually jettison X's Draw method and O's Draw method altogether. And I should do so; otherwise, X is generating the string "x" in two different places, which is wrong. All that's left now is Piece's Draw method, which goes like this:

```
dim h,w as integer
dim t as string // and g is the Graphics to draw into
t = self.type
```

```
if s.inThreeInARow then // s is the Space parameter
    g.foreColor = rgb(255,0,0)
else
    g.foreColor = rgb(0,0,0)
end
g.textfont = "sand"
g.textsize = 48
h = g.textheight - g.textascent
w = g.stringWidth(t)
g.drawString t, g.width/2-w/2, g.height/2+h/2
```

Next, let's return to the problem of comparing two X instances with each other. This comes up, for example, in Row's HasTwo method:

```
if theSpaces(i).myPiece.type = p.type then // p is the incoming Piece
```

I don't like this. We should not have to ask a Piece for further information in order to learn what type it is; the classes X and O *are* types of Piece. One way to solve the difficulty is this: instead of generating each new Piece with new x or new o, we should have from the outset exactly one global X instance and exactly one global O instance, and all references to X and O throughout the program should then be references to one of these. As a result, comparison through pure equality *will* work, because all references to an X instance will be references to the *same* X instance.

So, I give the Game class two new Piece properties, TheX and TheO. These are initialized to a new X and a new O in Game's constructor, and that must be the only place in the program that a new X or a new O is generated. I run through the program looking for places where this happens now, replacing them with references to the Game's TheX and TheO. Now Row's HasTwo method can use direct equality comparison:

```
if theSpaces(i).myPiece = p then
```

Now a Piece's Type method is no longer called for comparison purposes; it is called only in order to get a string version of the Piece (to draw it in a Space or to put its name in the Message text). So it is misnamed; I change its name, and all references to it, to ToString.

The Game class needs a destructor, to break the circular references between Player1 and Player2 and prevent a memory leak:

```
if player1 <> nil then
    player1.nextPlayer = nil
end
```

The "magic numbers" 8 and 3 are hardcoded everywhere. These depend entirely upon the fact that the game is played on a three-by-three grid. This fact is not purely contingent, since Tic-Tac-Toe is usually played on a three-by-three grid; but we *might* want the game to be extendable to permit play on a larger grid, and in any case there is no need for there to be more than one "magic number," namely 3. (The number 8 is merely 3 squared minus 1, the highest index of the ASpace control array.) So for now let's have a constant in a module, GridSize, initialized to 3, and a global method in the same module, GridLast:

```
return gridSize * gridSize - 1
```

We then run through all the code, looking for occurrences of 3 and 8 and replacing them with GridSize and GridLast, respectively. For example, Down's NeighborOf method now looks like this:

```
dim i as integer
i = s.index
if i\gridSize = gridSize-1 then
    return nil
end
return window1.aSpace(i+gridSize)
```

Nor must we forget about array dimensions. Row's property TheSpaces needs to be dimensioned to GridSize. We can't do this in its declaration if GridSize is a constant, so we declare it to -1 and Redim it to GridSize in Row's constructor.

This completes our code. I like everything about it. I like the brevity and clarity of the handlers. I like how everything is a class. I like the organization of the classes and subclasses, the architecture of which classes "own" other classes as properties, and how certain classes are used as decision-making mechanisms. I like the choices about who does what: no object seems to me to be impinging in a confusing or inappropriate way on any other object's territory. I like the code's generality: the program finds the rows for itself, the grid could in theory be any size, either player can be human or computer. To me, this program doesn't feel like a set of commands for playing Tic-Tac-Toe; it feels like an object-oriented expression of the essence of Tic-Tac-Toe. That's how a well-structured program should feel. If the code has flaws, they are that some lines are probably unnecessary, and that there is a distinct lack of error checking. However, we could spend forever polishing one program and never get anything else done. Sooner or later, you simply have to declare the program finished. I hereby declare this program finished.

Exercises

The exercises are presented in order of difficulty.

1. (Easy.) Build the Tic-Tac-Toe game just described. Some details were omitted from the description; figuring these out is the point of the exercise. (If you want to skip this, you can just download the complete project from my web site.)

2. (Easy to intermediate.) Extend the Tic-Tac-Toe game so that when the computer is to play against itself, the user has an option to have it play continuously and to decide how many games it should play. Thus, for example, the computer might be asked to play 100 games against itself without stopping. (This extension is already built into the downloadable project at my web site.)

3. (Intermediate.) Extend the Tic-Tac-Toe game so that the user can pick a grid size before starting a new game. Let's say that the game can be played on a three-by-three, four-by-four, or five-by-five grid. I envision an architecture somewhat as follows: GridSize will no longer be a constant, but, rather a globally available property set in accordance with the user's wishes. The window will initially contain just one ASpace control; the others are generated dynamically (cloned) and positioned correctly, in code, depending on the requested grid size. Cloned controls can't be deleted, so to start a new game, we can close the window and open a new instance of it, or reuse the existing clones.

4. (Hard.) Extend the Tic-Tac-Toe game so that the computer learns from experience as it plays, and becomes a good Tic-Tac-Toe player. A backtracking strategy for doing this is as follows. You'll need a way of encoding and identifying an entire game board situation, and don't forget that board situations that are rotationally or mirror-wise symmetric count as identical. After each of its plays, the computer records the board situation. If the computer's opponent wins, the computer adds the last recorded board situation to a list of board situations to be avoided; this list should be persistent (as a file of some sort). In the PlayRandom method, the computer removes from the array of possible moves any move that would create one of the situations to be avoided (though of course it cannot eliminate every move, since it must play somewhere). If the computer's opponent wins and the computer's last move is already on the list of situations to be avoided, the computer's next-to-last move is added to the list, and so forth. Now have the computer play 1000 games against itself, as a way of building up some experience. After that, the computer should be a good player; in fact, on a three-by-three grid at least, it should be impossible for a human opponent to win.

5. (Wow.) Extend the Tic-Tac-Toe game to play on a three-dimensional game board (for example, three-by-three-by-three). This is going to need one heck of an interface. Have a good time, but don't give up your day job.

Index

We'd like to hear your suggestions for improving our indexes. Send email to *index@oreilly.com*.

About the Author

Matt Neuburg started programming computers in 1968, when he was 14 years old, as a member of a literally underground high school club, which met once a week to do timesharing on a bank of PDP-10s by way of primitive teletype machines. He also occasionally used Princeton University's IBM-360/67, but gave it up in frustration when one day he dropped his punch cards. He majored in Greek at Swarthmore College, and received his Ph.D. from Cornell University in 1981, writing his doctoral dissertation (about Aeschylus) on a mainframe. He proceeded to teach Classical languages, literature, and culture at many well-known institutions of higher learning, most of which now disavow knowledge of his existence, and to publish numerous scholarly articles unlikely to interest anyone. Meanwhile he obtained an Apple IIc and became hopelessly hooked on computers again, migrating to a Macintosh in 1990. He wrote some educational and utility freeware, became an early regular contributor to the online journal *TidBITS*, and in 1995 left academe to edit *MacTech Magazine*. He is also the author of *Frontier: The Definitive Guide* (O'Reilly, 1998). In August 1996 he became a freelancer, which means he has been looking for work ever since.

Colophon

Our look is the result of reader comments, our own experimentation, and feedback from distribution channels. Distinctive covers complement our distinctive approach to technical topics, breathing personality and life into potentially dry subjects.

The animal on the cover of *REALbasic: The Definitive Guide* is a greyhound. Greyhounds were first bred approximately 3,000 years ago in Egypt, making them one of the oldest breeds of domesticated dogs. Mummified greyhounds have been found in ancient Egyptian tombs. They were bred as hunting dogs. They hunt by sight, not smell, and have the keenest eyesight of all dogs. Their hunting strategy is to outrun their prey, a task they easily accomplish. Greyhounds are the fastest breed of dog, reaching speeds of up to 45 miles per hour. In recent times, this speed has led to the sport of greyhound racing. Numerous societies promote the adoption of retired racing greyhounds.

The distinctive silhouettes formed by their graceful, virtually fat-free bodies, their even temperaments, and their power and speed have long made greyhounds favorites of royalty. At one time in England it was against the law for "commoners" to own greyhounds. Greyhounds have also made their mark in art and literature. There are references to greyhounds in the Bible and in classical literature from Homer to Shakespeare.

Mary Brady was the production editor and Norma Emory was the proofreader for *REALbasic: The Definitive Guide*. Darren Kelly, Claire Cloutier, and Linley Dolby provided quality control. Kimo Carter provided production support. Matt Neuburg wrote the index.

Hanna Dyer designed the cover of this book, based on a series design by Edie Freedman. The cover image is an original engraving from *The Illustrated Natural History: Mammalia*. Emma Colby produced the cover layout with QuarkXPress 4.1 using Adobe's ITC Garamond font.

Melanie Wang designed the interior layout, based on a series design by David Futato. The design was implemented by Neil Walls using tools created by Mike Sierra. The text font is Linotype Birka; the heading font is Adobe Myriad Condensed; and the code font is LucasFont's TheSans Mono Condensed. The illustrations that appear in the book were produced by Robert Romano and Jessamyn Read using Macromedia FreeHand 9 and Adobe Photoshop 6. The tip and warning icons were drawn by Christopher Bing. This colophon was written by Clairemarie Fisher O'Leary.

Whenever possible, our books use a durable and flexible lay-flat binding. If the page count exceeds this binding's limit, perfect binding is used.